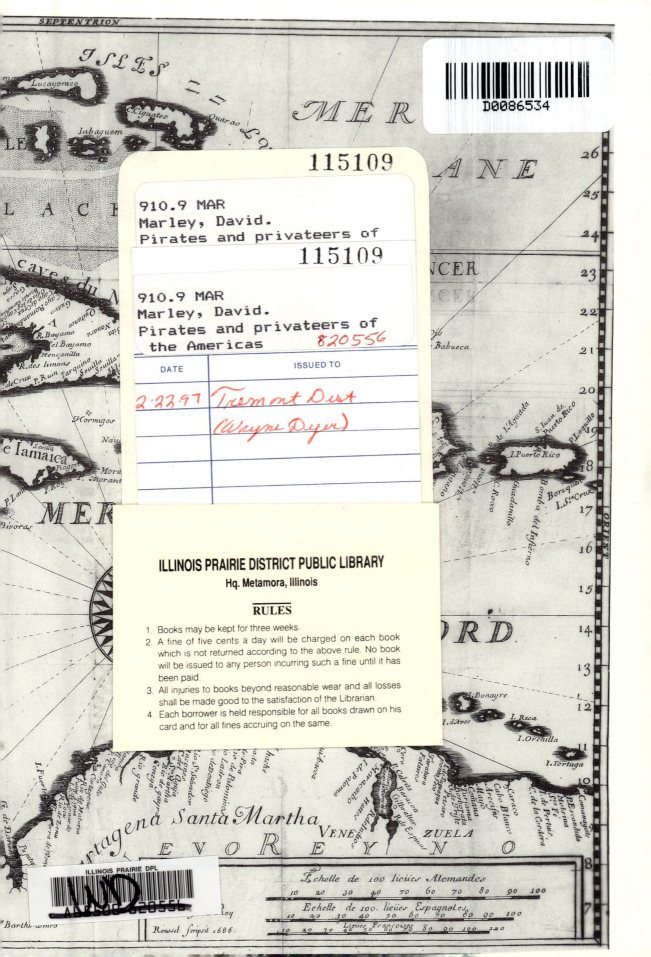

# PIRATES

## AND PRIVATEERS OF THE AMERICAS

# PIRATES

## AND PRIVATEERS OF THE AMERICAS

David F. Marley

**ABC-CLIO**

Santa Barbara, California
Denver, Colorado
Oxford, England

**Library of Congress Cataloging-in-Publication Data**

Marley, David F.
    Pirates and privateers of the Americas/David F. Marley
        p. cm.
        1. Pirates—America—History.    2. Privateering—America—History.
3. America, History, Naval.    I. Title.
E18.M44 1994   910'.9163—dc20   94-31348


ISBN 0-87436-751-4 (alk. paper)


00  99  98  97  96              10  9  8  7  6  5  4  3  2


ABC-CLIO, Inc.
130 Cremona Drive, P.O. Box 1911
Santa Barbara, California 93116-1911


This book is printed on acid-free paper ∞.
Manufactured in the United States of America

For my parents

*I saw new worlds beneath the water lie,*
*New people; yea, another sky*

Thomas Traherne
(1637?–1674)

# PIRATES

## AND PRIVATEERS OF THE AMERICAS

# PREFACE

More than three centuries ago, rovers prowled the length and breadth of the Americas. Most of the earliest Spanish conquistadors fought their way on to the continent, seizing the great kingdoms of Mexico and Peru while leaving a vacuum among the islands and torrid coastal regions of the Caribbean. Into this vast arena the seamen of rival European nations had followed, hoping to trade, poach, or do battle with Spain's new empire. In time, they found ample loopholes for their clandestine trade as well as scores of uninhabited Antillean isles on which to establish advance bases. By the early seventeenth century small French, English, and Dutch settlements were dotted throughout the Windward and Leeward Islands, spreading ever deeper through the archipelagos. The best-organized of these first interlopers were the Dutch—shrewd, tough traders whose *West Indische Compagnie* came to dominate commerce throughout the area.

In 1654, Oliver Cromwell dispatched an expedition into the West Indies to conquer a major stronghold for England as well, despite his uneasy peace with Spain. Although this force failed in its attempt to capture Santo Domingo, it nonetheless overran smaller Jamaica. Ten years of intermittent warfare ensued as the local Spanish American governments vainly strove to drive the English out and were in turn bedevilled by Jamaican counterraids. A similar friction developed on Hispaniola where French hunters (known as *boucaniers*, from their custom of curing meat in extemporized smokehouses called *boucans*) probed inland from the western and northern shores in pursuit of wild cattle. The Spanish inhabitants of Santo Domingo bitterly contested these border encroachments, thus feeding the surly undertone that came to characterize the region. Such frequent clashes bred a distinct class of mercenary—privateers, or *flibustiers*—who made seaborne descents against their enemies under any flag of convenience, motivated principally by greed and a thirst for violent reprisal.

European conflicts being carried over into the West Indies also added to the turmoil whenever they exploded back in the homelands. However, the free-spirited corsairs often reinterpreted these distant events to suit their own particular purpose, such as during the Second Anglo-Dutch War (1665–1667), when Jamaican privateers openly refused to attack the Dutch, saying "there was more profit with less hazard" to be gained against the neutral Spaniards, confining most of their subsequent operations against that traditional foe. Such a cavalier attitude extended to joint operations with expeditions sent out from Europe as well, making the privateers seem unreliable auxiliaries when compared with the more sternly disciplined regular troops. Soon the freebooters' propensity for unauthorized attacks began to exasperate home governments, as well as the growing class of their fellow merchant traders and planters in the West Indies, who required peace and stability in order to prosper. This intolerance led to the arrest of both Henry Morgan and Governor Sir Thomas Modyford of Jamaica following the spectacular peacetime raid against Panama in January 1671.

But the prolonged war which then ensued, pitting France against Spain and Holland during the remainder of the 1670s, provided ample employment for a whole new generation of mercenaries who continued to mount assaults even after peace had been restored back in Europe by the

Treaty of Nijmegen in spring 1679. Three years afterward, a citizen of the Spanish American port of Cartagena was to lament that during the intervening period:

> Trinidad has been robbed once; Margarita and Guayana burnt once and sacked twice; La Guaira, sacked once and its inhabitants sold, the ransom for its women and children amounting to more than 100,000 pesos, in addition to the 300,000 which [the pirates] seized in the city and other damages. [The raiders also] entered Puerto Caballos and sacked Valencia, which is more than 20 leagues inland. Maracaibo has been robbed many times, and in the occupation of 1678, the enemy remained more than six months, reaching Trujillo which is more than 16 days' travel inland ... and causing such heavy damage to its farms that whereas before they provided 20 shiploads of cacao [a year], today they produce no more than four. The city of Ríohacha has been abandoned, the city and garrison of Santa Marta sacked more than three times and burnt once, from which its citizens have yet to recover. And here in Cartagena, which formerly had more than 20 shipowners, today not a single one remains.

Worse was to follow, for in the next few years the buccaneers would reach their zenith under leaders such as Laurens de Graaf and the sieur de Grammont, capturing Veracruz and Campeche as well as penetrating the Pacific Ocean with relative impunity.

But the raiders' very success would eventually contribute to their extinction, as smaller Spanish-American outposts were abandoned while larger ones became more heavily fortified. Freebooter fleets became so numerous that no prize except the very richest could possibly satisfy all its participants when the booty had to be split so many different ways, but these targets were beyond their grasp. Instead, supply became a constant worry and the number of safe havens where rovers might dispose of their plunder and make repairs were less available with every passing year. Some rovers—men such as Michiel Andrieszoon and Jan Willems—even took to traveling as far north as Boston or Rhode Island to find a temporary sanctuary until this venue, too, was closed to them.

The War of the League of Augsburg (which lasted from 1689 to 1697, and was known in America as "King William's War") witnessed the greatest concentration of privateers, yet with disappointing results. Prizes proved scarce, and the richest financial hauls of that conflict were Thomas Tew and Henry Every's piratical forays around the world into the Red Sea, which had nothing to do with the course of hostilities, yet proved so profitable they spawned dozens of imitators. Meanwhile, huge buccaneer enterprises, such as the *flibustier* invasions of Jamaica in 1694, or Pointis and Ducasse's sack of Cartagena in 1697, showed little rewards despite their skilful execution. The high water mark of piracy had been reached and would begin to recede when the union between the French and Spanish crowns of 1700 at last started to heal the long struggle for Hispaniola. Peace was as yet far in the future, but cities would no longer quail before the might of cruel invaders.

David Marley
Windsor, Ontario, Canada,
September 1994

# A Note on Dates

During the seventeenth century, the English used a different calendar to that of the French, Spanish, and most of the United Provinces of the Netherlands. In 1582, Pope Gregory XIII had approved the introduction of a new calendar which advanced the ancient Roman version by ten days, thus bringing it into closer alignment with the movements of the planets, and which still serves as our modern calendar.

But the Protestant English stubbornly refused to adopt the Pontiff's reform, persisting with their older Julian calendars for another 170 years, so that throughout the period covered by this book their records did not coincide with those of the other major European powers, rather lagging behind by ten days. (When Henry Morgan reconquered Providencia Island from the Spaniards in December 1670, for example, he and his English cohorts considered the date to be the 15 December, while the French *flibustiers* accompanying his expedition knew it to be Christmas Day, and so made a special effort to prevent any desecration of the churches.) Those relatively rare occasions on which English and European dates had to be combined into a written form, such as on international treaties or conventions, these were rendered jointly—for example, Madrid, 19/29 October 1674—with the Old Style or English version occurring first, the New Style or Continental form appearing second.

For purposes of overall clarity, the dates given in this book are in New Style or modern Gregorian form, unless otherwise indicated. A few specifically English entries have been marked (O.S.), to signify Old Style. Another exasperating seventeenth century eccentricity among the English has also been dispensed with, that of sometimes beginning each new calendar year as of 25 March rather than 1 January. This is what led to such bizarre datings as "19 January 1654/55," which in reality meant 19 January 1655 (O.S.), or 29 January 1655 (New Style).

# Acknowledgments

The author would like to acknowledge the generous assistance provided by Dr. Basil Kingstone, Head of the French Department of the University of Windsor, Ontario, Canada; Dr. William Autry of the Newberry Library, Chicago; Lic. Leonor Ortiz Monasterio, Directrix of the Archivo General de la Nación, Mexico; Dr. Pedro González García, Director of the Archivo General de Indias, Seville; Prof. Joel H. Baer of the English Department, Macalester College, Saint Paul, Minnesota; Miguel Laburu Mateo of the Sociedad de Oceanografía de Guipúzcoa of San Sebastián, Spain; Walter Nebiker of the State of Rhode Island and Providence Plantations Historical Preservation Commission of Providence, Rhode Island; Dr. Ronald B. Prud'homme van Reine of the Nederlands Scheepvaartmuseum, Amsterdam, Holland; Capitán de Fragata Jorge Ortiz Sotelo of the Instituto de Estudios Histórico-Marítimos of Lima, Peru; Ms. Hendrika Ruger and Ms. Joan Magee of Windsor, Ontario; Dr. Jean Starr of Edinburgh, Scotland; M. Christian Pfister of Dunkerque, France; Dr. Charles T. Gehring of the New Netherland Project of Albany, New York; Ms. Maureen Souchuk, Ms. Janice Bell, and Ms. Cathy Maskell of the Inter-Library Loan Office of the University of Windsor; and many other countless friends and colleagues who have helped with this project.

# PIRATES

AND PRIVATEERS OF THE AMERICAS

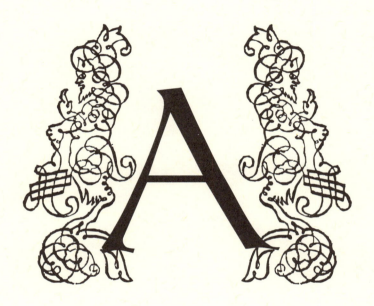

# ACOSTA, GASPAR DE

## (FL. 1683-1686)

Spanish *guardacosta* who raided the Bahamas, then operated along the southern shores of Cuba.

The first mention of Acosta's name occurred in May 1683, when he and Tomás Uraburru led a party of 200 corsairs against the Bahamas, attacking Charles Town (New Providence) with a single *piragua* and the galliot *Nuestra Señora del Rosario* (Our Lady of the Rosary). The English, under Governor Robert Lilburne, had already suffered through several invasions, and Acosta's assault effectively depopulated the islands for the next two-and-a-half years.

The following month, an English turtling sloop called *Providence,* Joseph Crockeyes master, was pursued off the south cays of Cuba "by two Spanish *piraguas* under Jean Costeau [*sic*]" and Crockeyes was forced to abandon his sloop, which was taken into Santiago. Acosta allegedly bragged that "he would have killed every man in her or any other vessel that he found turtling." In August 1683, the merchant sloop *Hereford* of Captain "Boucher Clauson" (i.e., Van den Clausen) was approaching Jamaica when its captain

> was driven by stress of weather to the Cuban coast, anchored four leagues to windward of Santiago, and sent a boat ashore for water, but made no attempt to trade [i.e., smuggle goods ashore]. While I was at anchor there came one Juan de Costa [*sic*] in a *piragua* of 50 men, who at once opened fire of small arms and dangerously wounded one man. I made no resistance, but they boarded and in spite of my protests that I had done no trade, forced me into Santiago, where the governor and Juan Costa detained both sloop and goods, to the value of £4,000.

Both English vessels had blundered into a war zone, hostilities having flared anew between the local French and Spanish privateers, who were bitterly contesting those waters. In the forefront of the fighting was Acosta, oftentimes confused in English reports with Juan Corso, who was also at Santiago around this time.

The following year Acosta transferred almost 300 miles west to the smaller Cuban port of Trinidad. There in late summer, the sloop of Derick Cornelison "was attacked without any warning by Don Juan Balosa [*sic*]" and carried into Trinidad for adjudication. Acting Jamaican governor Hender Molesworth dispatched Captain Edward Stanley of the tiny Royal Navy warship *Bonito,* four guns, to lodge a protest with his Spanish counterpart. Stanley "was forced by foul weather into a bay 25 leagues short" of Trinidad, sending a boat inshore on 16 November 1684 under the king's flag to ask for water. The boat failed to return, and at six o'clock the next morning the officer

> saw a galley rowing close under the shore and put into a creek about two miles to eastward of me. I at once got up sail, but had no sooner done so than I saw the galley and a *piragua* coming under sail and oars, the galley flying the Spanish flag with a red ensign, and the *piragua* the king's jack which he had taken [from] my boat. I fired at the galley when she came within range, and she at me, and we were engaged from 9 to 11, when they got into the creek where there was not water for me to follow them.

Acosta subsequently learned he had attacked a Royal Navy vessel and apologized to Stanley.

It was well that he did, for early in 1686 the pink *Swallow* of Captain Edward Goffe and sloop *Ann* of Captain William Peartree appeared off Trinidad. Both had been trading in the Bay of Honduras and, while returning toward Jamaica, had been carried so far to leeward that Goffe sent in a boat

> asking leave to wood and water, which was refused. I was therefore forced to go to the cays ten leagues from Trinidad for water, whither the governor of Trinidad sent two galleys out, one of 40 and one of 85 men, the latter of which, as the master confesses, was present at the sack of New Providence. Both galleys came up to my ship's side and without hailing poured in a volley, which killed two men and wounded five or six, and then making fast to my ship's side tried to board her. Having the sloop's crew on board we defended ourselves, and after about half an hour's engagement, there were about 16 Spanish pirates killed and 38 wounded. The smaller galley managed to clear herself, but the larger we captured and brought into Jamaica.

Acosta was carried into Port Royal on 22 February 1686 and within a month was "found guilty of piracy for robbing a sloop from Nevis, and stealing Captain Stanley's boat."

However, given his reputation for treating captives well and having apologized to Captain Stanley "soon after committing the fact," Acosta was pardoned. "I am since glad that I did so," Molesworth added, because numerous Spanish governors had written to request his release. Acosta's galley was incorporated into the Royal Navy, though, "being very well fitted to clear the south cays and that part of Cuba from such enemies as destroy our trade and fishery."

*See also* Corso, Juan; *guardacostas;* Lilburne, Robert; Uraburru, Tomás.

*References:* Craton, *Bahamas; C.S.P., Amer. and W.I.,* Vols. XI–XII; Sáiz; Weddle, *Wilderness.*

# AERNOUTS, JURRIAEN
## (FL. 1674-1676)

Dutch corsair from Curaçao who mounted expeditions against the French in North America and the Caribbean.

His name is often misspelled in non-Dutch sources, appearing as "Jurrien Arian" in some French documents and "Jurian Aronson" in English ones. In early 1674, Aernouts was commissioned by Governor Jan Doncker of Curaçao to attack the English and French, with whom the Netherlands had been at war for the past two years. He ventured northward with his frigate *Vliegende Postpaard* (Flying Post Horse), arriving at New York in early July. This former Dutch colony had been reconquered by Cornelis Evertsen's naval expedition the previous summer, but Aernouts learned that the Treaty of Westminster had since been signed with England, whereby the province was to be restored to London. He therefore decided to attack the French possessions farther north in Acadia (present-day Maine and New Brunswick).

### NORTH AMERICAN CAMPAIGN
### (AUGUST 1674)

While preparing for this enterprise he met Captain John Rhoades of Boston, an experienced pilot who was well acquainted with the French settlements. Aernouts enlisted Rhoades and several other Americans, sailing into the Bay of Fundy to land 110 men. Advancing against the French stronghold of Penobscot (Pentagoët), they easily overwhelmed the thirty-man garrison on 11 August 1674 after a one-hour firefight. Governor Jacques de Chambly was captured with a musket wound in one arm, and the defenses thrown down. Aernouts buried two glass bottles on the site that contained a copy of his commission and an account of the conquest. He ravaged several smaller outposts before entering the Saint Jean River and seizing the secondary French fort at Jemsec. Lieutenant Governor Joybert de Marson was also taken, and another pair of bottles buried. Aernouts renamed the province New Holland, then retired to Boston.

Before departing for the Antilles, he appointed Rhoades acting governor of the colony on 11 September, furnishing him with two small, armed vessels. (The Massachusetts authorities would later disavow all knowledge of this arrangement, claiming that Aernouts denied having granted such patents, adding that he would not "make himself responsible for others' actions.") Rhoades and his subordinates Cornelis Andreson, Pieter Roderigo, and the Cornishman John Williams soon created frictions with their New England neighbors by impounding trading vessels and fishing boats in a misguided attempt to enforce Dutch jurisdiction. A retaliatory force sortied from Boston under Captain Samuel Moseley and captured the two coast guard vessels in the Bay of Fundy, bringing in their commanders to be tried for piracy at Cambridge, Massachusetts, in April 1675. Although initially condemned to death for piracy, Roderigo and the rest were eventually reprieved.

### WEST INDIAN CAMPAIGN
#### (SUMMER 1675)

Meanwhile, Aernouts had returned to the Caribbean, where the following summer he, along with Jan Erasmus Reyning and about 100 other Dutch raiders, made a descent on the French island of Grenada. They quickly occupied the principal fort but failed to notice the arrival of enemy reinforcements, who in turn besieged and starved them into submission. Aernouts, Reyning, and other captives were conveyed to Martinique aboard the warship *Émerillon* (Merlin) of Captain Chadeau de la Clicheterre. They succeeded in escaping from the plantation

where they were being held by drugging the guards' wine, then stealing a *piragua*. Seven desperate men laid in a course for Curaçao but nearly died when their boat was carried westward by the winds and current, landing them on Cora Island (in present-day Venezuela). They eventually succeeded in reaching Maracaibo, where they were briefly incarcerated by the Spaniards who, although common foes against the French, remained suspicious of any trespassers on their territory. In 1676, Aernouts and his companions were restored to Curaçao.

*See also* Andreson, Cornelis; Evertsen de Jongste, Cornelis; Moseley, Samuel; Reyning, Jan Erasmus; Rhoades, John; Roderigo, Pieter.

*References:* Chapin; *C.S.P., Amer. and W.I.,* Vol. IX; Vrijman; Webster.


# ALFORD, LEWIS
## (FL. 1659)

English privateer who was mentioned in the journal of Colonel Edward D'Oyley, governor of Jamaica, as having been issued a "let pass" on 7 November 1659 (O.S.).

*See also* D'Oyley, Edward.

*Reference:* Pawson, *Port Royal.*


# ALLARD, CAPTAIN
## (FL. 1672)

English privateer hired "to seek a trade" with the Spaniards.

Following the general recall of Jamaican commissions in 1671, in the aftermath of Henry Morgan's sack of Panama, the new governor, Sir Thomas Lynch, cast about for gainful employment for privateers thus left idled. Allard was one, hired in late January 1672 along with John Morris "at £80 a month" to attempt some clandestine trade with the Spaniards, as well as capture the Dutch rover "Captain Yellowes"— Jelles de Lecat—who was making a nuisance of himself as a Spanish *guardacosta* in the "Bay of Campeche," or Laguna de Términos.

*See also guardacostas;* Laguna de Términos; Lecat, Jelles de; Lynch, Sir Thomas; Morris, John.

*Reference: C.S.P., Amer. and W.I.,* Vol. IX.

# ALLEN, CAPTAIN

## (FL. 1660)

English privateer who was mentioned in the journal of Colonel Edward D'Oyley, governor of Jamaica, as having been issued a "let pass" for his ship *Thriver* on 1 April 1660 (O.S.).

*See also* D'Oyley, Edward.
*Reference:* Pawson, *Port Royal.*

# ALLISON, ROBERT

## ALSO ALLISTON OR ALLESTON
## (FL. 1679-1699)

English privateer who led John Coxon's vanguard at Portobelo and piloted the Scottish emigrants to Darien.

In late December 1679—after England had been at peace for several years and France and Spain were winding down their hostilities in the New World—Allison attended a gathering of privateers at Port Morant, off the southeastern tip of Jamaica. Present were his own sloop of 18 tons, no guns, and 24 men, along with the barks of Coxon, Cornelius Essex, and Bartholomew Sharpe, as well as the sloop of Thomas Magott. All five agreed to unite under Coxon's leadership for an assault on Spanish

Portobelo, despite having only the sketchiest authorization for such a venture. They quit Port Morant on 17 January 1680 and less than 20 miles out at sea met the brigantine of French *flibustier* Jean Rose, who also joined the enterprise. The weather turning foul, Coxon hailed his vessels to make for Isla Fuerte, 90 miles south–southwest of Cartagena on the Spanish Main. Whoever got there first was "to leave a note on the Sandy Point, to satisfy the rest."

Only Essex and Sharpe failed to keep the rendezvous, while "four *piraguas* and six very good large canoes" were captured at the nearby San Bernardo or "Friends" Islands to provide landing craft for the forthcoming disembarkation. Essex had meanwhile rejoined, and the formation then proceeded toward *Isla de Pinos* (Island of Pines), 130 miles east of Portobelo in the Archipelago de las Mulatas. Only Coxon's bark was able to shoulder through the contrary winds and gain this place, the rest being forced to put into *Isla de Oro* (Golden Island) some miles away. There the pirates befriended the local Indians until Coxon ordered 250 buccaneers into the boats to row westward along the coast to fall upon Portobelo before the Spaniards could learn of their presence.

Nearing their destination they came upon "a great ship riding at anchor," which proved to be that of *flibustier* Capitaine Lessone, who added 80 Frenchmen to the force. Shortly thereafter, the buccaneers slipped ashore at Puerto del Escribano in the Gulf of San Blas, proceeding afoot to avoid Spanish coastal watchers. They marched three days "without any food, and their feet cut with the rocks for want of shoes," until they came upon an Indian village three miles from Portobelo on the morning of 7 February 1680. A native boy spotted them and shouted *"¡Ladrones!"* (Thieves!), setting off at a run toward the distant city. Coxon immediately ordered Allison and his advance unit—known as the "forlorn"—to hurry in pursuit.

Allison's buccaneers trotted gamely, but the boy arrived half an hour before them and raised the alarm. The approaching pirates could hear a signal gun being fired, and "then certainly knew that we were decried." Nevertheless, the vanguard swept in with only five or six wounded, the Spaniards scurrying inside their citadel and leaving the raiders to ransack Portobelo unopposed over the next two days. The freebooters then retired ten miles northeastward, entrenching themselves with their booty and a few prisoners on a cay half a mile offshore from Bastimentos. Allison was again called upon to perform a singular service, being sent in a boat to recall the vessels from further up the coast. By the time he returned three days later, several hundred Spanish troops had appeared and were firing on the pirates from the beach but retreated at the sight of reinforcements.

The pirates briefly blockaded Portobelo, and by "keeping very good watch at topmast head," saw a ship arriving from Cartagena:

Our ships and sloops weighed and went out and met her, as she was standing into Portobelo. Captain Allison coming up with her first in his sloop engages her, and Coxon seconding him claps her aboard and takes her without loss of any men. Some Spaniards fell, for they fought about one hour.

The vessel proved to be a new 90-ton ship of eight guns with valuable cargo. A general distribution of booty was then made, resulting in shares of 100 pieces of eight per man. Afterward, the flotilla retired to careen at Bocas del Toro (literally "bull's mouths" or "entrances of the bull") located at the northwestern extremity of present-day Panama, where the privateers also found Captains Richard Sawkins and Peter Harris.

Once refitted, all the buccaneers except the French decided to return to Golden Island to have the Darien Indians guide them overland to Panama so they could attack the Spaniards on their Pacific flank. Coxon, Allison, Cooke, Harris, Magott, Sawkins, and Sharpe all anchored close inshore on Golden Island, out of sight in a small cove. A watch was left aboard each vessel, with orders to rally to Coxon's and Harris's—the two largest—if their ships should be discovered. At six o'clock on Monday morning, 15 April 1680, 332 buccaneers went ashore to cross the isthmus. (Among their number were William Dampier, Basil Ringrose, and Lionel Wafer, all of whom would later write accounts of these adventures.)

But Allison and Magott, "being sickly were unable to march" and so remained behind. The rest of the buccaneers reached the mainland and disappeared into the jungle, overrunning the inland town of Santa María at the confluence of the Chucunaque and Tuira Rivers ten days later. From there the buccaneers pushed on into the Pacific, although Coxon showed himself increasingly reluctant. By the time the pirates captured some Spanish coastal craft and bore down upon Panama City, command had devolved upon Harris, Sawkins, and Sharpe. Coxon returned to Golden Island with 70 loyal followers; it is possible that Allison then sailed away with him, as Coxon was seen passing Point Negril, Jamaica, in late May 1680 with two smaller vessels, which he abandoned upon being chased.

### DARIEN EXPEDITION
### (1698-1699)

Nothing more is known about Allison's movements for almost two decades. Then the Scottish ship *Unicorn* and its tender *Dolphin* anchored at Saint Thomas in the Danish Virgin Islands on 11 October 1698. They were part of a larger flotilla conducting 1,200 colonists to establish a new commercial settlement at Darien for the Company of Scotland. Its leaders were unfamiliar with the Spanish Main and therefore required a pilot; upon being directed to a tavern, they found Allison "now sadly old, white haired and garrulous." Nonetheless, he promised to guide them to their destination, and four days later they weighed.

Off Crab Island (Isla de Vieques, due east of Puerto Rico) they overtook the other three vessels of their group, and Allison went aboard the flagship *Saint Andrew* to direct the helmsmen. The passage proved slow and arduous, through torrential downpours and muddy seas, until the night of 26 October, when Allison felt that land was near. "About two o'clock this morning," a passenger observed, "we saw with the lightning black, high stones like land." Dawn revealed the Nuestra Señora de la Popa headland outside Cartagena. Two weeks later the ships reached Golden Island, and on 15 November the Scots went into a mainland harbor, renaming it Caledonia Bay.

Allison remained at the new settlement, which soon succumbed to disease, isolation, and strife. In late February 1699, he put to sea again as supercargo of the tender *Endeavour,* with orders to guide Captain John Anderson to Jamaica for provisions. A few days later they were driven back by gale winds. It is not known whether the old privateer survived the next four months before the Darien colony was evacuated.

*See also* careen; Coxon, John; Crab Island; Dampier, William; Essex, Cornelius; Golden Island; Harris, Peter (fl. 1671–1680); Lessone, Capitaine; Magott, Thomas; pieces of eight; Ringrose, Basil; Rose, Jean; Sawkins, Richard; Sharpe, Bartholomew; Spanish Main; Wafer, Lionel.

*References:* Bradley, *Lure;* Gosse, *Who's Who;* Jameson; Prebble.

# ALMIRANTA

Spanish term for "vice-flagship."

*Capitana* is the equivalent word for a flagship; the two are often confused by foreigners, as they seemingly reverse the natural order whereby captains are subordinate to admirals. However, when the expressions first appeared in medieval Spain, it was customary for fleets to be commanded by a *capitán general,* while the designation *almirante* was later adapted from the Arabic *al-amir* (the emir). To north Europeans, though, *admiral* only meant senior naval officer. Thus, for example, when the buccaneers under John Coxon, Richard Sawkins, and Bartholomew Sharpe captured a Spanish flotilla before Panama in early May 1680, they asked their prisoner Francisco de Peralta

> which was the best sailors. He told us on his word the [400-ton *Santísima*] *Trinidad* was the best in the South Seas, so we pitched on her for admiral [i.e., flagship].

*See also* capitana; Coxon, John; Sawkins, Richard; Sharpe, Bartholomew.

*Reference:* Jameson.

# ALVAREZ, AUGUSTÍN
## (FL. 1683-1684)

Corsair from Havana who made his most notorious depredations off Hispaniola and the Spanish Main.

In early July 1683 (30 June 1683 O.S.), the English bark of Captain Robert Glover departed Jamaica on a peacetime voyage to Curaçao. Traveling aboard was the wealthy Jewish merchant Benjamin Baruch Carvallo, a naturalized Englishman, who was fetching his family from that Dutch island. Upon passing Santo Domingo they were intercepted by the *barco luengo* of Alvarez, who "cruelly treated, tortured and robbed" Baruch until he agreed to pay a ransom of 22,000 pieces of eight at Curaçao. Alvarez and his 25 men—16 of whom were Dutch—proceeded southeastward until they, in turn, were attacked off Curaçao by another *barco luengo* of 50 men. The second Spaniard tried to board Alvarez's craft by grappling but lost ten men and its captain in the attempt. Alvarez's *barco luengo* was driven onto the rocks outside Caracas Baai on Curaçao, where he and his men continued to fight until the attackers withdrew.

The Dutch governor, Joan van Erpecum, learned of this and Alvarez's extortionate demands late that August, professing to be "much troubled" and sending officers to examine the matter. Eventually Baruch's ransom was reduced to 3,500 pieces of eight and paid by his friends, and Glover's bark released. Baruch complained bitterly to the governor, demanding compensation from Alvarez for his lost merchandise, at least, "but the agreement having been settled," Van Erpecum opined, "he spoke too late." The Spanish corsair was allowed to retain his ill-gotten gains, while the Dutch official was later criticized in both Holland and England for having struck such a deal despite holding Alvarez in his power.

HMS *Bonito*, of four guns, afterward retrieved Alvarez's boat and two Spaniards from Curaçao, bringing them into Port Royal on 27 February 1684. There the corsair was convicted of piracy in an English court, for he had also taken "a New England ketch in the high seas." Nevertheless, Governor Sir Thomas Lynch reprieved Alvarez because his original commission had been legitimate, and he also wanted "to see if his security in Havana will pay damages."

*See also* barco luengo; Hispaniola; pieces of eight; Spanish Main.

**References:** *C.S.P., Amer. and W.I.,* Vol. XI; Goslinga, *1680–1791.*

# AMBLIMONT, THOMAS-CLAUDE RENART DE FUCH-SAMBERG, MARQUIS D'

## (1642-1700)

French naval officer who threw back Michiel de Ruyter's massive assault on Martinique with a handful of defenders, later becoming governor general of the French Antilles.

D'Amblimont was born on 21 March 1642 at Mouzon in the Ardennes, France, descended from an ancient Saxon line. He entered the king's service as an infantry captain, transferring to the navy as a *lieutenant de vaisseau* (senior lieutenant) in November 1663. He was promoted to ship's captain six years later, and in 1674, during the second summer of the Franco-Dutch War, was lying at Fort Royal, Martinique, with his 44-gun warship *Jeux* (Games). At three o'clock on the afternoon of 19 July, 20 Dutch men o' war and 28 troop transports hove into view, bearing a landing force of 3,400 soldiers. The French had known of this approach, but their strength was concentrated up the coast at St. Pierre. Instead, De Ruyter bore directly down upon Fort Royal, then became becalmed.

During the night the French worked frantically to shore up their defenses. In addition to d'Amblimont's warship, they had the 22-gun merchantman *Saint Eustatius* (Saint Eustache) and four lesser vessels in the roads. A garrison of 161 men was hastily scraped together to work the batteries, and booms were placed across the harbor mouth. When the Dutch disembarked the following morning, they encountered a position of great natural strength. Fortifications sat high atop rocky cliffs, and the assault columns became embroiled in a crossfire between the batteries and d'Amblimont's ships. The attackers had no artillery, scaling ladders, or supporting bombardment, and discipline collapsed when a warehouse full of rum was breached.

The Dutch commanders attempted to regroup in the shelter of a nearby cliff, but d'Amblimont quickly landed half a dozen guns and opened fire on this new position. The attackers' will broke and the Dutch drew off, returning that afternoon for a second try. Again they suffered heavily from combined fire and retired to their transports in defeat. Against seemingly impossible odds, d'Amblimont and the other defenders had won a spectacular victory. They killed or wounded 574 Dutchmen, at a cost of only five dead and ten injured. (Their most prominent fatality was Guillaume d'Orange, one of the founding fathers of the French settlements in the West Indies.)

Fifteen years later, d'Amblimont again fought successfully against the Dutch, destroying a squadron of five ships before the Texel on 27 July 1689 while commanding the *Profond* (Deep). He was promoted to commodore *(chef d'escadre)* in January 1693 and four years afterward became governor general of the Antilles in succession to the comte de Blénac, dying at Fort Royal on 17 August 1700.

*See also* Blénac, Charles de Courbon, comte de.

*References:* Crouse; Taillemite.

# ANDREIS, BERNART

## (FL. 1692)

Captain, perhaps of German, Dutch, or Flemish origin, who served on English Jamaica.

On 19 September 1692 (O.S.), Andreis was appointed by the Jamaica council "to command any sloop or sloops employed against Nathaniel Grubbing." The latter was

an English renegade who had gone over to the French of Saint Domingue, and following the outbreak of the War of the League of Augsburg (known in America as King William's War, or to history as the Nine Years War), had begun leading them on harassing raids against northern Jamaica.

There is no evidence that Andreis succeeded in catching this turncoat, and the captain was involved a couple of months later in court-martial proceedings against some of his officers.

*See also* Grubbing, William.

*Reference: C.S.P., Amer. and W.I.*, Vol. XIII.

# ANDRESON, CORNELIS

## ALSO ANDRIESZOON
## (FL. 1674-1675)

Dutch privateer who was charged with piracy on the coast of Maine.

In the summer of 1674, a Dutch naval expedition out of Curaçao commanded by Jurriaen Aernouts conquered French Acadia, renaming it New Holland. Before returning to the Antilles, Aernouts appointed Captain John Rhoades of Boston as acting governor of the colony, furnishing him with two small, armed vessels for coast guard patrol: the *Edward and Thomas* of Captain Pieter Roderigo and the shallop *Penobscot* of Captain Cornelis Andreson. Long accustomed to trading and fishing off Acadia, New Englanders requested permission from the new administration to continue doing so but were refused. As England was neutral in the Franco-Dutch conflict, though, they ignored this ban until Roderigo and Andreson began impounding vessels.

Incensed, the New Englanders retaliated by branding these as piratical acts and called upon the Massachusetts council to take strong action. On 15 February 1675 (O.S.), Captain Samuel Moseley of the ketch

*Salisbury* was ordered to sortie from Boston and apprehend the transgressors. Once at sea he fell in with a French ship that was also hunting the Dutch vessels as enemy privateers, and together they came upon the *Edward and Thomas* and *Penobscot* in the Bay of Fundy, lying with their latest prize, the English bark *Philip* of Captain George Manning. Moseley and his French consort immediately engaged, and once the battle was joined, Manning turned the *Philip*'s guns on Roderigo and Andreson as well, so that between them all they quickly battered the Dutch pair into submission. Moseley then carried the *Edward and Thomas* and *Penobscot* into Boston on 2 April 1675 (O.S.).

Roderigo produced a commission with three seals in his defense, and Andreson "another without seals for liberty to trade, keep the country and sail on the coast." Nonetheless, they and four companions were tried for piracy at Cambridge, Massachusetts, and all except Andreson were sentenced to death (although soon pardoned). During the Indian conflict later that same summer known as "King Philip's War," Andreson fought very bravely in defense of the English colony. A contemporary letter states:

He pursued Philip so hard that he got his cap and now wears it. The general, finding him a brave man, sent him with a command of 12 men to scout, with orders to return in three hours on pain of death; he met 60 Indians hauling their canoes ashore: he killed 13 and took 8 alive, and pursued the rest as far as he could go . . . and on his return burnt all the canoes . . . and a short time after was sent out on a like design and brought in 12 Indians alive and two scalps.

**See also** Aernouts, Jurriaen; Moseley, Samuel; Rhoades, John; Roderigo, Pieter.
**References:** Chapin; *C.S.P., Amer. and W.I.,* Vol. IX; Gosse, *Who's Who;* Jameson; Webster.

# ANDRIESZOON, MICHIEL

## (FL. 1683-1686)

Dutch rover who operated out of French Saint Domingue, often as a confederate to Laurens de Graaf.

He was commonly referred to as "Capitaine Michel" or "l'Andresson" by his *flibustier* followers and "Michel" or "Mitchell" by the English. His first recorded activity occurred in early 1683, when he was lying off the Bay of Honduras with De Graaf. Six months previously, the Spanish man o' war *Princesa* or *Francesa* (former French *Dauphine* or "Princess") had been captured off Santo Domingo and was now being careened at Bonaco Island. The buccaneers were joined there in early April by another band of *flibustiers* commanded by Nikolaas van Hoorn, the "chevalier" de Grammont, and Jan Willems, who had come in quest of reinforcements for a major campaign against the Spaniards. Van Hoorn had been cheated out of a large consignment of slaves at Santo Domingo, for which the governor of Saint Domingue (Jacques Nepveu, sieur de Pouançay) had granted him a letter of reprisal, despite the official peace prevailing with Spain. De Graaf and Andrieszoon incorporated their men and ships into this expedition, rounding the Yucatán peninsula en masse five weeks later.

### SACK OF VERACRUZ
### (MAY 1683)

On the night of 17 May, 800 buccaneers slipped into the sleeping city of Veracruz and attacked at dawn. The Spanish garrison and citizenry were surprised in their beds, and every house was ransacked over the next four days. The pirates then withdrew offshore to Sacrificios Island with 4,000 captives, dividing their booty and awaiting ransoms from Mexico's interior. Two weeks later these were paid and, after herding 1,500 blacks and mulattos aboard as slaves, the 13 pirate vessels weighed. Just as they were standing out from the coast, they encountered the arriving plate fleet, whose commander, Admiral Diego Fernández de Zaldívar, deferred combat, thus allowing the raiders to escape.

The buccaneers paused at Coatzacoalcos to take on water before shouldering their way back around Yucatán to Isla Mujeres, where by late June 1683 they had finished distributing the spoils. Each went his separate way, with Andrieszoon, Willems, and others following De Graaf into the maze of islands off Cuba's southern coast. There they sold their goods, smuggling the profits into Jamaica. After a few months the pirate contingent stood away toward the Spanish Main, arriving near Cartagena in late November 1683.

## VICTORY AT CARTAGENA
### (CHRISTMAS 1683)

When the local Spanish governor, Juan de Pando Estrada, learned that they were before his harbor, he commandeered the private merchant ships *San Francisco,* of 40 guns; *Nuestra Señora de la Paz* (Our Lady of Peace), of 34 guns; and a 28-gun galliot to chase them away. This trio exited on 23 December 1683, manned by 800 soldiers and sailors under the command of Andrés de Pez. The resultant battle was scarcely what the Spaniards had envisioned—the seven smaller pirate ships swarmed all over them, and in the confusion, the *San Francisco* ran aground. The *Paz* struck after four hours' fight, and Willems captured the galliot. Ninety Spaniards were killed in the fray, as opposed to only 20 pirates.

The triumphant buccaneers refloated the *San Francisco,* which De Graaf appropriated as his new flagship, renaming it *Fortune;* Andrieszoon received command of the *Paz,* calling it *Mutine* (Rascal); and Willems was

given De Graaf's old *Francesa,* or *Dauphine.* On 25 December the victors deposited their captives ashore, then settled down to blockade the port. In mid-January 1684, a small convoy of English merchantmen arrived to deliver a consignment of slaves, and the pirates let them pass. De Graaf, Andrieszoon, and Willems also entered a joint arrangement on 18 January with a Dutch Jew named Diego Maget (or Marquet), who was traveling with the English, in which they agreed to buy a large quantity of wine and meat. Significantly, this was to be delivered from Port Royal, Jamaica, to Roatan.

Shortly thereafter, the pirates quit their blockade and headed northwestward. En route, De Graaf captured a 14-gun Spanish vessel, then touched at Roatan with his flotilla before continuing to the south coast of Cuba. There they intercepted a Spanish *aviso,* or dispatch vessel, bearing news that Spain and France were once again at war. Realizing that he could renew his French privateering commissions, De Graaf left Andrieszoon and Willems to prowl the Cuban coast while he sailed his 14-gun Spanish prize into Petit Goâve to obtain new patents.

## VIOLATION OF THE DUTCH
## WEST INDIAMEN
### (MAY 1684)

After parting company with their leader, Andrieszoon and Willems rounded western Cuba and took up station near Havana. On 18 May 1684, while opposite the tiny hamlet of Santa Lucía, they saw two large vessels approaching, which they intercepted. The strangers identified themselves as the Dutch West Indiamen *Stad Rotterdam* (City of Rotterdam) and *Elisabeth.* Despite Holland's neutrality in the conflict, Andrieszoon led an 80-man boarding party across in two boats to inspect the West Indiamen's cargos. He discovered that they had sailed from Cartagena three weeks earlier, and because of the protection afforded by Dutch colors, the Spaniards had placed a great deal of money and several passengers on board, including a bishop. Andrieszoon laid claim to half the 200,000 pesos and all Spanish nationals being carried, removing these over the masters' objections.

In a heated argument, the West India commanders allegedly declared that if they had realized Andrieszoon's intent, they would never have allowed him on board. The latter supposedly retorted that he was willing to rejoin his ships and fight it out, winner take all, but the Dutch masters demurred. Instead, they reputedly took revenge by concealing the money he left behind, later claiming that Andrieszoon had stolen it all.

### NEW ENGLAND VISIT
### (AUGUST 1684)

From Cuba, the pair of buccaneer vessels worked their way up the Atlantic seaboard, and by the end of August 1684, Governor Edward Cranfield of New Hampshire was reporting to London:

> Since my last a French privateer of 35 guns has arrived at Boston. I am credibly informed that they share £700 a man. The Bostoners no sooner heard of her off the coast than they dispatched a messenger and pilot to convoy her into port in defiance of the King's proclamation [of March 1684, prohibiting aid and abetment to such rovers]. The pirates are likely to leave the greatest part of their plate [i.e., silver] behind them, having bought up most of the choice goods in Boston. The ship is now fitting for another expedition.

This was Andrieszoon's *Mutine*.

Two days later the governor wrote again, giving further details of this and a second French privateer—Willems's *Dauphine*—that had appeared off that coast as well. Spanish escapees from the former had sought sanctuary in New Hampshire, "which they shall have and all friendship besides," Cranfield piously declared. They told him they had been taken off Cartagena "by the men who plundered Veracruz" and identified the ship refurbishing in Boston's dockyard by its former Spanish name of *La Paz;* the second ship they identified as the *Francesa* (which the governor misheard as *Francis)*. "They are both extraordinarily rich ships," Cranfield concluded, "chiefly through spoil of the Spaniards, though they have spared none that they have met at sea." Once Andrieszoon's ship had completed refitting, Willems's was to be repaired.

However, a couple of weeks later the king's latest proclamation against piracy was promulgated in Boston, leading Governor William Dyre to attempt to seize

> a privateer of the first magnitude, famous in bloodshed and robberies, called *La Trompeuse* (commanded by one Michel Andreson, Bhra, or Lavanza, a reputed Frenchman). I have moved for justice against him but have been delayed, and much discouraged and severely threatened by many, and more especially by one Mr. Samuel Shrimpton, a merchant of this place, to have my brains beat out or a stab for seizing the said ship. He has supplied, succored, countenanced and encouraged her, and taken her into his custody and keeping at Nodles Island, the place and receptacle of all piratical and uncustomed goods, also the guns, ammunition and all, though under seizure by myself for the King's use, resolving and boasting to defend the same and fit the ship out again. He has also received clandestinely great quantities of their gold, silver, jewels, and cacao within the compass of my seizure and claim.

Dyre was in fact confusing Andrieszoon with at least two other pirate leaders, first by referring to his ship as *Trompeuse* (Trickster), which had actually been Jean Hamlin's vessel, sunk the previous year at Saint Thomas in the Danish Virgin Islands. Second, appending the pseudonym "Bhra" to the Dutchman's name implied that he might be Thomas Paine's confederate Bréhal, guilty of helping to assault Saint Augustine in 1683. Dyre went on to list the 198 French, Scotch, Dutch, English, Spanish, Portuguese, black, Indian, mulatto, Swedish, Irish, Jersey, and New England men who comprised the *Mutine*'s crew, and ended by saying he was sending "great quantities of the piratical plundered gold" to London.

## RETURN TO THE SPANISH MAIN
### (JANUARY 1685)

As the governor anticipated, Andrieszoon emerged unscathed from this brief impoundment at Boston, and by the end of that year was back in the Antilles. He parted company with Willems to patrol the Cuban coast with his own *Mutine* and De Graaf's flagship *Neptune* (formerly *San Francisco*, which had only briefly borne the name *Fortune*) while his chief remained busy in Petit Goâve. During the first days of the new year, Andrieszoon shifted southeastward, leading a small flotilla of *flibustiers* to the Spanish Main, where De Graaf was to overtake them. Captains Jean Rose, Vigneron, La Garde, and an English trader joined the *Mutine* and *Neptune* in blockading those shores. The night of 17 January they espied a ship, which the following morning they challenged. The response was in French, but the stranger's lines were Spanish, so Rose opened fire. In the growing dawn, Andrieszoon recognized it as the 14-gun Spanish prize captured by De Graaf the year before, and so realized that they were engaging their commander.

The mistake corrected, the next day De Graaf ordered his formation toward Curaçao. At two o'clock that afternoon, while within sight of Bonaire, they sighted a Flemish ship out of La Guaira, which they chased and captured that evening. On 20 January 1685, De Graaf detached La Garde to request permission from Governor Joan van Erpecum of Curaçao to buy masts for his ship, replacing those lost in a storm off Saint Thomas. "This was flatly refused and the gates of the city closed," Ravenau de Lussan later wrote, because of the sacking of the two Dutch West Indiamen off Havana the year before. Nevertheless, a couple hundred buccaneers managed to slip ashore in small groups to enjoy a liberty, until they were discovered and driven out "by beating drums" four days later.

On 27 January, De Graaf set sail for Cape de la Vela (present-day Venezuela), arriving three days later and posting a lookout on the headland, while below his ships began careening. Rose meanwhile sailed down the coast to Ríohacha, attempting to deceive the Spaniards into thinking that he was a peaceful English trader, but met with no success. Returning empty-handed on 8 February, the pirates decided to split up. De Graaf wanted to organize another major venture such as his Veracruz raid, but not everyone was in accord. They therefore redistributed themselves around the vessels and separated. De Graaf laid in a course for the Gulf of Honduras with *Neptune,* while Andrieszoon remained off the Spanish Main with Rose, being spotted on 23 February 1685 near Palmas Islands, then putting into Golden Island four days later.

He and Rose had unsuccessfully chased a trading vessel from Santiago de Cuba as it neared Cartagena and now required water. But on Golden Island they found an excited band of *flibustiers* preparing to march across the Isthmus of Panama to attack the Spaniards in the South Seas. Rose and his

64 men decided to scuttle their ship and join this enterprise, while 118 of Andrieszoon's crew also enrolled. With his complement thus drastically reduced, Andrieszoon had little choice but to make for Saint Domingue.

## CUBAN OPERATIONS
### (SPRING 1685)

In early May (24 April 1685 O.S.), Lieutenant Governor Hender Molesworth of Jamaica noted that

> Captain Michel, a French privateer, was recently beaten off by the Spaniards from Darien with loss of his prizes. The French continue to issue commissions against the Spaniard, on pretence of damage done them by *piraguas* set out from Havana before the making of the recent truce in Europe.

Andrieszoon quickly resumed his roving, for three weeks after this first letter, Molesworth was writing in a second letter, "Michel, the privateer, is gone to the south cays of Cuba to take three Dutch ships that are trading there." The corsair unwittingly aided the Jamaicans when his patrol boats chased a suspicious sloop into a creek. This was the *Speedwell,* Francis Powell master, which had been seized by a Spanish *guardacosta* flying false English colors and intended for a raid on the coastal plantations of Jamaica, which scheme was frustrated when he drove it ashore.

It is quite probable that Andrieszoon then took part in De Graaf and Grammont's great enterprise against Campeche, as the pirates were already gathering on nearby Pinos Island for such a purpose. They eventually shifted to Isla Mujeres to fully marshal their strength.

## ASSAULT ON CAMPECHE
### (JULY 1685)

Hovering off Cape Catoche for more than a month, the buccaneers advised passing freebooters of their plan but also alerted the Spaniards. Late in June they moved—the pirate fleet of 6 large and 4 small ships, 6 sloops, and 17 *piraguas*—materializing half a dozen miles off Campeche the afternoon of 6 July. A landing force of 700 buccaneers rowed to shore and overran the city the following day. Its citadel held out for a week, after which the invaders remained in undisputed possession of the port for the next two months. But as most of the Spaniards' wealth had been withdrawn prior to the assault, little plunder was found. Captives were threatened with death if ransoms were not forthcoming, but Yucatán's Governor Juan Bruno Téllez de Guzmân prohibited any such payments. Finally, late in August the pirates evacuated the city after putting it to the torch.

Protests were duly lodged with the French Crown, and Governor Pierre-Paul Tarin de Cussy of Saint Domingue felt compelled to act against some of the returning *flibustiers.* In a letter to his Spanish counterpart at Santo Domingo dated 8 January 1686, he explained that the commissions he had previously issued were to expire on 18 March 1685, after which the holders might be regarded as pirates:

> In proof of which, having learned that the one named Michel was anchored seven leagues from Petit Goâve with a ship of 36 guns and 150 men, I went there myself with a king's frigate to disarm them, which they did; after which, having learned they wished to carry off said frigate to become pirates, I had them arrested and confiscated the said frigate, prohibiting any *flibustier* or settler [*habitant*] from exiting to go privateering, under penalty of corporeal punishment and confiscation of their goods.

The Spaniard, Captain General Andrés de Robles, dismissed this as a hollow gesture, pointing out that "those with whom you should make this demonstration are Captain Grammont and Lorenzo [De Graaf] who are the ones who most infest these seas and lands of the king my Lord." Indeed, it seems more than likely that Andrieszoon simply decided to retire from the sea and settle down on Saint Domingue at this time, which allowed the governor to record this to his advantage.

*See also* aviso; Bréhal, Capitaine; careen; De Graaf, Laurens Cornelis Boudewijn; Golden Island; Grammont, "chevalier" de; *guardacostas;* Hamlin, Jean; La Garde, Capitaine; Lussan, Ravenau de; Paine, Thomas; Pez y Malzárraga, Andrés de; Pouançay, Jacques Nepveu, sieur de; Rose, Jean; South Seas; Spanish Main; Van Hoorn, Nikolaas; Vigneron, Capitaine; Willems, Jan.

*References: C.S.P., Amer. and W.I.,* Vols. XI–XII; Juárez; Lugo; Lussan; Marley, *Veracruz.*

# Apostles

Seventeenth-century military slang for the charges carried in a bandolier or cartridge belt, perhaps because these usually numbered a dozen.

*Reference:* Pope.

# Archaimbaud, Capitaine

## (FL. 1681)

French *flibustier* who operated off the Spanish Main.

In early June 1681, Archaimbaud was lying at Springer's Key in the San Blas Islands north of Panama with his vessel of 8 guns and 40 men in the company of John Coxon, Jan Willems, Jean Rose, George

Wright, and three other captains. Capitaine Tristan then joined, having rescued John Cooke's band of rovers at nearby La Sound's Key, after raiding in the South Seas. Among this group was William Dampier, who recorded that after their initial greeting, they were disposed of in the following manner:

> Captain Archembo [*sic*] wanting men, we that came out of the South Seas must either sail with him or remain among the Indians. Indeed we found no cause to dislike the Captain, but his French seamen were the saddest creatures that ever I was among; for though we had bad weather that required many hands aloft, yet the biggest part of them never stirred out of their hammocks but to eat or ease themselves.

The buccaneer commanders decided to make a descent on the Central American coast, for which they sailed toward San Andrés Island to procure boats. A gale scattered the formation, and Wright chanced upon a Spanish tartan armed with four *pedreros,* or swivel guns, and 30 men. After an hour-long fight, he captured it and learned that it was part of a larger *armadilla* sent from Cartagena to drive the pirates away. Cooke, Dampier, and the other English rovers who had arrived from the South Seas

desired Captain Wright to fit up his prize the tartan and make a man o' war of her for us, which he at first seemed to decline, because he was settled among the French in Hispaniola, and was very well beloved both by the governor of Petit Goâve and all the gentry; and they would resent it ill that Captain Wright, who had no occasion of men, should be so unkind to Capitaine Archembo [*sic*] as to seduce his men from him.

Nevertheless, the English insisted, and Wright relented on condition they "should be under his command, as one ship's company." Cooke and his comrades therefore had their ship and shortly thereafter crossed to Bluefields on the Mosquito Coast, where they finally quit Archaimbaud's company.

*See also* armadilla; barco luengo; Cooke, John; Coxon, John; Dampier, William; Hispaniola; Lussan, Ravenau de; pedrero; Pouançay, Jacques Nepveu, sieur de; Rose, Jean; South Seas; Spanish Main; Tristan, Capitaine; Willems, Jan; Wright, George.

*References:* Dampier; Lussan.

# ARMADILLA

Diminutive of the Spanish word *armada,* which signifies a fleet of warships; *armadilla,* consequently, refers to a flotilla of smaller vessels.

The term was often misapplied in English. For example, when a group of stranded interlopers surrendered in May 1680 to Captain Felipe de la Barrera's patrol boats in Mexico's Laguna de Términos, a survivor later related how the Spaniards "drove the whole of the English on board two small *armadillas,* where they were immediately clapped in the hold." In fact there were only two small Spanish warships, comprising a single *armadilla.*

*See also* Barrera y Villegas, Felipe de la; Laguna de Términos.

*Reference: C.S.P., Amer. and W.I.,* Vol. XI.

# ASH, ISLE OF

English mispronunciation of "Ile-à-Vache" (literally "cow island"), the French name for the island located off the southwestern tip of modern Haiti, which was a favorite pirate lair.

In one of many instances, the seaman Thomas Phips described how his ship, the Royal African Company slaver *Thomas and William,* was intercepted by Jean Hamlin's *Trompeuse* in late October 1683 "off Hispaniola, near the Isle of Ash."

*See also* Hamlin, Jean; Hispaniola.
*Reference: C.S.P., Amer. and W.I.,* Vol. XI.

# ASIENTO

Any contract to supply the Spanish Crown or its dependencies, although foreigners in the seventeenth century came to misinterpret this as exclusively meaning the providing of African slaves for Spain's American markets.

Actually, every year the Spanish government entered into countless such arrangements, for items as diverse as gunpowder or ships' biscuits, leasing each individual *asiento* to the highest bidders, provided they were Spanish subjects. One of the few exceptions to this rule was the cruel business of supplying slaves for the empire, because the Spaniards themselves maintained no stations in West Africa. Thus, while the actual owner of the slave *asiento* might be a Spanish national, slaves would have to be furnished by an international cartel. The latter were doubly attracted to this New World traffic, for beyond its obvious profitability, their vessels also gained access to Spanish-American ports that otherwise were closed to them. Thus, exporting slaves promised a lucrative sideline in contraband goods.

Soon the *asiento* came to be synonymous with slaving, such as when in March 1684 Governor Sir Thomas Lynch of Jamaica learned of the arrival of a new Venetian factor at Cartagena, representing the Dutch cartel of Baltasar Coymans. "If we can get Negroes," the governor assured his superiors in London, "it is very likely that, let who will have the *asiento,* they will likely come to us."

**Reference:** *C.S.P., Amer. and W.I.,* Vol. XI.

# AVESILLA, ALONSO DE
## (D. 1683)

Spanish renegade who served the French of Saint Domingue against his countrymen.

Avesilla was originally from Saint Augustine, Florida, but changed sides for unknown reasons. When in early May 1686 the pirate galliot of Nicolas Brigaut made a descent on Matanzas, 15 miles south of Saint Augustine, the Spaniards became convinced that the hand of Avesilla lay behind it. The raiders ran aground on the bar at the mouth of the bay, forcing them to abandon ship and retreat along the coast in hopes of being rescued by their consorts. The governor of Saint Augustine sent a column of troops in pursuit, who overtook the French in the vicinity of present-day Daytona Beach, and massacred them almost to the last man.

One of three survivors was Brigaut, who was carried before the governor for interrogation. When asked if he knew of Avesilla, he "replied that he had known him well, before his death two-and-a-half years ago in Petit Goâve."

**See also** Brigaut, Nicolas.
**Reference:** Weddle, *Wilderness.*

# AVISO

Spanish word for a dispatch vessel or mail boat, derived from the verb *avisar,* to advise or forewarn.

Whenever a fleet was scheduled to depart or some major event was about to occur, it was customary to send an *aviso* to give notice. These were usually small private vessels hired for the voyage, and at busy ports such as Cadiz, Cartagena, or Veracruz, their departures became so regular that they constituted a semiofficial mail service. Once at sea, the *avisos* carried their dispatches in small wooden chests, which were to be weighted and thrown overboard at any threat of capture. Because attacks happened with such frequency during the seventeenth century, both Crown officials and private citizens routinely wrote letters in triplicate, or even quadruplicate, sending copies on successive *avisos* to ensure safe delivery. In one such instance recorded in June 1663, the Mexican diarist Gregorio Martín de Guijo noted how an *aviso* arrived, pursued by English buccaneers, but "Our Lord was pleased that while fleeing from the enemy, it ran aground at Antigua Veracruz and so the people and letters were saved."

From the Spanish, the expression passed into English. In late May 1678, for example, the inhabitants of Jamaica were alarmed by news that a huge French fleet was marshaling in the Windward Isles under Vice Admiral comte d'Estrées. Although England had been at peace for several years, the Dutch and Spanish continued to fight the French. Fearful that this vast armada might be intended against Jamaica because of unknown policy shifts in Europe, Lieutenant Governor Sir Henry Morgan imposed martial law, closed Port Royal, and sent the sloop of Captain Thomas Wigfall to Hispaniola for intelligence. The sloop returned a few days later, reporting that d'Estrées's force had been sailing toward Dutch Curaçao when it was lost on Aves Islands. A relieved Jamaican council voted "the advice sloop having returned from Hispaniola, that she have £20 and Mr. Wigfall £10 for his particular good service and readiness to obey the governor's orders."

A similar use was made in June 1693, when Benjamin Skutt petitioned the Crown in London, that in consequence of the losses of West Indian merchants, he may have a license for his advice boat of 150 tons and 16 guns to sail to and from Barbados, also a commission for her as a private man o' war, and immunity from embargo or press gang.

**See also** Estrées, Jean, comte d'; Hispaniola.
**References:** *C.S.P., Amer. and W.I.,* Vol. X and XIV; Guijo.

# AYLETT, CAPTAIN

## (FL. 1668-1669)

English privateer who commanded the 14-gun *Lilly.*

On 12 January 1669, eight English and French corsair captains met aboard Henry Morgan's *Oxford,* anchored off Ile-à-Vache at the southwestern tip of Saint Domingue, to decide on a descent against the Spaniards. They had already been mustering for several weeks and numbered 900 freebooters. Their strength was such that the captains agreed to attempt the great port of Cartagena on the Spanish Main, after which "they began on board the great ship to feast one another for joy of their new voyage."

Morgan and Captains Aylett, Bigford, Edward Collier, John Morris the Elder, John Morris the Younger, Thornbury, and Whiting all sat down to dinner on the quarterdeck, while the men celebrated on the forecastle. "They drank the health of the king of England and toasted their good success and fired off salvoes," as the tropical darkness fell. Suddenly the *Oxford*'s magazine accidentally exploded. Ship's surgeon Richard Browne, who sat toward the foot of the officer's table on the same side as Morgan, later wrote:

I was eating my dinner with the rest, when the mainmasts blew out and fell upon Captains Aylett, Bigford and others, and knocked them on the head.

Out of a company of more than 200, only six men and four boys survived, including the lucky few sitting beside the admiral on the quarterdeck.

**See also** Morris, John.
**References:** *C.S.P., Amer. and W.I.,* Vol. IX; Earle, *Panamá;* Exquemelin; Pope.

# AZOGUE

Spanish word for mercury, or quicksilver, but which also came to be applied to the ships that conveyed it across the Atlantic for the Crown.

Mercury was a vital ingredient for refining American ores during the seventeenth century; it was used to separate silver from other unwanted materials. Peru had its own source of *azogue* at Huancavelica, but Mexico's had to be imported from the royal mines of Almadén in southwestern Spain. A pair of merchantmen were usually hired for this duty, selected on the basis of strength, speed, and soundness, and they sailed independently of the annual plate fleets. These *azogue,* or quicksilver ships, proved to be valuable prizes, as their cargos were in great demand in Spanish America; also, they occasionally shipped part of the king's bullion on their return passage toward Spain. The *María* was such a vessel, outward bound from Seville with a lading of 1,000 quintals of mercury and other merchandise, when it was intercepted by the privateer Captain Cooper and carried into Port Royal, Jamaica, in October 1663.

**See also** Cooper, Captain.

# BAMFIELD, JOHN

## (FL. 1665)

English privateer who commanded the 1-gun *Mayflower* in Colonel Edward Morgan's expedition against Dutch Sint Eustatius and Sabá during the Second Anglo-Dutch War.

This force departed Jamaica in two divisions, five sail putting out of Port Royal on 5 April 1665, and Morgan himself following with another four on 28 April. There were 650 men in all, described in a letter by Governor Sir Thomas Modyford as

> chiefly reformed privateers, scarce a planter amongst them, being resolute fellows and well armed with *fusils* [Spanish word for muskets] and pistols.

The Crown official was particularly pleased they would be serving "at the old rate of no purchase, no pay, and it will cost the King nothing considerable, some powder and mortar pieces." Their landing was successfully made, but the colonel, "being a corpulent man," died from heat exertion during the chase, and his expedition disbanded shortly thereafter.

*See also* purchase.

*References:* Cruikshank; *Interesting Tracts;* Pope.

# BANNISTER, JOSEPH

## (FL. 1680-1687)

English sea captain turned pirate.

Bannister was first mentioned while lying in Port Royal on 23 March 1680 (O.S.), when the log of HMS *Hunter,* 28 guns, recorded:

> At six this morning the *Golden Fleece* of 30 guns, Captain Bannister commander, overset at an anchor in the harbor, no current nor wind, but her men going over her side to scrape her made a sally that the guns and other weight aloft gave way at once. The captain saved himself out of the mizzen shrouds; the purser, gunner and doctor, with five others and a Negro were drowned.

Helped by the *Hunter,* Bannister refloated his ship and the following spring was again bringing passengers into that port.

His notoriety dates from 11 June 1684, however, when out of financial hardship he "ran away" with *Golden Fleece.* Supposedly bound for New England, he instead assembled a crew out of sloops about Jamaica, 115 of "the veriest rogues in these Indies," according to the outraged governor, Sir Thomas Lynch. Lynch further believed that Bannister had procured a French privateering commission, despite this being prohibited to English subjects. Lynch wrote his counterpart, Pierre-Paul Tarin de Cussy, governor of Saint Domingue, beseeching him "to give none to Bannister, Coxon or any other Englishman." Within two months Bannister was caught when HMS *Ruby,* 48 guns, and *Bonito,* four, visited the Cayman Islands accompanied by a *barco luengo.* They found the *Golden Fleece* close inshore with its crew turtling and easily secured all hands. The night of 25 August, the prize was brought back into Port Royal, and an admiralty court soon convened. "We conclude they'll be found guilty of piracy," Lynch wrote his superiors.

Bannister was charged with securing a commission at Saint Domingue, it being a felony then under Jamaican law "for any person to serve under any foreign prince or state" as a means of restricting privateer activities. Bannister had approached the French governor for such a patent, but it had been denied him. He was then accused of unlawfully attacking Spaniards regardless, as two from a captured canoe had been found aboard his *Golden Fleece.* But Bannister contrived to borrow money and pay off the two prisoners, who swore "backward and forward" in court that they had not been held against their will. The trial ended with all charges dropped.

Lynch was a sick man, and his vexation at this verdict created "such disturbance of mind" that a week later he died. His successor, Lieutenant Governor Hender Molesworth, attempted to persuade the jury to reconsider its decision. Making no headway, he bound Bannister "over in good security" until another court could be convened. He was especially galled to hear that Bannister had "threatened Captain David Mitchell [of HMS *Ruby*] with an action for damages, as though he were the honestest man in the world." Meanwhile, Bannister fitted out *Golden Fleece* with "another master and sent the ship to London, but without profit; then he was in treaty with the Spaniards, but without success." These failures compounded Bannister's financial woes, leading him to rush the harbor mouth "in a desperate, resolute manner" one dark night in early February 1685. The land batteries reacted slowly because of "carelessness of the sentries and darkness of the night," only managing to strike *Golden Fleece* three times. Bannister had allegedly placed about 50 men in his hold, with "plugs of all sizes wherewith to stop any breach."

Furious, Molesworth sent *Bonito* in pursuit, which found itself "unable to do more against a ship of her size and strength" than fire a few warning rounds. He then sent Bannister a note saying that he would be treated as a pirate unless he returned. Bannister replied that he had "done no piratical act as yet and intended to do none, but his design was for the Bay of Honduras for logwood." This was disproved three months later, when Mitchell

saw Bannister's ship lying among a huge throng of freebooters off Ile-à-Vache. The corsair gathering included the "chevalier" de Grammont, Laurens de Graaf, and Jan Willems, whose collective strength intimidated even *Ruby*'s commander. Mitchell visited Grammont and asked that Bannister be arrested for serving under a foreign commission, but the *flibustier* insisted that the English renegade had not entered French service, and Mitchell "thought it best not to insist further."

The freebooters were actually assembling for a raid on the Mexican port of Campeche, and by early June had transferred to the Yucatán coast to finalize their arrangements. It is almost certain that Bannister was among the pirates who appeared before Campeche the afternoon of 6 July 1685, overrunning the city the following day. Such was the raiders' strength that they remained in undisputed possession until early September, by which time Campeche had been stripped bare. Booty divided among so many was disappointing, and the ships worked their way back around Yucatán to Isla Mujeres before dispersing.

Bannister continued upwind and was sighted to leeward of Jamaica in late November 1685. *Ruby* was being careened, so Mitchell hired two sloops and manned them from his own crew; but by the time they sortied, *Golden Fleece* had disappeared northeastward. On 20 January 1686, Governor de Cussy wrote his Spanish counterpart at Santo Domingo: "I have been advised one named Bannister has arrived at Petit Goâve, with a ship of 36 guns." The French official promised to disarm this vessel, or at least prevent it from sailing under French colors, but the Spaniard remained skeptical. Soon Bannister was operating out of Samaná Bay, snapping up prizes in the Mona Passage.

When news of his activity reached Jamaica in May 1686, Molesworth sent out

Captain Charles Talbot's HMS *Falcon* and Captain Thomas Spragge's HMS *Drake,* which had replaced *Ruby* on that station. The two caught Bannister on 4 July 1686 as he was preparing to careen in a deep bay along with a small prize. The corsair had mounted two batteries ashore and gave the English frigates a hostile reception. They fought as close in as the water would allow, sinking and beating "almost to pieces the buccaneer's ships." *Drake* suffered 13 killed and wounded and the *Falcon* 10 killed and wounded in an exchange that ended only when the attackers ran out of ammunition. Returning to Port Royal in early July, Talbot and Spragge were censured for not having utterly destroyed Bannister. They rearmed and went back to Samaná Bay, where they discovered that the renegade had torched his shattered *Golden Fleece,* then sailed away in his prize. (Five months later, the treasure hunter William Phips came upon the remains, describing it as "a wreck in four fathom water, and burnt down to her gundeck, judging her to be a ship about 400 tons. Likewise found two or three iron shot which had the broad arrow [the device of the Royal Navy] upon them.")

Bannister apparently fled to the Mosquito Coast with some followers under an assumed name but a few months later was captured by Spragge. Having specific instructions from Molesworth, the Royal Navy captain sailed back into Port Royal on 28 January 1687 (O.S.) with the corpses of Bannister and his lieutenants dangling from the yardarms of the *Drake.* The delighted governor declared this to be "a spectacle of great satisfaction to all good people, and of terror to the favorers of pirates."

*See also* barco luengo; careen; Coxon, John; De Graaf, Laurens Cornelis Boudewijn; Grammont, "chevalier" de; logwood; Lynch, Sir Thomas; Modyford, Sir Thomas; Willems, Jan.

*References:* C.S.P., Amer. and W.I., Vol. XI; Earle, *Treasure;* Gosse, *Who's Who;* Lugo; Pawson, *Port Royal.*

# BARCO LUENGO

### ALSO BARCO LONGO

Spanish expression that translated literally means "long boat," but in fact referred to a type of galliot or oared sailing vessel.

Because of their shallow draft and combined means of propulsion, these were ideally suited for service along West Indian shorelines. The *Santiago* was one such vessel, launched specifically at Anoeta outside San Sebastián, Spain, in May 1686, to accompany the Biscayan privateers to the New World. It measured roughly 51 feet (28 *codos*) along its keel, 16-1/2 feet in breadth; it was pierced for 32 sweeps, rated at 30 tons, and bore a crew of 53 men. Significantly, it was most often described as a *galera* or "galley," in the subsequent records of that expedition. The proliferation of *barcos luengo* in the Americas led to the expression entering the English language, with many different spellings.

*See also* Biscayan privateers.
*References:* Garmendia; Laburu.

# BARLOVENTO, ARMADA DE

Spanish naval squadron (the name literally means "windward fleet") that defended the Caribbean against pirates and smugglers.

The Spaniards had stationed war fleets in the Americas as early as the sixteenth century, but following the English seizure of Jamaica and other setbacks of the late 1650s, felt a permanent naval presence was required even in peacetime. Therefore, in 1663 Madrid sent a special agent to Amsterdam to arrange the construction of four new galleons to serve in American waters. Poor financing threatened this project, until the Crown promised officers' commissions to anyone willing to advance money back in Spain. Many of the Armada de Barlovento's first commanders were individuals bent on recouping these investments or otherwise profiting from service in the New World. Agustín de Diústegui obtained overall command of the squadron in return for a loan of 50,000 pesos plus the use of two of his frigates; other appointments, such as those of Flag Captain Mateo Alonso de Huidobro or Ship's Captain Antonio de Layseca y Alvarado, resulted from lesser sums.

### FIRST FLEET
### (1667-1669)

Early in May 1664 the first new galleon reached Spain from Amsterdam, followed a few months later by the other three. A long delay ensued before the squadron could depart for the Americas, by which time only two of the Dutch vessels remained under Diústegui's command: the 572-ton flagship *San Felipe* and the 507-ton vice-flagship *Nuestra Señora de la Concepción* (Our Lady of the Conception). On 21 July 1667 they sailed from Seville, accompanied by the 412-ton *Magdalena,* plus the frigates *Concepción* and *Nuestra Señora de la Soledad* (Our Lady of Solitude, alias *Marquesa* or "Marchioness"). The armada also transported a large quantity of *azogue,* or quicksilver, for the Mexican mines. More than 100 of its 963 officers and men deserted during a stopover at the Canary Islands after being paid.

On 27 August 1667, the five ships reached Puerto Rico, from where *San Felipe* and *Magdalena* proceeded to Veracruz to deliver their quicksilver. Second-in-command Alonso de Campos remained with the other three to patrol the coasts of Santo Domingo and southern Cuba. He captured a single

sloop out of Jamaica before rendezvousing with Diústegui at Havana in February 1668. The reassembled armada then sailed through the Antilles toward Caracas before returning to what was supposed to become its permanent home base of San Juan, Puerto Rico. Judging these port facilities inadequate, Diústegui transferred to Havana for repairs. The local Spanish-American authorities, for their part, considered the large armada ships too cumbersome to chase pirates, so the flagship and vice-flag were almost immediately recalled to Spain for duty in the renewed wars against France. *Magdalena* and the two frigates were to remain at Santo Domingo, reinforced by local auxiliaries.

This recall order reached the armada once more at Puerto Rico, and Diústegui instantly set sail for Veracruz to load the king's treasure for his return passage to Spain. Campos and the three smaller ships hovered off Cuba's Cape San Antonio, inspecting three English ships under Captain Francis Stuart, as well as a Dutch vessel, but letting all four go (allegedly in return for bribes). Campos then retired to Havana, where he learned that buccaneers had assaulted the south Cuban port of Trinidad. He sent his newly acquired frigate *Nuestra Señora de los Remedios* (Our Lady of Remedies) and *Marquesa* to Veracruz for reinforcements. The *Remedios* was wrecked less than 50 miles from Campeche, but when the survivors reached Veracruz they found the Mexican exchequer had purchased another frigate, the 218-ton *San Luis.* Together with *Marquesa,* this frigate carried almost 300 reinforcements back into Havana on 5 January 1669.

Meanwhile, Diústegui had sailed toward Spain, leaving Campos as senior armada commander amid news of Henry Morgan's attack on Portobelo. Campos sortied with *Magdalena, San Luis,* and *Marquesa,* laying in a course for Puerto Rico, where he heard of a large freebooter gathering at Ile-à-Vache. From a Dutch merchantman he met in the

Mona Passage, Campos learned that five French ships from Martinique were allegedly preparing to raid Santo Domingo. He therefore backtracked, arriving there on 25 March 1669, to reinforce its garrison. This report proved false, but he was then correctly informed that more than a dozen buccaneer sail had passed by Santo Domingo on their way toward the Spanish Main. Sailing in their wake, he heard from another Dutch merchantman that they were in the Lago de Maracaibo, where he arrived by mid-April.

Inside lay the flotilla of Morgan, who had landed to ransack the interior. Campos reoccupied the fort guarding the approaches; after several days, he lightened his warships and crossed over the bar. The armada had trapped the raiders inside, but at dawn on 27 April 1669 they were rushed by Morgan, who destroyed the *Magdalena* with a fireship. The *San Luis* of De Huidobro ran aground attempting to shelter by the fort and was deliberately set ablaze to prevent its capture, while the 50-ton *Soledad* was taken by the buccaneers, who then slipped past the fort and sailed off in triumph.

## SECOND FLEET
### (1677-1678)

Following this annihilation, a half-hearted attempt was made to reconstitute the armada three years later but was deferred when Spain once more fell into conflict with France. It was not until late 1676 that the impoverished Spanish Crown could assemble five ships for the Caribbean: the 450-ton flagship *San José, Santa Rosa María, y San Pedro de Alcántara,* which was purchased by the governor-designate of Venezuela, Francisco Alberró, on the understanding that it would transport him to his destination and be reimbursed out of local taxes; the 350-ton vice-flagship *Nuestra Señora de Aranzazu y San Lorenzo,* which was sold by Antonio de Astina on condition he

be appointed *almirante,* or second-in-command, of the armada and might recoup its value at Puerto Rico; the 240-ton *San Juan,* formerly the French *Dauphine* (Princess), which had been captured in the North Atlantic the previous year and was more commonly known as *Princesa* or *Francesa;* the 200-ton *Nuestra Señora del Camino,* purchased from Doña Gracia de Atocha; and the 200-ton *Santo Cristo del Buen Viaje* (alias *Mogoleño*) bought from Pedro de Castro.

The flagship *San José* sailed from Cadiz early the following year and deposited the new Venezuelan governor at Caracas on 6 July 1677. It remained there while the *Francesa, Camino,* and *Mogoleño* reached Cartagena a few days later, having quit Cadiz on 26 May. Captains José de Arizmendi, Felipe de Diústegui, and Francisco López de Gómara reported there to their new *capitán general* or armada commander-in-chief, Antonio de Quintana, a veteran officer who had directed Cartagena's *guardacostas* for the past 20 years. The trio was immediately dispatched, along with two merchantmen and 500 troops, to rescue the nearby city of Santa Marta, which had been surprised by a French contingent under Captains La Garde, Coxon, and Barnes. Quintana's flotilla supposedly bombarded the invaders before being driven off by a storm, but Spanish observers charged that the men o' war reluctantly engaged because they were laden with merchandise. By the time they returned to attack a few days later, the enemy had withdrawn, taking the city governor, bishop, and other prominent hostages with them.

The three armada ships then proceeded to Portobelo to deliver the king of Spain's dispatches (along with their own wares), retiring very worn to Cartagena. There were no repair facilities there, and the crews began to fall ill and desert, not having been paid and receiving a daily ration of only a "pound-and-a-half of cassava and 12 ounces of meat." In October the flagship *San José* at last stirred forth from Caracas, sailing to Santo Domingo and Campeche, where it deposited the governor-designate of Yucatán, Antonio de Layseca, before reaching Veracruz. The vice-flagship *Aranzazu* also departed Spain in October 1677, conveying a quicksilver consignment to Veracruz, where it joined the flag. Fear of the huge French fleets of the comte d'Estrées, as well as material deficiencies and personnel losses, kept both armada units mostly idled throughout all of 1678.

### CRUISES OF 1679-1681

Early in 1679, the two capital ships at Veracruz were reinforced by the frigate *Santo Cristo de San Román* (Holy Christ of San Román, the patron saint of Campeche, where it had been built) and the 650-ton *Urca* or cargo ship *San Juan Bautista, San Antonio, y San Cayetano,* which had been expropriated for illegal trading at Puerto Rico. The acting Mexican viceroy then purchased two 6-gun *pataches,* the *San Antonio y las Animas* and *Jesús, María y José,* to act as fleet auxiliaries and recruited 800 men. When word arrived that the French *flibustiers* under the "chevalier" de Grammont had assaulted Maracaibo, Astina sortied on 25 February 1679 but limped into Havana on the last day of March after being battered during his gulf crossing by a storm that ripped the mast from *San Antonio y las Animas* and forced it back into Campeche.

A few days later, the annual plate fleet arrived at the Cuban capital from Cartagena, accompanied by Quintana with the *Francesa, Camino,* and *Mogoleño.* The latter was broken up at the Havana yards and its crew incorporated into the armada flagship, so that on 14 May 1679 the commander-in-chief led *San José, Aranzazu, San Juan Bautista, Francesa,* and *Camino* out to sea. The French having long since

withdrawn from Maracaibo, Quintana's mission was now to deliver the annual payrolls, or *situados,* for the garrisons of Puerto Rico and Santo Domingo, then sweep the coasts of the Spanish Main for foreign interlopers. After visiting San Juan, Puerto Rico, the armada intercepted a French sloop out of Petit Goâve bearing a cargo of cacao toward Cuba. This vessel was seized, although an English sloop encountered a few days later was released.

The French prize was sold at Santo Domingo, and upon exiting, the armada captured the Dutch sloop *Tigre* (Tiger), with a crew of 18 men, and charged them with smuggling. While cruising the Spanish Main they sighted an abandoned 80-ton English pink, which they boarded. (This was the vessel of Edmond Cooke who, having been victimized by Spanish *guardacosta* Philip FitzGerald many years before, hid ashore rather than risk mistreatment. Angered at the loss of this second ship, he then turned pirate.) The armada reached Caracas's port of La Guaira on 14 July 1679 and used it as a base for forays along that coast. One involved the *San Juan Bautista* and *Francesa,* which almost captured the Dutch *Witte Lam* (White Lamb) of Pieter Markus at nearby Puerto Cabello. The *Aranzazu* and *Camino* also sailed to investigate reports of a buccaneer landing near the Carguao Valley, followed a few days later by *Tigre,* which had become incorporated into the armada. Shortly thereafter, the *Tigre* fell victim to French *flibustiers* under Laurens de Graaf.

Quintana's flotilla transported reinforcements to Araya, then Coro, before returning to patrol the coasts of Santo Domingo and Cuba. By late October 1679 the flagship and vice-flag had reentered Havana for refit, which proved to be lengthy. They did not sail again until 21 June 1680, when they crossed the Gulf of Mexico to Veracruz. There, Quintana resigned his command because of advanced age and was replaced by Andrés de Ochoa y Zárate. The new commander sortied 13 September, escorting the annual plate fleet across to Cuba, reaching Havana on 23 October. On 28 November, the reunited armada exited but was driven back by foul weather. A month later they departed again and prowled through Nevis, Saint Christopher, Saint Barthélemy, Saint Martin, and Anguilla before visiting Puerto Rico. They then continued for the Spanish Main but were struck by a storm off Santa Marta and limped into Cartagena with three damaged ships. Because of numerous reports of French and English privateers blockading Portobelo and crossing the Isthmus of Panama from Golden Island, a patrol was detached into that area but found nothing. Ochoa's five ships then weighed on 19 February 1681 to return to Veracruz, arriving late in May in poor shape, with only a tiny fishing boat as a token prize. The *Camino* was broken up and *Santo Cristo de San Román* underwent repairs, while on 4 August the other three again departed to escort a plate fleet across to Havana and remained there.

## THIRD FLEET
### (1682)

Meanwhile, more vessels had been raised in Europe, so in the spring of 1681 the 350-ton *Nuestra Señora de la Soledad,* purchased in Spain and commanded by Antonio de Olza, put into Santa Marta with troops, artillery, and ammunition. After delivering this consignment, Olza touched at Cartagena, from where *Soledad* was detached on 29 May 1681 to carry dispatches for Havana, then returned at the end of that year with 350 black slaves from Curaçao as laborers for Cartagena's fortifications. A new *capitana* and *almiranta* also arrived at La Guaira on the last days of 1681, having been built at Amsterdam. The flagship was the 650-ton *Santo Cristo de Burgos,* and the vice-flagship the 550-ton *Nuestra Señora de la Concepción,*

both manned by a total of 305 sailors and 413 marines under a new commander-in-chief, Juan de Peredo.

They had quit Cadiz on 16 October 1681 with a cargo of quicksilver, pausing at the Canary Islands to take on 800 Spanish soldiers. The latter were deposited at La Guaira, with a contingent being forwarded to Maracaibo in a hired ship, while the two men o' war continued toward Cartagena a month later. Peredo died shortly after arriving, so temporary command devolved upon Olza, who delegated his *Soledad* under Captain Andrés de Arriola to conduct the quicksilver to Veracruz, while the flagship and vice-flag visited Portobelo. But Olza also died shortly thereafter, leaving the armada without a leader until Ochoa could join them.

He departed Havana on 25 March 1682 with *San José, Aranzazu, San Juan Bautista,* and *Santo Cristo de San Román.* (*Francesa,* which was still being careened, was to follow under Captain Manuel Delgado, but when it sailed on 8 July with the payrolls for Puerto Rico and Santo Domingo, fell prey to the pirate De Graaf off Aguada.) Ochoa reached Cartagena in May to discover Peredo was dead, after which he found *Santo Cristo de Burgos* and *Concepción* lying at Portobelo in early June, their crews very sickly and poorly supplied. He therefore replaced them on that station with the smaller *Aranzazu* and *San Juan Bautista* (which mustered only 317 men between them), withdrawing the others to Cartagena.

Ochoa also wished to return to Veracruz, as in the interim he had been promoted to *castellano,* or garrison commander, for its island fortress of San Juan de Ulúa, and his armada ships needed refurbishing. He therefore sent the flagship and vice-flag into Havana under his second-in-command, De Astina, while he sailed *San José* and *Santo Cristo de San Román* to Veracruz, arriving in mid-August. Because of Peredo and Olza's untimely deaths, the Mexican viceroy persuaded Ochoa to stay on as armada commander until new replacements could be sent from Spain. He also added two auxiliaries to the fleet: the 335-ton *Nuestra Señora del Honhón* and a new 8-gun *Jesús, María y José* (alias *Sevillano*), which had been launched at Campeche.

### CRUISE OF 1683

Ochoa did not sortie from Veracruz until March 1683, crossing to Havana where he reunited most elements of his squadron. He sailed on 26 May 1683 with the flagship *Santo Cristo de Burgos*, vice-flag *Concepción*, *San José* as *gobierno*, *Soledad*, *Sevillano*, and *Santo Cristo de San Román*, manned by a total of 1,239 officers, marines, and sailors. Putting into San Juan, Puerto Rico, he received a report of a French squadron threatening Portobelo. *Sevillano* and *Santo Cristo de San Román* were detached to reinforce *Aranzazu* and *San Juan Bautista* on the Panamanian coast, while the rest of the armada swept through the Caribbean before retiring toward Veracruz.

This was one of the most successful cruises in the armada's history, with six vessels and 110 French and English prisoners taken. At first the prizes were innocuous: the tiny six-man sloop *Margaret* of William Roberts, supposedly bound from Curaçao to Bermuda but caught off Puerto Rico as a suspected smuggler, and the ketch of Peter Carr, sailing from New England for Curaçao, intercepted near Santo Domingo with a cargo of dry goods. However, on 4 August 1683 Ochoa seized the *Prophète Daniel* (Prophet Daniel) of Antoine Bernard and *Dauphin* (Prince) of Pierre d'Orange at Little Cayman and learned that they had taken part in a massive pirate assault on Veracruz. The Spanish prize *Nuestra Señora de Regla* was also recovered, having been set ablaze by its pirate captors with 90 slaves aboard, who managed to extinguish the flames. Hastening

back toward his base, Ochoa combed the Laguna de Términos during his passage, driving off the New Englander William "Jualen" and capturing five of his men ashore who had been poaching logwood.

But Veracruz lay in ruins when the armada arrived 22 August, and one in four of its 6,000 inhabitants had been carried off into bondage. There was bitterness at the belated return of the armada with its prizes, especially when citizens learned that they would have to buy back their own goods at public auction. The pirate captives were executed, and the smugglers retained ashore.

### TAMPICO FORAY
### (MAY 1684)

Demoralized, Ochoa remained at Veracruz until 29 April of the following year, when news was received of a pirate attack six days earlier against Tampico, 300 miles up the gulf coast. Part of the armada sortied on 4 May 1684 and four days later caught the frigate *Presbyter* and a small sloop still inside the Tampico bar, with 104 freebooters. The original attackers had consisted of three frigates and eight sloops, which had come from New Providence in the Bahamas under Captain John Markham and others but had mostly dispersed by the time Ochoa arrived. The captives—77 Englishmen and New Englanders, 26 Dutchmen, and a Spaniard—included some who had participated in the sack of Veracruz. Upon returning to base two weeks later, 13 of the Englishmen and the Spaniard were sentenced to death; this was carried out on the Veracruz waterfront the morning of 14 June 1684.

Despite this isolated victory, the armada remained an object of universal scorn, and in Spain, Francisco García Galán was proposing that its elephantine flagship and vice-flag be replaced by his more nimble Biscayan privateers. Meanwhile, the *San José* had been broken up at Veracruz, followed shortly thereafter by *Aranzazu* at Portobelo. Ochoa did not put to sea again until April 1685, when he escorted two homeward-bound *azogues* across to Havana with *Santo Cristo de Burgos, Concepción, Honhón, Sevillano,* and the new tender *Santo Cristo y las Animas.* Upon arriving he was ordered to the Spanish Main because of the incursions of Peter Harris (the Younger), François Grogniet, Jean Rose, and others across the Isthmus of Panama. The armada reached Cartagena at the beginning of June but found hostilities well beyond their reach in the South Seas.

While lying at Cartagena, word arrived that the pirates "chevalier" de Grammont and De Graaf had captured the Mexican port of Campeche. Ochoa was to intercept and punish them as they withdrew. He set sail on 2 August 1685 with his flagship, vice-flag, *Soledad, Honhón, Sevillano,* an auxiliary called *Santo Cristo de Leso,* and a supply pink recently arrived from Spain. The latter separated the second night, and Ochoa wasted the next day trying to find it. Then *Soledad*'s mainmast collapsed, leaving it astern; and the night of 5 August, the *Santo Cristo de Leso* also became lost. The remainder of the armada checked the Cayman Islands for pirates before touching at Trujillo (in present-day Honduras) on 17 August. The buccaneer lair of Roatan was inspected offshore but found uninhabited. Ochoa then repaired to Trujillo for fresh provisions before resuming his course northward on 8 September.

## FAILURE AT ALACRÁN REEF
### (SEPTEMBER 1685)

At dawn three days later, five sail were sighted near Isla Mujeres off the Yucatán coast, and the armada gave chase. Two lagged behind and were captured, proving to be the corsair Pierre Bot's 22-gun *Nuestra Señora de Regla* and a sloop, which had been dividing the spoils of Campeche. With them was De Graaf's *Neptune.* The Spaniards desperately

hoped to take De Graaf, the greatest pirate of his day. They lost sight of him while securing their prizes and scuttling the sloop, but at two o'clock the following afternoon spotted more sail to the northwest. Ochoa sent *Honhón* and *Sevillano* to investigate; they recognized the largest of the vessels as De Graaf's, so *Honhón* shadowed while *Sevillano* returned to report.

By nightfall, *Honhón* lost contact, and the following morning made off toward Veracruz. *Sevillano,* however, regained *Santo Cristo de Burgos* and *Concepción* and led them toward De Graaf. At four o'clock on the afternoon of 13 September, they spotted him to the east of Alacrán Reef, and the two warships gradually closed on the heavily laden corsair. Enjoying both the advantage of the wind and a two-to-one superiority, Ochoa joined battle at dawn on 14 September 1685, despite being so infirm as to lie under an awning on his own quarterdeck. De Graaf fought his ship brilliantly, outmaneuvering and outshooting the Spaniards until nightfall. After dark the flagship hailed *almirante* Astina aboard *Concepción* to advise him that Ochoa had been given last rites and that command of the armada was now his. The next morning, *Neptune* was to windward, and as it fled, the battered armada gave up. Only Ensign Pedro de Iriarte, prizemaster aboard the *Regla,* argued in favor of renewing the pursuit, adding, "What would be said of them in Veracruz, and that he wished to be landed far from port, where the people could not see him." But the matter was decided when the flagship's weakened superstructure fell overboard.

Ochoa died two days later, and Astina limped back into Veracruz with his four vessels on the night of 28 September 1685. Having failed to check small, nimble corsairs, the armada ships had also shown themselves incapable of subduing larger opponents. A series of courts-martial ensued for Astina and the other senior officers, while back in Spain the Biscayan privateers were authorized to raise a private squadron.

## Search for La Salle and other Cruises (1685-1687)

From Bot and the other prisoners, the Spanish authorities learned that a French colonizing expedition had settled on the northern shores of the Gulf of Mexico the previous year under René Robert Cavelier, sieur de La Salle. Alarmed at this impingement on their territory, they detached the chief pilot of the *Soledad,* Juan Enríquez Barroto, and Antonio Romero of the *Concepción* to make a reconnaissance from Havana. They sailed from Veracruz on 21 November 1685 aboard Gaspar de Acosta's *Nuestra Señora del Carmen,* reaching the Cuban capital on 3 December. They hired a small frigate and explored the gulf coast, returning to Veracruz on 13 March 1686 without sighting any settlement.

Meanwhile, the courts-martial had been held and, although Astina had been sentenced to a two-year suspension of duties, he remained in command of the armada for lack of a substitute. The *Soledad* and *Honhón* had been sold off, while *Sevillano* sank at anchor during a norther. Captain Benito Alonso Barroso made a sally with the prize *Regla* (now incorporated into the armada), capturing a smuggler with an English and Dutch crew off Coatzacoalcos in April 1686. Then on 6 May, Astina sortied with his flagship, vice-flag, and *Regla* to escort the quicksilver ship *Santa Teresa* across to Havana. After completing this mission, he searched the Laguna de Términos, Isla Mujeres, Guanaja, Utila, and Roatan, returning to Veracruz more than four months later "mortified at not having found enemies with which to have encounters." A lengthy refit followed, further delayed when Captain

Francisco López de Gómara's pink, sent to Havana for spars, sank in a storm.

A second exploratory expedition was also organized with two specially constructed *piraguas*—*Nuestra Señora del Rosario* (Our Lady of the Rosary), commanded by Captain Martín de Rivas, and *Nuestra Señora de la Esperanza* (Our Lady of Hope), under Pedro de Iriarte. In addition to the two officers, the armada furnished 130 crewmen for these craft, which departed Veracruz in search of La Salle on Christmas Day 1686. The remaining men rioted several months later, in May 1687, angered at their lack of pay, enforced idleness, and the arrival of Biscayan privateers at Veracruz. Some 200 armada sailors and marines deserted en masse, and the rest were put down, with three fatalities. In order to keep them occupied, the flagship *Regla* and tender *Santo Cristo de Leso* put out on 14 June 1687, carrying the *situados* for Havana, Puerto Rico, and Santo Domingo. They sailed under Captain Andrés de Arriola, because Astina's suspension from duties had taken effect. (He spent it commanding one of the Pacific galleons that annually plied between Acapulco and Manila, making the fastest crossing in history.) The *Santo Cristo de San Román* and a *patache* also departed, under Captains Francisco Francisco López de Gómara and Andrés de Pez, as a third exploratory expedition for the Mississippi.

## Fourth Fleet (1687-1689)

In mid-September 1687, the new armada commander-in-chief, Jacinto Lope Gijón, escorting the plate fleet from Spain with his 300-ton frigates *San José* (alias *Marabuto)* and *San Nicolás,* arrived at Veracruz. After a few local forays, he sailed again on 29 June 1688, convoying the plate fleet across to Havana with his flagship *Santo Cristo de Burgos,* vice-flag *Marabuto, San Nicolás* as *gobierno* (under his son Sebastián Gijón), *Regla* commanded by Arriola, the auxiliary *Santo Cristo de San Román,* and two *piraguas.* They reached the Cuban port 40 days later, where they paused briefly before continuing to Aguada, Puerto Rico, with the *situados.* Here Gijón fell into a dispute with Governor Gaspar Martínez de Andino, refusing to help drive foreign interlopers from Vieques Island. Instead, he set sail for Santo Domingo on 29 September 1688, anchoring in Ocoa Bay while *Regla* and *Santo Cristo de San Román* entered to deliver the *situados.*

The armada then cleared toward the Spanish Main, arriving off Santa Marta and learning of a Dutch intruder near that coast. Arriola captured this vessel, which proved to be of 250 tons and 24 guns, so he incorporated it into the squadron with the name *San Francisco Xavier.* After touching at Cartagena, Gijón joined the annual *galeones* at Portobelo. In the latter days of 1688 his warships patrolled off Golden and Santa Catalina Islands, finding them uninhabited except for a small ketch at the latter place, which was captured. The armada returned to Veracruz in early January 1689, where it underwent a lengthy overhaul. *Santo Cristo de Burgos, Regla,* and *Santo Cristo de Leso* were all retired, leaving *Marabuto* as flagship, *San Nicolás, San Francisco Xavier,* and *Santo Cristo de San Román.*

Gijón did not sortie again until 30 July 1689, by which time news of the outbreak of the War of the League of Augsburg (King William's War) had reached New Spain. He convoyed two quicksilver ships across to Havana, afterward proceeding to San Juan, Puerto Rico, to deliver *situados.* Arriving 9 November, he was again enjoined to clear Vieques Island, for which he detached the men o' war of Sebastián Gijón and Pedro de Astina to make a reconnaissance. They found only abandoned huts, which they torched before the armada called at Santo Domingo with the remaining *situados,* then prowled the southern Cuban coast from Cape Cruz

past the Cayman Islands to Cape Catoche. After passing Campeche, they returned to Veracruz in early February 1690.

### FIRST SAINT DOMINGUE CAMPAIGN (1690-1691)

The new 140-ton *Nuestra Señora de la Concepción,* built at Campeche, was incorporated into the armada there, and Gijón put to sea once more on 19 July 1690. His flagship *Marabuto* was followed by vice-flag *San Francisco Xavier,* under López de Gómara; *San Nicolás* of Bartolomé de Villar; *Concepción,* commanded by Sebastián Gijón; and *Santo Cristo de San Román,* with a total complement of 827 men. The squadron accompanied the outward-bound Spanish plate fleet to Havana, then proceeded to Puerto Rico with *situados.* On 9 November 1690 Gijón reached Santo Domingo with a French prize of 16 guns to find the inhabitants in an uproar. An army under Pierre-Paul Tarin de Cussy, governor of the French half of the island, had recently occupied the inland town of Santiago de los Caballeros.

Faced with this crisis, the Spaniards were galvanized into action. A host of volunteers had already been mustered and trooped aboard the armada vessels. They departed on 21 December, circling eastward around the island, while another Spanish army advanced overland. The two met near Manzanillo Bay, and after landing were confronted by De Cussy, with inferior numbers. At the Battle of La Limonade on 21 January 1691, the invaders won a crushing victory, killing the French governor and more than 400 followers, against only 47 Spanish dead. The attackers then rampaged throughout the island, making off with 130 slaves and two vessels from Saint Malo of 28 and 24 guns, while burning several more. Flushed with this victory, the armada returned to Veracruz on 10 March 1691.

## CRUISES
### (1691-1693)

Gijón retired on this note, being then 70 years of age, and was replaced temporarily by Antonio de Astina, who had completed his two-year suspension from duty. After a refit, Astina sortied on 16 August 1691, escorting a plate fleet across to Havana. Arriving 6 September, he continued to Puerto Rico with *situados,* then departed San Juan on 16 October for Santo Domingo. Another expedition was being contemplated against French Saint Domingue but failed to materialize. Astina remained at anchor there until April 1692, when he sailed down the Cuban coast and reached Veracruz on the last day of May. The armada was now in desperate need of an overhaul, so one of the Saint Malo prizes (now renamed *Nuestra Señora de Atocha y Santo Tomás)* was sent to the Campeche yards, while others were repaired at Veracruz.

On 19 October 1692, Astina sailed with *San Nicolás, Concepción,* and *Santo Cristo de San Román* toward Havana, bearing the annual *situados.* He arrived a month later, and on 24 November his ships were damaged by a hurricane while in port. He departed for Puerto Rico in December, remaining at San Juan all of January 1693. He then continued to Santo Domingo, anchoring in Ocoa Bay while *Santo Cristo de San Román* stood into the capital with the payrolls. While waiting, Astina learned of a Dutch smuggler in the Macorís River, and sent *Concepción,* under Captain Tomás de Torres, with a sloop and two launches, to intercept. The interloper put up a stout resistance and was consumed in flames along with *Concepción*—49 Zeeland sailors perished in the action. The Spaniards were only able to raise 8 guns from the wreckage of both vessels.

Astina sailed to Santa Marta on the Spanish Main, then entered Cartagena on 14 March 1693. He made a sweep toward Portobelo, seizing a French *piragua* with seven crew members before returning to Cartagena. He quit the Spanish Main for Cape Catoche and Campeche, entering Veracruz on 8 May 1693. During his absence he had been superseded and the armada reconstituted.

## FIFTH FLEET
### (1693-1694)

On 23 October 1692, four days after Astina's departure, Francisco de Vivero Galindo had arrived in New Spain with the plate fleet, as new armada commander-in-chief. The local authorities assembled a force by purchasing the 450-ton, South American–built *Santo Cristo de Maracaibo* and Mexican-built *Nuestra Señora de Guadalupe* (alias *Tocoluta),* both part of that year's plate fleet, to serve with the armada. Vivero sailed on 14 July 1693 with his flag aboard *Maracaibo* and *San Nicolás* as vice-flag, accompanied by *Guadalupe, Atocha,* and *Santo Cristo de San Román.* His mission was to convoy the homeward-bound plate fleet, as well as deliver *situados* to Puerto Rico and Santo Domingo, then join a combined Anglo-Spanish assault against French Saint Domingue.

Reaching Havana on 11 August, he continued toward Puerto Rico but was struck by a hurricane in early September while traversing the Old Bahama Channel. *Atocha* and *Santo Cristo de San Román* were lost, and the remaining three vessels limped into San Juan badly damaged. After repairs, Vivero hastened to Santo Domingo, only to learn that the anticipated union with an English expedition had been canceled because the latter had returned to Europe after failing to overrun Martinique. Vivero therefore proceeded to the Spanish Main, making several small captures between

Cartagena and Portobelo before returning to Veracruz on 14 April 1694.

## SECOND SAINT DOMINGUE CAMPAIGN
### (1695)

During the next several months, both Vivero and Astina fell sick and died early the following year. When the three armada ships next put to sea in January 1695, they were commanded by Francisco Cortés. He deposited a *situado* at Havana, then reconnoitered Danish Saint Thomas in the Virgin Islands before putting into Puerto Rico. Crossing to Santo Domingo, he joined up with 24 vessels and almost 1,000 troops brought out from England by Colonel Luke Lillingston and Commodore Robert Wilmot. A large Spanish contingent from Santo Domingo also had assembled, so on 15 May 1695 this huge force descended on Cap François (modern-day Cap Haïtien), pushing aside the heavily outnumbered French defenders. One month later the invaders had fought their way to Port-de-Paix, besieging the garrison until 15 July, when they were annihilated. After leveling the town, the English and Spanish withdrew on 27 July.

Cortés's trio carried the Spanish wounded back along the northern shore as far as Guanaxibez before depositing them ashore and running downwind to Cuba. After patrolling the southern coast, the armada touched at Cape Catoche and Tabasco before reentering Veracruz on 2 September 1695. There they found three new men o' war awaiting them: *Santísima Trinidad y Nuestra Señora de Atocha,* 52 guns and 500 tons, built at Campeche; *Nuestra Señora del Rosario y Santiago,* 44 guns and 450 tons, launched at Alvarado; and *Natividad de Nuestro Señor Jesucristo* (Nativity of Our Lord Jesus Christ), a Dutch prize so called because it had been captured off Cartagena on

Christmas Day 1692 and was now being converted into the armada storeship, or *urca*.

## DEFEAT BEFORE SANTO DOMINGO
### (1697)

The armada soon received new senior officers as well when Andrés de Pez and Guillermo Murphy arrived 28 September aboard the plate fleet, the former to serve as commander-in-chief and the second as *almirante*. After a lengthy delay, the armada finally sailed on 4 August 1696, consisting of *Trinidad* (flag) with 56 guns and 350 men, *Maracaibo* with 46 guns and 250 men, *Rosario* with 42 guns and 240 men, *Guadalupe* with 26 guns and 130 men, and the recently launched *Jesús, María, y José* with 22 guns and 100 men. These vessels escorted the 26 sail of two plate fleets across to Havana, arriving 25 August. Traditionally the armada was to remain in company with the plate fleet until it entered the Straits of Florida on its homeward leg, but after a long layover, Pez decided to proceed alone.

He quit Havana on 11 November 1696, standing toward Puerto Rico, which was reached 15 December. On 29 December the armada departed for Santo Domingo, intercepting en route the French merchantmen *Saint Louis* and *Americaine*. On the morning of 6 January 1697, off Caucedo Point, four large sail were sighted, and the armada bore down upon the wind. The strangers hoisted English and Dutch colors, and after sending an officer aboard to make an inspection, Pez continued his voyage. However, he had been duped; the ships were actually the French royal warships *Bourbon,* 58 guns; *Bon,* 52 guns; *Favorite,* 36 guns; and *Badine* (Playful), 24 guns. They stole down upon his formation that night with the weather gauge, and the armada scattered in panic. Pez himself made directly toward Cuba, while Murphy's *Maracaibo* was captured, *Guadalupe* and *Jesús María* fled inshore, and Francisco Buitrón's *Rosario* headed for Santa Marta. Pez returned to Veracruz on 5 April 1697, having failed to deliver all his *situados* or reach the Spanish Main.

Almost a year later he sailed again, peace having meanwhile been declared in Europe. On 28 May 1698 he left Veracruz with *Trinidad, Rosario, Guadalupe,* and the 6-gun sloop *San José y las Animas,* with a total of 670 men, to escort another plate fleet across to Havana. He remained in the Cuban capital most of July before conducting the plate fleet out into the straits. He intercepted a small English brigantine, which he carried into Santiago, and from there his armada reconnoitered Saint Thomas before making a lengthy layover in San Juan, Puerto Rico. The armada visited Santo Domingo before heading for the Spanish Main, calling at Margarita, Araya, Cumaná, La Guaira, Ríohacha, and Santa Marta (where a small sloop was seized) before reaching Cartagena.

### DARIEN CAMPAIGN
#### (1699)

Following his arrival, Pez received intelligence of a new Scottish settlement at Darien. After attempting to reinforce the armada at Cartagena, he sailed for Portobelo, which he reached on 16 January 1699. Convinced that his four warships were inadequate for a seaborne assault, he instead proposed leading 500 men over the Isthmus of Panama to form the nucleus of a land attack. This was agreed to by the president of Panama, conde de Canillas, who added two companies of regulars to the expedition. Pez and his men left Panama on 9 March, gathering volunteers as they advanced. However, the jungle trails grew increasingly difficult, particularly when the rains set in, and progress halted two leagues short of their objective.

Pez was hurried in his retreat by rumors of an English squadron approaching Portobelo, where he had left the armada careening its vessels. This threat never materialized, but he had lost 90 men through desertion and another 80 to illness. Despite being ordered by Canillas to remain at anchor, Pez chose to sail to Cartagena that summer, arriving late in July. News was received that the Scots had abandoned Darien because of disease, so he was free to return to Veracruz. Upon reaching New Spain on 24 August 1699, however, Pez found that he was to be tried along with Murphy for the loss of *Rosario.* Both were incarcerated on San Juan de Ulúa to await transportation to Spain, while Buitrón assumed temporary command of the armada's remnants.

***See also*** Acosta, Gaspar de; *almiranta; azogue;* Barnes, Captain; Bernard, Antoine; Biscayan privateers; Bot, Pierre; Campos y Espinosa, Alonso de; *capitana;* cassava; Castro, Pedro de; Cooke, Edmond; Coxon, John; De Graaf, Laurens Cornelis Boudewijn; Estrées, Jean, comte d'; FitzGerald, Philip; Galán, Francisco; *galeones;* Golden Island; Grammont, "chevalier" de; Grogniet, Capitaine; *guardacostas;* Harris, Peter (fl. 1684–1686); Huidobro, Mateo Alonso de; La Garde, Capitaine; Laguna de Términos; Layseca y Alvarado, Antonio de; logwood; Markham, John; Orange, Pierre d'; *patache;* Pez y Malzárraga, Andrés de; Rose, Jean; South Seas; Spanish Main.

***References:*** Exquemelin; Prebble; Robles; Rodríguez, *1655;* Sáiz; Torres; Weddle, *Wilderness.*

# BARNES, WILLIAM
## (FL. 1676-1677)

English privateer who served under French colors.

Barnes presumably participated in the Third Anglo-Dutch War but shifted allegiance to the French once England withdrew from the hostilities in spring 1674. As such, he became one of those captains who embarrassed the Crown by continuing depredations against the Spanish and Dutch even after England's declaration of peace, leading to diplomatic protests on account of his nationality. On 22 November 1676 (O.S.), Barnes was identified by Governor Sir William Stapleton of the Leeward Islands as operating a vessel "with 12 guns and 150 men" in that region.

In June 1677, Barnes joined French Capitaine La Garde and John Coxon in a descent against Santa Marta on the Spanish Main. The *flibustier* force surprised the town at dawn and took many captives, including the governor and bishop, holding them for ransom until a trio of Spanish warships of the Armada de Barlovento appeared from Cartagena with 500 soldiers to drive them off. The raiders then retired toward Port Royal, Jamaica, and on 28 July 1677 Sir Thomas Lynch noted:

Five or six French and English privateers lately come to Jamaica from taking Santa Marta, Barnes being one and Coxon expected every hour. On board the governor and the bishop, and Captain Legarde [sic] has promised to put them on shore. The plunder of the town was not great, money and broken plate [i.e., silver] about £20 a man.

Three days later Coxon entered and personally escorted the bishop, Dr. Lucas Fernández y Piedrahita, and a Spanish friar into the presence of the new island governor, Lord Vaughan. The prelate was nobly housed, and royal officers sent aboard the buccaneer flotilla to attempt "to procure the liberty of the [Spanish] governor and others, but finding the privateers all drunk, it was impossible to persuade them to do anything by fair means." Vaughan therefore ordered the French to depart, advising Barnes and

the Englishmen that it was now against the law for them to serve under foreign colors. The French were "damnably enraged" at being deprived of their English consorts and sailed off without releasing their captives.

Barnes apparently retired from roving around this time.

*See also* Barlovento, Armada de; Coxon, John; La Garde, Capitaine; Spanish Main.

*References:* C.S.P., Amer. and W.I., Vols. IX–X; Gosse, *Who's Who;* Pope.

# BARRE'S TAVERN

One of the more genteel establishments at rollicking Port Royal, Jamaica, noted for its light refreshments, offered "silabubus [sic], cream tarts and other quelque choses," according to one satisfied patron. ("Sillabubs," or "syllabubs," were drinks or dishes made by curdling cream or milk with an admixture of wine, cider, or some other acid, producing a soft curd that was whipped or solidified with gelatin, then sweetened or flavored.) The name of this establishment may actually have been "Barré's Tavern," perhaps owned or operated by the family of Charles de la Barré, Governor Sir Thomas Lynch's French secretary.

*References:* C.S.P., Amer. and W.I., Vol.XI; Pawson, *Port Royal.*

# BARRERA Y VILLEGAS, FELIPE DE LA

## (1635-1705?)

Spanish officer who defended the Laguna de Términos and Campeche against pirates.

Born in the Toranzo Valley of the Santillana Mountains in Santander, Spain, De la Barrera arrived in Campeche as a 20-year-old soldier in the train of

Governor-designate Francisco de Bazán in 1655. Because his uncle was an influential member of the Council of Indies in Madrid, De la Barrera was able to marry the daughter of a prominent local figure and enroll in the company of garrison commander Captain Antonio Maldonado de Aldana. He was soon promoted to *alférez real* (king's ensign), then infantry captain. De la Barrera also served at sea, making cruises as far as the Bay of Honduras in pursuit of pirates aboard the coast guard vessel *Pescadora* (Fisher) and transporting stone slabs to Veracruz for the island fortress of San Juan de Ulúa aboard *Santa Teresa* and *Nuestra Señora del Carmen*.

## LAGUNA DE TÉRMINOS CAMPAIGN (1680)

He saw action in defense of Campeche as early as 1673, but his first important command occurred in 1680, after being elected *alcalde ordinario*, or town magistrate, when the reinstated governor of Yucatán, Antonio de Layseca y Alvarado, appointed him to sweep the English logwood cutters from the Laguna de Términos. De la Barrera sailed with a small flotilla of *piraguas*, and on 6 February took some prizes; bolstered by this success, his second expedition consisted of a *barco luengo*, two *piraguas*, and 115 men, which netted a 24-gun merchantman. Delighted, Governor de Layseca appointed him *teniente de capitán general* (lieutenant commander) for Campeche on 12 April, as De la Barrera prepared for a third raid.

At his own expense, he secured half ownership of the 24-gun prize and reinforced it with two brigantines and six *piraguas*, plus more than 500 troops: 200 mulatto militia from the capital of Mérida, 70 regulars, and 16 gunners from the Campeche garrison, plus 240 volunteers. His officers included the corsair captains Pedro de Castro and Juan Corso. De la Barrera

burst into the laguna on 17 April; more than 38 craft of all sizes were seized, along with 163 Baymen and numerous Spanish hostages and slaves. De la Barrera also learned that a force of 240 buccaneers had departed in seven vessels to waylay the annual cocoa harvest of Tabasco, so he sent a detachment in pursuit. His prisoners and prizes were carried triumphantly into Campeche, but De la Barrera himself did not arrive. Ironically, he had become separated from his expedition and was captured by English stragglers. Conveyed to London, he was allegedly detained in the Tower before being released. By January 1682 he was in Madrid reporting to the Crown and returned to Campeche the following year to resume his duties.

## SACK OF CAMPECHE (JULY 1685)

Two years later, reports began reaching De la Barrera of a large pirate formation gathering off the northeastern tip of Yucatán. Specifically, Captain Cristóbal Martínez de Acevedo arrived with his coast guard frigate *Nuestra Señora de la Soledad* (Our Lady of Solitude) to report that his two-ship convoy had been pursued on the high seas by hostile craft on 27 May 1685. De la Barrera ordered *Soledad* to remain in port as reinforcement for its garrison, while 25 sailors, along with 25 soldiers under Baltasar Navarro, were used to man a reconnaissance *piragua* and return around the peninsula. They spotted numerous interlopers prowling off Cape Catoche and Isla Mujeres and reported these sightings to both De la Barrera and Yucatán's provincial governor, Juan Bruno Téllez de Guzmân.

The buccaneer ships included those of Laurens de Graaf, "chevalier" de Grammont, Michiel Andrieszoon, Joseph Bannister, Jan Willems, and many others who, unknown to the Spaniards, were mustering for a descent against Campeche proper. By late June, De la Barrera learned that the enemy were advancing, creeping past Sisal toward his port. Fortifications were strengthened and noncombatants sent inland along with most valuables. Finally, on the afternoon of 6 July 1685, the pirate fleet of 6 large and 4 small ships, 6 sloops, and 17 *piraguas* hove into view half a dozen miles offshore. A landing force of 700 buccaneers took to the boats and began rowing in toward the beach, but De la Barrera was ready—four militia companies totaling roughly 200 men exited and positioned themselves opposite the intended disembarkation point. The surprised pirates put up their helms, not wishing to wade into the muzzles of Spanish infantry.

All night they remained in check by De la Barrera's deployment, until the next morning when they began to draw off toward their ships. But this proved to be a feint, as the freebooters suddenly rushed the outskirts of the city and stormed ashore before the defense could react. Several columns bore down on Campeche, scattering De la Barrera's men back into the city. Martínez prepared to scuttle *Soledad* out in the harbor, but instead of boring holes in its bottom as originally planned, the speed of the enemy advance made him run a trail of powder into the magazine and light a fuse. *Soledad* exploded with a deafening blast, collapsing the defenders' morale and sending them reeling into their citadel while the pirates entered unopposed. De la Barrera attempted to mount a counterattack but was beaten off into the countryside with his men and that night saw to the safety of his wife and family.

Over the next few days, the raiders subdued the isolated strong points within Campeche until only the citadel remained. They began bombarding this fortress at dawn on 12 July 1685, but at ten o'clock that morning two relief columns of Spanish militia appeared from Mérida de Yucatán. In the past, such troops had simply to appear for smaller bands of rovers to scuttle back out to

sea, so the overconfident volunteers ignored De la Barrera's call to assemble at the town of Santa Lucía, and instead rushed piecemeal into battle. Well-aimed volleys greeted them from a freebooter army that stood and fought behind Campeche's ramparts. All day the two sides struggled, De la Barrera throwing his troops into the fray only to have Grammont circle behind the Spaniards and catch them between two fires. The relief force drew off in defeat, leaving the citadel in such despair that it was abandoned during the night.

His city having fallen, De la Barrera was forced to wait until another expedition could be dispatched from the provincial capital. More than two weeks later he received an order from Governor Téllez, directing all troops to be marshaled at Tenabó, eight leagues outside Campeche. De la Barrera set out with his own 46-man company, only to be captured near Cholul on 28 July 1685 by two columns of buccaneer horsemen. The pirates had commandeered these mounts from outlying ranches and sent riders to ravage the countryside, and so brought De la Barrera and many other captives back into Campeche the following day. Their frustration at finding most of the Spaniards' wealth withdrawn led to numerous instances of cruelty. On 25 August the French *flibustiers* celebrated Louis XIV's saint day with fireworks and festivities, then the following morning began preparations to decamp.

A message was sent inland demanding a ransom of 80,000 pesos and 400 head of cattle for Campeche. Téllez's reply arrived a few days later, addressed to De la Barrera. He was forced to read aloud a sneering rejection of the pirates' demands, in which the governor said that

they would be given nothing and might burn down the town, as [Spain] had

39

ample funds with which to build or even buy another, and people with which to repopulate it.

Furious, Grammont had the houses torched the next dawn; one of the few houses to be spared was De la Barrera's, which lay outside the city limits and was occupied by the pirate leaders. The *flibustier* commander then sent another missive in which he threatened to massacre his captives but received the same response. The next day the captives were paraded in the main square, and the executions began. After half a dozen men had been hanged, De la Barrera and other leading citizens

> presented themselves before "Lorencillo" [De Graaf], whom they knew to be more humane than the Frenchman, and offered to serve him for the rest of their lives as slaves if he saved the rest of the inhabitants of Campeche. Lorenzo, after a lengthy discussion with Grammont, ordered a halt to the executions and that the remaining prisoners be carried out to the ships. Immediately after this incident, all the pirates evacuated the citadel, having spiked the guns.

De la Barrera was fortunate in that he was left behind when the raiders eventually quit Campeche in early September 1685. He was cleared at the subsequent inquest into the loss of his city, held two months later, but apparently retired from active campaigning.

He was last heard from in 1704, giving his opinion as to a new projected assault on the Laguna de Términos. He must have died shortly thereafter, as the next January his wife petitioned the Crown for a pension.

**See also** Andrieszoon, Michiel; Bannister, Joseph; *barco luengo;* Castro, Pedro de; Corso, Juan; De Graaf, Laurens Cornelis Boudewijn; Grammont, "chevalier" de; Laguna de Términos; Layseca y Alvarado, Antonio de; logwood; Willems, Jan.
   ***References:*** Eugenio; Juárez.

# BASQUE, MICHEL LE

## (FL. 1667-1670?)

*Flibustier* from Tortuga Island who served at the sack of Maracaibo.

According to the chronicler Alexandre Olivier Exquemelin, Le Basque was a man who by the late 1660s "had won so much by marauding he no longer went to sea." Nevertheless, when the rover Jean-David Nau l'Olonnais began to prepare an expedition in 1667 to attack the Spaniards, Le Basque offered to command the land contingent because of his considerable military experience in Europe. This offer was accepted, and Le Basque sailed with the expedition that eventually assaulted Maracaibo and other towns on the Spanish Main. Three years afterward, on 9 October 1670, a certain "Capitaine Michel" was delegated by Governor Bertrand d'Ogeron of the French West Indies Company at Saint Domingue to carry a missive to the Windward Isles, beseeching help in putting down a *boucanier* revolt, but whether this might have been a later allusion to Le Basque is impossible to determine.
   ***References:*** Exquemelin; Lugo.

# BEARE, JOHN PHILIP

## (FL. 1684-1697?)

English mercenary who served under three different flags in the West Indies.

## ENGLISH SERVICE
### (1684-1687)

Beare was first heard from in early October 1684 when he obtained a privateering commission from Governor Sir William Stapleton of the Leeward Islands; shortly thereafter, he put into neutral Willemstad, Curaçao, with his sloop *Betty,* where he found the Spanish privateer Manuel Rodríguez riding at anchor. Knowing this corsair to be wanted for seizing the Royal African Company sloop *Africa* between Tortola and Saint John in the Virgin Islands, Beare applied to the Dutch governor Joan van Erpecum for permission to detain Rodríguez and his ship, which was refused. Beare therefore stood out of the harbor, but so slowly as to allow the Spaniard to overhaul him and be overpowered. All the Spanish crew were set ashore, except one who "was kept to condemn the prize" (i.e., testify at its adjudication before an English court).

However, Beare then made the mistake of going ashore at the town of Sint Kruis on the western tip of the island, where he was detained on orders of the outraged Van Erpecum. The first mate of the *Betty,* Henry Cock, went ashore to exhibit Beare's commission but was himself held for two days. Upon the mate's release, Beare "sent orders secretly to the ship to sail to Nevis" and acquaint Stapleton of his predicament, which Cock eventually managed to do by late December 1684. Stapleton dispatched the frigate HMS *Guernsey* of Captain Matthew Tennant in mid-January of the following year to demand Beare's release, arguing that he bore "my commission to pursue pirates and Indians."

Beare was not heard of again until a year-and-a-half later, when he returned to Nevis after having traveled to England. On his westward passage, *Betty,* which was bearing stores, sprung a leak near Scilly, obliging Beare to complete the Atlantic crossing with the small frigate *James.* Upon entering Charlestown "with the king's colors flying," he was challenged to his right to wear such insignia by Captain George St. Loe of HMS *Dartmouth.* Beare presented his old patent before the council and explained the circumstances of his transfer to another vessel. A new commission was promptly granted him on 17 July 1686, over St. Loe's objections, and Beare sortied in pursuit of a Spanish corsair of about 20 to 30 guns and 150 mulattos that had raided the English settlements on Tortola that April. The ringleader was apparently an English doctor who had formerly been Beare's surgeon.

Although he failed to come up with this renegade, while cruising the Virgin Islands Beare was attacked by the Spanish vessel *Nuestra Señora de la Soledad* (Our Lady of Solitude). Turning the tables on his assailant, Beare captured the Spanish ship and carried it into Nevis at the end of October, where it was condemned as a legitimate prize in late January 1687. Beare then fitted out his new vessel and departed toward Saint Thomas, followed shortly thereafter by a vengeful St. Loe, who had returned from arresting Bartholomew Sharpe and traveling to New England and still considered Beare guilty of piracy. The Council of Nevis disagreed but reluctantly authorized the Royal Navy officer to take away Beare's commission if they should meet, which they did. Perhaps as a result of this incident, Beare transferred his allegiance to the Spaniards at Havana. One of his crew members later reported how "the Englishmen then refused to sail with him, but Beare embarked about 70 Spaniards, put it to the choice of the English to go with him, or go to prison."

## SPANISH SERVICE
### (1687-1695)

On 18 August 1687, Lieutenant Governor Hender Molesworth of Jamaica informed his superiors in London:

We hear that one Captain Beare, who formerly held a commission from Sir William Stapleton, is turned pirate and has robbed several of our fleet that sailed from hence. He took £1,000 from a New England man, besides what he took from the Londoners and other ships bound for Ireland, and has chosen his station so that no ships from hence can pass without discovery by him.

In addition to regarding Beare as a turncoat, Molesworth was prejudiced against his Catholicism, for this was a time when religious tensions were once again growing in England. He added spitefully that he had heard from Campeche

that Beare was married at Havana and gave himself out as a faithful subject of the king of Spain. I have therefore sent Captain [Thomas] Spragge [of HMS Drake] to Havana to demand him as a pirate and an English subject. He gave out that his wife was a noblewoman who ran away with him, and they actually fired the guns of the castle as a salute to her, while the governor and most of the chief men of the town were present at the wedding. The nobleman's daughter is a strumpet that he used to carry with him in man's apparel, and is the daughter of a rum-punch-woman of Port Royal. I have hopes that he may be surrendered to me, or at any rate not allowed to take his ship to sea again.

Such expectations were quickly dashed because the Spaniards were well pleased with their new *guardacosta,* whom they knew by the hispanicized name "Juan Felipe de Vera."

In addition to this initial round of captures, Beare also sailed to the salvage of a Spanish galleon that summer (allegedly one lost off Key Largo, Florida, although possibly William Phips's rich find north of Hispaniola). For this voyage he recruited some English captives from the Havana jail, including the carpenter of the frigate *Dark Wanderer,* a man named Ralph Wilkinson. During the voyage, the latter informed Beare of a mysterious French settlement on the shores of the Gulf of Mexico recently established by La Salle. Beare gave a formal statement of this discovery to the acting governor of Havana, Andrés de Muñibe, immediately following his return on 29 August 1687. Two years later Beare was still being consulted from Madrid about this intelligence report.

In the spring of 1688 he was reportedly at Veracruz, and in the last days of that year, evidently participated in a major Spanish effort to sweep foreign settlers from the islands of Anguilla and Vieques. More than one eyewitness reported that Beare was among the English, Irish, French, Turk, mulatto, and black rovers who comprised this force. After the outbreak of the War of the League of Augsburg (King William's War) the following year, Beare's frigate departed Havana in 1690 on an 11-month cruise. Putting into San Juan de Puerto Rico for five weeks, he was then delegated by Governor Gaspar de Arredondo to locate the Armada de Barlovento, which was expected on that island with the annual payrolls, or *situados.* Beare reached San Juan again in early November 1691 with this force and a few days later was once more ordered to sea by De Arredondo to convey dispatches to Spain. The rover set sail at ten o'clock on the night of 26 November, a circumstance that unwittingly contributed to the mutiny of the Puerto Rican garrison. Not having been paid in many months, the impoverished soldiery suspected that this nocturnal departure signaled the expropriation of a large part of their pay that the governor was removing from the island. These fears were seemingly confirmed when their pay was issued on 5 December and amounted to a paltry 40 pesos per man. The troops rebelled, and when De Arredondo called out the militia, it refused to act against the mutineers. Eventually Franciscan friars persuaded the soldiers to return to duty on Christmas Day 1691.

Meanwhile, Beare continued to Spain, unaware of the chaos left in his wake. Reaching Sanlúcar de Barrameda outside Seville early the following year, he remained in Spain for several months. On 5 June 1692 he was granted a royal privateering commission for all of Spanish America and sailed with his frigate *San José y San Diego* as part of that year's Mexican plate fleet, reentering San Juan de Puerto Rico early the following year. For the next two years he made several cruises throughout the Caribbean as an *aviso,* or dispatch vessel, until two boxes were decommissioned from his ship following a voyage to Cartagena. They were labeled as containing books but actually held expensive bolts of contraband cloth. Although neither belonged to Beare, he felt he would nonetheless be held responsible. When his ship was suddenly ordered to sortie from San Juan in March 1695 to chase away an enemy privateer, he sailed a mere dozen leagues out to sea before informing his Spanish passengers that he was quitting Spain's service to join the French. Upon setting the passengers ashore on the Puerto Rican coast, he added "that before falling into the power of the Spanish Exchequer, he preferred deserting."

## FRENCH SERVICE
## (1695-1697)

On 1 May 1695, Governor Jean-Baptiste Ducasse of Saint Domingue wrote:

> I have learned one named Jean de Wer [*sic*], English by nationality, captain of a coastguard vessel for Santo Domingo, coming from New Spain has put into the port of Saint Croix, where he has re-quested asylum saying he wishes to serve the king his master [presumably James II of England, exiled in Paris], of which he has apprised Monsieur le comte de Blénac.

Knowing a large Anglo-Spanish force was assembling on Santo Domingo to attack his colony, Ducasse urgently requested Beare be sent to him, so as to use his knowledge of the enemy camp. Before Beare could be dispatched, Saint Domingue was overrun by this invading host, so Blénac retained his services. It was not until the end of 1695 that Beare reached the devastated French island and gave Ducasse a detailed report of Spanish strengths. The governor was so impressed that he dispatched Beare to France in late March 1696 with a letter of recommendation to Minister Pontchartrain saying that

> he has a complete knowledge of the town [of Santo Domingo] and the way of taking it; he has given me a map and underscored there are more men on that island than I believed; his belief is the Spaniards can muster 3,000 men. He is traveling aboard the ship of Monsieur Dessangiers, and will have the honor of presenting [the map] and giving you a memorial for an attack, and the best season for making it; he has a very extensive knowledge of all the ports of Indies and enterprises one can mount here.

Apparently Beare also found favor with the royal minister, for late in 1697 he returned to the West Indies and led an assault on Caracas's port of La Guaira with four French vessels, surprising the Spanish garrison, who believed it was the Armada de Barlovento approaching from Cumaná. Beare's raid wreaked a good deal of havoc, destroying the *patache* that the Spaniards used to communicate with their offshore outpost at Margarita. This was one of the very last actions of the war and of Beare's career.

**See also** *aviso;* Barlovento, Armada de; Blénac, Charles de Courbon, comte de; Ducasse, Jean-Baptiste; *guardacostas;* Hispaniola; *patache;* Rodríguez, Manuel; Sharpe, Bartholomew; Tennant, Matthew.

**References:** *C.S.P., Amer. and W.I.,* Vols. XI–XIII; Lugo; Marley, *Pirates;* Torres; Weddle, *Wilderness.*

# BECQUEL, CAPTAIN
## (FL. 1659-1663)

Privateer commander—most probably French—who was mentioned under the name "Bequell" in the journal of Colonel Edward D'Oyley, governor of Jamaica, as having been issued a "let pass" on 3 December 1659 (O.S.).

He is presumably the same "Captain Buckell" listed as commanding an 8-gun French frigate with a crew of 70 men in 1663, being described as "belonging to Tortuga" but bearing a commission from the English authorities on Jamaica.

**See also** D'Oyley, Edward.
**Reference:** Pawson, *Port Royal.*

# BEEF ISLAND

A common place name in the seventeenth-century Caribbean, as the procuring of meat was a constant quest for many rovers.

One such "Beef Island" was in fact not an island at all, but rather a long, narrow strip of land today called Xicalango Point, connected to the Mexican mainland due west of Isla del Carmen. It encloses the western portion of the Laguna de Términos, which was then a popular destination for adventurers from Jamaica, who referred to it as the "Bay of Campeche." Some visitors were raiders come to plunder the Spanish coastal towns, others relatively honest merchantmen come to buy logwood from the resident poachers, or "Baymen." To all of them, Beef Island was a particular stretch of low coastline where, over the years, cattle had been rustled or slaughtered.

In November 1681, for example, an Englishman named Jonas Clough described how a year-and-a-half earlier he had been aboard one of a group of three New England sloops, when a Spanish expedition under Felipe de la Barrera suddenly appeared and "took two of the sloops and forced the third ashore on Beef Island, called by the Spaniards Jica Lanoga [Xicalango]." More than 80 interlopers remained marooned, he added, until they agreed to surrender more than a month later. The Englishmen thought they had been promised safe conduct to the Cayman Islands or Jamaica but were carried off as prisoners to Mexico City, where they were harshly treated.

## VIRGIN ISLANDS

Another Beef Island was at the eastern extreme of Tortola in the Virgin Islands, which still bears this name today. In early 1684, one of pirate George Bond's prizes—a Dutch ship he had seized at Suriname—was reportedly recaptured "at Beef Island, near Saint Thomas."

**See also** Barrera y Villegas, Felipe de la; Bond, George; Laguna de Términos; logwood.
**References:** *C.S.P., Amer and W.I.,* Vol. XI; Gerhard, *Southeast.*

# BEESTON, WILLIAM
## (1636-1702?)

English pirate hunter who became governor of Jamaica.

Beeston was born at Tichfield, Hampshire, England, in 1636. His elder brother Henry became master of Winchester School and warden of New College, Oxford. William emigrated to Jamaica in May 1660 and little more than three years later was elected to the first council as a member for Port Royal. He was made judge of the Court of Common Pleas in December 1664, and the following summer was sent by the new governor, Sir Thomas Modyford, with three ships to recall a group of privateers who were reportedly gathered off Cuba for an attack against the town of Sancti Spíritus. Beeston was to read them "a proclamation from the king to keep peace with the Spaniards" and recall them for defense of Jamaica, but after six weeks he returned to Port Royal empty-handed; he learned that in the interim the rovers had plundered Sancti Spíritus.

Modyford's successor, Sir Thomas Lynch, delegated Beeston on a similar commission three years later. Having brought out the peace treaty with Spain, Lynch and Modyford chose "Major Beeston and Captain Reid to carry the articles of peace" to the Spanish governor of Cartagena and bring back any English prisoners who were there. The frigates HMS *Assistance,* of 40 guns, and *Welcome,* of 36 guns, were placed at Beeston's disposal, sailing on 16 July 1671 (O.S.) but were hardly out of sight of Port Royal when Captain John Hubbart of *Assistance* fell ill. He died three days later and was succeeded in command by Lieutenant John Willgress. Cartagena was reached on 23 July (O.S.), where arrangements were made for the publication of the treaty and the Englishmen's release. By 7 August (O.S.), Beeston was back in Jamaica and five days later witnessed the arrest of Modyford for deportation toward England.

## PIRATE HUNTING
### (1671-1672)

On 8 December 1671 (O.S.) Wilgress was dismissed from command of HMS *Assistance* for "wicked, drunken behavior," being

replaced two days later by Beeston. On 16 December (O.S.), he set sail for Trinidad, returning to Port Royal in January of the following year. Then, as noted in Beeston's journal:

> January 31, 1672 [O.S.]—The *Assistance* sailed again to the south cays of Cuba after privateers and pirates, by the desire of the Governor of Santiago [de Cuba]; yet when she came there, he would not suffer them to have provision for their money, nor would he let them come into Santiago, though the captain [Beeston] brought and delivered him a ship he took from the privateers (which belonged formerly to the Spaniards) without any charge; therefore the 18th of March [O.S.] the *Assistance* again returned to Port Royal.

During this cruise Beeston had vainly pursued the renegade privateer ship *Seviliaen* of Jelles de Lecat and Jan Erasmus Reyning near Campeche, where he had also seized the rogue ship *Charity* of Francis Weatherbourne and the French vessel of Capitaine du Mangles, both for committing "great violence against the Spaniards." The latter two captains were tried for piracy and condemned to be shot to death aboard *Assistance* a couple of days after reentering Port Royal, yet eventually they were ordered deported to England aboard *Welcome* when that frigate departed Jamaica on 6 April 1672 (O.S.) with Henry Morgan as a prisoner.

Five days afterward Beeston sailed again with *Assistance,* this time "to Hispaniola to look for privateers, and thence to the Havana to fetch away the [English] prisoners, from whence she returned [to Jamaica] the 15th of June [O.S.]." Beeston then commanded the warship on its return passage to England, quitting Port Royal on 10 July 1672 (O.S.) with a convoy comprised of the merchantmen *Friesland,*

*Thomas and Charles, Huntsman,* and *Endeavour.* They reached the mouth of the Thames that October, and shortly thereafter Beeston relinquished his command, returning to Jamaica the following summer, perhaps aboard Captain Canning's 40-gun frigate HMS *Portland* or Captain Gollop's smaller *Thomas and Francis,* both of which entered Port Royal on 21 July 1673 (O.S.).

## SUBSEQUENT CAREER
### (1673-1702)

Two years later, when Lord Vaughan reached Jamaica as that island's new governor, Beeston was appointed one of its Commissioners of the Admiralty (along with the recently returned Lieutenant Governor Sir Henry Morgan and the latter's brother-in-law, Colonel Robert Byndloss). In April 1677, "Lieutenant Colonel" Beeston was chosen as Speaker of the Assembly of Jamaica and led the opposition to proposed changes in its government from London. Differences with the new governor, the earl of Carlisle, eventually reached such a pass that the Assembly was dissolved and Beeston, along with the island's Chief Justice Colonel Samuel Long, were ordered to travel to England and "answer for their contumacy." Beeston set sail on 6 July 1680 (O.S.), reaching England before either Carlisle or Long, both of whom had departed fourteen weeks previously. Together with the chief justice, Beeston then filed counter charges against the earl and after a lengthy proceedings was cleared of any wrongdoing.

Late in 1692, Beeston was knighted at Kensington and returned to Jamaica the following summer, in the wake of the dreadful earthquake that had devastated Port Royal shortly before noon on 7 June 1692 (O.S.). He found the island still suffering from terrible aftereffects and wrote a friend, "By the mortality which yet continues I have lost all my family but my wife and one child, and have not one servant left to attend me but my cook, so it is very uneasy being here." His discomfiture was further increased by the War of the League of Augsburg (King William's War), which left Jamaica vulnerable to an attack from the French on Saint Domingue. The next summer Jean-Baptiste Ducasse in fact led a massive descent on Jamaica, which Beeston managed to resist, although the French rampaged unchecked throughout the southern plantations for the better part of a month before retiring.

Beeston was superseded in his government at the end of January 1702 and must have died shortly thereafter, being survived by a single daughter.

*See also* Ducasse, Jean-Baptiste; Hispaniola; Lecat, Jelles de; Lynch, Sir Thomas; Modyford, Sir Thomas; Morgan, Sir Henry; Reyning, Jan Erasmus; Weatherbourne, Francis.

*References:* D.N.B.; *Interesting Tracts;* Pawson, *Port Royal;* Pope.

# BENNETT, JOHN
## (FL. 1670-1676)

English privateer who served in Henry Morgan's sack of Panama.

Late in 1670, Bennett joined the buccaneer fleet gathering at Ile-à-Vache off southwestern Hispaniola with his tiny *Virgin Queen,* of 50 tons and 30 men, to take part in the expedition against the Spaniards. He must have sailed to Providencia Island and Chagres, then led his contingent across the isthmus as part of Morgan's main body. Following this attack, little more is heard about Bennett's activities, although he presumably continued roving during the Third Anglo-Dutch War (1672–1674). When England withdrew from the confederation against the Netherlands, many West Indian corsairs shifted allegiance in order to continue privateering.

Bennett was one of these, obtaining a commission from Bertrand d'Ogeron, governor of French Saint Domingue, to make war against the Spaniards. His reputation became such that Bennett was the principal renegade to whom Morgan drafted a letter in March 1675, offering liberty to all English rovers who returned to Jamaica. This proposal was never sent, the Jamaican authorities preferring other measures to recall English subjects from foreign service. Meanwhile, Bennett remained busy, intercepting the *Buen Jesús de las Almas* (Good Jesus of the Souls), Bernardo Ferrer Espejo, master, as it approached the coast of Hispaniola with 46,471 pieces of eight as payroll, or *situado,* for that island garrison. The Spanish authorities were highly suspicious of this capture, noting Bennett had only a small brigantine with 20 men, while Ferrer Espejo's 50-ton frigate held three times that number. They believed Ferrer had colluded in the capture, allowing *Buen Jesús* to be carried into Saint Domingue in April 1675.

The Spanish officials even ordered the arrest of Ferrer, also believing him guilty of fraud on his previous voyage to Cartagena and Havana for the *situado.* They lodged a protest with London as well, which was rejected, it being pointed out that the English renegade had run away with his brigantine from Jamaica, "had Frenchmen on board, French commission, fought under French colors, had the prize condemned and adjudged in French ports." Nevertheless, the English would have happily detained Bennett, but chance intervened. On 9 February 1677 (O.S.), a Jamaican newsletter reported that

two French vessels lately well beaten by a Spanish hulk [an *urca*] in the Gulf of Mexico with the loss of 80 men, Captain Bennett killed in the engagement.

*See also* Hispaniola; Ogeron, Bertrand d'; pieces of eight.

*References:* C.S.P., Amer. and W.I., Vols. IX–X; Pope.

# BERNANOS, JEAN
## (1648-1695)

French *flibustier* who took part in the assault on Jamaica and died defending Saint Domingue.

Bernanos, the son of a butcher, was born in Metz, Lorraine, France, on 6 March 1648. His last name apparently derived from his great-grandfather, a Spanish soldier who had settled in the region a century earlier after serving in the armies of Emperor Charles V. It is not known when Jean Bernanos first arrived in the New World, nor in what capacity. He was in command of the ship *Schitée,* with 8 guns and 60 men, in 1684. In August of that year (hostilities against Spain having been temporarily revived), he sailed with three other French corsairs to the Spanish Main—some accounts say to make a descent on the Gulf of Paria; others, on the Gulf of Darien.

Six years later, with the War of the League of Augsburg (King William's War) raging against the English, Dutch, and Spanish, Governor Pierre-Paul Tarin de Cussy passed through Cap François on his way to attack Santiago de los Caballeros in Santo Domingo and found

the *flibustiers* awaiting him to obtain a commission; they were headed by Capitaine Bernanos, and their intention was to go take Santiago de Cuba.

A patent was issued, but there is no record of any attack having been made against this Cuban port, only a few English vessels taken by Bernanos. Following the death of

De Cussy in the devastating Spanish invasion of 1691, his successor Jean-Baptiste Ducasse sent Bernanos to make a reconnaissance of the English forces on Jamaica. In July 1692, Bernanos led 100 *flibustiers* aboard Capitaine Damon's *Emporté* (Intemperate), with orders to

> reconnoiter the enemy, and in case they have attacked any quarter, or were anchored off any roads, to land about 100 *flibustiers* under the command of Bernanos and make every effort to take them. In the event nothing is found, they are enjoined to cruise past the coasts of Jamaica and push on [round Cuba] into the Bahama Channel, trying to capture ships.

Damon and Bernanos returned the following month empty-handed.

On 11 July 1693, Bernanos was appointed *brevet major* of Port-de-Paix opposite Tortuga Island. The next summer he took part in the Jamaican assault under Ducasse and Laurens de Graaf. Bernanos and his men sailed aboard the flagship *Téméraire* (Fearless), 54 guns, commanded by the chevalier de Rollon. This vessel anchored with the main body in Cow Bay, 15 miles east of Port Royal, on 27 June 1694 but four days later, "the wind blowing very hard," dragged its anchors and, with one other vessel, was driven downwind into Bluefields Bay. Here Bernanos led a contingent of 60 *flibustiers* ashore, seizing a plantation. A unit of Jamaican militia appeared and a skirmish erupted, whereupon De Rollon, hearing the small-arms fire on board, ordered a round shot over the *flibustiers'* heads as a signal. At this

> they ran aboard in such haste that they left their meat they had killed, and some cattle they had tied up to carry aboard, and their bread and salt, and sailed away as soon as they could get up their anchors.

*Téméraire* could not find the French fleet again and stood away for Petit Goâve. Learning that Ducasse was still at Port Morant, De Rollon made a gallant attempt to rejoin, but the outbreak of an epidemic forced him back into Léogâne, where almost half his crew died.

The following spring, a huge Anglo-Spanish fleet appeared off northern Saint Domingue and deposited a considerable army. Ducasse had already hurried Bernanos northward with 100 troops to Port-de-Paix, with orders to assist De Graaf, who was *lieutenant du roi* (king's lieutenant) at nearby Cap François. When the latter called for help, Bernanos marched on 18 May 1695 with 130 men and reached him three days later, although this proved too little to check the enemy host. The French abandoned Cap François, retreating toward Port-de-Paix.

The invaders reached this place on 13 June, the Royal Navy landing 500 English soldiers to meet the Spanish army marching along the coast. Faced with overwhelming odds, the French again decided to abandon their defenses, although not without considerable dissent. By the time guns had been spiked, powder magazines flooded, and a train of refugees gathered, it was too late. The column was betrayed and attacked as it evacuated the town, disintegrating into chaos. Some called for an about-face into Port-de-Paix, others to cut their way through the enemy. Bernanos attempted to rally the vanguard by roaring, "They are but dogs, we shall easily run them through!" But it was he who fell, pierced through the body three times. It is said that he expired stretching out his hand to another dying officer, the "chevalier" de Paty, and was eulogized as "the bravest man there ever was in the colony."

*See also* De Graaf, Laurens Cornelis Boudewijn; Ducasse, Jean–Baptiste; Spanish Main.

*References:* Gosse, *Who's Who;* Tribout.

# BERNARD, ANTOINE

## (D. 1683)

French *flibustier* who took part in the sack of Veracruz.

On 5 March 1683, Bernard sailed from Martinique aboard his tiny 2-gun *Prophète Daniel* (Prophet Daniel), accompanied by the equally small *Dauphin* (Prince) of Pierre d'Orange. They intended to go turtling on the Cayman Islands, but a month later heard of a great pirate gathering off the Central American coast. Crossing to Guanaja Island, they learned of a Dutch rover named Nikolaas van Hoorn being defrauded of a consignment of slaves at Santo Domingo, and—as a French subject—obtaining a letter of reprisal from Jacques Nepveu, sieur de Pouançay and governor of Saint Domingue, to exact restitution. Van Hoorn had sortied with the "chevalier" de Grammont and other *flibustier* commanders to recruit at Roatan for a descent against the Mexican port of Veracruz.

Bernard and d'Orange joined this expedition, which eventually swelled to 13 vessels and roughly 1,400 men. Rounding Yucatán, a landing party of 800 freebooters slipped ashore near Veracruz the night of 17 May 1683, infiltrating the city and attacking at dawn. The garrison was quickly overwhelmed, and after four days' sack, the raiders withdrew to Sacrificios Island two miles offshore with several thousand hostages and vast quantities of booty. A fortnight later they weighed and staggered back around Yucatán to divide their spoils at Isla Mujeres.

The flotilla then broke up, Bernard and d'Orange being among the first to attempt to beat across toward Petit Goâve on Saint Domingue, although *Prophète Daniel* only got as far as the Cayman Islands before Bernard fell ill. He recuperated, but on 4 August 1683 was still lying with d'Orange's *Dauphin* at Little Cayman when the Armada de Barlovento suddenly appeared and captured both. The Spanish report described *Prophète Daniel* as a 35-ton sloop "with a crew of 17 men, two guns, two swivel guns, a blunderbuss, two carbines, three cutlasses, 80 pounds of gunpowder and 30 tons of cheese," although it is quite probable that more had already been pilfered by the light-fingered armada sailors.

They were carried into Veracruz three weeks later with other prizes, and a hearing convened aboard Andrés de Ochoa y Zárate's flagship, *Santo Cristo de Burgos* (Holy Christ of Burgos). Spanish law decreed that pirate leaders were to be tried at the scene of their crimes, and minions deported to Spain. It is therefore likely that Bernard remained in Veracruz when the plate fleet sailed for Cadiz a few days later to face judgment in the still-devastated Mexican port. Most probably he was executed on 22 November 1683, when his associate d'Orange is known to have died.

*See also* Barlovento, Armada de; Grammont, "chevalier" de; Orange, Pierre d'; Pouançay, Jacques Nepveu, sieur de; Van Hoorn, Nikolaas.

*References:* Juárez; Marley, *Veracruz;* Sáiz; Torres.

# BERNARDSON, ALBERT

## (FL. 1665)

Privateer who commanded the 6-gun *Trueman* in Colonel Edward Morgan's expedition against Dutch Sint Eustatius and Sabá during the Second Anglo-Dutch War. This force departed Jamaica in two divisions, five sail putting out of Port Royal on 5 April 1665 and Morgan himself following with another four on the 28 April. There were 650 men in all, described in a letter by Governor Sir Thomas Modyford as

chiefly reformed privateers, scarce a planter amongst them, being resolute fellows and well armed with *fusils* [Spanish word for muskets] and pistols.

The Crown official was particularly pleased they would be serving "at the old rate of no purchase, no pay, and it will cost the King nothing considerable, some powder and mortar pieces." Their landing was successfully made, but the colonel, "being a corpulent man," died from heat exertion during the chase, and his expedition disbanded shortly thereafter.

**See also** purchase.
**References:** Cruikshank; *Interesting Tracts;* Pope.

# Bilbo or bilboes

In the seventeenth century, *bilbo* was a nickname for any rapier or fine sword, apparently derived from Bilbao, the name of the Spanish port where many such blades were bought.

*Bilboes,* on the other hand, referred to a long iron bar with shackles used to confine the feet of prisoners. In the summer of 1686, for example, a coastal trader named Samuel Woodward complained of harsh treatment received off Maryland from Captain John Crofts of the Royal Navy ketch *Deptford.* This officer, he said, "had insulted him, called him into his cabin, boxed him severely, and ordered him to be put into bilboes. He remained in irons for an hour-and-a-half, during which time his [Woodward's] ketch was searched, but nothing irregular found."
**Reference:** *C.S.P., Amer. and W.I.,* Vol. XII.

# Billiards

Popular seventeenth-century pastime, particularly in English drinking establishments.

Several taverns at Port Royal, Jamaica, sported billiard rooms, which seem to have been situated in the yard, or otherwise removed from the main bar, to prevent frictions. The "George" tavern—which "fronted to the old market place" in town, according to a contemporary report—had a special room built for the game; the same was true at the "Feathers," whose billiard room was situated over another room in its yard.
**Reference:** Pawson, *Port Royal.*

# Billop, christopher

## (FL. 1682-1684)

Royal Navy captain who commanded the ketch *Quaker* at Nevis and was accused of fraud.

Governor Sir William Stapleton said of him that since coming out from England, Billop had "acted more like a merchant, and sometimes more like a piratical one," than a king's officer. When a merchant ship bound from La Rochelle to Antigua during peacetime was intercepted off Nevis, it was rumored that Billop did not release the Frenchman until allowed to keep "the things he took from her." But more blatant still was his very last coup in the Indies, when on 15 June 1682 a vessel "was seen tacking off and on" toward Nevis, before finally steering away toward Dutch Sint Eustatius. Billop set off in pursuit, and "upon firing a shot across her forefoot, to his great surprise found his fire returned." He therefore blasted the stranger with a broadside and boarded, discovering it to be the *Providence* of London, with one dead and six wounded among its crew. The master, George Nanton, confessed that he had no license to trade in the New World but was coming out from Africa as an interloper with 215 slaves plus roughly a ton each of "elephants' teeth" (ivory), copper, and redwood.

This engagement took place within plain view of everybody in Nevis's capital of Charlestown, who then saw the ketch stand away toward the French half of St. Kitts with its prize. When Billop returned five days later, the only merchandise left aboard the *Providence* was 96 slaves, a dozen of them with smallpox. He was charged with embezzling Charles II's bounty by profiting from this contraband, and when the verdict appeared to go against him, he refused to set foot ashore. The island council described him to the Lords of Trade and Plantations in London as "one of the worst men we ever saw in the king's service, and the most unfit to continue in it."

On 16 July, Governor Stapleton sent the provost marshal aboard Billop's ship, and Billop promised to present himself the next day. But the following morning he was already hull down, sailing away to England. Charges followed him across the Atlantic, but he was able to prolong the dispute by launching a countersuit of his own, alleging that the *Providence* had been adjudged legal prize, after which the "Negroes and other goods he [had been] sending to New York were illegally seized." His naval career ended, Billop moved to New York, where in late 1686 he was allowed to establish "a ferry upon the southwest side of Staten Island," and became the island's surveyor.

*Reference: C.S.P., Amer. and W.I.,* Vols. XI–XII.

# BINCKES, JACOB

## ALSO BENCKES
### (?-1677)

Frisian commander who led two expeditions into the West Indies.

Binckes was a veteran of the Second Anglo-Dutch War, having fought in the two day battle off Dunkirk in 1666 and the daring Medway raid the following year. At the outbreak of the Third Anglo-Dutch War in 1672, he was given command of the *Woerden,* 70 guns, by the admiralty of Amsterdam, fighting in the Battle of Sole Bay and off West Kapellen that June aboard *Groot Hollandia* (Great Holland). In September he, along with four other senior officers, was unjustly accused of having quit the Battle of Sole Bay but was quickly cleared.

## FIRST CARIBBEAN CAMPAIGN (1673)

After this trial, Binckes rejoined Admiral Michiel de Ruyter at the Texel. The Anglo-French invasion threat having been defused and summer campaigning drawing to a close, he was ordered to lead a small squadron into the West Indies. His flagship was the two-year-old frigate *Noordhollandt* (North Holland), 46 guns and 210 men, accompanied by three other men o' war. He quit the Texel on 18 December 1672 and by late May 1673 had taken two prizes and was blockading Cul de Sac Bay, Martinique. At noon on 22 May, he saw four ships approaching and turned toward them with French colors, hoping to lure them nearer. The strangers immediately hoisted Dutch flags, proving to be a Zeeland squadron under Cornelis Evertsen. Having left Vlissingen (Flushing) on an identical mission, they agreed to join forces; that night, they attempted to force the French harbor but were prevented by contrary winds. They then proceeded to Guadeloupe, seizing the merchantmen *Saint Joseph* and *Françoise,* as well as the island trader *Nouveau France* (New France) and Irish merchantman *Saint Michael* of Galway, from beneath the Monserrat batteries. Nevis and St. Kitts were bombarded before the former Dutch island of Sint Eustatius was overrun on 29 May 1673.

Binckes and Evertsen raided the Virginia coast in mid-July, reoccupying New York City (formerly New Netherland) at the end of the month. Having reinstated Dutch rule, they detached four ships to raid Newfoundland before sailing with the main body to the Azores and Europe. By the time they reached neutral Cadiz in December 1673, they had captured a total of 34 English and French prizes and destroyed at least 150 more. However, a peace treaty was just being concluded with the English, so New York was restored to English domination.

## SECOND CARIBBEAN CAMPAIGN
### (1676)

Binckes was promoted to vice admiral of Amsterdam and in March 1676 was sent back out to the West Indies with a fleet of three ships of the line of 44 to 56 guns, six frigates of 24 to 36 guns, a fireship, and numerous troop transports. On 4 May 1676, he dropped anchor off Cayenne, landing 900 men and taking Fort Saint Louis with almost no resistance. Leaving a garrison, he proceeded northward and visited a like treatment on Marie Galante, throwing down its fortifications and carrying off the French colonists. When he sighted Guadeloupe on 16 June, he considered the defenses too strong and so passed it by, instead pursuing (unsuccessfully) a trio of French vessels. A few days later he landed 500 men and overran Saint Martin, killing the French governor and seizing 100 slaves. From there Binckes continued toward Tobago; his instructions were to fortify Tobago and simultaneously detach his second-in-command Pieter Constant, who was to attempt to incite the *boucaniers* of Saint Domingue to revolt against the high tariffs imposed by the French West Indies Company.

A French counterattack was not long in developing. Louis XIV dispatched a large fleet into the New World under Vice Admiral Jean, comte d'Estrées. In December 1676 he recaptured Cayenne, then pressed on toward Martinique, where he gained intelligence and was heavily reinforced by *flibustiers*. On 12 February 1677, he again set sail for Tobago, which Binckes had transformed into a heavily fortified base, although the Dutch were outnumbered 4,000 to 1,700. On the evening of 21 February 1677, the French landed 1,000 soldiers near Rockly Bay and sent 14 light vessels to make a feint against its harbor mouth.

## FIRST BATTLE OF TOBAGO
### (MARCH 1677)

D'Estrées launched his major assault the morning of 3 March 1677. The fighting was intense both on land and sea, especially in the harbor, with Binckes eventually emerging victorious. However, he lost 10 of his 13 anchored vessels to spreading conflagrations (which also consumed 4 of the attacking French men o' war). Two French vessels were also captured, and d'Estrées was forced to retreat to Grenada and Martinique with over 1,000 casualties; by early July, he was back in Versailles reporting on his failure.

The Sun King immediately ordered his admiral to return to the West Indies and complete his mission. D'Estrées departed Brest on 27 September 1677 with 17 more ships. He arrived off Tobago on 6 December, having destroyed the Dutch slaving station of Gorée, West Africa, en route. Meanwhile, Binckes's squadron and garrison, which had been reduced to less than 500 effectives by the first battle and tropical disease, had not been reinforced from Holland. Binckes's sole advantage lay in the torrential weather, but despite this the French quickly threw a contingent of 1,000 troops ashore and installed siege artillery, refusing to be drawn into a suicidal charge like the last time. The harbor was no longer a consideration, as the Dutch had only two ships there.

### SECOND BATTLE OF TOBAGO
#### (DECEMBER 1677)

On 12 December 1677, the chief French gunner began firing ranging shots against the Dutch fortification, laying odds that he would blow it up at the third attempt. Incredibly, the third round landed in the magazine, killing Binckes and 250 defenders with a mighty blast. The French swarmed exultantly over the ruins, while Dutch resolve collapsed, and the island fell.

*See also* Estrées, Jean, comte d'; Evertsen de Jongste, Cornelis.

*References:* Buchet; Shomette, *Raid.*

# BISCAYAN PRIVATEERS

Squadron of corsairs raised in northeastern Spain to combat pirates and smugglers in the New World.

With the Armada de Barlovento unable to cope with peacetime hostilities in the Caribbean, Madrid accepted a proposal from some Guipuzcoan merchants on 6 November 1685 to raise a private force of four frigates in return for certain trade concessions. Ships and Basque crew members were assembled at the port of San Sebastián, and their commodore, Francisco García Galán, vowed in a letter to Charles II of Spain that, upon reaching the West Indies, he would "first of all seek out the pirate Lorencillo [De Graaf]." On 23 August 1686 the following vessels set sail:

| | Guns | Tons | Men |
|---|---|---|---|
| *Nuestra Señora del Rosario* | | | |
| *y las Ánimas* (flag) | 34 | 250 | 180 |
| *San Nicolás de Bari* (vice-flag) | 24 | 200 | 142 |

| | Guns | Tons | Men |
|---|---|---|---|
| *Nuestra Señora de la* | | | |
| *Concepción (gobierno)* | ? | 140 | 66 |
| *San Antonio (patache)* | ? | 60 | 36 |
| *Santiago* (32-oar galliot) | ? | 30 | 53 |

García Galán's second-in-command was Francisco de Aguirre; his third *(gobernador),* Miguel de Vergara; with José de Leoz y Echalar, Martín Pérez de Landeche, Sebastián Pisón, Silvestre Soler, and Fermín de Salaberría as individual ship captains. This formation, known collectively as the *Vizcaíno* (Biscayan), or *Guipúzcoa,* squadron, was poorly equipped; its two capital ships were old and useless, "more intended for carrying French cloths and trading with these in the Indies than doing harm to the enemy," according to an observer. The vessels touched at the Canary Islands before departing Lanzarote on 30 October with an additional 70 men.

At dawn on 10 November, they sighted a large ship towing a prize near Cape Verde, West Africa, and closed with their standard, "the cross of Borgoña," prominently displayed. The stranger proved to be the English East Indiaman *Caesar,* which refused to salute the Biscayan flag, even when a signal gun was fired to draw attention to it. *San Nicolás* therefore crashed a broadside at the Indiaman, who responded with such a withering counterfire that 12 Biscayans were killed and many others wounded in the exchange, including García Galán. He died two days later, and the chastened formation straggled on across the Atlantic. Once in Caribbean waters, the small frigate of Fermín de Salaberría parted company to convey dispatches to New Spain, while the rest of the formation cruised past the islands of Trinidad and Margarita. Off the Salt Tortugas (present-day Tortuga Island, Venezuela), they plundered the 100-ton sloop *Relief* of London, then seized the Bermuda sloop *Speedwell.* The latter and its 18 crew members were carried into La

Guaira, the port of Caracas, to be sold in early March 1687. Shortly thereafter, the Biscayans also found the Jamaican sloop *Phoenix* of Captain John Jennings stranded on a beach, and took it into Cartagena. The English authorities were outraged at this "most inhuman treatment" of their island traders.

Meanwhile, De Salaberría's vessel had reached Havana in early March and Veracruz by mid-April 1687, unwittingly contributing to a mutiny by the crews of the Armada de Barlovento six weeks later, on account of their competition. By this time De Salaberría had sailed again, only to face an even more hostile reception off Júcaro, on the southern coast of Cuba. While attempting to rejoin his squadron on the Spanish Main, he encountered the pirate flagship of De Graaf, who chased him into the shallows. Soon De Salaberría found himself aground in unfamiliar waters, in danger of being captured. A force of small Cuban coast guard vessels hurried out to his rescue, which De Graaf turned on as well, seizing a schooner and sinking a *piragua*. (During this fighting the brother of the Cuban corsair Blas Miguel died, leading him to later seek revenge against the pirate.) Having survived this ordeal, De Salaberría completed his passage and the reunited Biscayan squadron then traveled northeastward through the Caribbean in two contingents. One group reached Veracruz in early July 1687, followed by Captain José de Leoz's flagship *Rosario* and a consort, which arrived at midday on 24 July.

An inspection revealed all to be in poor condition, with little possibility of repair. Mexican officials were authorized to return any unfit vessels to Spain, or incorporate these into the Armada de Barlovento or coast guard duty off Santo Domingo. No one seemed very happy to greet them—Spanish American officials resented the Biscayan privateers' autonomy and divisive presence, while foreign authorities suspected their commission would encompass attacks against peaceful merchants or fishermen. Already by the end of August 1687 Lieutenant Governor Hender Molesworth of Jamaica was writing to his superiors, "I have heard a great deal more than I can yet prove of these Biscayers, so that they deserve to be called to account for it." At virtually the same time Spanish officials in Madrid were growing uneasy at the lack of news from this squadron, not having received any communication since it had quit the Canaries.

Early in 1688 the Biscayan flotilla departed Veracruz to roam eastward, intercepting the bark *Dragon* of Roger Whitfield as it was bound from Jamaica toward New York, and sending it into Santiago de Cuba for adjudication. Richard Whiffin's pink was also taken and carried into Santo Domingo, where its crew was soon released, and the Biscayans then apparently left a contingent to establish themselves there as local *guardacostas*. On 1 May 1688, Governor Pierre-Paul Tarin de Cussy of Saint Domingue learned they had taken two French barks, one loaded with foodstuffs and the other bearing "twelve or thirteen *flibustiers* of the crew of [Claude de Roux, chevalier de] Saint-Laurent, who were going to trade among the islands." Five of these men managed to escape onto Puerto Rico (which the Guipuzcoans also visited that summer after raiding the French establishments at Samaná Bay). In September the Biscayans heard rumors that 300 French, English, and Danish buccaneers were occupying Vieques Island but found the place uninhabited when they made a reconnaissance in January 1689. A second raid in December, led by Captain John Philip Beare, produced a number of prisoners, mostly harmless settlers.

English wrath over real or imagined depredations by this squadron had led a royal warrant to be drawn up in London at the end of 1688, authorizing the governor of Jamaica to employ Royal Navy warships "to suppress the Biscayans who prey upon British trade." This was never signed, as the "Glorious Revolution" intervened and sent James II into exile, followed by the outbreak of the War of the League of Augsburg (King William's War) the next year, in which England, Spain, and Holland fought together against France. Allegations of Biscayan assaults against foreign vessels continued to be received, however, although it is unlikely many of these were actually perpetrated by the now enfeebled force. By November 1690 its commander, Francisco de Aguirre, was in Havana, homeward bound with the remnants of his staff. Most of the crew had deserted in the Americas, and by 1692 the Biscayan squadron was officially disbanded.

*See also* Barlovento, Armada de; Beare, John Philip; De Graaf, Laurens Cornelis Boudewijn; Galán, Francisco; *gobernador de tercio; guardacostas;* Miguel, Blas; Spanish Main.

*References: C.S.P., Amer. and W.I.,* Vols. XII–XIII; Garmendia; Juárez; López; Lugo; Robles.

# BLACKBURNE, LANCELOT

## (1658-1743)

Archbishop of York who allegedly served aboard buccaneer ships in the West Indies as a young man.

Blackburne was educated at Westminster School, and in 1676 matriculated at Christ Church, Oxford, at age 17. Five years later, shortly after his ordination, he went to Antigua on a brief secret mission (the sum of £20 appears opposite his name in the record of "Moneys paid for Secret Services" for the

year 1681). By 28 January 1683 (O.S.) he was back in England, receiving his master of arts degree. He concentrated on his church career, slowly gaining preferments until he became archbishop of York in 1724. This rise, aided by political influence, made him the target of jealous enemies, who repeated many injurious rumors—the most persistent being that Blackburne had acted as chaplain aboard ships engaged in buccaneering and even shared in their loot. One joke of the day had a buccaneer returning to England after many years and asking what had become of his old chum, only to be told he was now archbishop of York.

Blackburne's jolly, earthy personality lent itself to this image. Another story said that on a visitation to St. Mary's, Nottingham, he ordered pipes with tobacco and liquor brought into the vestry "for his refreshment after the fatigue of confirmation." The merry old cleric passed away on 23 March 1743 (O.S.), "at a time of extreme cold," and was buried at St. Margaret's, Westminster, England.

*Reference: D.N.B.*

# BLAUVELT, WILLEM ALBERTSZOON

## (FL. 1649-1663)

Famous Dutch rover whose name was variously spelled "Bluefield" or "Blewfield" by the English, among whom he served.

One of the earliest known references to Blauvelt occurs in October 1649, when he brought a Spanish prize into Newport, Rhode Island, after having captured this vessel on 22 April off Tabasco, Mexico, with his vessel *Garse* [*sic;* perhaps *Gans* for "goose," or *Garza* for "heron"]. Because of bad weather, he was forced to seek shelter in Newport, from where he sent his prize with its cargo of "grains of paradise" (Malagueta pepper) to Manhattan to be condemned. In 1663, Blauvelt was reportedly living among the friendly Indians at Cape Gracias a Dios on the Central American coast, commanding a bark of 3 guns and 50 men, with an English commission from Jamaica. He was very active in the logwood cutting in Honduras, the town and river of Bluefields supposedly being named after him.

*See also* logwood.

*References:* Chapin; Gosse, *Who's Who;* Pawson, *Port Royal.*

# BLÉNAC, CHARLES DE COURBON, SEIGNEUR DE ROMEGOUX, COMTE DE

## (1622-1696)

Governor general of the French Antilles who on several occasions raised *flibustiers* for West Indian campaigns.

Blénac was born in Saintonge, France, in 1622, of a noble family. He married his cousin's widow Angélique de La Rochefoucauld in 1649, by whom he had 11 children. He served the infant Louis XIV throughout the Fronde rebellions, rising in military rank. In 1669 Blénac transferred to the nascent French Navy and commanded the *Infante* in the comte d'Estrées's expedition against the Barbary pirates, as well as the *Fort* (Strong) at the 1672 Battle of Sole Bay. Hot-tempered and quarrelsome, he was briefly incarcerated the following year for insulting a superior officer but again saw action against the Dutch that August, when he captained *Fortuné* (Fortunate) at the Battle of the Texel.

Late in 1676, Blénac sailed in d'Estrées's first Caribbean expedition, commanding

*Fendant* (Sword Stroke) in the unsuccessful assault on Dutch Tobago. Retreating to Grenada, the French learned of the death of Jean-Charles de Baas-Castelmore, governor general of the Antilles, whom Blénac was appointed to succeed. He returned to France with d'Estrées to have his nomination confirmed, then sailed back to Martinique with the admiral's second fleet in the autumn of 1677, assuming office that November. Blénac was instrumental in raising a large force of *flibustiers* for d'Estrées's subsequent venture against Curaçao, which ended in disaster when the force was wrecked on Aves Islands the evening of 11 May 1678.

Blénac also employed buccaneer contingents during the War of the League of Augsburg (King William's War), especially at its inception in 1689, when he launched offensive operations against English Saint Christopher and Dutch Sint Eustatius. His early successes were soon reversed, and he was so severely criticized by subordinates such as Jean-Baptiste Ducasse that he offered to resign. Blénac returned to France "on leave" aboard *Pont d'Or* (Golden Bridge) in 1690 and did not resume his duties at Martinique until 16 February 1692. He died of lingering dysentery the night of 8 June 1696 at Fort Royal and was succeeded by the marquis d'Amblimont.

*See also* Amblimont, marquis d'; Ducasse, Jean-Baptiste; Estrées, Jean, comte d'.

*Reference:* Baudrit.

# BLOT, CAPITAINE

## (FL. 1684)

*Flibustier* named in a French document of 1684 as commanding the *Quagone* of 8 guns and 90 men at Saint Domingue. As this particular list was drawn up by a third party, with misspelled or otherwise incomplete names, and no other known reference exists to a "Capitaine Blot," this may be an erroneous reference to Pierre Bot.

*See also* Bot, Pierre.

*References:* Gosse, *Who's Who;* Juárez; Lugo.

# BLUNDEN, ROBERT

## (FL. 1662-1664)

English privateer out of Jamaica.

When the new governor, Lord Windsor, arrived at Port Royal in August 1662, his instructions included the suggestion that an attempt be made to win over the *boucaniers* of Tortuga Island before they could threaten the burgeoning English colony. The idea was to make a peaceful overture, hoping to persuade them without antagonizing the French government. Windsor remained in office only ten weeks before returning to England, so the matter was left to the Council of Jamaica, which dispatched Colonel Samuel Barry and Captain Abraham Langford on this business aboard the privateersman *Charles* of Robert Blunden.

The trio set sail in January 1663, crossing to western Santo Domingo; upon arriving, they learned that the *boucaniers* of Tortuga were quite hostile to such a notion, and might contest their approach by force of arms. Blunden flatly refused to proceed, and the *Charles* was redirected—over Barry's objections—to the mainland settlement of Petit Goâve. Here, a different band of *boucaniers* acclaimed Blunden their chieftain, even raising the English flag. Langford apparently seconded Blunden, departing soon after for England to petition Charles II for appointment as governor of "Tortuga and the coasts of Hispaniola."

Barry returned to Jamaica several months later and reported this strange conclusion, which London never approved because Blunden's claim would not only have

annoyed the French government but also the Spaniards (who shared Santo Domingo).

*See also* Hispaniola; Langford, Abraham; Windsor, Thomas.

*References:* Pawson, *Port Royal;* Pope.

# BOND, GEORGE

## (FL. 1683-1684)

English master turned pirate.

Bond arrived in the West Indies commanding the *Summer Island* of London, but at Saint Thomas in the Danish Virgin Islands was persuaded to go a-roving, so in May 1683 was seen fitting out his ship, now renamed *Fortune's Adventure.* He was abetted by the local governor, Adolf Esmit, with "spars, sails, and provisions." Bond ventured on a cruise and returned with a Dutch prize, stopping at the east end of Saint Thomas to send Esmit word of his arrival. The governor met Bond at sea, offering "his sloop and storehouse [to land and hide] the captured goods," plus protection for the rovers. Soon Bond's depredations began to multiply, one being the English merchantman *Gideon,* which he sent into Saint Thomas. His prize crew (all English) were well received by the governor, the booty was stored in the castle, and the pirates themselves were "given an ounce of gold dust a man," presumably as payment for their plunder.

By 25 August 1683, things had reached such a pass that Governor Sir William Stapleton of the Leeward Islands sent a letter from Nevis, informing London that

> Captain Carlile goes this very day to look for one Cooke and one Bond, two English pirates fitted from Saint Thomas. I have furnished him with men and powder lest he should be overpowered.

Carlile evidently met with no success, because two months later—after it was falsely reported that the great corsair Laurens de Graaf had been hanged by the Spaniards—Stapleton was moved to add that

> there is now no pirate abroad but Bond with a small ship and 100 men. He is expected at Saint Thomas where Captain Carlile is ready for him.

But the English renegade continued to evade the Royal Navy, with only a few of his prizes intercepted. On one occasion Bond apparently purchased a Dutch ship at Saint Thomas, which was then seized by a trio of English privateers sent out in pursuit of him. In early 1684, another Dutch ship that Bond had taken off Suriname was recaptured at Beef Island, off east Tortola. Its English liberators carried it into Nevis but were disappointed to discover that the cargo had already been off-loaded at Saint Thomas.

The Jamaican sloop *Fox* underwent an even more complicated ordeal, first being taken by French *flibustiers* who carried it to Saint Croix, where it was then cut out by Bond and brought to Saint Thomas. He made a gift of it to Esmit, who in turn refused a Jamaican request to restore the sloop to its English owners. Instead, Esmit put a cargo of timber aboard and dispatched it to Barbados. On its return passage, the *Fox* dropped anchor off Saint John's Island "by Captain Hill's ship, who seized the sloop and took possession," sailing it into Nevis in June 1684.

*See also* Beef Island; Carlile, Charles; Cooke, John; De Graaf, Laurens Cornelis Boudewijn.

*References: C.S.P., Amer. and W.I.,* Vol. XI.

# BONIDELL, CAPTAIN

(FL. 1659)

Privateer commander, presumably French, who was mentioned in the journal of

Colonel Edward D'Oyley, governor of Jamaica, as having been issued a "let pass" on 24 November 1659 (O.S.).

*See also* D'Oyley, Edward.

*References:* Pawson, *Port Royal.*

# BOON, JOHN

(FL. 1687)

Member of the Council of Carolina under Governor Colleton, who was expelled in 1687 "for holding correspondence with pirates."

*Reference:* Gosse, *Who's Who.*

# BOT, PIERRE

ALSO BOTTE
(FL. 1672-1685)

Breton corsair who took part in the assaults on Veracruz and Campeche.

Bot apparently first went to sea in 1672, serving aboard fishing boats that visited both La Coruña and Martinique, as well as on a ship belonging to the Knights of Malta. Late in 1682 he joined the *flibustier* flotilla of Grammont off Cuba, proceeding to the Bahamas where—"being the bravest," according to him—he captured a Spanish ship commanded by "Martín de Melgar" [*sic;* more likely Martín de Echagaray, senior pilot at Saint Augustine, Florida]. Bot's share of this booty came to "60 pounds of silver," and the Spanish survivors were returned to Havana aboard a *barco luengo.* In March 1683 Bot intercepted the 22-gun Spanish merchantman *Nuestra Señora de Regla* off Cuba's southern coast, losing nine men in a bloody clash before this ship could be carried. He set its survivors ashore at Guantanamo Bay, sailing his battered prize toward Petit Goâve with the rest of

Grammont's squadron. Upon approaching, they were met by Nikolaas van Hoorn, who was exiting in Grammont's corvette *Colbert* to recall them for an enterprise against the Spaniards.

Bot then captained *Regla* across to Roatan, and afterward to Guanaja, before taking part in the huge assault on Veracruz led by Grammont, Van Hoorn, and Laurens de Graaf in May 1683. He returned to Saint Domingue and may be the "Capitaine Blot" listed as commanding the 8-gun *Quagone*, of 90 men, in 1684. Botte also served in Grammont and De Graaf's sack of Campeche in 1685, withdrawing at the end of August to Isla Mujeres with the rest of the freebooters to divide the spoils.

From there he departed with De Graaf's *Neptune* and three other pirate ships for Petit Goâve but on 11 September 1685 was sighted and pursued by the Armada de Barlovento. After four hours, *Regla* and a pirate sloop had lagged so far astern that they came under Spanish fire. A brisk cannonade ensued, but Antonio de Astina's vice-flagship *Nuestra Señora de la Concepción* closed inexorably, despite Bot's desperate attempts to lighten his ship by flinging articles overboard—beginning, according to one eyewitness, with the "three large canoes they had stolen from the Campeche fishermen."

Finally Bot hailed, offering to strike if granted quarter. This was conceded, and *Regla* hove to. The Spaniards found 130 French buccaneers on board, along with numerous captives from Campeche: 20 Spanish, 13 Indians, and some black slaves. In addition to its 22 guns, Bot's ship had been armed with 10 swivel guns and more than 200 firearms, plus those jettisoned during the chase or appropriated by the armada's light-fingered sailors. (The Spanish seamen behaved badly, seizing many weapons and items for themselves despite their officers' intervention. The purser, or *veedor*, Juan Nieto beat back one group with his cutlass, calling them "scoundrels, drunks and thieves"; another band was set upon by prizemaster Ensign Pedro de Iriarte. The situation worsened when boarders also arrived from the flagship *Santo Cristo de Burgos*, bitter rivals to the vice-flag. By the time this pilfering was done, scarcely 30 pounds of church ornaments were recovered, along with some dry goods in the hold and a little money.)

While *Regla* was being ransacked, Bot and his men were redistributed around the Spanish warships: 50 aboard the flagship, a like number aboard the vice, and 30 on the frigate *Honhón*. The pursuit of De Graaf then resumed, ending unsuccessfully four days later when his *Neptune* escaped. The armada limped back into Veracruz, entering the night of 28 September 1685. Although the French buccaneers had been promised clemency, Bot and his lieutenants were convicted and sentenced to death, along with half a dozen Spanish subjects who had been serving under them. These executions were carried out in Veracruz a few weeks later.

***See also*** Barlovento, Armada de; *barco luengo;* De Graaf, Laurens Cornelis Boudewijn; Grammont, "chevalier" de; Van Hoorn, Nikolaas.

***References:*** Juárez; Weddle, *Wilderness.*

# BOURILLON, FRANÇOIS

## (FL. 1669)

French adventurer from Marseilles who, according to a memorandum he submitted in November 1669, had "made many voyages in Spanish America, with the Spaniards and in their service, and lived many years both in the islands as well as Tierra Firme, always passing himself off as a Spaniard."

In a rather simplistic proposal for promoting French expansion overseas, Bourillon suggested that an expedition of ten large ships and 8,000 troops be sent to Tortuga, where it could be augmented by *boucaniers.* From there, part of this force could be used to overrun the Spanish stronghold of Santiago de los Caballeros on Santo Domingo, continuing overland to meet the rest of the formation, which would land at the island capital. Once this city fell, "the same army and same ships could make a descent on Cuba," he concluded. This was one of many such half-baked schemes submitted to the French Crown during the seventeenth century, and there is no indication it was ever acted upon.

*Reference:* Lugo.

# BRADISH, JOSEPH
## (1672-1700)

New Englander convicted of running away with a ship in the Far East.

Bradish was born at Cambridge, Massachusetts, on 28 November 1672 (O.S.). Pursuing a career at sea, he signed on as mate aboard the 350-ton ship *Adventure* of London in March 1698, bound on a trading voyage to Borneo. When the ship paused at the Spice Islands for water in September, its captain, Thomas Gullock, and most of the officers and passengers went ashore. Bradish seized the opportunity to lead the crew in a mutiny, setting loyal hands ashore in a boat before sailing away. When their booty was counted, he and his followers found that their shares came to £1,600 apiece, Bradish himself receiving two-and-a-half shares.

*Adventure* touched at Mauritius and Ascension Island to replenish supplies before appearing off Long Island at the end of March 1699 to strike a deal with Colonel Henry Pierson and store some of their loot.

Bradish then continued northward to Block Island, near Rhode Island, where he encountered two sloops. Their crews helped the pirates strip *Adventure* of everything of value before scuttling the ship. The men then attempted to disperse throughout New England, but the alarm had been raised. Bradish and ten others were detained in Boston's jail, but he and a companion managed to escape on 25 June with the collusion of jailer Caleb Ray, a relative. A reward of £200 was posted and search parties sent out, and the two fugitives were quickly recaptured at Saco, Maine, being returned to Boston.

Bradish was apparently sent to England in irons aboard HMS *Advice* in early 1700, along with William Kidd, James Kelley, and other pirates. He was tried and executed along with Kelley, their bodies exhibited in chains at Hope Dock near Gravesend "as a greater terror to others."

*See also* Kidd, William.

*References:* Gosse, *Who's Who;* Ritchie.

# BRADLEY, JOSEPH
## (FL. 1668-1671)

English privateer who operated out of Jamaica.

The first mention of Bradley's activities occurred in summer 1668, when he joined Henry Morgan's attack on Portobelo, then later quit his company after the loss of HMS *Oxford* to participate in an independent assault on the Spanish American port of Cumaná (Venezuela).

The next spring, Bradley sailed his 80-man frigate (*Mayflower?*) into the Gulf of Mexico along with the brigantines of Rok Brasiliano and Jelles de Lecat to campaign against the Spaniards in and around the Laguna de Términos. For two or three weeks this trio hovered off the port of Campeche without taking any prizes. They then attempted some disembarkations on the coast before Bradley finally captured a Cuban vessel laden with flour, and the raiders could retire into the Laguna de Términos to rest.

They remained in the laguna two months and Brasiliano careened his brigantine while De Lecat laid in a cargo of logwood. At the end of this interlude Bradley and Brasiliano returned to blockade Campeche, his frigate taking up station directly opposite that port while Brasiliano's brigantine hauled up close inshore off Las Bocas, four leagues to the southwest.

On 18 December 1669, the Spaniards sortied with three armed ships, chasing the intruders away. Brasiliano was shipwrecked on the north shores of Yucatán, from where he was later rescued by De Lecat, transferred aboard Bradley's frigate, and returned to Jamaica.

Shortly after arriving at his plantation, reports began to reach Bradley of renewed activities by Spanish corsairs in the West Indies, culminating with a series of raids against Jamaica itself by Manoel Rivero Pardal in summer 1670. The Jamaican governor and council therefore decided to organize a retaliatory strike under "General" Morgan, whom Bradley immediately joined. When it seemed that the 22-gun, 120-ton *Satisfaction* would not reappear in time to lead this expedition, Morgan selected Bradley's 70-ton *Mayflower* as his flagship. At the last moment *Satisfaction* returned, and Morgan transferred into it before setting sail from Port Royal on 11 August 1670 at the head of a fleet of 11 vessels and 600 men.

The fleet ventured to the south coast of Cuba on a brief sweep before touching at Tortuga Island to recruit more followers among the French *flibustiers,* and then reached the agreed rendezvous point off Ile-à-Vache by 12 September. Bradley played a prominent role in the subsequent series of

conferences, which eventually led to the decision to attack Panama, further being invested with the title *lieutenant colonel* for the forthcoming enterprise.

## CHAGRES ASSAULT
### (JANUARY 1671)

Toward the end of 1670, Morgan's huge fleet of 36 vessels and 2,000 buccaneers at last got under way, pausing on Christmas Day to recapture tiny Providencia Island from the Spaniards. Three days afterward, Bradley was sent ahead with 470 men aboard his own ship, "Major" Richard Norman's 10-gun *Lilly,* and De Lecat's *Seviliaen* to capture the crucial San Lorenzo castle at the mouth of the Chagres River, which was to be used as the pirates' advance base for their overland march against Panama.

Bradley and his consorts landed within sight of this fortification at noon on 6 January 1671, 400 freebooters disembarking and approaching "with flags and trumpets" to make their initial assault that afternoon. The 360 Spanish defenders waited confidently under their *castellano* (garrison commander), Pedro de Elizalde, who had written, "Even if all England were to come, they would not capture this castle."

Bradley's first and second charges were halted by a deadly hail of bullets, but as dusk fell he led his men forward through some gullies, creeping up to toss grenades and fire-pots inside, which ignited the wooden stockades. Fire spread gradually throughout the night, consuming the defenses and detonating San Lorenzo's magazines. In the darkness, some 150 Spanish soldiers deserted, but enough remained to break Bradley's first assaults the next day. Finally, a contingent of *flibustiers* from Tortuga fought their way inside on the third attempt, swords in hand, so that a badly wounded Bradley could hear them shouting *"Victoire! Victoire!"* above the din. Elizalde and his remaining 70 defenders fought bravely to the last man. At least 30 buccaneers had been killed and another 76 injured during the assault, including Bradley, who was shot through both legs. Norman assumed overall command while Bradley convalesced, but five days later—as Morgan's ships hove into view—he died of his wounds.

**See also** Brasiliano, Rok; careen; Laguna de Términos; Lecat, Jelles de; logwood; Morgan, Sir Henry; Rivero Pardal, Manoel.

**References:** Earle, *Panamá;* Pope.

# BRANDENBURG PRIVATEERS

Despite their name, these were actually Dutch frigates commissioned by the elector of Brandenburg to raid the Spanish West Indies.

During the fighting in the Low Countries of the 1670s, Spain had incurred a considerable debt with Friedrich Wilhelm, elector of the German duchy of Brandenburg, which it was unable to meet once peace was concluded with the Treaty of Nijmegen in late 1678. With budding overseas ambitions of his own, Friedrich Wilhelm decided to exact restitution by issuing letters of reprisal to two unemployed Dutch privateers at Zeeland in the spring of 1679. When the French government learned that these two men o' war were preparing to sail, they objected, not having finalized their own terms with the elector, which meant this pair might also attack French interests. Colbert therefore threatened to send Admiral comte d'Estrées with a squadron of 14 vessels "to seize or sink" these intruders, thus constraining them to remain in port until peace with France was finalized at the end of June 1679. By this time, the season was too far advanced to consider any departure for the New World that year.

Over the winter the original pair was reinforced with two more Dutch frigates and a fireship. This flotilla sailed from Königsberg on 14 April 1680, its commander, Cornelis Reers, flying the elector's standard aboard his flagship *Kurprinz* (Prince Elector). This small force comprised frigates of 16 to 32 guns, while the fireship *Salamander* mounted 2 guns, and a total of 500 men served aboard all the craft. Outside Oostende (off the Belgian coast) they made their first capture, a Spanish merchantman bound for Cadiz with dry goods. They sent this ship back to Brandenburg, then crossed the Atlantic in August, searching for further prey in the West Indies.

At Santa Marta (in present-day Colombia) they saw a galliot and merchant vessel lying at anchor and employed a cunning trick. The merchant ship had originally been the *William and Anne* of London, which had sailed to Bilbao in Spain and exchanged part of its English crew for Spaniards. It had then continued to the Canary Islands, where the remainder were replaced by Spanish seamen, save the first mate (who became master) and ship's carpenter Samuel Button of Boston, Massachusetts. Loaded with Canary wine and brandy, the ship then cleared for Cartagena on the Spanish Main. They had entered Santa Marta to take on water but were delayed by the local governor to provide escort for the galliot, which was also bound for Cartagena.

"After we had been two or three days in the road," Button later declared:

> We espied five ships lying off and on, by the space of two or three days. At length they sent in their pinnace with Dutch colors to the governor, to get liberty to wood and water, pretending to be Dutchmen come to clear the coast of privateers.

The unsuspecting Spaniards allowed them into port, but four or five nights later, when the *William and Anne* was preparing to put to sea on the land breeze, it was boarded in the dark. The mysterious captors secured the Spaniards, then asked Button if he was the ship's carpenter. When he replied yes, they told him, "That's good, you be an Englishman. That doeth no harm." The ship was snuck out and the next morning, prizemaster Marsilius Cock of *Salamander* gleefully informed Button that "they would show me such colors as I never saw, and then spread their Brandenburg colors."

The *William and Anne* and galliot taken, the Dutch also intercepted a Spanish merchantman called *Torito* (Bull Calf), before arriving at Port Royal, Jamaica, toward the end of that year (20 December 1680 O.S.). Acting governor Sir Henry Morgan allowed them in to refit and later reported to London how the privateers "urged the Duke [of Brandenburg's] alliance with England for permission to sell their prizes, that by the produce thereof they might purchase all necessary refreshments for their present expedition." Morgan agreed, even allowing *William and Anne* to join a convoy assembling for England, as Reers hoped to return it to Brandenburg. The privateers remained in Port Royal a month, where curiosity seekers noted the strange blue uniforms and bonnets of the elector's soldiers. Eventually Reers set sail with his four frigates in early February 1681, "bound eastward to cruise and search the coast of Hispaniola first," Morgan noted, "then the [Spanish] Main." But luck now abandoned the Dutch, as few sightings were made and their one sure prize never reached its destination.

The *William and Anne* had apparently been renamed *Salamander*. A fireship of this name was sold off at Port Royal, then sailed with the convoy some weeks after Reers's departure. But in early April 1681, Cock put into "Piscataqua" (New Hampshire), complaining of leaks and lack of provisions and remaining more than three months to

make repairs. Finally, the English authorities began to suspect that "he intended to sell the said ship and deceive the duke," and his crew grew surly at the enforced idleness and lack of pay. Cock "cruelly beat 12 of the ship's company at the capstan and otherwise, as made them weary of their lives," and on 21 July 1681 the *Salamander* was ordered to sail to Boston and anchor within range of the harbor guns, sending its sails ashore.

Meanwhile, Rears had returned to Prussia by May 1681, inspiring the elector to dispatch other expeditions. That same summer a little establishment was begun on the West African coast, and Brandenburghian vessels would continue to visit the West Indies. At the end of June 1684, Governor Sir Thomas Lynch of Jamaica reported "two or three pirate [ships] have been lately taken," one of which claimed to be a Brandenburger, while in March 1691 three Brandenburg vessels touched at Nevis, bound for Danish Saint Thomas.

*See also* Estrées, Jean, comte d';
Hispaniola; Spanish Main.
*References:* *C.S.P., Amer. and W.I.*, Vols. XI–XIII; Jameson; Marley, *Pirates*.

# BRANLY, CAPTAIN

(FL. 1685)

English buccaneer.

Branly commanded a 36-man bark in the flotilla of Edward Davis as it was lying off the Panamanian coast in the South Seas during April to May 1685, awaiting the arrival of the Peruvian silver ships. The chronicler Ravenau de Lussan misspelled his name as "Brander."

*See also* Lussan, Ravenau de; South Seas.
*References:* Bradley, *Lure;* Lussan.

# BRASILIANO, ROK

## (FL. 1654-1673)

Dutch-born rover who settled among the English of Jamaica.

According to the chronicler Alexandre Olivier Exquemelin, Brasiliano was originally from Groningen in the Netherlands, from where he emigrated to the Dutch West India Company colony of Bahía, Brazil. When this outpost was lost to the Spanish and Portuguese in 1654, he found his way to Jamaica. He thus became known as "Rock the Brazilian" to his English colleagues and soon began serving aboard privateers as a common seaman. He eventually rose to command of a small bark, with which he reputedly captured a rich prize from New Spain "and in the end became so audacious he made all Jamaica tremble." On one of his first cruises he was taken prisoner at Campeche and deported to Spain, although he managed to regain his freedom and return across the Atlantic to Jamaica.

Detailed accounts of Brasiliano's activities begin early in 1668, when the French *flibustier* Jean-David Nau l'Olonnais touched at Jamaica with an 80-ton, 12-gun Spanish brigantine he had taken in order to sell it. Brasiliano was installed as captain, with Jelles de Lecat as his first mate. They ventured to the Mosquito Coast and joined Henry Morgan's attack on Portobelo that July, after which they participated in another assault on the Spanish American port of Cumaná (Venezuela). Returning to Port Royal with a second captured brigantine, Brasiliano assumed command of this new vessel, while De Lecat remained aboard the old one.

## GULF OF MEXICO CAMPAIGN (1669-1670)

In spring 1669, both accompanied the 80-man frigate (*Mayflower?*) of Joseph Bradley into the Gulf of Mexico to campaign against the Spaniards in and around the Laguna de Términos. Brasiliano's 40-man crew consisted of 34 Dutchmen and 6 Englishmen, and for two or three weeks this trio of vessels hovered off the port of Campeche without making any prizes. Forays were then attempted ashore, Brasiliano losing two men during a disembarkation at the town of Lerma before Bradley captured a Cuban vessel laden with flour, and so the raiders retired into the Laguna de Términos to rest.

They remained in the laguna for the next two months—Brasiliano careened his brigantine while De Lecat laid in a cargo of logwood. At the end of this interlude, Bradley and Brasiliano returned to blockade Campeche again, the frigate taking up station directly opposite that port, while the brigantine hauled up closer inshore off Las Bocas, four leagues to the southwest. Here Brasiliano seized three fishermen and tortured one who revealed that a ship from Veracruz would soon be bringing "a new governor" for the province. (Actually, the *oidor* Lic. Fructos Delgado was scheduled to arrive, who had been sent out from Mexico City as *visitador*, or auditor, for the outgoing administration; a new governor would not be appointed in Spain for yet another year.)

On 18 December 1669, the Spaniards suddenly sortied with three armed ships, chasing the intruders away. Brasiliano then became caught in a stiff norther that forced him to claw northeastward, hoping to get clear of Yucatán. He managed to round the northwestern tip of the peninsula but eventually wrecked on Chicxulub beach, a thin strip of barrier sand just east of the present-day town of Progreso. One of his prisoners escaped, carrying word to the Spanish authorities at the provincial capital of Mérida that the rovers were ashore, prompting the immediate dispatch of a cavalry patrol to that site. The patrol found the pirates hastily burying their artillery, tools, and other heavy items rescued from the wreck in the sand and immediately bore down upon them. Brasiliano's men scattered for their boat, leaving two behind as they pulled frantically away from shore. These two surrendered to the Spaniards, who then dug up Brasiliano's trove—a bronze cannon bearing the arms of Spain's King Philip II, two bronze *pedreros* or swivel guns, and 60-odd iron balls—before returning to the capital at the end of that month.

### PANAMA CAMPAIGN
### (1670-1671)

Meanwhile, Brasiliano and his surviving crewmembers were rescued by De Lecat, who transferred them to Bradley's frigate for the return passage to Jamaica. Shortly after arriving there, the English colony became agitated by the growing depredations of Spanish corsairs, particularly the nuisance raids of Manoel Rivero Pardal against their coastline. Consequently, in August 1670 Brasiliano sailed with Bradley and De Lecat to incorporate themselves into Morgan's retaliatory strike against Panama, which was rendezvousing at Ile-à-Vache first for supplies and reinforcements. This corsair fleet descended on Providencia Island, overwhelming its tiny Spanish garrison, before Morgan sent Bradley on ahead with his two cohorts to seize San Lorenzo castle, at the mouth of the Chagres River, as a foothold for their overland approach to Panama. Brasiliano and De Lecat were among the 470 buccaneers who served in the three ships of this advance force, which departed Providencia on 30 December 1670.

The buccaneers disembarked a few days later and stormed the castle despite heavy opposition. Both Brasiliano and Bradley were wounded during this assault, the latter fatally, and the Spanish defenders were ruthlessly massacred. It is believed Brasiliano then recuperated sufficiently to participate in Morgan's epic march across the isthmus a

few weeks afterward, where in spite of the harsh climatic conditions and shortages of food and water, the freebooters fought their way into Panama and occupied that city for a month. Nevertheless, booty proved disappointing and the raiders further found upon their return to Jamaica that they no longer enjoyed official sanction, as the new governor, Sir Thomas Lynch had arrived and begun to recall commissions.

As late as October 1673, when Mateo Alonso de Huidobro captured a Dutch brigantine in the Laguna de Términos, its Captain Jan Lucas reported that Brasiliano was still active in the West Indies.

*See also* Bradley, Joseph; careen; Lecat, Jelles de; logwood; Morgan, Sir Henry; Mosquito Coast; Rivero Pardal, Manoel.

*References:* Earle, *Panamá;* Exquemelin; Vrijman; Weddle, *Spanish.*

# BRÉHAL, CAPITAINE

### ALSO BRÉAL
### (FL. 1683-1684)

French *flibustier* out of Saint Domingue whose name has often been misspelled: "Bhra," "Braha," "Brahan," "Braugham," "Brea," "Breha," "Brouage," etc.

Perhaps he bore the name of the tiny village of Bréhal near Saint Malo, France, although this is mere speculation.

### SAINT AUGUSTINE RAID
### (1683)

The first notice of Bréhal's activities occurred in March 1683, when he was lying at the Bahamas with the privateer vessels of Captains Conway Woolley, John Markham, and Jan Corneliszoon (commander of a New York brigantine), preparing "to fish for silver from a Spanish wreck." The next arrival was the bark *Pearl* of Thomas Paine, bearing a commission from the Jamaican governor Sir

Thomas Lynch to hunt pirates, so the five captains conspired instead to raid the nearby Spanish outpost of Saint Augustine, Florida, despite the peace prevailing with that nation and having no other authorization than Paine's commission.

The attackers landed on the Florida coast flying French colors but found the Spaniards forewarned. After releasing some captives they had brought and looting the surrounding countryside, they withdrew. (The Spanish garrison commander referred to Bréhal as the leader of this expedition, calling him "Capitán Braha" in his official report of 28 June 1683.) Bréhal, Paine, and Markham then returned to New Providence in the Bahamas, where Governor Robert Lilburne allegedly wished to impound the two English ships "but failed for want of a force." Bréhal and Paine went wrecking, and by the time the governor manned a large ship that had arrived and followed them to the wreck site, the rovers had sailed northward to New England.

## RHODE ISLAND VISIT
### (1683-1684)

Several weeks later, the two entered Newport, Rhode Island, leading Governor Edward Cranfield of neighboring New Hampshire to write in mid-October 1683:

> During my stay at Rhode Island two pirates came in. Pain [sic] was one of them, with a counterfeit commission from Sir Thomas Lynch styling him [i.e., the Jamaican governor] one of the gentlemen of the king's bedchamber, instead of his privy chamber, whereby I knew it to be forged. Colonel Dongan and I asked the government to arrest them, but they refused.

*Pearl* was detained, but Bréhal was allowed to depart undisturbed. Because of his notoriety, though, his name came to be attached to

another pair of freebooters who visited New England that following summer, Michiel Andrieszoon and Jan Willems, the former being temporarily identified as "Bhra."

## CUBAN BLOCKADE
### (1684)

Meanwhile, Bréhal had returned to Saint Domingue and possibly participated in Markham's Tampico raid of late April 1684. A French document from this same year lists Bréhal as commanding the ship *Fortune,* of 14 guns and 100 men. In early November—following the renewal of hostilities between Spain and France—he was blockading the southern coast of Cuba along with a pair of sloops. When his flotilla began to run low on supplies, he dispatched his consorts to impress the services of Jamaican turtlers in the region. Anthony Griffin, master of the sloop *Prosperous,* later declared:

> I was leaving the South Cays with turtle when two sloops, which I had thought to be English, ordered me to anchor, and some Frenchmen came on board and took me prisoner. Anthony Hawkes of the sloop *Elizabeth* was also taken a few hours later, and we were all carried to Boga Pavillione [?], six leagues off which Captain Breha [sic] was lying with his ship. He took all our turtle and detained us.

Daniel Pindar of the sloop *Greyhound* had already been "boarded by a *piragua* with several men, commanded by Captain Breha, who cut our cable and compelled us to catch turtle for them for several days." The same had happened a little earlier to Henry Smith of the *Seaflower,* while John Griffin's *True Love* had been relieved of 30 turtles before being released, and Francis Powell's *Speedwell* had managed to escape despite being pursued.

Shortly afterward, the tiny Royal Navy warship *Bonito,* four guns, appeared and learned the turtlers' fate. Gathering a convoy of seven frightened sloops around him, Captain Edward Stanley sailed in search of the raider flagship, which he described as "a French privateer of 16 guns and 180 men, commanded by one Captain Braugham [*sic*]." At nine o'clock on the morning of 19 November 1684, he found *Fortune* at anchor with its prizes and sent a message across to Bréhal asking "why the four sloops with him did not hoist their English colors?" The *flibustier* chieftain boarded *Bonito* to personally explain that he had been forced to impress their services to feed his crews and intended to release the sloops. "He promised to end all difference next morning," Stanley concluded, "but the wind blowing fresh in the night he hove up anchor and went to sea."

### COMPLAINT AT PETIT GOÂVE
#### (1684)

Less than a month later, Acting Governor Hender Molesworth of Jamaica dispatched Captain David Mitchell's HMS *Ruby*, 48 guns, with a complaint to the French authorities at Petit Goâve. Although mostly concerned with Willems's capture of the English sloop *James* off Cartagena, he added:

A privateer, Captain Brahan [*sic*], belonging to your port, has lately robbed several of our turtling sloops to the value of £500. I trust that you will grant us satisfaction, or give us leave to take it.

Mitchell arrived off Petit Goâve the morning of 16 December, sighting both Willems's *Dauphine* (Princess) and Bréhal's *Fortune* in the roads, as well as other privateers. He immediately sent his message ashore, but Governor Pierre-Paul Tarin de Cussy was absent, being represented by Captain Boisseau. The latter returned a polite answer to the Royal Navy officer's submission, saying:

With regard to your complaints against Captain Breha, it is true that with a ship full of people he met the frigate commanded by Captain Stanley, and asked him for provisions, of which he was much in need, and which Captain Stanley was so good as to give him. As to the restitution which you request, I doubt if it can be made, and I do not see that I can compel it.

*Ruby*'s master could only acquiesce in this interpretation of events off south Cuba and four days later reported back to Port Royal.

**See also** Andrieszoon, Michiel; Corneliszoon, Jan; Lilburne, Robert; Markham, John; Paine, Thomas; Willems, Jan; Woolley, Conway.
*Reference: C.S.P., Amer. and W.I.*, Vol. XI.

# BRENNINGHAM, CAPTAIN
#### (FL. 1663)

English privateer described as commanding a frigate of 6 guns and 70 men at Jamaica in 1663.
**References:** Gosse, *Who's Who;* Pawson, *Port Royal.*

# BRIGAUT, NICOLAS
#### (C. 1653-1686)

*Flibustier* who served in the assaults on Maracaibo, Campeche, and Saint Augustine, Florida.

Brigaut was born a Huguenot (French Protestant) on the Ile de Ré near La Rochelle, France, sometime around 1653. He went to sea at a young age, and in 1679 embarked for Martinique. His ship was lost

"50 leagues from Puerto Rico," but he was rescued by another vessel and carried into Saint Domingue, where the following year he signed on with the "chevalier" de Grammont's freebooter flotilla bound for Cumaná. After this campaign, Brigaut traveled to New England (perhaps with Capitaine Bréhal in 1683 or Michiel Andrieszoon and Jan Willems in 1684), where he purchased a 40-ton sloop. Returning to the Caribbean, Brigaut rejoined his comrades off Isla Orchila near Caracas before heading northward and joining the formations of Grammont and Laurens de Graaf in their descent on the Mexican port of Campeche.

This assault took place in July 1685, after which Brigaut received command of a 40-man Spanish galliot lying in the roads and followed Grammont when the raiders withdrew two months later. This galliot, Grammont's *Hardi* (Audacious), and a sloop went to Roatan off the Central American coast to careen, after which Grammont decided to attack the Spanish outpost of Saint Augustine, Florida, perhaps in alliance with the English settlers of Carolina. The *flibustier* trio worked its way into the Atlantic, and on 30 April 1686, Brigaut's galliot stood in alone toward Matanzas, Florida, flying Spanish colors. Grammont's flagship and sloop remained concealed at anchor farther south.

The pirates wished to gather intelligence on the main garrison of Saint Augustine, 15 miles north, and at first everything seemed to go well. Four Spanish soldiers rowed out in a boat and with a friendly hail were invited aboard Brigaut's galliot. Once in the pirates' power, however, two soldiers were tortured while the rovers set a landing party ashore to obtain an Indian interpreter and pillage supplies. The landing party returned some hours later with another Spanish prisoner, several Indian captives, and provisions. But soon more Spanish soldiers appeared on the beach, and the raiders

realized they had been discovered from Saint Augustine. The following morning, 1 May, two boats filled with buccaneers rowed ashore and fought a four-hour battle against the Spanish soldiers, killing one and wounding four. During the night the weather worsened, grounding the galliot on a bar in a heavy ground swell. The next day, Brigaut's men, "carrying their arms in their mouths, waded ashore and dug holes in the beach from which they poured a heavy fire into the Spanish troops." Although outnumbered, they were able to drive off the Spaniards because of superior firepower, killing four and wounding seven, but their galliot remained fast.

That night Brigaut decided on a desperate expedient: He sent a launch with five men to advise Grammont that he and his crew would march almost 40 miles south to "Mosquitos Bar" (near modern-day Daytona Beach), asking the sloop to pick them up within five days. In the darkness and a heavy downpour, Brigaut and his remaining 40 men abandoned their galliot, stealing ashore undetected with their captives and beginning the trek. Dawn of 3 May found them clean away, the rain having erased their footsteps from the sand. However, this same night Grammont had anchored close to Matanzas searching for his lost consort and consequently never received Brigaut's plea for help. Within 15 miles of their destination, the buccaneers were approached by a band of 50 or 60 Indians, who beckoned them to board canoes and join them for a meal. Brigaut was suspicious and warned his men to be careful; suddenly, the natives shot arrows, and six buccaneers fell wounded. When they returned fire with their muskets, the Indians vanished.

Shaken, Brigaut and his men gained the offshore bank and awaited rescue. One of their captives, a Spanish-speaking native of Tallahassee named Juan López, bolted and gained the mainland despite being fired upon as he swam away. Three days later he was reporting to Governor Juan Márquez Cabrera of Saint Augustine, saying that the raiders were led by the turncoat Alonso de Avesilla. A column of 50 soldiers sallied in pursuit, chancing upon the *flibustiers* at a weak moment, when 19 had "left the bar to swim ashore, carrying their muskets and powder in waterproof bags." The Spaniards ambushed and massacred them all before proceeding to the bank and visiting a like treatment on the rest. Even the Spanish captives were mistakenly slain; only Brigaut, a black pirate named Diego, and a nine-year-old boy were carried off as prisoners. At Saint Augustine the *flibustier* captain and his lone companion were interrogated on 30–31 May 1686, and hanged shortly thereafter.

*See also* Andrieszoon, Michiel; Avesilla, Alonso de; Bréhal, Capitaine; careen; De Graaf, Laurens Cornelis Boudewijn; Grammont, "chevalier" de; Willems, Jan.

*Reference:* Weddle, *Wilderness.*

# BROWNE, JAMES

### (FL. 1676-1677)

Scottish privateer hanged for capturing a Dutch slaver.

Browne left Jamaica in October 1676 with a crew comprised mostly of "English, the rest French and Dutch" sailors, and an old commission issued by the French governor of Saint Domingue, Bertrand d'Ogeron. Browne used this license to take the Dutch *Goude Zon* (Golden Sun) in early 1677 while it was standing into Cartagena with a consignment of 200 slaves belonging to the Dutch West India Company. The Dutch master and several of his crew were killed in the fray.

By May 1677, Browne was once again off Jamaica, where he landed 150 blacks "in a

remote bay on this island," hoping to sell them to the planters. Word of this was carried to Lord Vaughan, governor at Port Royal; although the governor learned that Browne's ship was gone, some of the seamen left behind were nevertheless apprehended and interrogated. Discovering through them the particular circumstances surrounding this depredation, Vaughan then sent a frigate, which seized about 100 of the slaves "concealed in several planters' hands," as well as Browne and eight of his crew members. The governor further apprised the Dutch authorities at Curaçao, who filed a complaint and demanded return of their slaves.

The English governor, plagued by unruly privateers who refused to restrict their activities, decided to make an example of Browne. Captain and crew were tried for piracy because their French commission was patently out of date, Governor d'Ogeron having "been dead above a year." The crew were pardoned, but Browne was condemned to be executed. The captain appealed to the House of Assembly to have the benefit of the "Act of Privateers," and the assembly twice sent a committee to the governor to beg a reprieve. Lord Vaughan refused and ordered the immediate execution of Browne. Half an hour after the hanging, the provost marshal appeared with an order, signed by the Speaker, to stop the execution.

*See also* Ogeron, Bertrand d'; Vaughan, John.

*Reference: C.S.P., Amer. and W.I., Vol X;* Gosse, *Who's Who; Interesting Tracts;* Pope.

# BUCKINGHAM, CAPTAIN

### ALSO BOCKINGHAM OR BUCKENHAM (FL. 1679-1680)

English master captured in the Laguna de Términos for attempting to poach logwood.

Buckingham set sail from London, England, in 1679 with his ship *John,* of 300 tons, 20 guns, and 70 men, bound on a trading voyage to the West Indies. According to his surgeon's mate, Lionel Wafer:

> when we came to Jamaica, the season of sugars being not yet come, the captain was willing to make a short voyage in the meanwhile to the Bay of Campeche, to fetch logwood; but having no mind to go further with him, I stayed in Jamaica.

Unfortunately, the Spanish authorities chose to send an armed patrol into the laguna at this time, and the *John* was taken in January 1680, along with the pink *Loyal Farmers* of Boston, ketch *Susan* of London, a ship belonging to Hugh Pering of New England, and numerous lesser craft. All were carried into Campeche; from there, the captives were forwarded to Mexico City to be tried, arriving in early July. Having long suffered at the hands of the Baymen, the Spaniards were little inclined to mercy. The prisoners were condemned to *obrajes* (public works), where they could be hired out as forced labor at six pieces of eight per head (to help defray the costs of their incarceration). The work was often grueling, the conditions akin to slavery. Russell, an English seaman who managed to escape, later told Wafer he last saw "Captain Buckenham with a log chained to his leg and a basket on his back, crying bread about the streets of Mexico for his master, a baker."

***See also*** Laguna de Términos; logwood; pieces of eight; Wafer, Lionel.

***References:*** *C.S.P., Amer. and W.I.,* Vol. XI; Gosse, *Who's Who;* Robles.

# Burk, captain
## (FL. 1699)

An Irish commander who committed many piracies on the coast of Newfoundland before drowning in an Atlantic hurricane in 1699.

***Reference:*** Gosse, *Who's Who.*

# CABALLERO, ANDRÉS

### (D. 1673)

Spanish colonial official victimized by pirates.

A lawyer, Caballero began as *corregidor* of Salamanca, Spain, and was promoted to the Royal Audiencia of Santo Domingo in October 1654. He set sail for the New World accompanied by his wife and two children on 13 February 1655, in the train of Governor-designate conde de Peñalba. They arrived 8 April, only 15 days before the huge English expedition of William Penn and Robert Venables disembarked. Caballero played a minor role in the ensuing campaign, which ended with the invaders' withdrawal three weeks later.

In August 1659, Caballero was suspended from office and returned to Spain to clear his name. He succeeded partially after a four-year suit and by June 1664 was one of the judges on the Canary Islands. In December 1671 he won reappointment to the Audiencia of Santo Domingo, departing Cadiz on 27 February 1672. He stopped at Puerto Rico to conduct official inquiries, most especially about the former governor of Cumaná, Sancho Fernández de Angulo. This finished, Caballero took ship in June 1673 to complete his voyage toward Santo Domingo.

But during the passage he "was made prisoner by the English, who took from him his clothes, money, silverware and a slave that accompanied him." The freebooters set most of their victims ashore but retained Caballero, his son Francisco (a cleric), and other "people of worth," hoping to extort ransoms. When these were not forthcoming, they set their captives ashore at an uninhabited stretch of the coast near Coro (Venezuela), where the unhappy Spaniards "underwent great discomfort, hunger and nakedness." Eventually Caballero and his son reached Coro proper, but were

so weakened by their ordeal that the father died on 30 August 1673, "being buried in a pauper's grave."

*Reference:* Rodríguez, *Invasión* (Montalvo).

# CACHEMARÉE, CAPITAINE

### (FL. 1684)

*Flibustier* listed in an anonymous French document of 1684 as commanding the ship *Saint Joseph,* of 6 guns and 70 men, out of Saint Domingue.

His name, also spelled "Caché Marée," would seem to be a pseudonym, *ketch marin* being the modern French term for a small two-masted vessel. In northern Spain such a craft was called a *quechemarín* or *cachemarín,* while in English it would be a simple ketch.

*References:* Gosse, *Who's Who;* Laburu; Lugo.

# CAGWAY

### ALSO CAGAWAY, CAGUA

English distortions of *Cayagua,* the original Carib-Spanish name for Port Royal, Jamaica.

The first English invaders of 1655 mistook the name of the tip of Palisadoes Spit for that of the entire cay, thus calling their new port "Cagway." The name was officially changed to Port Royal in 1660, in honor of the restoration of Charles II to the English throne, although old hands continued to refer to it by its original name for quite some time thereafter. Commodore Christopher Myngs, for example, wrote to Governor Lord Windsor on his return passage from Santiago de Cuba in late October 1662, "We are now in safety in the harbor, on our return to Cagaway." Robert

Searle had also fitted out a privateering ship for this same expedition, calling it *Cagway.*

***See also*** Myngs, Sir Christopher; Searle, Robert; Windsor, Thomas.

***References:*** Dyer, *Myngs;* Pawson, *Port Royal;* Pope.

# CAMPOS Y ESPINOSA, ALONSO DE

## (1620s?-1678)

Spanish admiral defeated by Henry Morgan at the bar of Maracaibo.

Campos, the son of Admiral Juan de Campos Cervantes, was born in the Canary Islands sometime in the 1620s. His older brother Gaspar commanded a military company in Galicia, which Alonso joined in 1640, soon being promoted to ensign. In 1655 he transferred to the Royal Spanish Navy as an arquebusier, quickly rising to command a *patache,* then a company of marines, followed by a galleon. In 1663 he raised 6,000 pesos toward the construction in Amsterdam of four new galleons for the Armada de Barlovento, which won him appointment as *almirante,* or second-in-command, of the fleet. He assumed command of the 507-ton vice-flagship *Nuestra Señora de la Concepción* (Our Lady of the Conception) when it reached Cadiz the following summer.

He saw some action against the French off Spain before the armada sailed from Seville for the New World on 21 July 1667 under Agustín de Diústegui. More than a month later the five ships reached Puerto Rico, where the flagship and *gobierno Magdalena* parted company to convey a cargo of quicksilver to Veracruz. Campos remained with his vice-flagship and the frigates *Concepción* and *Nuestra Señora de la Soledad* (Our Lady of Solitude, alias *Marquesa* or "Marchioness") to patrol the coasts of Santo Domingo and southern Cuba before rendezvousing with Diústegui at Havana. During this sweep Campos made a single capture, a sloop sailing from Jamaica to the Laguna de Términos to warn of the armada's arrival in Caribbean waters.

In February 1668 Campos was reunited with Diústegui at Havana, and together the armada sailed through the Antilles toward Caracas before returning to Puerto Rico. The squadron then transferred to Havana for repairs and shortly thereafter revisited Puerto Rico, where it was lying when the flagship and vice-flag were recalled to Spain. Campos was to remain behind as commander of the force, now comprised solely of *Magdalena* and two frigates. Diústegui meanwhile sailed to Veracruz to pick up a load of silver bullion before heading for Spain, while Campos hovered off Cuba's Cape San Antonio, inspecting passing ships. He allegedly detained three English ships under Captain Francis Stuart, as well as a Dutch ship, letting all four go in exchange for bribes. Campos then proceeded to Havana, where word arrived of an attack on the southern Cuban port of Trinidad. Campos sent his newly acquired frigate *Nuestra Señora de los Remedios* (Our Lady of Remedies) and *Marquesa* to Veracruz for reinforcements. *Remedios* was wrecked less than 50 miles from Campeche, but when the survivors reached Veracruz, they found that the Mexican authorities had purchased another frigate, the 218-ton *San Luis.* Together with *Marquesa,* this frigate carried almost 300 reinforcements back into Havana on 5 January 1669.

Meanwhile, news had been received of an enemy attack on Portobelo as well. Campos sortied with *Magdalena, San Luis,* and *Marquesa,* laying in a course toward Puerto Rico, where he heard of a large freebooter gathering at Ile-à-Vache. From a Dutch merchantman he met in the Mona Passage, he was told that five French ships from Martinique were preparing to raid Santo Domingo. He therefore backtracked, arriving at that Spanish island on 25 March 1669 to reinforce its garrison. This report proved false, but he was then correctly advised that more than a dozen buccaneer sail had passed by Santo Domingo on their way to the Spanish Main. Sailing in their wake, he learned from another Dutch merchantman that they were in the Lago de Maracaibo, where he arrived by mid-April.

Inside lay the flotilla of Morgan, who had landed to ransack the interior. Campos first reoccupied the fort guarding the approaches, then several days later lightened his warships and crossed over the bar. The armada had trapped the raiders inside, but at dawn on 27 April 1669, they were rushed by Morgan, who destroyed *Magdalena* with a fireship. The *San Luis* of Mateo Alonso de Huidobro ran aground attempting to shelter beside the fort and was deliberately set ablaze, while the 50-ton *Soledad* was captured by the buccaneers, who then slipped past the fort and sailed off in triumph.

Campos was eventually exonerated at his court-martial in Spain, and in October 1674 he was appointed governor of Puerto Rico. He assumed office in April 1675, was promoted to *maestre de campo* the following year, and in June 1677 was elevated to the governorship of Havana, although his Puerto Rican term still had two more years to run. Departing San Juan toward Cuba, Campos disappeared en route, his ship presumably lost with all hands.

**See also** *almirante;* Barlovento, Armada de; *galeones; gobierno;* Huidobro, Mateo Alonso de; Laguna de Términos; *patache;* Spanish Main.
**References:** López; Torres.

# CAPITANA

Spanish term for "flagship," *almiranta* being the word for "vice-flagship."

The two terms are often confused by foreigners, as they seemingly reverse the natural order whereby captains are subordinate to admirals. However, when these expressions first made their appearance in the language of medieval Spain, it was customary for fleets to be commanded by a *capitán general,* while the designation *almirante* was later adapted from the Arabic *al-amir* (the emir). To north Europeans, though, "admiral" only ever meant senior naval officer.

**See also** *almiranta.*

# CAREEN

Expression meaning to tilt a stationary vessel so as to expose its underside for cleaning, caulking, or repairs.

The term came from the Latin word *carina,* for ship's keel. When carefully beached, a lightened vessel would come to rest with its hull exposed as the tide receded, allowing the crew to scrub off barnacles and other impediments to swift sailing, as well as protecting against worms or other forms of wood rot. During this period the ship, lying immobile with its guns removed, would be at its most vulnerable. Pirate commanders, who seldom enjoyed the sanctuary of a protected harbor, had to careen with great caution in isolated bays. It was while engaged in such an operation on the northeastern coast of Hispaniola in summer 1686, for example, that Joseph Bannister's 36-gun *Golden Fleece* was destroyed by the Royal Navy, virtually ending his career.

**See also** Bannister, Joseph; Hispaniola.

# CARLETON, MARY

## (?-1673)

The most celebrated prostitute in old Port Royal, Jamaica, nicknamed the "German princess" and hanged at Tyburn in 1673.
**Reference:** Pawson, *Port Royal.*

# CARLILE, CHARLES

## (FL. 1683)

Royal Navy pirate hunter who ran Jean Hamlin to ground at Saint Thomas in the Danish Virgin Islands.

At three o'clock on the afternoon of 8 August 1683, Carlile—described as "a brave discreet young commander" by Governor Sir William Stapleton of the English Leeward Islands—appeared with HMS *Francis* before the port of Saint Thomas (modern-day Charlotte Amalie), seeing a large ship inside "with white color flying, jack, ensign, and pendant." Although these were the insignia of an English man o' war, Carlile knew there was no such warship in those waters, and his pilot confirmed it was *Trompeuse* (Trickster), a pirate frigate of 32 guns and 6 "patararoes" *(pedreros,* or swivel guns), which had been hijacked ten months earlier by a band of buccaneers under Hamlin, then sailed all the way to West Africa and back on a rapacious cruise that had made it the most infamous raider in the Caribbean.

Carlile stood into port, but both the pirate ship and shore batteries opened fire, forcing *Francis* to retreat. He sent a boat ashore with a letter requesting cooperation from the Danish governor, but this was Adolf Esmit, notorious collaborator to pirates. Esmit invited Carlile ashore the next day, but the Royal Navy officer demurred, believing Esmit might be attempting to buy time for a pirate consort to arrive, which was "daily expected." Therefore, on 9 August after nightfall, Carlile took *Francis*'s pinnace and another boat into harbor with 14 men. They exchanged shots with *Trompeuse*'s anchor watch, but most of the pirates had already quit Hamlin's service with their booty. The remaining few now fled ashore, leaving the Royal Navy boarders to set fire to the frigate before withdrawing. Carlile and his men lay on their oars

to see that none came off [from shore] to put out the fire. When she blew up she kindled a great privateer that lay by, which burned to the water's edge.

This second vessel was Bartholomew Sharpe's *Santísima Trinidad* (Most Blessed Trinity), which he had abandoned there the previous year after his return from the South Seas; it had been converted into a depot for buccaneers.

With the two wrecks smouldering within the harbor, the next morning *Francis* got under way but had only tacked about a league to eastward when it sighted "a ship aground, a Flemish vessel of 300 tons, full of good ship's stores for the pirates." Carlile's men cut down its masts and set it on fire, "but could not stay long, the people coming to oppose me." (This may have been the prize Hamlin seized two months previously off West Africa, a Flushinger of 20–24 guns, which had been given over to one of his English subordinates masquerading under the alias "Captain Morgan." Three months later, it was reported at Antigua and Barbados "that Morgan, the pirate who parted from Hamlin of *La Trompeuse,* is now in these parts. He was seen at anchor at Saint Thomas, where he had taken some ships and sloops.")

Carlile returned to blockade the port of Saint Thomas; a few days later, the weather changed and he was forced to depart, having learned Hamlin and his principal confederates had transferred "to another part of the island in an open boat." Retiring to Nevis, Carlile replenished his supplies and on 25 August sortied again "to look for one Cooke and one Bond, two English pirates fitted from Saint Thomas."

***See also*** Bond, George; Cooke, John; Hamlin, Jean; Morgan, Captain; Sharpe, Bartholomew; South Seas.

***References:*** *C.S.P., Amer. and W.I.,* Vol. XI; Howse.

# CASSAVA

Slender, erect shrub of the spurge family, native to tropical America and the West Indies, whose tuberous roots were harvested in the seventeenth century to provide sustenance for slaves and indentured servants, usually in the form of bread or tapioca. Because of this, it came to have a negative connotation. For example, in a letter dated 19 November 1681, the governor general of the French Antilles, comte de Blénac, declared:

The manner in which *engagés* are treated is enough to make one tremble; it has to be seen to be believed. Of 600, not 50 will survive. A settler treats his *engagé* in the following manner: he usually puts him on a diet of cassava, water and three pounds of stinking beef a week. The *engagé*, who is unaccustomed to such a life, falls prey to colic, swelling of the legs, fever, and stomach ache. The settler believes his money lost, as the agreed indenture continues to expire, so no matter how sick will beat him to make him work.

From such treatment emerged many runaways to swell the ranks of *flibustiers*—presumably with a lifelong distaste for cassava.

**See also** Blénac, Charles de Courbon, comte de; *engagé*.

**Reference:** Baudrit.

# CASTRO, PEDRO DE

## (FL. 1676-1685)

Spanish captain who became a *guardacosta* in the Gulf of Mexico.

De Castro was apparently first mentioned in the summer of 1676; a man of this name sold his 200-ton frigate, *Santo Cristo del Buen Viaje* (Holy Christ of the Good Voyage, alias *Mogoleño*), to the Crown in Spain as one of five vessels that were to be used to reconstitute the Armada de Barlovento. It is unknown whether De Castro then traveled to the Americas with this force the following year, perhaps aboard the flagship *San José, Santa Rosa María y San Pedro de Alcántara,* which deposited the governor-designate of Yucatán, Antonio de Layseca y Alvarado, at Campeche on 30 November 1677. In any event, De Castro was soon operating as a coast guard out of that port under Captain Juan González Moreda.

## INITIAL CAPTURES
## (1680)

On 7 January 1679, De Castro obtained his own privateering commission from Governor Layseca in Mérida and began cruising on the account. He took part in the expedition mounted by Captain Felipe de la Barrera in April 1680 to sweep the English logwood cutters from the Laguna de Términos. After returning, De Castro sailed again in mid-July with his two *piraguas* to patrol the Yucatán coast as far as the Bay of Honduras. Off Cocinas Island, he saw a large vessel at anchor and another small frigate nearby, which he suspected of poaching logwood. Boarding the smaller vessel at night, he captured eight or nine Englishmen and marched inland to destroy their logging operation; he killed two cutters and scattered the rest, then burned their huts. The larger ship then surrendered and De Castro released three Spanish captives, transferred on board, and burnt the frigate. While putting to sea, he believed he had too many prisoners to guard—some 50 English men, women, and children—so he deposited the still "bellicose" captain and eight hands on a nearby island (which suggests that this must have been Robert Oxe of the *Laurel,* although De Castro called his prize *León Colorado,* or "Crowned Lion").

When De Castro reached Campeche, he was informed by the pilot boat that another large intruder lay at the Laguna de Términos; it had seized a coaster with salt near Sisal. De Castro immediately went in pursuit and found the 36-gun ship inside the bar. Unable to enter with *León Colorado,* he nonetheless persuaded its French captain and few crew members to surrender. De Castro learned that it was *Nuestra Señora del Honhón,* which had been captured by John Coxon's flotilla off Portobelo 11 months earlier. Rather than return with these prizes to Campeche, De Castro then decided to put into Veracruz, sending his lieutenant Juan Corso back in a single *piragua* to request supplies. The Campeche authorities were greatly annoyed at this, arresting Corso and sending 50 soldiers aboard a *piragua* in pursuit.

Meanwhile, De Castro reached Veracruz on 19 October 1680, a day after *Honhón* had anchored outside between Sacrificios and Blanca Islands under its prizemaster. The two ships were examined by Crown officials: *León Colorado* was found to be a brand-new 300-ton vessel with 40 gunports (although mounting only 20 cannon) and reputedly "built in Virginia." *Honhón* was much the same size, pierced for 36 guns (although only mounting 22), "and well supplied with arms, powder, cannon balls, grenades and other explosives." After a lengthy proceeding in Mexico City, these were deemed legitimate prizes, on which De Castro did not have to pay duty, in accordance to the terms of his commission. Furthermore, on 26 March 1681, the Mexican viceroy appointed him "coast guard captain" for the province of Yucatán, arranging to have his two new frigates maintained out of public funds.

This arrangement did not last long, as the impoverished port of Campeche could not meet such heavy costs, nor were large vessels suitable for inshore patrols. Within a year, *Honhón* was transferred to the Armada de Barlovento, and De Castro and Corso shifted operations to the southern coast of Cuba. Here Corso acquired a reputation for brutality among his English victims, while De Castro was seldom mentioned, presumably because he left such rough-and-tumble work to his lieutenant.

## SEARCH FOR LA SALLE
### (1685)

In the spring of 1685, De Castro was one of the first Spaniards to learn of a secret new French colony being established in the Gulf of Mexico by René Robert Cavelier, sieur de La Salle. Realizing that this was an unwelcome encroachment on Spain's hegemony and knowing that its destruction would be well received by the Crown, he went in quest of this settlement. He and Corso sailed their galliot to Tuxpan and Tampico (Mexico) that April, hoping to take on provisions and a pilot for the uncharted gulf waters. On 4 May 1685, four days after leaving Tampico on an east–northeasterly heading, they were driven by a storm close inshore "two leagues to windward of Espíritu Santo Bay." While riding out the weather, they saw signs of white habitation; going ashore, they met a party of six Indians, who informed them through sign language that many people with muskets had proceeded inland.

De Castro led 50 well-armed men and three Indian guides in search of the intruders. A day-and-a-half later they reached the shores of the bay proper, where they saw "barefoot tracks in the sand and many broken casks and bottles." Half a dozen canoes could be distinguished on the far side, but it was impossible to recognize people at that distance. De Castro retired to his galliot, and on 19 May stood out to sea, only to be driven into another unknown inlet by contrary winds and currents, where he lost his anchor. Desperate to keep off the rocks, he put 25 men in the water to fashion a mooring, then abandoned them when the wind veered. Three days later he returned in rough weather, rescuing 16, but the rest had gone foraging for food. By the time they reappeared, the surf was too dangerous, so De Castro hailed them to meet the galliot at Apalache Bay, many miles along the coast.

This was the last time he was ever seen. The nine men survived their grueling trek, but the galliot was lost with all hands. In early July 1687, it was reported at Mexico City that two vessels had returned to Veracruz from a reconnaissance along the gulf coast, having failed to find any sign of La Salle. However, they did "bring back a scarred Spanish boy, of the Merced district of this city of Mexico, who was lost with the two ships of Corso and Castro on those shores, the others being drowned or eaten by the Chichimec Indians."

*See also* Barlovento, Armada de; Barrera y Villegas, Felipe de la; Corso, Juan; Coxon, John; *guardacostas;* Laguna de Términos; Layseca y Alvarado, Antonio de; logwood; Oxe, Robert.

*References:* Juárez; Robles; Torres; Weddle, *Wilderness.*

# CHARTE-PARTIE

## ALSO CHARTER PARTY

Freebooter covenant, drawn up prior to a cruise to determine the division of spoils.

The term was originally a commercial one, used when two or more merchants agreed to share a hired vessel. If only a single individual was involved, the question of cargo space was not a pressing concern; but in the case of a *charte-partie* (literally "split charter"), each consignor's portion had to be carefully allotted. The seventeenth-century *flibustiers*—many of whom were veteran merchant sailors—adopted this expression for their own affairs, agreeing on a proportional distribution of booty

beforehand, with special provisos for the wounded, senior commanders, etc.

*See also* purchase.

# CINCUENTENA

Spanish irregular cavalry on Santo Domingo, greatly feared by French *boucaniers.*

These riders were all volunteer militia raised in companies of 50—*cincuenta* in Spanish—hence their name. They were organized specifically to contain the encroachments of French *boucaniers* and settlers pushing in from the northwestern coast. As many were local, well-to-do Spanish planters or their followers, they viewed such encroachments as land grabs. The *boucaniers,* who had to hunt wild cattle singly or in small bands, dreaded falling into their hands and told lurid tales of their cruelty.

*Reference:* Lugo.

# CLARKE, ROBERT

## (FL. 1681-1684)

English governor of the Bahamas, dismissed for granting letters of marque against the Spaniards in peacetime.

A Bahamian settler described as "one of Cromwell's officers," Clarke had been appointed governor by the colony's Lord Proprietors back in England sometime prior to 1681. (His predecessor, Charles Chillingworth, had so provoked the inhabitants that they "assembled tumultuously, seized him, shipped him off for Jamaica, and lived every man as he thought best for his pleasure and interest.") Despite this seeming autonomy, the Bahamas actually depended upon Jamaica for its survival, so when Governor Sir Thomas Lynch learned that John Coxon had been raiding Portobelo and the South Seas—allegedly with a commission granted by Clarke—he wrote the latter to complain.

Clarke replied in July 1682, explaining he had never sanctioned such actions and citing recent Spanish depredations against two English ships in the Bahamas, plus the carrying off of planters from the southern islands to Cuba as prisoners. He would therefore continue authorizing attacks against the local Spaniards. A New York merchant arriving at Jamaica in late September 1682 reported that the Bahamians had just "taken a *piragua,* a *barco luengo,* diverse Indians from Florida and 17 from Cuba, whom they have sold for slaves." When he learned of these seizures, Lynch wrote, "I am more than ever apprehensive of the consequences of this folly and rapine." The Crown having grown increasingly intolerant, Clarke's commissions were invalidated and a warrant was issued in London for his arrest. The Lord Proprietors also disavowed him, ordering Clarke home and replacing him with another settler, Robert Lilburne, late in 1682.

But before Clarke could be deported back to England, the Spaniards took matters into their own hands. In January 1684, a large force sortied from Havana and attacked English shipping off Andros Island, capturing one William Bell to serve as their pilot. Juan de Larco then led 150 picked men in two *barcos luengos* to New Providence, landing on the east end of the island and—guided by Bell, wearing a halter around his neck—marching against Charles Town, as Nassau was then called. Clarke and his son Judah brought out some men to investigate the commotion but were met by musket fire, in which the former governor was wounded and captured. He died in Spanish captivity, allegedly being roasted over a spit, although this tale was likely invented by the Bahamians to justify their continuing hostilities against the Spaniards.

*See also barco luengo;* Coxon, John; letter of marque; Lilburne, Robert; Lynch, Sir Thomas; South Seas.
**References:** Craton; *C.S.P., Amer. and W.I.,* Vol. XI; Gosse, *Who's Who.*

# CLOSTREE, CAPITAINE
### (FL. 1663)

French *flibustier.*

He was named in an English document of 1663 as commanding a 9-gun ship with a crew of 68 men and holding a commission from the governor of Tortuga. The name may have been merely a pseudonym, perhaps more properly spelled "Claustré."
**Reference:** Pawson, *Port Royal.*

# COATES, CHARLES
### (FL. 1696)

English privateer whose ship *Exchange* carried the *Experiment* into Barbados sometime prior to 1696, presumably for illegal trading on the Barbary Coast.
**Reference:** Chapin.

# COBHAM, NATHANIEL
### (FL. 1666)

English privateer who commanded the 2-gun *Susannah* in Colonel Edward Morgan's expedition against Dutch Sint Eustatius and Sabá during the Second Anglo-Dutch War.

This force departed Jamaica in two divisions, five sail putting out of Port Royal on 5 April 1666, and Morgan himself following with another four on 28 April.

There were 650 men in all, described in a letter by Governor Sir Thomas Modyford as

chiefly reformed privateers, scarce a planter amongst them, being resolute fellows and well armed with *fusils* [Spanish word for muskets] and pistols.

The Crown official was particularly pleased they would be serving "at the old rate of no purchase, no pay, and it will cost the King nothing considerable, some powder and mortar pieces." Their landing was successfully made, but the colonel, "being a corpulent man," died from heat exertion during the chase, and his expedition disbanded shortly thereafter.

*See also* purchase.

*References:* Cruikshank; *Interesting Tracts;* Pope.

# COFFIN, CAPTAIN

## (FL. 1683)

English privateer issued a commission by Governor Sir Thomas Lynch of Jamaica in early 1683 to cruise the leeward (western) portion of that island, clearing it of pirates. Coffin's patent was one of many granted by the governor around this time, ostensibly to clear the sea lanes of raiders such as Jean Hamlin, but also to give employment to privateers idled by the peace (as well as turning them against one another). John Coxon, George Johnson, and Thomas Paine were among others so designated.

Toward mid-March 1683 Coffin—who had sortied in a sloop with 70 men—returned to Port Royal to report he had engaged two rogue privateers. He had killed the captain and seven crew members of one, wounding 20 more, and damaged the second considerably; "but both got away with oars." He brought in three French prisoners, two

of whom were executed. The third had been a gunner aboard Hamlin's notorious *Trompeuse* (Trickster), and so was held over for a later trial.

*See also* Coxon, John; Hamlin, Jean; Johnson, George; Paine, Thomas.

*Reference: C.S.P., Amer. and W.I.,* Vol. XI.

# CONWAY, CAPTAIN

## (FL. 1686)

English privateer issued a warrant by the governor of Jamaica on 24 November 1686 (O.S.), along with Captain Rich Cubitt, "to apprehend John Coxon the pirate, said to be logwood cutting in the Bay of Campeche [or Laguna de Términos]."

*See also* Coxon, John; Cubitt, Rich; Laguna de Términos; logwood.

*Reference: C.S.P., Amer. and W.I.,* Vol. XII.

# COOKE, EDMOND

## ALSO EDMUND
## (FL. 1673-1683)

English master turned corsair.

Cooke commanded the 130-ton merchantman *Virgin* of London when it was seized by the Spanish *guardacosta* Philip FitzGerald in May 1673 on its way from Jamaica to England. It was condemned in Havana for carrying "prohibited" cargo—logwood—which its captor argued could only have been obtained from Spain's American dominions. Upon his return to Europe in the autumn of 1674, Cooke and his owners instituted a £15,000 lawsuit against this illegal seizure, which the captain pursued at the court of Madrid. Nine months later, the aggrieved Englishmen petitioned Charles II for letters of reprisal, which were denied, and the case languished for several more years.

Meanwhile, Cooke resumed his sea career, making another voyage to Jamaica in 1679, during which he apparently called at Mexico's Laguna de Términos for a cargo of logwood. But while lying off Aruba, Cooke saw the Armada de Barlovento bearing down, so he and his men abandoned ship and went ashore in their boats. The armada seized his ship and sailed it off. Governor Lord Carlisle of Jamaica later observed that the English preferred

> to sacrifice their ship rather than fall into the hands of the Spaniards by whom they knew so many to have been ill treated and undone. This caused Cook [sic] to turn privateer, he never having been so before.

Marooned on that island, master and crew waited until a Spanish bark approached, which they rowed out and seized. Finding it ladened with cacao, hides, and money, Cooke sailed his prize to Jamaica, smuggling the cargo ashore and selling it in October 1679.

## PORTOBELO ATTACK

Determined to wreak vengeance on the Spaniards, in January 1680 Cooke followed an unofficial expedition that had quit Port Morant, Jamaica, to attack Portobelo. Sailing to the rendezvous of Isla de Pinos, 130 miles east of Portobelo in the Archipelago de las Mulatas on Panama's northern shores, Cooke saw a bark approaching in heavy weather that proved to be the chief commander, John Coxon. The freebooters were "glad of his company," because the rest were at Golden Island, some miles away. Coxon detached Cooke to carry the order for this flotilla to join up before the Spaniards discovered their presence. Cooke, new to the business, almost ruined matters when on his way across to the main body he met

a Spanish galliot from Cartagena, bound to Portobelo with Negroes, but there being a dissension among the company, some desirous to board him, others not, so that in fine they lost him. The current under shore setting strong to the eastward and having hard westerly winds, Captain Cooke could not get the Golden Islands, but was drove down into the Bay of Darien.

Despite this setback, Coxon was able to get 250 buccaneers into boats and row westward along the coast. The raiders slipped ashore at the Gulf of San Blas, proceeding afoot until they surprised Portobelo. The city was ransacked over two days, the freebooters retiring ten miles northeastward to be picked up by their ships. A brief blockade ensued, after which a general distribution of booty was made, resulting in shares of 100 pieces of eight per man. The flotilla retired to Bocas del Toro (literally "bull's mouths" or "entrances of the bull") at the western extremity of present-day Panama to careen; once refitted, the pirates decided to return to Golden Island "to travel overland to Panama" and attack the Spaniards on the Pacific side.

## PACIFIC CAMPAIGN

Coxon, Cooke, Robert Allison, Peter Harris, Thomas Magott, Richard Sawkins, and Bartholomew Sharpe all anchored close inshore in a small cove on Golden Island, out of sight of any Spanish ship that might chance to pass. An anchor watch was left aboard each vessel, with orders to rally to the two largest—Coxon's and Harris's—if they should be discovered. At six o'clock on Monday morning, 15 April 1680, 332 buccaneers went ashore and began to obtain Indian guides to cross the isthmus. Ten days later the pirates came upon the Spanish stockade of Santa María at the confluence of the Chucunaque and Tuira Rivers.

Sawkins led a dawn attack that stormed the place.

The buccaneers then pressed on into the Pacific, capturing Spanish coastal craft until they had a small flotilla, with which they bore down upon Panama. The Spaniards sent out a hastily assembled force to do battle, and the raiders captured it after a three-hour fight. Coxon's reluctance to go further resulted in his being deposed, and he sailed away on 5 May 1680 with 70 loyal hands to retrace his steps across the isthmus. Sawkins became chief commander aboard the captured Spanish flagship *Santísima Trinidad* (Most Blessed Trinity), while Cooke commanded a bark of about 80 tons, and Sharpe a slightly smaller one.

The next day a large ship arriving from Lima, Peru, was intercepted to become Sharpe's new command. The flotilla roamed westward past Coiba Island, where Sawkins went aboard Cooke's bark with 60 men two days later to attempt a landing at the town of Remedios. Sawkins was killed in the disembarkation, and Cooke brought off the survivors. Upon quitting this river mouth on 11 May (1 May 1680 O.S.), the pirates seized a Spanish bark ladened with pitch, into which Cooke transferred, renaming it *Mayflower*. Rejoining the main body, he found circumstances altered, Sawkins's death having created an upheaval, with 60 of his followers abandoning the enterprise altogether to sail away in Cooke's former bark toward the Caribbean. Sharpe was now promoted to principal commander aboard *Trinidad,* while Cooke was turned out of *Mayflower* by his own crew.

The merchant captain had never displayed the proper touch for privateering, "and went on board the great ship [*Trinidad*] as a private soldier." Sharpe named his old friend John Cox, a New Englander, to command *Mayflower* in his stead. Cooke served out the remaining two years of the voyage in a minor capacity, apparently roving up and down the South American coast, and may have been aboard when *Trinidad* eventually rounded the Strait of Magellan and reached the English West Indies in late February 1682. A buccaneer noted that a merchant captain they had met "went away with one Cook, our [sailing] master, to the governor of Antigua [to ask] liberty to come in." The pirates scattered at this point, each according to his inclination.

It was said that Cooke's pirate flag had been red striped with yellow, on which was a device of a hand and sword.

***See also*** Allison, Robert; Barlovento, Armada de; careen; Coxon, John; FitzGerald, Philip; Golden Island; *guardacostas;* Harris, Peter (fl. 1671–1680); Laguna de Términos; logwood; Magott, Thomas; pieces of eight; Sawkins, Richard; Sharpe, Bartholomew.

***References:*** *C.S.P., Amer. and W.I.,* Vols. IX–XI; Gosse, *Who's Who; Interesting Tracts.*

# COOKE, JOHN
## (FL. 1679-1684)

English buccaneer who twice raided the Spaniards in the Pacific Ocean.

Cooke was apparently born on the West Indian island of Saint Christopher, and his first documented exploit came during Bartholomew Sharpe's incursion into the South Seas. In April 1681 Cooke led a splinter group of some 50 buccaneers—including William Dampier, Edward Davis, and Lionel Wafer—who parted company and marched back across the Isthmus of Panama to Point San Blas, where they were rescued by Capitaine Tristan. Later at Dominica, Cooke and some other Englishmen made off with Tristan's ship while the *flibustier* chieftain was ashore.

About 20 of this group went to Virginia in July 1682, which is where Cooke met them the following April, having taken two

French ships laden with wine. He used the profits from this coup to plan a second raid against Peru. Cooke and his reunited followers left Chesapeake Bay on 23 August 1683 aboard his 18-gun *Revenge* with a crew of 70 men. It soon became apparent that this vessel would not be sufficient to round the Horn, so the buccaneers steered to the West African coast, where in November they seized a 36-gun Danish ship off Sierra Leone, renaming it *Bachelor's Delight*. At Sherbro, a little farther along that coast, they burnt *Revenge* so that "she should tell no tales," according to their pilot William Ambrose Cowley. Cooke then laid in a course for the Horn, sighting the Seebald de Weert Islands on 28 January 1684 and simultaneously "great shoals of small lobsters, which colored the sea in red spots." He passed Isla de los Estados (Staten Island) on 7 February, emerging into the Pacific about a month later.

On 19 March 1684, *Bachelor's Delight* pursued a sail in the vicinity of Valdivia, Chile, which proved to be the *Nicholas* out of London, commanded by John Eaton. Although originally intended as a trader, Eaton's mission had quickly degenerated into simple plundering, so the two rovers decided to join forces. They repaired to the Juan Fernández Islands for fresh supplies and on 8 April headed northward in hopes of surprising the Peruvian coastal traffic. They seized a vessel on 3 May bearing timber from Guayaquil toward Lima, from whose crew they learned that their presence in those waters was already known.

Withdrawing to the Lobos de Afuera Islands on 9 May to careen and revise their plans, the buccaneers could only muster 108 men between them, having many sick, including Cooke himself. While lying there, they sighted three sail, which were pursued and overhauled the next day. These proved to be Spanish supply ships bearing flour, "seven or eight tons of quince marmalade" and other goods for Panama, which Cooke and

Eaton diverted to the remote Galápagos Islands and unloaded as a reserve supply. They remained there from 31 May to 12 June, when they proceeded farther northward toward New Spain, hoping news of their depredations had not yet reached that far. As they approached the Gulf of Nicoya (off present-day Costa Rica) to raid for beef, Cooke died and was succeeded in command of *Bachelor's Delight* by Edward Davis.

*See also* careen; Dampier, William; Davis, Edward; Eaton, John; maroon; Sharpe, Bartholomew; South Seas; Tristan, Capitaine; Wafer, Lionel; Willems, Jan.

*References:* Bradley, *Lure;* Gosse, *Who's Who;* Lussan.

# COOPER, CAPTAIN

## (FL. 1663)

English privateer who on 29 October 1663 brought two Spanish prizes into Port Royal, Jamaica. One was the *María* of Seville, a royal *azogue* ship carrying 1,000 quintals of quicksilver for the mines of Mexico and trade items such as oil, wine, and olives. A number of prisoners were also included, among them several friars bound for Campeche and Veracruz. In a separate document dated this same year, Cooper's ship was described as a frigate of ten guns with a crew of 80 men.

*See also* azogue.

*References:* Gosse, *Who's Who;* Pawson, *Port Royal.*

# CÓRDOBA Y ZÚÑIGA, LUIS BARTOLOMÉ DE

## (C. 1650-1706?)

Spanish governor of Veracruz during the pirate invasion of May 1683.

De Córdoba was born in Veracruz during the service of his father, Admiral Lorenzo de Córdoba y Zúñiga, Knight of the Order of Santiago, as *castellano,* or garrison commander, of its island fortress of San Juan de Ulúa. After going abroad to serve the king, Don Luis returned with his own appointment as governor early in 1677. He was considered the puppet of his older, corrupt brother-in-law, Diego Ortiz de Largacha, Knight of the Order of Santiago, whose unpopularity soon encompassed De Córdoba as well. The governor's prestige was considerably diminished when Ortiz de Largacha was extradited to stand trial in Mexico City in 1681.

At three o'clock on the afternoon of Monday, 17 May 1683, De Córdoba was attending a banquet in Veracruz when word arrived of two sails out at sea. Such arrivals were dealt with by San Juan de Ulúa's commander, so Don Luis resumed his meal; but upon quitting the banquet hall more than an hour later, he was approached by Don Juan Morfa (John Murphy) with the suspicion that the ships were behaving oddly by not entering on the prevailing wind. This opinion was seconded by the city's *sargento mayor* or military commander, Mateo Alonso de Huidobro, but dismissed by the governor.

That evening De Córdoba received a message from nearby Antigua Veracruz of strange ships out at sea, and San Juan de Ulúa's commander advised him that the island was being placed on full alert. The governor ordered his own city troops into barracks rather than individual billets but did not alert his militia; furthermore, he ignored the fact that his regulars had not received their monthly allotment of powder and shot. That night a false report was brought in of a signal flare being made on San Juan de Ulúa, so Don Luis ordered more sentries posted along the waterfront, then visited each of his separate barracks "wrapped in a cape."

Satisfied, he went back to bed, little realizing that his inspection had been observed by pirates from the shadows. They had infiltrated the city from the landward side under Laurens de Graaf and the "chevalier" de Grammont, preparing to attack at first light.

Gunfire awakened the governor at dawn on 18 May; he scrambled downstairs with sword and baton to rally his household company, but they lacked powder. Outside, Grammont led two columns of heavily armed *flibustiers* against the palace, firing volleys. Those Spaniards brave enough to form a line were mowed down, the survivors fleeing back inside to bar the door. De Córdoba ran upstairs with his troops, then emerged onto a balcony to call for quarter, but a soldier behind him warned him "not to do so with a naked blade in his hand, for he might be killed." Withdrawing hastily, the governor tried to dispose of his official papers by sweeping these off his desk into a couple of baskets, with orders to hurl them down the well. His wooden writing case with its correspondence was tossed underneath a rolled awning.

He joined his panic-stricken men on the rooftop, flinging himself over the wall to the adjacent private homes. Soon, the invaders cut off this escape, but De Córdoba had disappeared. He hid for 24 hours in the palace stables with an injured leg, but was discovered the morning of 19 May by an English buccaneer (reputedly Captain Spurre), and the pirates beat him mercilessly. Bloodied, Don Luis was kept hostage along with a dozen leading citizens. He offered ransom, writing a pitiful letter to his sister Doña Ana María (wife of Ortiz de Largacha) in Puebla, asking her to obtain the sum. Eventually 150,000 pesos were paid for all the captives, and Don Luis was released along with the rest.

He was then arrested on charges of neglect of duty and cowardice. On 14 June

1683, he was transferred from the Veracruz jail to San Juan de Ulúa, vilified by a jeering mob. On 11 August he was sentenced to death at his court-martial, but a year later the Mexican viceroy commuted this verdict to "perpetual destitution of office and banishment from the Indies, plus ten years imprisonment in Mamora or some other African *presidio.*" Outrage caused petitions, calling for the execution to be carried out, to be raised in Veracruz. The ex-governor languished on San Juan de Ulúa for many years, until finally a *real cédula* (royal decree) authorized his release in 1706.

*See also* De Graaf, Laurens Cornelis Boudewijn; Grammont, "chevalier" de; Huidobro, Mateo Alonso de; Murphy Fitzgerald, John; Spurre, George.

*References:* Juárez; Marley, *Veracruz.*

# CORNELISZOON, JAN

### (FL. 1683)

Rover of Dutch descent who operated out of New York.

In March 1683 Corneliszoon was lying at New Providence in the Bahamas with his brigantine and Captains Markham, Conway Woolley, and the French *flibustier* Bréhal, preparing to jointly "fish silver from a Spanish wreck." But then Captain Thomas Paine arrived in his bark *Pearl,* of 8 guns and 60 men, with a license from Governor Sir Thomas Lynch of Jamaica to hunt pirates. The five decided to raid the nearby Spanish outpost of Saint Augustine, Florida, using Paine's commission as authorization despite the official peace with Spain. They landed flying French colors but found the Spaniards forewarned. After releasing some captives they had brought and looting the surrounding countryside, they withdrew.

Once back in the Bahamas, Corneliszoon and Woolley apparently proceeded directly to the wreck site, while the other three reentered New Providence. When Governor Robert Lilburne visited the site of the sunken galleon a few weeks later, he found all the rovers gone.

*See also* Bréhal, Capitaine; Lilburne, Robert; Markham, John; Paine, Thomas; Woolley, Conway.

*Reference: C.S.P., Amer. and W.I.,* Vol. XI.

# CORSAIR

Synonym for privateer, meaning an individual or vessel licensed to commit hostilities.

The word is believed to derive from the Latin *cursus* or *corsa,* for "course" or "cruise." It remained commonplace among the Latin-speaking peoples—particularly the Spanish—even after the English introduced "privateer" into their language, and the Dutch *kaper* into theirs. The Spaniards retained the classic usage, referring to "sailing on the account" as *andar a corso* or a privateering commission as *patente de corso.* Some even appended the term to their own names, such as the raider Blas Miguel Corso, or Juan Corso.

*See also* Corso, Juan; *kaper;* Miguel, Blas.

# CORSO, JUAN

### ALSO CORZO
### (FL. 1680-1685)

Famous Spanish corsair, greatly feared and hated by his victims.

In all likelihood the name Juan Corso was merely a pseudonym, being roughly equivalent to "John Privateer" in English. His real name and origins are unknown, although he may have been Italian or from the Mediterranean, as Governor Sir Thomas Lynch of Jamaica was to describe the *guardacostas* of his day as "Corsicans, Slavonians, Greeks, mulattoes, a mongrel parcel of thieves." Certainly Corso was subordinate to the Spaniard Pedro de Castro throughout his West Indian career, which would suggest that he was not Spanish himself but rather a foreign mercenary. Corso's own first mate, "Jorge Nicolás" (Giorgio Niccolo) was known to be a native of Venice.

It is possible that Corso took part in De Castro's early cruises, but the first direct reference to his activities occurred in April 1680, when both sailed in the expedition that Captain Felipe de la Barrera mounted against the English logwood cutters of the Laguna de Términos. After returning from this highly successful sweep, De Castro and Corso departed in mid-July with two *piraguas* to patrol the Yucatán coast as far as the Bay of Honduras. Off Cocinas Island they saw a large vessel at anchor, then another small frigate nearby, which they suspected of poaching logwood and therefore captured. The larger ship was likely Robert Oxe's *Laurel*, renamed *León Colorado* (Crowned Lion) and carried back toward Campeche. Upon approaching their base, De Castro and Corso were informed that another large intruder lay at the Laguna de Términos, so they immediately went in pursuit and found a 36-gun ship inside the bar. Unable to enter with *León Colorado*, De Castro nonetheless persuaded the enemy captain to surrender. They learned that it was *Nuestra Señora del Honhón*, which had been captured by John Coxon's flotilla off Portobelo 11 months earlier.

Rather than return with these prizes to Campeche, De Castro decided to put into Veracruz, sending Corso back in a single *piragua* to Campeche. The local authorities were greatly annoyed at this decision; they arrested Corso and sent 50 soldiers aboard a *piragua* in pursuit of De Castro. The matter was not resolved until March 1681, when De Castro's action was deemed legitimate and Corso released. The two then resumed coastal patrols with *León Colorado* and *Honhón* until the latter was incorporated into the Armada de Barlovento in 1682, and the corsairs shifted operations to the southern coast of Cuba. This was a very active arena, the Spaniards waging a bitter peacetime feud with the French *flibustiers* of Saint Domingue, as well as with English smugglers, hunters, and fishermen. Corso's name soon became prominent, both because De Castro left much of the work to him and because some captures made by other rovers were erroneously attributed to him. The English in particular—neutral in the conflict but with many ships at sea—became incensed at his growing number of depredations.

By April 1683, Governor Lynch of Jamaica was writing to

> the governor of Havana complaining of the piracies of Juan Corso, and desiring to know if he owned them; but neither he nor the governor of Santiago de Cuba would ever answer. This Juan a month since [late June or early July 1683] took a boat of ours bound to New Providence [in the Bahamas]; he has killed diverse of our people in cold blood. In one case he cut off a man's head because he was sick and could not row so strongly as he expected. Barbarities like these and worse he commits daily.

The governor also reported that a New England ketch that had gone turtling to the Salt Tortugas (Isla La Tortuga, off Venezuela) had been seized by some French corsairs and carried toward Saint Domingue but was intercepted by Corso before it could arrive. Sailing it into Santiago de Cuba, the French prize crew were condemned to death as pirates, but the vessel and the Englishmen detained. As the French pirates were marched to execution the town mutinied and reprieved them from fear of the Frenchmen's revenge, and paid the governor 200 pieces of eight in composition. This is the manner in which they do everything.

A few weeks later, in early August 1683, Lynch again advised his superiors that it was Corso

who by landing off the coast of Hispaniola and carrying away many prisoners, slaves, etc., caused the French government to grant commissions of war, and it is feared that on the privateers' return [from the sack of Veracruz under Laurens de Graaf, the "chevalier" de Grammont, and Nikolaas van Hoorn] they will destroy Santiago de Cuba, where Corso shelters himself.

On 28 August, Lynch enumerated his complaints against the corsair in a letter to the Spanish governor of Havana, saying:

This Juan Corso, or some such villains, have killed Captain Prenar, pretending to come to trade with him in a canoe.

He or some others came aboard one Bodeler and one Wall, when at anchor in an uninhabited bay, killed both of them and several [other] men, and carried the sloops to Santiago de Cuba.

The same surprised Captain Van den Claus[en] in an uninhabited bay, and tortured the men to make them confess that they were trading. The governor [of Santiago de Cuba], bribed by a share, condemned her.

These pirates constantly rack their prisoners, and the governors make no effort to stop it.

Corso having captured an English boat with four men, killed one with his own hand because he was sick.

He or others have lately taken a vessel bound for New Providence without cargo.

He has often declared that he will serve us as he served the French, and threatens to come and take Negroes from the north side of Jamaica.

Lynch ended his disquisition by telling the governor of Havana that if "you could receive anybody at Havana, I could much strengthen my case against Juan Corso."

In early March 1684, Lynch again wrote his superiors in London:

It is reported that Juan Corso attacked a Frenchman with three *periagos* [*sic; piraguas*] and was killed, but that the French were taken and all killed to the number of 100. The Spaniards are said to have lost as many. This is reported to have taken place off Havana, Corso having come from New Providence, which he had destroyed.

This information was incorrect, as both Corso and De Castro continued to operate out of Cuba. In the spring of 1685, they were among the first Spaniards to learn of a secret French colony being established in the Gulf of Mexico by René Robert Cavelier, sieur de La Salle. Realizing that Madrid would welcome the destruction of this intrusive settlement, they went in quest of it. Sailing in a galliot to Tuxpan and Tampico (Mexico) that April, they hoped to take on provisions and a pilot for the uncharted gulf waters. On 4 May 1685, four days after leaving Tampico on an east–northeasterly heading, they were driven by a storm close inshore "two leagues to windward of Espíritu Santo Bay." While riding out the weather they saw signs of white habitation and going ashore met a party of six Indians, who informed them through sign language that many people with muskets had proceeded inland.

De Castro led 50 well-armed men and three Indian guides in search of the intruders, but returned empty-handed a few days later. On 19 May he and Corso stood out to sea, only to be driven into another unknown inlet by contrary winds and currents, where they lost their anchor. Desperate to keep off the rocks, 25 men were put in the water to fashion a mooring, then abandoned when the wind veered. Three days later Corso and De Castro returned in rough weather, rescuing 16 men, but the rest were absent, foraging for food. By the time they reappeared, the surf was too dangerous, so they were hailed to meet the galliot at Apalache Bay, many miles along the coast. The nine men survived this grueling trek, but the galliot was never seen again, being lost with all hands—including Juan Corso.

**See also** Barlovento, Armada de; Barrera y Villegas, Felipe de la; Castro, Pedro de; Coxon, John; De Graaf, Laurens Cornelis Boudewijn; Grammont, "chevalier" de; *guardacostas;* Hispaniola; Laguna de Términos; logwood; Lynch, Sir Thomas; Oxe, Robert; pieces of eight; Van Hoorn, Nikolaas.

**References:** *C.S.P., Amer. and W.I.,* Vol.XI; Robles; Weddle, *Wilderness.*

# COWARD, WILLIAM
## (FL. 1689-1690)

In November 1689, with three men and a boy, he rowed out to the ketch *Elinor,* William Shortrigs, master, lying at anchor in Boston harbor, seized the vessel, and took her to Cape Cod. The crew of the ketch could make no resistance, as they were all down with smallpox. The pirates were caught and locked up in the new stone jail in Boston. Coward was hanged on 27 January 1690 (O.S.).

**Reference:** Gosse, *Who's Who.*

# COXON, JOHN
## (FL. 1676-1688)

English privateer who prowled the West Indies for many years.

The first mention of Coxon's name appears to have occurred on 2 August 1676 (O.S.), when Peter Beckford wrote from Port Royal, Jamaica:

> Captain Coxen [*sic*] about the island with a French commission. My Lord [Vaughan, governor of Jamaica] uses all possible means to take him, and proclaimed mercy to all his men if they delivered their captain up, who was declared a pirate, but they refused, so my lord sent to take him, but he ran away immediately.

England being then at peace, it was illegal for Jamaican privateers to participate in the ongoing hostilities between France, Spain, and Holland, yet Coxon was one of several who ignored this stricture and in June 1677 sailed with his French commission under Capitaine La Garde to Santa Marta on the Spanish Main.

### CAPTURE OF SANTA MARTA
### (JUNE 1677)
The *flibustier* force surprised Santa Marta at dawn and took many captives, including the governor and bishop, holding them for ransom until a trio of Armada de Barlovento warships appeared from Cartagena with 500 soldiers and drove them off. The raiders then retired toward Port Royal and on 28 July 1677 Sir Thomas Lynch noted:

Five or six French and English privateers lately come to Jamaica from taking Santa Marta, Barnes being one and Coxon expected every hour. On board the Governor and the Bishop, and Captain Legarde [sic] has promised to put them on shore. The plunder of the town was not great, money and broken plate [silver] about £20 a man.

Three days later Coxon entered port and personally escorted the bishop, Dr. Lucas Fernández y Piedrahita, and a Spanish friar into the presence of the new island governor, Lord Vaughan. The prelate was nobly housed, and English officers went aboard the buccaneer flotilla to attempt "to procure the liberty of the [Spanish] Governor and others, but finding the privateers all drunk, it was impossible to persuade them to do anything by fair means." Vaughan therefore ordered the French to depart and officially advised Coxon and his English followers it was against the law for them to serve under foreign colors. The French were "damnably enraged" at being deprived of their English companions and sailed off without releasing the captives.

## Indigo Seizure
### (September 1679)

Coxon soon resumed his activities anyway, leading a mixed party of English, French, and other privateers on a foray into the Bay of Honduras in summer 1679. On 26 September they captured a Spanish merchantman ladened with valuable cargo and again approached Jamaica to dispose of it. By late October it was being reported at Port Royal:

There has been lately taken from the Spaniards by Coxon, Bartholomew Sharpe, Bothing and Hawkins [sic; Richard Sawkins?] with their crew, 500 chests of indigo, a great quantity of cacao, cochineal, tortoise shell, money and plate. Much is brought into this country already, and the rest expected.

The English governor tried to prevent its introduction, but the rovers threatened "they would leave their interest in Jamaica and sail to Rhode Island or to the Dutch, where they would be well entertained." Despite naval patrols, the goods were smuggled ashore and sold, to the noticeable benefit of both the island's economy and treasury.

## Portobelo Campaign
### (February 1680)

Coxon then held an illegal assemblage in late December 1679 at Port Morant, off the southeastern tip of Jamaica, which was attended by the barks of Captains Cornelius Essex and Sharpe, as well as the sloops of Robert Allison and Thomas Magott, all of whom agreed to unite under Coxon's leadership for an assault on Spanish Portobelo. The authorization for such a venture was very sketchy, the privateers holding a mixture of outdated French and English commissions, including "let passes" from the new Jamaican governor Lord Carlisle "to go into the Bay of Honduras [modern Belize] to cut logwood." They quit Port Morant on 17 January 1680 and less than 20 miles out at sea met the brigantine of French *flibustier* Jean Rose, who also joined the expedition. The weather turning bad, Coxon hailed his vessels to make their best way to Isla Fuerte, 90 miles south–southwest of Cartagena on the Spanish Main. Whoever got there first was "to leave a note on the Sandy Point, to satisfy the rest."

Only Essex and Sharpe failed to keep the rendezvous, and Coxon raided the nearby San Bernardo or "Friends" Islands for landing craft. He returned three days later with "four *piraguas* and six very good large canoes," discovering that Essex had rejoined in the meantime. The formation then proceeded toward *Isla de Pinos* (Island of Pines, 130 miles east of Portobelo in the Archipelago de las Mulatas), although only Coxon's bark was able to shoulder through the contrary winds and gain this isle, the rest being forced into *Isla de Oro* (Golden Island) some miles away. There the pirates befriended the local Indians, while Coxon learned that Sharpe had been there before him, and that the privateer Edmond Cooke had come to join him, for which he was grateful because his force "wanted men."

The winds continuing foul, Coxon took 250 buccaneers into boats and rowed westward along the coast, hoping to strike before the Spaniards could learn of his presence. Near his goal he came upon "a great ship riding at anchor," which proved to be that of *flibustier* Capitaine Lessone, who added 80 Frenchmen to the boat parties. Shortly thereafter, the buccaneers slipped ashore in the Gulf of San Blas, proceeding afoot to avoid the Spanish coastal watchers. They marched three days "without any food, and their feet cut with the rocks for want of shoes," until they came upon an Indian village three miles short of Portobelo. A native spotted them and shouted "*¡Ladrones!*" (Thieves!) before setting off at a run toward the city.

"Good boys," Coxon called to his men, "you that are able to run, get into town before we are descried!" The buccaneers trotted in pursuit, but the Indian arrived half an hour before them and raised the alarm. Nevertheless, the vanguard under Allison was able to sweep in unopposed. The Spaniards withdrew in fear inside their citadel and left the raiders to ransack Portobelo unchecked over the next two days. Coxon then retired ten miles northeastward, entrenching himself with his booty and a few prisoners on a cay half a mile offshore of Bastimentos, while Allison sped in a boat to recall the anchored ships. Three days later, several hundred Spanish troops appeared and began firing

upon the pirates from the beach but were unable to exact vengeance before the vessels arrived.

Coxon instituted a blockade of Portobelo, and Sharpe—who had reappeared in the interim—intercepted a *barco luengo* from Cartagena; three days later Coxon and Allison combined to take a new 90-ton ship of eight guns, which also came from Cartagena, bearing 30 slaves, timber, salt, corn, and allegedly 500 pieces of gold in a jar of wine (which Coxon "wronged the party of by keeping it to himself," according to a disgruntled follower). A general distribution of booty was then made, resulting in shares of 100 pieces of eight per man. Afterward, Coxon's confederates agreed to retire to Bocas del Toro (literally "bull's mouths" or "entrances of the bull"), located at the northwestern extremity of present-day Panama, "to make clean our ships, there being the best place to careen our ships, by reason there is good store of turtle and manatee and fish."

Coxon found the *barco luengo* of Richard Sawkins already inside, who in turn advised him that Captain Peter Harris was careening at Diego's Point on nearby Isla Solarte. Coxon transferred into his new Spanish prize, abandoning his old bark; once refitted, he suggested that the pirates return to Golden Island and avail themselves of their friendship with the Indians "to travel overland to Panama" and attack the Spaniards on their Pacific flank. The English all agreed; only the French under Lessone and Rose refused, preferring to prowl the Gulf of San Blas again. Thus the two contingents parted, in true brotherhood fashion.

## PACIFIC INCURSION
### (APRIL 1680)

Coxon, Allison, Cooke, Harris, Magott, Sawkins, and Sharpe all anchored their ships close inshore in a small cove on Golden

Island, out of sight of any Spaniards who might chance to pass. An anchor watch was left aboard each, with orders to rally to Coxon's and Harris's ships—the two largest—if any attack should occur. At six o'clock on Monday morning, 15 April 1680, Coxon led 332 buccaneers ashore and obtained guides from the local Indians to cross the isthmus. Ten days later, the pirates came upon the Spanish stockade of Santa María at the confluence of the Chucunaque and Tuira Rivers. This fort had no artillery, so at dawn Sawkins led a mad rush of buccaneers; after a heated half-hour exchange of small arms fire they penetrated the palisades. Seventy of the 200 Spanish defenders were killed outright, and the rest were massacred later by the Indians.

Flush with their cruel victory, the buccaneers pressed on toward the Pacific, although it was noted that "our general, Captain Coxon, seemed unwilling, but with much persuasion went." It seemed to him that they did not possess sufficient strength to emulate Henry Morgan's feat of subduing Panama, so they should be satisfied with smaller gains. But his "people was eager for more voyage" despite the dangers, and other captains assumed the lead. Once on the Pacific side, the pirate boats captured an anchored Spanish bark one night, and Sharpe went aboard with 135 men. The next night Harris captured a second, and soon the buccaneers enjoyed a small flotilla, with which they bore down upon Panama. The Spaniards sent out a hastily assembled force to do battle, and the raiders captured it after a three-hour fight.

By this time, Coxon's prestige was so eroded that he was deposed. "Our former admiral not behaving himself nobly in time of engagement," a pirate wrote, "was something hooted at by the party, that he immediately went away to go overland." On 5 May 1680, Coxon quit the campaign with 70 loyal hands in a small bark, retracing his steps across the isthmus. Sharpe, Sawkins, and Cooke remained in command of the expedition, which began its epic two-year campaign of terror along the South American coast. Meanwhile, Coxon forged back up the Chucunaque river and regained the Caribbean, appearing a few weeks later before Jamaica. Retiring governor Carlisle met with the corsair and 55 men

> off Point Negril on my passage home. We gave chase with the *Hunter* frigate in company for 24 hours, but he outsailed us and we could not come up with him, but we took two vessels belonging to him forsaken by their crews who were all aboard his vessel.

The following spring Coxon was rumored to be calling for another assembly of pirates "somewhere in the Gulf of Honduras," perhaps at Roatan, and is also known to have raided the Spanish outpost of Saint Augustine, Florida. By early June 1681 he was lying at Springer's Key in the San Blas Islands again, with a ship of 10 guns and 100 men in company with Rose, Jan Willems, George Wright, and four other captains. They were joined there by Capitaine Tristan, who had just rescued John Cooke's band of rovers at nearby La Sound's Key, fresh from their South Seas adventures. William Dampier, who was among the latter group, recorded how Coxon and the others were overjoyed to see them, having "never heard what became of us." The whole band then decided to make a descent on the Central American coast, for which they sailed toward San Andrés Island to procure boats. But a gale scattered the formation, and an *armadilla* of a dozen tiny men o' war sent from Cartagena drove others away. Coxon put into Bocas del Toro to careen, his expedition having disintegrated.

## JAMAICAN SERVICE
### (1682-1683)

Apparently tiring of his nomadic existence, in May 1682 Coxon approached yet another new governor of Jamaica, Sir Thomas Lynch, and showed him his commission—issued by Captain-General Robert Clarke of the Bahamas—to operate against the Spaniards. Lynch was appalled, considering this a violation of the peace with Madrid, but did not hold it against Coxon personally. Instead, he wrote reprovingly to Clarke, who replied on 16 July of this same year:

> Captain John Coxon being denied a commission to take Saint Augustine, Florida, went hence in contempt of any orders and contrary to law and custom, carrying away some persons that are indebted to the inhabitants [of the Bahamas]. All that he did in landing and plundering on Spanish territory was done by his own power. I thought fit to inform you of this, since I hear he is now at Jamaica.

Lynch was unconvinced and continued to put his trust in the privateer. Four months later (6 November 1682 O.S.), he reported to his superiors that he had recently sent

> Coxon and two other vessels to the Bay of Honduras to bring away our logwood cutters. So far from doing so, he was in danger of losing his ship and his life. His men plotted to take the ship and go privateering, but he valiantly resisted, killed one or two with his own hand, forced eleven overboard and brought three here, who were condemned last Friday. I shall order one or two to be hanged for an example to others and encouragement to him. I am hiring him to convey a Spaniard to Havana.

In February 1683, Lynch again entrusted Coxon with a special commission, dispatching him in search of Jan Willems to mount a joint pursuit of Jean Hamlin, the French renegade who had been making captures with the hijacked vessel *Trompeuse* (Trickster). The governor was willing to offer Willems, "(who commands an admirable sailer), men, victuals, pardon, naturalisation and £200 in money to him and Coxon, if he will go after *La Trompeuse.*"

The Dutchman being otherwise engaged, Coxon was unsuccessful. Returning toward Port Royal, he met the corsair flagship *Saint Nicholas* to leeward (westward) of that island, bearing Nicholas Van Hoorn and the "chevalier" de Grammont, who informed him that they were "trying to unite all the privateers for an attack on Veracruz." Although he must have been tempted, Coxon refused and reentered Port Royal in mid-March. He subsequently learned the buccaneers had met with Laurens de Graaf, Michiel Andrieszoon, George Spurre, Jacob Hall, Pierre Bot, Antoine Bernard, Pierre d'Orange and others, and had made a spectacular assault on that Mexican port, obtaining enormous amounts of booty with almost no casualties. Such a missed opportunity must have galled the old rover, and by 12 November Lynch was writing, "Coxon is again in rebellion," having resumed his former calling.

## RENEGADE
### (1683-1688)

Nothing more was heard of Coxon for some years, until in late January 1686 Lieutenant Governor Hender Molesworth of Jamaica reported:

> Captain John Coxon, a notorious privateer, who took advantage of a clause in the act for restraining and persuading pirates to return to the honest life, became weary

of it and reverted to piracy, has wearied again of that and returned here. His bond for good behavior, when required, could not be found, but I have evidence against him and have ordered him to be apprehended. The place of trial will be Santiago de la Vega, where there will be fewer sympathisers among the jury.

The veteran commander apparently remained as wily as ever, however, for by mid-November 1686 Molesworth was complaining:

I hear that Coxon is cutting logwood in the Gulf of Campeche [*sic;* Laguna de Términos], and has written to his friends that he has given up privateering and means to earn an honest living. I shall nonetheless send the proclamation declaring him a pirate to those parts by first opportunity.

He followed this up by issuing a warrant on 24 November 1686 (O.S.), commissioning "Captains Rich Cubitt and Conway to apprehend John Coxon, the pirate, said to be logwood-cutting in the Bay of Campeche."

Even so, Coxon could not be caught, although when Royal Navy Captain Thomas Spragge returned to Port Royal in August of the following year, with 71 English prisoners restored to him by the Spanish governors of Campeche and Veracruz, he also "brought in six French pirates who had robbed some [Jamaican] vessels, and eleven of Coxon's men." The latter were tried on 18 August, eight being convicted after the other three turned informers. But it was not until October 1688 that Coxon himself and several of his men finally surrendered to the new Jamaican governor, the duke of Albemarle, who in turn handed them over to Stephen Lynch, Sir Robert Holmes's agent in the Americas. Coxon's *barco luengo,* called the *Dorado* (Spanish for "Golden

One"), was taken over "by one Lisle, whose company numbered 80 English, three French and five Flemings," and was later seized off Ile-à-Vache by the French authorities on 16 November 1688.

***See also*** Allison, Robert; *barco luengo;* Barlovento, Armada de; Barnes, William; careen; Clarke, Robert; Cooke, Edmond; Cooke, John; Dampier, William; Essex, Cornelius; Golden Island; Grammont, "chevalier" de; Hamlin, Jean; Harris, Peter (fl. 1671–1680); La Garde, Capitaine; Laguna de Términos; Lessone, Capitaine; logwood; Lynch, Sir Thomas; Magott, Thomas; pieces of eight; Rose, Jean; Sharpe, Bartholomew; South Seas; Spanish Main; Van Hoorn, Nikolaas; Willems, Jan.

***References:*** *C.S.P., Amer. and W.I.,* Vols. X–XIII; Jameson; Juárez; Marley, *Pirates;* Pope.

# CRAB ISLAND

English name for present-day Vieques Island, east of Puerto Rico, noted for its large crabs.

In a letter dated 28 October 1684 (O.S.) at Nevis, Governor Sir William Stapleton of the Leeward Islands described Crab Island as "the best of all the Virgins, if not better than them altogether. It is a small traject [i.e., distance] off Puerto Rico." Although the island was occasionally occupied by foreigners, the Spaniards were able to retain ownership of this outpost, thanks largely to its proximity to Puerto Rico.

***References:*** *C.S.P., Amer. and W.I.,* Vol. XI; Prebble.

# CRANE, WILLIAM

### (FL. 1675)

English privateer who sailed under French colors.

In the summer of 1675, Crane approached Captain John Edmunds of Point Negril, on the western extremity of Jamaica, to ask whether he might safely come in with his ship even though he held a French privateering commission. Until the previous year, England had been allied with France in the wars against the Dutch; now, peace had been declared by London, and English subjects were discouraged from participating in hostilities. Edmunds wrote on Crane's behalf to the recently returned Sir Henry Morgan, deputy governor of the island, who replied on 25 August 1675 (O.S.) that Crane "will be very welcome in any harbor."

*Reference: C.S.P., Amer. and W.I.,* Vol. IX.

# CRIJNSSEN, ABRAHAM

## (FL. 1667)

Dutch commodore who led a daring raid during the Second Anglo-Dutch War.

After seizing the English colony of Suriname on the Wild Coast in February 1667, Crijnssen (or "Crimson," as the English called him) led his Zeeland squadron northward and retook the island of Sint Eustatius. From there he appeared unexpectedly off Chesapeake Bay in the first days of June, where his four warships and an 8-gun dogger quickly snapped up a small Carolina-bound shallop, plus another English merchantman. Learning of a convoy assembling up the James River to convey the annual tobacco crop to market in London, Crijnssen hoisted English colors and followed his captured shallop in past Point Comfort.

English-speaking crew members were used to call out soundings as the Dutch advanced, and passing vessels were hailed in the same language, so everyone was deceived. Three leagues upriver they came upon the sole Royal Navy vessel for that station, the 20-year-old frigate HMS *Elizabeth,* 46 guns,

which had just arrived the previous month from its trans-Atlantic crossing. It was being repaired and had a 30-man skeleton crew on board, so Crijnssen blasted it with a broadside, then boarded. But Crijnssen could not haul the warship off, so he burned it at its mooring. The Dutch then reversed course downriver, seizing everything in their path.

The English attempted to mobilize a defense but even after hastily arming a dozen merchantmen found the masters reluctant to match broadsides with Crijnssen. The raiders burned half a dozen tobacco ships and manned more than a dozen others before sailing away.

*Reference:* Shomette, *Raid.*

# CUBITT, RICH

## (FL. 1686)

English privateer issued a warrant on 24 November 1686 (O.S.), by the governor of Jamaica, along with Captain Conway, "to apprehend John Coxon the pirate, said to be logwood cutting in the Bay of Campeche [Laguna de Términos]."

*See also* Conway, Captain; Coxon, John; Laguna de Términos; logwood.

*Reference: C.S.P., Amer. and W.I.,* Vol. XII.

# CUSACK, GEORGE

## (FL. 1668-1675)

Irish pirate, allegedly intended for the priesthood, who briefly operated in the West Indies.

In 1668 Cusack seized the *Hopewell* of Tangier and renamed it *Valiant Prince,* sailing to the Leeward Islands, where it was retaken. He and his men were imprisoned at Barbados but escaped in a small boat and then captured the *San Josef* of Lisbon. Calling it *Flying Devil,* they sailed to New England, burnt it, transferred to small boats, and reached Virginia. From there they recrossed the Atlantic, resuming attacks off the Irish and English coasts. Cusack's final captures were the *Robert* and *Saint Anne,* the latter disposed of at Aberdeen. Coming down into the Thames estuary, Cusack was captured by Colonel Kennedy off Leigh. There is a small, contemporary quarto entitled *The Grand Pyrate: or, The Life and Death of Capt. George Cusack, the Great Sea-Robber* (London: Jonathan Edwin, 1676), which describes his trial at the Old Bailey in January 1675 and subsequent execution.

**Reference:** *Piracy and Privateering.*

# CUSSY, PIERRE-PAUL TARIN DE

## (FL. 1676-1691)

Sixth French governor of Saint Domingue and Tortuga Island, who reluctantly repressed its privateers and then lived to regret it.

De Cussy was an old-time resident of Saint Domingue, serving as interim governor as early as March 1676, when both Bertrand d'Ogeron and his nephew Jacques Nepveu, sieur de Pouançay, were absent on business in France. That year De Pouançay succeeded his uncle as governor when d'Ogeron died, just as seven years later De Cussy would succeed De Pouançay in the same office, when the latter passed away. De Cussy's three-year term technically began to run as of 1 September 1683, although it was unlikely this official appointment reached him from France until early the next year.

Initially, De Cussy continued the policy of his predecessors regarding the *flibustiers,* considering them necessary both for that colony's defense and prosperity. He promulgated France's 1684 Treaty of

Ratisbon with Spain while simultaneously maintaining a suspiciously hostile attitude toward the local Spanish Americans, who reciprocated in full. But as the decade wore on, depredations such as the "chevalier" de Grammont's unprovoked sack of Campeche in July 1685 became increasingly embarrassing to the royal authorities, until finally on 9 March 1687—on direct orders from Paris—De Cussy was forced to publish an amnesty for that island's *flibustiers,* "on conditions that they return into ports and cease their piratical acts and become inhabitants, or give themselves over to the business of the sea." The greatest rover, Laurens de Graaf, had already been settled with the title of *mayor* of one of Saint Domingue's districts or *quartiers,* as well as possessing membership in the Order of Saint Louis, and it was hoped that other *flibustiers* would follow his example. Privateering gradually receded, amid De Cussy's deep suspicions of the Spanish.

When the War of the League of Augsburg (King William's War) exploded in April 1689, France was ranged against the combined forces of England, Holland, and Spain, and De Cussy felt his fears amply vindicated. "I destroyed privateering here because the court so willed it," he wrote bitterly from Port-de-Paix on 24 August of that same year, adding that if he had not succeeded "there would be ten or twelve stout ships on this coast, with many brave people aboard to preserve this colony and its commerce." In summer 1690 he led a small army across the border into Santo Domingo, capturing the Spanish town of Santiago de los Caballeros and unwittingly precipitating a massive counteroffensive. A host of Spanish volunteers mustered and trooped aboard the ships of the Armada de Barlovento. The armada departed the capital of Santo Domingo on 21 December, circling eastward around the island while another Spanish army advanced overland.

The two forces rendezvoused near Manzanillo Bay on the north coast and were confronted shortly after advancing into French territory by an overconfident De Cussy with inferior numbers. At the Battle of La Limonade on 21 January 1691, the Spanish invaders won a crushing victory, killing more than 400 Frenchmen against only 47 Spanish dead. When the naval officer Jean-Baptiste Ducasse stepped ashore amid the burnt remains of Cap François and visited the nearby battlefield two weeks later, he found De Cussy's corpse lying among the dead, "their bodies not yet buried, being rotted and half desiccated."

**See also** Barlovento, Armada de; Ducasse, Jean-Baptiste; Ogeron, Bertrand d'; Pouançay, Jacques Nepveu, sieur de.

**References:** Crouse; Lugo.

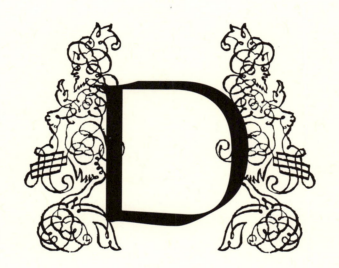

# DAMPIER, WILLIAM

## (1652-1715)

English buccaneer, chronicler, and circumnavigator.

The son of a tenant farmer, Dampier was born at East Coker, near Yeovil, England. He was baptized on 8 June 1652 (O.S.). His father died when he was ten years old, and his mother when he was 16. He was sent to sea in charge of a Weymouth trader, making a voyage to France and then Newfoundland. After a brief spell at home, he sailed to Bantam aboard the East Indiaman *John and Martha,* returning to England just as the Third Anglo-Dutch War broke out in 1672. The following year he was rated able seaman aboard HMS *Royal Prince,* 100 guns, Sir Edward Spragge's flagship at the battles of Schooneveldt and the Texel. Dampier missed this latter engagement, having been sent home sick.

His health restored and hostilities with the Dutch ended, in 1674 Dampier accepted the offer of his father's old landlord, Colonel Helyar, to go to Jamaica as assistant manager for his plantation. Tiring of this, Dampier made local trading voyages and in August 1675 shipped on a ketch into the "Bay of Campeche" [Laguna de Términos] with a cargo of rum and sugar to exchange for logwood. So taken was he with the Baymen's life that after the ketch returned to Jamaica, he made his way back to the laguna in February 1676 and remained for more than two years. In the autumn of 1678 he traveled to England with a good amount of money and married a young woman named Judith "out of the family of the duchess of Grafton."

In the spring of 1679, he sailed again for the West Indies in the *Loyal Merchant,* leaving his wife at Arlington House. He remained at Jamaica for some months and by Christmas, just on the point of returning home, was persuaded to go on a short voyage to the Mosquito Coast. Putting into Negril Bay at the western end of Jamaica, he joined a party of buccaneers led by Captain Richard Sawkins. They crossed to Bocas del Toro (on the northwestern shores of present-day Panama), where they incorporated into the pirate fleet of John Coxon, then ventured to Golden Island. Dampier was one of more than 300 buccaneers who traversed the isthmus, captured some Spanish coasters, and terrorized the Pacific coast. In February 1681 they were repulsed with heavy losses at Arica and withdrew in disarray. That April Dampier went with a contingent of about 50 buccaneers to recross the Isthmus of Panama, emerging near Point San Blas, where they found the French corsair ship of Capitaine Tristan lying off La Sounds Cay. Dampier remained with this commander about a year, then in July 1682 went with 19 companions to Virginia.

In August 1683 he and his comrades joined Captain John Cooke's *Revenge.* Cooke had served in the previous expedition and intended to return to the South Seas. Finding their craft too small, the raiders crossed to Sierra Leone on the West African coast, where they seized a Danish ship of 36 guns and renamed it *Bachelor's Delight.* With this they rounded Cape Horn and touched at Juan Fernández Island, rescuing a Mosquito Indian who had been marooned three years earlier. They then proceeded northward as far as New Spain, where in July 1684 Cooke died off Cabo Blanco, being succeeded by Edward Davis. The pirates ravaged the Pacific coast of South America for another year, most particularly in the company of Captains John Eaton and Charles Swan, until Dampier parted from Davis on 27 August 1685 (O.S.) off Peru, in favor of Swan's *Cygnet.* "It was not from any dislike to my old captain," Dampier later explained, but rather because Swan intended to "pass over for the East

Indies, which was a way very agreeable to my inclination."

First *Cygnet* prowled the Mexican coast for a few months, hoping to intercept the fabulously wealthy Manila galleon, which usually reached Acapulco around the end of each year. The *Santa Rosa,* forewarned of the enemy presence, slipped safely into harbor on 14 December 1685, and the buccaneers gave up in frustration. On 31 March 1686 (O.S.), they set out from Cape Corrientes and reached Guam almost two months later. Dampier cruised Far Eastern waters for the next five years, finally returning to England aboard the East Indiaman *Defence* in September 1691. He published his *Voyage Around the World* six years later, which became an immediate success, and in 1699–1700 led an exploration of Australia. In 1703, during the War of the Spanish Succession (Queen Anne's War), he commanded the 26-gun privateer *Saint George* into the South Pacific, again failing to take the Manila galleon. In 1708 he made a third attempt, acting as pilot aboard Woodes Roger's *Duke and Duchess,* which succeeded in capturing one of the Philippine ships and returned via the Cape of Good Hope to England in October 1711. Dampier died in London four years afterward in March 1715.

*See also* Cooke, John; Coxon, John; Eaton, John; Golden Island; Laguna de Términos; logwood; Sawkins, Richard; South Seas; Swan, Charles; Tristan, Capitaine.

*References:* Dampier; *D.N.B.; Piracy and Privateering;* Robles; Wafer.

# DARIEN COLONY

Short-lived Scottish settlement on the northeastern shores of Panama.

During the summer of 1698, a flotilla of five ships left Scotland with 1,200 people in an ill-conceived attempt to establish a

trading outpost on the Spanish Main. Having hired the retired privateer Robert Allison as pilot, they reached the Gulf of Darien by mid-November and had established themselves ashore. Although able to fend off an overland assault by Spain's Armada de Barlovento, they nonetheless quickly succumbed to disease, lack of profits, and internal strife, withdrawing the next summer.

*See also* Allison, Robert; Barlovento, Armada de; Spanish Main.

*Reference:* Prebble.

# DAVIS, CAPTAIN

## (FL. 1663)

English privateer described in 1663 as operating a 6-gun Dutch ship out of French Tortuga with a crew of 40 men and a Portuguese commission.

*Reference:* Pawson, *Port Royal.*

# DAVIS, EDWARD

## (FL. 1680-1693)

English pirate who twice roamed the South Seas and rounded Cape Horn.

Davis began as a simple freebooter among the contingents of John Coxon and other English commanders, who penetrated the Isthmus of Panama from Golden Island in April 1680 and began raiding the Spaniards on their Pacific coast. Eventually, Bartholomew Sharpe assumed overall command, until a faction of 50 buccaneers—including Davis, William Dampier, and Lionel Wafer—quit his company under John Cooke a year afterward to attempt to regain the Caribbean.

They emerged near Point San Blas in early June 1681, where they found the French corsair ship of Capitaine Tristan, lying off La Sounds Cay, who rescued them. Incorporated into the crew of Capitaine Archaimbaud, they then served under both George Wright and Jan Willems in succession before arriving off Ile-à-Vache in summer 1682, where they fell out with the latter commander over a prize and became marooned. Tristan nonetheless took eight or ten of them—including Cooke, Davis, and Wafer—into his ship and carried them to Petit Goâve, where they repaid his kindness by running off with his vessel when he and his men went ashore.

Returning to Ile-à-Vache to rescue their English companions, the band then seized a ship recently arrived from France carrying wines and another French ship "of good force," which they renamed *Revenge* and which they decided to use for another foray into the South Seas. They sailed to Virginia, disposed of their goods, reunited with Dampier, Ringrose, and other shipmates and ventured across the Atlantic to West Africa. Here they seized a 36-gun Danish ship, renaming it *Bachelor's Delight* and rounded the Horn to cruise into the Pacific.

## PACIFIC COMMAND
### (1684-1688)

When Cooke died from illness as they were approaching the Gulf of Nicoya (off present-day Costa Rica) in summer 1684, Davis assumed command of this powerful vessel, which would give him precedence over any rovers he met. On 2 October 1684 he encountered the vessels of Charles Swan and Peter Harris (the younger) off Isla de la Plata (literally "Silver Island," also referred to as "Drake's Island"), and finding that together they mustered close to 200 men, sailed for the South American mainland on 20 October. Paita was assaulted the morning of 3 November 1684, but nothing much of

value was found before this town was put to the torch. The Lobos Islands were visited next, after which a second abortive raid followed against Guayaquil in early December. A few small prizes were taken off the coast, but Davis realized that they were too weak for greater enterprises, so he headed northward for Panama in hopes of meeting other buccaneers crossing over the isthmus. At the end of December he captured an *aviso* off Gallo Island bound for Callao, and although its correspondence had been flung overboard, some letters were retrieved quickly enough from the water to reveal that the annual plate fleet had arrived at Portobelo on 28 November, which the Peruvian silver ships would very soon have to meet. On 8 January 1685 his buccaneers further intercepted the 90-ton *Santa Rosa* before repairing to the Pearl Islands to careen.

On 14 February a fresh contingent of 200 French *flibustiers* and 80 English buccaneers reached the islands in canoes, under Capitaines François Grogniet and Lescuyer. The *flibustiers* were offered *Santa Rosa* by Davis, while the Englishmen were to be incorporated into his *Bachelor's Delight* and Swan's *Cygnet*. In appreciation, Grogniet presented Davis with a blank privateering commission from the French governor of Saint Domingue and informed him more buccaneers were apparently on their way, so a party was sent to await them in the Gulf of San Miguel. On 3 March they met Captain Francis Townley with 180 men, mostly English, in two captured barks. A few days later another bark bearing about a dozen Englishmen entered the Gulf of Panama from the west, having separated from William Knight off the coast of New Spain. On 11 April another band of 264 mainly French *flibustiers* arrived across the isthmus under Capitaines Jean Rose, Pierre le Picard, and Desmarais. These three remembered Davis as one of the Englishmen who had stolen Tristan's ship, but they nevertheless joined his flotilla and settled down to await the arrival of the Peruvian convoy.

The convoy slipped past Davis's lookouts, deposited their treasure in Panama City, and sortied to do battle. On 7 June 1685, the six Spanish men o' war suddenly emerged from a morning shower off Pacheca Island and caught the pirates unprepared. An indecisive, long-range engagement ensued, with the lightly armed buccaneer craft unwilling to close with the mightier vessels of the Armada del Mar del Sur, who in turn could not overtake such nimble opponents. The next day ended with a Spanish victory, Davis being driven off.

The buccaneers then fell out among themselves along national lines, with Davis, Swan, Townley, and Knight sailing northwestward as a single group and raiding Realejo and León (Nicaragua) in early August 1685 with little spoils. Davis proceeded southward from Realejo with three other vessels, visiting the Gulf of Fonseca (Honduras) and the Galápagos Islands before raiding the Peruvian coast with Knight in July 1686. The latter parted from him after careening at the Juan Fernández Islands, "making the best of his way round Tierra del Fuego to the West Indies" while Davis returned to Mocha Island around Christmas 1686. He continued on that coast for another year before finally rounding the Horn himself.

After touching at the River Plate, Davis rounded Brazil and met a Barbados sloop commanded by Edwin Carter. The latter informed Davis and his men of James II's recent "proclamation to pardon and call in the buccaneers [most probably that of 22 May 1687 O.S.]," and so sailed with Carter's sloop to Philadelphia, where they arrived in May 1688. After a brief layover, Davis, Wafer, and a few other rovers traveled to their former sanctuary of Virginia, but immediately upon reaching there in June

1688, they were arrested by Captain Simon Rowe of HMS *Dumbarton,* on suspicion of piracy because of the £1,500 worth of battered silver that they had brought with them. Davis and his men insisted that this silver was procured in the South Seas merely to help them "spend the remainder of their days honestly and quietly" but were nonetheless cast into irons. When Rowe questioned a black slave that they had also brought from the Pacific, he came to the conclusion the rovers should have been hanged as multiple murderers.

In fact Davis and the rest of his men were allowed to travel to England aboard the merchantman *Effingham* in late 1690 to stand trial, their appearance in court guaranteed by dispatching all of their treasure separately. Although cleared of the charges after lengthy proceedings, in March 1693 Davis and the others were forced to cede £300 of their booty toward building a college in Virginia, which became William and Mary College.

*See also* Archaimbaud, Capitaine; careen; Cooke, John; Coxon, John; Dampier, William; Grogniet, Capitaine; Harris, Peter (fl. 1684–1686); Lescuyer, Capitaine; Mar del Sur, Armada del; maroon; South Seas; Swan, Charles; Townley, Francis; Tristan, Capitaine; Wafer, Lionel; Willems, Jan; Wright, George.

*References:* Bradley; *C.S.P., Amer. and W.I.,* Vol. XIII; Dampier; Lussan.

# DE GRAAF, LAURENS CORNELIS BOUDEWIJN

### (FL. 1682-1704?)

Gifted Dutch seaman who became the greatest corsair of his day.

Legend has it that De Graaf began his West Indian career as a gunner aboard the Armada de Barlovento, then turned against the Spaniards and used his firsthand knowledge to outwit them at every turn. At the height of his powers he was described as tall, blonde, and handsome, with a spiked Spanish-style moustache, "which suited him very well." It was noted that

> he always carries violins and trumpets aboard with which to entertain himself and amuse others, who derive pleasure from this. He is further distinguished amongst filibusters by his courtesy and good taste. Overall he has won such fame that when it is known he has arrived at some place, many come from all around to see with their own eyes whether "Lorenzo" is made like other men.

He was married to a Spanish woman on the Canary Islands named Petronila de Guzmán, and according to Spanish historians made his first recorded assault at Campeche.

On the night of 31 March 1672, the citizens of that Mexican port awakened to a huge conflagration from nearby San Román beach, where a vast quantity of timber had been stockpiled for a *guardacosta* frigate under construction and two new armed launches. Pirates had slipped ashore to set this ablaze, then infiltrated the city and directed their ships into the illuminated harbor, while the panic-stricken defenders fled. The next morning an unsuspecting merchantman arrived, sailing straight in with rich cargo and 120,000 pesos in silver. The raiders immediately decamped thereafter, disappearing over the horizon before a relief column could arrive from Mérida de Yucatán.

Ten years elapsed before De Graaf's name was mentioned again, which would seem to cast serious doubt on his role in this particular affair. In September 1682, Governor Jacques Nepveu, sieur de Pouançay of Saint Domingue, reported that De Graaf was a native of "Boost [?] in Holland," who had been roving on the account for five or six years (i.e., since 1676–1677), "never having wanted to take out a commission from anyone," nor "put into the port of any nation." His rise as a pirate, the governor added, had been, "From a small bark, he took a small ship; from this a bigger one, until at last there came into his power one of 24 to 28 guns." This was apparently *Tigre,* wrested from the Armada de Barlovento in the autumn of 1679 off the Spanish Main. By the spring of 1682, De Graaf had become so notorious that Acting Governor Sir Henry Morgan of Jamaica had described him as "a great and mischievous pirate," further warning Captain Peter Heywood of the frigate HMS *Norwich* when he departed on patrol "to look out for one Laurence ... who commands a ship of 28 guns and has 200 men on board." As an added precaution, Morgan even reinforced the Royal Navy warship with 40 soldiers from the Port Royal garrison.

## CAPTURE OF THE SITUADOS (1682)

De Graaf's first famous coup came in July 1682, when the frigate *Princesa* of the Armada de Barlovento (formerly the French *Dauphine,* commonly called *Francesa* by the Spaniards) stood into the Mona Passage out of the northwest. It was bound from Havana under Captain Manuel Delgado to deliver 120,000 pesos in Peruvian silver as the annual *situados,* or payrolls, for the garrisons of Puerto Rico and Santo Domingo, as well as sundry other goods. Its decks cluttered in anticipation of making landfall at Aguada, Puerto Rico, *Francesa* was surprised by De Graaf's *Tigre,* and 50 of its 250-man crew were killed or wounded in the ensuing battle. The triumphant buccaneer and his crew, most of them French *boucaniers,* repaired to Samaná Bay on the northern shores of Hispaniola with their prize, where they allegedly "made 140 shares and shared 700 pieces of eight a man." The Spanish prisoners and wounded were transferred to a pink for return to Cuba, while *Francesa* became De Graaf's new flagship.

When news of this depredation reached Santo Domingo, the outraged authorities retaliated by expropriating a consignment of slaves brought into port that November by Nikolaas van Hoorn, another Dutch adventurer with French ties. Furious, Van Hoorn escaped, and in February 1683 obtained a letter of reprisal from the French governor at Petit Goâve, to exact vengeance. In order to recruit freebooters for this purpose, Van Hoorn left Petit Goâve with the "chevalier" de Grammont, steering toward the pirate haunts on the Central American coast to find De Graaf and his Dutch confederate Michiel Andrieszoon, who were both reputedly lying there with "two great ships, a bark, a sloop . . . and 500 men."

The latter two, after seizing and refurbishing *Francesa,* had sailed to Cartagena but encountered only small coastal craft, so they returned into the Bay of Honduras where two large Spanish merchantmen— *Nuestra Señora de Consolación* (Our Lady of Consolation) and *Nuestra Señora de Regla*—were anchored. These were part of the regular traffic out of Cadiz, having landed their cargo some months earlier to be transported overland to Guatemala. Soon profits would be brought back over the jungle trails, along with valuable bundles of indigo, to be stowed aboard the empty vessels. Both would then weigh for Havana, to join the Mexican plate fleet on its homeward leg to the Old World.

De Graaf cleverly retired to Bonaco Island to careen his flagship while waiting for the Spaniards to load their treasure. A few weeks later, he was annoyed to find Van Hoorn noisily entering the roadstead, having taken the two unladen vessels at anchor. De Graaf departed in anger, but was

overtaken at Roatan by Grammont and Van Hoorn. On 7 April 1683, a huge gathering of pirates met on the beach to hear Grammont and Van Hoorn propose an assault on Veracruz. De Graaf and his cohorts agreed, quickly shifting the pirate fleet to nearby Guanaja Island for further reinforcements, then scurrying northward to round Yucatán before word of their design should reach Spanish ears. De Graaf led the way in the captured *Nuestra Señora de Regla* and Jan Willems's Spanish prize, while the main body of three ships and eight sloops trailed astern, out of sight.

## SACK OF VERACRUZ
### (MAY 1683)

On the afternoon of 17 May 1683, De Graaf's two advance scouts approached Veracruz, then broke off after closing within ten miles to determine that the plate fleet had not yet arrived. The port lookouts assumed these Spanish-built craft were merchantmen fearful of navigating the shoals after dark and did not become alarmed. That night De Graaf piloted his two vessels close inshore and landed a force of 200 buccaneers. While leading these on a reconnaissance of the sleeping city, Grammont and Van Hoorn brought another 600 ashore further away and stealthily marched to join him. Veracruz held 6,000 inhabitants, of whom 300 were regular troops and another 400 civilian militia; there were an additional 300 soldiers on the outlying island fortress of San Juan de Ulúa. But the landward stockades were low and neglected, with sand dunes drifted up against them, so the pirates stole over these and into the city.

At dawn on 18 May they attacked, firing indiscriminately so as to stampede the defenders. Within half an hour Veracruz was theirs, and several thousand half-dressed captives were herded into the principal church. The city was ransacked for four days, and numerous prisoners were tortured to reveal their hidden treasures. De Graaf and Grammont then marched the bulk of the captives down the coast to transfer them two miles offshore to Sacrificios Island, beyond rescue. There the pirates began loading their booty while waiting for the payment of a final ransom out of Mexico's interior. Despite the atrocities perpetrated, the Spaniards regarded De Graaf as the more humane of the buccaneer commanders, a reputation that was confirmed by an incident on Sacrificios.

Van Hoorn, impatient because the ransoms were not forthcoming, decided to send a dozen captives' heads ashore. According to Spanish eyewitnesses, De Graaf arrived from his flagship to prevent this, and when his countryman rounded on him with drawn sword, De Graaf wounded Van Hoorn and sent him aboard *Francesa* in chains. Shortly thereafter the ransoms were received, and after herding 1,500 blacks and mulattos aboard as slaves, the pirate fleet weighed. They encountered the annual plate fleet just as they were standing out from the coast, but its commander Admiral Diego Fernández de Zaldívar deferred combat, so the raiders escaped scot-free. De Graaf and the rest of the formation paused at Coatzacoalcos to take on water before shouldering their way back round Yucatán to Isla Mujeres, where by late June 1683 they had split the spoils. Each then went their separate ways, De Graaf and his followers sailing into the maze of islands off Cuba's southern coast to sell off their goods and smuggle the profits onto Jamaica.

## First English Overture
### (September 1683)

While lying at "Petite-Gouaîne" (*sic*; perhaps Petit Goâve) on 3 September, De Graaf wrote a letter in French to Governor Sir Thomas Lynch of Jamaica, thanking him for some small favor and adding:

I beg you to believe me the most humble of your servants, and to employ me if there be any place or occasion in which I can be of service to you. You will see how I shall try to employ myself. If by chance I should go to your coast in quest of necessities for myself or ship, I beg that my interests may be protected and no wrong done me, as I might do so if the opportunity presented itself for doing you service.

Lynch recognized that De Graaf was offering England his allegiance, which "would be a mighty service to the Spaniard, for if he pieces with the French they will go near to attack Cartagena." Such words proved prophetic, for shortly thereafter De Graaf and his cohorts Andrieszoon, Willems, François Le Sage, and others made for the Spanish Main, arriving near Cartagena late in November 1683. In London, meanwhile, the Lords of Trade and Plantations were empowering Lynch "to treat with Laurens the pirate, in order to pardon him and let him settle on [Jamaica] on giving security for his good behavior for the future."

## Cartagena
### (Christmas 1683)

When Governor Juan de Pando Estrada learned that the pirates were before his harbor, he commandeered the private ships *San Francisco*, 40 guns; *Paz*, 34 guns; and a 28-gun galliot to chase them away. This trio exited on 23 December 1683, manned by 800 soldiers and sailors under the command of Andrés de Pez. The result was scarcely as the governor envisioned—the seven smaller pirate ships swarmed all over his vessels and in the confusion *San Francisco* ran aground. *Paz* struck after four hours, and Willems took the galliot. Ninety Spaniards were killed, as opposed to 20 pirates. De Graaf refloated the *San Francisco* as his new flagship, renaming it *Fortune* (later *Neptune*);

Andrieszoon received the *Paz,* calling it *Mutine* (Rascal); and Willems was given De Graaf's old *Francesa* or *Dauphine.* On 25 December the triumphant buccaneers deposited their Spanish prisoners ashore, along with a message for the governor, thanking him for the Christmas presents. De Graaf then settled down to blockade the port.

In mid-January 1684, a small convoy of English slavers arrived escorted by HMS *Ruby,* of 48 guns. De Graaf let them pass, even inviting their officers aboard for a visit. Among the visitors was a trader named Diego Maquet, who bore a letter from De Graaf's wife on the Canary Islands, promising him a pardon if he gave up his piratical career and rejoined the King of Spain's service. Instead De Graaf, along with Andrieszoon and Willems, entered into an arrangement to buy wine and meat from Maquet, which was to be sent from Port Royal, Jamaica, to Roatan.

## SECOND ENGLISH OVERTURE
### (MAY 1684)

Shortly thereafter the pirates quit their blockade, traveling northwestward. En route, De Graaf spotted a 14-gun Spanish vessel and another ship, following both from a great distance until nightfall. He quietly closed and boarded the Spaniard in the dark, seizing it with only two shots being fired and finding it laden with "quinine and 47 pounds of gold." Next morning he took its consort as well, discovering it to be an English ship which the Spanish had captured and were carrying into Cuba. De Graaf restored this vessel to its crew and on 6 May 1684 wrote to Lynch again from "Saint Philip's Bay" [*sic*]:

I present my humble respects and hope that your health is good. I have a few details to give you about a small English ship laden with sugar, which I found in the hands of a Spaniard. I took both ships in the night, kept the Spaniard and set the Englishman free. The English captain told me that the Spaniard was taking him and his ship into Havana, but I gave him the ship back without doing him any harm. I send this short note only to show you that I am far from injuring your nation, but on the contrary, am anxious always to do it service.

The Jamaican governor replied some time later:

I have received your three letters, and thank you most particularly for letting the poor Irishman go. I shall show my gratitude to you when I have opportunity, for anyone who treats the English well lays me under obligation, and I expect no less from you who hold a patent from the Most Christian King [i.e., of France]. François Le Sage behaves very differently, for he has frequently injured and insulted our ships, and has by present report 60 pirates on board his ship from [Jean Hamlin's] *La Trompeuse.* I shall inform M. de Cussy of this. While you behave with such respect to the justice and friendship that exist between the French and English Crowns, I am always your friend.

The English would eventually be prepared to offer the rover "a pardon for all offences and naturalisation as an Englishman," provided De Graaf was to swear an oath of allegiance and buy a plantation on the island. The Crown authorities were further willing to "procure the necessary letters for the safe-conduct of his wife from the Canaries, provided Laurens pays the fees and the expenses of the passage," while the English ambassador would secure him a pardon from the king of Spain.

But in the meantime De Graaf's flotilla had intercepted a Spanish dispatch-vessel off the south coast of Cuba bearing news of a renewal to the fighting between Spain and France (at least partly on account of his destructive raid against Veracruz). De Graaf therefore left Andrieszoon and Willems to blockade Cuba with his other ships, while he sailed the 14-gun Spanish prize into Petit Goâve to dispose of its cargo and enter the French service. He apparently remained several months, during which he was given a *brevet de grâce,* or honorary commission. Also during his absence, Andrieszoon and Willems ransacked the Dutch West Indiamen *Stad Rotterdam* (City of Rotterdam) and *Elisabeth* as these approached Havana on 18 May, and in July a Spanish privateering *piragua* espied De Graaf's *Neptune* at anchor off Pinos Island on the southern Cuban coast. With part of its crew ashore wooding, the Spaniards landed and snuck up to ambush the unwary buccaneers, killing or capturing all while the *Neptune* was forced to cut its cables and flee back out to sea. De Graaf was still at Petit Goâve by mid-November when Willems brought in the Jamaican sloop *James* for trading with the Spanish, and its crew noted, "Laurens the pirate, who gave Yankey [*sic;* nickname for Jan Willems] his commission, took three barrels of flour from our ship."

## CRUISE TO THE SPANISH MAIN
### (JANUARY 1685)

The reason for this was that De Graaf was about to at last quit Petit Goâve, setting sail on 22 November 1684 with his 14-gun Spanish prize. Among his 120-man crew was a new recruit, Ravenau de Lussan, who has left a record of this voyage. He described his commander as "a man of good character" and relative newcomer to Saint Domingue, whom he admired very much. Intending to reunite with his corsairs off Havana, De Graaf worked into the Windward Passage

but did not clear it until New Year's Day 1685. Because of this slow progress, he veered round for the Spanish Main, reaching South America two weeks later. On the night of 17 January, Lussan recorded:

> toward the setting moon we sighted two ships and four small vessels only a cannon's shot to windward. This caused us to come about and clear our decks for action.

Next morning one of the small vessels hailed, and De Graaf responded that his was a French ship. Its Spanish lines made the other commander suspicious, though, so the stranger fired a pair of rounds and ordered De Graaf to heave to. Thinking he had blundered into a Spanish *armadilla,* De Graaf had two powder kegs stove in so as to be able to blow up his vessel, for such a fate was preferable "to falling into the hands of men who gave no quarter and would inflict on us hideous tortures, beginning with the captain." At that moment one of the more distant ships signalled, and the two identified themselves as *Neptune* and *Mutine,* with Andrieszoon in command. The tartan that had fired was captained by Jean Rose, who had not recognized De Graaf's vessel. He and two other small French corsairs had joined Andrieszoon off that coast, along with an English trader.

Next day De Graaf ordered this formation toward Curaçao. At two o'clock that afternoon, while within sight of Bonaire, they sighted a Flemish ship out of La Guaira, which they chased and captured that evening. On 20 January, De Graaf detached one of his consorts to request permission from the governor of Curaçao to buy masts for his ship, replacing those lost in a storm off Saint Thomas. This was refused, and the city gates closed, because of Andrieszoon and Willems's ransacking of the two Dutch West Indiamen the year before. Nevertheless, a couple hundred buccaneers managed to enjoy individual liberties ashore, until they were driven out "by beating drums" four days later.

On 27 January De Graaf set sail for Cape de la Vela (Venezuela), arriving three days later to post a lookout on the headland and begin careening his ships. Meanwhile, Rose visited Ríohacha and attempted to convince the Spaniards that he was a peaceful English trader, to no avail. Returning empty-handed on 8 February, the pirates decided to split up. De Graaf hoped to organize another major venture such as his Veracruz raid, but not everyone was in accord. Thus the buccaneers redistributed themselves around the vessels, and Lussan and 87 others sailed away in the 14-gun prize that had been brought from Petit Goâve. De Graaf laid in a course for the Gulf of Honduras with *Neptune,* hoping to recruit freebooters for his project.

His fame ensured plenty of willing spirits, and at a reunion on Cuba's Pinos Island in April 1685, a vast assemblage of 22 sail gathered, including Grammont, Willems, Joseph Bannister, and Jacob Evertsen. But this mob insisted on a repeat assault against Veracruz, which De Graaf patiently explained would not be caught napping a second time. Finally, he sailed away in frustration to the Mosquito Coast, where he was overtaken by Grammont and the others, and it was eventually decided to make a descent on the smaller Mexican port of Campeche. The pirates then shifted to Isla Mujeres to marshal their strength.

## CAMPECHE
### (JULY 1685)

Compared to two years earlier, the preparations were a clumsy affair, with buccaneers maintaining their watch off Cape Catoche for more than a month advising passing freebooters of the scheme, but this also forewarned the Spaniards. The build-up grew so notorious that the deputy governor

of Campeche, Felipe de la Barrera y Villegas, even had time to dispatch lookouts and spy-boats up the coast to give advance warning of their approach. In late June 1685, a stream of reports began reaching De la Barrera of unidentified vessels creeping closer to his port. On the afternoon of 6 July 1685, the pirate fleet of six large and four small ships, six sloops, and 17 *piraguas* appeared half a dozen miles off Campeche. A landing force of 700 buccaneers took to the boats and began rowing in toward shore, but the Spaniards were prepared—four militia companies totaling roughly 200 men exited and positioned themselves opposite the intended disembarkation point. The surprised pirates put up their helms, not wishing to wade ashore into the muzzles of Spanish infantry.

All night they remained bobbing on the swell, until the next morning they began to draw off toward their ships, which were standing in to meet them. But this proved merely a feint, and before the Spanish defenders could react, buccaneers came swarming ashore at the very outskirts of the city itself. A hundred formed up behind Captain Rettechard as the vanguard; 200 joined De Graaf and marched directly toward the city center; another 200 advanced under Captain Foccard along a street parallel to De Graaf's; and the final 200 followed Grammont in an encircling maneuver. The Spaniards fell back, while out in the harbor Captain Cristóbal Martínez de Acevedo prepared to scuttle his coast guard frigate *Nuestra Señora de la Soledad* (Our Lady of Solitude), as per instructions. Originally, he had intended to bore holes in its bottom, but given the speed of the invaders' advance, he directed his boatswain to run a trail of powder into the magazine. From the frigate's boat, Martínez lit the fuse, and *Soledad* exploded with such a mighty blast that it broke the defenders' morale, sending them scurrying into their citadel while the pirates entered Campeche uncontested.

Over the next few days, the invaders subdued isolated strong-points until only the citadel remained. The pirates began bombarding this fortress at dawn on 12 July 1685, but at ten o'clock that morning two relief columns of Spanish militia appeared on the beach, having hastened down from Mérida. In the past, the simple appearance of such troops had been enough to send smaller bands of raiders scuttling back out to sea, but this time the freebooter host stood and fought from behind Campeche's ramparts, and the first ranks of overconfident Spaniards went down to well-aimed volleys. All day the two sides battled, until Grammont circled behind the militiamen and caught them between two fires. The Spanish relief force drew off in dismay, and that night the garrison mutinied. Their officers begged them to remain until daybreak when they might seek terms, but the soldiers replied "pirates keep faith with no one" and threatened to shoot any officer who got in their way. By eleven o'clock that night the citadel was deserted, and a couple of English prisoners shouted word to the besiegers. The buccaneers called back for them to discharge the fort's artillery so that they might advance knowing the guns to be empty. Once done, they poured over the walls, led by De Graaf and Grammont in person.

The pirates then dispatched riders to ravage the surrounding countryside and remained in undisputed possession of Campeche for the next two months. However, as most of the city's wealth had been withdrawn prior to the assault, little plunder was found. Captives were threatened with death if ransoms were not forthcoming, but Yucatán's Governor Juan Bruno Téllez de Guzmân strictly prohibited such payments. Finally, late in August, Grammont had the Spanish prisoners paraded in the Plaza

Mayor and began carrying out executions. Six men had been hanged when De la Barrera and other leading citizens approached De Graaf, "whom they knew to be more humane than the Frenchman," and beseeched him to intervene. After a long discussion with Grammont, the brutality stopped and the pirates evacuated the city after putting it to the torch.

### BATTLE OFF ALACRÁN REEF
### (SEPTEMBER 1685)

Pausing briefly at Sisal, the raiders rounded Yucatán to their base of Isla Mujeres to divide the loot. De Graaf then set sail for Petit Goâve with his heavily laden *Neptune,* accompanied by Pierre Bot in *Nuestra Señora de Regla* and three other freebooter vessels. On 11 September 1685, they were sighted by a powerful contingent of the Armada de Barlovento under elderly Admiral Andrés de Ochoa y Zárate, who gave chase. Bot's *Regla* and a pirate sloop fell astern and were captured, the Spaniards heaving-to to take possession of these prizes. The following afternoon the royal frigate *Nuestra Señora del Honhón* sighted De Graaf inside the Gulf of Mexico, and sent the 8-gun tender *Jesús, María y José* (alias *Sevillano*) beating upwind to advise Ochoa. The Spanish admiral did not locate *Neptune* until four o'clock on the afternoon of 13 September, by which time *Honhón* was no longer in sight. The Spanish flagship *Santo Cristo de Burgos* (Holy Christ of Burgos) and vice-flagship *Nuestra Señora de la Concepción* (Our Lady of the Conception) pressed down upon their opponent.

Outnumbered and outgunned, De Graaf frantically tried to gain the weather gauge by lightening his ship, to no avail. That night he tensely awaited the Spanish onslaught, which began at dawn on 14 September, when *Santo Cristo* drove down and received De Graaf's opening broadside. All day the three vessels maneuvered, firing repeatedly at one another.

The Spanish flagship loosed off "fourteen full broadsides" and many other shots, while *Concepción* spent 1,600 rounds. But *Neptune* continued to avoid being crippled, thanks to the great skill with which it was handled. De Graaf on occasion fought both sides of his ship simultaneously and supplemented his fire with musket volleys, so that only a couple of his spars were shot away.

As daylight faded, so did Ochoa's will. The aged Spanish admiral had begun the day in a canvas chair upon his quarterdeck, and by nightfall was so enfeebled and delirious he was given last rites. In the darkness *Santo Cristo* hailed Vice Admiral Antonio de Astina to inform him that he was now in command at almost the same time as De Graaf was jettisoning his artillery and every other nonessential to gain the wind. The next morning the Spaniards found themselves to leeward of *Neptune* and began a half-hearted upwind beat as their opponent clawed away toward the Yucatán channel. With a rising southeasterly wind, *Santo Cristo*'s weakened superstructure fell overboard, and *Concepción* heaved to, so as to remain by its damaged consort. Miraculously, De Graaf had escaped, dealing the armada's pride a shattering blow. For years, their huge warships had been described as unsuitable for pursuing nimble corsairs; now, when they had finally caught a major enemy on the high seas, their elephantine strength had also been found wanting. Ochoa died a few days later, thus being spared the disgrace of a court-martial. De Graaf soon resumed his activities, going ashore at Cuba in December 1685 to rustle cattle and careen his five vessels, seemingly unfazed by his lucky escape.

## VALLADOLID
### (1686)

In spring the following year, De Graaf organized yet another raid, perhaps motivated by the fact that in February more than 100 of his slaves had been carried off

from Saint Domingue by the local Spaniards. Apparently in retaliation, he rallied freebooters round his flag and led a flotilla of seven ships into Ascensión Bay (present-day Emiliano Zapata Bay) on Yucatán's eastern shores. Five hundred buccaneers disembarked and marched inland against the town of Tihosuco, which was abandoned by its terrified inhabitants before being ransacked and burnt. De Graaf then penetrated deeper toward the city of Valladolid, while frightened refugees streamed ahead of the invaders, sowing panic throughout the countryside. By the time the buccaneers arrived within half a dozen miles of Valladolid, only 36 Spaniards remained to defend the city.

Suddenly De Graaf gave the order to wheel about and return to the coast. This inexplicable retreat led to a legend being born in Yucatán—that the withdrawal was the work of a clever mulatto named Núñez. Noticing that the weary refugees littered their trails with items they could no longer carry (and which the pirates eagerly snapped up), Núñez added a fake set of instructions to one such pile, purporting to be from Luis de Briaga, military commander of the province, saying that the pirates were to be enticed farther inland into a deadly trap.

Whatever the truth behind this tale, by April 1686 De Graaf had retired to Ascensión Bay, soon after making away for Roatan. By July, Lieutenant Governor Hender Molesworth of Jamaica was reporting, "Laurens passed our north coast the other day, bound for Tortugas, but not in command [of a French freebooter fleet], as he himself told the master of one of our sloops."

## CARTAGENA SHIPWRECK
### (AUTUMN 1686)

This was to be De Graaf's last major invasion of Spanish territory, as the French government was no longer as tolerant of indiscriminate raids against Spain's colonies. However, he did continue plying the sea, and in early October 1686 reentered Petit Goâve aboard a 14-gun Spanish bark called *Santa Rosa,* which Governor Pierre-Paul Tarin de Cussy learned had cost him two men killed and eight wounded off the coast of the Spanish Main. The exact circumstances, as related to Molesworth one month later, were that

> Laurens was wrecked off Cartagena while in pursuit of a small bark, but nevertheless took her with his boat and saved his people. It is uncertain whither he is gone, but certainly my letter offering him terms has never come to his hand.

This news was confirmed early the following year, when the Royal Navy frigate *Falcon* of Captain Charles Talbot, bound toward Portobelo, intercepted one of De Graaf's sloops and removed six of his English crewmembers to stand trial in Jamaica.

## Battle with the Biscayans
### (May 1687)

At the beginning of 1687, there arrived in the West Indies a squadron of Biscayan privateers that had been purposely raised in Spain to combat pirates and interlopers in the New World. Before departing San Sebastián, its commander Francisco García Galán had sworn "to go in search of the pirate Lorencillo ['Little Lawrence,' as the Spanish called De Graaf] before anything else." But when in May 1687 the lone Biscayan frigate of Fermín de Salaberría at last encountered the rover off Júcaro, on the southern coast of Cuba, it was promptly driven into the shallows. De Salaberría found himself aground in unfamiliar waters and in serious danger of being captured, when a force of small Cuban coast guard vessels hurried out to his rescue. De Graaf turned

on these as well, seizing a schooner and sinking a *piragua*. During this fighting numerous Cubans were killed, wounded, or carried off.

## Blas Miguel's Counterraid
### (August 1687)

Blas Miguel, brother to one of the Cubans who died, vowed to seek revenge against the pirate. Despite the uneasy truce existing with the French on Saint Domingue, Miguel came gliding into the roadstead of Petit Goâve at daybreak on 10 August 1687. He had chosen this date with care, as it is when Saint Lawrence's day is celebrated on the Church calendar, and he hoped to catch his enemy off-guard about to celebrate his holiday. Although accompanied by no more than 85 men in a brigantine and *piragua,* Miguel stormed ashore and launched his attack but could not find De Graaf before being surrounded and captured. The rover actually was present during this battle, fighting bravely and even wading out personally into the surf to slay the corsair left guarding Miguel's boat before the Cuban captain was taken and broken alive on the wheel.

## Ile-à-Vache Stronghold
### (September 1687)

Shortly thereafter the governor of Saint Domingue ordered De Graaf to sail with 250 *flibustiers* in two small vessels to Ile-à-Vache, supposedly to confirm French dominion over this island, which De Cussy then advised Molesworth in a letter. The Jamaican governor learned "no more of our ships might be sent to fish nor hunt on that coast," or else it would be regarded as a breach of the treaty of neutrality between the two countries. Molesworth made inquiries and was informed

> that few of our ships do fish there, and then not for the edible turtle but for the

tortoise shell, and as to hunting, the thing is unknown; so I issued a proclamation ordering compliance with Monsieur de Cussy's request.

In reality the French governor wanted De Graaf's presence to scare away treasure hunters from an old Spanish shipwreck recently uncovered near Cap Carcasse, for which he also appointed him *major,* or royal adjutant, of that *quartier.* He said De Graaf promised "to acquit himself with the same zeal and fidelity as he had done during the ten years he has served under the French standard."

## TREASURE-HUNTING EXPEDITION
### (1689)

Little more than a year later, the French captured a Spanish captain who had been sent with an 18-gun ship and *patache* to work another ancient wreck on the Serranilla Bank, 180 miles south–southwest of Jamaica. De Cussy therefore proposed that De Graaf work this site, for which he recruited four small vessels and set sail at the beginning of March. By the end of April, the new acting governor of Jamaica, Sir Francis Watson, was noting, "A number [of French vessels] under Laurens have left Petit Goâve after a wreck, as they give out." The English doubted the veracity of this report as the War of the League of Augsburg (King William's War) was then breaking out back in Europe, and they assumed the corsair chieftain intended some mischief.

But in fact De Graaf had departed before the full scope of hostilities had become known and remained blissfully unaware in his enforced isolation. Upon his arrival at the Serranilla Bank he found the remains of a galleon being worked by an English salvor, and after several weeks' diving succeeded in raising four cannon and three *pedreros.* De Graaf then sent his largest vessel back to Saint Domingue for more supplies and an additional 15 to 20 divers, but this vessel became delayed by contrary winds and did not return to the site until two months later. By this time De Graaf had been forced to retire to the southern cays of Cuba in order to obtain provisions on his own and did not reappear at Serranilla until two-and-a-half months later. When he learned the true state of affairs in Europe, he began to tack toward Saint Domingue.

In early November 1689 Watson wrote:

> Laurens with a ship and 200 men touched at Montego Bay the other day and did no harm, but said that he would obtain a commission at Petit Goâve and return to plunder the whole of the north side of the island. The people are so affrighted that they have sent their wives and children to Port Royal.

One month later the corsair made good on his threat.

## JAMAICAN BLOCKADE
### (1689)

De Graaf returned at the beginning of December with some other French vessels, instantly taking eight or ten Jamaican merchant sloops off the north coast. His raiders also landed and plundered at least one plantation ashore, generally sowing panic throughout the island. An official declaration of war had not yet been received from London, so the English defenders were caught by surprise. Trading ships were ordered to remain in port while a flotilla was hastily assembled and sent out under Captain Edward Spragge of HMS *Drake* to drive the *flibustiers* away, but to little effect. A second sortie had to be mounted against De Graaf in early March 1690, and it was not until the end of May that the embargo on Jamaican shipping was at last lifted.

## ENGAGEMENT OFF THE CAYMANS
### (JUNE 1690)

Nevertheless, De Graaf still remained in the offing, and when HMS *Drake* was deemed unfit for further service, Jamaica's armed sloop had to sail alone to the Cayman Islands as protection for English turtling vessels. There it had the misfortune to encounter him, and in the words of the new governor, earl of Inchiquin:

Laurens, the great pirate of Petit Goâve, engaged the sloop, and the rest of the [turtling] craft escaped. The firing was heard continuing till eleven at night, and as this was a month since and nothing has been heard of the sloop, we conclude that Laurens has taken her, he having two men against one in his *barco luengo*. We have therefore no ships now except HMS *Swan*, which is so bad a sailer that she is little better than nothing.

De Graaf hurried back to Saint Domingue before the middle of June, as his prisoners had informed him the English authorities were proposing to the Spaniards a joint military operation against that colony. But De Cussy discounted this danger, although he did order De Graaf to transfer from Ile-à-Vache to the much larger *quartier* of Cap François on the north coast of that island, "so as not to risk further a person so zealous in his service in such a feeble quarter."

## LA LIMONADE
### (1691)

The French governor also used his *flibustier* vessels to transport a small army to the north shores of Santo Domingo, from where De Cussy marched inland to attack the town of Santiago de los Caballeros. The Spaniards responded wholly unexpectedly in January 1691, when a fleet of six Armada de Barlovento warships under Admiral Jacinto

Lope Gijón deposited 2,600 Spanish troops near Cap François, to meet up with another 700 marching overland from Santo Domingo under *maestre de campo* Francisco de Segura Sandoval. The French under De Cussy decided to meet the invaders on the open plain called Sabane de la Limonade, despite being outnumbered three-to-one, for they felt confident they could defeat the Spaniards. However, this time they were not dealing with some surprised Spanish garrison caught amid their loved ones; rather, it was the reverse. The resultant battle of 21 January (called the "Victory of Sábana Real" by the Spanish) turned into a crushing rout, in which as many as 500 Frenchmen died, including De Cussy and many of his officers. One of the few survivors who fled into the hills was De Graaf, much to the attackers' annoyance. The Spaniards then rampaged unchecked through his new *quartier* before withdrawing in triumph some weeks later.

The French gradually recuperated their strength under a vigorous new governor, Jean-Baptiste Ducasse. As one of the few remaining royal officers, De Graaf now achieved greater prominence among his adoptive countrymen, being described in French records of 1692 as "sieur de Graffe, *lieutenant du Roi* [king's lieutenant] for the government of Ile la Tortue and coast of Saint Domingue," with residence at Cap François. As such, De Graaf played a prominent role in the French deployments of February–March 1692, when it appeared the Spaniards might again overrun his territory, although they eventually contented themselves with remaining on their own side of the frontier. Nonetheless, Ducasse noticed how "he is a man who would fulfill his duty much better in a ship" than on land, going on to advise the king's minister, Pontchartrain, "I am obliged to tell you, Monseigneur, that he is one of the finest sea officers there is in Europe and if you should employ him as such, he will give you ample proofs."

## JAMAICAN RAID
### (1694)

Cap François was put on alert again in 1693, but nothing happened. The following summer the French launched a counteroffensive of their own, when Ducasse and De Graaf led a seaborne raid against Jamaica. In June 1694, more than 3,000 *flibustiers* and seamen swarmed ashore from Ducasse's 22 ships to ravage the eastern tip of that island before feinting toward the Jamaican capital. When the English marched out to meet them, the invaders quickly reembarked and sailed under De Graaf to Carlisle Bay, west of Port Royal. He brought his 1,500 men ashore the night of 28 July 1694, and the next day advanced upon the 250 soldiers and twelve artillery pieces guarding the town. Holding fire until they were within point-blank range, the French then loosed a murderous volley that drove the English out of their trenches and across the river.

English reinforcements arrived from Port Royal after a desperate overnight march, preventing an utter defeat. Still, De Graaf remained in control west of the river, sending 500 *flibustiers* out to strip the adjoining countryside. This proved more difficult than anticipated, as each plantation constituted a miniature fortress, impossible to breach without artillery. As the French did not have any heavy guns ashore, they satisfied themselves with whatever they could carry off. Ducasse rejoined a few days later, and De Graaf gave the order to withdraw. More than 1,600 slaves were carried away when the French finally departed that coast on 3 August.

## SAINT DOMINGUE
### (1695)

The next spring, the French suffered when the expedition of Commodore Robert Wilmot and Colonel Luke Lillingston arrived to unite with Spanish Admiral Francisco Cortés and General Gil Correoso. On 24 May 1695, this huge combined force descended on the north coast of the French colony, where De Graaf was once more commanding a small detachment at Cap François. Heavily outnumbered, he called for reinforcements from Ducasse in the south, while continually falling back before the invading host—much to the disgust of his French followers, who watched as their homes and farms went up in flames.

When the enemy closed in on Cap François, De Graaf abandoned it without a fight, and the Spaniards even captured his French wife and two daughters. The Anglo-Spanish force then pressed on toward Port-de-Paix, which was overrun in July after a bungled defense. Satisfied with this havoc, the enemy withdrew, leaving the French to exchange heated recriminations. Blame was laid on De Graaf and the commander of Port-de-Paix, it even being alleged that the Dutchman may "have had some secret understanding with the enemy" because of his birth, Holland being aligned with the Anglo-Spanish coalition against France. Both De Graaf and his French counterpart were relieved of their commands, and sent to France to stand trial. The resultant courts-martial completely exonerated De Graaf, but by the time he returned to Saint Domingue, the war was over and his prestige greatly diminished. His wife—the former widow Le Long, called "Marie Anne Dieu-le-Veut" (Marianne God-Wills-It) by the Spaniards—was not freed from Santo Domingo with her children until the final prisoner exchange of October 1698. Thus when Pierre Le Moyne d'Iberville touched at Saint Domingue at the end of that same year on his way to colonize Louisiana, De Graaf agreed to join his expedition.

## EMIGRATION TO LOUISIANA
### (1699)

On a foggy morning in January 1699, the tiny Spanish settlement of Pensacola, Florida, was startled to find five French ships outside its bar, calling for a pilot. The Spanish officer who went aboard the 58-gun flagship *François* (Francis) was even more perturbed at recognizing d'Iberville's enormous interpreter as "Lorencillo." When the visitors requested permission to put into harbor, this was denied, and at dawn French boats could be seen taking soundings in the channel under the direction of De Graaf. Worried, the Spanish garrison commander sent out a protest and the boats withdrew. Shortly thereafter the French flotilla stood away to the west, establishing their new colony at what is today Biloxi, Mississippi. A census taken there on 25 May 1700 lists, under staff officers, "Le sieur Graffe, clerk for the King." It is believed De Graaf was later to have been one of the original settlers of Mobile, Alabama, but apparently never made this trip, dying sometime in early 1704.

*See also* Andrieszoon, Michiel; *armadilla;* Bannister, Joseph; Barlovento, Armada de; Barrera y Villegas, Felipe de la; Biscayan privateers; Bot, Pierre; careen; Ducasse, Jean-Baptiste; Foccard, Jean; Grammont, "chevalier" de; *guardacostas;* Hamlin, Jean; Hispaniola; Le Sage, François; Lussan, Ravenau de; Lynch, Sir Thomas; Miguel, Blas; Pez y Malzárraga, Andrés de; pieces of eight; Pouançay, Jacques Nepveu, sieur de; Rose, Jean; Spanish Main; Van Hoorn, Nikolaas; Willems, Jan.

*References:* Crouse; *C.S.P., Amer. and W.I.,* Vols. XI–XIII; Juárez; Lugo; Marley, *Veracruz;* Robles; Weddle, *Wilderness.*

# DEANE, JOHN

## (FL. 1676)

English privateer who commanded the *Saint David* out of Jamaica.

In the spring of 1676, Deane was accused by John Yardley of having intercepted his merchant ship, *John Adventure,* on the high seas, "drunk out several pipes of wine and taken away a cable value £100," before forcibly carrying this vessel into Jamaica. When Governor Lord Vaughan learned of these violations, he decided to make an example of Deane, as the Crown had been attempting to curtail the activities of privateers since the end of the Third Anglo-Dutch War two years earlier. As a result Vaughan instructed his deputy governor, Sir Henry Morgan, "to imprison the offenders," which the latter only did grudgingly. Morgan felt—as did many others—that Deane's mischief did not warrant charging him with piracy. Nevertheless, the captive was brought before Vaughan in his capacity of judge on 27 April 1676 (O.S.), at which it was revealed that he had also frequently sailed "wearing Dutch, French, and Spanish colors without lawful commission" and so was condemned to death.

This verdict did not sit well with the public, and the governor was soon hearing how "since the trial Sir Harry has been so impudent and unfaithful at the taverns and in his own house, to speak some things which seemed to reflect upon my justice, and to vindicate the pirate." But Morgan was not alone, and Vaughan's resolve began to waver. Finally, in early October 1676, after Deane's "great repentance, confession of his faults and often petitioning," the governor pardoned him. It was well he did, for within a few weeks a stay of execution arrived from London, the trial having been considered "not warranted by the laws of this kingdom." Vaughan was forced to explain away his original charges as merely a warning to other privateers, ending his report, "So if I was not right in the law no great harm is done, it being very prudential and reasonable at that time to do what I did, however, I humbly beg your Lordships particular directions for the future."

*References:* C.S.P., Amer. and W.I., Vol.IX; Gosse, *Who's Who.*

# DEDENON, CAPITAINE

## (FL. 1684)

French *flibustier.*

He is listed as commanding the 20-gun *Chasseur* (Hunter) at Saint Domingue in 1684, with a crew of 120 men. His name is sometimes misspelled "Dednau," or even "De Drain."

*Reference:* Gosse, *Who's Who;* Juaréz; Lugo.

# DELANDER, ROBERT

## (FL. 1668-1671)

English buccaneer who served under Henry Morgan during his attacks on Portobelo and Panama.

Delander allegedly hated the Spaniards because once, having sprung his mast off the Cuban coast, he requested permission to enter Havana for repairs. The Spanish governor agreed, then seized his ship, sold it, and incarcerated Delander and his crew. He later participated in the sack of Portbelo and commanded a *chata* or small coasting craft ahead of Morgan's main body when in January 1671 they marched from San Lorenzo on the great assault against Panama.

*References:* Earle, *Panamá;* Gosse, *Who's Who;* Pope.

# DELBOURG, JEAN

## (FL. 1696)

Listed in a French document dated 26 March 1696 as a *flibustier* from the island of Guadeloupe.

Little is known about his activities beyond the fact that he was married to Madeleine Chaumont, by whom he had three children.

*Reference:* Goddet-Langlois.

# DEMPSTER, EDWARD

## (FL. 1668)

English buccaneer who in 1668 was in command of several vessels and 300 men blockading Havana, and who afterward joined Henry Morgan.

*Reference:* Gosse, *Who's Who.*

# DESSAUDRAYS, CAPITAINE

## (FL. 1692)

Saint Malo shipmaster issued an emergency commission by Governor Jean-Baptiste Ducasse.

In the early days of 1692, when the French colony of Saint Domingue was struggling to recover from the trauma of the previous year's Spanish invasion, its vigorous new governor, Ducasse, dispatched the frigates of Captains Dessaudrays and Duhamel

> to cruise off Cape Tiburon with orders that when they discover the enemy ships returning, they are to advise me in order to gather everyone who is scattered over 20 or 30 leagues of countryside.

Dessaudrays's name may have been more properly spelled "De Sauldre."

*See also* Ducasse, Jean-Baptiste; Duhamel, Capitaine.

*Reference:* Lugo.

# DEVEREUX, COLONEL

## (FL. 1689)

Scottish freebooter.

Late in 1689, at the onset of the War of the League of Augsburg (King William's War), Devereux was placed in command of a sloop built and outfitted by Lieutenant Governor Isaac Richier of Bermuda, with a commission to seize pirates and sea rovers.

*Reference:* Chapin.

# DEW, GEORGE

## ALSO DREW
## (FL. 1691-1693)

Bermuda freebooter who prowled the New England coast.

In 1691, during the third year of the War of the League of Augsburg (King William's War), Dew was issued a privateering commission and permit to impress seamen by Lieutenant Governor Isaac Richier of Bermuda, along with Captain Thomas Griffin. Prizes proving scarce, both commanders roamed northward and appeared off New England that summer, intercepting the pink *Three Brothers* of Captain Thomas Wilkinson near Piscataqua, as it was arriving from a commercial voyage to Cadiz, Spain. Dew and Griffin pretended they had mistaken this merchantman for a French vessel, then "discovered" it was transporting prohibited goods. Realizing their actions "should be unkindly dealt with" by the local authorities, Dew and Griffin took the *Three Brothers* to the Isles of Shoals and afterward into the river near Portsmouth (New Hampshire), where they held a mock trial at which the ship and its cargo were duly "condemned."

When the local collector of customs, Jahleel Brenton, learned of this travesty, he attempted to impound the pink, whereupon Dew and Griffin resisted "with force of arms." Eventually Brenton succeeded in gaining possession of the *Three Brothers* and part of its cargo, while the privateer *Swan* of Captain Christopher Goffe was sent out of Boston to pursue the raiders, who easily eluded him, Goffe reporting later, "they could sail two feet to his one." Off Cape Cod, Dew and Griffin boarded another English vessel, which was bound for Virginia with a valuable cargo of oil, brimstone (sulfur), gold, and silver. They claimed its captain did not have the requisite papers and sailed this prize back to Bermuda.

Two years later Dew ventured to sea again in the company of Rhode Island Captain Thomas Tew, setting out from Bermuda in January 1693, ostensibly to attack the French slaving factory of Gorée, West Africa. But a few days out into the Atlantic, Dew's sloop sprang its mast in a storm, and he was compelled to put back for repairs. Tew continued his journey to Africa and the Red Sea, but what became of Dew is unknown.

*See also* Goffe, Christopher; Griffin, Thomas; Tew, Thomas.

*References:* Chapin; Gosse, *Who's Who*.

# DEY, DENNIS

## (FL. 1683)

One of a trio of privateers—Andries van de Velde and Laurens Westerband being the others—who were commissioned by Sir William Stapleton, governor of the English Leeward Islands, "to look after pirates" in late 1683.

Specifically, they were to hunt the renegade George Bond. After learning he had recently bought a Dutch ship at Saint Thomas in the Virgin Islands, the trio went there and seized it, over the objections of the

Danish governor, Adolf Esmit. They then sailed their prize back to Nevis.

*See also* Bond, George; Van de Veld, Andries; Westerband, Laurens.

*Reference: C.S.P., Amer. and W.I.,* Vol. XI.

# DOCKYER, RICHARD
## (FL. 1656)

English captain commissioned by the Council of Bermuda as a salvager.

In 1656 he sailed to the Bahamas to salvage the remains of a Spanish treasure galleon "for the benefit of the Lord Protector [Cromwell], the Honorable [Somers Island] Company and of the recoverers that shall adventure therein." The council had learned of this shipwreck from Spanish survivors, who had been rescued at sea and carried into Bermuda.

*Reference:* Crump.

# DOTSON, THOMAS
## ALSO DUDSON OR DIEDSON
## (FL. 1673)

Boston privateer who unwittingly precipitated a confrontation with the Dutch.

On 3 November 1673, during the closing stages of the Third Anglo-Dutch War, Dotson chanced upon the dismasted merchantman *Expectation,* stranded near Nantucket. This vessel had been taken by the Dutch in their recent reconquest of New Netherland (modern New York, New Jersey, and Delaware) by Cornelis Evertsen, who had dispatched this vessel on 2 September under Captain Maerten Jansse Vonck to carry news of this victory to the Netherlands. Struck by a storm, it had been driven aground. Dotson boarded the *Expectation* from his own tiny brigantine of

2 to 4 guns and 14 to 20 crew members, refloating and sailing the prize home to Boston along with its Dutch captain and crew, who had been lodging ashore with the inhabitants of Nantucket. This seizure, although fully warranted by Dotson's commission and the ongoing war against Holland, was nonetheless unwelcome to the Massachusetts authorities, who thus far had refrained from any direct involvement in the fighting to the south.

Meanwhile, Captain Cornelis Eewoutsen had sortied from New York with the 6-gun snow *Zeehond* (Sea Lion) to aid the stranded *Expectation,* and upon learning that it had been carried off by Dotson, retaliated by capturing four New England ketches and carrying these into New York on 15 November. The Dutch sent the masters and crews to Boston in an express boat, receiving Vonck and his men by way of return; but they refused to restore either the ketches or their cargos, leading to heightened tensions that culminated with an armed confrontation at Southold, Connecticut, in late February 1674.

*See also* Evertsen de Jongste, Cornelis; Vonck, Maerten Jansse.

*Reference:* Shomette, *Raid.*

# DOUBLOON

Term for the largest of Spanish gold coins, derived from the word *doblón,* signifying an *escudo,* or piece of gold currency, worth double the regular face value.

In the seventeenth century, the *doblón,* or doubloon, was the most valuable Spanish gold coin, although its purity varied. The *ducado,* or ducat, was a lesser Spanish gold coin worth 11 *reales,* while the *escudo* was worth 10. The silver *pesos,* or pieces of eight, struck in the Americas were infinitely more plentiful. Their name reflected the fact that each was worth 8 *reales.*

**See also** ducat; pieces of eight.

# DOUGLAS, JOHN

## (FL. 1662-1664)

English privateer who roamed the West Indies in peacetime with a Portuguese commission.

On 20 September 1662, Douglas was lying at Lisbon where he became empowered by Charles de Bils, holder of a patent that allowed him "to make war with the enemies of this Crown of Portugal." The Portuguese had revolted against Spanish rule more than two decades earlier, and hostilities still persisted between the two, although without much intensity. Armed with this permit, Douglas sailed his 4-gun *Saint John* to Spain's Canary Islands, remaining there four or five months "without taking any prize." Discouraged, he crossed the Atlantic to the Lesser Antilles, where within a few days *Saint John* had a bloody encounter with a man o' war off Martinique. Many of his men were killed or wounded, Douglas himself receiving a musket round in the arm, which forced him to retire to the English-held island of Montserrat. He remained there most of 1663, until the *Saint John* foundered at anchor.

Douglas then traveled to Jamaica, where early in 1664 he bought and armed a frigate, sallying forth once more with his Portuguese commission. After an uneventful cruise of three months, he learned of a sloop called the *Blue Dove,* which the privateer John Morris had carried into Port Royal on suspicion of intending to smuggle contraband into Cuba. The sloop's papers indicated it was coming from Amsterdam to Jamaica, and *Blue Dove* was released. However, it became widely believed that Morris was correct, his prize claim having been rejected solely because of the intervention of the sloop's consignors, influential Jewish merchants Isaac Cardozo and Benjamin Musket.

Lying at the Cayman Islands, Douglas decided to seize this sloop once it sailed again, not as a smuggler but as a transporter of Spanish cargo, hence liable to Portuguese capture. His scheme was doubtless fueled by poor hunting, so he shifted to Bluefields Bay at the west end of Jamaica, anchoring close inshore to await *Blue Dove's* departure. The sloop quit Port Royal soon after, accompanied by the merchantman *Lucretia,* commanded by Captain Charles Hadsell. Both put into Bluefields Bay to take on wood and water for their upcoming voyage, and while Hadsell and Captain Robert Cooke of *Blue Dove* went ashore, Douglas visited the *Lucretia* to determine whether its crew would defend their consort.

That evening at seven o'clock, the two masters returned aboard, and half an hour later Hadsell saw Douglas's bark gliding out on the land breeze. He hailed to inquire where this vessel was from and whither bound; from Barbados to the Caymans, Douglas replied. When Hadsell shouted that he himself was headed for New England, Douglas mischievously responded he would be there before him. "In what ship?" the bewildered master asked. No matter what ship, came the ominous reply, and with that Douglas clapped his helm hard to starboard and bore down on *Blue Dove,* boarding in the gloom. Thirty privateersmen swarmed over the side, firing a ragged volley that wounded Captain Cooke in one arm. *Blue Dove's* Scottish crew, outnumbered three to one, were driven below while its cables were cut and sails hoisted. The *Lucretia's* crew simultaneously deserted Hadsell, rowing across to join Douglas and disappear into the night.

Three days later, a small English bark from the Caymans put into Bluefields Bay bearing the injured Cooke, along with his passengers and a few loyal hands, who had been transferred out of *Blue Dove* off Point Negril, being given "some victuals and a case of spirits" for their return to Port Royal but nothing else. Douglas's privateers then "lashed their bark aboard of the prize and took most of their things out of her, and let her [their bark] go adrift." Afterward, the rover laid in a course for the Windward Passage and Old Bahama Channel, heading the *Blue Dove* northward. Douglas later declared his intention had been "to sail into Portugal with this his said prize, to give knowledge to the King," but called first at New England for provisions. The more likely explanation was that he wished to dispose of the sloop's West Indian cargo—notably its sugar and cocoa—at this ready market. *Blue Dove* appeared before Portsmouth (New Hampshire) in early July 1664, requesting permission to take on water and "sell some goods for to buy victuals." This was granted, and Douglas further had legal depositions drawn up from his remaining captives as to the nature of their cargo.

He particularly sought to stress that Port Royal merchant Isaac Cardozo had supervised the loading of 30 chests of quicksilver, or *azogue,* which could only have been Spanish in origin. This substance was mined in southern Spain for use in their American colonies, where it was used to refine silver ores. (It is likely Cardozo's consignment was part of a much larger shipment brought into Jamaica late in 1663, when the *María,* bound for Mexico, had been intercepted by Captain Cooper.) The Spaniards were known to pay handsomely to retrieve this element, which had no other large-scale application than their mining operations, and therefore must have been intended as contraband.

But despite Douglas's intimation, the Portsmouth authorities soon became suspicious of his activities, and a few weeks

later (18 July 1664 O.S.) his sloop was seized. Douglas and his crew were taken to nearby Boston aboard *Blue Dove*—now described in the records as a pink—where they were incarcerated. Three weeks later they were released and given back their clothes, along with a few score shillings "to preserve them alive till they can provide some honest employ for themselves." However, the capture at Bluefields Bay was declared illegal and *Blue Dove* forfeit. Late in September 1664, the ship's owner, Sir William Davidson, royal commissioner at Amsterdam, drew up a writ in London demanding *Blue Dove's* return, saying it had been "villainously and roguishly taken by pirates, rovers and thieves." By the time this complaint reached North America, Douglas and his men had vanished.

*See also* azogue; Cooper, Captain; Morris, John.

**References:** Jameson; Zahedieh, *Contraband*.

# D'OYLEY, EDWARD
## (1617-1675)

First governor of Jamaica, who greatly encouraged privateering.

D'Oyley was born at Albourne, Wiltshire, England, and as a young man trained as a lawyer at the Inns of Court, fighting on the Parliamentary side in the English civil war. In December 1654 he sailed as a lieutenant colonel in the expedition of William Penn and Robert Venables, and was promoted to full colonel of a regiment raised in Barbados the following March. He rose to commander-in-chief and de facto governor after the conquest of Jamaica, when disease killed 4,500 officers and men from the original 7,000 within the first year, and many other leaders fled back to England. The new colony was left in a precarious state, beset by Spanish counterattacks, while its naval defenses shrank from 30 to less than 10 warships by 1656. Nevertheless, D'Oyley, a brave and active man, was able to defeat enemy forces at Ocho Rios in autumn 1657, and at Rio Nuevo the following summer.

Under such difficult circumstances, D'Oyley began granting commissions to privateers, English or foreign, hoping to keep the local Spaniards off balance. He further sold government prizes on easy terms, as when in May 1659 Maurice Williams bought the Spanish frigate *Abispa* (Wasp) for £120, renaming it *Jamaica.* D'Oyley issued Williams a patent as well and sold him five cannon from the state warehouses to help arm the vessel. He then published a proclamation allowing Williams to recruit sailors out of Christopher Myngs's flagship, with the words

> that such seamen aboard the *Marston Moor* frigate that will go along with the aforesaid Captain Maurice Williams may have liberty to go on board the said *Jamaica* frigate at their pleasure.

But more importantly still, D'Oyley made Jamaica a haven for corsairs of all nationalities, where they might dispose of their booty, obtain supplies, and effect repairs in relative safety.

By 1661 his policy had become almost too successful, for the privateers refused to restrain their activities even when the colony was prospering and a tentative peace had been signed with the Spaniards back in Europe. D'Oyley noted that his attempts to rein in the rovers merely vexed the Jamaican populace, who had come to "live only upon spoil and depredations." His position was further eroded by the restoration of Charles II who, although he briefly confirmed D'Oyley as governor, soon superseded him with Royalist Lord Windsor. When the new representative reached Port Royal on 21 August 1662, he was barely civil to his predecessor and obliged D'Oyley to sail for England a scant month later aboard the *Westergate,* notwithstanding the latter's petition to remain on the island. D'Oyley lived out the remaining 13 years of his life quietly at St. Martin's in the Fields, London, dying about March 1675.

*See also* Myngs, Sir Christopher; Williams, Maurice; Windsor, Thomas.

*References:* Buisseret, *D'Oyley; Dictionary of National Biography* (England), Supplement; *Interesting Tracts;* Pawson, *Port Royal.*

# Dry gripes

English name for a West Indian "disease" of the seventeenth century—actually a kind of poisoning caused by drinking large quantities of rum distilled in lead pipes.

*Reference:* Pawson, *Port Royal.*

# Dry tortugas

Seventeenth-century English nickname for the shoals at the western extremity of the Florida Keys.

According to the buccaneer chronicler William Dampier, turtling was such a frequent activity among Caribbean seafarers, that this particular group of isles was so called to distinguish it from the Salt Tortuga off Venezuela, and the French island of Tortuga (Ile de la Tortue) off Hispaniola. Quite possibly the Dry Tortugas got their name from the method employed in curing this meat, as opposed to the Salt Tortuga, which drew upon the vast natural pans of the nearby Araya Peninsula, opposite Cumaná.

*Reference:* Dampier.

# DUCASSE, JEAN-BAPTISTE

## (1646-1715)

Seventh governor of French Saint Domingue, who led its *flibustiers* on major assaults against Jamaica in 1694, and Cartagena three years later.

Ducasse was born on 2 August 1646 into a Huguenot (French Protestant) family in the tiny town of Saubuse, near Dax in southern France, not far from the Bay of Biscay. He first went to sea as a young boy in slavers of the *Compagnie du Sénégal*. Starting in 1677, he made several voyages from West Africa to Saint Domingue, Canada, and the "coast of Florida," and in September 1678, during the final stages of the Franco-Dutch War, captured a Dutch slaving station on the African coast, thus winning appointment as one of the directors of his company two years later.

In March 1686, Ducasse was admitted into the French Royal Navy as a *lieutenant de vaisseau* (full lieutenant) and the following year conducted a lengthy campaign against pirates and Dutch slavers along the African coast in *Tempête* (Tempest). Promoted to *capitaine de frégate* (junior captain) at the outbreak of the War of the League of Augsburg (King William's War), Ducasse led an unsuccessful assault against the Dutch colony of Suriname in November 1688 and the following year played a conspicuous part in the conquest of the English portion of St. Christopher.

### CAPTURE OF FORT CHARLES
#### (AUGUST 1689)

In command of a contingent of 120 *flibustiers,* Ducasse quit Martinique as part of Governor General comte de Blénac's six warships, 14 merchantmen, and 23 sloops, arriving off Basseterre, St. Christopher, on 27 July 1689. The French landed "and laid the southern part of the island in ashes,"

driving Colonel Thomas Hill and 400 to 500 English defenders inside tiny Fort Charles at Old Road Town. Blénac instituted a formal siege, digging an approach trench while his batteries and warships bombarded the gate, although the fortress itself had no moat and its walls sloped gently. More importantly, a hill overlooked its interior, and after two weeks' fruitless firing, Ducasse convinced Blénac that a battery should be installed there. The governor general finally agreed, and during the night of 14 August, Ducasse's men dragged six heavy pieces to the top. The following morn they opened fire, and once the besieged found that their counterfire could not reach the summit, they surrendered.

Early next year Ducasse was given command of three warships, a brigantine, and a sloop to convey 700 reinforcements to the island of Saint Martin, which was being attacked by Sir Timothy Thornhill's expedition. Ducasse arrived in the nick of time to save the French colony from being overrun, trapping the English contingent on shore. The latter were rescued in late January 1690 by Thomas Hewetson, who fought a running two-day battle with Ducasse before evacuating Thornhill's men to Nevis. Upon hearing of a devastating Spanish attack against Saint Domingue's French inhabitants, Ducasse sailed there late in January 1691. Stepping ashore amid the burnt remains of Cap François, he visited the nearby Limonade battlefield, where he found more than 300 French dead, "their bodies not yet buried, being rotted and half desiccated." Shortly thereafter, he proceeded to France, where he reported on this defeat, and by the end of March left La Rochelle for the West Indies once more.

### GUADELOUPE OPERATION
#### (MAY 1691)

Upon his return to Martinique, it was learned that a large English force under Governor Codrington of the Leeward

Islands and Royal Navy Captain Lawrence Wright was besieging Guadeloupe. Ducasse conveyed two companies of infantry and 600 *flibustiers* aboard his *Hasardeux* (Daring), *Mignon* (Dainty), *Émerillon* (Merlin), *Cheval Marin* (Sea Horse), and three 20-gun merchantmen to reinforce the beleaguered garrison. Being heavily outnumbered, he intended to avoid combat by stealthily depositing his troops. During the passage, the French freed Marie Galante from English occupation, then began landing their reinforcements on 23 May 1691 at Grosier, Guadeloupe. The English withdrew two days later, their morale sapped by torrential rains and the enormous sick lists; Wright refused to remain offshore or even engage Ducasse, despite his numerical advantage.

Returning triumphantly to Martinique, Ducasse transferred his ships, infected with yellow fever, to Saint Croix on 2 August. On 7 August, he sailed again for Port-de-Paix on the north shore of Hispaniola, where his two warships and single corvette lost 250 men before the disease abated. On 1 October a letter arrived from Paris appointing him governor of Saint Domingue, in succession to Pierre-Paul Tarin de Cussy, killed eight months earlier during the Spanish invasion. The colonists were still frightened and confused in the wake of this disaster, but Ducasse was able to restore their spirits. On 20 February 1692 he conveyed a company of infantry from Petit Goâve to Port-de-Paix aboard two corsair vessels, sending ahead another company under sieur Dumesnil to Cap François, where they disembarked along with the 120 *flibustier* crew members to reinforce Laurens de Graaf and Charles-François Le Vasseur de Beauregard, thus discouraging a second Spanish incursion from Santo Domingo.

Gradually, Saint Domingue recovered its strength, and in January 1693 Ducasse was promoted to *capitaine de vaisseau* (senior naval captain). In April of the following year he

dispatched Beauregard with six privateer vessels to raid the eastern coast of Jamaica. They took a New England ship, but the next day, HMS *Falcon* sighted the interlopers and chased them, recovering the prize. When Beauregard reentered Petit Goâve, the men o' war *Téméraire* (Fearless), 54 guns; *Envieux* (Envious); and *Solide* (Well-Found) had just arrived with a merchant convoy from France, so Ducasse employed them to return to *Falcon*'s patrol area and seize the Royal Navy vessel despite a stout resistance. He then marshaled all his forces for a descent on the English island.

## JAMAICAN CAMPAIGN
### (SUMMER 1694)

Early in June, Ducasse sortied from Petit Goâve with *Téméraire,* under its captain, chevalier du Rollon, as his flagship, accompanied by *Hasardeux* and *Envieux*. Off Cape Tiburon he gathered a fleet totaling 22 sail and more than 3,000 men, appearing off the eastern tip of Jamaica on the morning of 27 June 1694 "in a fresh gale." Eight vessels remained off Port Morant, while 14 others anchored 15 miles east of Port Royal. The French learned that the English had been forewarned by Captain Stephen Elliott, their defenses being fully prepared. Therefore, Ducasse's plan of storming Port Royal directly had to be altered, as Du Rollon refused to risk any of the king's ships in such an undertaking.

Ducasse consequently landed 800 men under Beauregard, who marched eastward, plundering and destroying everything in his path. Boats were sent from Port Morant to ravage the northern shores as well, the English under Governor William Beeston being reluctant to sally for fear of dividing their smaller forces with the enemy still to windward. On 1 July a sudden gust made *Téméraire* drag its anchors, carrying it and another French vessel downwind to Bluefields Bay. However, Ducasse was already encamped ashore, and continued to direct land operations until 27 July, when he mustered the bulk of his fleet to threaten Port Royal.

When Beeston sortied to contest this French maneuver, Ducasse quickly reembarked his men under cover of darkness and sent all but the three largest ships with his deputy De Graaf to assault Carlisle Bay, 35 miles west. This contingent dropped anchor the afternoon of 28 July, landing 1,400 to 1,500 *flibustiers* that night. The next morning they assailed the small English garrison, Beauregard commanding the vanguard, De Graaf directing the main body. After driving back the English, foraging parties were sent out to scour the countryside, and when Ducasse joined them a few days later, the booty was transferred aboard his flotilla. The French then weighed on 3 August and by 14 August were back in Petit Goâve, having spent a month-and-a-half rampaging throughout Jamaica.

## ANGLO-SPANISH COUNTERATTACK (1695)

Late the following month, Beeston sent a small force of three men o' war, a fireship, and two barks to exact vengeance. They bombarded the village of l'Esterre near Léogâne on 11 October 1694, then bore down on Petit Goâve, sheering off when they realized Beauregard was prepared to receive them. A few huts were burned on Ile-à-Vache before the Jamaicans disappeared over the horizon.

The next spring, however, an expedition arrived in the Antilles from England—two dozen vessels and almost a thousand troops under Colonel Luke Lillingston and Commodore Robert Wilmot—which joined forces with the Spaniards of Santo Domingo and Armada de Barlovento. On 15 May 1695 this huge force descended on Cap François (modern-day Cap Haïtien),

pushing aside the heavily outnumbered French defenders commanded by De Graaf. One month later the Royal Navy squadron reached Port-de-Paix, skirmishing with its defenders until the invading armies arrived overland. The garrison became besieged and attempted to evacuate two hours before dawn on 15 July, but was caught in an ambush. After leveling Port-de-Paix, the English and Spanish then sailed away on 27 May.

No major campaigns could be mounted the following year, although Ducasse was advised that a counterexpedition would be sent out from France under Bernard-Jean-Louis de Saint Jean, baron de Pointis, for which he should prepare by raising a large contingent of *flibustiers*. This fleet did not actually appear off Cap François until early March 1697; on 16 March, the 84-gun flagship *Sceptre* dropped anchor before Petit Goâve. When Ducasse went aboard, Admiral De Pointis was infuriated to learn that only a few hundred buccaneers awaited him, the rest having dispersed on their own pursuits. Relations worsened a day later when a French naval officer arrested an unruly *boucanier* ashore, touching off a riot in which two or three others died. Only the intervention of Ducasse succeeded in calming the mob.

The freebooters were offended by the secondary role they were being offered in the enterprise, the question of their shares being kept deliberately vague and Ducasse excluded from any command position. Nonetheless, they enlisted in good numbers once De Pointis published a proclamation stating that they would participate "man for man" with the crews of the royal warships. Ducasse offered to go as an individual ship captain with his 40-gun *Pontchartrain,* commanding only the island contingent. A force of 170 soldiers, 110 volunteers, 180 free blacks, and 650 buccaneers was promptly raised, sailing aboard the *Serpente,*

18 guns; *Gracieuse* (Graceful), 20 guns; *Cerf Volant* (Kite), 18 guns; *Saint Louis,* 18 guns; *Dorade* (Golden One), 16 guns; *Marie; Françoise;* and one other vessel. They rendezvoused off Cape Tiburon with the royal fleet and by 8 April 1697 were in sight of the Spanish Main. Five days later they dropped anchor before Cartagena.

### CARTAGENA CAMPAIGN
#### (APRIL–MAY 1697)

An immediate landing of the buccaneers near the city was proposed, but canceled once Ducasse and De Pointis reconnoitered the shore in a boat and found it lined with dangerous reefs. (Their own craft overturned, and they barely escaped drowning.) It was therefore decided to force the harbor entrance known as Bocachica farther east, and on 15 April Ducasse and De Pointis disembarked with 1,200 men. While preparing their siege operations, the buccaneers captured a coaster arriving from Portobelo and drove off Spanish reinforcements, which were stealing down from Cartagena in boats. During this latter fray, some freebooters came under fire from the fortress itself, which caused them to immediately scatter. Mistaking this for military indiscipline, De Pointis fell upon them with a cudgel and treated them with ever-increasing contempt. Bocachica surrendered after the initial assault on 16 April, with six French soldiers and seven buccaneers having been killed and 22 wounded, Ducasse among the latter.

The *flibustier* contingent was now under his second, Joseph d'Honon de Gallifet, a relative newcomer to Saint Domingue who was not well known. When De Pointis ordered them into the boats to seize the Nuestra Señora de la Popa high ground while the main army advanced overland, there was considerable hesitation. Gallifet seized a buccaneer by the arm but was thrown off. De Pointis had the offender tied

to a tree and blindfolded, in anticipation of being executed by regular musketeers. Gallifet publicly interceded and, in a contrived gesture, De Pointis released the man so as to ingratiate Gallifet with his followers. The buccaneers occupied the heights unopposed and linked up with the army on 20 April.

A formal siege ensued, with approach trenches being dug and heavy artillery landed from the fleet. De Pointis was wounded in the leg by a sharpshooter's round and supervised the works from a litter. On 28 April a heavy bombardment began against the Getsemaní suburb, and during a lull on 30 April, Ducasse—recuperated from his injury—visited a Spanish officer at the gate and noticed that a breach had been made. At his urging De Pointis ordered the final assault at four o'clock that same afternoon, and in bloody fighting, the French grenadiers and buccaneers fought their way through to the very edge of Cartagena itself. The defenders' morale collapsed, and on the evening of 2 May, white flags were hoisted on the walls. While finalizing terms, De Pointis received word that a Spanish relief column of more than 1,000 men was approaching, so he sent Ducasse and his buccaneers with several hundred soldiers to oppose them.

They never appeared, and meanwhile De Pointis occupied Cartagena on 4 May. By the time Ducasse and his men returned, they found the gates closed and were billeted in the impoverished, devastated suburb of Getsemaní. The French commander-in-chief feared that they would violate his carefully arranged capitulation terms, so he kept them outside the walls and away from where the booty was being tallied. The few remaining Spanish inhabitants were obligated to surrender most of their wealth as tribute, and the total plunder eventually came to eight million French crowns. The buccaneers expected a quarter of this, but were outraged at the end of that month to discover that they were to receive only 40,000 crowns. Unknown to them, the crews aboard De Pointis's warships had been serving for only a small percentage of the whole, which is what he had meant when he had deceitfully offered them shares "man for man."

By now the plunder was aboard his men o' war, ready to depart. Furious at being duped, the buccaneers swarmed back into Cartagena on 30 May, despite Ducasse's attempts to dissuade them, and rounded up every Spaniard they could find. These unhappy victims were herded into the principal church and sprinkled with gunpowder, which the buccaneers threatened to light unless an additional five million crowns was forthcoming. This was clearly impossible, but through torture and extortion, the buccaneers raised a thousand crowns per man before weighing on 3 June. De Pointis had meanwhile departed, but four days later encountered the large fleet of Vice Admiral John Neville and his Dutch allies hastening to Cartagena's rescue. Outnumbered and with most of his crews dead or diseased, De Pointis reversed course and evaded his pursuers for the next two days, until finally shaking them off by sunup on 10 June.

This chase had carried Neville very near Cartagena, which he visited briefly before roaming eastward and, on 25 June, he sighted Ducasse anchored with eight buccaneer vessels off Sambay. The English captured the *Gracieuse* and 50-gun *Christe* (perhaps a Spanish prize originally called *Santo Cristo*) and drove the *Saint Louis* of Capitaine Charles aground, where he and his crew escaped ashore, only to be hunted down and eventually put to work rebuilding Cartagena's defenses. Neville detached four men o' war to pursue Ducasse's remaining vessels, which scattered in the direction of Saint Domingue. The *Cerf Volant* of

Capitaine Macary was driven aground on that coast, but the rest arrived safely. On 8 July 1697, Ducasse wrote Pontchartrain from Léogâne, complaining bitterly of De Pointis's deceitfulness and the destruction of his *flibustiers*. A prolonged litigation ensued even after hostilities were concluded a few months later, which eventually resulted in a slightly larger share being paid. By 1700, Ducasse had resigned his post as governor and returned to France.

## SUBSEQUENT CAREER (1701-1715)

Upon the outbreak of the War of the Spanish Succession, he was promoted to *chef d'escadre* (commodore) in the remobilizing royal navy in July 1701 and dispatched into Spain to secure the slave *asiento* for French interests now that the two countries had become united. Appointed *capitán general,* or admiral, by the new Bourbon monarch Philip V of Spain, Ducasse quit Cadiz escorting a Spanish convoy with his flagship *Heureux* (Happy) and three other French warships—ironically reentering Cartagena as an ally five years after having helped lay it to waste. Then in a running fight off Santa Marta from 29 August to 3 September 1702, he beat off a superior English force in what has become known as Admiral John Benbow's "Last Fight."

Returning to Europe, Ducasse participated in the large scale Battle of Vélez-Málaga on 24 August 1704, in which he was wounded. Recuperated from his injuries, he resumed his escort duties of Spanish treasure fleets, successfully guiding these across the Atlantic in 1705, 1708, and 1711. As a reward for these services, he was promoted to *lieutenant général* (rear admiral) in the French royal navy in 1707 and invested with Spain's *Toisón de Oro* (Golden Fleece) in April 1712. In March 1714 Ducasse was placed in command of the Spanish royalist forces besieging Barcelona but was forced to retire the following year because of ill health. He died in Bourbon l'Archambault, France, on 25 June 1715.

**See also** *asiento;* Barlovento, Armada de; Beeston, William; Blénac, Charles de Courbon, comte de; De Graaf, Laurens Cornelis Boudewijn; Dumesnil, sieur; Elliott, Stephen; Hewetson, Thomas; Pointis, Bernard, baron de; Spanish Main.

**References:** Crouse; *C.S.P., Amer. and W.I.,* Vol. XIII; *Interesting Tracts;* Lugo; Taillemite.

# Ducat

English name for a Spanish gold coin originally called a *ducado,* worth 11 *reales.*

The *doblón,* or doubloon, was the most valuable Spanish gold coin, while the *escudo* was worth only ten *reales.* The silver *pesos,* or pieces of eight, struck in the Americas, were infinitely more plentiful, their name derived from the fact that each was worth eight *reales.*

**See also** doubloon; pieces of eight.

# Duchesne, Capitaine

## (FL. 1685)

*Flibustier* commander almost arrested by the English while careening his ship at Lucea, Jamaica.

On 26 November 1685, Lieutenant Governor Hender Molesworth wrote his superiors in London:

a week since one Dushean [*sic*], a French privateer, was careening in Porto Lucia [*sic*] on the north side of this island. Hearing that many people were consorting to him, I pressed a sloop, manned her with [HMS] *Ruby*'s men, and sent her to bring the vessel in, which she did; but

the captain and several men escaped ashore.

Duchesne was subsequently rescued by the English renegade Joseph Bannister, who carried his French colleague safely to Saint Domingue upon his return passage from the sack of Campeche.

**See also** Bannister, Joseph; careen.
**Reference:** *C.S.P., Amer. and W.I.,* Vol. XII.

# Ducking

Naval punishment whereby a malefactor was dropped from a great height into the sea, being "ducked" beneath the surface.

A particularly vivid example occurred in late September 1683. HMS *Falcon* was riding at anchor in Port Royal, Jamaica, when the cooper of a nearby merchantman came aboard and offered to enlist. Captain George Churchill of *Falcon* demurred until contacting its master, Francis Mingham, whom he sent for; but the latter "insolently replied that he would not come, but that he dined at such and such places, and that Churchill might come to him." Irked, the Royal Navy officer entered the cooper in his ship's books and sent a boat to fetch the man's clothes; but Mingham's mate rebuffed this approach with such "ill words and affronts" that Churchill angrily ordered five merchant sailors impressed. Mingham's son and the mate of a nearby merchant vessel then spoke such harsh words to Churchill's coxswain that the captain sent his boat back to take off Mingham's mate.

He was carried aboard *Falcon* "and there hoisted up to the very top of the 'gunbill,' and shamefully exposed as a criminal for more than an hour, to the derision and scorn of the ship's company, in all readiness to be ducked." At this point the mate of the second merchant ship, William Flood, came aboard to protest and was seized in the other's stead. Flood was "hoisted up to the yardarm and three times ducked, with a gun fired over his head;" when even this failed to curb his tongue, a furious Churchill ordered that he be given 20 lashes and sent ashore.

*Reference:* C.S.P., Amer. and W.I., Vol. XI.

# DUHAMEL, CAPITAINE

## (FL. 1692)

Saint Malo shipmaster issued an emergency commission by Governor Jean-Baptiste Ducasse.

In the early days of 1692, when the French colony of Saint Domingue was struggling to recover from the trauma of that previous year's Spanish invasion, its vigorous new governor, Ducasse, dispatched the frigates of Captains Dessaudrays and Duhamel

> to cruise off Cape Tiburon with orders that when they discover the enemy ships returning, they are to advise me in order to gather everyone who is scattered over 20 or 30 leagues of countryside.

*See also* Dessaudrays, Capitaine; Ducasse, Jean-Baptiste.
*Reference:* Lugo.

# DUMESNIL, SIEUR

## (FL. 1684-1692)

*Flibustier* and defender of Saint Domingue.

Dumesnil's name was first mentioned in 1684, when he was listed in a report to the Marquis de Seignelay as one of the senior buccaneer captains on that island, commanding the ship *Trompeuse* (Trickster), of 14 guns and 100 men. Eight years later, following the disastrous losses incurred during the Spanish invasion of 1691, Dumesnil and his men were pressed into a more active role in the colony's landward defenses. On 16 February 1692 he and his company set sail from Petit Goâve with the new Governor Jean-Baptiste Ducasse, aboard two small *flibustier* vessels, to bolster the northeastern frontier against an anticipated Spanish return. Ducasse landed with some militia contingents at Port-de-Paix on 20 February, forwarding Dumesnil and his freebooters to Cap François to reinforce Laurens de Graaf and Charles-François Le Vasseur de Beauregard. The expected Spanish attack never developed, and in the words of Ducasse, "From the moment the *flibustiers* knew that the Spaniards' design had been aborted, they exited with five or six vessels." The frustrated governor added:

> They are very bad subjects, who believe they have not been put in the world except to practice brigandage and piracy. Enemies of subordination and authority, their example ruins the colonies, all the young people having no other wish than to embrace this profession for its libertinage and ability to gain booty.

*See also* De Graaf, Laurens Cornelis Boudewijn; Ducasse, Jean-Baptiste.
*References:* Gosse, *Who's Who;* Lugo.

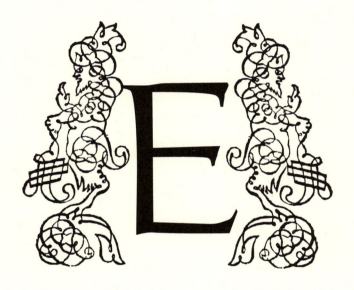

# EARRING

Although often associated with pirates in popular fiction, earrings and other jewelry were in fact commonplace among seamen since the very earliest times, being a simple yet effective means of carrying personal wealth aboard ship. The association with pirates may have become particularly vivid during the seventeenth century because of their predilection for the theft of such items, as well as the incongruity of hard-bitten rovers wearing these exquisite pieces. Spanish officials estimated that the booty carried away from Veracruz in May 1683 by Laurens de Graaf and the "chevalier" de Grammont's raiders consisted of 800,000 pesos in coin, 400,000 in wrought silver, and 200,000 in "gold chains, charms, jewels and pearls."

**See also** De Graaf, Laurens Cornelis Boudewijn; Grammont, "chevalier" de.

**Reference:** Marley, *Veracruz*.

# EATON, JOHN

## (FL. 1683-1686)

English rover who prowled the South Seas.

Eaton left London during the latter half of 1683 in command of the private vessel *Nicholas,* supposedly bound to conduct clandestine peacetime trade on the Pacific coast of South America, although more likely to emulate the piratical exploits of Bartholomew Sharpe by plundering hapless Spaniards. Certainly, Eaton left a trail of destruction during his passage down the Brazilian coast, raiding the River Plate and capturing a Portuguese prize, which subsequently sank in a storm. At the entrance to the Strait of Magellan he encountered the 16-gun *Cygnet* of Charles Swan (with the pirate chronicler Basil Ringrose aboard), also out of London on a similar mission. The two ships rounded the Horn in company but became separated by bad weather.

On 19 March 1684, *Nicholas* was pursued in the vicinity of Valdivia, Chile, by another sail, which proved to be the 36-gun *Bachelor's Delight* of John Cooke (with William Dampier aboard). Together they repaired to the Juan Fernández Islands to refresh provisions and on 8 April headed northward in the hopes of surprising the Peruvian coastal traffic. They seized a vessel bearing timber from Guayaquil toward Lima on 3 May but learned their presence was already known to the Spaniards. Withdrawing to the Lobos de Afuera Islands on the 9 May to careen and revise their plans, the 108 remaining buccaneers sighted three sail passing by, which were pursued and overhauled the next day. These proved to be Spanish supply ships headed for Panama, bearing flour, "seven or eight tons of quince marmalade," and other goods, which Eaton and Cooke sailed to the remote Galápagos Islands to unload.

They remained there from 31 May to 12 June, when they proceeded farther north toward New Spain, hoping news of their depredations had not yet penetrated that far. As they approached Nicoya (off present-day Costa Rica) to raid for beef, Cooke died and was succeeded by Edward Davis. The latter did not get along well with Eaton, and after spending August 1684 refreshing themselves on the coast of Mexico, they returned independently toward Peru and anchored off *Isla de la Plata* (literally "Silver Island," also known as "Drake's Island") on 21 September. But after failing to win a ransom for two prizes containing black slaves and a cargo of sugar off Paita, Eaton finally headed out across the Pacific, where his crew eventually disbanded. He then returned to England, apparently in 1686.

See also careen; Cooke, John; Dampier, William; Ringrose, Basil; Sharpe, Bartholomew; South Seas; Swan, Charles.
Reference: Bradley, Lure.

# ELLIOTT, STEPHEN
## (FL. 1692-1694)

English master who saved Jamaica.

It is not known whether Elliott was in command of the private sloop *Pembroke* in 1692, the third year of the War of the League of Augsburg (King William's War), when this vessel was hired by the Council of Jamaica, but it seems likely. Specifically, 10 or 12 French corsair craft had been reported in mid-April prowling to windward (eastward) of that island, and the renegade "Nathaniel Grubbing on his way to make a second raid." As a result, *Pembroke* was hired and Captain Edward Oakley of HMS *Guernsey* was instructed to put 60 men on board and press 10 more, so that his lieutenant might "take command and in company with the sloop *Greyhound* cruise round the island." These two sloops were joined by a third a few days later but did not come up with the enemy. In the first days of September a similar crisis occurred, when the order was given "for payment to the master of the sloop *Pembroke,* and that he at once go in pursuit of Nathaniel Grubbing."

However, it was not until two years later that Elliott truly distinguished himself. In April 1694, he was sent from Port Royal with a cargo of £8,000–£10,000 worth of merchandise "to trade upon the coasts of Cartagena and Portobelo." There in a bay he was captured by two French privateers and carried to Petit Goâve on Saint Domingue. While being held captive, he witnessed the arrival of a French convoy escorted by three 50-gun men o' war under the chevalier du Rollon. The island governor, Jean-Baptiste

Ducasse, used this trio to surprise the lone Jamaican coast guard frigate, HMS *Falcon,* then decided to mount a full-scale assault against unsuspecting Jamaica, which the French knew to be weakened because of the aftereffects of the earthquake two years earlier and desertion by many privateers. Consequently, a huge force began to muster, soon swelling to 20 sail and 3,000 men.

Alarmed, Elliott and two companions stole a canoe and put out to sea on the night of 5 June 1694. They reached Jamaica five days later, arriving in the evening at the house of Governor William Beeston as he sat with visitors. Beeston was astonished at the sight of Elliott, "in a very mean habit and with a meager weather-beaten countenance," but more astounded still at his news. The council was immediately convened, and at nine o'clock that night declared a state of emergency. Work was rushed on the harbor fortifications, guns were mounted, troops marshaled, ships secured, and reinforcements dispatched to outlying areas. By the time Ducasse appeared off Port Morant with 22 sail on 27 June, the defenders had used the intervening two-and-a-half weeks to great advantage. Although outnumbered by the invading host, they were able to discourage any direct assault on Port Royal, and the French contented themselves with ravaging the coastal plantations.

As a reward for his bravery, the Lords of Trade and Plantations in London voted that November

that the services of Captain Elliott and two men who escaped from Petit Goâve and gave warning of the coming attack on Jamaica be represented to the king, and that His Majesty be moved to grant Captain Elliott £500, a medal and chain, and the two men £50 apiece.

See also Beeston, William; Ducasse, Jean-Baptiste.

*References:* *C.S.P., Amer. and W.I.,* Vols.
XIII–XIV; *Interesting Tracts.*

# ENGAGÉ

French indentured servant, brought out as a
worker for hire in the Americas.

Although it is generally conceded that
*engagés* enjoyed better terms of service than
their English counterparts—signing up for
only three to four years' servitude on
average, for example, as opposed to seven—it
was nonetheless a deeply resented position
that fed a steady stream of recruits into
freebooter ranks. Alexandre Olivier
Exquemelin and Ravenau de Lussan were
only two of many young adventurers who
began their privateering careers this way,
fleeing "cruel" West Indian masters to go
a-roving.

Many became runaways simply because
they despised manual labor, although there
were also frequent instances of ill usage. The
written instructions given by Governor
Bertrand d'Ogeron to the captain of his ship
*Nativité* (Nativity) in August 1665, "for the
preservation of *engagés* and their health,"
reveals a host of potential abuses. The
transportees were not to be struck by
seamen, d'Ogeron wrote, but only by "the
captain, pilot, or quarter-master;" they were
to be allowed ashore once land was reached,
not kept on board where "sadness might
make them fall ill, as I have often witnessed."
They were to be provided adequate sleeping
and storage space during the passage, their
belongings well protected from sailors "who
are ordinarily very given to thieving." Fresh
food and drink were also to be supplied, not
some "wretched, rotten meal" that would
make them sicken and die; and they were
not to be overcharged for their provisions.

*See also* Exquemelin, Alexandre Olivier;
Lussan, Ravenau de; Ogeron, Bertrand d'.

*Reference:* Lugo.

# ERASMUS, CAPTAIN

## (FL. 1688)

Minor rover. On 5 April 1688 (O.S.), the
governor of Jamaica, duke of Albemarle
related how he

> had news of Erasmus, a pirate, at Blue-
> field's Bay, and sent [Royal Navy] Cap-
> tains Wright and Monk to take him, but
> he had escaped before they came.

*Reference:* *C.S.P., Amer. and W.I.,* Vol. XII.

# ESSEX, CORNELIUS

## (FL. 1679-1680)

English rover who participated in John
Coxon's raid against Portobelo.

The first mention of Essex's name
occurred in early November 1679, when
Governor Lord Carlisle of Jamaica delegated
HMS *Hunter,* 28 guns, to patrol the coasts of
that island and arrest any rogue privateers
attempting to land indigo from a depredation
made in late September against the Spaniards
by Coxon and Bartholomew Sharpe in the
Bay of Honduras. The Royal Navy frigate
returned a few days later

> with one Cornelius Essex, commander
> of the *Great Dolphin,* who was tried with
> 20 of his men for riotously comporting
> themselves and for plundering Major
> Jencks of St. James' parish in this island,
> and two of them sentenced to death.

Despite this harsh verdict, Essex was absolved
of the more serious charge of piracy and
released.

Unfazed by his ordeal, he attended an
illegal gathering of privateers late the
following month at Port Morant, off the

southeastern tip of Jamaica. Besides his own bark, there were the barks of Coxon and Sharpe, as well as the sloops of Robert Allison, and Thomas Magott. All five agreed to unite under Coxon's leadership for an assault on Spanish Portobelo, although they had little authorization for such a venture. They quit Port Morant on 17 January 1680, and less than 20 miles out at sea met the brigantine of French *flibustier* Jean Rose, who also joined the expedition. The weather turned foul as they made toward Isla Fuerte, 90 miles south–southwest of Cartagena on the Spanish Main. Essex's bark was very old and in such poor shape that it had been "woolded" (wrapped around with two hawsers to help keep its hull intact). Falling behind, he and Sharpe failed to keep the rendezvous, although Essex managed to rejoin the main body at Isla Fuerte only a couple of days late. The formation then cleared for *Isla de Pinos,* 130 miles east of Portobelo in the Archipelago de las Mulatas. Coxon's was the only vessel capable of gaining this place, the rest being forced into *Isla de Oro* (Golden Island) some miles away. There the pirates befriended the local Indians until Coxon ordered 250 buccaneers into the boats to row westward along the coast in order to fall upon Portobelo before the Spaniards could learn of their presence.

Nearing their destination, they came upon "a great ship riding at anchor," which proved to be that of *flibustier* Capitaine Lessone, who added 80 Frenchmen to the force. Shortly thereafter, the buccaneers slipped ashore at Puerto del Escribano in the Gulf of San Blas, proceeding afoot to avoid any Spanish lookouts. They marched three days until they came upon an Indian village three miles short of Portobelo on the morning of 7 February 1680; a native boy spotted them and set off at a run toward the distant city.

The buccaneers trotted in pursuit, but the boy arrived half an hour before them and raised the alarm. The approaching pirates could hear the signal gun being fired, but nevertheless swept in. The freebooters suffered only five or six wounded; the Spaniards hiding inside their citadel and leaving the raiders to ransack Portobelo over the next two days. They then retired ten miles northeastward, entrenching themselves with their booty and a few prisoners on a cay half a mile offshore of Bastimentos, from where they were rescued three days later by their ships.

A brief blockade of Portobelo ensued, after which a general distribution of booty was made, resulting in shares of 100 pieces of eight per man. The flotilla then retired to careen at *Bocas del Toro* (literally "bull's mouths" or "entrances of the bull"), located at the western extremity of present-day Panama, where the privateers Richard Sawkins and Peter Harris were found lying. When a general refit began, Essex decided to simply abandon his bark, "she being so rotten." Henceforth his name disappears from the narratives; whether he and his men were incorporated into another crew and served in the subsequent incursion into the South Seas is unknown.

**See also** Allison, Robert; Coxon, John; Golden Island; Harris, Peter (fl. 1671–1680); Lessone, Capitaine; Magott, Thomas; pieces of eight; Rose, Jean; Sawkins, Richard; Sharpe, Bartholomew; Spanish Main.

**References:** Bradley, *Lure; C.S.P., Amer. and W.I.,* Vol. X; Gosse, *Who's Who;* Jameson.

# ESTRÉES, JEAN, COMTE D'

### LATER DUC D'
### (1624-1707)

French admiral who commanded several expeditions into the West Indies, reinforcing these with large contingents of *flibustiers.*

## EARLY CAREER

D'Estrées was born on 3 November 1624 at Soleure in present-day Switzerland, the son of an ancient family out of Picardy. He joined the French army and campaigned in Flanders from 1644 to 1647, being promoted to colonel of the Navarre Regiment. He served under the legendary Condé against the Spaniards at Lens on 20 August 1648, and was promoted to field marshal the following year. He remained loyal to the infant Louis XIV during the revolt known as the "Fronde of the Princes," serving under Turenne in Lorraine during 1652–1653, then once again in Flanders.

D'Estrées was promoted to lieutenant general in June 1655, but imprisoned in Valenciennes the next summer, where he remained until the conclusion of the Franco-Spanish War in 1659. It was during this period that he apparently became interested in nautical studies. When the so-called War of Devolution began in the spring of 1667, d'Estrées joined the French armies invading the Spanish Netherlands but soon quarreled with the senior commander, Louvois, and quit the service. Haughty and difficult with superiors and underlings alike, d'Estrées has been described as "a brave man but a bad leader, and worse subordinate."

## NAVAL SERVICE

Transferring to France's royal navy, d'Estrées made his maiden voyage to the Antilles in 1668. Because of his seniority, noble birth, and influential connections, he was promoted to *vice-amiral du ponant* (vice admiral of the west) in May 1671, sweeping down the West African coast with Admiral Abraham Duquesne. On the outbreak of the Franco-Dutch War in the spring of 1672, d'Estrées was given overall command of the 26 French ships of the line sent to join the English fleet. He commanded the allied vanguard aboard his 78-gun flagship *Saint Philippe* during the Battle of Sole Bay on

6–7 June 1672 against Dutch Admiral Michiel de Ruyter. The inexperienced French squadron performed poorly, contenting itself with long-range-gun exchanges, while the English and Dutch hammered out a draw at close quarters, resulting in a postponement of their projected invasion of the Netherlands.

D'Estrées was again in command of the French contingent the following summer, when the allies resumed their offensive. He held the center aboard his flagship *Reine* (Queen) at the two Battles of Schooneveldt, or Walcheren (7–14 June 1673), where once more the raw French ships acquitted themselves indifferently, having their line broken by De Ruyter and an allied landing frustrated. The same occurred on 21 August, when the French were driven out of the vanguard at the Battle of the Texel, having their line pierced. In no small part because of d'Estrées's conduct, England made peace with Holland the coming winter, forcing the French navy back into its ports by 1674.

D'Estrées nonetheless retained his command, not being held entirely culpable for these defeats. He sortied again two years later when the Dutch began making conquests in the French West Indies. Admiral Jacob Binckes sailed to the New World in spring 1676, seizing Cayenne, Marie Galante, and Saint Martin. In response, Louis XIV dispatched d'Estrées with four 50-gun ships, four 30- to 40-gun frigates, and some lesser craft, plus 400 hastily raised troops. The Crown provided ships and soldiers, while private investors subscribed funds in an arrangement called *en course de compte et demi* (which roughly translates to "shared cost" or "joint venture privateering"), whereby both sides agreed to split any prize money.

D'Estrées set sail from Brest on 6 October 1676 with his flag aboard *Glorieux* (Glorious), 60 guns, pausing for five days in early November at Cape Verde to take on provisions. He then appeared before Cayenne on the afternoon of 17 December, landing 800 men at two different places under cover of darkness and launching his assault once the moonlight faded, supported by fire from his frigates. The 300 Dutch defenders were overwhelmed, with 33 killed and 37 wounded, as opposed to 40 dead and 95 injured among the French. D'Estrées then proceeded to Martinique, where he was reinforced by several hundred men raised by the local governor, Jean-Charles de Baas-Castelmore. The French admiral also obtained intelligence about Dutch dispositions at Tobago.

## First Battle of Tobago
### (March 1677)

Binckes had transformed this island into a heavily fortified base. On the evening of 21 February 1677, d'Estrées landed 1,000 soldiers near Rockly Bay and sent 14 light vessels ahead to feint against the harbor mouth. He mounted his major assault the morning of 3 March 1677, the fighting being fierce both on land and within the harbor. The Dutch emerged victorious, although they lost 10 of their 13 anchored vessels to conflagrations that raged throughout the harbor (and also consumed four of the heaviest French men o' war). Two French vessels were also captured, and d'Estrées retired to Grenada and Martinique with 1,000 losses. By early July, he was back in Versailles reporting this failure to the monarch.

## Second Battle of Tobago
### (December 1677)

The Sun King immediately ordered his admiral to return to the West Indies and complete his mission. D'Estrées departed Brest on 27 September 1677 with 17 more ships. He arrived off Tobago on 6 December, having paused en route to destroy the Dutch slaving station of Gorée in West Africa. The weather at Tobago was rainy, but despite this the French quickly threw a large contingent

ashore and installed siege artillery, refusing to be drawn into a suicidal charge like the last time. The Dutch were much reduced by hunger and disease, only two of their ships remaining in the harbor.

On 12 December 1677, the French chief gunner began firing ranging shots against the Dutch fortification, laying odds that he would blow it up at the third attempt. Incredibly, the third round landed squarely in the magazine, killing Binckes and 250 defenders with a mighty blast. The French swarmed exultantly over the ruins, while Dutch resolve collapsed.

## Shipwreck on Aves Islands
### (11 May 1678)

Curaçao, the last Dutch outpost in the West Indies, braced for d'Estrées's inevitable assault. On this occasion, though, fortune smiled on the Dutch, for when the French expedition of eighteen royal warships—heavily reinforced by more than a dozen *flibustier* craft—confidently headed out of St. Kitts toward Curaçao five months later, d'Estrées chose a course closely parallel to the Spanish Main, despite warnings from local pilots that these were dangerous waters.

At nine o'clock on the evening of 11 May, one of the Admiral's *flibustier* consorts suddenly began firing musket shots, followed immediately by a gun, signalling that the fleet was sailing onto the reefs surrounding the Aves Islands group. This warning came too late, though, as seven ships of the line, three transports, and three corsair vessels ran aground and were destroyed, including d'Estrées's own flagship *Terrible,* with a total loss of 500 lives. His forces thrown away, the admiral had no choice but to retire toward Saint Domingue with the survivors, further embittered to see *flibustiers* openly scavenging among the wreckage of his fleet. (Rather than retreat with d'Estrées, the *flibustiers* preferred to continue with a project of their own, attacking Maracaibo under their leader the "chevalier" de Grammont.) By the time the admiral departed for France in early June, the wars were virtually ended.

Nevertheless, d'Estrées returned into the West Indies the next summer with another squadron, ostensibly to demand prisoners from the Spanish American authorities at both Cartagena and Havana, but more likely to reestablish French naval prestige by showing the flag. The appearance of his eight men o' war off Jamaica on 18 July 1679 caused considerable alarm, with Governor Lord Carlisle manning the defenses while its citizenry fled inland. But one of d'Estrées's subordinates, the comte d'Erveaux, knight of Malta, merely came ashore to request permission to take on water and provisions at Bluefields Bay, which was readily granted. The French squadron then worked its way through the Greater Antilles, piloted by the Marquis de Maintenon, before returning to Europe.

### LATER CAREER
### (1680-1707)

In March 1681, d'Estrées's seniority ensured his promotion to marshal of France, and four years later he was sent to campaign against the Barbary States in the Mediterranean, bombarding Tripoli in June 1685 and securing the release of numerous captives. Three years later he performed a similar service against Algiers, bombarding that port in July 1688. He became a duke in March 1687, lieutenant general of Brittany in 1701, and died in Paris on 19 May 1707.

*See also* Binckes, Jacob; Spanish Main.

*References:* Buchet; Crouse; *C.S.P., Amer. and W.I.,* Vol. X; Taillemite.

# EVERTSEN, JACOB

## (D. 1681)

Dutch privateer killed on Sir Henry Morgan's orders for illegally visiting Jamaica.

On a Saturday night in Port Royal, 29 January 1681 (O.S.), Morgan was advised of the arrival off that coast "of one Captain James Everson [*sic*], commander of a sloop, a notorious privateer," with a brigantine prize he had seized. Doubtless this seemed an ideal opportunity for Morgan to prove the honesty of his administration, as he was temporarily serving as governor because of the death of Sir Thomas Modyford and had often been suspected of collusion with pirates in the past. He therefore

> secured all the wherries on the Point and manned a sloop with 24 soldiers and 36 sailors, which at midnight sailed from hence, and about [Sunday] noon came up with him in Bull Bay. Then letting the king's jack fly they boarded him; they received three musket shot, slightly wounding one man, and returned a volley killing some and wounding others of the privateers. Everson [*sic*] and several others jumped overboard and were shot in the sea near shore.

The victors brought back the sloop and 26 prisoners, reentering Port Royal Monday night. All the captives were English except for six Spaniards, whom Morgan forwarded to the authorities at Cartagena, Evertsen's 70-man crew having been largely comprised of Englishmen. The names of those who had slipped ashore were obtained and warrants issued for their arrest, while the prisoners were confined aboard HMS *Norwich* to await trial. "Such is the encouragement which privateers receive from my favor," Morgan wrote to the secretary of state in London, with no small satisfaction.

Evertsen's survivors were tried at the admiralty court in late March 1681, most being convicted of piracy and sentenced to hang. However, Morgan decided "it [was] not fit to post them to execution, lest it should scare all others from returning to their allegiance," and so they were spared. Evertsen's sloop was incorporated into the Royal Navy as an auxiliary, or "tender," to the *Norwich,* Morgan pointing out that it could sound "dangerous places and is able to pursue pirates where the frigate cannot go." He also judged it useful to carry messages "of such accidents as happen."

**References:** *C.S.P., Amer. and W.I.,* Vol.XI; Gosse, *Who's Who;* Pope.

# EVERTSEN, JACOB
### (FL. 1685-1688)

Dutch freebooter who acted as Jan Willems's consort.

Evertsen was first mentioned in April 1685, when Laurens de Graaf and the "chevalier" de Grammont assembled a huge throng of pirates off Isla de Pinos, on Cuba's southern coast, to launch a peacetime raid against Campeche. Evertsen commanded one of the vessels in a buccaneer fleet of 6 large and 4 small ships, 6 sloops, and 17 *piraguas* that appeared off that Mexican port on the afternoon of 6 July. A landing force of 700 buccaneers rowed in toward shore and the following day overran the city. The citadel held out for a week, after which the invaders were left in undisputed possession of Campeche for two months. But as most of the Spaniards' wealth had been withdrawn prior to the assault, little plunder was found and the disappointed pirates evacuated the city in late August, after putting it to the torch.

### JAMAICAN OVERTURE
#### (SEPTEMBER 1687)

Evertsen was not heard of again until autumn 1687, when he reappeared off the northwestern shores of Jamaica with Willems, their force being described as follows:

Yankey [Willems] has a large Dutch-built ship with 44 guns and 100 men; Jacob [Evertsen] has a fine bark with ten guns, 16 "patararoes" [*sic; pedreros,* or swivel guns] and about 50 men. They have also a small sloop.

Having recently returned from North America, the rovers hoped to refresh their provisions, for which Willems smuggled a letter ashore to a Jamaican he had dealt with previously. This man advised Acting Governor Hender Molesworth, who declared that the privateers could not be resupplied, but if they were to come in and renounce roving, they might be made welcome. At the same time, Molesworth secretly instructed Captain Charles Talbot of the frigate HMS *Falcon* to circle round the north coast of the island and seize Willems, who was wanted for having captured an English sloop three years earlier. This scheme came to naught when the frigate had to turn back into Port Royal because of dilapidated sails and rigging.

Unaware of this treacherous attempt, Willems and Evertsen entered Montego Bay and drafted a formal petition to the governor on 3 September 1687 (O.S.), saying:

We have arrived from Carolina and brought several people thence who have been driven from the colony by the trouble with the Spaniards. In all sincerity we present ourselves, our ships and company to the service of the king of England, and hope for your assurance that our ships and men shall not be troubled or molested, as we are ignorant of the laws and customs of this island. We can satisfy you that we have never injured any British subject.

Molesworth replied nine days later, offering a royal pardon and letters of naturalization if the rovers would break up their ships and renounce privateering. Willems and Evertsen responded in late September that to do so would leave them "destitute of all livelihood in present and future," and that neither had "money to purchase an estate ashore." The governor remained unmoved, writing on 19 October, "If you will accept the condition, make the best of your way to Port Royal; if not, leave the coast at once, for I shall consider the treaty to be at an end." The two captains made off, although a number of their men deserted ashore.

## HONDURAN ATTACK
### (FEBRUARY 1688)

Four months later, the new Jamaican governor, the duke of Albemarle heard

that the pirates Yankey and Jacobs have fallen upon a great Spanish ship in the Bay of Honduras called the Hulk [sic; urca, or cargo ship], and that they had been in sight of her twelve hours. If Yankey failed in this attempt he is ruined, for it is said that he was very ill provided before.

Evidently the buccaneers succeeded in their aim, for two months later Albemarle received confirmation that they had fought the Spanish ship "in the port of Cavana [sic; Puerto Cabello?] from seven in the morning till three in the afternoon, and took her." This was to be their last hurrah, however, for shortly thereafter both commanders died.

Later that same summer Captain Peterson appeared off New England with "the remainder of Yankey's and Jacobs' company," and possibly Willems's ship as well, as his craft was described as "a barco luengo of ten guns and 70 men."

**See also** De Graaf, Laurens Cornelis Boudewijn; Grammont, "chevalier" de; Peterson, Captain; Willems, Jan.

**References:** C.S.P., Amer. and W.I., Vol. XII; Juárez.

# EVERTSEN DE JONGSTE, CORNELIS
### ALIAS "KEES THE DEVIL"
### (1642-1706)

Dutch commodore who reconquered Sint Eustatius and New York during the Third Anglo-Dutch War.

Cornelis Evertsen came from a proud naval tradition, being a direct descendant of one of the first Sea Beggars. Born at Middelburg on 16 November 1642, he saw his first major action as 23-year-old captain of the 32-gun *Eendraght,* which, with one other Dutch ship, fought a pitched battle against a trio of British men o' war in February 1665, before the official declaration of the Second Anglo-Dutch War. Evertsen's childhood nickname of "Kees" (short for Cornelis) became transformed into "Kees the Devil" for his ferocity, although he was captured and carried off to England. The diarist John Evelyn records how late in March he conducted the young captive before Charles II, who "gave him his hand to kiss, and restored him his liberty." The king's younger brother James, duke of York, was impressed when Evertsen commented offhandedly about a bullet that had passed through his hat during the battle, "that he wished it had gone through his head, rather than be taken."

Restored to Zeeland, Evertsen served with distinction at the Battle of Lowestoft in 1665, the Four Days' Fight in 1666, and Michiel de Ruyter's Medway raid in 1667. He also fought in the opening engagement of the Third Anglo-Dutch War five years later, helping defend the Smyrna convoy against Sir Robert Holmes, as well as later that summer at the Battle of Sole Bay. Once the 1672 campaigning season had ended, the admiralty of Zeeland decided to send Evertsen with a small squadron to attempt to intercept the homeward-bound English East India Company convoy off St. Helena.

| Name | Guns | Men | Captain |
|---|---|---|---|
| *Swaenenburgh* (flag, ex-HMS *St. Patrick*) | 44 | 186 | Evert Evertsen Corneliszoon |
| *Schaeckerloo* | 30 | 157 | Passchier de Witte |
| *Suriname* (ex-English *Richard and James*) | 25 | 158 | Evert Evertsen Franszoon |
| *Zeehond* (Sea Lion, snow) | 6 | 22 | Daniel Thijssen |
| *Sint Joris* (ketch) | 6 | 34 | Cornelis Eewoutsen |
| *Eendracht* (victualler) | 4 | 30 | Maerten Andriessen |

## WEST INDIAN CAMPAIGN
### (1673)

Evertsen quit Vlissingen (Flushing) on 5 December 1672 with the ships listed in the table above.

He proceeded to Madeira, the Canaries, and Cape Verde Islands, where in February 1673 he blundered into an English force. Realizing that this dimmed his hopes of surprising the East Indiamen, Evertsen now turned to his alternate plan, which called for venturing into the Caribbean and reinforcing the Dutch colonies while attacking Anglo-French interests.

He arrived off Suriname in March, landing troops and provisions, after which he chanced to meet an Amsterdam squadron under Jacob Binckes off Martinique, and together they rampaged through the Lesser Antilles. In June they paused at Sint Eustatius to remove it from English control, and in mid-July they raided the Virginia coast, being bravely resisted in Chesapeake Bay by the Royal Navy's hired vessels *Barnaby* and *Augustine*. No such defense was mounted when they reached New York at the end of that same month, and the city was quickly occupied. Having reinstalled Dutch government, Evertsen and Binckes then detached Captain Nikolaas Boes with four ships to raid Newfoundland, later rendezvousing with the main body at the Azores.

When the two Dutch commodores finally reached the neutral port of Cadiz in December 1673, they had captured a total of 34 English and French prizes and destroyed at least 150 more. However, Evertsen's actions did not meet with approval at The Hague, which was in the final stages of concluding a peace treaty with the English. New York was to be restored to English domination and nothing said about the damage he had wrought. Unlike Binckes, who was promoted to vice admiral of Amsterdam and sent back out to fight the French, Evertsen did not receive appointment as rear admiral of Zeeland until 1675, nor serve again in this particular conflict.

## LATER CAREER

Once peace with France was restored in 1679, Evertsen was promoted to vice admiral, then lieutenant admiral in 1684, and finally supreme admiral of Zeeland in 1688. That autumn he served as second-in-command to the incompetent Lord Torrington in the fleet that carried William and Mary to England for the "Glorious Revolution," and the following summer he fought the French most gallantly at Beachy Head. Kees the Devil finally retired from sea command in 1690 and died at Middelburg 16 years later on his birthday.

*See also* Binckes, Jacob; Holmes, Sir Robert.

*Reference:* Shomette, *Raid*.

# EVERY, HENRY
## (1659-1696?)

English mutineer and pirate, last seen at New Providence in the Bahamas.

Every—whose name has sometimes been erroneously rendered "John Avery," or even "Long Ben" Every—was apparently born to John and Anne "Evarie" in the village of Newton Ferrers, a few miles southeast of Plymouth, England, in August 1659. The details of his early career are unknown, until he enters the books of HMS *Rupert,* of 64 guns, as an experienced midshipman under Captain Francis Wheeler in March 1689. In all likelihood Every must have taken part in the capture of a large French convoy off Brest that summer, the first year of the War of the League of Augsburg (King William's War), and at the end of July was promoted chief mate to *Rupert's* sailing master. In June 1690, Every transferred to HMS *Albemarle* of 90 guns, when Wheeler became its commander, doubtless seeing action in the disastrous Battle of Beachy Head two weeks later. In August of that same year Every was discharged from the Royal Navy.

He next appears in 1693 as mate aboard the heavily-armed private frigate *Charles II* lying at Gravesend, in anticipation of making a salving expedition into the West Indies. An Irish officer named Arturo O'Byrne, after long service in the Royal Spanish Navy, had secured permission from King Charles II of Spain to work wrecks in the Americas. O'Byrne then sought financial and technical support in London, as England and Spain were temporarily allied against France. The command of this flagship—named after the Spanish monarch and flying his colors—was held by John Strong, who had served with Sir William Phips in a highly lucrative operation on the treasure-ship *Concepción* six years earlier. This latest expedition was also intended to attack French possessions and trade with Spanish-American ports and so was to sail well armed. In addition to the flagship, there were the frigates *James, Dove,* and the pink *Seventh Son.*

After lengthy delays, the flotilla put into the Spanish port of La Coruña in early 1694,

only to remain at anchor for another three months. Strong died and was succeeded as flag-captain by Charles Gibson with Every as his first mate. The English crews grew restless at being unpaid and at nine o'clock on a Monday night, 7 May 1694, finally rose with their flagship and slipped past the harbor batteries, Every acting as ringleader. The next morning he set Captain Gibson and some sixteen loyal hands adrift in a boat, saying, "I am a man of fortune, and must seek my fortune." Every then convened a meeting of the 85 mutineers left aboard *Charles II,* whom he persuaded to embark on a piratical cruise into the Indian Ocean (doubtless in emulation of the well-known exploits of the Rhode Island freebooter Thomas Tew that very same year).

The ship was renamed *Fancy* and fell down the West African coast to round the Cape of Good Hope. After a year-and-a-half of adventures in the East, Every succeeded in boarding the enormous Moghul trader *Ganj-i-sawai* off Bombay on 8 September 1695, pillaging it of the immense sum of £200,000. He and his men then sought a means of escape with their ill-gotten booty by returning into the Atlantic and making for the West Indies.

In late April 1696, the weather-beaten *Fancy* dropped anchor at Royal Island off Eleuthera, some 50 miles from New Providence (Nassau) in the Bahamas. Every sent a boat with four men to call on the corrupt local governor, Nicholas Trott, ostensibly saying his name was "Henry Bridgeman" and his ship an "interloper" or unlicensed slaver come from the Guinea Coast with ivory and slaves. Privately, this official was offered a bribe of £1,000 to allow the vessel into port and the pirates to disperse. He signalled his acceptance and Every quickly sailed *Fancy* into harbor, where he and the governor further struck a deal as to the disposal of the craft itself. Still maintaining the fiction that this was a legal transaction, Every made over the ship into the governor's safe-keeping, "to take care of her for use of the owners." Once this deal was struck, *Fancy* was stripped of everything of value—including 46 guns, 100 barrels of powder, many small arms, 50 tons of ivory, sails, blocks, etc.—and allowed to drift ashore two days later, to be destroyed by the surf.

With this evidence erased, Every and the majority of his followers disappeared from the Bahamas aboard different passing ships, hoping to blend back into civilian life. He was one of the few rovers who ever fully succeeded in eluding justice, which may be why so many myths have attached themselves to his name, both during his lifetime and since. More typical perhaps was his crewman Joseph Morris, left behind on the Bahamas when he went mad after "losing all his jewels upon a wager."

*See also* Strong, John; Tew, Thomas.
*Reference:* Baer.

# EXQUEMELIN, ALEXANDRE OLIVIER

## (c. 1645-1707?)

*Flibustier* surgeon who became famous as a chronicler of buccaneers.

He was apparently born around 1645 at the seaport of Honfleur, in France's Baie de la Seine, and raised as a Huguenot, or French Protestant. In 1666, with war having just been declared against England, Exquemelin departed France as an *engagé,* or indentured servant, for the Antilles. He set sail from Havre on 2 May aboard the West Indian Company ship *Saint Jean* (Saint John), of 28 guns. This vessel joined a convoy of 30 merchantmen assembling at Barfleur, which struck out into the Atlantic one foggy morning escorted by the Commodore chevalier de Sourdis. A relatively uneventful

passage ensued, Barbados, Martinique, Guadeloupe, and Puerto Rico being sighted before Tortuga Island was reached on the north coast of Saint Domingue 7 July. Here Exquemelin was sold into indenture to "the wickedest rogue in the whole island," the deputy governor or lieutenant general. Falling sick, he was in turn resold to a surgeon, "and when I had served him for a year he offered to set me free for 150 pieces of eight, agreeing to wait for payment until I had earned the money."

Exquemelin seems to have joined the *flibustiers* in the late 1660s, possibly serving under Jean-David Nau l'Olonnais in 1667–1668, for he compiled a most detailed account of the latter's raids on Maracaibo and Central America. In later writings, Exquemelin stated he remained with the buccaneers "until the year 1670," although he must have meant only among the *flibustiers* of Saint Domingue, for he certainly participated in Henry Morgan's sack of Panama in January 1671. Disappointed in the meager booty from this enterprise (as many freebooters were), Exquemelin returned to Europe some time later, and by the late 1670s was studying medicine in Amsterdam. While in Holland, he wrote an account of the buccaneers of the West Indies entitled *De Americaensche Zee-Roovers* (Jan ten Hoorn, publisher, 1678), which became a celebrated best-seller. A German edition appeared the following year, a Spanish one in 1681, and two rival English editions in 1684. (Morgan, who figured prominently in Exquemelin's work, sued the latter two publishers for £10,000 on account of his negative portrayal and succeeded in winning £200 with damages from each plus a public apology.)

Little else is known definitely about the life of Exquemelin, beyond the fact he qualified as a doctor with the Dutch Surgeons's Guild on 26 October 1679, and 17 years later served aboard Admiral Bernard de Pointis's 84-gun flagship *Sceptre,* when it set sail from France in January 1697 to participate in the sack of Cartagena. Exquemelin evidently returned from that enterprise, for it is believed he was still alive in France ten years afterward.

*See also* engagé; Morgan, Sir Henry; Nau l'Olonnais, Jean-David;

**References:** Camus; Exquemelin; *Piracy and Privateering;* Taillemite.

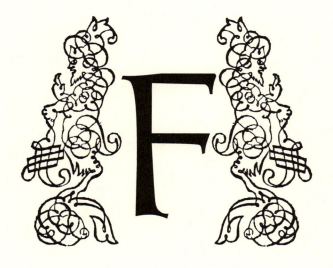

# Fernando, Luis

## (fl. 1699)

Spanish corsair mentioned as having captured a sloop belonging to Samuel Salters of Bermuda in 1699.

**Reference:** Gosse, *Who's Who.*

# Filibuster

Synonym for privateer or corsair, meaning a private vessel or individual licensed to make war.

The commonly accepted root for this name is the Dutch word *vrijbuiter* or freebooter. However, a more plausible suggestion might be *vliebooter,* the name originally given to sailors who plied the Zuiderzee to the offshore island of Vlieland in very tiny craft. During the Netherlands' struggle for independence from Spain in the sixteenth century, this term came to be applied—as a form of ridicule—to the small war vessels of the Dutch rebels, or Sea Beggars. They in turn transformed *vliebooter* into an expression of pride, so that by the end of that century, "flyboat" had come to mean any "fast sailing vessel used for warlike purposes or voyages of discovery." The word certainly was known in a similar context during the seventeenth century. For example, on 14 November 1675, Governor Sir Jonathan Atkins of Barbados wrote, "This day came in a flyboat, bound to New England to fetch masts for the king." But it also came to denote seaborne raiders, particularly among the French, who rather significantly spelled the word *flibustier,* omitting the initial *i.*

With the passage of time, this expression came to imply invaders, warmongers, or pirates in general. It also developed a special meaning in the United States, where a U.S. congressman accused a nineteenth-century opponent of acting as a "filibuster" by halting all business through continuous speaking. From this incident came the concept of congressional filibusters, whereby bills are delayed through long-winded, rambling speeches.

*See also* corsair.

**Reference:** *C.S.P., Amer. and W.I.,* Vol. IX.

# FitzGerald, Philip

## (fl. 1672-1675)

Irish corsair who served the Spaniards at Havana and Campeche.

FitzGerald was apparently first issued a local *guardacosta* commission by the authorities at Havana late in 1672, when such patents once again began to be authorized by the Spanish Crown after a brief hiatus. He operated under the Hispanicized name "Felipe Geraldino," and one of his most notorious early captures was that of Matthew Fox's *Humility* out of London, which he intercepted and carried into Havana in December 1672. Timothy Stamp and other members of this crew were so ill treated that they died at FitzGerald's hands. Another of his captures from around this same time that caused a diplomatic furor was that of the 130-ton merchantman *Virgin* of London, commanded by Edmond Cooke, which was seized before Havana in May 1673 as it was bound from Jamaica for England. FitzGerald bore this prize into port, where it was condemned for carrying "prohibited" cargo—logwood—which the Spaniards always assumed came from their American dominions. After more than a year of hardships and tribulations, Cooke succeeded in reaching home and demanding satisfaction from the government in Madrid; it was conceded only grudgingly. He later turned pirate in retaliation for this abuse, raiding the Spaniards in the South Seas.

In November 1673, when Spain was drawn into the Franco–Dutch War on the side of the Netherlands, FitzGerald found his scope of activities increased, and early the following year he was dispatched by the governor of Havana to patrol Mexico's Laguna de Términos. FitzGerald sailed to Campeche with 80 Spanish soldiers as reinforcements (in addition to his own 150-man crew), capturing two English vessels en route. By summer he was back in Havana, where an English prisoner working on the fortifications claimed to have seen

> Don Philip FitzGerald, commander of a Spanish man o' war of 12 guns, come into the harbor with a New England bark as prize, whose lading was only provisions, liquor and money; and he had five English tied ready to hang, two at the main yardarms, two at the fore yardarms and one at the mizzen peak, and when he came near El Morro castle he caused them to be turned off, and they hanged till they were dead, and FitzGerald and his company shot at them from the deck of the frigate.

A few days later FitzGerald visited the English captives ashore, hoping to recruit more hands for his ship. He showed them his commission to take all English and French vessels, and when they refused to join him, allegedly stabbed one to death with his sword.

England had by then been neutral in the European conflicts for several months, and FitzGerald's continuing depredations against their craft led to increasing animosity. He became the most hated corsair in all the Caribbean (in no small part because of English anti-Irish sentiment), until finally in October 1675 the Lords of Trade and Plantations in London authorized the authorities to "bring in the head of FitzGerald the Pirate from the Havana."

Charles II issued a proclamation "for the discovery and apprehension of Captain Don Philip Hellen, alias Fitz-gerald," but there is no evidence the elusive Irish rover was ever caught.

**See also** Cooke, Edmond; *guardacostas;* Laguna de Términos; logwood; South Seas.

**References:** *C.S.P., Amer. and W.I.,* Vol.IX; Marley, *Pirates; Piracy and Privateering;* Sáiz.

# Flag of truce

In addition to its obvious meaning of a white standard displayed to request a military parley, this term was also applied to any vessel delegated to visit a hostile coast or port with peaceful intent.

The Council of Jamaica, for example, ordered its "French prisoners to be sent away under flag of truce" in late April 1692, restoring these to Saint Domingue despite the ongoing hostilities with that nation. Such exchanges were relatively commonplace and attractive to privateers, for in addition to whatever stipends might be paid for their hire, there were usually ample opportunities for illegal trade as well—all at little risk, as both sides normally honored such commissions.

One of the few instances when a flag of truce was not respected occurred in spring 1694, when Lieutenant Colonel Thomas Clarke and Major Low sailed from Jamaica to Petit Goâve, to complain of the activities of the English renegade William Grubbing. Upon approaching that island, they were seized and detained because a royal squadron had arrived unexpectedly from France, and Governor Jean-Baptiste Ducasse was determined to use this windfall to launch a surprise attack against Jamaica. After the conclusion of this campaign, the English plenipotentiaries were released.

The Spaniards absorbed this term phonetically into their language as *fragatrus,* much as the French did.

See also Grubbing, William.

References: C.S.P., Amer. and W.I., Vols. XIII–XIV; Interesting Tracts; Lugo.

# Flip

English nickname for a nautical drink made chiefly with "hot small beer and brandy, sweetened and spiced upon occasion" ("small" beer being a light or watered beer).

This curious name is believed to have derived, obscurely, from the name "Philip." The pirate Henry Every was once described as "lolling at Madagascar with some drunken sunburnt whore, over a can of flip."

See also Every, Henry.

References: Baer; Penguin.

# Flota

Seventeenth-century Spanish expression for the annual plate fleets sailing to and from Veracruz (Mexico).

The other great convoys were the galeones that serviced Cartagena (Colombia) and Panama. Both were fleets comprised of galleons, so in order to avoid confusion when referring to either one, it became customary in Spain and its overseas possessions to speak of those headed for Veracruz as flotas, while those making for Cartagena were the galeones.

# Foccard, Jean
## (fl. 1682-1685)

French flibustier who repeatedly raided the Mexican coast.

Details are sketchy regarding Foccard's activities, but on 18 June 1683 the surviving Spanish authorities at Veracruz submitted a report to Madrid, describing the devastating assault their city had suffered at the hands of pirates the previous month. They listed the four principal perpetrators as follows (misspelling each man's name, which they had never seen written down, merely spoken by the foreign invaders during their four days of occupation):

Nicolás Bonor [i.e., Nikolaas van Hoorn], of Dutch nationality, admiral of the 12 vessels; Captain Lorenzo [Laurens de Graaf], Flushinger; Monsiuir de Agrammont [sic; "chevalier" de Grammont], of French nationality, rear admiral; and Captain Juan Foxor [Jean Foccard?], of the same nationality, who is the one who took Tampico.

Apparently Foccard had also been responsible for the landing at the gulf port of Tampico in August 1682, when some 30 Spanish captives were seized and a large quantity of cattle slaughtered.

He then participated in the Veracruz attack, which began when Van Hoorn obtained a letter of reprisal from the French Governor Jacques Nepveu, sieur de Pouançay of Saint Domingue in retaliation for the Spaniards having seized a consignment of slaves at Santo Domingo in peacetime. Reinforced with boucaniers commanded by Grammont and Jan Willems, Van Hoorn set sail into the Bay of Honduras to recruit further help from De Graaf and Michiel Andrieszoon. This freebooter throng, including Foccard, paused off Yucatán to gather greater strength before descending on the unwary city the night of 17 May 1683. The inhabitants were caught sleeping in their beds, and resistance crumbled after a few heavy volleys. Veracruz was ruthlessly ransacked before the raiders sailed back around the Yucatán Peninsula to rendezvous off Isla Mujeres and disperse.

The following year, Foccard (or "Joccard") was listed as commanding the *Irondelle* of 18 guns and 120 men at Saint Domingue. He is known to have played a leading role in the assault on the Mexican port of Campeche, once more serving under De Graaf and Grammont. Late in June 1685, a pirate fleet of six large and four small ships, six sloops, and 17 *piraguas* again rounded Yucatán into the Gulf of Mexico. Among its captains were Andrieszoon, Joseph Bannister, Willems, and Foccard. This host materialized half a dozen miles off Campeche the afternoon of 6 July, and a landing force of 700 buccaneers took to the boats, to row in toward shore. A company of Spanish troops exited the city and stationed themselves opposite the intended disembarkation point before the raiders could land, forcing them to remain offshore that night.

The next morning the boats stood out to sea as if withdrawing, then suddenly bore down on the outskirts of Campeche. Before the startled Spaniards could react, the buccaneers came ashore, forming up into four distinct columns. According to eyewitnesses, Capitaine Rettechard commanded the vanguard of 100 men, while Grammont led 200 buccaneers in an encircling maneuver around the city. De Graaf marched at the head of another 200 up Campeche's principal avenue toward the central plaza, while Foccard brought a like number along a parallel street. The pirates swiftly overran the city, although its citadel held out for another week. The invaders remained for the next two months, but as most of the Spaniards' wealth had been withdrawn prior to the assault, relatively little plunder was found. Captives were threatened with death if ransoms were not forthcoming, but Yucatán's Governor Juan Bruno Téllez de Guzmân, prohibited any such payments. Finally, late in August 1685, Foccard and the rest of the pirates abandoned the city after putting it to the torch.

*See also* Andrieszoon, Michiel; Bannister, Joseph; De Graaf, Laurens Cornelis Boudewijn; Grammont, "chevalier" de; Pouançay, Jacques Nepveu, sieur de; Van Hoorn, Nikolaas; Willems, Jan.

**References:** Gosse, *Who's Who;* Juárez; Robles.

# FORBAN

French synonym for "pirate" or lawless sea rover, as opposed to the licensed *corsaire* or *flibustier.*

In a report addressed to Minister Colbert by Jacques Nepveu, sieur de Pouançay and governor of Saint Domingue, dated 4 May 1681, the colonial official justified his decision to allow privateering sorties against the Spaniards of Hispaniola to continue—even after publication of a general peace in Europe—with the argument, "It is certain that if one wishes to prevent these sort of voyages, they [the *flibustiers* or freebooters] will become *forbans,* and one could never dispose of them again."

*See also* Hispaniola; Pouançay, Jacques Nepveu, sieur de.

**Reference:** Lugo.

# FORD, ANTHONY

## (FL. 1697)

English privateer whose ship, *John's Bonadventure,* in consort with the Dutch privateer *Dolfijn* (Dolphin) of Middelburg, captured the French *Concorde* or *Conquête* (Conquest) in 1697, during the closing stages of the War of the League of Augsburg (King William's War) and carried it into Barbados.

**Reference:** Chapin.

# FORLORN

Seventeenth-century English military slang for any advance unit or vanguard, the French equivalent being *les enfants perdus* (literally "the lost children").

When the pirate fleet of Laurens de Graaf, "chevalier" de Grammont, and Nikolaas van Hoorn appeared before Veracruz the night of 17 May 1683, a hand-picked force of 200 freebooters slipped ashore to reconnoiter the Spanish defenses before the main body of 600 additional buccaneers disembarked. This advance party was known as the forlorn, as when Governor Sir Thomas Lynch of Jamaica later reported, "In the action the Spaniards killed but one man. Some three more, all English that were of the forlorn, were killed by the French themselves."

In this same sense, the Jamaican privateer Thomas Rogers apparently commanded a small ship called the *Forlorn* (Vanguard) in Henry Morgan's 1669 victory at the bar of Maracaibo.

**See also** De Graaf, Laurens Cornelis Boudewijn; Grammont, "chevalier" de; Rogers, Thomas; Van Hoorn, Nikolaas.

**References:** *C.S.P., Amer. and W.I.*, Vol.XI; Juárez; Marley, *Veracruz*.

# FRANCIS, CAPTAIN

## (FL. 1676)

Mulatto privateer who operated in the Lesser Antilles.

On 22 November 1676 (O.S.), Governor Sir William Stapleton of the English Leeward Islands described Francis as one of a handful of privateers frequenting those coasts in a vessel "with 12 guns and 60 men." Presumably Francis served under a foreign commission, for although England had been at peace for more than two years, the French were still at war against both the Dutch and the Spanish.

**Reference:** *C.S.P., Amer. and W.I.*, Vol.IX.

# FRANCO, CAPITAINE

## (FL. 1686-1694)

French or Dutch corsair who roamed the South Seas.

Franco's tiny expedition originally sailed from the coast of New England for the Guinea Coast (West Africa), from whence it again departed on 11 December 1686, presumably to join the French privateering forces known to be already in the Pacific under Capitaines François Grogniet, Pierre le Picard, Jean Rose, and others. Franco himself was later described in Spanish records as French, or possibly Dutch but operating with a French commission.

Franco's small ship entered the Strait of Magellan in early March 1687, emerging one month later into the South Pacific. By 27 June he was off Tumbes, at the mouth of the Gulf of Guayaquil, after which he touched at Coiba Island on 20 July before entering the Gulf of Panama on 4 August. The *flibustiers* he had hoped to meet were already being driven out of those waters by the Armada del Mar del Sur, so Franco—with only 41 crew members—elected to proceed even further northwestward and prowl the coast of New Spain. He may have been the rover who landed at Acaponeta (Mexico) more than a year later, on 14 November 1688, "and carried off 40 women, much silver and people," including a Jesuit and Mercedarian friar. This same intruder was chased by ships from Acapulco early the next year, and the enemy vessel was described as "old and with few people on it."

By June 1689, Franco had returned to Isla de la Plata (Ecuador) and shortly thereafter visited the remote Galápagos Islands, which he was to use as a base for sweeps along the mainland between the Gulf of Guayaquil and Trujillo. The raiders' numbers were insufficient for any land raids, however, as was revealed when Franco captured the ship *San Francisco Xavier* out of Puná on 15 October 1689. The Spanish captives discovered he only had 89 men on board, 34 of them French, four Dutch, an English pilot, and the rest Spanish American blacks or Indians. By April 1690, Franco was back at the Galápagos, where he burnt his old vessel and transferred into the prize. He then sailed northward to New Spain, remaining off that coast from July 1690 through August 1691.

Returning to the Galápagos, he seized *Santa María y Hospital de los Pobres* (Saint Mary and Hospital of the Poor) off Isla de la Plata on 25 August 1691, with a cargo of cloth, sails, ropes, and 70 black slaves. Next he intercepted the Jesuit-owned *Santo Tomás* off Punta Pariñas (Peru) on 2 September, with only timber aboard. Franco then ran southward, touching at the Juan Fernández Islands on 31 October, before capturing the Valdivia-bound *Nuestra Señora de Begonia* three days later, with a welcome cargo of flour, biscuit, cheese, and wine. The rovers then retired to Juan Fernández, making occasional forays to the Chilean coast until 1 March 1692, when they struck northward again toward Peru. This cruise took them as far as the Galápagos and back to Juan Fernández but proved unsuccessful, with few prizes or plunder won. Franco therefore decided to exit by the straits and parted company with his quartermaster and 22 other companions in late December 1692, who had chosen to remain cruising in the South Seas with one of their prizes.

By early March 1693 Franco's ship was as far south as the island of Chiloé (Chile), when he inexplicably veered around and headed up the South American coastline

again, this time employing different tactics. He took the *Santiago de Mendía* off Iquique at the end of that same month, which he sailed to Arica and offered to restore to the Spaniards, if they would pay a ransom of 7,000 pesos. This was refused, and he burnt *Santiago* within sight of that port; but when he returned in June with *Magdalena* and *Nuestra Señora del Rosario* (Our Lady of the Rosary), which he had intercepted carrying a cargo of Chilean wheat for Lima, he received payments of 4,000 and 9,000 pesos respectively. In a final act of duplicity, Franco cheated the merchants of Arica by sailing away with this latter prize to the Galápagos, where he prepared it for return into the Atlantic and abandoned *San Francisco.*

Three more Spanish vessels were plundered (mostly of wine) off Pisco, before Franco at last disappeared into the Strait of Magellan in early December 1693. Once through he set course for Brazil, then sought refreshment and provisions at the French colony of Cayenne. From there he ran the Anglo-Dutch blockades across the Atlantic, ironically running aground as he approached La Rochelle on 4 September 1694.

*See also* Grogniet, Capitaine; Mar del Sur, Armada del; South Seas.

*References:* Bradley, *Lure;* Robles.

# FREEBOOTER

General term for any individual doing military or naval service without salary, rather for plunder or prize money alone (which was a common arrangement for seventeenth-century West Indian privateers). The word is believed derived from the Dutch *vrijbuiter,* which probably entered the English language during the frequent wars in the Low Countries of the late sixteenth and early seventeenth centuries.

# GAINES, HUGH

## (FL. 1692)

English captain issued a privateering commission by the Council of Jamaica on 12 February 1692 (O.S.).

**Reference:** *C.S.P., Amer. and W.I.*, Vol. XIII.

# GALÁN, FRANCISCO

## (FL. 1680-1686?)

Spanish captain mentioned in French records as having visited the Cayman Islands in 1680 with a 40-gun ship; there, he seized a vessel from Nantes and sent it into Havana for adjudication.

This was possibly an early reference to Francisco García Galán, a Guipuzcoan sailor from San Sebastián who five years later was given command of the Biscayan squadron of privateers, raised to hunt pirates in the West Indies. García Galán died on 12 November 1686, after an ill-considered attack on the English East Indiaman *Caesar* off Cape Verde, West Africa.

**See also** Biscayan privateers.
**References:** Garizmendia; Lugo.

# GALEONES

Seventeenth-century Spanish expression for the annual plate fleets sailing to and from Cartagena.

The other great convoys were the *flotas* that serviced New Spain. Both were composed of fleets of galleons, so to avoid confusion when referring to either one, it became customary in Spain and its overseas colonies to speak of those headed for Cartagena as the *galeones,* while those making for Veracruz were *flotas.*

# GALESIO, FRANCISCO

## (FL. 1670-1673)

Spanish corsair, slaver, and trader.

Galesio obtained a privateering commission against the English for his ship *San Nicolás Tolentino* on 5 February 1670 from the governor of Santiago de Cuba, one of several issued by Spanish American authorities around this time. Queen Regent Mariana of Spain had inaugurated this aggressive new policy on 20 April of the previous year as an angry reaction to news of Henry Morgan's assault against Portobelo. There is no indication Galesio ever captured any prizes with his license, but Governor Mathias Beck of the neutral Dutch colony of Curaçao obtained a copy, forwarding it to Governor Sir Thomas Modyford of Jamaica as a piece of intelligence. The Englishman was annoyed to discover an undeclared war existing with Spanish corsairs in the West Indies, especially as Manoel Rivero Pardal then interpreted his patent so broadly as to make raids on Jamaica itself. Modyford had spent the previous months attempting to curtail English hostilities, even issuing a public proclamation of peace with the Spaniards at Port Royal on 24 June 1669, only to learn that circumstances had changed. English displeasure over the granting of Spanish American commissions such as Galesio's would lead directly to Morgan's retaliatory strike against Panama in early 1671.

A year-and-a-half later, in August 1672, Galesio arrived at the port of Veracruz with a consignment of slaves. There he met the Dutch mercenary Jan Erasmus Reyning, whose ship *Seviliaen* had been temporarily impounded by the Mexican authorities, despite having Spanish papers. Galesio informed Reyning that war had broken out back in Europe between England, France, and Holland, prompting the Dutchman to sail off—once his ship was released at the end of that month—to join the fighting on behalf of his homeland. Reyning traveled by a roundabout route to Caracas, where he again met Galesio and escorted the Spaniard's vessel across to Curaçao in early 1673.

**See also** Reyning, Jan Erasmus; Rivero Pardal, Manoel.

**References:** Earle, *Panamá;* Marley, *Pirates;* Sáiz; Vrijman.

# GARRETSON, GARRET

## (FL. 1665)

English privateer who commanded the 16-gun *Civilian* in Colonel Edward Morgan's expedition against Dutch Sint Eustatius and Sabá during the Second Anglo-Dutch War. This force departed Jamaica in two divisions, five sail putting out of Port Royal on 5 April 1665 and Morgan himself following with another four on the 28 April. There were 650 men in all, described in a letter by Governor Sir Thomas Modyford as

> chiefly reformed privateers, scarce a planter amongst them, being resolute fellows and well armed with *fusils* [Spanish word for muskets] and pistols.

The Crown official was particularly pleased they would be serving "at the old rate of no purchase, no pay, and it will cost the King nothing considerable, some powder and mortar pieces." Their landing was successfully made, but the colonel, "being a corpulent man," died from heat exertion during the chase, and his expedition disbanded shortly thereafter.

**See also** purchase.
**References:** Cruikshank; *Interesting Tracts;* Pope.

# GOBERNADOR DE TERCIO

Spanish officer charged with raising and maintaining the military regiment *(tercio)* that served as marines or shipborne infantry aboard the Armada de Barlovento.

As such, this officer also became de facto third-in-command for the entire squadron, subordinate only to the *capitán general* and *almirante,* and with his own individual flagship known as the *gobierno.* The Spaniards traditionally maintained large contingents of troops aboard their ships, so *gobernador de tercio* was an important position. Unfortunately, it also perpetuated the age-old practice of subordinating naval officers, thus hampering the evolution of a skilled and independent class of seagoing commander such as the Dutch and English would do.

During the seventeenth century, the *gobernadores de tercio* for the Armada de Barlovento were as follows (including years of their appointments):

| | |
|---|---|
| Francisco de Vivero Galindo | 1664 |
| Antonio de Layseca y Alvarado | 1667 |
| Francisco de Alberró | 1677 |
| Pedro Lamaza de la Peña | 1680 |
| Andrés de Ochoa y Zárate | 1681 |
| Antonio de Olza | 1681 |
| Martín de Zuzoaregui | 1683 |
| Francisco Moreno de Villareal | 1683 |
| Pedro Guzmán Dávalos | 1684 |
| Francisco de Buitrón | 1695 |

**See also** Barlovento, Armada de; *gobierno;* Layseca y Alvarado, Antonio de.
**Reference:** Torres.

# GOBIERNO

Name for the warship bearing the third-in-command of any Spanish naval formation.

In the Armada de Barlovento, for example, the overall commander was the *capitán general* serving aboard his *capitana,* or flagship; the second-in-command was the *almirante* aboard his *almiranta,* or vice–flagship; the *gobernador de tercio* was the third-in-command, responsible for the military companies scattered throughout the fleet and flying his flag aboard the *gobierno.* This form of designation was also used in other Spanish squadrons, such as Peru's Armada del Mar del Sur, or the privately raised Biscayan privateers.

**See also** *almiranta;* Barlovento, Armada de; Biscayan privateers; Campos y Espinosa, Alonso de; *capitana; gobernador de tercio.*

**References:** Garizmendia; Pérez; Torres.

# GOFFE, CHRISTOPHER

## (FL. 1685-1691)

Rhode Island privateer who in summer 1685 appeared before Bermuda with Captain Thomas Henley in a Dutch prize they had taken. The new Royal Governor Richard Cony attempted to detain this ship and cargo, but was prevented by his recalcitrant colonists. On 28 May (O.S.), while all of this was transpiring, one Christopher Smith attested before the governor, "That it was commonly reported at the Bahama Islands in April that Thomas Henley and Christopher Goffe had been proclaimed pirates at Jamaica." Confirmation soon followed, specifying that Henley had been proclaimed so at Jamaica, but Goffe at New England. Nevertheless Cony was unable to prevent either one from departing.

Two years later, in early June 1687, a large ship appeared off New Providence in the Bahamas, setting a boat ashore to say she was come from the South Seas under Captain Thomas Woollerly. The local Bahamian magistrate, Thomas Bridge, instructed one man to remain ashore while the boat returned to the ship, then learned Goffe and some of his cohorts were aboard. Bridge therefore advised the strangers that

> it was the King's order that they [pirates] should not be entertained, and as she continued standing in, I fired a shot across her forefoot. She then anchored, and next day Woolerly told me that he was come to wood and water, that he had Colonel Lilburne's commission and had done nothing contrary to it, and that he had taken in Goffe and his companions in extremity of distress. I refused him leave to come in, and he sailed away next day. I am told that they burnt the ship at Andrew's Island and dispersed, leaving only six or seven men in the Bahamas.

Despite Bridge's apparent compliance with the king's instructions, it was suspected he had merely allowed Woollerly's prize a convenient place to be scuttled, and the captors opportunity to scatter back into civilian life, most likely in exchange for a hefty bribe. This impression was reinforced when Bridge delayed three months before writing to his immediate superiors at Jamaica, by which time Woollerly and Goffe had long since left the Islands.

In fact, Lieutenant Governor Hender Molesworth of Jamaica was to learn of their presence in the Bahamas by chance through secondhand sources, and on 17 August 1687 (O.S.) was informing London he had heard the buccaneers

> quarrelled and burnt the ship, but some of them had bought a vessel and intended to sail for New England, but were detained by want of provisions. It is said that some of these pirates have [so much money] at times [they pay] half a crown a pound for flour.

Molesworth therefore dispatched Captain Thomas Spragge of HMS *Drake* to the Bahamas with specific orders "to take the pirate Woollerly" but arrived to find the rovers already gone. It is presumed they had sailed to Boston, where Goffe is known to have surrendered himself in November of that year, obtaining a royal pardon.

In August 1691, during the War of the League of Augsburg (King William's War), Goffe was commissioned by the governor of Massachusetts to cruise with his ship *Swan* between Cape Cod and Cape Ann to protect that coast from the depredations of the rogue Bermuda privateers George Dew and Thomas Griffin, who were illegally seizing New England traders on trumped-up charges. Goffe sighted the pair and attempted to overhaul, but the *Swan* was easily outdistanced, Goffe reporting later "they could sail two feet to his one."

*See also* Dew, George; Griffin, Thomas.

*References: C.S.P., Amer. and W.I.,* Vol. XII; Gosse, *Who's Who.*

# GOLDEN ISLAND

Located in the Golfo de San Blas due east of Nombre de Dios, Panama; used as a staging place for buccaneers crossing over the isthmus to attack Spaniards in the Pacific Ocean.

On 19 December 1684 (O.S.), Acting Governor Hender Molesworth of Jamaica ordered Captain David Mitchell of the Royal Navy frigate *Ruby*, 48 guns, to escort the Spanish slaver *Santa Rosa* back to Portobelo with a cargo of 302 slaves purchased at Port Royal. Before returning to Jamaica, Molesworth added, Mitchell was to

visit Golden Island off the coast of the [Spanish] Main, through which a passage has lately been found to the South Sea.

Four hundred Englishmen are said to have been conveyed that way in small parties by Darien Indians, and it would be well to spread report that they have been cut off, in order to discourage others.

In a letter written 11 days later, the governor added that this place was at "Sambalos [*sic;* San Blas], a cluster of islands between Portobelo and Cartagena."

*See also* Spanish Main.

*Reference: C.S.P., Amer. and W.I.,* Vol. XI.

# GONZÁLEZ PERALES, JUAN
## (FL. 1665-1669)

Spanish *guardacosta* who operated out of La Guaira, the port of Caracas.

In conjunction with Captain Esteban de Hoces, González was designated to patrol the Spanish Main by the governor and captain-general of Venezuela, Admiral Félix Garci-González de León, knight of the Order of Santiago. Their *armadillas* made numerous captures, including the pirate ship *Caballero Romano* (*sic;* French *Chevalier Romain* or "Equestrian").

*Reference:* Sucre.

# GOODSON, WILLIAM
## (?-1680?)

Puritan merchant-adventurer who became the first commander-in-chief of the Jamaica station.

Goodson is believed to have been from Yarmouth, England, and seems to have traveled to the New World at a young age. He reputedly lived at Cartagena around 1634, although not long enough to acquire a perfect knowledge of that language. He entered the protectorate's service in 1649, and the following year contracted one of his ships—the *Hopeful Luke* of London—to the state, and in October 1651 petitioned for a license to transport shoes to Barbados. His first direct involvement in the navy seems to have occurred in January 1653, when he was appointed captain of the *Entrance* and took part in the Battle of Portland against the Dutch. Promoted to rear admiral aboard *Rainbow* after this victory, Goodson served in the hard-fought triumphs of Gabbard Bank and Scheveningen later that summer, for which he and the other flag officers received a gold chain and medal.

Upon the cessation of the First Anglo-Dutch War in the spring of 1654, Goodson became vice admiral of the blue under William Penn. (He was also a major naval contractor, supplying clothes for the seamen.) Toward the end of that year he was appointed to *Paragon,* vice-flagship of the fleet intended to gain a foothold in the West Indies. This ill-prepared formation of 17 warships and 21 transports left Portsmouth on 24 December 1654 (O.S.), with General Robert Venables sailing aboard Goodson's vessel. Thirty-five days later, they reached Barbados, where a convoy of victuallers awaited and 3,500 volunteers were raised over the next two months, supplementing the 2,500 soldiers brought out from England. In addition to his other duties, Goodson was appointed colonel of "a regiment of seamen" intended to serve on land, with Robert Blake's brother Benjamin as his lieutenant colonel. The whole expedition materialized before Santo Domingo in late April 1655; while Penn bore down on the defenses to create a diversion, Goodson led the bulk of the fleet westward, seeking a disembarkation point. Because of uncertainty regarding the shoals, he deposited the army 30 miles away, an absurdly long distance that contributed to the defeat of the enterprise. The troops spent several days struggling back through the

jungle, while the outnumbered Spaniards recovered from their shock and beat off the enfeebled English assaults until the invaders withdrew with the loss of 1,000 men.

Goodson served ashore with some distinction, but his personal bravery hardly compensated for poor strategic judgment. Hoping to salvage something from the fiasco, the English turned their attention on smaller Jamaica, landing unopposed that May. Penn immediately prepared to return to England, leaving Goodson as the general commander of nine small men o' war and four converted victuallers, his flag aboard *Torrington.* The main body departed in early July 1655, and a month later Goodson sailed for the Spanish Main, leaving a few ships to defend Jamaica. He tacked 450 miles upwind to Santa Marta, which he took, sacked, and burned, although for scant booty. Moving down the coast toward Cartagena, he discovered that his force was insufficient to attempt this place, so he returned to Jamaica by mid-November 1655 "to refit and consider of some other design."

The next spring Goodson again assaulted the Spanish Main, sailing from Jamaica with a diminished force in late April 1656 to fall upon Ríohacha. After devastating it, he proceeded down the coast to water at Santa Marta before once more anchoring impotently off Cartagena for a day, then returning to Jamaica by early June 1656. Unsuccessful attempts followed on the Spanish plate fleets. By August several of Goodson's vessels were deemed unfit for duty, including his own flagship, so they were ordered home while he transferred to *Marston Moor.* In January 1657 he moved into *Mathias* and sailed for England, arriving in late April complaining of ill health. His tenure had been an uninspiring one, for despite undoubted courage and many logistical problems, Goodson lacked the flair for independent command. His successor,

Christopher Myngs, was to shine by comparison.

Goodson assumed command of a squadron in the Downs that same summer of 1657 and continued in important sea commands for the next couple of years, then fell out of favor and left the navy entirely following the restoration of Charles II in the spring of 1660. His Roundhead sentiments made him a suspect in a plot to kill the king three years later, although nothing ever came of this. Because of his connection with Penn, it is believed that he was also the father of John Goodson, "the first English physician that came to Pennsylvania."

*See also* Myngs, Sir Christopher; Spanish Main.

*References: D.N.B.;* Pope.


# GOODY, CAPTAIN

## (FL. 1663)

English privateer from Jamaica who in 1663 was described as commanding a pink with 6 guns and 60 men.

*References:* Gosse, *Who's Who;* Pawson, *Port Royal.*


# GRAHAM, CAPTAIN

## (FL. 1684-1685)

English corsair mentioned in a letter of Governor Sir Thomas Lynch of Jamaica, dated at Port Royal on 20 June 1684 (O.S.). Speaking of several pirate vessels that had been operating in the West Indies, the governor noted that

> many of the men are of this island, but the chief pirate, Graham, is not. It is said that they mean to sail for the South Seas.

This may have been the same Captain Graham who commanded a shallop with 14 men in 1685, sailing up and down the coast of Virginia and New England in company with Captain Veale.

*See also* South Seas; Veale, Captain.

*References: C.S.P., Amer. and W.I.,* Vol. XI; Gosse, *Who's Who.*


# GRAMMONT, "CHEVALIER" DE

## OR SIEUR DE
## (C. 1650-1686)

French adventurer and greatest of *flibustier* commanders.

Little is known about his early life, and there is even some doubt regarding his first name, which has variously been reported as François, Michel, or Nicolas; the Spanish called him "Agrammont" or "Ramón."

Legend has it that Grammont was born in Paris around 1650, although as he was later described by a man who met him in 1683 as an "honest old privateer," he may have been born earlier. The son of a French officer, he allegedly killed a man in a duel when he was 14, then ran away to sea. He made his way to Saint Domingue, where his bravery, quick wit, and openhandedness soon made him popular among the hard-bitten *boucaniers.* "He has a particular secret for winning their hearts," an observer wrote, "and insinuating himself into their spirits." Small, dark and active, the "chevalier" was primarily a land commander (like his contemporary Sir Henry Morgan), using ships principally to reach his military objectives and undergoing several wrecks. In the field he was invincible, however, and he was greatly feared by the Spaniards for his cruelty to prisoners.

During France's wars with Holland and Spain in the 1670s, Grammont rose to prominence among the *flibustiers* and was the leader of the Saint Domingue contingent which sailed as auxiliaries for Vice Admiral comte d'Estrées's expedition against Curaçao, the last major Dutch stronghold in the West Indies. This formidable French armada quit Martinique on 7 May 1678, but four days later suffered disaster when most of its royal warships ran aground off Aves Islands. The admiral turned back with his few survivors, but Grammont and the *flibustiers* decided to make an alternate attack of their own.

## MARACAIBO CAMPAIGN (1678)

Leapfrogging past Curaçao, the freebooters materialized unexpectedly in the Gulf of Venezuela during the first days of June, a host 2,000 strong aboard 6 large ships and 13 smaller ones. Grammont disembarked half his men and marched along the San Carlos peninsula toward the fort guarding its approaches, whose artillery he knew to be mostly pointed seaward. The garrison commander Francisco Pérez de Guzmán was only able to stave off an immediate assault by stationing 100 arquebusiers outside its walls, but heavy guns were then landed from the buccaneer flotilla, and after a brief bombardment the Spanish defenders surrendered. Grammont passed his ships over the bar, leaving the six largest to blockade the entrance while he pressed on for Maracaibo with the other thirteen.

The city and its outlying area were thrown into panic by this fearsome incursion, and the ancient, sickly governor—Jorge Madureira Ferreira, who had only been in office a week—was unable to inspire any confidence in the troops. People began fleeing in every direction, soon followed by Madureira himself, who retired to the inland town of Maicao with his handful of regulars. Thus Grammont

occupied Maracaibo largely unopposed on 14 June and gave it over to plunder. A Spanish eyewitness said of him, "this French enemy was so tyrannical that after taking everything people had, he would torture them unto death, something which not even a Turk nor a Moor would do."

*Flibustier* columns struck out in pursuit of the Spanish governor and other notables, scattering them even further afield. On 28 June, Grammont abandoned the gutted remains of Maracaibo, crossing to the eastern shores of the laguna and falling upon Gibraltar. This town too was already quite deserted, and after bombarding its walls, the garrison of only 22 soldiers gave up. Emboldened by this lack of opposition, Grammont marched almost 50 miles inland to the town of Trujillo, defended by a fort with 350 troops and four artillery pieces. Again he prevailed, storming this fortification from the rear on 1 September "by some hills where it seemed impossible to do so," according to one defender. Once more, terrified Spanish citizens crowded the roads, straggling 75 miles southwestward into Mérida de la Grita to escape from the rapacious raiders.

Having defeated or dispersed every Spanish concentration he met, Grammont deliberately retraced his steps toward the laguna, eventually reentering Gibraltar. This unfortunate town was stripped bare and put to the torch on 25 September. The invaders then remained in undisputed possession of the entire region till almost the end of that year, for it was not until 3 December 1678 that Grammont finally sailed away from the Laguna de Maracaibo, his ships heavy laden with booty and captives. They arrived at Petit Goâve on Christmas Eve, and Grammont was given a hero's welcome. The war was officially winding down in Europe, but local hostilities would continue to smoulder for a long time against the Spaniards in the Americas.

## LA GUAIRA RAID
### (1680)

A year-and-a-half later, Grammont reappeared off the Spanish Main and led an exceptionally daring assault against La Guaira, the port of Caracas. On the night of 26 June 1680, he came ashore with a mere 47 followers and infiltrated the sleeping city. At dawn the next morning its garrison commander and 150 soldiers were taken without a struggle and the inhabitants awakened to find that their city had been occupied during the night. Grammont and his *flibustiers* quickly set about looting before a relief force could arrive.

A small company of Spanish soldiers under Captain Juan de Laya Mujica had escaped capture and dispatched a warning to Caracas while at the same time marching around to Peñón de Maiquetía, just outside the port, to rally its outlying defenders. When word of the freebooter attack reached Caracas that same morning, there was such widespread concern that mule trains immediately began travelling inland with the royal treasure and other valuables. Meanwhile, every able-bodied militiaman fell in to resist the invaders, and a large host set off toward the beleaguered port under Governor Francisco de Alberró. Before these could arrive, however, Captain de Laya launched his own counterattack, encouraged by the small number of *flibustiers* visible in broad daylight. Grammont was forced to make a fighting retreat to the beach, during which nine of his buccaneers were killed and several others wounded—including himself, being slashed across the neck with a machete.

Although repelled, this raid had been successful in that it produced a goodly amount of booty and numerous hostages for the *flibustiers,* as well as shaking the Spaniards' morale by its breathtaking audacity. Grammont's stock soared even higher among the Brethren of the Coast and was scarcely diminished when he lost most of his captives and profits in a shipwreck off Petit Goâve during a hurricane.

## CUBAN BLOCKADE
### (1682)

Considerably less success was enjoyed when Grammont led a flotilla of eight pirate vessels along the northern shores of Cuba in the summer of 1682. After spending two months vainly hovering off Hicacos Point east of Matanzas Bay, hoping to snap up a homeward bound Spanish galleon, he was obliged to retire to Saint Domingue empty-handed. His flotilla remained prowling westward as far as Santa Lucía with ships such as *Diligente* and *Cagone,* commanded by Pierre Bot and Jan Willems. After careening a pink on that coast, the force veered round for the Bahamas, then stemmed the Windward Passage early in 1683. Bot captured a Spanish merchantman and set its survivors ashore at Guantanamo before the whole flotilla headed for Petit Goâve.

Meanwhile, a Dutch rover called Nikolaas van Hoorn had been cheated out of a large consignment of slaves at Santo Domingo and fled to the French half of that island with twenty crewmembers aboard his ship, the *Saint Nicholas.* Governor Jacques Nepveu, sieur de Pouançay, granted him a letter of reprisal against the Spaniards and put him in contact with Grammont, who agreed to help the rover gain revenge. He lent Van Hoorn his own corvette *Colbert* to recall the flotilla from Cuba, meeting this just as it was reentering Petit Goâve. *Saint Nicholas'* complement was then increased to more than 300 with the infusion of Grammont's men and cleared for Roatan on the Central American coast to obtain further reinforcements for a projected attack on the main Mexican port of Veracruz.

They paused outside Port Royal on 27 February 1683 to deliver letters to the

Jamaican authorities, assuring them no hostilities were contemplated against the English. Governor Sir Thomas Lynch sent out his French secretary, Charles de La Barré, to visit the *Saint Nicholas,* who found Grammont nominally serving as lieutenant to Van Hoorn but regarded as captain by his *flibustiers,* who resented the Dutchman's "insolence and passion." They bore away to westward and a few days later met Captain John Coxon, telling him they were "trying to unite all the privateers for an attack on Veracruz." Then they proceeded into the Bay of Honduras, where the legendary Dutch corsair Laurens de Graaf and his consort Michiel Andrieszoon were reputed to lie, with "two great ships, a bark, a sloop . . . and 500 men." As Van Hoorn and Grammont prowled the bay, they spotted two Spanish merchantmen lying at anchor, the *Nuestra Señora de Consolación* and *Nuestra Señora de Regla,* which they promptly seized. Little did they realize De Graaf had been careening his flagship *Dauphine (Princess,* also known by its Spanish nickname *Francesa)* at nearby Bonaco Island, patiently waiting for the Spaniards to bring their profits back aboard from the commercial fair at Guatemala.

Annoyed at this clumsy intrusion into his plans, De Graaf made away for Roatan, where he was overtaken by the *Saint Nicholas* with its two prizes. On 7 April 1683, a huge gathering of buccaneers met on the beach to hear of the proposed assault on Veracruz. This port had not been attempted in living memory, but doubters were swayed when Grammont reputedly declared, "I would believe it almost impossible, except for the experience and valor of those who hear my words." Heartened, the freebooters endorsed this plan by acclamation, and after pausing at Guanaja Island to raise more men, a pirate fleet of five ships and eight lesser craft stood into the Gulf of Mexico, bearing 1,300–1,400 raiders.

## SACK OF VERACRUZ
### (1683)

On the afternoon of 17 May, De Graaf cunningly reconnoitered the port with two ships, then led an advance force of 200 buccaneers ashore under cover of darkness to infiltrate the city from its landward side. Grammont and Van Hoorn landed the main body of 600 men at nearby Punta Gorda some time later, following De Graaf's trail through the dunes, over Veracruz's low stockades and directly into the darkened streets. There the buccaneers silently redistributed themselves, Grammont personally assuming command of the crucial column of 80 *flibustiers* that was to snuff out Spanish resistance around the governor's palace. The attack commenced at four o'clock in the morning and easily overwhelmed the startled garrison.

Van Hoorn immediately saw to the amassing of booty, while Grammont and De Graaf looked to the city defenses, anticipating a Spanish counterattack from the outlying areas. In a brilliant stroke, Grammont organized a company of mounted buccaneers from the stables within Veracruz. At dawn on 19 May, the second day of pirate occupation, first light revealed a large body of horsemen drawn up to the west of the city. Grammont responded by sending out a flying column of more than 100 mounted *flibustiers.* The Spanish irregular cavalry were astonished at the sight of heavily armed men bearing down upon them "with a flag and trumpet in regular order," and melted away without a fight. The buccaneer riders followed up their sally by making a reconnaissance far afield, finding no other Spanish concentrations in the region.

Grammont also played a prominent role in extorting money from the thousands of captives within Veracruz. In addition to the wealth already stolen from their homes and warehouses, the freebooters demanded ransoms be raised in Mexico's interior to spare the city and its inhabitants once they withdrew. In order to inspire the proper tone of terror in the prisoners' letters for help, Grammont made a grand show of stockpiling wood all around the principal church where the captives were being held, and loudly calling for the death by fire of every man, woman, and child inside. Thanks to these cruel threats, a sum of 150,000 pesos was agreed upon as ransom.

On 22 May, the raiders evacuated Veracruz, Grammont riding his horse directly into the church to marshall the 4,000 prisoners into bearers. These carried massive amounts of booty a mile down the coast and were transferred offshore to Sacrificios Island, beyond any hope of rescue. A week later the ransoms were paid, and after herding 1,500 blacks and mulattos aboard as slaves, Grammont and the rest of the pirate flotilla weighed. They encountered the annual plate fleet just as they were standing out from the coast, but its commander Admiral Diego Fernández de Zaldívar deferred combat, and so the buccaneers escaped. They then paused at Coatzacoalcos to take on water before shouldering their way back around Yucatán to Isla Mujeres. There they completed dividing the spoils and Van Hoorn died, having been wounded in a brawl with De Graaf.

In late June 1683 the commanders began going their separate ways, Grammont sailing the 52-gun *Saint Nicholas* (which he was apparently soon to rename *Hardi,* or "Audacious") toward Tortuga Island. His progress was greatly hampered by contrary winds to the extent that his crew and 236 prisoners were in danger of starving. This problem was solved by a chance encounter in late July with the Spanish merchantman *Nuestra Señora de la Candelaria* out of Havana, which he detained to rob of its cargo of flour. Seeing he still could not beat upwind

to Tortuga, Grammont eventually decided to make for Petit Goâve, releasing the *Candelaria* after having impressed five of its seamen and removed most of the sails. He also transferred 22 Veracruz prisoners on board and gave its captain Luis Bernal a pass "so that no other corsair would harm him."

Rumors abounded throughout the Caribbean during 1684 of Grammont and De Graaf getting together for another major exploit, but this did not actually occur until April 1685, when another huge pirate gathering was held off Isla de Pinos on Cuba's southern coast. The captains could not concur on an objective, however, a majority insisting on a repeat assault against Veracruz, while De Graaf patiently explained this city would not be caught napping a second time. Finally, the Dutchman sailed away in frustration to Central America's Mosquito Coast, where he was followed by Grammont and the others, who eventually agreed to a descent on the smaller Mexican port of Campeche.

The pirate host shifted to Isla Mujeres to gather greater strength, maintaining vessels off Cape Catoche for more than a month to advise passing freebooters of their scheme but also alerting the Spaniards. These preparations grew so notorious the deputy governor of Campeche, Felipe de la Barrera y Villegas, had ample time to dispatch spy-boats up the coast to give advance warning of the buccaneers' approach. Finally, in late June 1685, a steady stream of reports began reaching him of unidentified vessels creeping ever closer to his port.

### SACK OF CAMPECHE
### (1685)

On the afternoon of 6 July, a pirate fleet of 6 large and 4 small ships, 6 sloops, and 17 *piraguas* appeared half a dozen miles off Campeche. A landing force of 700 buccaneers took to the boats and began rowing in toward shore, but four Spanish militia companies totalling 200 men exited and positioned themselves opposite the intended disembarkation point. The pirates put up their helms and waited, until the next morning they began to draw off toward their ships in a feint. Before the Spaniards realized it, the pirate boats sped inshore and disgorged at the very outskirts of the city itself.

A hundred buccaneers quickly formed up behind Captain Rettechard as the vanguard; 200 joined De Graaf and marched directly toward the city center; another 200 advanced under Captain Foccard along a street parallel to De Graaf's; and the final 200 followed Grammont in an encircling maneuver. The Spaniards fell back, as out in the harbor Captain Cristóbal Martínez de Acevedo prepared to scuttle his coast guard frigate *Nuestra Señora de la Soledad* (Our Lady of Solitude) as per his instructions. Originally, he had intended to bore holes in its bottom, but given the speed of the invaders' onrush, he directed his boatswain to run a trail of powder into the magazine. When the fuse was lit, *Soledad* exploded with such a mighty blast that it collapsed the defenders' morale, sending them scurrying into their citadel and other strongholds while the pirates entered Campeche uncontested.

Over the next few days Grammont subdued these outposts until only the citadel remained. The pirates began bombarding this fortress at dawn on 12 July 1685, but at ten o'clock that morning two relief columns of Spanish militia appeared on the beach, hastening down from the provincial capital of Mérida de Yucatán. In the past, such troops simply had to appear for smaller bands of raiders to scuttle back out to sea; but this time Grammont's *flibustiers* stood and fought from behind Campeche's ramparts, and the first ranks of Spaniards went down to well-aimed volleys. All day the two sides fought, until Grammont circled

behind the relief force and caught it between two fires. The Spaniards drew off in confusion, and that night the garrison abandoned their citadel. By 11 o'clock that night the building was deserted, and a couple of English prisoners shouted to the besiegers. These called back for the guns to be discharged, and once this was done, poured over the walls led by Grammont and De Graaf in person.

Again, Grammont organized troops of mounted buccaneers, who were dispatched to reconnoiter and ravage the surrounding countryside as far as 25 miles inland. As at Maracaibo, the invaders were then left in undisputed possession of the city for the next two months, but as most of Campeche's wealth had been withdrawn prior to the assault, the buccaneers found little plunder. Their frustration led to numerous instances of cruelty. On 25 August, Grammont's *flibustiers* celebrated Louis XIV's saint day with fireworks and festivities, and then began preparations to break camp the following morning. A message was sent inland demanding a ransom of 80,000 pesos and 400 head of cattle for Campeche. Governor Juan Bruno Téllez de Guzmán's reply arrived a few days later, addressed to the captive De la Barreda. He was forced to read aloud a sneering rejection of the pirates' demand, in which the governor averred that

> they would be given nothing and might burn down the town, as [Spain] had ample funds with which to build or even buy another, and people enough with which to repopulate it.

A furious Grammont had the houses torched the next dawn, then sent another missive inland threatening the captives. He received the same response, and the day after paraded the prisoners in the main square, where the executions began. Half a dozen had been hanged when De la Barreda and other leading citizens approached De Graaf, "whom they knew to be more humane than the Frenchman," and offered

> to serve him for the rest of their lives as slaves if he saved the rest of the inhabitants of Campeche. Lorenzo, after a lengthy discussion with Grammont, ordered a halt to the executions and that the remaining prisoners be carried out to the ships. Immediately after this incident, all the pirates evacuated the citadel, having spiked the guns.

The raiders quit Campeche in early September 1685, pausing briefly at Sisal before rounding Yucatán to Isla Mujeres, where they dispersed. Grammont's *Hardi,* Nicolas Brigaut's captured Spanish galliot, and a sloop sailed together to Roatan to careen, after which Grammont decided to make an attack on the Spanish colony of Saint Augustine, Florida, perhaps in alliance with the English settlers of Carolina.

### SAINT AUGUSTINE RAID
#### (1686)

This trio of *flibustier* vessels worked its way into the Atlantic, and on 30 April 1686 Brigaut's galliot stood in alone toward Matanzas, Florida to gather intelligence, flying Spanish colors. Grammont's flagship and the sloop remained concealed at anchor further south, awaiting his scout's return. When the scout failed to reappear, Grammont sailed to Matanzas himself three days later, examining the shoreline from his quarterdeck. The galliot had sunk in heavy weather, and now Grammont also was driven northward by the same storm, never to be seen again.

More than a year-and-a-half later, a *flibustier* captain called Du Marc escaped from a Spanish prison and reported a rumor to Governor Pierre-Paul Tarin de Cussy of Saint Domingue, that "the 'chevalier' de Grammont has perished with approximately 180 men that were aboard his ship."

**See also** Andrieszoon, Michiel; Barrera y Villegas, Felipe de la; Bot, Pierre; careen; Coxon, John; De Graaf, Laurens Cornelis Boudewijn; Estrées, Jean, comte d'; filibuster; Foccard, Jean; letter of reprisal; Pouançay, Jacques Nepveu, sieur de; Spanish Main; Van Hoorn, Nikolaas; Willems, Jan.

**References:** *C.S.P., Amer. and W.I.,* Vol.XI; Juárez; Lugo; Marley, *Veracruz;* Robles; Sucre; Weddle, *Wilderness.*

# GREAVES, CAPTAIN

Also known as "Red Legs," this West Indian pirate was born in Barbados of parents who were prisoners sent there as slaves by Cromwell. Most of these slaves were natives of Scotland and Ireland and, owing to their bare knees, generally went by the name of "Red Legs."

Young Greaves was left an orphan but had a kind master and a good education. When his master died, the boy was sold to a cruel master. He ran away and swam across Carlisle Bay, but by mistake clambered onto the wrong ship, a vessel commanded by a notoriously cruel pirate called Captain Hawkins. Finding himself driven to the calling of piracy, Greaves became very efficient and quickly rose to eminence. He was remarkable for his dislike of unnecessary bloodshed, torture of prisoners, and killing of noncombatants. These extraordinary views brought about a duel between himself and his captain, in which he was victorious, and he was at once elected leader.

Greaves now entered a period of the highest piratical success, but always preserved very strictly his reputation for humanity and morality. He never tortured his captives, nor robbed the poor, nor maltreated women. His greatest success was the capture of the Island of Margarita, off the Venezuelan coast. On this occasion, after capturing the Spanish fleet, he turned the guns of their warships against the forts, which he then stormed, and was rewarded by a huge booty of pearls and gold.

Red Legs retired to the respectable life of a planter on Nevis, but one day was denounced as a pirate by an old seaman. He was cast into a dungeon to await execution when a great earthquake destroyed and submerged the town in 1680; one of the few survivors was Greaves. He was picked up by a whaler, on board which he served with success; later on, he received a pardon as a reward for his assistance in capturing a gang of pirates.

He again retired to a plantation and was noted for his many acts of piety and his generous gifts to charities and public institutions. When he died, he was universally respected and grieved for.

*Reference:* Gosse, *Who's Who.*

# GREGGE, THOMAS

## (FL. 1659)

English privateer mentioned in the journal of Colonel Edward D'Oyley, governor of Jamaica, as having been issued a "let pass" for his ship *Aime* (or *Aimée*) on 28 September 1659 (O.S.).

*See also* D'Oyley, Edward.
*Reference:* Pawson, *Port Royal.*

# GRENADE

One of the favorite assault weapons used by seventeenth-century pirates.

Oftentimes buccaneers found themselves outnumbered, so they had to rely on surprise, mobility, and superior firepower in order to gain their objectives. Not wishing to be encumbered with artillery, they substituted hand grenades in order to sow confusion and panic among large enemy concentrations. For example, the contingent of 40 buccaneers that rushed the northern Caleta bastion of Veracruz at dawn on 18 May 1683, as part of Laurens de Graaf and the "chevalier" de Grammont's concerted attack against that entire city, tossed grenades through the apertures before swarming onto its rooftop. The detonations could be plainly heard three-quarters of a mile away on San Juan de Ulúa Island and caused the bastion to surrender without a struggle.

Grenades were made of iron or glass. The French chronicler and priest Jean-Baptiste Labat recorded an instance of the latter's usage of grenades, when the *flibustiers* of Capitaine Pinel swarmed over the bows of an 18-gun English ship off Barbados in early 1694, during the War of the League of Augsburg (King William's War). The English barricaded themselves inside the forecastle, but Pinel's boarders found a small hatch through which they flung a glass jar filled with gunpowder and surrounded by four or five lit fuses, which ignited the powder when the jar burst and burnt seven or eight Englishmen so horribly, they called for quarter.

*See also* De Graaf, Laurens Cornelis Boudewijn; Grammont, "chevalier" de; Labat, Jean-Baptiste; Pinel, Capitaine.
*References:* Labat; Marley, *Veracruz.*

# GRIFFIN, JOHN

## (FL. 1692)

English captain issued a privateering commission by the Council of Jamaica on 4 February 1692 (O.S.).

*Reference:* C.S.P., Amer. and W.I., Vol. XIII.

# GRIFFIN, THOMAS

## (FL. 1691)

English freebooter who in 1691, during the War of the League of Augsburg (King William's War), was issued a privateering commission and permit to impress seamen by Lieutenant Governor Isaac Richier of Bermuda; another was issued to his colleague Captain George Dew.

However, both commanders misused them; appearing off the New England coast later that summer, near Piscataqua they attacked the pink *Three Brothers* of Captain Thomas Wilkinson, just arriving from a trading voyage to Cadiz, Spain. Upon capturing this vessel, Griffin and Dew pretended they had mistaken it for a French ship, then charged Wilkinson with transporting illegal goods. Knowing that their actions "should be unkindly dealt with" by the local authorities, Griffin and Dew took the *Three Brothers* to the Isles of Shoals and afterward into the river near Portsmouth, New Hampshire, where they held a mock trial at which ship and cargo were both "condemned."

When the local collector of customs, Jahleel Brenton, learned of this travesty of justice, he attempted to impound the pink, whereupon Griffin and Dew resisted "with force of arms." Eventually Brenton succeeded in obtaining possession of the ship and part of its cargo, while the privateer *Swan* of Captain Christopher Goffe was sent out from Boston in pursuit of the raiders. They easily eluded him, Goffe reporting later that "they could sail two feet to his one." Then, off Cape Cod, Griffin and Dew boarded another English vessel that was bound to Virginia with a cargo of oil, brimstone (sulfur), gold, and silver. The privateers again trumped up false charges, claiming that its captain did not have proper clearance papers, and so sailed this prize back to Bermuda.

*See also* Dew, George; Goffe, Christopher.
*Reference:* Chapin.

# GRILLO, DIEGO

## (FL. 1670-1673)

Mulatto corsair originally from Havana, sometimes confused with Diego de los Reyes or "Diego Lucifer," an earlier mulatto pirate also from Cuba, but who operated during the 1630s and 1640s.

After the general amnesty given to pirates in 1671 by the new governor of Jamaica, Sir Thomas Lynch, Grillo was mentioned as one of those (along with Humphrey Thurston and Jelles de Lecat) who continued to act as renegades, attacking Spanish ships and carrying these into his lair at Tortuga Island, most likely under a French commission. Grillo apparently commanded a vessel mounting 15 guns and succeeded in defeating three armed ships that had been sent to take him in the Bahama Channel, massacring all of the Spaniards of European birth that he found among their crews. As late as October 1673, when Mateo Alonso de Huidobro captured the brigantine of Dutch captain Jan Lucas outside Mexico's Laguna de Términos, Grillo was still reportedly operating in the West Indies, although shortly thereafter he was caught and hanged.

*See also* Lecat, Jelles de; Lynch, Sir Thomas; Thurston, Humphrey.
*References:* Gosse, *Who's Who;* Juárez; Weddle, *Spanish.*

# GROGNIET, CAPITAINE

## (FL. 1683-1687)

French freebooter who roamed the South Seas for two years.

Early in 1685, Grogniet and his fellow commander Lescuyer led a contingent of 200 French *flibustiers* and 80 English buccaneers from Golden Island across the Isthmus of Panama into the Pacific Ocean, hoping to meet up with other rovers under Francis Townley, who had already penetrated that area the previous month. Seizing coastal craft with which to transport themselves, Grogniet and Lescuyer reached Taboga Island south of Panama City, where on the night of 13 February they sighted a burning vessel to the north. The next morning a force of English buccaneers under Edward Davis and Charles Swan appeared (including William Dampier). They offered the *flibustiers* the 90-ton *Santa Rosa,* which they had recently captured, while their English companions were to be incorporated into *Bachelor's Delight* and *Cygnet.*

In appreciation of this gift, Grogniet (Lescuyer having died) presented the two English commanders with blank commissions issued by the French governor of Saint Domingue. More *flibustiers* were also known to be on their way, so Grogniet sent a boat eastward to await them in the Gulf of San Miguel. On 3 March this craft met Francis Townley with 180 men, mostly English, in two captured barks, and a few days later another bark bearing about a dozen Englishmen entered the Gulf of Panama from the west, having separated from William Knight off the coast of New Spain. Then on 11 April the band that Grogniet was expecting arrived across the isthmus, consisting of 264 mainly French *flibustiers* under Jean Rose, Pierre le Picard, and Desmarais (as well as Ravenau de Lussan). The pirate assemblage of six vessels and almost 1,000 men then determined to blockade Panama in hopes of intercepting the Peruvian treasure fleet.

But those vessels slipped past, delivered their cargo, then sallied to engage the buccaneers. Toward noon on 7 June 1685,

the rovers were lying off Pacheca Island when Grogniet

who was anchored further away from the island gave us the signal that he had sighted the Spanish fleet composed of seven sails. He indicated how many were coming by hoisting his flag seven times.

A squadron of six Spanish men o' war and a tender bore down upon the pirates, who were caught ill prepared. Grogniet in particular had to delay weighing because large numbers of his men were still ashore at two small chapels, so he fell behind his consorts. An indecisive, long-range engagement ensued between Davis and Swan versus the Spaniards, with the buccaneer pair unwilling to close with the more heavily armed vessels of the Armada del Mar del Sur, who in turn feared being boarded by their more nimble opponents. Nevertheless, the next day ended with a Spanish victory, and the pirates were driven off.

The buccaneers fell out amongst themselves along national lines, each group blaming the other for this defeat. A failed attack on the coastal town of Remedios (Pueblo Nuevo) followed at the beginning of July, after which both contingents headed northwestward as separate groups. Grogniet refused to join the English raid on León (Nicaragua) of early August 1685, preferring to take 120 men in five boats for a repeat attempt against Remedios. The attack was repulsed, and he rejoined his remaining 200 men aboard *Santa Rosa* on 3 September. Realejo was entered on 1 November, but the *flibustiers* found it and the surrounding countryside devastated from an earlier English assault, so obtained little booty. Reversing course, Grogniet hesitated to march inland and sack Esparta (in present-day Costa Rica) on 9 December, pressing on instead into the Gulf of Chiriquí by the end of that year.

On 9 January 1686 his *flibustiers* captured the tiny coastal town of Chiriquita (Panama), which was abandoned a week later. At the end of this same month a Spanish squadron passed by out at sea, and when Grogniet's men approached Remedios again the night of 5 March to forage for supplies, they were ambushed by a small frigate, *barco luengo,* and *piragua,* suffering more than 30 casualties. They roamed westward once more, anchoring off Esparto on 19 March, sighting Francis Townley's small flotilla four days later.

Despite some residual ill will, the two groups combined for a joint attempt against the inland city of Granada (Nicaragua), landing a force of 345 men on 7 April and fighting their way into the city three days later. Little loot was found, however; the Spaniards had been forewarned and had transferred their valuables offshore to Zapatera Island, so the pirates withdrew empty-handed five days later. They endured numerous ambushes before passing Masaya and regaining their ships, after which they traveled to Realejo.

Having enjoyed such limited success, on 9 June 1686 half of Grogniet's French followers voted to join Francis Townley in his eastward progress toward Panama. The remaining 148 *flibustiers* agreed to remain with Grogniet while he sailed westward, and the two contingents parted company a fortnight later. Grogniet operated for a time in the Gulf of Amapala (present-day Gulf of Fonseca), until a majority of his men again voted to quit his leadership. These 85 *flibustiers* sailed *Santa Rosa* northwestward for New Spain and California to await the annual galleon from Manila, while Grogniet retraced his passage down the Central American coast with 60 followers aboard three *piraguas.* He rediscovered Townley's contingent, now commanded by George Hutt, in the Gulf of Nicoya on 23 January

1687. After ravaging that area for a month, they weighed together for a surprise attack on the equatorial port of Guayaquil.

On 16 April 1687 the rovers arrived opposite Puná Island, and two hours before dawn on Sunday (20 April) landed to march inland. Grogniet led his company through a marsh toward the heart of Guayaquil, while Hutt advanced on one small fort and Le Picard directed his men against another. The Spaniards had been advised of strange sails off Puná, but when no attack developed, assumed it was a false alarm. Between three and four o'clock on a rainy morning, the buccaneers burst upon the city, and a vicious house-to-house struggle ensued. Between 34 to 60 Spaniards were killed and many others captured in eight hours of fighting, as opposed to only nine pirates dead and a dozen wounded. But among the latter was Grogniet, who was carried back to the ships when the triumphant raiders evacuated Guayaquil four days later. He died off Puná on 2 May, while waiting for the Spanish to ransom their captives.

***See also*** *barco luengo;* Dampier, William; Golden Island; Hutt, George; Jolly Roger; Knight, William; Lescuyer, Capitaine; Lussan, Ravenau de; Mar del Sur, Armada del; Picard, Pierre le; Rose, Jean; South Seas; Swan, Charles.

***References:*** Bernal; Bradley, *Lure; C.S.P., Amer. and W.I.,* Vol. XII; Dampier; Gosse, *Who's Who.*

# GRUBBING, WILLIAM

## (FL. 1694)

English turncoat who led French marauding raids against Jamaica.

Grubbing was born on that island of English parents, but perhaps being Roman Catholic or otherwise loyal to the exiled James II, chose to flee to Saint Domingue and take up service with the French during the War of the League of Augsburg (King William's War). His knowledge of Jamaica stood him in good stead in

landing in the night upon lone settlements near the sea, and robbing them of all they had, and away again before any notice could be given for any strength to come against him.

These depredations escalated after Grubbing's French wife was captured off Hispaniola by a Jamaican sloop. The English wished to release her, but she allegedly preferred to "be quit of her husband who, she said, used her very ill," so remained in Jamaica.

In revenge, Grubbing vowed to make off with every Jamaican woman "he met with till he had his wife again." One such victim was Rachel, the 14-year-old daughter of a minister's widow named Mrs. Barrow, whom Grubbing carried off to Petit Goâve after ransacking her mother's plantation. Another was Major Terry's wife, whom Grubbing "stripped to her shift and beat" on board his ship after a nocturnal descent. Governor William Beeston wrote to his French counterpart Jean-Baptiste Ducasse to complain of these and other "inhumanities beyond the customs of Christian warfare," but the matter was interrupted by the massive French invasion of Jamaica in the summer of 1694.

*See also* Beeston, William; Ducasse, Jean-Baptiste; Hispaniola.

*References: C.S.P., Amer. and W.I.,* Vol. XIV; *Interesting Tracts.*

# GUARDACOSTAS

Privateers commissioned by the Spanish-American authorities to operate coast guard vessels in the West Indies.

For a long time, Crown officials in the New World were restricted from issuing patents in peacetime, but when piratical raids, logwood poaching, and foreign smuggling became too intense in the early 1670s, Madrid relented. Ironically, many of the first and most successful *guardacostas* were foreign-born mercenaries, such as Philip FitzGerald, who was based at Havana before transferring to Campeche; Jelles de Lecat, who patrolled Mexico's Laguna de Términos; and John Philip Beare, who served at Havana and Puerto Rico. As distinct from the Armada de Barlovento—a royal squadron assigned to patrol the entire Caribbean—*guardacostas* were usually authorized to operate only along a specific stretch of shoreline, returning to a particular port. This somewhat limited their activities, although it also meant their vessels were usually heavily manned with fresh crews.

As the Spaniards had so often been victimized by seaborne raiders, they took a dim view of any foreign vessels they encountered. Legally, foreign ships were not even allowed to enter Spanish-American ports, so many honest merchants and fishermen were waylaid by *guardacostas.* Such activities increased the animosity already felt against Spain in the New World. In early August 1683, for example, Governor Sir Thomas Lynch of Jamaica wrote his superiors in London, complaining that the Spaniards had

armed some small craft and ordered them to take all ships that have on board any *frutos de esas Indias* [fruits of these Indies], whereby they make all fish that come to net. They have committed barbarous cruelties and injustices, and better cannot be expected, for they are Corsicans, Slavonians, Greeks, mulattoes, a mongrel parcel of thieves and rogues that rob and murder all that come into their power without the least respect to humanity or common justice.

The *guardacostas* were unpaid mercenaries who lived off their takings. Colonel Hender Molesworth, acting governor of Jamaica, has left an unflattering portrait of one such group operating off the southeastern coast of Cuba in 1684:

These galleys and *piraguas* are mostly manned by Greeks, but they are of all nations, rogues culled out for the villanies that they commit. They never hail a ship; and so they can but master her, she is certain prize. They lurk in the bushes by the shore, so that they can see every passing vessel without being seen. When our sloops are at anchor they set them by their compasses in the daytime, and steal on them by night with so little noise that they are aboard before they are discovered.

The captors often colluded with local Spanish judges as well, to ensure that every vessel they brought in was condemned as a prize. The Spanish Crown further abetted this policy by claiming that it was prohibited for foreign vessels to carry such items as logwood or pieces of eight (presuming that these could only be gained illegally). As a result, traders wandering too close to Spanish waters became liable to seizure, their vessels and cargos being deemed entirely forfeit if so much as a single Spanish coin or piece of logwood were found aboard.

*See also* Barlovento, Armada de; Beare, John Philip; FitzGerald, Philip; Laguna de Términos; Lecat, Jelles de; logwood; pieces of eight.

*Reference:* C.S.P., Amer. and W.I., Vol. XI.

# GUY, RICHARD

### (FL. 1659-1663)

English privateer who sortied from Port Royal, Jamaica, with his ship *Hopewell Adventure,* bearing a "let pass" dated 24 November 1659 (O.S.) from Governor Edward D'Oyley. Guy enjoyed considerable fortune on this cruise, capturing a prize in May 1660 with 14,775 pieces of eight on board and another the following month for which he paid "133 lbs. 9 ozs. of bullion" as royal tenth of its value. Four years later Guy was listed as commanding the frigate *James,* of 14 guns and 90 men.

*See also* D'Oyley, Edward; pieces of eight.

*References:* Gosse, *Who's Who;* Pawson, *Port Royal.*

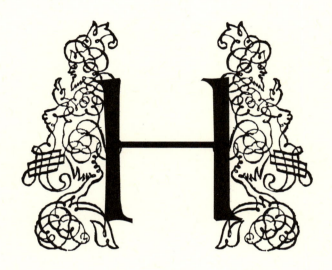

# HALL, JACOB

### (FL. 1683-1684)

English freebooter who took part in the French peacetime raid against Veracruz.

Early in 1683, a Dutch rover named Nikolaas van Hoorn arrived at Saint Domingue and obtained a letter of reprisal from the French governor Jacques Nepveu, sieur de Pouançay, because the Spaniards had impounded a consignment of slaves Van Hoorn had delivered at Santo Domingo. Reinforced with a heavy contingent of *flibustiers* commanded by the "chevalier" de Grammont and Jan Willems, Van Hoorn set sail into the Bay of Honduras to recruit further help from such pirate chieftains as Laurens de Graaf and Michiel Andrieszoon. Together they decided to assault the Mexican port of Veracruz but felt they needed still more men; consequently, the raiders visited Guanaja Island and paused briefly off Yucatán's Cape Catoche to gather greater strength, at which point Hall and several other freebooter ships joined the expedition. The pirate fleet then descended on the unsuspecting city of Veracruz the night of 17 May 1683.

The Spanish inhabitants were surprised in their beds, and the city was occupied for four days by the pirates, during which time it was ruthlessly ransacked. The freebooters then withdrew back around the Yucatán peninsula, although Hall appears to have been one of the few to stand away directly toward the Straits of Florida and Carolina, rather than toward the rendezvous at Isla Mujeres. When word of this assault reached Port Royal in early August 1683, Governor Sir Thomas Lynch of Jamaica wrote his superiors in London, saying that among the pirate commanders were "no English, except one [George] Spurre, and Jacob Hall in a small brig from Carolina." He later learned that the latter had proceeded to Carolina

where he is free, as all such are; and therefore call it *Puerto Franco* [Spanish for "free port"]. The colonists are now full of pirates' money, and from Boston I hear that the privateers have brought in £80,000.

However, the earl of Craven replied on 27 May 1684 (O.S.), "On inquiry I learn that one Jacob Hall did touch there [Carolina] to wood and water on his way from Veracruz, but he did not belong to the place, and had no inhabitants of Carolina with him. After a very few days' stay he sailed for Virginia." The earl added that Hall had served under Van Hoorn's French commission, it not then being known in Carolina that English privateers were forbidden to serve under foreign princes, which "accounts, I conceive, for his not being secured."

**See also** Andrieszoon, Michiel; De Graaf, Laurens Cornelis Boudewijn; Grammont, "chevalier" de; Pouançay, Jacques Nepveu, sieur de; Spurre, George; Van Hoorn, Nikolaas; Willems, Jan.

**Reference:** *C.S.P., Amer. and W.I.,* Vol. XI.

# HAMLIN, JEAN

### (FL. 1682-1684)

French pirate who went on a ten-month rampage with his frigate *Trompeuse* (Trickster).

### FIRST CRUISE
### (1682-1683)

The *Trompeuse* (Trickster) was a 30-gun French royal frigate that had been hired for a peacetime commercial venture by Pierre LePain, who sailed it into Port Royal, Jamaica, in January 1682 and decided to remain. Consequently, he prepared the frigate for return to Europe that autumn by loading it with a valuable consignment of merchandise for Hamburg, then dispatching it into the Bay of Honduras for an additional cargo of logwood. The ship was surprised off the Central American coast by two sloops carrying a band of 120 "desperate rogues," most of them French, who commandeered it as their flagship.

They began making captures with *Trompeuse,* and after seven or eight English losses, Governor Sir Thomas Lynch of Jamaica commissioned the privateer Captain George Johnson to sortie in late October and recapture the frigate, equipping him with "a ship of 35 or 40 guns and 180 men." Off Cape Tiburon, Johnson came upon an English sloop from Antigua and Tobago that had recently been robbed by the pirates. He learned from its survivors that the pirates were talking "of going to Mona to intercept Irish and New England vessels." Johnson therefore hurried toward this passage, further believing the *Trompeuse* to be "in bad condition and ready to sink, for they cannot get victuals to enable them to go and careen."

But this intelligence proved faulty. The pirates' commander, Hamlin, was still operating around Ile-à-Vache, the island off the southwestern tip of French Hispaniola, which Johnson bypassed. On the morning of 25 January 1683, while this first English pursuer was searching as far east as Puerto Rico, the *Trompeuse* was almost caught at anchor by another Jamaican pirate hunter, Captain Matthew Tennant of HMS *Guernsey,* when he put into "Jaqueene." However, with the wind growing calm, Tennant could not get near Hamlin "for want of oars," and when a wind finally did spring up, it became such a gale that the pirates easily eluded him, for the *Trompeuse* could sail "three feet to his one."

Governor Lynch began commissioning a growing number of privateers to bring in Hamlin, including such men as John Coxon and Thomas Paine, but despite their best efforts, vessels continued to be looted. The most valuable of 18 ships taken was the Royal African Company slaver *Thomas and William,* of between 20 and 30 guns and commanded by Richard North. This vessel had been traveling from Barbados to Jamaica when its crew

> spied a ship standing towards us, which coming up ordered Captain North to strike, hoist out his boat and come aboard, at the same time firing a volley of small shot and the great guns. North answered the fire but was perplexed, some of the crew saying that this was an English frigate firing to make him strike his topsail yard. Some of the crew hauled down the colors, while others presently rehoisted them.

Amid the confusion, North sent his mate over in a boat, who was clapped in the hold while the bombardment continued, and North finally surrendered. Hamlin's pirates then manned their prize, transferred the prisoners to *Trompeuse,* and sailed into a quiet bay on the coast where they tortured their principal captives by "squeezing their thumbs and privy members in vices, hanging them up in the brails by their hands tied behind them; and so found out what riches they carried."

Hamlin looted the *Thomas and William* of 65 pounds of gold and other valuable items, including slaves and skilled seamen, before releasing the vessel. He then took a small pink from New England (to which some of his men transferred), and quit Saint Domingue before any more English men o' war could find him. He sailed to Saint Thomas in the Danish Virgin Islands, capturing a Jamaican sloop and speaking with a French convoy just outside its harbor before sending a message ashore inquiring whether *Trompeuse* might enter. The governor was the notorious Adolf Esmit, who readily acceded to the pirate's request and sent out refreshments. Hamlin "in return sent him silks and satins, and arranged with him a private signal."

The pirates tallowed their ship and took on provisions before setting out once again with a new pilot for West Africa. They arrived off Sierra Leone in May 1683 and began working their way down the coast, "generally anchoring at night." They took a Dutch trader, exchanging its cargo ashore for gold, then turning the vessel itself into a fireship. The *Trompeuse* was now masquerading as a Royal Navy man o' war, flying "the king's jack and pendant," and so was able to sail right in on an anchored vessel next day, which struck its colors in salute. Hamlin returned the greeting, but after anchoring athwart its bows let fly with a full volley and broadside. The stranger cut its cable and attempted to escape, but was soon captured and discovered to be a 20-gun Flushinger "with 70 pounds of gold on board and abundance of liquor." Hamlin joyfully made it his consort.

Next, the English vessel *Sevenoaks* was sunk, and three ships and a pink ransacked in quick succession near Cape Coast castle (off present-day Ghana). Hamlin then laid in a course for Accra but overshot and reached Ouidah instead, robbing and sinking some coastal boats. Spying three Royal African Company ships anchored close inshore, he employed the same ruse as before, approaching under Royal Navy colors, then loosing a broadside. His pirates captured and tortured the crew of the first vessel, shooting the gunner dead and flogging the rest to make them confess where their gold was hidden. The second was found abandoned, while the third deliberately cut its cable and wrecked on shore. Hamlin then refitted his two craft and proceeded to "Cape Lopus," where within a few days he intercepted a large 20-gun Dutch West Indiaman. According to an eyewitness, "She surrendered without resistance, but had

little on board but slaves. The pirates did not torture the Dutch, favoring them more than the English."

The raiders then landed near Cape St. John's to divide their booty and part company. The spoils came to around "30 pound weight of gold a man," and the jubilant rovers redistributed themselves on the two ships according to inclination. Hamlin remained in command of the *Trompeuse* with 120 men; an anonymous Englishman from Jamaica became captain of another 70 aboard the consort. While rounding Cape Lopus again together in early June 1683, the latter boarded the Royal African Company ship *Eaglet* one evening, obtaining still more plunder when they "stretched [its Captain John] Waffe and his officers, and put screws on their thumbs to make them confess what gold they had." Having robbed the *Eaglet,* the pirates then warned Waffe to make shift during the night, lest Hamlin "take all he had." Determined to disappear back into civilian life, the rovers refused to reveal their names, "and punished one of Waffe's sailors who asked the pirate captain's name" (he had apparently adopted the pseudonym "Morgan").

Hamlin chose to sail *Trompeuse* back across the Atlantic to Dominica. Here at least 46 of his men voluntarily left him, so that eventually only 16 white men and 22 black slaves remained aboard when he set out for Saint Thomas. The blacks rose against the whites during this crossing, "but were beaten back with loss of three killed." On 6 August 1683 *Trompeuse* appeared before Saint Thomas, "made the private signal, and was admitted." Hamlin's booty was stored in the harbor castle for safekeeping, and a scant two days later HMS *Francis* of Captain Charles Carlile appeared off the harbor mouth at three o'clock in the afternoon, sealing the pirate vessel's doom. Although still disguised as a Royal Navy warship "with white color flying, jack, ensign, and pendant," Carlile was undeceived. When Governor Esmit showed himself unwilling to cooperate against Hamlin, the following night the English officer sent in two boats, which boarded *Trompeuse* while the corsair captain and his men fled ashore, then set it alight. The frigate exploded after the victorious English withdrew. Hamlin and half a dozen companions reputedly escaped from the harbor castle in an armed boat provided by Esmit.

## SECOND CRUISE
### (1683-1684)

Within weeks, reports began reaching the English authorities at Nevis that Hamlin had bought a sloop from Esmit and abandoned the Danish Virgin Islands altogether. "It is thought that he is gone to Petit Goâve," Governor Sir William Stapleton of the Leeward Islands wrote, "where there are enough of that trade [i.e., piracy] to protect him, and from thence to Campeche to get some good ship." It was also known that several of Hamlin's followers had remained on Saint Thomas; John Poynting, master of an English sloop who visited several times, claimed to have met them. But of Hamlin nothing more was heard for several months, until he made a spectacular reappearance, for once again English intelligence was faulty.

On 3 April 1684 the sloop *Three Sisters* of Captain John Thomas lay at Tortola, having been dismasted and forced back after attempting to reach St. Kitts. "While he lay at anchor, a three-master vessel came in under a commander supposed to be Hamlin, who boarded the sloop, plundered it and threatened to kill [Thomas], telling the governor of Tortola he would cut him into meat for the pot." After his *Trompeuse* had been burned at anchor, the French corsair had manned a Dutch frigate lying in the roads of Saint Thomas and in September 1683 set out on a cruise for Brazil. There he took several vessels, including a large Portuguese prize, which he sailed back to

Cayenne. Once more some of his people left before Hamlin himself continued to Tortola with his prize, chancing upon the *Three Sisters*. The raiders remained in possession of the sloop for a day and a night, then left it in the roads when Hamlin sailed away to Saint Thomas. He and the Portuguese ship arrived shortly thereafter, being welcomed by Esmit. Meanwhile, the *Three Sisters'* captain reclaimed his sloop, repaired its mast, and sailed to Nevis to report the pirate chieftain's return into Caribbean waters at the end of that month.

Within two more months, Governor Lynch of Jamaica was recording a somewhat garbled version of this report:

> Hamlin, captain of *La Trompeuse,* got into a ship of 36 guns on the coast of the [Spanish] Main last month [i.e., May 1684], with 60 of his old crew and as many new men. They call themselves pirates and their ship *La Nouvelle Trompeuse,* and talk of their old station at Isle des Vaches [*sic;* Ile-à-Vache]. I have consequently sent to apprise the French governor [of Saint Domingue] and warn our merchantmen.

***See also*** Carlile, Charles; Coxon, John; Hispaniola; Johnson, George; LePain, Pierre; logwood; Lynch, Sir Thomas; Morgan, Captain; Paine, Thomas; Tennant, Matthew.
***Reference:*** *C.S.P., Amer. and W.I.,* Vol. XI.

# HAMLYN, WILLIAM

### ALSO HAMLIN
#### (C. 1651-C. 1676?)

Adventurer, originally from Plymouth, England, who emigrated to Antigua and in December 1674 was pressed with his sloop *Betty* by the deputy governor of that island, Colonel Philip Warner, to carry dispatches to nearby Nevis.

Upon Hamlyn's return, Colonel Warner had 34 troops placed aboard the *Betty* and ordered Hamlyn to accompany him with another two ships and 300 men to the island of Dominica. Arriving on Christmas Day (O.S.), the colonel met his half-breed bastard brother, Thomas Warner, head of one of the local tribes, and asked him to assist in a retaliatory strike against some Indians who had supposedly raided Antigua. This was merely a ruse, however, for once Thomas's followers assembled, the colonel "made them very drunk with rum, gave a signal" and had them slaughtered, presumably to eradicate all traces of his unwanted sibling and nephews.

To his credit, Hamlyn attempted to intervene and even "took an Indian boy in his arms to preserve him, but the child was wounded in his arms and afterward killed." Upon the dispersal of the expedition, Hamlyn proceeded to Barbados and laid a deposition before Governor Sir Jonathan Atkins, who was outraged at Warner's action. Aside from its inhumanity, it had cost the English the loyalty of many native islanders, "whose friendship was so necessary in time of war, to the great damage of the French." Atkins judged Hamlyn to be "a serious and intelligent man of his quality" and duly ordered Warner deposed, arrested, and forwarded to the Tower of London in chains to stand trial.

Once these proceedings began, however, a lack of material witnesses hampered the prosecution, while the colonel portrayed his ambush as a legitimate tactic of war and cast aspersions on the absent Hamlyn. Warner was acquitted in September 1675 and restored to his offices, having—in his own words—"proved Hamlin a perjured rogue." This verdict was reinforced by a report received later from Atkins's chief rival, Governor Stapleton of the Leeward Isles, who justified Warner's use of such a "stratagem to destroy a skulking heathen enemy" and stigmatized Hamlyn as

"a fellow of an evil life [who] dare not return to Plymouth, and has since run away to Jamaica, and is now master in a Dutch privateer [England's recent enemy], and has chased and fired on an English boat."

Stapleton's resentment against Hamlyn led him to file a complaint with the governor of Curaçao, accusing the young renegade of "stealing 30 odd Negroes from the English part of St. Christopher's, which he did twice, and other felonious acts." As Hamlyn had allegedly committed these depredations while holding a Dutch privateering commission from Curaçao, but only to operate against the French, Stapleton was delighted to learn in late November 1676 that Hamlyn had been "sent to Holland in irons" to be punished.

*Reference:* C.S.P., Amer. and W.I., Vol. IX.

# HANDLEY, THOMAS
## (FL. 1684)

English privateer commissioned by Governor Robert Lilburne in late March 1684 "for defence of the Bahama Islands" with his frigate *Resolution*.

This measure was adopted two months after the devastating Spanish assault on Charles Town (New Providence), capital of that colony, and proved entirely futile, for soon after the Spaniards drove the English out of the archipelago by a series of raids throughout that summer.

*See also* Lilburne, Robert.
*Reference:* C.S.P., Amer. and W.I., Vol. XI.

# HARDUE, CAPTAIN
## ALSO HERDUE
## (FL. 1663)

Privateer listed in an English document of 1663 as commanding a 4-gun frigate (originally a Spanish prize) with a crew of 40 men and holder of a Jamaican commission.

*References:* Gosse, *Who's Who;* Pawson, *Port Royal.*

# HARMAN, JOHN

## (FL. 1665-1667)

English privateer who commanded the 12-gun *Saint John* in Colonel Edward Morgan's expedition against Dutch Sint Eustatius and Sabá during the Second Anglo-Dutch War. This force departed Jamaica in two divisions, five sail putting out of Port Royal on 5 April 1665 and Morgan himself following with another four on the 28th. There were 650 men in all, described in a letter by Governor Sir Thomas Modyford as

> chiefly reformed privateers, scarce a planter amongst them, being resolute fellows and well armed with *fusils* [Spanish word for muskets] and pistols.

The Crown official was particularly pleased they would be serving "at the old rate of no purchase, no pay, and it will cost the King nothing considerable, some powder and mortar pieces." Their landing was successfully made, but the colonel, "being a corpulent man," died from heat exertion during the chase, and his expedition disbanded shortly thereafter.

Two years later the better known naval officer, Admiral Sir John Harman, reconquered the Guianas from the Dutch, not realizing the war had already ended back in Europe with these territories being ceded to the Netherlands under the provisions of the Treaty of Breda. Harman's squadron first fell upon and sacked Cayenne, then assaulted Suriname. Fort Zeelandia was taken after a savage battle, and the entire colony decimated, with most of its mills being destroyed. It was only then that the English learned of the peace, and while they submitted to its terms, much pressure was brought to bear upon the former English colonists to transfer to Jamaica. Some resisted, and it was not until the last group of 500 was shipped off under Major James Banister that tranquility was fully restored.

*See also* purchase.

*References:* Cruikshank; *Interesting Tracts;* Pope; Shomette, *Raid.*

# HARRIS, PETER

## (FL. 1671-1680)

English privateer who joined John Coxon's pioneering expedition into the South Seas.

At the end of November 1679, Governor Lord Carlisle of Jamaica heard "of the capture of a valuable ship of 28 guns, belonging to the United Provinces, by one Peter Harris, a privateer ever since the taking of Panama [by Henry Morgan more than eight years previously]." Doubtless Harris had since been operating with a variety of French commissions, this nation having been at war with both Holland and Spain during the interval; but these hostilities were at last winding down. Furthermore, it was now against Jamaican law for privateers to serve under foreign colors. The governor therefore dispatched HMS *Success,* 32 guns, to cruise the south cays of Cuba for Harris, the news of his latest depredation being confirmed a few days after the Royal Navy frigate's departure, "by the arrival of 11 men belonging to the Dutch ship in their long boat."

At first everything went well. Captain Thomas Johnson of *Success* intercepted the brigantine of another renegade, Richard Sawkins, and sent it into Port Royal for adjudication. Upon sighting Harris off the Cuban coast in the first days of December, however, the frigate blundered into shoal waters and tore its bottom out on a sand bank. Thus the *Success* was "irrecoverably lost," and Harris made good his escape.

The rover was next heard from in early March 1680, careening his 150-ton prize at Diego's Point on Isla Solarte, within the maze of islands known as *Bocas del Toro* (literally "bull's mouths" or "entrances of the bull"), located at the northwestern extremity of the present-day Panamanian Republic. While lying there, Harris had met the *barco luengo* of Sawkins, who had also eluded the Jamaican authorities, and was then further joined by Coxon's flotilla fresh from its sack of Portobelo. The raiders refitted their vessels, then suggested returning to Golden Island to avail themselves of their newfound friendship with the local Indians, "to travel overland to Panama" and attack the Spaniards on their vulnerable Pacific flank. Harris agreed to join the expedition with his 107 men, and on 2 April the freebooters weighed.

## PACIFIC INCURSION

Coxon, Harris, Sawkins, Robert Allison, Edmond Cooke, Thomas Magott, and Bartholomew Sharpe all anchored their ships close inshore at Golden Island, out of sight in a small cove. An anchor watch was left aboard each, with orders to rally to Coxon's and Harris's ships—the two largest—if any attack should occur. At six o'clock on Monday morning, 15 April 1680, 332 buccaneers went ashore and obtained guides to cross the isthmus. Ten days later they came upon the Spanish stockade of Santa María, at the confluence of the Chucunaque and Tuira Rivers. This fort had no artillery, so at dawn Sawkins led a rush of buccaneers that penetrated the palisades. Seventy of the 200 Spanish defenders were killed outright, the rest being massacred later by the Indians.

Flush with their victory, the buccaneers determined to press on into the Pacific, although it was noted that "our general, Captain Coxon, seemed unwilling, but with much persuasion went." Henceforth, other captains began to assume the lead, most particularly Sawkins, Harris, and Sharpe. Reaching the Pacific, the pirates traveled westward along the coast in their river boats, until one night they captured an anchored Spanish bark, of which Sharpe took command with 135 men. The next night Harris came upon a second bark

in his canoe, and took [it]. She had on board her about 20 armed men. They fought about a quarter of an hour, wounded one of our men.

Soon the buccaneers had assembled a small flotilla and bore down upon Panama. The Spaniards sent out a hastily mustered force to do battle, and the raiders engaged it in a three-hour fight. During this action, "Brave, valiant Captain Peter Harris was shot in his canoe through both his legs, boarding of a great ship."

The day ended with all the Spanish vessels taken, but Harris was grievously injured. He was transferred aboard the 400-ton *Santísima Trinidad* along with the other wounded to be tended, as this now became the buccaneer flagship. The surgeons removed one of his legs, but the stump became "fester'd, so that it pleased God he died."

***See also*** Allison, Robert; *barco luengo;* Cooke, Edmond; Coxon, John; Golden Island; Sawkins, Richard; Sharpe, Bartholomew; South Seas.

***References:*** Bradley, *Lure; C.S.P., Amer. and W.I.,* Vol. X; Jameson; Pawson, *Port Royal.*

# Harris, peter

## (fl. 1684-1686)

Nephew of Peter Harris (fl. 1671–1680), who also led a buccaneer incursion into the South Seas.

Toward the end of June 1684, Harris arrived at Golden Island from the Mosquito Coast with 99 men aboard a bark and two sloops, which he scuttled and then headed inland to attack the Spaniards. In alliance with 300 Darien Indians, he fell upon the Santa María stockade at the confluence of the Chucunaque and Tuira Rivers one dawn, massacring the defenders and sharing about 24 ounces of gold dust per man among his buccaneers, leaving "the other gross plunder to the Indians." More importantly, Harris seized a bark armed with four *pedreros,* or swivel guns, as well as eight large canoes, which he and his men used to reach the Pacific Ocean. Off that coast they took a trading bark laden with provisions and wine, which they then sailed to Isla del Rey and snapped up some pearling vessels. While prowling off Punta Chame just south of Panama City, a flotilla of five Spanish barks suddenly sortied, killing five of Harris's men in an all-day fight but eventually retiring in defeat.

The buccaneers veered westward for the Gulf of Nicoya (off present-day Costa Rica), intending to secure a larger craft and knowing this to be "a place where the Spaniards built their ships." Within sight of that coast, they came upon a ship at anchor on 3 August, which proved to be Charles Swan's *Cygnet,* of sixteen guns, 150 tons, but a relatively small and unhappy crew. Swan had originally entered the South Seas as a merchant trader, not a raider, but meeting with continual rebuffs from the Spaniards, his crew now wished to go a-roving.

Confronted with Harris's much more numerous freebooters, Swan finally acceded, else he would have "no one to sail the ship." Nonetheless, he insisted on exchanging part of his cargo for some of the buccaneers' Santa María gold, and that *Cygnet*'s owners receive a share in any prize money. Harris grudgingly agreed, after which all but one of his prize barks was set adrift, and they sailed together to rendezvous with John Cooke's 36-gun *Bachelor's Delight* off Isla de Plata (Ecuador).

Harris and Swan arrived there on 2 October to discover Cooke had died and been succeeded by Edward Davis, who now assumed general command of the flotilla. Between them they mustered close to 200 men, so on 20 October sailed for the South American mainland. Paita was assaulted the morning of 3 November 1684, but nothing much of value was found before the town was put to the torch. The Lobos Islands were visited next, followed by an abortive raid against Guayaquil in early December, which ended when the pirates' captive Indian guide escaped as they were approaching overland. A few small prizes were taken off that coast, but Harris and the other rovers realized they were too weak for greater enterprises and so headed northward for Panama in hopes of meeting other buccaneers crossing the isthmus. At the end of December they captured an *aviso* off Gallo Island bound for Callao, which revealed that the annual plate fleet had arrived at Portobelo on 28 November, and the Peruvian silver ships would soon arrive.

The buccaneers therefore established a blockade south of Panama in January 1685, where they were joined over the next few months by fresh contingents under Captains François Grogniet, Francis Townley, Jean Rose, Pierre le Picard, and a bark bearing about a dozen Englishmen separated from William Knight's expedition. Harris and his men were transferred into this latter vessel, and he was in command of it when a fleet of six Spanish men o' war suddenly emerged from a morning shower off Pacheca Island on 7 June 1685, catching the pirates by surprise. An indecisive engagement ensued, after which the buccaneer forces fell out among themselves and separated. Harris attached himself to Davis and in 1686 was still serving as his lieutenant off the South American coast.

*See also* aviso; Golden Island; Harris, Peter (fl. 1671–1680); Mosquito Coast; plate fleet; South Seas; Swan, Charles.

*References:* Bradley, *Lure; C.S.P., Amer. and W.I.,* Vol. XII; *Interesting Tracts.*

# Harris, thomas

## (fl. 1670-1671)

English buccaneer who participated in raids on Colombia, Nicaragua, and Panama.

In summer 1670, Harris served along with Captain Ludbury under the senior rover Laurens Prins, sailing on a peacetime expedition against the Spanish Main. In a singularly bold stroke, this flotilla headed up the Magdalena River (in present-day Colombia), attempting to reach the inland town of Mompós, 150 miles from the sea. This daring attempt was foiled by a fort that had been recently built on an island in that river, so the trio was obliged to venture westward in August to the Mosquito Coast, hoping to find better fortune there.

Ascending the San Juan River (despite the fort which had also been installed on that river, following Henry Morgan's raid of five years previously), Prins and his cohorts stole across the Lago de Nicaragua and surprised the city of Granada with only 170 men. According to a Spanish account, these pirates "made havoc and a thousand destructions," but because the city had been so recently victimized, their plunder only came to £20 per man.

A few weeks later, the flotilla was back in Port Royal, William Beeston noting in his journal for 19 October 1670 (O.S.), "Arrived the ships that had taken Grenada [*sic*], who were Captains Prince, Harris and Ludbury." Jamaica's Governor Sir Thomas Modyford mildly reproved the trio for attacking Spaniards without commissions but thought it prudent not "to press the matter too far in this juncture." Instead he ordered them to join Morgan's own expedition, which was gathering off Ile-à-Vache to attack Panama, "which they were very ready to do."

Harris incorporated his ship *Mary* into Morgan's fleet late that year and evidently participated in the subsequent captures of Providencia Island and Chagres, as well as the epic march overland through isthmian jungles in January 1671. The city was quickly captured and looted over the next four weeks, producing a disappointingly small booty because much of its wealth had been evacuated prior to the assault. He then returned to Port Royal in April 1671, along with Morgan aboard Joseph Bradley's *Mayflower,* Prins's *Pearl,* and John Morris's *Dolphin.*

*See also* Beeston, William; Modyford, Sir Thomas; Mosquito Coast; Prins, Laurens; Spanish Main.

*References:* Exquemelin; Gosse, *Who's Who;* Pope.

# Harvey, captain

## (fl. 1685)

Arrived at New London in 1685, accompanied by another pirate, Captain Veale; posed as an honest merchant, but being recognized, left in great haste.

*See also* Veale, Captain.

*Reference:* Gosse, *Who's Who.*

# HATSELL, CAPTAIN

## (FL. 1666-1668)

Buccaneer who served as an officer during Edward Mansfield's successful and daring night attack on the island of Providence (or Santa Catalina), when with only 200 men the fort was captured and the Spanish governor taken prisoner.

Captain Hatsell was left behind with 35 men to hold the island, while Mansfield sailed to the mainland with his captives, who had surrendered on condition that they would be granted safe conduct.

Hatsell may also have been the "Captain Hansel" who behaved so courageously at the taking of Portobelo two years later that a party of some 400 men in four ships chose him to be their admiral in an attempt on the town of Cumaná (in eastern Venezuela). This attack was a most complete failure, the pirates being driven off "with great loss and in great confusion." When the party arrived back at Jamaica, they found that the rest of Henry Morgan's men had returned before them, who "ceased not to mock and jeer at them for their ill success at Comana, after telling them: 'Let us see what money you brought from Comana, and if it be as good silver as that which we bring from Maracaibo.'"

*See also* Mansfield, Edward; Morgan, Sir Henry.

*References:* Earle, *Panamá;* Gosse, *Who's Who;* Pope.

# HENLEY, THOMAS

## (FL. 1683-1685)

English privateer who in 1683 sailed from Boston "bound for the Rack," afterward going to the Red Sea, where he plundered Arab and Malabar ships.

Two years later he was operating with a commission from Governor Robert Lilburne of the Bahamas and that same summer appeared before Bermuda with a prize, where the new governor, Richard Cony, was struggling to impose royal rule over the recalcitrant colonists. On 4 June 1685 (O.S.), Cony reported to London:

> Captain Henley, a privateer, lately arrived here in a Dutch ship and as is reported, landed £3,000 or £4,000 worth of Dutch goods. He was piloted in by one Zachariah Burrows, but the country [i.e., inhabitants] would not permit his ship to come under my command. I laid hold of Henley, however, and imprisoned him; but the country forced me to set him at liberty. My very Council and captains of militia, though all protesting that they would bring him under my command, yet would not, nor would the sheriff lay his broad arrow [i.e., the symbol of his royal stamp] on the goods he landed, that account might be given to the King in case the Dutch should redemand them.

On 28 May 1685 (O.S.), while all of this was transpiring, one Christopher Smith attested at Bermuda "that it was commonly reported at the Bahama Islands in April that Thomas Henley and Christopher Goffe had been proclaimed pirates at Jamaica." Confirmation soon followed, specifying that Henley had been proclaimed at Jamaica, while Goffe at New England.

The hard-pressed official was unable to detain either one and concluded his account with the words:

> It is the intention of the people to make this island a pirates' refuge. I expect two more pirates by what Henley said, and daily dread the capture or plunder of the country.

See also Goffe, Christopher; Lilburne, Robert.

References: C.S.P., Amer. and W.I., Vol. XII; Gosse, Who's Who.

# HEWETSON, THOMAS

## (FL. 1688-1690)

English commander who failed to establish a colony in Chile but fought well as a privateer in the West Indies.

Hewetson departed England with a small flotilla during 1688, intending to found a settlement on the Pacific coast of South America, but was unable to beat his way through the Strait of Magellan. Instead, he retreated to Tobago with his 50-gun flagship Lion and two other vessels, where he learned England's James II had been deposed in favor of William and Mary, and he then reached Barbados where one of his ships exploded at anchor toward the end of July 1689. Discouraged, and with most of his men having deserted, Hewetson sailed for home as escort for a merchant convoy, touching at Bermuda where he learned that the War of the League of Ausburg (King William's War) had broken out back in Europe. In cooperation with Bermuda's Governor Sir Robert Robinson, Hewetson was furnished with a commission dated 19 October 1689 and sufficient strength to bring Lion's strength up to "350 lusty men," causing him to decide to return to Antigua by the middle of the following month and offer his services against the French.

Governor Christopher Codrington promptly appointed Hewetson "commander-in-chief of all vessels fitted in the Leeward Islands," and when word arrived that the comte de Blénac had commenced attacks against the island of St. Kitts, Codrington retaliated by sending Hewetson with his three ships and two sloops to Marie Galante to "reduce it, securing the plunder for himself and his fellow adventurers." (Among the latter was William Kidd, commanding the 20-gun Blessed William of 80–90 men.) Hewetson made a successful descent against this French island on 30 December 1689 (O.S.), ransacking it over the next five days. Upon returning to Nevis, his squadron was hurried out again to rescue the squadron of Sir Thomas Thornhill, which had become cut off after assaulting the French colony on Saint Martin. Hewetson arrived off that island in late January 1690 to finds the English troops besieged ashore by five French warships under Jean-Baptiste Ducasse. The two squadrons exchanged broadsides throughout much of the day, until Ducasse withdrew at nightfall. Thornhill's men were rescued and restored to Nevis, after which Hewetson transferred to Barbados, where he was issued yet another commisssion by Governor Edwyn Stede on 11 April (O.S.) to protect that island as well.

Once reinforcements arrived from England, Hewetson apparently chartered Lion to the factor of the Spanish slave asiento and sailed away.

See also asiento; Blénac, Charles de Courbon, comte de; Ducasse, Jean-Baptiste.

References: Chapin; C.S.P., Amer. and W.I., Vol. XIII; Ritchie.

# HISPANIOLA

English name for the Antillean island today shared by the Dominican Republic and Haiti.

Christopher Columbus originally gave this name to the island, which he visited on his first trans-Atlantic voyage. Having encountered exotic new flora and fauna during his passage through the Bahamas and eastern Cuba, the explorer found its rugged coastline reassuring. According to his son, seeing that the new island was

> very large, and that its fields and trees are like those of Spain and that in a net that they had made the crew caught many fish like those of Spain—that is to say sole, skate, salmon, shad, dories, gilthead, conger, sardines and crabs—the admiral decided to give the island a name related to that of Spain; and so on Sunday 9 December [Saint Dominic or Santo Domingo's feast day] he called it *Isla Española* [literally "Spanish Island"].

With the passage of time, the Spaniards shortened this in conversation to *Española,* from which it passed into English in its phonetic equivalent, "Hispaniola."

# Hoar, john

## also Hore
### (fl. 1694-1695)

Irish privateer and brother-in-law to Richard Glover, both of whom operated in the West Indies and then turned pirate in the Far East.

Hoar first appeared before Newport, Rhode Island, in the early days of 1694 with his frigate *Dublin,* bearing a commission from Governor Sir William Beeston of Jamaica and a French prize called the *Saint Paul.* England then being involved in the War of the League of Augsburg (King William's War) against France, Hoar asked to have this prize lawfully condemned so he might change ships. As there was still no Admiralty court in the colony, the general assembly agreed on 7 January 1694 (O.S.) to approve such a measure, allowing their general council to act in such a capacity "until His Majesty's pleasure be further

known." *Saint Paul* was duly condemned and renamed *John and Rebecca* by Hoar. Some months later he sailed it south to New York, where he obtained yet another privateering commission from the pliant Governor Benjamin Fletcher, then departed Narragansett Bay in early 1695, apparently without clearance papers.

Hoar openly turned pirate by subsequently working his 100-man ship around the Cape of Good Hope and attacking neutral shipping in the Arabian Sea and Persian Gulf, finally capturing a 300-ton ship near Surat and retiring with it in February 1697 to the island of Saint Marie, off the east coast of Madagascar. Five months later the local natives fell upon the rovers, killing 30 and driving the rest to seek shelter at Fort Dauphin, the abandoned French settlement at the southeastern tip of that island. There their ship foundered, but Hoar's quartermaster Abraham Samuel—a former slave from the French West Indian island of Martinique—was proclaimed king by the local tribal queen, ruling under the title "Tolinor Rex" with a bodyguard of 20 of his old shipmates.

*See also* Beeston, William.
**References:** Chapin; Gosse, *Who's Who;* Ritchie.

# Hoces, esteban de
### (fl. 1665-1669)

Spanish *guardacosta* who operated out of La Guaira, the port of Caracas.

In conjunction with Captain Juan González Perales, De Hoces was designated to patrol the Spanish Main by the governor and captain-general of Venezuela, Admiral Félix Garci-González de León, knight of the Order of Santiago. Their *armadillas* made numerous captures, including the pirate ship

*Caballero Romano* (*sic;* French *Chevalier Romain* or "Equestrian?").

**See also** González Perales, Juan; Spanish Main.

**Reference:** Sucre.

# HOLMAN, WILLIAM
## (FL. 1694)

English privateer who was lying at Ferryland, Newfoundland, with his 16-gun letter of marque galley *William and Mary* in 1694 during the War of the League of Augsburg (King William's War), when news was received of an impending French attack. Holman encouraged the inhabitants to arm the forts with 30 guns taken from ships in the harbor, and when two French men o' war appeared on 1 August 1694 (O.S.), drove them off after a day-long fight. The Admiralty later gave Holman a medal and chain for this gallant service.

**See also** letter of marque.

**Reference:** Chapin.

# HOLMES, SIR ROBERT
## (1622-1692)

English admiral commissioned to expropriate "all wares, merchandises, etc., piratically taken on board in any part of America."

Holmes was born in Mallow, County Cork, Ireland, and served as a cavalier during the English civil war. After Charles I's execution, he went abroad with Prince Rupert's squadron and attached himself to James, duke of York. At the restoration of Charles II, Holmes entered the Royal Navy, his patron having become lord high admiral. He sailed to the Guinea coast in October 1660 to protect English trade and returned to England the following summer with "a great baboon" aboard. In the autumn of 1663, Holmes was appointed to HMS *Jersey,* 40 guns, to lead another peacetime expedition to the coast of Africa in support of the English slave factories competing with the Dutch. Although instructed to avoid hostilities, he was forced to take possession of several Dutch settlements.

Holmes then led his squadron across the Atlantic, ransacking the Dutch island of Sint Eustatius in passing, although not bothering to occupy it. Upon his return to England in 1664, he was detained in the Tower of London to answer Dutch protests regarding his conduct. In the meantime, Admiral Michiel de Ruyter sailed to Africa and reconquered the Dutch forts; he then crossed over into the West Indies and took many prizes. The Second Anglo-Dutch War resulted, much of the blame being leveled at Holmes, although at the inquest he showed that he had merely obeyed instructions.

Holmes fought with rare distinction at Lowestoft, the Four Days Fight, and St. James's Day, and in August 1666 burned between 150 and 160 Dutch East Indiamen at the Texel in what became known as "Holmes's Bonfire." He ended the war in 1667 with a knighthood and seat in Parliament, as well as appointment as admiral of Portsmouth and governor of the Isle of Wight. He became very wealthy, lavishly entertaining the king at his new mansion at Yarmouth. In early 1672, Holmes again commanded the English squadron that launched hostilities by being sent out to attack the homeward-bound Dutch Smyrna convoy off the Isle of Wight, thus inaugurating the Third Anglo-Dutch War.

After the cessation of these hostilities two years later, Holmes seldom went to sea again. In late August 1687 he was supposedly given "command of a squadron of ships sent to America for suppressing pirates," but it does not appear as if any such force actually set sail. Instead, Holmes delegated a man called Stephen Lynch to visit the West Indies in his place, with plenary powers to have pirates arrested and their goods impounded by local Crown authorities. This individual reached Jamaica in April 1688, where his powers were much resented, the Governor Duke of Albemarle observing: "Had he not been deputed by the King, I should have given him deserved correction." When James II was deposed at the end of that year in favor of William and Mary, Lynch found himself no longer welcome in the Caribbean and returned home.

Holmes's last venture occurred when Edward Davis and colleagues were deported to England from Virginia in 1690 to stand trial for piracy in the South Seas. Holmes impounded their money and petitioned to keep it, writing in August 1691: "The robberies of Daves [sic] and his crew were unparalleled, and I am sorry to hear that he is countenanced in England, when the gallows is too good a reward for him." Holmes promised to visit London "as soon as my health enabled me to leave Bath," but was evidently never able to do so, dying there on 18 November 1692 (O.S.) and being buried in Yarmouth church.

**References:** *C.S.P., Amer. and W.I.,* Vols. XII–XIII; *D.N.B.;* Piracy and Privateering; Shomette, *Raid.*

# HUIDOBRO, MATEO ALONSO DE

## (FL. 1663-1683)

Spanish naval officer who spent many years hunting pirates in the Caribbean.

The first mention of De Huidobro's name occurs in 1663, when he is listed as having lent 2,000 pesos to the Spanish Crown toward the construction of four new

galleons in Amsterdam for the Armada de Barlovento. As a reward for this contribution, De Huidobro was named captain of the new 572-ton flagship *San Felipe,* and early the following year was in Malaga recruiting crew members for the fleet. However, this armada did not actually depart for the New World until July 1667, nor did the flagship remain in the Caribbean any more than a few months before being ordered back to Spain. Consequently, De Huidobro transferred to the newly acquired armada frigate *Nuestra Señora de los Remedios* so as to be able to remain in the West Indies.

## CRUISES
## (1668-1669)

While lying at Havana in autumn 1668, word was received of an English attack on Trinidad, Cuba. De Huidobro was dispatched by Admiral Alonso de Campos to advise the Mexican viceroy and request reinforcements. Exiting Havana in September 1668 with his own frigate and the 50-ton fleet auxiliary *Nuestra Señora de la Soledad* (Our Lady of Solitude, better known as the *Marquesa* or "Marchioness"), De Huidobro sailed past west Cuba until his *Remedios* was wrecked in a storm "sixteen leagues" from Campeche.

Reaching Veracruz, De Huidobro found that the 218-ton frigate *San Luis* had been recently purchased for the armada by the Crown, and so he assumed command. Together with the *Marquesa* and almost 300 troops, he returned to Havana on 5 January 1669. Meanwhile, news had been received of another enemy attack on Portobelo, so Campos sortied with *Magdalena, San Luis,* and *Marquesa.* These three laid in a course for Puerto Rico, where it was learned a large freebooter gathering had recently been held at Ile-à-Vache. A false report of the French preparing to raid Santo Domingo was received from a Dutch merchantman encountered in the Mona Passage, so the Spaniards backtracked to that island on 25 March 1669 to reinforce its garrison. They were then correctly advised that more than a dozen buccaneer sail had passed by for the Spanish Main some weeks previously, and following in their wake, they heard from another Dutch merchantman that the raiders were already inside the Lago de Maracaibo.

## DEFEAT OFF MARACAIBO
### (1669)

The armada vessels stemmed the entrance by mid-April, discovering the flotilla of Henry Morgan still within, having landed his men to plunder the interior. The Spaniards reoccupied the fort guarding the approaches, then several days later lightened their warships and crossed over the bar. The armada had trapped the raiders within the laguna, but at dawn on 27 April were rushed by Morgan, who attacked Campos's *Magdalena* with a fireship. De Huidobro's *San Luis* had at first steered to help the flagship, but when he saw flames shoot up, turned toward the shelter of the fortress instead, hounded by three enemy privateers. Although managing to reach the safety of its guns, *San Luis* grounded on a sandbank with the falling tide, and De Huidobro ordered his 140-man crew to take all the weapons and provisions ashore to reinforce the garrison. Meanwhile, he and a small party set the frigate ablaze to prevent its falling into enemy hands. The buccaneers completed their sweep of the armada by capturing Diego del Barrio's *Marquesa* before slipping triumphantly past the fort and back out to sea.

The demoralized Spaniards bought a small *barco luengo* at Maracaibo and sailed back to Mexico with only 56 men, the rest having died or deserted. Campos blamed the *Marquesa*'s captain for the disaster, and Del

Barrio made the voyage in chains. After touching at Campeche for water, they arrived at Veracruz, where an official inquiry was convened on 12 August 1669 and decided to deport all the senior officers to Spain aboard that year's plate fleet to face a general court-martial. This eventually resulted in some guilty verdicts, but after a few years these were overturned, and each man resumed his career.

## LAGUNA DE TÉRMINOS CAMPAIGN
### (AUGUST 1673)

De Huidobro was then appointed *sargento mayor*, or garrison commander, for the city of Veracruz, from where he made several patrols against the English logwood-cutters in the Laguna de Términos. Following a particularly audacious raid by a small English vessel into Coatzacoalcos (Mexico), in which three native villages were ransacked and eight Indians carried off as hostages, the Viceroy Marqués de Mancera ordered De Huidobro to pursue these interlopers with a frigate and three *piraguas*. He overtook the corsairs near Santa Ana bar (Tabasco), forcing them to beach their vessel and set it ablaze before disappearing into the jungle.

Upon his return to Veracruz, further accounts of nuisance raids continued to arrive and two enemy ships were reported inside the Laguna de Términos. A second, larger enterprise was then mounted, with De Huidobro quitting Veracruz again on 14 August 1673 with a force of three frigates, a sloop, and 300 soldiers from the San Juan de Ulúa garrison.

This expedition arrived undetected off Xicalango Point (known as Beef Island to the English Baymen), where they were boldly approached by three *piraguas*. Belatedly realizing the danger, the *piraguas* suddenly veered around and fled into the

laguna spreading the alarm while De
Huidobro's men stormed ashore behind
them. One interloper was killed and several
wounded, abandoned huts and boats were
set ablaze, but the Spanish men o' war drew
too much water to pass over the bar. A
brigantine was seen heading deeper into the
lagoon, but De Huidobro had no other
choice but to continue up the coast toward
Campeche. En route he chased another
*piragua* manned by a mixed crew of
Englishmen, Frenchmen, and Indians, but
these escaped when a storm set in.

After visiting Campeche, De Huidobro
reversed his course back toward Veracruz,
and this time had the good fortune to
intercept the brigantine that had eluded him
outside the laguna with a Spanish prize. Its
Dutch captain, Jan Lucas, was carried back
into Veracruz along with his crew and prize
when De Huidobro returned there
triumphantly in late October 1673.

## PIRATE RAID
### (MAY 1683)

Ten years later, De Huidobro underwent a
much more terrible ordeal at the hands of
the buccaneers. The port of Veracruz had not
been attacked in more than a century, but at
three o'clock on the afternoon of 17 May
1683, two sails were seen approaching from
out at sea. De Huidobro was attending a
banquet along with Governor Luis de
Córdoba and the other city dignitaries in
anticipation of the appearance of that year's
plate fleet. Arriving vessels were traditionally
received offshore at the island fortress of San
Juan de Ulúa, so there was no immediate
call for De Huidobro's involvement; but
upon quitting the banquet hall more than
an hour later, the governor and his staff
were approached by Don Juan Morfa
(John Murphy), who expressed the fear
that this pair was behaving suspiciously
because they did not enter, despite having
a favorable wind.

De Huidobro seconded this opinion, even
getting into an argument with one of his
captains, who downplayed such apprehensions.
The arrogant young governor dismissed the
question entirely by presuming the ships to
be merchantmen from Caracas, who would
essay another attempt next morning at first
light. De Huidobro remained unconvinced
and at seven o'clock that evening was at the
city wharf when a messenger landed from San
Juan de Ulúa, reporting the island was being
placed on full alert. Governor de Córdoba
grudgingly followed suit, ordering Veracruz's
300 city troops into barracks, although he
did not alert the 400-man militia; worse, he
ignored the fact De Huidobro's regulars had
not received their monthly allotment of
powder and shot, as he was still unconvinced
of any pressing danger.

The two vessels were actually Spanish
prizes being piloted by the Dutch
freebooters Laurens de Graaf and Jan
Willems, who in turn were serving as
advance scouts for a much larger *flibustier*
formation over the horizon under the
"chevalier" de Grammont and Nikolaas
van Hoorn. These pirates circled back and
deposited 800 men near the city that night,
infiltrating it from its landward side under
cover of darkness. At four o'clock in the
morning, gunfire erupted throughout the
streets, and the Spanish garrison was caught
utterly by surprise. De Huidobro rushed to
the governor's palace, baton and sword in
hand, hoping to rally its guardhouse
company. These were almost without
ammunition, so De Huidobro bravely
ordered them to form up with cold steel
only, as twin columns of heavily armed
*flibustiers* under Grammont closed in,
firing murderous volleys. "*¡Ea!* sons," De
Huidobro bellowed above the din, "it
only remains for us to sell ourselves dearly
according to our obligations!" Moments later
he was struck and died before sunrise on
that fateful 18 May 1683.

**See also** Barlovento, Armada de; Campos y Espinosa, Alonso de; De Graaf, Laurens Cornelis Boudewijn; Grammont, "chevalier" de; Laguna de Términos; logwood; Morgan, Sir Henry; Murphy Fitzgerald, John; Van Hoorn, Nikolaas; Willems, Jan.

**References:** Earle, *Panamá;* Eugenio; Juárez; Marley, *Veracruz;* Sáiz; Torres; Weddle, *Spanish.*

# HUTT, GEORGE

ALSO HOUT
(FL. 1686)

English buccaneer captain who succeeded Francis Townley, when the latter was mortally wounded during a gallant fight against three Spanish galleons near Panama in 1686.

**References:** Gosse, *Who's Who.*

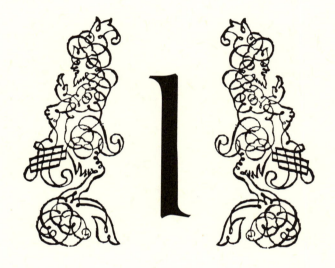

# INCH OF CANDLE

An expression used to denote—quite literally—the fixing of a time limit by marking a line on a lit candle.

This device was commonly employed at the auctioning of prize vessels at Port Royal, Jamaica. For example, the well-known privateer Captain Maurice Williams bought the Spanish prize *Abispa* (Wasp) for £120 in May 1659, "by inch of candle." In other words, after proclaiming the highest price, Williams waited while a candle was lit and scored an inch from the top; when no higher bid was received before the flame burned down past this mark, the ship legally became his.

***See also*** Williams, Maurice.
***References:*** Pawson, *Port Royal*.

# INDIGO

Blue dye produced from the genus *Indigofera (Leguminosae)* plants, a valuable crop for the West Indies and Spanish America during the seventeenth century.

Once harvested and refined, these plants produced a bluish-purple powder that was a coveted commercial dye in Europe, just as logwood was for tinting dark colors. The great permanence and rarity of these dyes meant they commanded a high price, and shipments therefore attracted the attention of privateers. Maurice Williams brought a Spanish prize loaded "with logwood, indigo and silver" into Port Royal, Jamaica on 23 November 1664 (O.S.), and fifteen years later John Coxon and consorts made an even more spectacular haul when they returned with 500 chests of indigo from a Spanish merchantman they had seized loading in the Bay of Honduras, leaving a like amount to rot on the beach.

***See also*** logwood.
***Reference:*** *Interesting Tracts*.

# IRELAND, JOHN

### (FL. 1695)

"A wicked and ill-disposed person," according to the royal warrant granted in King William III's name in 1695 to "our truly and dearly beloved Captain William Kidd" to seize him and other pirates who were doing mischief to the ships trading off the coast of North America.

***See also*** Kidd, William.
***Reference:*** Gosse, *Who's Who*.

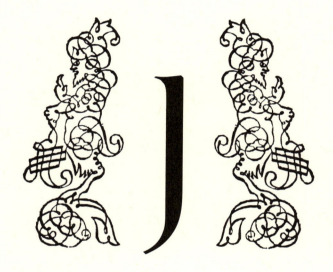

J

# JACKMAN, CAPTAIN

## (FL. 1664-1666)

Jamaican privateer who participated in raids against New Spain and Central America.

Late in 1664, Jackman joined John Morris, David Martien, Henry Morgan and Captain Freeman in mounting a small peacetime expedition against the Spaniards in the Gulf of Mexico. Strictly speaking, such ventures were illegal, as the new governor, Sir Thomas Modyford, had proclaimed as far back as 16 June 1664 (O.S.) "that for the future all acts of hostility against the Spaniards should cease." However, the privateers ignored this injunction, later arguing that "having been out 22 months" (i.e., since Commodore Christopher Myngs's sack of Campeche in early 1663), they knew nothing of the cessation of hostilities with the Spaniards, and so continued operating under two-year-old commissions from Governor Lord Windsor.

## MEXICAN RAID
### (SPRING 1665)

Morris and Martien were the apparent leaders of this venture, which mustered a few vessels and 200 men, departing Jamaica in January 1665. Rounding Yucatán, they moved gingerly down the gulf coast until arriving opposite Campeche, where one night in mid-February they cut out an 8-gun Spanish frigate from the roads. Sailing this prize past the Laguna de Términos, they anchored on 19 February before the tiny town of Santa María de la Frontera at the mouth of the Grijalva River. Some 110 to 120 buccaneers disembarked and traveled 50 miles upriver through marshy channels until coming within sight of the provincial capital of Villahermosa de Tabasco. At four o'clock on the morning of the 24 February they fell

upon the sleeping city, capturing most of the inhabitants in their beds. A general sack ensued, with booty and captives being loaded aboard a coaster in the river. The raiders then headed downriver, seizing a second coaster bearing flour.

Near the river mouth, they discovered their anchored ships had been captured during their absence by a Spanish naval patrol. Three Spanish frigates and 270 men had been sent out from Campeche by Lieutenant Governor Antonio Maldonado de Aldana, which sighted the interlopers' trio of vessels on 22 February and boarded them without a fight. A few Englishmen fled on a single vessel, abandoning their 10-gun flagship and 8-gun prize to the Spaniards. Seven buccaneers were left behind, revealing to their captors that "Captain Mauricio [sic; Morris] and David Martin [sic; Martien]" had led the bulk of the raiders inland.

Retreat cut off, the main body of freebooters released their remaining hostages and began moving westward with the two coasters, hoping to find another river channel whereby to escape. On the afternoon of 17 March they were overtaken by the Spanish guardacostas opposite Santa Ana Cay, this time sailing the privateers' former 10-gun flagship and 8-gun prize, having crewed these with 300 volunteer militia from Campeche. José Aldana, the Spanish commander, sent a messenger in a boat to call upon the buccaneers to surrender, but they pretended not to understand. When an interpreter approached shore the following morning, the buccaneers replied they would not give up without a fight, and the Spaniards reluctantly disembarked. They discovered the raiders had entrenched themselves behind a palisade reinforced with sandbags, bristling with seven small cannon. The Spanish force, mostly armed civilians, showed little stomach for an assault and were easily repelled without a single loss among the freebooters. The next day, 19 March, the Spanish ships were found conveniently run aground, thus allowing the raiders to exit undisturbed with their two coasters.

### CENTRAL AMERICAN CAMPAIGN
#### (SUMMER 1665)

Jackman and the other privateers proceeded northward along the coastline, capturing smaller boats and occasionally landing to obtain supplies. Off Sisal they looted a vessel laden with corn, whose crew was allegedly released with a message to the governor of Yucatán, vowing to return and lay waste the province. They then rounded Yucatán and traversed the Bay of Honduras as far south as Roatán, where they paused to take on water. Striking next at Trujillo [Honduras], they overran this port and seized a vessel from the roads before continuing to Cape Gracias a Dios and the Mosquito Coast. Native guides were hired, and the buccaneers continued southward to Monkey Point (Punta Mico, Nicaragua), where they hid their ships before heading up the San Juan River in lighter boats. They emerged in the great Lago de Nicaragua, crossing this by travelling at night and thus sneaking up on Granada, taking it by surprise on 29 June 1665 when they

> marched undescried into the center of the city, fired a volley, overturned 18 great guns in the Plaza de Armas, took the *sargento mayor* [or garrison commander's] house wherein were all their arms and ammunition, secured in the great church 300 of the best men prisoners, abundance of which were churchmen, plundered for 16 hours, discharged all the prisoners, sunk all the boats, and so came away.

Retracing their course across the lake, at the southeastern extremity "they took a vessel of 100 tons and an island as large as Barbados, called Lida [*sic*; Solentiname?], which they plundered."

Eventually they regained their anchored vessels, and by the end of August 1665, William Beeston noted in his journal at Port Royal:

> Captain Fackman [*sic*] and others arrived from the taking of the towns of Tabasco and Villahermosa, in the bay of Mexico, and although there had been peace with the Spaniards not long since proclaimed, yet the privateers went out and in, as if there had been an actual war without commission.

***See also*** Beeston, William; Huidobro, Mateo Alonso de; Laguna de Términos; logwood; Maldonado de Aldana, Antonio; Martien, David; Morgan, Sir Henry; Myngs, Sir Christopher.

***References:*** Cruikshank; Eugenio; *Interesting Tracts;* Juárez; Pope.

# JACOBS, CAPTAIN
#### (FL. 1690-1694)

Possibly a Dutch mercenary who served both the French and English in the Greater Antilles during the War of the League of Augsburg (King William's War).

Late in 1690, Governor Pierre-Paul Tarin de Cussy of Saint Domingue sent a flag-of-truce bark to Jamaica, hoping among other things to arrange the exchange of "Capitaine Jacob" and his crew, who had been captured after a pitched battle with two English armed barks, one of 10 guns and 75 men, the other of 8 guns and 65 men. De Cussy added Jacobs had been wounded three times in this engagement and that the English regarded him "with much admiration and held him in high esteem."

Perhaps for this reason they refused to part with their prisoner, for on 16 January

1694, during a period of particularly low English fortunes, the island council ruled that

since the men in the [two hired sloops] of war refuse to go to sea, ordered that Captain Jacobs have leave to go out in the vessel lately captured from the French, on terms of "no purchase, no pay," and that the tenths and fifteenths on captures be remitted to them.

**Reference:** *C.S.P., Amer. and W.I.,* Vol.XIV; Lugo.

# JAMES, WILLIAM

## (FL. 1660-1663)

English privateer named in the journal of Colonel Edward D'Oyley, governor of Jamaica, as having been issued a "let pass" for his frigate *America* or *American* on 16 May 1660 (O.S.).

Three years later, James was apparently still in command of this same vessel, which is described as having 6 guns and a crew of 70 men. He evidently sailed as part of Commodore Christopher Myngs's expedition against Campeche, exiting Port Royal with 11 other ships on 21 January 1663. However, James's frigate never reached its destination, for some months later it was reported by Captain Mitchell of the *Blessing*

that about 90 leagues this side of Campeche, he met three sail of the fleet, viz. Captain William James his ship, sunk in the sea by foul weather, who was the best ship in the fleet next the Admiral, and that many of their men in the fleet were dead.

Notwithstanding such setbacks, Myngs had succeeded in carrying Campeche, although James was apparently not present at this victory.

Legend has it James may have also been the privateer who "discovered" the commercial value of logwood for the Brethren of the Coast, thus inaugurating the poaching of this product in Mexico's Laguna de Términos and the Bay of Honduras. According to the story, a certain "Captain James carried off a Spanish prize full of logwood, being astonished upon reaching port at the high price his cargo fetched;" until then, he had supposedly "known so little of its real value that he had burned much of it for fuel on the voyage." When news of this spread, hundreds of poachers began descending on the Campeche coast, setting up logging camps and launching a protracted guerrilla struggle with the local Spaniards.

*See also* D'Oyley, Edward; Laguna de Términos; logwood; Mitchell, Captain; Myngs, Sir Christopher.

*References:* Cruikshank; Gosse, *Who's Who; Interesting Tracts;* Pawson, *Port Royal.*

# JOHNSON, GEORGE

## (FL. 1682-1683)

English privateer sent in pursuit of the renegade *Trompeuse.*

Early in 1682, the Huguenot sea captain Pierre LePain arrived at Port Royal, Jamaica, requesting citizenship because of the increasing religious intolerance in his native France. He brought with him the French royal frigate *Trompeuse* (Trickster), which—it being peacetime—he had hired for a commercial voyage to Cayenne. LePain's petition for English naturalization was granted, and he prepared to return *Trompeuse* to Europe by lading a valuable cargo of merchandise for Hamburg, then dispatching the ship across to the Bay of Honduras for an additional consignment of logwood. Unfortunately, *Trompeuse* was surprised there by some 120 pirates under the Frenchman Jean Hamlin, who seized it as their flagship.

When news of this reached Port Royal in early November 1682, Governor Sir Thomas Lynch commissioned George Johnson to set out and recapture the frigate. He was provided with a ship of 35 or 40 guns and a crew of 180 men, plus £100 and provisions, "all of which has been raised by merchants and traders here," Lynch later informed his superiors in London. The governor further instructed Johnson that upon encountering the *Trompeuse,* he was to try "to preserve the ship as the French king's property," although privately doubting whether this could be done, as the pirate vessel was reportedly "in bad condition and ready to sink, for they cannot get victuals to enable them to go and careen."

*See also* Hamlin, Jean; LePain, Pierre; logwood; Lynch, Sir Thomas.

*Refernces:* C.S.P., Amer. and W.I., Vol. XI.

# JOLLY ROGER

English euphemism for a pirate flag, believed derived from the French expression *joli rouge* (jolly red), itself an ironic reference to the blood-red ensigns flown in battle when no quarter was to be expected or given.

One example of this occurred after the sacking of Granada (Nicaragua) in May 1686, when a *flibustier* force under Captains François Grogniet, Jean Rose, and Francis Townsley began fighting their way back toward their anchored ships off the Pacific coast. At the town of Masaya they found 500 Spanish militia barring their path, and the chronicler Ravenau de Lussan noted:

They were flying the red flag, thus giving us to understand there would be no quar-

ter. Upon seeing this we hauled down our white [French] colors and exposed a red flag like theirs.

Such displays, however, were more usually made in conjunction with national standards; for instance, when Captain Edward Stanley's Royal Navy warship *Bonito,* with four guns, was attacked off the southern Cuban coast by a *guardacosta* in November 1684, the enemy galley bore down upon him "flying the Spanish flag with a red ensign." A similar account was given by a Spaniard who witnessed the "chevalier" de Grammont's *flibustiers* celebrating their capture of Veracruz in May 1683, cheering "the King of France with white flags and fleurs-de-lis and a red one."

Some privateer commanders apparently refined this practice even further by devising personal banners that they flew in addition to whatever national flag they were serving under. Thus veteran Spanish officers noticed that the mixed pirate force of Laurens de Graaf and Grammont marched out of devastated Veracruz led by "five French flags, four English, a green and a flowered one," the latter two presumably being individual ensigns. Red backgrounds seem to have been favored for such banners in the seventeenth century, as they added the appropriate touch of menace. Black backgrounds, with the skull and crossbones and other such variants, appear to have been a later development, dating from the early eighteenth century.

*See also* Grogniet, Capitaine; Lussan, Ravenau de.

*References:* Juárez; Gosse, *Who's Who;* Lussan; Marley, *Veracruz.*

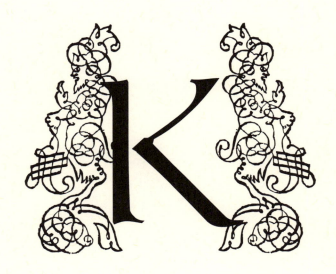

# KAPER

Dutch word for "privateer" or "corsair," a private man o' war outfitted with a legitimate commission to conduct hostilities.

Just as in English, the word *kaper* could be applied either to the privateers themselves or to the vessels in which they served. The word was usually transcribed as "caper" in either French or English; thus, the *London Gazette,* reporting from the United Provinces in February 1673, said that they were having difficulty recruiting men for the states' fleets because of competition from their own privateers. "These capers being so numerous, do make Middleburg and Flissingen so dead, and so unpeopled them of men, that it appears not how our Fleet can be manned," the report read.

**References:** Gehring; Shomette, *Raid.*

# KEELHAULING

Savage form of naval punishment, even for such a cruel age.

Perhaps the most graphic instance occurred at the Dutch colony of Sint Eustatius in June 1673, when the Zeeland squadron of Commodore Cornelis Evertsen (Kees the Devil) arrived to reconquer the island from the English. After securing the settlement following a brief firefight, Evertsen learned that during the occupation, three Dutch sailors had treacherously murdered the former governor of the outpost, Jan Symonsen de Buck. Determined to make an example of these men, the commodore ordered all three tried within the next few days, who were duly found guilty. The prisoners were then made to draw lots, as only one was to be hanged; the other two were condemned to be keelhauled, flogged, and marooned on a desert isle.

On execution day, all three were paraded to the gallows and had nooses placed around their necks—but only one was actually turned off to die. The remaining two were rowed out to the anchored flagship, where one by one they were hoisted out to dangle from their wrists at the tip of the mainyard. A weighted line was tied to their feet, the other end passed under the hull and run up to the opposite tip of the yardarm. An oil-soaked rag was tied over their mouths and noses to prevent drowning, after which each was dropped into the sea and the line hauled in; thus, each was tugged beneath the ship in suffocating agony, dragging over sharp barnacles, until he emerged barely conscious and upside-down on the far side of the vessel. This exercise was repeated three times for both men, after which the rest of their sentences were carried out.

With such officially sanctioned barbarity, pirates had little trouble devising fiendish tortures for their own victims, and indeed, themselves resorted to keelhauling on more than one occasion.

**See also** Evertsen de Jongste, Cornelis; maroon.

**Reference:** Shomette, *Raid.*

# KIDD, WILLIAM
## (c. 1645-1701)

Scottish rover and pirate hunter, who ironically became the most notorious pirate of them all.

Legend has it that Kidd was born at Greenock, Scotland, around 1645, the son of a Presbyterian minister. He first figured in official records in 1689, when he was an officer of a mixed crew anchored off Saint Christopher in the Leeward Islands. Learning of the outbreak of the War of the League of Augsburg (King William's War) back in Europe, Kidd and his English and

Dutch colleagues overpowered their French comrades and carried the 20-gun ship into Nevis. The vessel was renamed *Blessed William,* with Kidd himself either elected or appointed captain. Additional volunteers were raised to bring the crew to 80 to 90 privateersmen, after which it was incorporated into the small squadron that Captain Thomas Hewetson was to lead against the French.

A descent was made against Marie Galante on 30 December 1689 (O.S.), and the French island was ransacked over the next five days. Upon returning to Nevis, the squadron hurried out again to rescue Sir Thomas Thornhill's expedition, which had become cut off after attacking the French colony of Saint Martin. Hewetson and Kidd arrived in late January 1690 to find the English troops besieged ashore by five French warships under Jean-Baptiste Ducasse. The two squadrons exchanged broadsides throughout much of that day, until Ducasse withdrew at nightfall. Thornhill's men were rescued and restored to Nevis. Kidd was praised by Hewetson as a "mighty man" who fought as well as any he had ever seen. But his freebooters felt differently, muttering about Kidd's "ill behavior" and resentful at finding themselves involved in a line-of-battle engagement with scant booty to be won. When Kidd went ashore on 2 February 1690 (O.S.), a group of mutineers led by William Mason made off with *Blessed William* and £2,000 worth of Marie Galante loot.

Governor Christopher Codrington presented Kidd with a recently captured French vessel renamed *Antigua,* and after raising a new crew, he set off in search of his lost ship. *Blessed William* had been sailed to New York, where Kidd eventually went in pursuit. He arrived by March 1691, too late to overtake the mutineers (who had served briefly as New York privateers before departing for the Indian Ocean), but just as

royal rule was about to be restored to this city. The previous governor had been driven out when James II fled into exile in France and the new monarchs, William and Mary, had dispatched Colonel Henry Sloughter to assume this office, but he had not yet arrived. Meanwhile, an usurper government had entrenched itself in power under Jacob Leisler, and because Mason had served under this administration with *Blessed William,* Kidd sided with the royalist faction. He used *Antigua* to ferry arms and ammunition to the troops preparing to assault insurrectionist Fort James just as Sloughter arrived to carry the day for the Crown.

Kidd's loyalty was rewarded with £150 from the new provincial assembly, and he profited from the adjudication of the French prize *Saint Pierre,* which had been seized by *Blessed William* under one of Leisler's commissions. More importantly, Kidd married Sarah Bradley Cox Oort, who was recently widowed for the second time. Their marriage license was dated 16 May 1691 (O.S.), just days after John Oort died, leaving her a sizable estate. Kidd quickly sortied eleven days after his wedding to pursue a French privateer reportedly lurking off Block Island, Rhode Island. None was encountered, and he soon seems to have settled down in New York, selling property in 1693 on Dock Street and the next year moving into a fine house with his wife at 119–121 Pearl Street, as well as purchasing a pew in Trinity Church where the new Governor Benjamin Fletcher was also a congregant.

Kidd still maintained contact with his former calling, however, for on 27 May 1694 (O.S.) Captain John Evans of HMS *Richmond* noted in his log how Captain Kidd, a "privateer," left New York harbor in his brigantine; and shortly thereafter Kidd appeared as foreman of the jury which acquitted his friend Robert Livingston's ship *Orange* of trading with the French enemy on

Captain William Kidd on the deck of the frigate-galley *Adventure*, 1902
watercolor by Howard Pyle. Delaware Art Museum.

Notorious for his cruelty, French *flibustier* Jean-David Nau l'Olonnais, having cut the heart from a Spanish prisoner in the Honduran jungle, pushes it into the mouth of another victim. Exquemelin, *Buccaneers of America*. Library of Congress.

Sr HEN: MORGAN

*Part. 2. Page. 60.*

Portrait of the English buccaneer leader Sir Henry Morgan. Exquemelin, *Buccaneers of America*. Library of Congress.

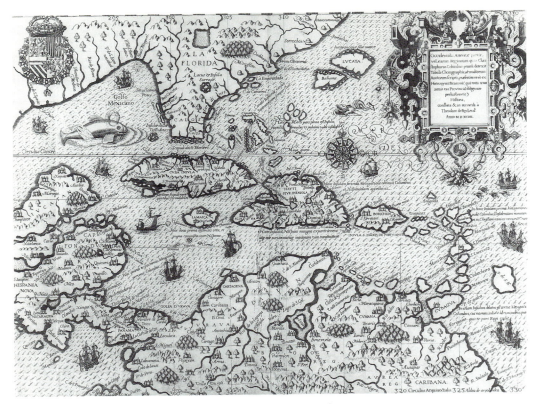

Map of the Caribbean, 1594. Theodore DeBry, *Historia Americae,* 1590–1634.
Library of Congress.

A seaborne assault on the Spanish Main. Exquemelin, *Buccaneers of America.*
Library of Congress.

FRANCIS LOLONOIS.

*Part. 2. Page. 1.*

The French *flibustier* Jean-David Nau l'Olonnais, also known as Francis l'Olonois and l'Ollonais the Cruel. Exquemelin, *Buccaneers of America*. Library of Congress.

French corsairs sack a Spanish settlement. Theodore DeBry, *Historia Americae,* 1590–1634. Library of Congress.

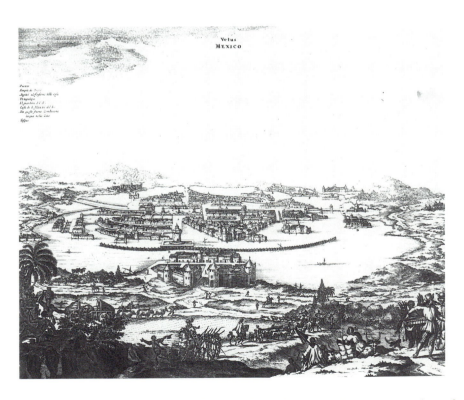

Imaginary view of Mexico City, capital of the wealthy viceroyalty of New Spain, surrounded by the central highlands and waters of Lake Tenochtitlán. Author's collection.

Pirates ride priests about the deck. Roman Catholic clergy could expect little but mistreatment at the hands of Protestant buccaneers. *The Pirates Own Book*, 1856. Library of Congress.

Cartagena on the Spanish Main, as envisioned by a Dutch artist in the 1670s, twenty years before it was devastated by the French assault of Pointis and Ducasse. Author's collection.

Frontispiece to a seventeenth-century Dutch book on the Americas, showing some of the exotic riches that drew adventurers to the New World. Author's collection.

English pirate Joseph Bannister, hanged from the yardarm of HMS *Drake* after his capture by Captain Thomas Sprague in 1687. *The Pirates Own Book,* 1856. Library of Congress.

Depiction of the Honduran port of Trujillo, raided by John Morris, David Martien, and Henry Morgan in 1665, as well as Jean-David Nau l'Olonnais three years later. Author's collection.

Imaginary view of the port of Acapulco during the latter half of the seventeeth century, with Mexican merchants arriving to meet the annual galleon from Manila. Author's collection.

*The Buccaneer Was a Picturesque Fellow,* 1905 oil painting by Howard Pyle.
Delaware Art Museum.

A Caribbean planter flogs a slave tied to a tree. Ill treatment of slaves and indentured servants drove some to escape to a life of buccaneering. Exquemelin, *Buccaneers of America*. Library of Congress.

*Extorting Tribute from the Citizens,* 1905 oil painting by Howard Pyle. Delaware
Art Museum.

*So the Treasure Was Divided*, 1905 oil painting by Howard Pyle. Delaware Art Museum.

French seamen defend their ship against a boarding party of eastern pirates. This woodcut illustrates the typical ferocity of these encounters. Library of Congress.

English buccaneer, chronicler, and circumnavigator William
Dampier. A. T. Story, *British Empire,* 1898. Library of Congress.

A confrontation aboard a pirate vessel. *The Pirates Own Book,* 1859.
Library of Congress.

French corsairs attack the port of Cartagena. Theodore DeBry, *Historia Americae,*
1590–1634. Library of Congress.

Hispaniola, despite overwhelming evidence to the contrary.

In 1695 Kidd sailed *Antigua* to London, England, ostensibly on a trading voyage, but also hoping to obtain a privateering commission. These were not readily available, so he and his fellow New York Scot, Livingston—who was also in London that summer—entered into a scheme with the influential earl of Bellomont, whereby such a patent might be granted. The earl was in need of money and about to be appointed governor of New England: he would therefore gather investors and secure a patent from his friends in the Whig government to allow Kidd to outfit a ship and hunt pirates in the Far East. These were making a rich haul in those unguarded waters, and through a special proviso Kidd would be allowed to carry his prizes back to New England for adjudication, where the investors need pay no royal duties.

A privateering commission was duly issued to Kidd on 11 December 1695 (O.S.) against the French, and a few days later the brand new frigate-galley *Adventure* of 34 guns, 287 tons, and 46 sweeps was bought at Deptford, with 70 seamen being recruited on the basis of "no purchase, no pay." A second patent was issued to Kidd on 26 January 1696 (O.S.), allowing him specifically to hunt for such rovers as Thomas Tew or William Mayes, a most unusual concession for any but a Royal Navy warship.

*Adventure* quit London at the end of February 1696 but did not get far. Kidd had acquired a reputation for conceited boastfulness because of his influential patrons, and instead of saluting a warship at the mouth of the Medway, had his men man the yards and "clap their backsides in unison" over some minor slight. *Adventure* was detained and Kidd's seamen taken aboard HMS *Duchess* of 90 guns, not being released to him until April, when he

continued his voyage. He captured a small French fishing boat while traversing the Atlantic, before putting into New York to recruit a full complement. Announcing a cruise to the Red Sea, he quickly had 152 men on board—some coming from as far away as Philadelphia—and on 6 September 1696 (O.S.) bid farewell to his wife and daughters to get under way.

*Adventure* reached Madeira by mid-October, then visited the Cape Verde Islands. Proceeding southward, he fell in unexpectedly with the Royal Navy squadron of Commodore Thomas Warren on 12 December 1696 (O.S.). Sailing together toward the Cape of Good Hope for a week, Kidd bragged of his prospects while fearful Warren would impress many of his seamen. When the ships became becalmed, Kidd availed himself of this opportunity to row out of sight. Warren entered the Cape Colony convinced Kidd intended to turn pirate, while the latter reached Madagascar on 27 January 1697 (O.S.).

These suspicions were confirmed only a few months later, when *Adventure* attacked the peaceful Mocha trading fleet in August, being driven off by the 36-gun English East Indiaman *Sceptre*. Other attacks followed, until at the end of January 1698 Kidd finally succeeded in capturing a rich prize, the 400-ton *Quedah Merchant* out of Surat, India. It took him a few weeks to dispose of the goods, and then several months before he touched at the pirate lair off Madagascar, where he beached and burnt *Adventure* before heading home in his prize.

In early April 1699 *Quedah Merchant* (or *Adventure's Prize*) made its landfall off Anguilla Island in the West Indies, and Kidd took on fresh provisions. He now learned his numerous clumsy attempts to capture merchantmen in the Far East had spread alarm throughout the East India Company, which had declared him a pirate and instituted a global manhunt. He sought asylum at Danish Saint Thomas, but this was denied, so he hovered off Mona Island between Puerto Rico and Santo Domingo, selling off his Indian wares while attempting to buy another ship. He eventually purchased the sloop *San Antonio* and abandoned his prize, creeping stealthily into lower Delaware Bay in early June, hoping to avoid attention. His wife and daughters met him off Oyster Pond Bay a few days later, and Kidd learned the full scope of his notoriety. Honest merchants felt he was a villainous pirate, while others believed he was returning fabulously wealthy, so he sent a message to his patron Bellomont—who had been installed as New England's governor little more than a year previously—to find out where he stood.

Bellomont returned a letter from Boston assuring Kidd of protection but hinting at unforeseen complications. *San Antonio* put into port, where Kidd met the Governor on the weekend, 1–2 July 1699 (O.S.). On Monday, the rover presented himself before the Massachusetts council, and although all seemed to go well at first, Kidd was arrested when he returned to testify on Thursday, 6 July, despite rushing into the chamber and calling out for Bellomont's assistance as the constables closed in on him. The governor did not intervene as Kidd was dragged away and jailed, nor when he was deported to England the following spring. After a sensational trial, Kidd was executed at Wapping, along the banks of the Thames, on 23 May 1701 (O.S.).

*See also* Ducasse, Jean-Baptiste; Hewetson, Thomas; Hispaniola; Mayes, William; purchase; Tew, Thomas.

*References: C.S.P., Amer. and W.I.,* Vol. XIII; Ritchie.

# KILDUIJVEL

Literally "kill-devil," a seventeenth-century Dutch euphemism for rum.

When the 30-gun *Schaeckerloo* of Captain Passchier de Witte captured a large English merchant yawl on 18 May 1673, outward bound from Barbados toward Maryland, De Witte gleefully reported to his superior, Commodore Cornelis Evertsen, that it was carrying a cargo of "*kilduijvel* and molasses."

*See also* Evertsen de Jongste, Cornelis.
*Reference:* Shomette, *Raid.*

# KNIGHT, WILLIAM

English privateer who roamed the South Seas.

In March 1685, Knight's bark with a dozen men aboard came from the coast 'of New Spain to join the pirate fleet of Edward Davis, François Grogniet, Charles Swan, and others off the coast of Panama. After an unsuccessful engagement with the Armada del Mar del Sur on 7 June, the buccaneers fell out among themselves along national lines. Knight at first sailed northwestward as a part of the English contingent, raiding Realejo and León (Nicaragua) in early August 1685, for little gain. Returning southward, he raided the Peruvian coast with Davis in July 1686, before parting from him after careening at the Juan Fernández Islands and "making the best of his way round Tierra del Fuego to the West Indies."

*See also* Mar del Sur, Armada del; Swan, Charles; South Seas.

*References:* Bradley, *Lure;* Dampier; Gosse, *Who's Who;* Lussan.

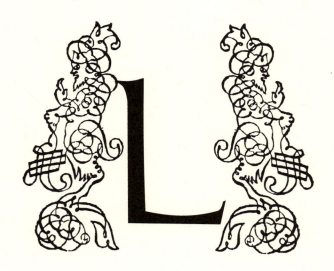

# LAARS

Dutch name for a "cat o' nine tails," a whip used to administer floggings aboard ships. The one used in meting out punishment aboard Cornelis Evertsen's squadron in 1673 was described as "a one-yard length of unraveled four-inch rope, tipped with felt."

**See also** Evertsen de Jongste, Cornelis.
**Reference:** Shomette, *Raid*.

# LA GARDE, CAPITAINE
## (FL. 1677-1684)

*Flibustier* who raided the Spanish Main.

In June 1677, during France's war against both Holland and Spain, La Garde led an attack on the Spanish American port of Santa Marta, seconded by the English freebooters John Coxon and William Barnes. This force surprised the town at dawn and took many captives, including its governor and bishop, holding them for ransom until a trio of Spanish warships of the recently reconstituted Armada de Barlovento appeared from Cartagena, with 500 soldiers to drive them off. The raiders then retired toward Port Royal, Jamaica, and on 28 July 1677 Sir Thomas Lynch noted:

Five or six French and English privateers lately come to Jamaica from taking Santa Marta, Barnes being one and Coxon expected every hour. On board the Governor and the Bishop, and Captain Legarde [sic] has promised to put them on shore. The plunder of the town was not great, money and broken plate [i.e., silver] about £20 a man.

Three days later Coxon entered, and personally escorted the Bishop Dr. Lucas Fernández y Piedrahita and a Spanish friar into the presence of the Jamaican Governor,

Lord Vaughan. This prelate was nobly housed, and royal officers sent aboard La Garde's flotilla to attempt "to procure the liberty of the [Spanish] Governor and others, but finding the privateers all drunk, it was impossible to persuade them to do anything by fair means." Vaughan therefore ordered the French to depart, advising Barnes and the Englishmen it was now against the law for them to serve under foreign colors. La Garde and his followers were "damnably enraged" at thus being deprived of their English consorts and sailed off without releasing their captives.

Seven years later, La Garde was listed as still commanding a *flibustier* vessel out of Saint Domingue, the ship *Subtille* of two guns and 30 men.

**See also** Barnes, William; Barlovento, Armada de; Coxon, John; Spanish Main; Vaughan, John.
**References:** *C.S.P., Amer. and W.I.*, Vol. X; Gosse, *Who's Who;* Juárez; Lugo; Sáiz; Torres.

# LABAT, JEAN-BAPTISTE
## (1663-1738)

French missionary who lived on Martinique in the seventeenth century and later wrote an interesting account of the West Indies.

Labat left his Jacobin monastery in Paris on 5 August 1693, traveling to La Rochelle to embark as a missionary for the Antilles. He took passage on the *flûte Loire,* a royal vessel of 40 gunports (but only mounting 20 cannon, to make room for more passengers and cargo), commanded by Capitaine de la Héronnière. This ship sailed as part of a 38-vessel convoy at the end of November, escorted by the 44-gun royal warship *Opiniâtre* (Obstinate), because the War of the League of Augsburg (King William's War) was then raging against England, Holland, and Spain. On the afternoon of 28 January 1694 the *Loire* approached Martinique alone, having become separated, when it was engaged by HMS *Chester,* 50 guns. The French had been able to beat off the attack despite their few cannon because the English initially believed they were encountering *Opiniâtre.* Darkness fell with *Loire* still bravely defending itself.

Labat disembarked on Martinique at three o'clock the following afternoon and two weeks later began his missionary work. An intelligent and inquisitive observer, he visited numerous West Indian islands during the next 12 years, making careful note of everything he encountered. Upon his return to France, he wrote a six-volume treatise entitled *Voyages aux Iles de l'Amérique,* which was published in Paris in 1722. It contains valuable information on Antillean life and frequently mentions the activities of such privateers as Capitaine Pinel and George Roche.

*See also* Pinel, Capitaine; Roche, George.
*Reference:* Labat.

# LAGUNA DE TÉRMINOS

Huge shallow bay on the gulf coast of Mexico that became a sanctuary for sea rovers during the seventeenth century.

Located amid steamy tropical mangroves, within easy striking distance of the Spanish towns of Campeche and Tabasco, the laguna became known as the "Bay of Campeche" to English interlopers. The first of these had infiltrated the area as early as 1658, shortly after the conquest of Jamaica. They found the region largely uninhabited, the Spaniards never having settled these torrid backwater inlets, which they believed to be unhealthy. But what really attracted foreign trespassers were the large stands of logwood trees, whose resin fetched handsome profits in Europe as a dye for tinting cloth. (Legend has it that the raiders first learned of its

profitability when a certain Captain James carried off a Spanish prize full of logwood and was later astonished at the price it commanded; until then, he had supposedly "known so little of its real value that he had burned much of it for fuel on the voyage.")

Soon poachers began streaming into the laguna, where hundreds established themselves ashore, eking out livings as loggers. They existed much the same as the *boucaniers* of Saint Domingue, except that rather than hunt wild cattle for their livelihood, they felled and hauled trees to the coast in anticipation of selling these to merchant traders who came to call. Like their French counterparts, they were rugged individualists content to live beyond government rule, supplementing their sporadic income with raids on the local Spaniards. William Dampier, who lived for two years among the English loggers during their heyday, wrote:

they often made sallies out in small parties amongst the nearest Indian towns, where they plundered and brought away the Indian women to serve them in their huts, and sent their husbands to be sold at Jamaica; besides they had not forgot their old drinking-bouts, and would still spend £30 or £40 at a sitting on board the ships that came hither from Jamaica, carousing and firing of guns three or four days together.

*See also* Dampier, William; James, William; logwood.
*References:* Dampier; Gerhard, *Southeast.*

# LANGFORD, ABRAHAM

## (FL. 1659-1682)

English naval officer who almost became governor of the *boucanier* stronghold of Petit Goâve.

Langford had been one of the first settlers at "Point Cagway," on Palisadoes spit at the entrance to Jamaica's main harbor, where he received a small plot of land in July 1659. He was apparently the "naval officer" of that station, a position that called for him to survey men o' war "and report upon their fitness for doing service in the island." In the overheated political climate of those early days, he had no shortage of enemies, being described in the council minutes for August 1661 as a "promoter of mutiny."

In January 1663, Langford accompanied Colonel Samuel Barry and privateer Captain Robert Blunden on a peaceable attempt to reduce the *boucaniers* of Tortuga Island to English rule. The new Jamaican governor, Lord Windsor, had brought out specific instructions from Whitehall, suggesting that an attempt be made to win over these rugged individualists, although without provoking a reaction from the French government. This trio sailed across to western Santo Domingo aboard Blunden's ship *Charles,* but upon arriving, learned that the *boucaniers* of Tortuga were hostile to any such notion and might well resist, at which Blunden flatly refused to proceed with the project. Instead, over Barry's objections, the delegates visited the mainland camp of Petit Goâve, where a different band of *boucaniers* was persuaded to acclaim Blunden their chieftain, and even raised an English flag.

A disapproving Barry returned to Jamaica several months later, while Langford sailed for England to petition Charles II to be appointed governor of "Tortuga and the coasts of Hispaniola." This was denied, the opinion on Langford at that time being that he

speaks no French, nor does he understand it; he is a man of no wisdom, his interest in Jamaica and person is despicable, his fortune forlorn, his honesty questionable. Fears lest all his contrivance amounts to no more than a desire to

repay out of the King's purse debts he has contracted by his debonair life and defrauding, as 'tis said, his principals. Denies not he is a good seaman and skilled in those parts, but so opiniative he will boast of much more than he knows.

His dreams of advancement dashed, Langford sank back into relative obscurity. He apparently returned to the West Indies, remaining in minor postings for the next decade-and-a-half. On 28 August 1682 (O.S.) he again petitioned the king, explaining that being clerk of the navy office at Barbados, he had deputized his son and now wished him to succeed "after his own death." Evidently in weak health, Langford died before anything could be resolved. A rather tantalizing note appended to his petition said the king would "remember him if he be told this was the man who prosecuted him with the Guaicum powder."

***See also*** Blunden, Robert; Cagway; Hispaniola; Windsor, Thomas.

***References:*** *C.S.P., Amer. and W.I.,* Vol. XI; Pawson, *Port Royal;* Pope.

# Laques, captain
## (FL. 1659)

Privateer captain mentioned in the journal of Colonel Edward D'Oyley, governor of Jamaica, as having been issued a "let pass" for his bark on 31 December 1659 (O.S.).

***See also*** D'Oyley, Edward.

***Reference:*** Pawson, *Port Royal.*

# Lartigue
## (FL. 1696)

French rover who is described in a document dated 22 June 1696 as a "*flibustier* of Béarn," then residing at Mont Carmel

(Basse Terre), on the West Indian island of Guadeloupe. Nothing is known about his privateering activities.

*Reference:* Goddet-Langlois.

# Laurens, Pieter

### (FL. 1693-1694)

Dutch privateer who operated with an English commission out of Rhode Island during the War of the League of Augsburg (King William's War), under the Anglicized name "Peter Lawrence."

In summer 1693, following the capture of John Godfrey's sloop off that coast, Governor John Easton authorized Laurens to sortie with his brigantine and engage the enemy raider. Laurens failed to come up with the French vessel but did chase it away before returning to Newport. He was granted another commission more than a year later by Deputy Governor John Greene, Jr., with which he captured two French fishing boats off the Banks. His greatest success would come in Queen Anne's War.

*Reference:* Chapin.

# Layseca y Alvarado, Antonio de, Conde de la Laguna de Términos

### (1638-1688)

Spanish naval officer who later became governor of Yucatán.

Layseca was born in Madrid on 16 January 1638, the son of one of King Philip IV's royal secretaries. Little is known about his early career, although he apparently saw his first service in the Americas at a very young age, in 1650. Thirteen years later he

made a loan to the Spanish Crown toward the construction of four new warships in Amsterdam, for the Armada de Barlovento, a contribution that won him appointment as one of these vessels' future captains. By the time this armada sailed from Seville for the New World in July 1667, Layseca was serving as *gobernador de tercio,* or third-in-command, of the of the entire force, aboard his 412-ton *gobierno* called *Magdalena.* This vessel and the armada flagship both transported a large quantity of *azogue,* or quicksilver, for the Mexican mines, and after reaching Puerto Rico on 27 August 1667, proceeded to Veracruz together while the other three men o' war swept the coasts of Santo Domingo and Cuba under *almirante,* or second-in-command, Alonso de Campos. The armada then reassembled at Havana in February 1668 before patrolling through the Antilles toward Caracas and returning to what was supposed to become its permanent home base of San Juan, Puerto Rico. Judging these port facilities inadequate, though, they instead transferred to Havana for repairs.

Shortly thereafter, the flagship and vice-flag were recalled to Spain for the renewed war against France. *Magdalena* and two smaller frigates were to remain at Santo Domingo, reinforced by local auxiliaries. This order reached the armada when it was once again lying at Puerto Rico, and its *capitán general,* or commander-in-chief, Augustín de Diústegui immediately set sail for Veracruz, to load a shipment of the King's bullion before returning to Spain. Campos and the three smaller ships hovered off Cuba's Cape San Antonio, inspecting passing vessels before putting into Havana. While there, Diústegui touched at that port and made his final dispositions before relinquishing command of the armada. Layseca was promoted *almirante* over Diústegui's objections and as such must have accompanied Campos when *Magdalena, San Luis,* and *Marquesa* sortied to counter enemy activities.

## MARACAIBO CAMPAIGN
### (SPRING 1669)

The trio first laid in a course for Puerto Rico, where it was learned a large freebooter gathering had recently been held at Ile-à-Vache. The men o' war then reached Santo Domingo on 25 March 1669, where they learned more than a dozen buccaneer sail had passed by for the Spanish Main some weeks previously and so followed in their wake. The Spanish warships stemmed the entrance to the Laguna de Maracaibo by mid-April, discovering the flotilla of Henry Morgan inside, whose men had landed to plunder the interior. At dawn on 27 April 1669 the Spaniards were rushed by Morgan, who destroyed *Magdalena* and Mateo Alonso de Huidobro's *San Luis* while capturing the *Marquesa*. The defeated Spaniards sailed a small *barco luengo* back to Mexico with only 56 men, the rest having died or deserted. After touching at Campeche for water, they arrived at Veracruz, where an official inquiry was convened on 12 August 1669, and decided to deport all the senior officers to Spain to stand trial. The subsequent courts-martial eventually resulted in some guilty verdicts, but after a few years these were overturned and each man resumed his career. Campos became governor of Puerto Rico in October 1674, and two years later Layseca was appointed *almirante* of a new quintet of warships destined to replace the shattered armada.

While lying at Cadiz preparing to depart, Layseca was then promoted to a five-year term as governor of the Mexican province of Yucatán, by a *real cédula* dated 12 November 1676 and which reached him before the ships had sailed. He therefore transferred to the 450-ton armada flagship *San José, Santa Rosa María y San Pedro de Alcántara* as a passenger, which was also transporting the governor-designate of Venezuela, Francisco de Alberró, Knight of the Order of Santiago, to his own destination. This vessel quit Cadiz

early the following year and deposited De Alberró at Caracas on 6 July 1677. After a lengthy layover, *San José* at last stirred forth from Caracas in October of that year, touching briefly at Santo Domingo before depositing Layseca at Campeche on 30 November 1677. He arrived in the capital of Mérida de Yucatán on 18 December to assume office.

## CAMPECHE ASSAULT
### (SUMMER 1678)

A scant few months later, the province's principal port was seized by pirates. An hour before daybreak on Sunday, 10 July 1678, a large group of people appeared at one of Campeche's small landward gates, answered the sentinel's challenge, and were allowed to enter. Rather than native worshipers come to early morning church services, however (as the sentry had thought), these were actually 160 buccaneers under Captains George Spurre and Edward Neville, come to plunder. The attackers advanced swiftly through the streets, and once in front of the lieutenant governor's residence, "with a great shout fired a heavy volley." The garrison was taken utterly by surprise, and virtually every prominent citizen captured. These were terrified into paying ransoms, and their buildings ransacked. Two sloops and eight *piraguas* appeared from out at sea, and the freebooters remained in possession of the town until evening on Tuesday, 12 July, when they began to withdraw with their loot. The raiders additionally carried off three craft and 250 black, mulatto and Indian townspeople to sell as slaves.

Layseca's response had been slow, as he did not arrive with a relief column until long after the enemy had disappeared. This led to angry recriminations being forwarded to Mexico City, accusing the governor of incompetence and other charges. A special prosecutor, or *visitador,* was sent out to investigate, who died en route, so it was not until 20 February 1679 that a replacement could arrive and suspend Layseca from office. These inquiries lasted a year, resulting in exoneration and restitution to his post as governor; but Layseca was anxious to regain his reputation as well, so he promptly visited Campeche and delegated the veteran Captain Felipe de la Barrera y Villegas to begin sweeps against the English logwood-cutters in the Laguna de Términos.

### SPANISH COUNTEROFFENSIVE
### (SPRING 1680)

De la Barrera sailed with a small flotilla of *piraguas* and on 6 February 1680 took some prizes. Bolstered by this success, his second expedition consisted of a *barco luengo,* two *piraguas,* and 115 men, which netted a 24-gun merchantman. Delighted, Layseca appointed him *teniente de capitán general* (lieutenant commander-in-chief) for Campeche on 12 April and helped prepare a third raid. The 24-gun prize was reinforced with two brigantines and six *piraguas,* plus more than 500 troops—200 mulatto militia from Mérida, 70 regulars and 16 gunners from the Campeche garrison, and another 240 volunteers, including the corsair captains Pedro de Castro and Juan Corso—who burst into the laguna on 17 April. More than 38 craft of all sizes were seized, along with 163 Baymen and numerous Spanish hostages and slaves. De la Barrera also learned a force of 240 buccaneers had departed in seven vessels to waylay the annual cocoa harvest of Tabasco, so he sent a detachment in their pursuit. His prisoners and prizes were sent triumphantly into Campeche, but De la Barrera himself did not return. Ironically, he had become separated from his expedition and fell into the hands of English stragglers, who bore him off as a captive.

Layseca of course was unfazed by the loss of his champion, instead busily writing to his superiors in Mexico City and Spain to claim that the Laguna de Términos had at last been cleared of foreign interlopers. This was not entirely true, but the Baymen had certainly been dealt a major blow, and the governor followed up his advantage by maintaining regular patrols into the region with *guardacostas* such as Baltasar Navarro. When Layseca's term expired in summer 1683, he returned to Spain and three years later was ennobled with the title "Count of the Laguna de Términos" in honor of his services. He then died in Seville two years later, being succeeded in the title by his son Félix Francisco, product of a union with Josefa de Alberró y Cangas.

***See also*** *azogue; barco luengo;* Barlovento, Armada de; Barrera y Villegas, Felipe de la; Neville, Edward; Spurre, George.

***References:*** Marley, *Pirates;* Rubio, *Jurisdicciones* and *Ocupación;* Sucre; Torres.

# LE GOLIF, LOUIS-ADHÉMAR-TIMOTHÉE

Also known as "Borgnefesse." Fictional French corsair who supposedly operated out of Saint Domingue during the 1660s–1680s, later writing a lurid account of these adventures. His manuscript was allegedly discovered among the burned remains of Saint Malo's public records in August 1944, following the German retreat after the D-Day invasion. But it is merely a fabricated document, a forgery based upon plagiarized sources.

# LE SAGE, FRANÇOIS
### (FL. 1684)

French *flibustier* captain listed in an official government document of 1684 as being in command of the ship *Tigre,* of 30 guns and 130 men, at Saint Domingue.

Le Sage may have been a former lieutenant or confederate of Laurens de Graaf, as the *Tigre* had been the latter's flagship until the *Dauphine (Princess,* more commonly known as *Francesa)* was taken from the Spaniards in autumn 1682.

Le Sage was also mentioned in a letter written by Governor Sir Thomas Lynch of Jamaica, dated 25 August 1684 and addressed to De Graaf. After De Graaf freed a small English merchantman captured and being carried into Cuba by the Spanish, the governor wrote to thank the pirate admiral for his kindness. He then added, "François Le Sage behaves very differently, for he has frequently injured and insulted our ships, and has by present report 60 pirates on board his ship taken from *La Trompeuse* [Trickster]." This latter vessel had looted numerous English merchantmen during a ten-month rampage under Jean Hamlin before being destroyed in August 1683 at anchor at Saint Thomas in the Danish Virgin Islands. Virtually all the pirate crew had escaped ashore and were still being sought by the English.

*See also* De Graaf, Laurens Cornelis Boudewijn; Hamlin, Jean.

*References: C.S.P., Amer. and W.I.,* Vol. XI; Gosse, *Who's Who;* Lugo.

# LEAGUE

Measurement of distance, roughly equivalent to three miles.

In the seventeenth century, English nautical leagues were gauged at 20 to a degree of latitude, roughly equivalent to 6,000 total yards. Each league was further subdivided into three nautical miles. The Spaniards used the same measurements at sea (5.57 kilometers), although on land a *legua* of 17.5 to a degree was sometimes employed, equivalent to 6.35 kilometers.

*Reference:* Howse.

# LECAT, JELLES DE

### (FL. 1668-1672)

Dutch freebooter who served both the English and Spanish.

De Lecat's unusual first name probably indicates a Frisian origin; it was often garbled in official records of his day as "Yallahs," "Yelles," or "Yellowes" by the English and "Hels" or "Ycles" by the Spaniards. The first notice of his activities occurred shortly after the French raider Jean-David Nau l'Olonnais reached Jamaica in 1668, bringing in an 80-ton, 12-gun Spanish brigantine. This was sold and Rok Brasiliano was installed as its captain with De Lecat as first mate. They cruised to Cartagena and Portobelo on the Spanish Main, capturing another Spanish brigantine before returning to Port Royal, where Brasiliano took command of the new vessel while De Lecat remained aboard the old one.

### LAGUNA DE TÉRMINOS CAMPAIGN
### (1669)

The two brigantines then ventured into the Gulf of Mexico in the spring of 1669 in the company of Joseph Bradley's privateer frigate to operate around the Laguna de Términos. Plunder proving scarce, De Lecat began loading logwood, while Bradley and Brasiliano blockaded Campeche. The Spaniards finally sortied with three armed ships on 18 December 1669, chasing the rovers away. A norther wrecked Brasiliano on the Yucatán peninsula, from where he was rescued by De Lecat, who transferred him to Bradley's frigate for return to Jamaica. Soon after, De Lecat and his mate Jan Erasmus Reyning seized a Spanish merchantman, which they renamed *Seviliaen,* scuttling the brigantine to sail this prize back to Port Royal.

Upon arriving, they found the English colony in an uproar because of the nuisance raids of the Spanish privateer Manoel Rivero Pardal. In August 1670 they sailed as part of Morgan's retaliatory strike against Panama, pausing at Ile-à-Vache for supplies and reinforcements. From there the corsair fleet descended on Providencia Island, overwhelming its tiny Spanish garrison. Morgan then sent Bradley ahead to seize San Lorenzo castle at the mouth of the Chagres River as a base camp for the forthcoming attack on Panama. De Lecat, Reyning, and Brasiliano were all part of this advance force, which disembarked into heavy opposition, but finally carried the fort in a bloody assault in which the Spanish defenders were massacred and Bradley was fatally wounded.

## SACK OF PANAMA
### (1670-1671)

De Lecat then took part in Morgan's epic march across the isthmus where, despite hunger, disease, and repeated jungle ambushes, the freebooters fought their way into Panama and looted the city for a month. Retiring to the Atlantic coast, they were disappointed at the subsequent division of spoils, feeling that Morgan had cheated them by making off with the lion's share. Sailing in his wake toward Jamaica, De Lecat and Reyning had a brush with the Cartagena coast guard vessel *Santa Cruz* and another Spanish vessel before gaining Montego Bay, where Reyning disembarked. He found the political climate greatly altered. The new governor, Sir Thomas Lynch, arrived on 1 July 1671 (O.S.) with the warships *Assistance* and *Welcome* to arrest his predecessor and revoke all anti-Spanish privateering commissions. Reyning was asked to bring in *Seviliaen,* but when he met up with De Lecat at their prearranged rendezvous off the Caymans, they simply sailed away together to Cuba. There they rustled cattle until a trio of Spanish warships

exiting Havana prompted them to cross the Gulf of Mexico to their old hunting grounds.

Immediately upon reaching the Mexican coast, they seized a small Spanish coast guard vessel, De Lecat assuming command while Reyning captained the *Seviliaen*. Shortly thereafter, HMS *Assistance* hove into view, having been detached under William Beeston to bring in rogue privateers. De Lecat and Reyning withdrew close inshore, beyond the reach of their powerful antagonist, so the English sailed to nearby Campeche to hire shallow-draft vessels to cut them out of their anchorage. The wily Dutchmen frustrated this scheme by following the frigate into the Spanish port, whose neutrality offered protection, until the Royal Navy grew tired of the game and left.

## SPANISH SERVICE
### (1671-1672)

Realizing how risky it was to continue prowling the Caribbean, De Lecat and Reyning purged their crews of English seamen, marooning these on the island of Tris (where they were eventually rescued by the former privateer *Lilly* in January 1672). Meanwhile, the two Dutchmen struck a deal with the Campeche authorities and were issued Spanish commissions. The Spaniards, desperate to stem the foreign incursions into that region but without funds for a defense, overlooked the rovers' checkered past because they were willing to serve for prize money alone. Because they were being hunted by the English, De Lecat and Reyning agreed to these terms and further cemented the deal by beginning indoctrination in the Catholic faith.

On their first patrol into the Laguna de Términos, they captured four English vessels, auctioning these off at Campeche. Soon a routine developed whereby De Lecat took care of the rough-and-tumble aspects of coast guard duty, while Reyning remained in port attending to business. Within a few months they seized 32 prizes, and at Jamaica the logwood trade declined because of fears of "Captain Yellowes."

On 28 April 1672, while De Lecat was patrolling in a captured sloop, Reyning exited Campeche with the *Seviliaen* to transport retiring governor Fernando Francisco de Escobedo to Tabasco. Reyning contracted a rich cargo of cacao and logwood from that port, departing Tabasco on 18 July. He reached Veracruz five days later, where his ship was briefly impounded because of irregularities regarding its ownership. While waiting to be released, he learned from the Spanish slaver and privateer Francisco Galesio that war had broken out back in Europe between England, France, and Holland. Thus, once *Seviliaen* was cleared in late August 1672, Reyning hurried back to Campeche in ballast to pay off his Spanish hands and reassemble his Dutch crew. The *Seviliaen* was careened, and Reyning hoped De Lecat would rejoin him, but Reyning eventually left Mexico without him. Nothing more is known about De Lecat's activities.

*See also* Beeston, William; Bradley, Joseph; careen; Laguna de Términos; logwood; maroon; Reyning, Jan Erasmus; Rivero Pardal, Manoel; Spanish Main.

*References: C.S.P., Amer. and W.I.;* Vrijman; Weddle, *Spanish.*

# LENHAM, GEORGE

(FL. 1687)

English privateer and pirate hunter.

In autumn 1687, Lenham sailed to New Providence in the Bahamas with a special peacetime commission from Lieutenant Governor Hender Molesworth of Jamaica to seek out pirates. This patrol had been prompted by news of Thomas Woollerly illegally disposing his booty at those islands.

When Lenham arrived, he learned of another band of pirates "who had burnt their ship and raised a fort of eight guns on a neighboring island for their security." In the words of Molesworth's report, dated 7 December 1687 (O.S.):

> He [Lenham] accordingly sailed thither, beat them out of it and brought off the men with their goods, and three or four Portuguese negroes who were the only witnesses that could be produced against them. It appeared from their account that they had taken a Portuguese ship off the coast of Brazil, and on this evidence the men were condemned. Though pardon had been promised, not one of them singly would make the least confession. At last the pardon was offered to all, when it appeared that they belonged to three sloops which left Carolina in company, with the resolution to take some good ship and sail with her to the South Seas. At last they got a Dutch vessel of good force, with which they took another and sailed away south, but were beaten back by foul weather at Magellan's Strait, and forced into [New] Providence. There they burnt their ship (as Woollerly had done before them) and hearing of the proclamation for pardon of pirates, were intending to go to New England. Their spoil was condemned, though it was of little value . . .

Almost five months later, the citizens of the Bahamas complained to the Council of Jamaica that Lenham and Royal Navy Captain Thomas Spragge had plundered their houses during this operation, which both commanders denied, attributing this charge to the islanders' well-known sympathy for such rovers.

*See also* South Seas.
*Reference: C.S.P., Amer. and W.I.,* Vol. XII.

# LePain, Pierre

### (FL. 1682-1684)

Huguenot sea captain who carried a French royal frigate into Port Royal, Jamaica, in a misguided attempt to acquire English citizenship.

Late in January 1682, LePain appeared before Acting Governor Sir Henry Morgan and the Council of Jamaica, presenting a petition that described "the inhuman treatment of the Protestants in France, of which he is one," and asking to settle in Jamaica. His vessel was the royal frigate *Trompeuse* (Trickster), which LePain had hired from the peacetime French navy "at 500 francs a month," for a commercial venture to Cayenne. Aware of increasing anti-Huguenot sentiments in France, where Protestants were being forced to convert to Catholicism, the council "unanimously resolved that he should be received into the king's protection and naturalized, on his engaging to use his best endeavors to return his ship to the French king."

This latter point proved LePain's undoing, for three months later France's ambassador complained to Charles II that the captain had "disposed of the ship and cargo," rather than return these. An order was issued in London during the summer of 1682 for the arrest of "Peter Paine," as he was now styled, which was enacted at the end of October by the new Jamaican governor, Sir Thomas Lynch. Unfortunately, the *Trompeuse*'s cargo of sugar and wine had already been sold off and the proceeds dispersed, while the vessel itself had been "sent to the Bay of Honduras to load logwood" for a voyage to Hamburg. However, it had been captured by a band of 120 "desperate rogues" under Jean Hamlin, who turned it into a formidable pirate vessel. Captain George Johnson and other privateers were sent out to recapture it, while the unfortunate LePain was held over and stripped

of his new English citizenship in late October 1683, being ordered deported to Petit Goâve.

**See also** Hamlin, Jean; Johnson, George; logwood.

**References:** *C.S.P., Amer. and W.I.,* Vol.XI; Gosse, *Who's Who.*

# Lepene, Jacques

### (FL. 1659)

French *flibustier* who in May 1659 bought the prize *Nieuwe Tuin* (New Garden) of Flushing for £300 at Port Royal, Jamaica, along with its cargo of 110 hides and ten barrels of rosin.

Lepene renamed the ship *Bonaventure* and sold its cargo back to the "state" (i.e., the English government) at £3 per barrel, for which he was paid in cacao nuts. In late September (17 September 1659 O.S.) he departed, armed with a privateering commission issued by the English governor, Colonel Edward D'Oyley.

**See also** D'Oyley, Edward.
**Reference:** Pawson, *Port Royal.*

# Leroux, Jean

### ALSO Le Roux
### (FL. 1692-1693)

French privateer captured near New York City.

Leroux, raised a Huguenot, or French Protestant, emigrated to New York and became a naturalized English citizen in spring 1692, presumably to escape religious persecution by his Catholic compatriots. Master of a coastal trading sloop, he made a voyage to Boston during which he allegedly sank his vessel "and ran away with £600 or £700 in money," for which he was imprisoned. Breaking out of Boston's jail, he contrived to escape to Canada with some

French prisoners (the War of the League of Augsburg or King William's War, then being in its fourth year). Leroux crossed the Atlantic to France and claimed to have been interviewed in February 1693 by Jean Gabaret, "lieutenant general of the French forces by sea," as to a potential descent on New York by ten men o' war and six fireships, which he discouraged despite being offered the position of pilot.

Instead, Leroux quit La Rochelle in July 1693 in command of a privateer bark of 4 guns and 35 men, arriving off the coast of New England, where he seized a Boston ketch and on 16 October a Rhode Island sloop. Shortly thereafter he anchored his bark on the north side of Nassau Island and led a landing party ashore "to take his wife and [five] children on board." Leroux's group was discovered and captured, and a vessel sent out after his bark in the Sound. This bark easily outsailed its pursuer, but the captain remained in English hands, being kept "close prisoner till the king's pleasure is known." Several of those defrauded by Leroux's earlier Boston voyage called for his immediate execution, but a month-and-a-half later, passions had cooled sufficiently for the city council to order "John Reaux [sic] to be released from irons and lodged in New York jail."

The following spring, Leroux offered to serve aboard the provincial man o' war, and on 15 March 1694 (O.S.) was accepted, "provided that Captain Evans take care that he shall not escape"—again.

*Reference: C.S.P., Amer. and W.I.,* Vol. XIV.

# LESCUYER, CAPITAINE

(FL. 1685)

French freebooter who died in the South Seas.

Early in 1685, Lescuyer and his fellow captain François Grogniet led a contingent of 200 French *flibustiers* and 80 English buccaneers from Golden Island across the Isthmus of Panama into the Pacific Ocean, hoping to join other rovers under Captain Francis Townley—who had preceded them into those waters a month earlier—in attacking the Spaniards. Commandeering more than two dozen coastal craft and canoes with which to transport themselves, Lescuyer and Grogniet reached Taboga Island south of Panama City, where on the night of 13 February they sighted a burning vessel to the north. The next morning a force of English buccaneers under Edward Davis and Charles Swan appeared, offering to give the new French arrivals the 90-ton *Santa Rosa,* which they had recently captured, while the English contingent was to be absorbed into *Bachelor's Delight* and *Cygnet.* (The chronicler William Dampier, who was sailing aboard Davis's flagship, later identified the two French commanders as "Captain Gronet [sic] and Capt. Lequie [sic].")

Lescuyer apparently died soon after, for when another band of French *flibustiers* arrived two months later, one of its members, Ravenau de Lussan, noted how only one of ten vessels in the pirate fleet—*Santa Rosa*—was captained by a Frenchman, the rest having English commanders. This ship, he added, had been given "to Capitaine Grogniet and Lescuier's [sic] crew, who had recently lost their captain."

*See also* Dampier, William; Golden Island; Grogniet, Capitaine; Lussan, Ravenau de; South Seas; Swan, Charles.

*References:* Bradley, *Lure;* Dampier; Gosse, *Who's Who;* Lussan.

# LESSONE, CAPITAINE

(FL. 1680)

French *flibustier* who joined John Coxon's assault on Portobelo.

In early February 1680, Lessone was lying at anchor with his ship in the Archipiélago de las Mulatas (or San Blas Islands) north of Panama, when a large flotilla of 250 buccaneers appeared in boats, heading westward to attack the Spanish American town of Portobelo. Lessone added 80 of his crew to this force, which shortly thereafter slipped ashore at Puerto del Escribano in the Gulf of San Blas and proceeded afoot for three days, surprising the Spaniards the morning of 7 February. After ransacking Portobelo over the next two days, the raiders retired ten miles northeastward, entrenching themselves with their booty and a few prisoners on a cay half a mile offshore from Bastimentos, until they were rescued by their vessels.

Lessone continued in company with Coxon and his consorts while they briefly blockaded Portobelo, made a general distribution of booty, then retired to careen at Bocas del Toro (literally "bull's mouths" or "entrances of the bull") at the northwestern extremity of present-day Panama. But once refitted, all the English commanders decided to return to Golden Island and have the Darien Indians guide them over the isthmus to attack the Spaniards on the Pacific coast, while Lessone and his French colleague Jean Rose preferred remaining in the Caribbean.

*See also* Allison, Robert; careen; Coxon, John; forlorn; Golden Island; Harris, Peter (fl. 1671–1680); pieces of eight; Sawkins, Richard.

*Reference:* Jameson.

# LET PASS

Simplest form of license issued to English vessels in the West Indies, merely identifying the bearer and requesting he be allowed to pass to a particular destination. Privateer captains such as Richard Guy, William James, and Edward Mansfield often sortied with no more authorization than this, while the freebooter flotilla of John Coxon, Cornelius Essex, Bartholomew Sharpe, Robert Allison, and Thomas Magott, who made a violent peacetime assault on Spanish Portobelo in March 1680, attempted to justify their depredation by a combination of outdated French commissions and "let passes" from the new Jamaican governor, Lord Carlisle, "to go into the Bay of Honduras [modern Belize] to cut logwood."

This sort of abuse and misrepresentation meant that sometimes little faith could be placed in such documents, while the Spaniards further objected to even legitimate "let passes" being issued to destinations—like Honduras—which they regarded as within their territory, hence off limits to foreigners. Captains such as Robert Oxe often found their passes being contemptuously flung aside when boarded by *guardacostas,* thus adding to ill will on both sides.

*References:* C.S.P., Amer. and W.I., Vols. X–XI; Jameson.

# LETTER OF MARQUE

Another name for a privateer or corsair vessel, but apparently distinct in that its crew received regular wages "as any merchant marine sailors," in addition to shares from captures, while privateersmen served for booty alone.

Up until 1701, English merchant and privateering vessels both flew a Union Jack "with a white escutcheon in the centre." This was later changed so that letter-of-marque and letter-of-reprisal vessels wore a two-pointed red burgee flag "with the Union Jack described in a canton at the upper corner near the staff." Only Royal Navy warships were allowed to fly the full Union Jack.

*See also* letter of reprisal.
*Reference:* Chapin.

# LETTER OF REPRISAL

Special type of privateering commission issued to redress a wrong that could not be satisfactorily resolved through legal means and thus allowed the bearer to seek restitution through the capture of foreign vessels.

For instance, when English merchant captains such as John Cooke or Joseph Zohy were unjustifiably detained and pillaged by Spanish *guardacostas,* yet could not later obtain satisfaction by appealing to Madrid through proper channels, they requested letters of reprisal from the English government to exact their own form of compensation by seizing and disposing of Spanish ships on the high seas. Such permits were relatively rare, and unique in that they did not constitute an official declaration of war, nor allow the bearer to accumulate more than a specific amount of prize money.

# LIGHT MONEY

Seventeenth-century English euphemism for clipped or poor-grade coinage worth less than its purported face value.

For example, the minutes of a meeting of the Lords of Trade and Plantations in London on 14 February 1683 (O.S.) read, "The gentlemen of Jamaica added that light money may be refused in payments."
**Reference:** *C.S.P., Amer. and W.I.,* Vol. XI.

# LILBURNE, ROBERT

### (FL. 1680s)

Governor of New Providence in the Bahamas at the time of the Spanish invasions of 1684.

Lilburne, himself a resident of the Bahamas, had succeeded Robert Clarke as governor of the islands in 1682, when his predecessor was dismissed for issuing privateering commissions against the Spaniards in peacetime. It was feared that Lilburne would prove just as bad, only more devious, so a strong set of instructions was sent out from London dated October 1683. Before these could be enacted, however, the Spaniards attacked the Bahamas in retaliation for Thomas Paine's landings at nearby Saint Augustine, Florida, and numerous other infractions.

In January 1684, the first of a series of expeditions from Havana suddenly descended on English shipping off Andros Island, scattering it; one William Bell was seized to act as pilot. The Spaniards then pressed on to New Providence, disembarking 150 men half a mile from Charles Town (as Nassau was then called), and advancing upon the settlement. Lilburne was seated in the Wheel of Fortune Inn when he heard gunfire and fled into the woods with most of the inhabitants. Charles Town was taken almost without resistance and thoroughly ransacked, while the lone ship in the harbor—the frigate *Good Intent,* of ten guns—fled out to sea. The raiders departed at dusk, leaving the frightened citizenry to creep back and assess the damage.

Other assaults followed, including a second major descent on Charles Town by Gaspar de Acosta and Tomás Uraburru a few months later, which convinced many settlers to emigrate. New Providence would remain uninhabited until December 1686, when a new group of English colonists arrived. Lilburne sent a message to his Spanish counterpart at Havana, inquiring as to the reason for these attacks and was told that it was because the inhabitants of the Bahamas were all "pirates proven."
**See also** Acosta, Gaspar de; Clarke, Robert; Paine, Thomas; Uraburru, Tomás.
**Reference:** Craton.

# LILLY, THOMAS

## (FL. 1698)

English privateer who in October 1698 was ordered arrested at St. Kitts for persisting in attacks against French subjects, despite the cessation of the War of the League of Augsburg (King William's War) the previous year. Lilly had once served under the notorious James Weatherhill of Jamaica.

**Reference:** Chapin.

# LISLE, CAPTAIN

## (FL. 1688-1689)

English freebooter captured off French Hispaniola.

Early in November 1688, after the English authorities on Jamaica had detained a group of French *flibustiers,* Governor Pierre-Paul Tarin de Cussy received word that Lisle had arrived at Ile-à-Vache off the southwestern tip of Saint Domingue with a *barco luengo* called *Dorado* (Golden One), "heretofore commanded by one [John] Coxon." Lisle's crew consisted of 80 English, 3 French, and 5 Dutch or Flemish buccaneers. Governor de Cussy issued orders for this ship's detention

> which was punctually done on the 16th of November. A few days later 38 men, 24 of them English, were brought to me at Petit Goâve, several now [5 February 1689] being left ashore miserably wounded.

Lisle had meanwhile been condemned to perpetual punishment aboard France's galleys and his companions sentenced to long terms, by which the French governor intended to demonstrate to his English counterparts that

he too "shall show no mercy to those that I catch."

**See also** *barco luengo*; Coxon, John; Hispaniola.

**Reference:** *C.S.P., Amer. and W.I.,* Vol. XIII.

# LOGWOOD OR DYEWOOD

Dark-red tropical tree native to the West Indies *(Haematoxylum campechanium L.),* which was harvested to produce a black or brown dye that became highly prized in Europe for tinting cloth, because—in the words of the pirate chronicler Alexandre Olivier Exquemelin—it does "not fade like ours."

The secret of this product had been long known to the Indians, who imparted it to the Spanish shortly after their conquest of the Americas. Small local industries developed, until European traders began to realize its potential market overseas. As early as 7 July 1654, the directors of the Dutch West India Company in Amsterdam were writing to their representative on Curaçao, ordering him "to promote the cutting of dyewood as much as possible" on that island, "but paying attention nevertheless that the young saplings are spared." English rovers venturing out of Jamaica a few years later stumbled upon large stands in the uninhabited coastal regions of both Campeche and Belize, where they set up their own independent camps and began cutting trees. The Spanish Crown feared these poaching settlements would eventually develop into full-fledged colonies and so sent occasional patrols to attempt to drive the interlopers out, provoking counterraids by foreign rovers.

Despite such dangers, many peaceful merchants also visited the outposts in hopes of obtaining a potentially valuable cargo at very low cost (oftentimes saving money by harvesting the trees with their own crews, although preferring them already cut and seasoned). Within a few decades the price of a ton of logwood in Port Royal, Jamaica, was £20, although worth twenty times as much in London, England—a powerful temptation for homeward-bound masters.

**References:** Dampier; Exquemelin; Gehring, *Curaçao;* Gerhard, *Southeast;* McJunkin; Marley, *Pirates.*

# LUSSAN, RAVENAU DE
## (FL. 1679-1705?)

*Flibustier* chronicler famous for his eyewitness accounts of raids in the South Seas.

Born on the outskirts of Paris on an unknown date, Lussan set sail from Dieppe on 5 March 1679 as an *engagé,* or indentured servant, destined for three years' servitude on the West Indian island of Saint Domingue. He hated his master, so much so he later refused to even mention his name in his memoirs. Once this indenture was complete, Lussan joined the household of Deputy Governor Monsieur de Frasquenay, where he remained another six months. Then, wishing to earn money to meet his obligations, he "conceived the idea of joining the buccaneers, sailing away with them [and] seizing what money I could from the Spanish." He therefore enlisted in the 120-man crew of the legendary Dutch-born *flibustier* Laurens de Graaf, departing Petit Goâve on 22 November 1684 aboard a 14-gun Spanish prize.

Lussan sailed with De Graaf to the Spanish Main, where De Graaf reunited with his colleagues Michiel Andrieszoon, Jean Rose, and other consorts in January 1685 before agreeing to split up at a conference held off Cape de la Vela (Venezuela) on 8 February, thus allowing

Lussan and 87 others to sail away with the 14-gun Spanish prize.

Three days later this vessel called at Golden Island off the northeastern coast of Panama and learned that a large force of *flibustiers* had already traversed the isthmus under Captains François Grogniet and Lescuyer to join an even bigger contingent of English buccaneers who were already operating in the South Seas. Lussan and his companions, after reuniting with Rose, Pierre le Picard, and Capitaine Desmarais, decided to follow the first groups across to the Pacific, and on 1 March 1685, "after commending our journey to God," 264 mainly French *flibustiers* set off on foot.

## PACIFIC CAMPAIGN
### (1685-1688)

Emerging on the far side of the isthmus on 11 April, they were met by a boat that Grogniet had sent back for them. The new arrivals were conducted to a pirate assemblage off Isla del Rey, where they were incorporated into the fleet of English Captains Edward Davis, Charles Swan, William Knight, and Francis Townley, who offered the *flibustiers* the 90-ton *Santa Rosa* they had recently captured from the Spaniards. The French were to serve under Grogniet, and the six vessels and almost 1,000 men of the freebooter fleet then settled down to blockade Panama in the hope of intercepting the Peruvian treasure fleet. But these vessels slipped past, delivered their cargo, and sallied to engage the buccaneers on 7 June 1685, catching the rovers unawares off Pacheca Island. An indecisive engagement ensued, with the buccaneers eventually being driven off. They then fell out amongst themselves along national lines, each group blaming the other for this defeat.

A joint attack was made next on the coastal town of Remedios (Pueblo Nuevo), after which both contingents headed northwestward as separate groups. Lussan and the other *flibustiers* refused to join the English raid on León (Nicaragua) of early August 1685, preferring to take 120 men in five boats for a repeat attempt against Remedios. This was repulsed and Realejo attempted on 1 November, but the French found it already devastated from an earlier English assault, and so obtained little booty. Reversing course, on 9 January 1686 they captured the tiny coastal town of Chiriquita (Panama), which they abandoned a week later. At the end of this same month a Spanish squadron passed them out at sea, and when the *flibustiers* approached Remedios again the night of 5–6 March to forage for food, they were ambushed by a small frigate, *barco luengo,* and *piragua,* suffering more than 30 casualties. They then roamed westward once more, anchored off Esparta on 19 March, and sighted Townley's small flotilla four days later.

Despite some residual ill will, the two groups combined for a joint attempt against the inland city of Granada (Nicaragua), landing a force of 345 men on 7 April and fighting their way into that city three days later. Again, little plunder was found as the Spaniards had transferred their valuables offshore to Zapatera Island and the pirates withdrew empty-handed five days later. They endured numerous ambushes before passing Masaya and regaining their ships, after which they traveled to Realejo. Having enjoyed such limited success thus far, the French voted on 9 June 1686 to divide their forces. Lussan's group eventually rediscovered Townley's contingent, now commanded by George Hutt, in the Gulf of Nicoya on 23 January 1687, and after ravaging that area for a month, weighed together for a surprise attack on the Equatorian port of Guayaquil.

On 16 April, the rovers arrived opposite Puná Island, and two hours before dawn on Sunday, 20 April, landed to march inland against Guayaquil. The Spaniards had been advised of strange sails off the coast, but when no attack developed, they had assumed this to be a false alarm. Between three and four o'clock on that rainy Sunday morning, the buccaneers burst upon them and a vicious house-to-house struggle ensued. Between 34 to 60 Spaniards were killed in eight hours of fighting, and many others captured, as opposed to only 9 pirates dead and 12 wounded. Among the latter was Grogniet, who died a few days later and was succeeded by Picard. A few days later Davis joined, bringing word of a squadron of Peruvian privateers on their way to attack the raiders. Another inconclusive engagement was held with these vessels off Puná between 27 May–2 June, after which the bands separated.

Lussan sailed with Picard's five vessels as far north as Tehuantepec (Mexico), captured on 30 August 1687, and then looked into Acapulco bay before reversing course into the Gulf of Fonseca. There the *flibustiers* boldly scuttled their vessels on 2 January 1688 and marched overland into Nueva Segovia province. In the interior highlands they constructed rafts and sped down the Coco River, emerging at Cape Gracias a Dios on 9 March. A Jamaican ship was persuaded to carry them to Saint Domingue, which they reached on 8 April.

## LATER CAREER
### (1688-1705?)

Picard and the *flibustier* commanders were somewhat leery of any official reaction to their campaign—peace having long since been reestablished between France and Spain—and feigned not knowing this because of their lengthy absence. Governor Pierre-Paul Tarin de Cussy was not present at the capital of Petit Goâve, being then on an inspection tour of that island's northern districts, so there were no immediate recriminations for the returnees, although it became obvious the Crown's policy had changed drastically with regard to roving. Many of the freebooters therefore elected to continue even further afield, although Lussan was fortunate in that being a subordinate—as well as author of a meticulous journal of these events—he was able to approach the governor without hesitation.

Pleased with his account, De Cussy issued Lussan a certificate on 17 May 1688 at Port-de-Paix, commending his "zeal and courage" and recommending him both to the authorities and Lussan's father in Paris. The young adventurer must have returned there very shortly thereafter, for his *Journal du voyage fait à la Mer du Sud avec les flibustiers de l'Amérique* (Journal of the Voyage made to the South Sea with the Filibusters of America) was published in 1689 and reissued in 1705.

**See also** Andrieszoon, Michiel; De Graaf, Laurens Cornelis Boudewijn; *engagé;* Grogniet, Capitaine; Mar del Sur, Armada del; Rose, Jean; Spanish Main; Townley, Francis.

**References:** Bradley, *Lure;* Lugo; Lussan.


# LYNCH, SIR THOMAS
## (1632-1684)

Fourth Governor of Jamaica, who labored ceaselessly to restrain its privateers.

Lynch was born in Cranbrook, Kent, England, and came to the West Indies as a junior officer in the Cromwellian expedition sent out in 1654 under Admiral Sir William Penn and General Robert Venables. By 1660 he was back in England on furlough and seems to have adapted well to the restoration of Charles II, despite being an Old Stander. On 28 November (O.S.) of that same year, Lynch petitioned the government for passage back to Jamaica aboard one of the king's ships, describing himself as a captain,

and in January 1661 he was appointed provost-marshal of the island for life. When Lord Windsor arrived to inaugurate Royalist rule and administrative reforms the following year, Lynch secured appointment as lieutenant colonel of the newly created Fifth Regiment of Militia in December 1662, and in April 1663 he was sworn in as a member of Jamaica's first council.

A year later he was elected its president and acted as interim governor for two months until Sir Thomas Modyford could transfer from Barbados. Lynch was also a slaving agent for the Royal African Company, which meant he—unlike Jamaica's privateers and planters—hoped to establish peaceful trade with Spanish America. The first tentative contacts had been dashed by Commodore Christopher Myngs's descents on Santiago de Cuba and Campeche, which in turn had inspired such rovers as John Morris and Henry Morgan to continue their depredations, despite the official truce with Spain. "What compliance can be expected from men so desperate and numerous," Lynch wrote in late May 1664, "that have no element but the sea, nor trade but privateering?"

Within the first few weeks of Modyford's administration, Lynch also confronted other problems. The new governor was soon writing privately to London to suggest Lynch be created sheriff rather than marshall, "for he is a pretty understanding gentleman and very useful here; he has an estate and would be very well beloved were he sheriff instead of marshall." But such changes were not being sought by Lynch nor many other members of the council, and they bristled when Modyford began forcing the issue. Lynch was dismissed both from the council and as chief justice of the island, protesting that the reason was his "uncourtly humor of speaking plain and true" to Modyford. Nonetheless, he was obliged to return to England, something he resented as it had been his intent to marry, send for his relations, and make Jamaica his permanent home.

He spent much of this exile visiting Spain, where he learned the language "and to perfect it spent a whole winter in Salamanca, not talking to foreigners, learning much about the things of the Indies through his own studies and by talking to merchants and others there and in Andalusia." Gradually, his reputation grew with such ministers as the Secretary of State Lord Arlington, who also believed England's best policy would be to forsake hostilities and develop trade with Spanish America. By late 1670 this faction was in the ascendant at Whitehall, and Lynch was being groomed to replace Modyford. He was knighted on 3 December 1670 (O.S.), being described as "of Rixton Hall in Great Sonkey Lane," and a few days later married Lady Vere, the daughter of Sir Edward Herbert and sister of the Earl of Torrington. By January 1671, Lynch was designated the new governor and naval commander-in-chief for Jamaica, as well as being secretly issued a royal warrant to arrest Modyford, on the charge that he had, "contrary to the King's express commands, made many depredations and hostilities against the subjects of His Majesty's brother, the Catholic King."

## FIRST TERM
### (1671-1675)

Lynch sailed for Jamaica aboard HMS *Assistance* and *Welcome,* officially entering Port Royal on 1 July 1671 (O.S.). He was greeted with full honors and invited to a banquet at Modyford's house. There the revocation of the old governor's commission was read out, and Lynch noted, "The people seemed not much pleased." Modyford's aggressive policy against the Spaniards had proved quite popular on the island, Morgan having recently returned from his spectacular success at Panama, so that Lynch feared a

backlash. His situation was made more awkward by a bout of illness and the fact he was being generously accommodated in Modyford's own home. Finally, he lured his host aboard *Assistance* six weeks later, on the pretext he had "something of import to him from the King," and informed Modyford of the arrest warrant. The latter behaved with great dignity, wishing he might have been given the opportunity to show his loyalty "by his voluntary submission to His Majesty's pleasure," and an embarrassed Lynch promised him "his life and estate was not in danger," but that a show of sternness was needed to assuage Spanish complaints.

Lynch had to placate the Council of Jamaica and privateers as well, assuring the latter they would be pardoned if they returned to Jamaica and submitted. There was no immediate uprising, but many muttered privately the new governor was "a trepan [snare or trap]" who had "betrayed the good general." Modyford departed for England ten days later as a prisoner aboard the *Jamaica Merchant,* and rovers such as Jan Erasmus Reyning and Alexandre Olivier Exquemelin began avoiding Jamaica, preferring to seek service with the French or even the Spanish. Meanwhile, Madrid had reacted angrily to the news of Morgan's raid, and by November it was feared an invasion of Jamaica was imminent. At this same time Lynch received orders from London to arrest Morgan, which he was loath to do for it would further alienate the privateers, upon whom he now relied for the island's defense. He therefore decided to send the freebooter home in such a manner "as he shall not be much disgusted," and deferred the actual arrest because of Morgan's ill health. It was not until mid-April 1672 that the great privateer was conducted aboard the 36-gun royal frigate *Welcome* of Captain John Keene, along with the condemned prisoner Captain Francis Weatherbourne, to sail for England with a three-ship convoy.

This was virtually the same time as the Third Anglo-Dutch War was erupting back in Europe, with England and France ranged in an unlikely alliance against the Netherlands. Hostilities against the Protestant Dutch were not very popular, especially when the French proved inept allies and then went to war against Spain next year— all of which resulted in a complete reversal of policy at Whitehall, with surprising consequences. On 5 March 1675 (O.S.), the 40-ton privateer *Gift* of Captain Thomas Rogers entered Port Royal with Morgan on board, now bearing a knighthood and commission as lieutenant governor of the island. The following day Lynch resigned, and seven days afterward his successor Lord Vaughan arrived aboard the 522-ton frigate HMS *Foresight*. By 24 May (O.S.), William Beeston was noting in his journal, "Sir Thomas Lynch sailed from Jamaica in the *Saint Thomas,* Captain [Joseph] Knapman commander, and with him Captain [Hender] Molesworth." Nevertheless Lynch was not entirely out of favor, carrying dispatches from Vaughan as to his "prudent government and conduct of affairs."

## SECOND TERM
### (1682-1684)

Six years later, the English Crown policy again reversed and Lynch's pro-Spanish sentiments came into vogue once more. Following numerous complaints against the Jamaican privateers and Morgan, Charles II opted to appease the Spaniards by reappointing Lynch to that post. A confidential report from London added that

the Spanish Ambassador has given his thanks with great solemnity for this mark of His [Majesty's] friendship to the King of Spain, and he has complimented the ministers likewise upon the occasion and it is certain that as he is satisfied Sir T.

Lynch will be a good Governor for the satisfaction of the Spaniard, so he will be a nursing father for the improvement of that plantation.

Lynch's new commission was dated 28 July 1681 (O.S.), and by the end of October he and his family had gone aboard the 42-gun frigate HMS *Sweepstakes*. Winter gales forced this vessel to seek shelter in Plymouth, and it was not until mid–February 1682 that the frigate could put to sea again.

He arrived at Port Royal on 14 May (O.S.) with only his five-year-old daughter, Philadelphia; his wife and ten-year-old son, Charles, had been left behind at Madeira to recuperate from illness. That same day Lynch sent a letter ashore to Morgan, who was acting as governor, informing him his commission was cancelled. Finding the official residence uninhabitable, Lynch then lodged with his old friend Colonel Hender Molesworth, now the Royal African Company's chief agent for Jamaica. Less than two weeks later, Lynch convened his first council meeting and plunged into business. He found the island's clandestine trade to the Spanish Main very promising

were we not undersold by the great Dutch ships that haunt the coast of the [Spanish] Main and islands, and were we not fearful of pirates, which is the reason why the ships are so strongly manned. Those and other expenses and hazards carry away much of the profit.

As during his previous administration, he vigorously discouraged privateering because of its deleterious effects on commerce and hunted pirates ruthlessly.

But Lynch was a dying man, who complained of gout and "the disorders of my head," his spirits further receiving a heavy blow when he learned his wife and son had both died at Madeira. On 24 June

1684 (O.S.) he wed Mary Temple, the 17-year-old sister-in-law of the speaker of the assembly, but did not live to enjoy this second marriage. When the pirate Joseph Bannister was acquitted by a Jamaican jury, Lynch's vexation reputedly created "such disturbance of mind" that a week later he died, on 24 August 1684 (O.S.). His friend Molesworth succeeded him as interim governor, burying Lynch the next day in the church at Spanish Town, and four years later married his widow.

**See also** Bannister, Joseph; Morris, John; Myngs, Sir Christopher; Rogers, Thomas.

**References:** *D.N.B.;* Earle, *Panamá;* Exquemelin; *Interesting Tracts;* Pope.

# MAGOTT, THOMAS

## (FL. 1679-1680)

English privateer who served under John Coxon at Portobelo.

Late in December 1679—England having been at peace for several years, while France and Spain were winding down their hostilities in the New World—Magott attended a gathering of privateers at Port Morant, off the southeastern tip of Jamaica. Along with his own sloop of 14 tons and 20 men were the barks of Coxon, Cornelius Essex, and Bartholomew Sharpe, as well as the sloop of Robert Allison. All five agreed to unite under Coxon's leadership for an assault on Spanish Portobelo, although they had no clear authorization for such a venture. They quit Port Morant on 17 January 1680, and less than 20 miles out at sea met the brigantine of French *flibustier* Jean Rose, who also joined the force. When the weather turned bad, Coxon hailed his vessels to make toward Isla Fuerte, 90 miles south–southwest of Cartagena on the Spanish Main.

Only Essex and Sharpe failed to keep the rendezvous. Coxon stole "four *piraguas* and six very good large canoes" from the nearby San Bernardo, or "Friends," Islands to serve as landing craft. Essex meanwhile rejoined, and the formation proceeded toward Isla de Pinos 130 miles east of Portobelo. Only Coxon's bark was able to beat through the contrary winds and gain this isle; the rest were forced to put into Isla de Oro (Golden Island) some miles away. There they befriended the local Indians, until Coxon ordered 250 buccaneers into the boats to row westward along the coast, hoping to surprise Portobelo before the Spaniards could learn of their presence.

Nearing their destination, they came upon "a great ship riding at anchor," which proved to be that of *flibustier* Capitaine Lessone, who added 80 Frenchmen to the boat party. Shortly thereafter, the buccaneers slipped ashore at the Gulf of San Blas, proceeding afoot to avoid Spanish coastal watchers. They marched three days until they came upon an Indian village three miles short of Portobelo, where a native spotted them and set off at a run toward the distant city. Coxon called on his advance unit (the "forlorn") to hurry after the Indian before the Spaniards could mount a defense. The native arrived half an hour before them, but the pirates nevertheless swept in largely unopposed. The Spaniards withdrew inside their citadel and left the raiders to ransack Portobelo over the next two days. The freebooters then retired ten miles northeastward to be picked up by their ships.

A brief blockade ensued, and after a few more captures, a general distribution of booty was made, resulting in shares of 100 pieces of eight per man. Afterward, the flotilla retired to Bocas del Toro (literally "bull's mouths" or "entrances of the bull" located at the western extremity of present–day Panama) to careen, where the privateers Richard Sawkins and Peter Harris were found. Once refitted, all the pirates except the French decided to return to Golden Island and obtain guides from the Indians "to travel overland to Panama," and attack the Spaniards on the Pacific side. Coxon, Magott, Allison, Cooke, Harris, Sawkins, and Sharpe all anchored close inshore in a small cove on Golden Island, out of sight of any Spanish ship that might chance to pass. An anchor watch was left, and at six o'clock on Monday morning, 15 April 1680, 332 buccaneers went ashore to cross the isthmus.

But "Captain Allison and Captain Magott being sickly were unable to march" and therefore remained behind. The rest of the buccaneers disappeared into the jungle and ten days later took the inland town of Santa María at the confluence of the Chucunaque and Tuira Rivers. From there the buccaneers pushed on into the Pacific, although Coxon proved hesitant. By the time the expedition captured some Spanish coastal craft and bore down upon Panama, command had devolved upon Harris, Sawkins, and Sharpe. Coxon returned with 70 men to Golden Island, and it is possible that Magott may have sailed away with him, although nothing more is known about his movements.

*See also* Allison, Robert; Coxon, John; Essex, Cornelius; forlorn; Golden Island; Harris, Peter (fl. 1671–1680); Lessone, Capitaine; pieces of eight; Rose, Jean; Sawkins, Richard; Sharpe, Bartholomew; Spanish Main.

*References:* Gosse, *Who's Who;* Jameson.

# Maintenon, Charles-François d'Angennes, Marquis de

## (1648-post 1698?)

French nobleman who became a rover, smuggler, slaver, and plantation owner in the West Indies.

Maintenon was born at Chartres on 5 December 1648 into an ancient but impoverished family. He sold his marquisate at l'Eure-et-Loir, Maine, to Louis XIV in 1674, so that the king might bestow this title on his favorite mistress, Françoise d'Aubigné. As a reward, Maintenon was granted considerable leeway to seek his fortune in the New World. He arrived in the West Indies as a naval officer in 1676, when France was at war with Holland and Spain. His service does not seem to have been particularly distinguished; a newsletter dated 19 February 1677 at Jamaica reads, "The Marquis de Maintenon likely to do nothing, although he has all the French on Hispaniola and all their vessels ready for a design." On

2 March 1678 he married Catherine Giraud, the beautiful daughter of Louis Giraud, sieur du Poyet, a wealthy militia captain from the island of Saint Christopher.

This same year Maintenon commanded the royal frigate *Sorcière* (Sorceress), which with some *flibustiers* from Tortuga cruised the coast of Caracas on the Spanish Main. They ravaged the islands of Margarita and Trinidad but apparently gained little plunder, for soon after, the fleet scattered. The chronicler Ravenau de Lussan later related a lurid tale about the marquis's adventures to highlight the ferocity of American natives:

> [Maintenon] had taken a prize carrying 14 cannon. On this he embarked and having been separated from his warship found himself one day forced to take on water at Bocas del Dragón ["Dragon's Mouths," between Trinidad and Venezuela] on the mainland, a place inhabited by a tribe similar to those on Cape Vela. Having brought his vessel as close in as possible, he lined up his cannon on deck and under cover of these sent his small boat ashore with 22 armed men to fill their casks. The savages, who were hiding near the shore, did not even give the boat a chance to land, but jumping suddenly into the sea, attacked. In spite of the incessant fire from the ship's cannon they pushed the boat more than 50 feet up on shore where, after killing them, they threw them over their backs and departed. Then they swam out into deep water to cut the ship's cables and so force it to founder, hoping in the same way to annihilate those on board. The crew, fortunately, had time to unfurl their sails and push out from shore.

In the summer of 1679, peace having been restored, Maintenon was hired by the governor general, comte de Blénac, to cruise the Caribbean with Vice Admiral comte d'Estrées, judging Maintenon to be "most experienced and very knowledgeable of the places which monsieur the Vice Admiral wishes to visit." After visiting France, on 2 November 1680 Maintenon was granted exclusive privilege to trade clandestinely with the Spaniards in the West Indies for four years. This was backed by a *lettre de cachet* under Louis XIV's privy seal, instructing French officials in the New World to prevent trade missions to Tierra Firme that did not enjoy the marquis's approval. (When informed of this, the governor of Saint Domingue, Jacques Nepveu, sieur de Pouançay, puckishly observed, "I do not think this order can apply to the *flibustiers,* as they never approach Spanish lands to trade.")

Nevertheless, he dispatched Capitaine Tucker to advise John Coxon, Jean Rose, Jan Willems, and other French corsairs who were already operating off the Spanish Main. Tucker came up with these off the northeastern shores of Panama, and in the early days of June 1681, the English and French contingents held a series of conferences at Springer's Key in the San Blas Islands, during which the pirate chronicler William Dampier noted:

> the French seemed very forward to go [attack] any [Spanish] town that the English could or would propose, because the Governor of Petit Goâve (from whom the privateers take commissions) had recommended a gentleman lately come from France to be general of the expedition, and sent word by Captain Tucker, with whom this gentleman came, that they should if possible make an attempt on some town before he returned again. The English when they were in company with the French seemed to approve of what the French said, but never looked on that general to be fit for the service in hand.

Maintenon in fact never sought such a command, henceforth preferring to dabble in commercial ventures. He had also been granted special license to import 400 African slaves into the French Antilles every year to be resold to the Spaniards; but he openly disposed of them instead to French plantation owners, to the detriment of royal customs. He also profited from trade in ebony wood, and in 1683 secured the governorship of the island of Marie Galante, which he scarcely bothered to visit before making it over to his sister's new husband as a wedding present in 1686. He often issued passports for returning merchantmen to call at Dunkirk or Holland rather than France, thus breaking the Crown monopoly on trade. It is little wonder that Maintenon has been described as "more of a *flibustier* than a marquis." In 1687 he retired from public life by purchasing the "Montagne" plantation on Martinique, one of two that he maintained with a work force of 300 slaves, as well as a sugar refinery valued at 250,000 *livres.*

***See also*** Blénac, Charles de Courbon, comte de; Estrées, Jean, comte d'; Hispaniola; Lussan, Ravenau de; Pouançay, Jacques Nepveu, sieur de; Spanish Main.

***References:*** Baudrit; Gosse, *Who's Who;* Lugo; Lussan.

# MAL DE SIAM

Literally "Siamese disease" in French, a seventeenth-century nickname for yellow fever.

According to the chronicler-priest Jean-Baptiste Labat, this disease was so called because it was believed that the royal vessel *Oriflamme* had contracted it at Brazil upon its return leg from Bangkok and so introduced it to the French West Indian island of Martinique.

***See also*** Labat, Jean-Baptiste.
***Reference:*** Labat.

# Malarka, Abraham

## also Malarkey
### (fl. 1665)

Privateer who commanded a 1-gun galliot in Colonel Edward Morgan's expedition against Dutch Sint Eustatius and Sabá, during the Second Anglo-Dutch War. This force departed Jamaica in two divisions, five sail putting out of Port Royal on 5 April 1665 and Morgan himself following with another four on the 28 April. There were 650 men in all, described in a letter by Governor Sir Thomas Modyford as

> chiefly reformed privateers, scarce a planter amongst them, being resolute fellows and well armed with *fusils* [Spanish word for muskets] and pistols.

The Crown official was particularly pleased they would be serving "at the old rate of no purchase, no pay, and it will cost the King nothing considerable, some powder and mortar pieces." Their landing was successfully made, but the colonel, "being a corpulent man," died from heat exertion during the chase, and his expedition disbanded shortly thereafter.

*See also* purchase.

*References:* Cruikshank; *Interesting Tracts;* Pope.

# Maldonado de Aldana, Antonio

### (fl. 1663-1665)

Spanish defender of Campeche.

Originally born in the town of Esparragosa in Extremadura, Spain, Maldonado emigrated to the Mexican port of Campeche where he married the wealthy widow Juana de Vargas and settled down. Over the years he came

to finance numerous expeditions against pirates along the gulf coast, and as a *regidor,* or alderman, general treasurer of the *Santa Cruzada* (Holy Crusade), and officer in the local militia, was charged with the defense of the city's tiny inland keep of Santa Cruz.

## Myngs and Mansfield's Raid
### (February 1663)

At dawn on 9 February 1663, a cluster of anchored vessels was sighted three miles to leeward of Campeche, and its garrison hastily stood to arms. From his outpost at Santa Cruz, Maldonado beheld the advance of Christopher Myngs and Edward Mansfield's host toward the city walls but could not deflect their progress despite firing off the bulk of his fortress' scanty supply of ammunition. The English went on to carry Campeche by storm, Myngs being badly wounded in the street fighting. During the night Maldonado spiked his artillery and abandoned Santa Cruz, and on the morning of the 10 February—being the only Spanish official left—approached the triumphant invaders under a flag of truce to discuss terms. He met personally with Mansfield, and both agreed the 42 Spanish dead inside the city "should be cast into the sea and the [14] wounded treated, which had not yet been done," and all fires extinguished. Maldonado then retreated inland and observed the invaders' activities from a safe distance. On 17 February he received a message offering to spare the city and its prisoners, if the raiders could draw water from the nearby Lerma wells. He acceded, and on the 23 February the enemy fleet finally departed after releasing their captives and amassing an impressive booty.

## Spanish Pursuit
### (March 1663)

Shortly thereafter, word was received that a smaller landing of approximately 50 buccaneers had been made on the coastal town of Sisal, 80 miles north of Campeche. This was possibly a laggard element from Myngs's force, and on 2 March Maldonado was ordered by the acting governor of Yucatán to march to that town's relief. At the head of 200 Spanish regulars and 600 Indian auxiliaries, he arrived in time to catch these intruders still on land, where they had burned a hacienda. An English officer and seven buccaneers were seized, while their comrades fled back out to sea. The prisoners were then brought victoriously into Campeche, where they were incarcerated and interrogated.

## MORRIS AND MORGAN'S RAID
### (FEBRUARY 1665)

Less than two years later, Maldonado organized another strike against what he assumed were the logwood-cutters of the Laguna de Términos, after a cutting-out expedition had stolen an 8-gun Spanish frigate from Campeche's roads one night. During the intervening period, his cousin Rodrigo Flores de Aldana had assumed office as the new governor of Yucatán and designated Maldonado his deputy governor for Campeche. Three frigates were assembled with 270 troops on board, setting sail on 20 February 1665 under the command of Maldonado's nephew José Aldana. Two days later the latter came upon three ships anchored opposite the tiny town of Santa María de la Frontera at the mouth of the Grijalva River. These only had anchor watches left on board, one of which escaped in a single vessel while seven of their comrades remained on the 10-gun flagship and 8-gun Spanish prize. The prisoners revealed their ships were unmanned because "Captain Mauricio [sic; John Morris] and David Martin [sic; Martien]" had marched most of their force inland to sack the town of Villahermosa de Tabasco.

Surprised, Aldana returned immediately to Campeche with his prizes, which were fitted out with 300 men to replace the Spanish frigates, sallying again on 11 March. Near the Laguna de Términos he sighted six people ashore—citizens of Villahermosa released by the raiders—who indicated that the enemy had found their retreat cut off and so had continued westward in two captured river boats to look for another avenue of escape. Aldana sailed in pursuit and on the afternoon of 17 March spotted the interlopers on Santa Ana Cay. He sent a messenger close inshore, calling to the English from his launch to surrender, but the buccaneers pretended not to understand. When an interpreter approached the beach the following morning, Morris and Martien replied they would not give up without a fight, and the Spaniards discovered they had used the interval to entrench themselves behind a palisade reinforced with sandbags and seven small cannon brought from Villahermosa.

The Spanish troops reluctantly disembarked, but being mostly volunteer civilian militia, showed little stomach for the fight despite outnumbering the English almost three-to-one. A faint-hearted assault was made but repelled without a single injury among the freebooters. The next day, 19 March, the Spanish ships were found mysteriously run aground, thus allowing the raiders to exit unchallenged in their two small boats. Later that same morning, Aldana found the decrepit Spanish frigate *Patarata* wrecked a mile-and-a-half away, having been dispatched by Maldonado with another 100 men under Captain Carlos Vocardo. The intruders were nonetheless allowed to escape undisturbed.

This was the last action Maldonado seems to have been involved in; his cousin was soon after deposed as governor of Yucatán, and Maldonado no longer figured in the campaigns against the pirates. It is believed he may have still been living in Campeche when George Spurre attacked on 10 July 1678, although this is not entirely certain.

*See also* Laguna de Términos; logwood; Mansfield, Edward; Martien, David; Myngs, Sir Christopher.

*References:* Calderón; Eugenio; Juárez.

# MANSFIELD, EDWARD
## (FL. 1660-1667)

English privateer who commanded some of the earliest raids against Spanish America.

Mansfield may be regarded as one of the first freebooter "admirals" in the West Indies, a leader capable of rallying other captains for joint enterprises against the Spaniards. He was described in the 1678 book of Alexandre Olivier Exquemelin as "an old buccaneer called Mansveldt [*sic*]" and listed in the journal of Jamaican governor Colonel Edward D'Oyley as having been issued a "let pass" as early as 4 December 1660 (O.S.) to sortie with his vessel. Mansfield possibly took part in Commodore Christopher Myngs's large scale assault against Santiago de Cuba two years later and definitely served in that officer's raid against the Mexican port of Campeche of early 1663. During this latter campaign Mansfield led the privateer contingent but became *de facto* commander-in-chief when Myngs was wounded during the initial assault.

## SACK OF CAMPECHE
### (1663)

Encouraged by his success against Santiago de Cuba, Myngs had called for another expedition against the Spaniards on 22 December 1662, refitting his flagship HMS *Centurion,* 40 guns, and vice-flagship HMS *Griffin,* 14 guns (with a crew of 100 men under Captain Smart), while the freebooters once again began to marshal. Among the

latter was Mansfield, with his brigantine of 4 guns and 60 men, along with other captains such as William James and many others. Soon a dozen ships were being made ready and on Sunday, 21 January 1663, they got under way from Port Royal. Myngs quickly rounded Yucatán and worked his flotilla down into the Gulf of Mexico, losing contact with Smart's *Griffin* and several other privateersmen along the way. Nonetheless, he pressed on and skillfully snuck almost 1,000 men ashore at Jámula beach, four miles west of Campeche, on the night of 8–9 February to begin his stealthy overland advance against the city.

At first light Spanish lookouts saw the smaller vessels lying opposite this disembarkation point, with two larger ships riding farther out to sea. They sounded the alarm, but too late, for the buccaneer army burst out of the nearby woods at eight o'clock that morning and rushed the city. Despite being surprised and heavily outnumbered, the 150 Campeche militiamen put up a stout resistance, especially from their "strong built stone houses, flat at top." A bloody firefight ensued, in which Myngs received serious wounds in his face and both thighs while leading the charge. He was carried back aboard *Centurion* while Mansfield—given the absence of Smart—assumed overall command of the expedition. The Spanish defenders were eventually subdued after two hours' heated battle, suffering more than 50 fatalities as opposed to 30 English invaders slain. Some 170 Spanish captives were then rounded up, while many of the city's thatched huts went up in flames.

Next morning the sole remaining Spanish official, Antonio Maldonado de Aldana, entered Campeche and agreed to a truce in exchange for good treatment of the prisoners. As he dealt directly with Mansfield, this raid has gone down as "Mansfield's assault" to Spanish historians, the few cryptic references to Myngs further misidentifying him as "Cristóbal Innes [*sic*]." The buccaneers under Mansfield then looted the city and withdrew two weeks later, on 23 February, carrying off great booty and fourteen vessels found lying in the harbor, described by a Spanish eye-witness as "three of 300 tons, the rest medium or small, and some with valuable cargo still on board." The heavily laden formation slowly beat back around Yucatán against contrary winds and currents, until *Centurion* eventually reached Port Royal on 23 April 1663 under the command of flag-captain Thomas Morgan, being followed "soon after [by] the rest of the fleet, but straggling, because coming from leeward every one made the best of his way."

## SANCTI SPÍRITUS RAID
### (DECEMBER 1665)

Two years later news of the outbreak of the Second Anglo-Dutch War back in Europe reached Jamaica, and Mansfield was one of those who sallied again to take advantage of these hostilities. However, most privateers still preferred attacking their traditional Spanish foe rather than the Dutch—notwithstanding the fact Madrid had remained neutral in the conflict—until finally the new Jamaican governor Sir Thomas Modyford was obliged to recall them to their duty.

Realizing the rovers would never willing reenter Port Royal and place themselves at the mercy of the Crown, Modyford convened a rendezvous at Bluefields Bay off the southwestern shore of Jamaica for November 1665. Eventually 600 buccaneers answered his summons and responded to the governor's call for renewed efforts against the Dutch by assuring him they were "very forward to suppression of that enemy" and accepting instruction for a descent against the Dutch West Indian colony of Curaçao.

Instead, the buccaneers immediately laid in a course for the south coast of Cuba, supposedly to obtain provisions for their forthcoming campaign. A Spanish bark was intercepted and its 22 crewmembers murdered among the Cayos, after which the rovers reached the tiny port of Júcaro around Christmas. There their demand of "victuals for their money" was allegedly refused, furnishing them with an excuse to pillage. Two to three hundred buccaneers

> marched 42 miles into the country, took and fired the town of Santo Spírito [*sic;* Sancti Spíritus], routed a body of 200 horse, carried their prisoners to their ships, and for their ransom had 300 fat beeves [*sic;* beef-cattle] sent down [to the coast].

The raiders later justified this depredation by arguing some among their number held Portuguese commissions (issued by the French governor of Tortuga), which authorized such attacks.

Having thus disposed of their supply problems, the privateers then chose Mansfield as their admiral and in mid-January 1666 reassured an emissary from the Jamaican governor that they now "had much zeal to His Majesty's service and a firm resolution to attack Curaçao." But this quickly evaporated once they began the long upwind beat toward that Dutch island, until eventually even Mansfield's crew refused to go any further, "averring publicly that there was more profit with less hazard to be gotten against the Spaniard, which was their only interest." Consequently, Mansfield fell away to leeward and steered his ships to the buccaneer haunt at Bocas del Toro (literally, "bull's mouths" or "entrances of the bull"), on the northwestern shores of present-day Panama. There a fleet of 15 privateer vessels soon gathered, 8 of them sailing eastward to make a descent on the town of Natá in the Panamanian province of Veragua, while Mansfield led the remaining 7 vessels westward toward Costa Rica.

### CARTAGO CAMPAIGN
#### (APRIL 1666)

Arriving off Portete on 8 April 1666, the buccaneers were able to capture its coastal lookout before any alarm could be carried inland and anchored their ships off Punta del Toro. It was Mansfield's intent to take the provincial capital of Cartago by a surprise overland march and commenced this enterprise well by bursting upon the nearby town of Matina at the head of several hundred men, snapping up all its 35 Spanish citizens. But then an Indian called Esteban Yaperi fled from the smaller hamlet of Teotique, carrying word of the invasion to the Costa Rican governor *maestre de campo* Juan López de Flor. By 15 April hundreds of militiamen had begun mustering at the mountain stronghold of Turrialba, ready to dispute the invaders' passage, although the Spaniards were only lightly armed. Mansfield was experiencing even greater hardships in the jungle, his men succumbed to hunger and fatigue. When they encountered some natives bearing bags of ground wheat, the buccaneers fell to fighting among themselves over this meager prize.

Governor López, heartened by this report, advanced with his troops and Mansfield was forced to retreat. By 23 April his survivors had staggered back aboard their ships at Portete, "exhausted and dying of hunger," and shortly thereafter retired to Bocas del Toro. Here another two ships deserted Mansfield, and he was left in the unenviable position of being regarded as a failure both by the mercurial privateers as well as the king's officials on Jamaica. In an effort to vindicate himself, Mansfield therefore decided to mount an attack against the tiny Spanish garrison on the island of Providencia or Santa Catalina, which had belonged to the English more than twenty years earlier.

### CAPTURE OF PROVIDENCIA ISLAND
#### (MAY 1666)

Mansfield's two remaining frigates and three sloops raised this island at noon on 25 May 1666, gliding down on its northern coast unobserved that evening to drop anchor offshore by ten o'clock. Around midnight the moon rose, and 200 buccaneers rowed in through the reefs by its faint glow: more than 100 Englishmen, 80 Frenchmen from Tortuga, as well as Dutch and Portuguese. These marched across the island, rounding up isolated Spanish residents, and stormed the lone citadel at first light of 26 May without suffering a single loss. Only 8 Spanish soldiers were found asleep inside, the remaining 62 being scattered around their civilian billets. Mansfield granted all the inhabitants quarter, and the French *flibustiers* prevented the English from ransacking the church.

Ten days later, Mansfield set sail again with 170 Spanish captives, whom he had promised to restore to their compatriots. Captain Hatsell was left in command of the island with 35 privateers and 50 black slaves, until Mansfield or some other English authority returned. On 11 June 1666 Mansfield paused at Punta de Brujas (Witches Point) on the north coast of Panama, depositing his prisoners ashore before standing away for Jamaica. He arrived at Port Royal with just two ships on 22 June and there encountered a piece of good fortune—for three-and-a-half months previously, Modyford and the council had resolved "that it is the interest and advantage of the island of Jamaica to have letters of marque granted against the Spaniard." Thus, although Mansfield had never been authorized to attack any nation except the Dutch, he found his seizure of Providencia now enjoyed a retroactive veneer of legality. "I have yet only reproved him for doing it without order," Modyford wrote the English Secretary of State Lord Arlington four days later, "which I should suppose would have been an acceptable service had he received command for it."

### MYSTERIOUS DEMISE
#### (1667)

This operation was to prove the old buccaneer's last, for the following year he shifted to the French of Tortuga Island after Modyford ceased granting commissions at Port Royal. Shortly thereafter Mansfield died, the exact circumstances being somewhat disputed. A contemporary English report indicated he had been captured by the Spaniards and carried to Havana, where he was "suddenly after put to death." Spanish historians, on the other hand, insist he died at Tortuga in early 1667, apparently poisoned.

*See also* D'Oyley, Edward; let pass; letter of marque; Maldonado de Aldana, Antonio; Modyford, Sir Thomas; Myngs, Sir Christopher.

*References:* Crump; Earle, *Panamá;* Exquemelin; *Interesting Tracts;* Juárez; Pawson, *Port Royal;* Pope; Sáiz.

# MANSO DE CONTRERAS, ANDRÉS

### (FL. 1660s)

Cuban corsair who had good success fighting the English in the years immediately after the conquest of Jamaica. In one action he beat off an enemy ship and *patache* that had attacked a merchant convoy he was escorting to Veracruz, and later he enjoyed other triumphs as well.

*See also patache.*
*Reference:* Sáiz.

# MAR DEL SUR, ARMADA DEL

Peruvian squadron based at Callao, whose principal duty was to escort consignments of silver to Panama. Starting in the 1680s, this force also had to contend with foreign intruders in the South Seas.

The Armada del Mar del Sur (literally the "South Sea Fleet") was created in the late sixteenth century as a result of Sir Francis Drake's incursion into the Pacific. It fell under the administration of the Peruvian viceroys through their military adjutants, the *tenientes de capitán general.* Over the years, this latter position evolved into a well-paid sinecure, usually occupied by viceregal relatives; for example, the fleet that the conde de Lemus dispatched to repel Henry Morgan's invasion of Panama in 1671 was nominally under the orders of the Marqués de Zurria—the viceroy's seven-year-old son. Actual command functions were exercised by the captains of the flagship *(capitana)* and vice-flagship *(almiranta),* who were military rather than naval officers, drawn from the Callao garrison and addressed as *general* and *almirante,* respectively. In fact, the principal duty of the five companies garrisoning Callao was to provide seagoing infantry for the armada; at any given time, 200 or 300 of them could be found aboard the warships on cruises of many months' duration.

Early each year, the armada would sail southward from Callao to Chincha to load the mercury extracted from the *azogue* mines at Huancavelica. It would then convey this quicksilver farther south, unloading it at Arica (in present-day Chile), to be used for ore refinement at the Potosí fields, and then take on that region's silver production, which it would carry back to Callao to be transported inland to the royal mint in Lima for assaying and the striking of coinage. In May or June, the fleet departed again, this time northward toward Panama, bearing the king's bullion and a convoy of Peruvian merchantmen to meet the annual plate fleet from Spain and celebrate its commercial fair. The passage from Callao to Panama usually took only three weeks, but the armada remained at anchor until the fair concluded, then made the slow upwind beat back to Callao, normally arriving late in the year. Sometimes passengers disembarked at Paita and traveled the last few hundred miles overland, this being swifter than the slow-moving ships.

Over the course of the seventeenth century these vessels became quite large and cumbersome, more like Indiamen than men o' war. Their tactics were completely defensive, relying principally on the remoteness of their routes, as the ships often removed some artillery in peacetime to accommodate greater cargos. Senior commanders were also under orders that if the armada should be approached by enemy vessels while bearing the king's treasure, they were to defer combat until the silver could be placed ashore.

## STANDING FLEET
### (1654-1679)

When the new Peruvian viceroy arrived to assume office in 1656, only two men o' war were available to the armada: the 900-ton vice-flagship *Santiago* (Saint James), of 40 guns, in need of extensive repairs, and the 360-ton *San Francisco Solano,* of 20 guns. The former flagship *Jesús María de la Limpia Concepción* (Jesus Mary of the Immaculate Conception), an enormous vessel of 1,200 tons and 44 guns, had been shipwrecked on the Chanduy sand banks at the mouth of the Guayaquil River on 26 October 1654. As a result, the viceroy ordered two new galleons constructed, each of 825 tons and capable of mounting 32 to 44 cannon. They were completed by 1659 with the names *San José* (Saint Joseph) and *Nuestra Señora de*

*Guadalupe* (Our Lady of Guadalupe) and would remain in service for many years.

A few years later *Santiago* was scrapped, while the aged *San Francisco Solano* was reduced to making only the Arica run. Private merchantmen were also frequently hired to supplement the armada's duties, such as the *San Antonio* that sank off Itata (near Concepción) in the early 1660s while bearing the annual *situado* or payrolls for Chile.

After a long period of relative tranquility, Henry Morgan's sack of Portobelo in 1668 served to reawaken the armada. When the *San José* next sailed to Panama, it mounted 32 guns—10 more than had been customary—and carried an expanded complement of 400 men. Morgan then devastated Panama itself in 1671, and the armada was hastily used to dispatch 2,400 reinforcements to the isthmus. A new 20-gun *patache* called *San Lorenzo* (Saint Lawrence) was launched to replace *San Francisco Solano,* and other smaller auxiliaries were built as well. In 1675 a report was received that an English settlement had been established in the Strait of Magellan; on 21 September, Captain Antonio de Vea and the Biscayan privateer Pascual de Iriarte were dispatched with two vessels to investigate. They found no signs of any colony but lost a boat and 17 men when Iriarte's son attempted to place a bronze plaque with Spain's royal crest on those shores. The survivors returned to Callao on 20 April 1676.

After another peaceful interlude, the Spaniards were astonished when a foreign ship and two launches appeared off Callao on 13 February 1679, cutting out a loaded vessel from the roads. These rovers had worked their way northward from the strait, robbing vessels off Chile and Arica, so that a force of 150 soldiers and 70 arquebusiers were sent out from Callao under Captain Diego de Frias to give chase. After a brief pursuit, the interlopers released their prize and sailed away.

## FIRST MAJOR INCURSION
### (1680)

In April of the following year, John Coxon, Richard Sawkins, and Bartholomew Sharpe led a contingent of 332 buccaneers across the Isthmus of Panama into the Pacific, seizing coastal craft and instituting a blockade of Panama. The acting viceroy of Peru, Archbishop Melchor de Liñán y Cisneros, was unable to dispatch his regular armada warships as a relief force because these were being careened. Instead he hired private vessels and manned them with sailors and troops. On 6 July 1680, there set sail from Callao the 12-gun *Nuestra Señora de la Concepción* as flagship, with three companies of regulars, 17 gunners, and 24 seamen on board; the 10-gun *Nuestra Señora del Viejo* as vice-flag, with two companies of soldiers, 12 gunners, and 22 sailors; the 8-gun *San José* as *gobierno,* with one company of troops, 12 gunners, and 18 seamen; and the tender *Santa Rosa.* The whole was commanded by Santiago Pontejos, with Pedro Díaz Zorrilla as his *almirante.*

They ventured northward and paused at Lobos Island, sending *Santa Rosa* on ahead to Paita with a consignment of ammunition, and to gain intelligence of the enemy. Learning these had not yet been sighted, Pontejos pressed on to Santa Clara Island, again detaching *Santa Rosa* into Guayaquil on a similar mission. The flotilla then continued northward in similar fashion, carefully probing the coastline as far as Panama City itself but without encountering the pirates.

The flotilla remained on patrol for another three months, not realizing that the raiders were operating further out to sea. It was the *San Lorenzo* of Manuel Pantoja that finally discovered the intruders, after having returned from Arica too late to join the original expedition. His vessel had instead been sent south from Callao with the Crown auxiliary *Santísima Trinidad* (Most Blessed Trinty) to take up station off Pisco. While there they discovered the enemy had raided Ilo further to the south, which they visited but found no enemy, so returned to Callao with this information.

Meanwhile, the hired ship *San Juan de Dios* had been dispatched on 13 February 1681 under Captain Diego Barrasa to convey the *situado* to Valdivia (Chile). In light of this news of an enemy attack on Ilo, however, the Peruvian authorities decided to send Pontejos's *Concepción* out a few days later as well, having since given up its fruitless search of the Gulf of Panama. At the same time the hired ship *San Juan Evangelista* (Saint John the Evangelist) and *Santa Rosa* under Captain Francisco Salazar Alvarado were delegated with two armed launches to carry the *situados* from Callao to Panama and Portobelo, after which they were to remain off the Gulf of San Miguel and prevent the pirates from retracing their steps into the Caribbean. All these dispositions proved to be for naught when the last buccaneer commander, Sharpe, sailed his prize out of the Pacific around Cape Horn. With this danger removed, the flagship *San José* and vice-flag *Guadalupe* made their routine voyage to Panama in 1682 with the king's bullion, returning to Callao by December of that year.

Upon arriving, both vessels were found to be in need of extensive repairs, the 23-year-old *San José* lacking its rudder and its hull seriously eroded by teredo worms (a common complaint after lying several months in the warm waters off Panama). However, there were not enough construction materials available at Callao for both warships, so it was decided to dispatch *San Lorenzo* to Guayaquil for an overhaul, after which it could transport timbers back to Callao for the completion of the *San José* and *Guadalupe. San Lorenzo* set sail on 26 July 1683 but did not return until eleven months later, having been almost completely rebuilt in the Ecuadorian yards. Its cargo of lumber was then used to supplement the wood that had already been expropriated from Lima's Carmelite nunnery, so that repairs on the flagship and vice-flag could be rushed to their conclusion on 23 September 1684.

## Second Major Incursion
### (1684)

The reason for this haste was that earlier that same year, the vessels of John Cooke, John Eaton, and Charles Swan had entered the Pacific through the Strait of Magellan and begun raiding their way northward. Their depredations had become so notorious that by autumn Lima's merchants were reluctant to consign their silver and goods for shipment to the commercial fair at Panama. After lengthy conferences with Duque de la Palata, the new viceroy, the merchants were persuaded to do so, especially after news was received on 3 March 1685 that the Spanish plate fleet had arrived safely at Portobelo on 28 November. It was now urgent to meet these vessels, so preparations were pushed forward, but before these could be completed further reports arrived, indicating a fresh wave of buccaneers had crossed the Isthmus of Panama under Captains Desmarais, François Grogniet, William Knight, Lescuyer, Pierre le Picard, Jean Rose, and Francis Townley to join Edward Davis (Cooke's successor) and Swan. Faced with such heavy odds, the Peruvian merchants flatly refused to embark their silver, and the Duque de la Palata was forced to dispatch a largely military expedition.

On 7 May 1685, the armada set sail from Callao under the command of Lieutenant General Tomás Palavacino, the viceroy's brother-in-law. He was to be advised by the veteran flag captain, Santiago Pontejos,

aboard the *San José,* its armament having been increased from 24 to 40 cannon and its crew to 405 men. The vice-flagship *Guadalupe* departed under Captain Antonio de Vea, with 36 guns and 374 men, while Manuel Pantoja commanded the 26-gun *patache, San Lorenzo,* and a 6-gun tender also joined. The armada was seconded by the private merchantmen *Nuestra Señora del Pópulo* and *Nuestra Señora del Rosario* (Our Lady of the Rosary), both mounting 20 guns, plus a 6-gun fireship. The whole enterprise consisted of 1,431 men (their wages fully paid for eight months' service) and carried supplies and arms to reinforce the garrison at Panama, along with a *situado* of 533,434 pesos and some private silver.

## Victory Off Isla del Rey
### (June 1685)

These vessels entered the roadstead at Panama on 3 June, having slipped past the buccaneer blockaders, who were lazing unsuspectingly near Isla del Rey. After delivering their cargo, the Spanish men o' war sallied to engage the rovers, and toward noon on 7 June 1685 emerged from a morning shower to find their enemy lying off small Pacheca Island. The pirates were caught off guard, particularly Grogniet, who had to delay weighing because a large portion of his men were ashore at two small chapels and so fell behind his consorts. The pirates had eleven vessels, but only Davis and Swan's mounted guns, the rest being unarmed Spanish prizes. An indecisive, long-range engagement ensued, with the buccaneers unwilling to close with the armada vessels, who in turn feared being outmaneuvered and boarded by their more nimble opponents. All afternoon the two formations wheeled around each other in the Gulf of Panama, firing until darkness fell.

During the night Palavacino employed a stratagem of extinguishing and rekindling lights on his ships, which deceived the buccaneers into believing he had shifted position. Instead, the Spanish ships were still in good order next morning, while it was the pirates who were scattered, and the pursuit resumed. The day ended with a Spanish victory, as the raiders were driven off westward toward the sanctuary of Coiba Island. Although the armada had failed to make any captures, the buccaneers soon after fell out amongst themselves along national lines and lifted their blockade of Panama.

Flushed with this success, Palavacino began tacking back to Peru. He had reached as far as Paita by early September, where he went ashore with his staff, allegedly sick but more likely intending to complete the trip in greater comfort overland. Shortly after coming ashore, his flagship *San José* accidentally caught fire on 5 September and exploded at anchor, killing 241 men, among them Pontejos. The death of so many experienced officers and sailors was a devastating blow to the armada, as was the loss of the ship's irreplaceable artillery and accoutrements. Worse still, Peru's treasury was so drained it was impossible to replace the flagship while simultaneously maintaining any campaign against the dispersed pirates, who began striking at vulnerable points all up and down the Pacific coast.

## ENGAGEMENT WITH DAVIS
### (APRIL 1687)

On 9 July 1686, *maestre de campo* Francisco de Zúñiga, Knight of the Order of Santiago, sortied from Callao with three hired merchantmen: the 12-gun *San Francisco de Paula,* the 6-gun *Santa Catalina* commanded by Captain Gaspar Bernabeu de Mansilla, and the *patache* of Pedro García de San Roque with 80 black militiamen on board. This trio conducted the annual *situado* to Panama, then slowly worked its way back toward Peru, searching for pirates. Upon nearing their home port *Santa Catalina*

became separated by a storm and on 23 April 1687 headed into Huarmey to obtain fresh supplies. But at the entrance to the port it encountered Davis's ship, and being heavily outgunned, was forced to flee into the shallows. De Mansilla was killed early in the fight and his 145-man crew deliberately ran the ship aground, thus hoping to escape. Nonetheless, the Spaniards were badly mauled, suffering as many as 50 drowned, 7 or 8 killed, and another 10 or 12 wounded. Four days later de Zúñiga's two other merchantmen reentered Callao, unaware of the disaster that had befallen their consort.

## TRIUMPH OF THE PERUVIAN PRIVATEERS
### (1687-1688)

During their absence, a consortium of rich Peruvian merchants had agreed to finance a private *armadilla,* which they called the *Compañía de corso "Nuestra Señora de Guía"* (Privateering Company "Our Lady as Guide"). The viceroy contributed guns and ammunition, allowing the corsairs to retain full shares in any prize they took. Shortly thereafter the merchants had three purchased vessels ready to sail: the 20-gun *San José* and *San Nicolás,* commanded by the Biscayan privateers Dionisio López de Artunduaga and Nicolás de Igarza respectively, plus a small *patache.* In mid-May 1687 they sortied hurriedly, upon receipt of a report that pirates had captured Guayaquil, and were holding its citizens for ransom offshore. On 27 May they came in sight of this enemy formation, consisting of almost twenty medium and small craft under Davis, Picard, and George Hutt. A long-range-gun duel ensued over the next five days with the Peruvian privateers eventually scattering the raiders and recuperating some prizes.

During this action *San Nicolás* ran hard aground on a sandbank off Atacames and limped back into Callao making water. It was quickly substituted by *San Francisco de*

*Paula* and another *patache,* who joined López de Artunduaga and resumed the pursuit of the retreating buccaneers. Davis departed round the Horn and the Peruvians were able to hound the remaining rovers as far as New Spain, bringing them to a confrontation in late December 1687 wherein the pirates were worsted. Another contingent of six buccaneer ships and many *piraguas* was defeated in Amapala Bay during summer 1688, obliging the raiders to retreat overland. For the first time in almost a decade, the Pacific coast was free of any large concentration of enemy vessels, and the armada resumed its former peacetime duties.

The convoy, with recently promoted General Antonio de Vea, was escorted to Panama with the vice-flagship *Guadalupe* early in 1691, was one of Peru's biggest, beginning its return passage on 7 July. *Guadalupe* and one other man o' war protected 12 merchantmen all the way to Callao, arriving on 1 December and being followed by another warship and five more merchantmen that had lagged behind. The *Guadalupe* was more than 30 years old and in need of being replaced. The 40-gun private ship *Jesús, María y José* (Jesus, Mary and Joseph) was purchased in 1692 as a stop-gap measure, but new warships needed to be built. The viceroy therefore approached the merchant backers of the "Nuestra Señora de Guía" Privateering Company, who agreed to dissolve their enterprise and instead channel funds into the construction of a new armada.

## REBUILT FLEET
### (1693-1694)

By early 1693, two warships capable of mounting roughly 40 guns apiece were taking shape in the Guayaquil yards, and that summer de Vea traveled there to assume command of the new 845-ton flagship *Santísimo Sacramento* (Most Holy Sacrament). Unfortunately, he died on the last leg between Puná and Guayaquil, being replaced by José de Alzamora, who sailed this 40-gun vessel back into Callao on 25 September 1693. The following summer, on 8 June 1694, the new 36-gun, 700-ton vice-flagship *Nuestra Señora de la Concepción* arrived with a small new frigate, the *San Miguel* (Saint Michael), which was to serve as *patache* along with the 250-ton, 18-gun *Santa Cruz* (Holy Cross). The older auxiliary *Santo Toribio* was scrapped, and this was to remain the basic constitution of the armada for the remainder of the seventeenth century.

***See also*** *azogue;* Biscayan privateers; careen; Cooke, John; Eaton, John; Grogniet, Capitaine; Morgan, Henry; *patache;* South Seas; Swan, Charles.

**References:** Bradley, *Lure;* Earle, *Panamá;* Lussan; Pérez.

# MARKHAM, JOHN
## (FL. 1683-1684)

New York privateer who raided the Spaniards in the West Indies.

In March 1683 Markham was lying at New Providence in the Bahamas with Captains Jan Corneliszoon, Conway Woolley, and the French *flibustier* Bréhal, preparing to go "fish silver from a Spanish wreck." Then Captain Thomas Paine arrived with a license from Governor Sir Thomas Lynch of Jamaica to hunt pirates, so the five decided to unite and raid the nearby Spanish outpost of Saint Augustine, Florida, under Paine's commission (although England and Spain were then officially at peace). The raiders, in any event, landed flying French colors, but found the Spaniards forewarned, and so withdrew after releasing some captives they had brought and looting the surrounding countryside.

Returning to the Bahamas, Markham, Paine, and Bréhal reentered New Providence, while the other two proceeded directly to the wreck site. Governor Robert Lilburne allegedly wished to detain Markham and Paine for violating England's peace with Spain but could not do so "for want of a force." Shortly thereafter, the three rovers sailed away to the site and began working the wreck, although apparently with limited success, for by September 1683 Markham was back at New Providence, and Paine bound for Rhode Island.

Some months later, Markham organized a freebooter force of three frigates and eight sloops for a descent on the Mexican port of Tampico. This assault took place at dawn on Sunday, 23 April 1684, Spanish survivors relating later how "Captain Juan Marcan [*sic*] led his men in an encircling maneuver and firing musketry at the Spaniards" until other buccaneers could overrun the town. Tampico was but an impoverished fishing village, and the raiders announced they had come from "diving on a wreck in the Mimbres [Bahamas]" to obtain supplies. They then stole "wheat, fish, sugar, the church's ornaments and its silver, as well as clothing," plus indulging in their usual wanton destruction. (An English buccaneer called John Tudor boasted he had been with Laurens de Graaf at the sack of Veracruz the previous year, receiving a full share of 800 pesos as booty, and then "burned down a house and with his companions drank a barrel of spirits" in Tampico.) The unhappy Spanish captives also noticed it was Markham who gave the orders for them to be fed.

Markham loaded his plunder quickly aboard the ships, realizing it was best not to tarry. Six days later news of this attack reached the Armada de Barlovento at Veracruz, which sortied on 4 May and four days later caught the frigate *Presbyter* and a small sloop still inside the Tampico bar with 104 freebooters on board. Markham and most of his cohorts had already departed, but these laggards—77 Englishmen and New

Englanders, 26 Dutchmen and a Spaniard—were carried to Veracruz in chains. Two weeks later, 13 Englishmen and the lone Spaniard were condemned to death, these sentences being carried out on the Veracruz waterfront the morning of 14 June 1684.

**See also** Barlovento, Armada de; Bréhal, Capitaine; Corneliszoon, Jan; Lilburne, Robert; Paine, Thomas; Woolley, Conway.

**References:** *C.S.P., Amer. and W.I.,* Vol. XI; Juárez; Robles; Torres.

# MAROON

Term meaning to abandon someone on a desolate island or beach, usually as a punishment for undesirable elements.

This expression was originally derived from the Spanish word *cimarrón,* which before accents became standardized in that language was often spelled *cimaroon* or *cimarroon.* (The same occurred with terms such as *tifón,* which from *tifoon* or *tiphoon* became transformed into *typhoon* in English; *doblón* became *doubloon; picarón* became *picaroon,* etc.)

*Cimarrón* is a Spanish adjective that denotes anything wild, rogue, or untamed. Thus, *ganado cimarrón* means wild cattle; *indio cimarrón,* a renegade Indian; *negro cimarrón,* a runaway slave. It was this latter group that was most often referred to in Spanish America as *cimarrones* and is probably where the word passed into English. Many Africans who eluded their Spanish masters sought refuge in coastal areas, as these were normally shunned as unhealthy by Castillian Spaniards, and so became a sparsely populated haven that was reminiscent of West Africa to the runaways along the coasts. Buccaneers and other seamen who chanced upon these isolated settlements, hidden in remote inlets all the way from the Spanish

Main to the Gulf of Mexico, assumed their inhabitants had been driven there—marooned—for their rebelliousness.

A classic example of European seamen getting rid of an unwanted rogue element occurred when the Dutch Commodore Cornelis Evertsen (Kees the Devil) reconquered Sint Eustatius from the English in late May 1673. When one of his soldiers committed a serious infraction of the military rules, Evertsen ordered him keelhauled and then "dragged up on the land at some island or another, as a rogue."

*See also* doubloon; Evertsen de Jongste, Cornelis; keelhauling; picaroon.

*Reference:* Shomette, *Raid*.

# MARTIEN, DAVID

### ALSO MAARTEN
### (FL. 1664-1671)

Rover from the Netherlands who served under English and French colors.

Martien appears to have been a veteran commander in the West Indies when in late 1664 he joined four other Jamaican captains to mount a small peacetime raid against the Spanish in the Gulf of Mexico. Strictly speaking, such ventures were illegal, as the new governor, Sir Thomas Modyford, had proclaimed on 16 June 1664 (O.S.) "that for the future all acts of hostility against the Spaniards should cease," a policy that had been repeatedly underscored. However, the privateers chose to ignore this injunction, later arguing somewhat disingenuously that "having been out 22 months [i.e., since participating in Commodore Christopher Myngs's sack of Campeche in early 1663] and hearing nothing of the cessation of hostilities between the King and the Spaniards," they had continued operating under their two-year-old commissions from Lord Windsor.

## MEXICAN RAID
### (SPRING 1665)

John Morris and Martien were the apparent leaders of this venture, seconded by Captains Henry Morgan, Freeman, and Jackman. Together they mustered a few vessels and 200 men, departing Jamaica in January 1665. Rounding the Yucatán peninsula, they moved gingerly down the treacherous gulf coast until arriving in the vicinity of Campeche, where one night in mid-February they cut out an 8-gun Spanish frigate lying in the roads. Sailing their prize past the Laguna de Términos, they came to anchor on 19 February opposite the tiny town of Santa María de la Frontera, at the mouth of the Grijalva River. Some 110–120 buccaneers disembarked and traveled 50 miles upriver through the marshy channels until coming within sight of the provincial capital of Villahermosa de Tabasco. At four o'clock on the morning of the 24 February they fell upon the sleeping city, capturing most of the inhabitants in their beds. A general sack ensued, after which the booty and captives were loaded aboard a coaster lying in the river. The raiders then paused at nearby Santa Teresa ranch to release the women captives, retaining the men, for whom they demanded a ransom of 300 head of cattle. Farther downriver they came upon a second coaster bearing flour, which they also seized.

Nearing the river mouth, they discovered their waiting ships had been captured during their absence by a Spanish naval patrol. Three Spanish frigates and 270 men had been sent out from Campeche by Lieutenant Governor Antonio Maldonado de Aldana in quest of the prize taken from that port. This *armadilla* had sighted the interlopers' trio of vessels anchored offshore on 22 February, boarding them without a fight. A few Englishmen had fled on a single vessel, abandoning their 10-gun flagship and 8-gun prize to the Spaniards. Seven buccaneers were left behind in the panic and revealed to their captors that the ships had been left unmanned because "Captain Mauricio [*sic;* Morris] and David Martin [*sic;* Martien]" had led the bulk of the raiders inland.

Their retreat cut off, the main body of freebooters released their remaining hostages and began moving westward with their two coasters, hoping to find another river channel whereby to escape. On the afternoon of 17 March they were overtaken by the Spanish *guardacostas* opposite Santa Ana Cay, this time sailing the privateers' former 10-gun flagship and 8-gun prize, having crewed these with 300 volunteer militia from Campeche. José Aldana, the Spanish commander, sent a messenger in a boat to call upon the buccaneers to surrender, but they pretended not to understand. When an interpreter approached offshore the following morn, Morris and Martien replied that they would not give up without a fight. The Spaniards reluctantly disembarked, discovering that the raiders had used the interval to entrench themselves behind a palisade reinforced with sandbags and seven small cannon from Villahermosa. The Spanish force, mostly armed civilians, showed little stomach for an assault and were easily repelled without incurring a single loss among the freebooters. The next day, 19 March, the Spanish ships were found to have run aground, allowing the raiders to exit undisturbed with their two coasters.

## CENTRAL AMERICAN CAMPAIGN
### (SUMMER 1665)

Morris and Martien proceeded northward hugging the coastline, capturing smaller boats and making occasional landings to obtain supplies. Off Sisal they looted a vessel laden with corn, whose crew they allegedly released with a message to the governor of Yucatán, vowing to return and lay waste his province. They then rounded Yucatán and traversed the Bay of Honduras as far as

Roatan, where they paused to take on water. Striking next at Trujillo, on the north coast of Honduras, they overran this port and seized a vessel lying in the roads before continuing to Cape Gracias a Dios and the Mosquito Coast. Nine native guides joined them there, sailing southward to Monkey Point (Punta Mico, Nicaragua), where the buccaneers hid their ships in an inlet before heading up the San Juan River with their lighter boats. More than 100 miles and three waterfalls later, they emerged in the great Lago de Nicaragua. Crossing this by travelling at night and resting by day, they snuck up on Granada and took it by surprise on 29 June 1665, when they

> marched undescried into the center of the city, fired a volley, overturned 18 great guns in the Plaza de Armas, took the *sargento mayor* [garrison commander's] house wherein were all their arms and ammunition, secured in the great church 300 of the best men prisoners, abundance of which were churchmen, plundered for 16 hours, discharged all the prisoners, sunk all the boats [to prevent pursuit], and so came away.

Retracing their course across the lake, at the southeastern extremity "they took a vessel of 100 tons and an island as large as Barbados, called Lida [*sic;* Solentiname?], which they plundered."

The raiders then regained their anchored vessels and by the end of August, William Beeston was writing in his journal at Port Royal, "Captain Fackman [*sic;* Jackman] and others arrived from the taking of the towns of Tabasco and Villahermosa, in the Bay of Mexico." They had traveled almost 3,000 miles in seven months, assaulting five Spanish towns and undergoing countless lesser engagements. However, Martien did not return to the English island, for during the intervening period the Second Anglo-Dutch

War had erupted back in Europe, with Holland and France ranged against England and Spain. Thus "being a Dutchman and fearing his entertainment at Jamaica," Martien had sailed directly to the French *boucanier* stronghold of Tortuga Island, off the northwestern tip of Saint Domingue. His ship, it was said, still carried some of the Indians he had brought away from Granada.

This withdrawal appears to have been shortlived, for Governor Modyford actively recruited freebooters of every nationality to his colony's defense by freely issuing licenses. A year later, at the end of August 1666, he wrote:

> Had it not been for that seasonable action [of liberally granting commissions] I could not have kept this place against French buccaneers, who would have ruined all the seaside plantations, whereas I now draw from them mainly, and lately David Marteen [*sic*], the best man of Tortuga, that has two frigates at sea, had promised to bring in both.

There exist few details about Martien's remaining career, but on 17 December 1671 (O.S.) the new Jamaican governor, Sir Thomas Lynch, reported that there were but three privateers still operating, "One Captain Diego [Grillo], and Yhallahs [*sic*; Jelles de Lecat] and Martin." Early the following year, Beeston captured the renegade privateer ship *Charity* of Francis Weatherbourne at Campeche, describing this vessel as having "been formerly Captain David Martyn's [*sic*] man o' war."

**See also** Beeston, William; *guardacostas*; Huidobro, Mateo Alonso de; Jackman, Captain; Laguna de Términos; Maldonado de Aldana, Antonio; Morris, John.

**References:** *C.S.P., Amer. and W.I.,* Vol. IX; Eugenio; Gerhard, *Southeast; Gosse, Who's Who; Intersting Tracts;* Pawson, *Port Royal;* Pope; Sáiz.

# MARTÍN, ALONSO

(FL. 1684)

Spanish privateer who operated out of Santo Domingo.

On 20 June 1684 (O.S.), Governor Sir Thomas Lynch of Jamaica reported, "Last week a sloop from Nevis and two of our fishermen were all robbed, their boats taken by one Alonzo Martin of Santo Domingo. The [Spanish] governor would not condemn the sloops, for these rogues awe and hector them, so they carried them off to trepan others. This is what makes our men turn pirates."

**Reference:** *C.S.P., Amer. and W.I.,* Vol. XI.

# MARTIN, CHRISTOPHER

(FL. 1656-1673)

West Country sea captain who defended St. John's, Newfoundland, against attack in the closing stages of the Third Anglo-Dutch War.

Martin, originally from Cockington, Devon, had resided in St. John's for many years, and long served as its "vice admiral," when in October 1673 he received word of a powerful Dutch squadron under Captain Nikolaas Boes attacking nearby French and English fisheries. These raiders consisted of three warships of 40 guns apiece and another of 36, which had been detached by Commodore Cornelis Evertsen (Kees the Devil) following his recent reconquest of New York.

Improvising hastily, Martin stripped the vessel *Elias Andrews,* which was anchored in the roads, of its six light pieces of ordnance; with the help of 30 men, he installed these in the small earthen fort guarding the approaches to the harbor. When the Dutch men o' war bore down menacingly a few days later, Martin greeted them with such brisk fire that Boes assumed the place was defended in strength. He preferred to veer off and sweep the Grand Banks fisheries before returning to Europe.

*See also* Evertsen de Jongste, Cornelis.
*Reference:* Shomette, *Raid*.

# MATROSS

Seventeenth-century English expression for a gunner's mate, doubtless derived from the Dutch word *matroos* or "sailor."

In June 1681, for example, the Assembly of Barbados entered into its minutes: "On the petition of Captain Samuel Norris, gunner of Hole Fort, ordered that 5,000 lbs. of muscovado [*sic*] sugar be paid to him, and 3,000 lbs. to John Chilcott, his matross." *Mascabado* is the Spanish word for unrefined or brown sugar.

*Reference:* C.S.P., America and W.I., Vol. XI.

# MAYES, WILLIAM

## ALSO MAZE, MACE, OR MAISE
## (FL. 1694-1699)

Rhode Island seaman who emulated his fellow countryman Thomas Tew by making a piratical foray into the Red Sea.

Mayes was the son of a tavernkeeper and well connected in Rhode Island politics because his wife Sarah was the daughter of Samuel Gorton, former president of that colony. When Tew returned to Newport in the spring of 1694 with an immense booty acquired from one of the Great Mogul's treasure ships, Mayes was one of many locals dazzled by this easy success. On 7 September 1694 (O.S.), he obtained clearance from the customs house at Newport to sail his own 60-ton brigantine *Pearl,* of 6 guns and 50 men, "on a trading voyage to Madagascar." As the English Board of Trade later noted, there was no commerce on that island, so the best

reason one could have for going there was "to buy goods captured by pirates." At worst, Mayes intended to try his hand at piracy himself.

This was seemingly confirmed when on 20 December of this same year, he obtained a privateering commission from the dishonest deputy governor of Rhode Island, John Greene, Jr. (an official described by a contemporary source as "a brutish man of very corrupt or no principles in religion"). London complained that Greene was not empowered to issue such patents, nor did he extract a bond against Mayes's good behavior. Greene argued that he was unaware of these laws, to which the Board of Trade responded disbelievingly that "such an ignorant person" should never have been put in office.

By this time, Mayes had long since sailed for the Cape of Good Hope. It was rumored that after trading at Madagascar, he was robbed by Henry Every; but the Board of Trade refused to believe this, saying the Rhode Island captain had actually helped that pirate rob the Great Mogul's ship, *Ganj-i-Sawai*. For this reason, Mayes was specifically mentioned in the royal warrant authorizing Captain William Kidd to capture certain "wicked and ill-disposed persons" a few years later. Meanwhile, Mayes had apparently returned to New York in 1699 in command of a big ship loaded with booty taken in the Red Sea.

*See also* Every, Henry; Kidd, William; Tew, Thomas.

*References:* Chapin; Gosse, *Who's Who*.

# MIGUEL, BLAS

## (D. 1687)

Cuban corsair, possibly a mulatto, who attempted to kill Laurens de Graaf at Petit Goâve.

In May 1687, the frigate of the Biscayan privateer Fermín de Salaberría became embroiled in a lopsided battle with De Graaf's pirate flagship off Júcaro on the southern Cuban coast. The Spaniard was soon driven aground and in serious danger of being captured, when a flotilla of small *guardacosta* vessels hastened out to his rescue. De Graaf immediately turned on these as well, seizing a schooner and sinking a *piragua*. During the fighting, Blas Miguel's brother died, and the Cuban swore vengeance against the notorious pirate.

A few months later, Miguel launched his scheme. Despite the unofficial truce existing with the French of Saint Domingue, he decided to make a nocturnal assault on the *flibustier* capital of Petit Goâve, hoping to catch its defenders unawares. Moreover, he chose his date with particular care, selecting 10 August because he knew this to be the day on the church calendar when the festival of Saint Lawrence was observed, and he hoped to find De Graaf in port celebrating his holiday.

At first light on 10 August 1687, the officer of the watch overlooking Petit Goâve's harbor, Capitaine Vigneron, saw a large *piragua* gliding into the roads, and he challenged it. A terrified French captive was made to reply, but when Vigneron suspiciously hailed a second time, a warning cry ensued. Before the French defenses could react, the Cubans swarmed ashore, rampaging throughout the town. In the home of Mayor Dupuis, they hacked both him and his young manservant to death with machetes, then bayoneted the mayor's pregnant wife when she wept that she could not live without her husband. The small fortress was occupied without resistance and many homes ransacked (some by local "Negros, Negresses and free mulattos," a French official angrily noticed). But in the growing dawn, the defenders realized that Miguel had but a few score men with him, no more than 85 overall, 20 of whom remained aboard his brigantine and *demi-galère* (half-galley) out in the harbor.

French reinforcements began pouring in from outlying areas, shooting down isolated groups of looters and Cubans who had few firearms among them.

Miguel's men were soon forced back inside the fortress, then forsaken by their two craft out in the harbor as the batteries opened fire. Only the *piragua* still rocked idly in the surf, with a single Cuban corsair on board, until De Graaf personally waded out, "machete in hand," and took it. The attackers were now trapped inside the fortress and sent out a message with "a woman of ill repute they had captured," offering to restore their booty if allowed to sail away. The enraged *flibustiers* scorned the offer, storming the walls and taking the remaining 47 Cubans prisoner. Another 17 already lay dead on the streets of Petit Goâve.

The next day a summary trial was held, at which Miguel and his two principal lieutenants were condemned to be "broken alive" on the wheel, while another 42 corsairs were sentenced to be hanged, and only two, "a young boy and a Negro," were spared because they had been forced to join the raiders. On 12 August 1687, these terrible punishments were carried out, Miguel being slowly battered to death as the "whites, mulattos, Indians, and blacks who had accompanied" him were strung up all around.

*See also* Biscayan privateers; De Graaf, Laurens Cornelis Boudewijn; *guardacostas;* Vigneron, Capitaine.

*Reference:* Lugo.

# MITCHELL, CAPTAIN

## (FL. 1663)

English privateer who operated out of Jamaica.

On 28 February 1663 (O.S.), Mitchell's *Blessing* arrived at Port Royal with the first news of Commodore Christopher Myngs's expedition against Campeche. This large force had quit Jamaica more than a month-and-a-half earlier and nothing had been heard during this time. Mitchell reported that while cruising in the "Bay of Campeche" (i.e., eastern Gulf of Mexico), he had met three privateering ships that had become separated from the main body, after which Captain William James's vessel had sunk in a storm. Worse, the Spaniards had allegedly received advance warning of the attack and evacuated all their noncombatants and valuables to Mérida de Yucatán. They had then mustered

> 1,500 men in the town to oppose their [the privateers'] landing, and had unrigged all the ships in the harbor, that they might not carry them away, and had hauled them on shore, and landed their guns on batteries; had sent one ship to windward and another to leeward, to give advice that no ships might come thither, and set watches along the sea coast, to give intelligence of their approach.

This alarming report filled Jamaica with concern as to the fate of their colleagues and loved ones but was utterly unfounded. In fact, Campeche had been carried by surprise a month earlier, and on 2 March (O.S.) a true account reached Macarry Bay of this victory.

*See also* James, William; Myngs, Sir Christopher.

*References:* Gosse, *Who's Who; Interesting Tracts.*

# MODYFORD, SIR THOMAS

## (c. 1620-1679)

First Royalist governor of Barbados and second of Jamaica, dismissed from the latter post for encouraging privateers.

Modyford was probably born about 1620, the first of five sons of the mayor of Exeter, England. He became a barrister at Lincoln's Inn in London, married Elizabeth Palmer of Devonshire about 1640 (by whom he fathered three children: Elizabeth, Thomas, and Charles), and then served in the Royalist armies during the English Civil War. In June 1647, toward the latter stages of the conflict, he took his family and became a planter on the West Indian island of Barbados, bought half an estate (500 acres) for £7,000 and assumed a leading role in that little community.

After the execution of Charles I, he played a prominent part in the Royalist resistance to Parliamentary rule on that island but eventually succumbed and convinced his regiment to change sides, so that the king's governor, Lord Willoughby, was forced to yield. Despite this service, Modyford was never fully trusted by the Parliamentarians, who deprived him of his regimental command in 1653. He was restored and also appointed to the Council of Barbados after directly petitioning Cromwell.

Following the Restoration of Charles II in spring 1660, a commission was issued in London appointing Modyford to the post of governor of Barbados, which he enacted soon after receiving it in late June, reestablishing royal government without difficulty. By December, word had arrived that Willoughby was to be restored to his former position, and Modyford might face charges for "his treachery in betraying the island to the usurper, and his persecution of Royalists ever since." Consequently, he resigned and remained as speaker of the assembly only, while awaiting a resolution from England. He was never charged, thanks to his influential kinsman George Monck, duke of Albemarle, who in February 1664 proposed that Modyford succeed Lord Windsor as governor of Jamaica. This was approved, and Modyford was instructed to take as many settlers from Barbados as were willing to accompany him and was also created a baronet on 18 February 1664 (O.S.).

## GOVERNOR OF JAMAICA
### (1664-1671)

By the end of May 1664, HMS *Westergate* and the ketch *Swallow* had arrived at Port Royal, bearing Modyford's lieutenant governor, Colonel Edward Morgan, who immediately assumed office until his superior appeared. The *Blessing* of Captain James Gilbert followed on 1 June 1664 (O.S.) with 400 people from Barbados, and another 200 settlers came with Modyford on 4 June (O.S.) aboard Captain Stokes's HMS *Marmaduke*. The new governor forthwith "caused his commission to be publicly read" and set about launching his administration. One of Modyford's first acts was to issue a proclamation on 16 June (O.S.) announcing "that for the future all acts of hostility against the Spaniards should cease," a policy which was to become increasingly tenuous during his years in office. On the one hand, neither Whitehall nor Jamaica's commercial traders wished to have petty buccaneer raids dictate their relations with Spain; on the other, planters and ordinary citizens depended upon the privateers for their prosperity and defense, as did the Crown's own garrison in times of war. Thus, Modyford was compelled to restrain the freebooters' activities without openly driving them to seek French, Dutch, Portuguese, or even Spanish commissions.

He began in September 1664 by impounding two rich Spanish prizes brought in by the veteran Captain Robert Searle, in part prompted by a recent letter from the king that reiterated the prohibition of violence against the Spaniards and ordered "entire restitution and satisfaction made to the sufferers." In light of this reminder, Modyford and the Jamaican council agreed "that Captain Searle's commission be taken

from him and his rudder and sails taken ashore for security," while the prizes were returned intact to Santiago de Cuba. But later the governor discreetly allowed Maurice Williams and Bernard Nichols to bring in prizes, while privately communicating to London that the buccaneers must be allowed to dispose of their captures as they straggled back in to surrender their commissions, "otherwise they will be alarmed and go to the French at Tortuga, and His Majesty will lose 1,000 or 1,500 stout men." He added they might even be tempted to attack ships bound for Jamaica, as Captain Munro had already done, "for they are desperate people, the greater part having been men o' war for twenty years." He concluded on the rather optimistic note that they might instead be set "a-planting," and if afterward "His Majesty shall think fit to have Tortuga or Curaçao taken, none will be fitter for that work than they."

This suggestion was shortly put to the test when in spring 1665 word arrived of the outbreak of the Second Anglo-Dutch War back in Europe. With Modyford's backing, Lieutenant Governor Morgan assembled a force of ten privateer vessels and more than 500 men, leading these in the conquest of Dutch Sint Eustatia and Sabá. However, Morgan died during the assault, and the buccaneers then refused to follow his second-in-command Colonel Theodore Cary—"a man of too easy disposition," according to Modyford—in the projected attack against Curaçao. Instead they dispersed, preferring to raid their traditional Spanish foes rather than the Dutch. By November 1665, Modyford was obliged to send "for the leading men of the privateers," asking them to rendezvous at Bluefields Bay, where he again proposed they sail against Curaçao under Edward Mansfield. The buccaneers agreed, but once out of sight of Jamaica they turned upon the Spaniards again. Even Mansfield's crew refused to beat upwind for Curaçao, "averring publicly that there was more profit with less hazard to be gotten against the Spaniard, which was their only interest."

Such sentiments were not limited to the privateersmen, for late in February 1666 the Jamaican council presented Modyford with a resolution outlining twelve reasons why it was to the interest of that colony to grant letters of marque against the Spaniards, claiming "said commissions did extraordinarily conduce to the strengthening, preservation, enriching and advancing the settlement of this island." Modyford concurred, justifying this belligerence by the hostility met from the Spanish Americans, adding, "it must be force alone that can cut in sunder that unneighborly maxim of their government to deny all access of strangers." After complaining repeatedly to London about the depredations of Spanish *guardacostas,* he was given "latitude to grant or not to grant commissions against the Spaniards," despite the official peace prevailing with that nation in Europe.

The governor continued to issue licenses even after the first Treaty of Madrid was signed in May 1667, motivated in part by constant local friction with the Spanish Americans, as well as the profits to be had from this low-grade warfare. He contrived to appoint his brother James to replace Edward Morgan as lieutenant governor and chief justice of the Admiralty Court at Port Royal, and he commissioned Henry Morgan in February 1668 "to draw together the English privateers" and determine whether the Spanish Americans intended to invade Jamaica.

This threat was supposedly confirmed, then used to justify Morgan's descent on Portobelo, which he seized in late June 1668 and held for ransom. The next spring Modyford furnished the frigate HMS *Oxford,* of 34 guns, to serve as Morgan's flagship in his campaign against Maracaibo and later welcomed the raiders upon their victorious return. At this

point the licensed privateering might have begun to taper off, for Modyford had once more been ordered to put an end to hostilities against the Spaniards, and he proclaimed this throughout the streets of Port Royal on 24 June 1669 (O.S.). However, the Spanish Americans again provided him with a convenient excuse when they began issuing commissions of their own to corsairs such as Manoel Rivero Pardal, who raided Jamaica in summer 1670. In retaliation, Modyford commissioned Morgan on 2 July (O.S.) to gather a force and "use his best endeavors to surprise, take, sink, disperse or destroy the enemy's vessels, and in case he finds it feasible, to land and attack Santiago [de Cuba] or any other place." Morgan sailed to Ile-à-Vache, off the southwestern tip of Saint Domingue, and spent several months recruiting men. Meanwhile, Modyford was advised that a second Treaty of Madrid had been signed with the Spaniards that July but allegedly could not then get word to Morgan before his freebooter host devastated Panama.

Equally significant, Albemarle had died in January 1670, thus depriving Modyford of his patronage and protection. It had already been decided to replace Modyford with his old Jamaican rival, Sir Thomas Lynch, who believed in developing peaceful trade relations with Spanish America. Lynch was instructed to "cause the person of Sir Thomas Modyford to be made prisoner and sent home under a strong guard, [because] he has, contrary to the King's express commands, made many depredations and hostilities against the subjects of His Majesty's good brother, the Catholic King." On 1 July 1671 (O.S.) HMS *Assistance,* 40 guns, and *Welcome,* 36 guns, reached Port Royal bearing Lynch, who immediately read his patent and the revocation of that of Modyford at a banquet given in his honor at the latter's home. "The people seemed not much pleased," Lynch noted in a letter, for Modyford had presided over a period of considerable growth and successful military ventures in Jamaica's history.

## LATER CAREER
### (1671–1679)

Six weeks later, Lynch completed the second part of his instructions when he inveigled Modyford aboard *Assistance* on the pretext that he had "something to import to him from the King," and Modyford was arrested. Modyford learned that his younger son Charles had already been detained in the Tower of London against his father's good behavior and reacted with great dignity to his own detention. He only objected to the underhand method employed, wishing he might have been allowed to show "his obedience by his voluntary submission to His Majesty's pleasure." An embarrassed Lynch assured him "his life and estate was not in danger," but there was a need to make a convincing show of royal displeasure for the Spaniards' benefit. On 22 August 1671 (O.S.), Modyford set sail for England, a prisoner aboard the *Jamaica Merchant* of Captain Joseph Knapman.

Upon his arrival in London, Modyford was incarcerated in his son's cell at the Tower on 17 November (O.S.). Less than a year afterward, on 14 August 1672 (O.S.), he was ordered to have the liberty of the prison and remained in relatively easy confinement for a couple more years without ever being brought to trial. When the Crown's diplomatic priorities once again changed, he was released and restored to Jamaica as chief justice of the island in 1675. He died on 2 September 1679 (O.S.), being buried in the cathedral at Spanish Town.

*See also* guardacostas; letters of marque; Lynch, Sir Thomas; Mansfield, Edward; Morgan, Henry; Nichols, Bernard; Rivero Pardal, Manoel; Williams, Maurice.

*References: D.N.B.;* Earle, *Panamá;* Exquemelin; *Interesting Tracts;* Pawson, *Port Royal;* Pope; Thornton, *Modyfords.*

# MOIDORE

Term moved into English, originally derived from the Portuguese phrase *moeda d'ouro* (gold coin), which came to be applied to any finely wrought piece of gold currency in the seventeenth century.

# MOONE, SAILING MASTER

### (FL. 1683)

Sailing master, apparently originally from Bristol, England, who was serving aboard Jean Hamlin's notorious pirate vessel *Trompeuse* (Trickster), when it seized the Royal African Company ship *Thomas and William* off French Hispaniola in January 1683. The pirates reputedly obtained 65 pounds in gold from this one haul, leading some to quit Hamlin's service shortly thereafter and attempt to disappear back into civilian life. When he learned of the incident, Governor Sir Thomas Lynch of Jamaica wrote, "I have taken the description of this Moone and of 13 or 14 more English rogues, and shall send it to Bristol (whence he comes) and to all the colonies in America," to alert the authorities.

*See also* Hamlin, Jean; Hispaniola.
*Reference: C.S.P., Amer. and W.I.,* Vol. XI.

# MORGAN, CAPTAIN

### (FL. 1682–1683)

Apparently a pseudonym adopted by an anonymous English confederate of pirate Jean Hamlin to facilitate his escape into civilian life.

In October 1682, the 30-gun frigate *Trompeuse* (Trickster) was seized off the Central American coast by a band of 20 pirates,

"20 or 30 of them English." They sailed this prize to Ile-à-Vache off French Hispaniola, and under Hamlin's leadership began looting passing merchantmen until forced to abandon this hunting ground. They then traveled to Saint Thomas in the Danish Virgin Islands before crossing the Atlantic to sweep down West Africa's Gold Coast. While operating there, Hamlin captured a Flushinger of 20 to 24 guns, which he converted into a consort, and gave the command to his unnamed English subordinate.

After completing their sweep, the raiders landed near Cape St. John's to divide the booty and retire from roving. The spoils amounted to "30 pound weight of gold a man," and they jubilantly redistributed themselves on the two ships according to personal inclination. Hamlin remained in command of *Trompeuse* with 120 men; the Englishman became captain of another 70 aboard the consort. While standing away from the coast together in early June 1683, the latter intercepted and boarded the Royal African Company ship *Eaglet,* obtaining yet more plunder. Having robbed the slavers, the English pirates then released them, letting it slip that they intended to proceed next "for the East Indies, and if they could, for the South Sea."

This would appear to have been a deliberate lie, planted to confuse any pursuers. The rovers thus far had carefully concealed their identities, even punishing one captive "who asked the pirate captain's name"; yet the commander then obligingly said that he "owned himself a Jamaican, and said he had a good plantation there," in casual conversation with the slaver captain. All of this seems to have been a ruse to disappear back into civilian life, for in fact Hamlin sailed directly across the Atlantic to Dominica and Saint Thomas, followed closely by his English consort. On 9 August 1683, Captain Charles Carlile of HMS

*Francis* caught and destroyed the *Trompeuse* at anchor in Saint Thomas's harbor and the next day boarded and crippled "a ship aground, a Flemish vessel of 300 tons" a league away, which was purportedly Hamlin's consort.

The last reference to this mysterious pirate commander occurred on 22 November 1683, when the deputy governor of Barbados wrote his superiors in London:

> Since my last a vessel is come from Antigua, which reports that it is believed there that Morgan, the pirate who parted from Hamlin of *La Trompeuse,* is now in these parts. He was seen at anchor at Saint Thomas, where he had taken some ships and sloops.

Nothing else is known of "Morgan's" activities.

***See also*** Carlile, Charles; Hamlin, Jean; Hispaniola.

***Reference:*** *C.S.P., Amer. and W.I.,* Vol. XI.

# MORGAN, EDWARD
## (FL. 1664-1665)

Lieutenant governor of Jamaica who died fighting the Dutch in the West Indies.

Edward Morgan was uncle to the famous Henry Morgan, having been born in the village of Llanrhymny (modern-day Rhymney), near Tredegar, Wales. As a young man, Edward Morgan ventured abroad as a professional soldier of fortune, serving during the Thirty Years War among the Dutch in the Low Countries, to whom he became known as "Heer van Lanrumnij." He also saw action in Germany, and while stationed in Westphalia married Anna Petronilla, daughter of the governor of Lippstadt, by whom he would have six children. When the English Civil War erupted, Edward joined the Royalist forces and by 1649 had risen to captain-general of the king's forces in South Wales, under the Earl of Carberry. Following the collapse of the Royalist cause, he fled into exile to his wife's family estate at Aschbach, near Bamberg, Germany.

After the Restoration of Charles II, an impoverished Edward Morgan returned to London with his wife, who died there in 1662. He was then rewarded for his years of loyalty by being appointed lieutenant governor of Jamaica in February 1664, to second Sir Thomas Modyford, and set sail with his children aboard HMS *Westergate* and the ketch *Swallow.* Morgan's eldest daughter died en route, allegedly of "a malign distemper by reason of the nastiness of the passengers." He then paused at Santo Domingo to deliver an official message to the Spanish governor, proposing that the two nations "forbear all acts of hostility, but allow each other the free use of our respective harbors and the civility of food, water and provisions for money." The Spaniard returned a polite but evasive reply, and on 18 May 1664 (O.S.) Morgan arrived off Jamaica. Next day he entered Port Royal and "as soon as he came a shore, took the government into his hands and dissolved the Assembly," until Modyford could appear two-and-a-half weeks later aboard HMS *Marmaduke.*

The governor fully approved of his subordinate's energy and craft, writing to London, "I find the character of Colonel Morgan short of his worth and am infinitely obliged to His Majesty for sending so worthy a person to assist me, whom I really cherish as my brother." In addition to his administrative duties, Morgan also received a new plantation on the island, which he and his son Charles began to clear. In February 1665, news of the outbreak of the Second Anglo-Dutch War reached Port Royal, and Modyford determined to send an expedition

of privateers under Morgan against the Dutch West Indian islands of Sint Eustatius, Sabá, Curaçao, and Bonaire. The Colonel drew up a will and departed on 28 April 1665 aboard Maurice Williams's 18-gun flagship *Speaker,* eventually mustering a force of nine vessels and more than 500 men, although the rovers showed little enthusiasm for campaigning against the Dutch. Nevertheless, a long upwind beat followed toward this destination, during which Morgan put into Santo Domingo to ask permission to buy provisions, firewood, and water, but was refused by the Spanish.

Eventually Morgan appeared off Sint Eustatius and led a charge of 350 buccaneers ashore. This island was easily overrun, but in the words of his second-in-command Colonel Theodore Cary, "The good old Colonel, leaping out of the boat and being a corpulent man, got a strain, and his spirit being great he pursued overearnestly the enemy on a hot day, so that he surfeited and suddenly died."

*See also* Modyford, Sir Thomas; Williams, Maurice.

*References:* Crouse; Cruikshank; *Interesting Tracts;* Pope.

# MORGAN, SIR HENRY
## (1635-1688)

Greatest of freebooter commanders, who operated out of Jamaica.

Morgan was born either in Penkarne or Llanrhymny (modern-day Rhymney), Wales. He grew up in the tradition of a military family, observing years later, "I left school too young to be a great proficient in [Admiralty] or other laws, and have been more used to the pike than the book." His uncles Edward and Thomas were both professional soldiers of fortune on the Continent, achieving high ranks during the

Thirty Years War. When the English Civil War erupted in 1642, Edward joined the Royalist cause, Thomas the Parliamentary side. Following the execution of Charles I, Edward fled into exile while Thomas remained in England as a major-general in the New Model Army. He was second-in-command of the large scale Flanders expedition, being described as "a little, shrill-voiced choleric man" in action.

When 19 years of age, Henry Morgan apparently embarked as a subaltern in Oliver Cromwell's Western Design, sailing under General Robert Venables and Admiral William Penn. This expedition failed to capture Santo Domingo but overran the smaller Spanish island of Jamaica in early 1655. Several years of abject misery followed for the soldiers, with thousands succumbing to disease, guerrilla warfare, and general neglect. Morgan was one of the few to survive this difficult period, and when the new Royalist governor, Lord Windsor, reorganized the remnants of that army into five militia units in 1662, Morgan became a captain in the Port Royal Regiment. He also received a privateering commission for a tiny vessel lying in the roads and sailed as part of Commodore Christopher Myngs's retaliatory strike against the Spaniards.

## SANTIAGO DE CUBA RAID
### (OCTOBER 1662)

Myngs's flotilla quit Port Royal on 1 October 1662, comprised of HMS *Centurion,* 40 guns, HMS *Griffin,* 14 guns, and ten freebooter vessels, bearing a total of 1,300 men—many of them, like Morgan, former soldiers. Slowly rounding Point Negril at the west end of Jamaica, they arrived off eastern Cuba and incorporated the corsair ship of Sir Thomas Whetstone into their number, as well as seven more Jamaican stragglers. This force came within sight of Santiago de Cuba at daybreak on 16 October but could not close because of the

faint, erratic breezes. Finally, late that afternoon Myngs decided to steer directly toward land and by nightfall had put 1,000 men ashore. They fought their way into the town the next day and took possession of the vessels lying in the harbor, after which they sent columns in pursuit of the fleeing Spaniards. Five days later, the fortifications and principal buildings were razed, and the raiders made off with their booty. Myngs's expedition returned triumphantly into Port Royal on 1 November, having suffered only 6 men killed during this singularly successful campaign, with another 20 men dying due to accidents or illness.

Encouraged by this easy success, the privateers reputedly "all went to sea" for more plunder, while Myngs called for yet another expedition against the Spanish on 22 December of that same year. It is not known whether Morgan was present in Port Royal for the second enterprise, but this seems plausible. Soon, a dozen ships were being made ready and on Sunday, 21 January 1663, they left for the Mexican port of Campeche. Myngs quickly rounded Yucatán and worked his flotilla down into the Gulf of Mexico, losing contact with the vice-flagship *Griffin* and several other privateersmen en route. Nonetheless, he snuck almost 1,000 men ashore four miles west of Campeche on the night of 8–9 February and advanced against the sleeping city.

At first light Spanish lookouts saw his smaller vessels lying opposite the disembarkation point, with two larger ships riding farther out to sea. They sounded the alarm, but too late, for the buccaneer army burst out of the nearby woods at eight o'clock that morning and rushed Campeche. Despite being surprised and heavily outnumbered, the 150 Spanish militiamen put up a stout resistance, especially from their "strong built stone houses, flat at top." A bloody firefight ensued, in which Myngs received serious wounds in his face and both thighs while leading the charge. He was carried back aboard *Centurion* while the privateer leader Edward Mansfield assumed overall command.

The defenders were eventually subdued after a two-hour heated battle, suffering more than 50 Spanish fatalities as opposed to 30 English invaders slain. Some 170 Spanish captives were rounded up while many of the city's thatched huts went up in flames. The attackers then looted Campeche and withdrew two weeks later, on 23 February, carrying off great booty and 14 vessels from the harbor. These slowly beat back around Yucatán against contrary winds and currents, until *Centurion* reached Port Royal on 23 April 1663, followed "soon after [by] the rest of the fleet, but straggling, because coming from leeward every one made the best of his way."

Morgan and some colleagues later claimed they remained roving continuously for the next 22 months after this return, although this seems highly unlikely. What is known is that toward the end of 1664, the veteran Jamaican commanders John Morris and David Martien mounted a small peacetime expedition of their own into the Gulf of Mexico, seconded by Captains Jackman, Morgan, and Freeman. Strictly speaking, such ventures were now illegal, as the new governor, Sir Thomas Modyford, had proclaimed "that for the future all acts of hostility against the Spaniards should cease." However, the privateers ignored this injunction, disingenuously arguing they knew nothing of this cessation of hostilities and so had continued operating under their two-year-old commissions from Lord Windsor.

## TABASCO RAID
### (SPRING 1665)

Together, the five captains mustered a few vessels and less than 200 men, departing Jamaica in January 1665. Once more circling around Yucatán, they moved down the gulf coast until opposite Campeche, where one night in mid-February they cut out an 8-gun Spanish frigate from the roads. On 19 February they then anchored before the tiny town of Santa María de la Frontera at the mouth of the Grijalva River. Some 110–120 buccaneers disembarked and traveled 50 miles upriver through marshy channels until coming upon the provincial capital of Villahermosa de Tabasco. At four o'clock on the morning of 24 February, they fell upon the city, capturing most of the inhabitants in their beds. A general sack ensued, with booty and captives being loaded aboard a coaster in the river. The raiders then headed downriver, seizing a second coaster bearing flour.

Near the river mouth, they discovered their anchored ships had been captured by a Spanish naval patrol during their absence. Three Spanish frigates and 270 men had been sent out from Campeche by Lieutenant Governor Antonio Maldonado de Aldana, which sighted the interlopers' trio on 22 February and boarded them without a fight. A single English vessel fled, abandoning their 10-gun flagship and 8-gun prize to the Spaniards. Seven buccaneer captives revealed that "Captain Mauricio [*sic; Morris*] and David Martin [*sic; Martien*]" had led the bulk of the raiders inland. Their retreat cut off, Morgan and the main body of freebooters released their hostages and began moving westward with the two coasters, hoping to find another river channel whereby to escape. On the afternoon of 17 March they were overtaken by the Spanish *guardacostas* opposite Santa Ana Cay, this time with the privateers' former 10-gun flagship and 8-gun prize crewed by 300 volunteer militia from Campeche. José Aldana, the Spanish commander, sent a messenger in a boat to call upon the buccaneers to surrender, but they pretended not to understand. When an interpreter approached shore the following morning, the rovers replied they would not give up without a fight, and the Spaniards reluctantly disembarked. They discovered the raiders had entrenched themselves behind a palisade reinforced with sandbags and bristling with seven small cannon. The Spanish force, mostly armed civilians, showed little stomach for an assault and were easily repelled without a single loss among the freebooters. The next day, 19 March, the Spanish ships were found conveniently run aground, thus allowing the raiders to exit undisturbed.

## CENTRAL AMERICAN CAMPAIGN
### (SUMMER 1665)

Morgan and the other privateers proceeded northward along the coast, capturing smaller boats and occasionally foraging ashore to obtain supplies. Off Sisal, they looted a vessel laden with corn, whose crew was allegedly released with a message to the governor of Yucatán, vowing to return and lay waste the province. They then rounded Yucatán and traversed the Bay of Honduras as far south as Roatan, where they paused to take on water. Striking next at Trujillo (Honduras), they overran this port and seized a vessel in the roads before continuing to Cape Gracias a Dios and the Mosquito Coast. Native guides were hired there, and the buccaneers continued southward to Monkey Point (Punta Mico, Nicaragua), where they hid their ships before heading up the San Juan River in lighter boats. They emerged into the great Lago de Nicaragua, crossing this by travelling at night and sneaking up on Granada, which they took by surprise on 29 June 1665 when they

marched undescried into the center of the city, fired a volley, overturned 18 great guns in the Plaza de Armas, took the *sargento mayor* [or garrison commander's] house wherein were all their arms and ammunition, secured in the great church 300 of the best men prisoners, abundance of which were church-

men, plundered for 16 hours, discharged all the prisoners, sunk all the boats, and so came away.

Retracing their course across the lake, at the southeastern extremity "they took a vessel of 100 tons and an island as large as Barbados, called Lida [*sic;* Solentiname?], which they plundered." Eventually they regained their anchored vessels and by the end of August 1665, William Beeston was noting in his journal at Port Royal:

Captain Fackman [*sic;* Jackman] and others arrived from the taking of the towns of Tabasco and Villahermosa, in the bay of Mexico, and although there had been peace with the Spaniards not long since proclaimed, yet the privateers went out and in, as if there had been an actual war without commission.

Toward the end of this same year Morgan apparently married his first cousin Mary Elizabeth Morgan (who had come out from England that previous summer with her father, Lieutenant Governor Edward Morgan) and in February 1666 was promoted to colonel of the Port Royal Volunteer Militia and assigned to supervise the expansion of its harbor defenses. The chronicler Alexandre Olivier Exquemelin later wrote that Morgan also participated in Edward Mansfield's final campaign against Providencia Island in May 1666, but this appears to have been an error.

## PUERTO PRÍNCIPE RAID
### (APRIL 1668)

Nevertheless, Morgan did inherit Mansfield's mantle as unofficial leader of the colony's buccaneers, so that late in 1667—during a period of renewed anti-Spanish fears—he was commissioned by Modyford "to draw together the English privateers and take prisoners of the Spanish nation, whereby he might inform of the intention of that enemy to invade Jamaica." Such an open-ended license meant rovers flocked to Morgan's rendezvous off the South Cays of Cuba, including John Morris and Edward Collier, as well as numerous French *flibustiers* (whose own country, unlike England, was at least at war with Spain). After holding consultations, Morgan led this formation of a dozen ships and 700 men into the Gulf of Ana María, setting a large party ashore on 28 March 1668 to raid the inland town of Puerto Príncipe (modern-day Camagüey).

The Spaniards attempted to dispute their passage with militia cavalry and native lancers, but these were helpless before the superior firepower of the buccaneers, who inflicted almost 100 casualties before carrying the town by storm. Fifteen days of pillage ensued, although the raiders withdrew with only 50,000 pieces of eight, a disappointing sum when distributed among so many. Nonetheless, the Spaniards also provided several hundred head of cattle as ransom for their hostages, so that Morgan left the Cuban coast well supplied and headed his force toward Cape Gracias a Dios on the Mosquito Coast. Here the two contingents parted company when Morgan suggested that a descent on the Panamanian port of Portobelo be made next. The French, already resentful at the small purchase obtained, "wholly refused to join with us in that action," Morgan later reported, "as being too full of danger and difficulty."

## PORTOBELO RAID
### (JULY 1668)

With four frigates, eight sloops, and less than 500 men left to him, Morgan sailed down the Central American coast and anchored at Bocas del Toro (literally, "bull's mouths" or "entrances of the bull") off the northwestern shores of Panama. He transferred his men into 23 *piraguas* and smaller boats, rowed 150 miles eastward in four nights, and arrived in the vicinity of Portobelo on the afternoon of 10 July 1668. That night the flotilla disgorged its men and Morgan led them in a swift overland march, taking the stunned Spanish citizenry by surprise at daybreak. An eyewitness reported the buccaneers fired "off their guns at everything alive, whites, blacks, even dogs, in order to spread terror" and so secured Portobelo without suffering a single loss. The 80-man citadel held out for a couple of hours longer, until Morgan rounded up a group of captives—including the *alcalde mayor,* two friars, several women and nuns— to act as a human shield for a party of buccaneers that approached the main gate with torches and axes. The Spanish defenders reluctantly opened fire, wounding two friars and killing an Englishmen, but were unable to prevent the buccaneers from reaching their gate. While thus distracted, another band of buccaneers used scaling ladders to enter on the far side of the fortress, planting "their red flag on the castle walls" and carrying the building. At least 45 Spanish soldiers died in this bloodbath, the rest being wounded.

The next morning, Morgan led 200 buccaneers across the bay and, after a token resistance, forced the surrender of the 50 Spanish soldiers still holding out in Portobelo's harbor castle. This allowed his ships to anchor in the shelter of the roads once they arrived from Bocas del Toro, and at the cost of 18 buccaneer dead, Portobelo was theirs. Wealthy citizens were tortured to reveal their hidden riches and other excesses committed. On 14 July, Morgan wrote a letter in Spanish to the President of Panama, saying:

> Tomorrow we plan to burn this city to the ground and then set sail with all the guns and munitions from the castles. With us we will take all our prisoners . . . and we will show them the same kindness that the English prisoners have received in this place.

Morgan offered to spare the city if a ransom of 350,000 pesos was paid. Acting President Agustín de Bracamonte, marching to Portobelo's relief at the head of 800 Panamanian militia, responded, "I take you to be a corsair and I reply that the vassals of the King of Spain do not make treaties with inferior persons." Morgan unabashedly wrote back:

Although your letter does not deserve a reply, since you call me a corsair, nevertheless I write you these few lines to ask you to come quickly. We are waiting for you with great pleasure and we have powder and ball with which to receive you. If you do not come very soon, we will, with the favor of God and our arms, come and visit you in Panama. Now it is our intention to garrison the castles and keep them for the King of England, my master, who since he had a mind to seize them, has also a mind to keep them. And since I do not believe that you have sufficient men to fight with me tomorrow, I will order all the poor prisoners to be freed so that they may go to help you.

Much to his chagrin, Bracamonte's army was too weak to assault Morgan's positions when he arrived outside Portobelo next day, and the Spaniards remained unhappily bogged down for a week in the jungle. Finally, on 24 July, Bracamonte ordered a retreat, leaving a subordinate to negotiate the ransom. This was set at 100,000 pesos and paid in the first days of August, at which Morgan loaded up his ships and sailed away, returning to Port Royal in triumph by 27 July.

## OXFORD EXPLOSION
### (JANUARY 1669)

He sortied again in early October 1668, calling on freebooters to join him at Ile-à-Vache for another enterprise against the Spaniards. When the 34-gun frigate

HMS *Oxford* reached Port Royal shortly thereafter, to be maintained by Jamaica and used against piracy, Modyford decided to send it as a reinforcement for Morgan "to face Cartagena." The ship's captain paused at Port Morant that November, where he culminated a dispute with his sailing master by killing the man and fleeing, so that the governor appointed veteran privateersman Edward Collier in his place and fleshed out the crew to a total of 160 men. The new captain then sailed on 20 December, with additional instructions to detain the 14-gun French corsair *Cerf Volant* (Kite) out of La Rochelle, which had recently plundered a Virginia merchantman.

Upon arriving at Ile-à-Vache with the aggrieved master, Collier found this culprit lying among Morgan's flotilla and invited the French captain aboard. Identified by the Virginian, Capitaine Vivien and his 45-man crew were arrested and sailed back to Port Royal along with their ship for adjudication. *Cerf Volant* was quickly condemned, renamed *Satisfaction,* and incorporated back into Morgan's fleet.

On 12 January 1669 (2 January O.S.), Morgan and his colleagues decided that since 900–1,000 freebooters had gathered, their strength was sufficient to try the great port of Cartagena on the Spanish Main, after which they began a feast to celebrate both their forthcoming voyage and the New Year. Captains Aylett, Bigford, Collier, Morris, Thornbury, and Whiting all sat down to dinner with Morgan on the quarterdeck, while seamen caroused on the forecastle. "They drank the health of the King of England and toasted their good success and fired off salvoes," until suddenly the *Oxford's* magazine exploded. Ship's surgeon Richard Browne, who sat toward the foot of the officer's table on the same side as Morgan, later wrote, "I was eating my dinner with the rest, when the mainmasts blew out and fell upon Captains Aylett, Bigford and others, and knocked them on the head." Only six men and four boys survived the accident out of a company of more than 200 that were aboard.

Miraculously, Morgan lived through this blast, but the loss of so many others ended any prospects for a Cartagena campaign. Collier departed with *Satisfaction* to make an independent cruise against Campeche, while Morgan transferred into the 14-gun frigate *Lilly* and led his remaining forces eastward, hoping to raid smaller Trinidad or Margarita (Venezuela). By the time he reached Saona Island at the eastern end of Santo Domingo, three more of his best ships had deserted, leaving only 8 and 500 men. (His loyal captains were John Morris, Jeffery Pennant, Edward Dempster, Richard Norman, Richard Dobson, Adam Brewster, and one other.) It was then that one of his French followers suggested a repeat of Jean-David Nau l'Olonnais's feat of two years earlier by raiding the rich Laguna de Maracaibo.

## MARACAIBO RAID
### (MARCH 1669)

Morgan and the rest of his consorts agreed, so after touching at Aruba a few weeks later to stock up on provisions, the buccaneer fleet stood into the Gulf of Venezuela. On 9 March 1669 they were nearing the Bar of Maracaibo, a string of islands and shoals marking the entrance to the laguna proper, when they saw it had been fortified since Nau l'Olonnais's foray. A small 11-gun castle covered the channel, so the freebooters landed and besieged the defenders. Despite the stout resistance offered, there were only an officer and eight Spanish soldiers within the keep, and they slipped out of the fort that night after leaving a long slow fuse burning into the magazine. Morgan and an assault column meanwhile inched into the darkened fortress, gradually "amazed to find no defenders," until a search revealed the fuse, which was extinguished ("about an

inch away from the powder," according to Exquemelin).

After spiking the guns, Morgan's ships navigated through the shoals to Maracaibo, which was abandoned by its terrified citizenry despite the garrison commander's insistence all militiamen must present themselves "on pain of their lives as traitors to the kingdom." When only twelve actually reported, he too took to his heels. The buccaneers then sent raiding parties out into the surrounding countryside "with complete liberty and no resistance," rounding up scores of prisoners who were brutally tortured to reveal their riches. After three weeks, Morgan crossed to the east side of the laguna, visiting a like treatment on the town of Gibraltar. By 17 April, he was back at Maracaibo with a captured Cuban merchant ship and five smaller *piraguas* from Gibraltar, ready to head out to sea again.

## BATTLE OF THE BAR OF
## MARACAIBO
### (APRIL 1669)

While Morgan's freebooters had been ransacking the interior, Spain's Armada de Barlovento arrived outside the laguna, bottling them up inside. Admiral Alonso de Campos y Espinosa had with him the 412-ton *Magdalena* of 38 guns, the 218-ton *San Luis* of 26 guns, and the 50-ton *Nuestra Señora de la Soledad* (Our Lady of Solitude, alias *Marquesa* or "Marchioness") of 14 guns, all manned by 500 officers, troops, and sailors. Finding the fortress guarding its channel devastated, the Spanish Admiral immediately reoccupied it with 40 arquebusiers, repaired six of its guns, and sent messages to the inland provinces calling for assistance. After several days he lightened his warships and crossed over the bar, sending a letter to Morgan calling on him to surrender, as else he had

orders to destroy you utterly and put every man to the sword. This is my final resolution: take heed, and be not un-grateful for my kindness. I have with me valiant soldiers, yearning to be allowed to revenge the unrighteous acts you have committed against the Spanish nation in America.

When Morgan read this aloud to his followers in Maracaibo's deserted marketplace, they roared back they would rather fight to the death than hand over their spoils, as having risked their lives for it once, they were willing to do so again.

After a week's preparation, Morgan's 13 vessels sailed for the bar, arriving within sight of the anchored Spaniards on 25 April 1669. Two days later they rushed toward the armada at nine o'clock in the morning, led by their large Cuban prize flying an admiral's regalia. This ship bore down on Campos's flagship as if to board, and indeed grappled; but when the Spanish surged over the bulwarks they found its decks lined with wooden dummies, and a party of only twelve buccaneers decamping over the side. Just then the Cuban ship burst into flames and *Magdalena* became completely engulfed, forcing Campos to leap into the water with his panicstricken men. Seeing this spectacle, the smaller *San Luis* and *Marquesa* cut their cables and ran for the shelter of the fort's guns, pursued by an angry swarm of buccaneers. Both Spanish vessels ran aground in the shallows and deliberately set themselves ablaze to prevent capture, although the latter was boarded, saved, and refloated by the buccaneers.

Despite this stunning victory, however, Morgan's flotilla could still not pass the fort. Its garrison had been heavily reinforced by 70 militiamen from the interior, as well as most of the armada crews. When Morgan attempted a land assault the next day, this was beaten off with ease, and his ships returned to Maracaibo. He proposed a cease-fire and free passage in exchange for his Spanish captives, but this was refused by Campos. When Morgan learned that only six of the fort's guns were still functional, he had found his way. Returning to the bar a few days later, his boats busily plied back and forth inshore, seemingly depositing a large landing party. The Spaniards, who had observed this activity from a distance, manhandled their guns into position and braced for a nocturnal assault. Morgan, however, had again deceived them, his boat crews merely hiding men in their bottoms during the return trips, and none had disembarked. Under cover of darkness, his ships weighed and slipped past the fort, depositing their prisoners outside and sailing off in triumph.

By 27 May 1669 Morgan was back in Port Royal, apparently destined to retire from roving. During his absence Secretary of State Lord Arlington had once more reiterated the Crown's directive against anti-Spanish hostilities, which was proclaimed throughout Jamaica by Modyford on 24 June, the governor adding he had been instructed "that the subjects of His Catholic Majesty be from now until further order treated and used as good neighbors and friends." However, Madrid in the interim had also countered with a more aggressive policy of their own, authorizing Spanish American officials to issue local commissions against the English. When the first of these corsairs began making attacks the following year, Jamaicans became outraged, especially by the nuisance raids of Manoel Rivero Pardal in summer 1670. By way of retaliation, Modyford met with the island council on 9 July and passed a unanimous resolution that Morgan be commissioned "to be Admiral and Commander-in-Chief of all the ships of war belonging to this harbor," drawing them together into one fleet "to attack, seize and destroy all the enemy's vessels that shall come within his reach."

Morgan set sail from Port Royal on 11 August, at the head of a fleet of 11 vessels and 600 men, his flag flying aboard *Satisfaction* of 120 tons, now armed with 22 guns. He had further called for a freebooter gathering at Ile-à-Vache for greater strength, but first ventured to the south coast of Cuba, where he left Morris's *Dolphin* on watch before touching at French Tortuga Island, and therefore not reaching Ile-à-Vache until 12 September. Four days later, Morgan detached another six vessels under Collier to gather provisions and "get prisoners for intelligence" on the Spanish Main. These appeared off Ríohacha (Colombia) at daybreak on 24 October 1670, landing and marching against the tiny 4-gun fort with such a discipline that the Spaniards assumed they were regular troops out of England. This impression faded once they drew closer, as the garrison included the crew of Rivero Pardal's consort *Gallardina* (which was lying in the roads), and these *gaurdacostas* were terrified at falling into the buccaneers' hands. The fort held out a day and night before surrendering, after which Collier conducted a pair of executions and tortured captives for their wealth. "In cold blood they did a thousand cursed things," a Spanish eyewitness noted, before weighing almost four weeks later with meat, maize, 38 prisoners, *Gallardina,* and another ship.

## RECONQUEST OF PROVIDENCIA ISLAND
### (CHRISTMAS 1670)

Meanwhile, Morgan's fleet had been scattered by a storm off Ile-à-Vache and was slowly regaining its strength. Morris rejoined with Rivero Pardal's *San Pedro* (alias *Fama),* which he had seized after killing that Spanish corsair off Cuba. Many other captains arrived, and by the time Morgan weighed on 18 December he had 38 vessels and more than 2,000 English, French, and Dutch freebooters under his command—the largest buccaneer enterprise ever mounted. Their intended target was Panama, but first Morgan paused en route to reclaim tiny Providencia Island, which on two previous occasions had belonged to the English. Early on 24 December his fleet appeared before that place, forcing its Spanish garrison to surrender next day by sheer weight of numbers.

Morgan then detached three ships and 470 men (including Rok Brasiliano and Jan Erasmus Reyning) to sail ahead of his fleet and seize the fort guarding the mouth of the Chagres River, where he intended to land and advance across the isthmus to Panama. The bulk of his fleet followed a few days afterward, coming within sight of Chagres on 12 January 1671, which the buccaneers had already secured. But as *Satisfaction* led the rest of the fleet in, it struck a hidden reef and was destroyed, along with the next four vessels in line. Ten men were drowned but otherwise the loss was minimal. After a week spent refurbishing the fort and installing 300 defenders under Captain Richard Norman, Morgan ventured upriver with 1,500 men, 7 small ships and 36 boats.

## SACK OF PANAMA
### (JANUARY 1671)

An epic seven-day trek through the jungles ensued, although the Spaniards shrank away before this invading host. Nonetheless, the climate, terrain, and lack of provisions proved sufficiently grueling, despite the lack of any military opposition. Finally at nine o'clock on the morning of 27 January, Morgan's vanguard crested a hill and "saw that desired place, the South Sea," with a galleon and several smaller vessels riding on it. Toward noon they came upon a great plain filled with cattle, which they slaughtered and paused to eat. Thus refreshed, they pressed on and that afternoon sighted the tiled roofs of

Panama, with a Spanish army drawn up to bar their path. Morgan began his final advance at sunrise on 28 January with his remaining 1,200 men marching behind "red and green banners and flags, clearly visible to the Spaniards." The governor of Panama, Juan Pérez de Guzmán, had his own 1,200 militia infantry drawn up in a long line, six deep, with two militia cavalry companies of 200 riders apiece on both flanks—but his inexperienced troops had few firearms and no artillery, so that despite their bravery they would prove no match for the better armed freebooters.

Morgan's vanguard was advancing upon the right flank of the Spaniards, when Pérez de Guzmán's unwieldy throng suddenly launched an undisciplined dash against the buccaneer lines. The buccaneers broke the Spanish charge with steady fusillades, more than 100 militiamen being killed in the initial volley. This murderous fire, to which the Panamanians could make scant reply, broke their spirit and caused them to flee, leaving 400–500 dead or wounded on the battlefield, as opposed to only 15 buccaneers. Panama was occupied, but many of its buildings were set ablaze as the raiders entered, and most of its riches had already been removed to the ships offshore. Thus, although Morgan was to remain in undisputed possession of Panama for the next four weeks, he found its wealth largely gone. Despite cruel tortures inflicted by the frustrated invaders, relatively little more could be extracted from the city or its outlying areas, especially considering the large number of his followers. When the army marched back to Chagres and made a final division of spoils, these received only £15 or £18 a head, so that there was much ugly talk that they had been cheated.

## ARREST
### (1672)

Morgan departed Chagres on 16 March 1671 aboard Bradley's *Mayflower*,

accompanied by three other vessels. He reached Port Royal a couple of weeks later to find English policy completely reversed. A new treaty had been signed with Madrid, so attacks against the Spaniards were now most definitely out of favor. Three months afterward, HMS *Assistance* and *Welcome* entered Port Royal with a new governor for that island, Sir Thomas Lynch. Some time later he informed Modyford that he was to be arrested, although assuring him "his life and estate was not in danger," but that London had merely felt a show of sternness was needed to assuage Spanish complaints. A like gesture was required when news of Morgan's Panama raid reached Europe a little while later, so that in November, Lynch was ordered to arrest him as well. This the new governor was loath to do, for it would further alienate the privateers on whom he was relying for the island's defense. He therefore decided to send the admiral home in such a manner "as he shall not be much disgusted" and deferred the actual arrest because of Morgan's poor health. It was not until mid-April 1672 that the great freebooter was conducted aboard the 36-gun royal frigate *Welcome* of Captain John Keene to sail for England with a three-ship convoy.

Three months later they arrived at Spithead, and because Morgan continued "very sickly," was not imprisoned when he reached London in August 1672, but rather housed at his own expense. This was also the same summer as the Third Anglo-Dutch War erupted, with England and France fighting against the Netherlands. Hostilities against the Protestant Dutch proved not very popular, especially when the French were inept allies, and then went to war against Spain the next year. All of this gradually resulted in another full circle to Whitehall's policies, with the most surprising consequences—instead of being tried, Morgan was able to use his liberty to meet the young duke of Albemarle, who intervened on his behalf with Charles II. By the end of July 1673, Morgan's position was so improved he was asked to submit a memorandum describing what was needed to ensure Jamaica's security.

In January 1674, the Council of Trade and Plantations decided to recall Lynch and replace him with the Earl of Carlisle, son to the earl of Carberry, with Morgan as his deputy governor. Such a position called for a title, so that in November Morgan was knighted and the next spring set sail for Jamaica.

## LIEUTENANT GOVERNOR
### (1675-1688)

On 5 March 1674 (O.S.), the 40-ton privateer *Gift* of Captain Thomas Rogers entered Port Royal with Morgan on board. The following day Lynch resigned, and one week afterward his successor arrived aboard the 522-ton frigate HMS *Foresight*. For the remaining 13 years of his life, Morgan lived quietly as a plantation owner, growing fatter and embroiled in nothing more dangerous than the cut and thrust of local politics. He died of dropsy in 1688, the result of being "much given to drinking and sitting up late," according to his physician. He left a personal estate of over £5,000 and several properties, being buried with a 22-gun salute from all the ships in Port Royal harbor.

**See also** Barlovento, Armada de; Beeston, William; Campos y Espinosa, Alonso de; Exquemelin, Alexandre Olivier; Lynch, Sir Thomas; Maldonado de Aldana, Antonio; Mansfield, Edward; Martien, David; Morgan, Edward; Morris, John; Modyford, Sir Thomas; Myngs, Sir Christopher; Pérez de Guzmán, Juan; *piraguas;* purchase; Reyning, Jan Erasmus; Rivero Pardal, Manoel; Rogers, Thomas; Spanish Main; Whetstone, Thomas; Windsor, Thomas.

**References:** Cruikshank; Earle, *Panamá;* Eugenio; Exquemelin; *Interesting Tracts;* Juárez; Pope.

# MORRIS, JOHN
### (FL. 1658-1672)

Morris was first mentioned in summer 1658, after Commodore Christopher Myngs returned to that island from a raid against the Spanish Main with three prizes. These were all sold to men who would prove formidable corsairs in their day: the largest, of 8 guns and 60 tons, was bought by Robert Searle and renamed *Cagway;* one of 4 guns and 50 tons was purchased by Dutch-born Laurens Prins, who changed its name to *Pearl;* while the third later became Morris's *Dolphin*. It is believed Morris may have participated in Myngs's attacks against both Santiago de Cuba and Campeche a few years later, and in 1663 he was listed as commanding a 7-gun brigantine (perhaps the *Virgin Queen)* with a crew of 60 men and holding a commission from the former governor of Jamaica, Lord Windsor.

In January of the following year, Morris escorted the merchant sloop *Blue Dove* into Port Royal "upon suspicion that she was to trade with the Spaniards as a Hollander [i.e., conduct clandestine trade with the Spanish pretending it was of Dutch rather than English registry, thus avoiding Jamaican duties]." He had intercepted this vessel with his *Virgin Queen* between Hispaniola and Jamaica and detained it because the sloop was sailing toward Cuba laden with "ammunition and goods suitable to the Spanish trade." The *Blue Dove* had in fact cleared Amsterdam and carried papers declaring its final destination to be Port Royal, so it had to be freed by the Court of Admiralty because there was no proof its master intended to break any law. Morris complained later that he got nothing for his troubles but "an English ensign and a hogshead of strong beer."

In June 1664 a new governor reached the island, Sir Thomas Modyford, who immediately proclaimed "that for the future all acts of hostility against the Spaniards should cease," as the English Crown hoped to promote a more benign policy with Spanish America. Morris and four other privateer captains soon chose to ignore this injunction, later arguing—somewhat disingenuously—that "having been out 22 months [i.e., since participating in Myngs's sack of Campeche in early 1663]," they had not known of the cessation of hostilities and so continued operating under their old commissions.

## MEXICAN RAID
### (SPRING 1665)

Morris and the Dutch-born David Martien were the leaders of this new venture, seconded by Captains Henry Morgan, Freeman, and Jackman. Together they mustered a few vessels and 200 men, departing Jamaica in January 1665. Rounding Yucatán, they moved gingerly down the treacherous gulf coast until arriving opposite Campeche, where one night in mid-February they cut out an 8-gun Spanish frigate lying in the roads. Then sailing past the Laguna de Términos, they came to anchor on 19 February before the tiny town of Santa María de la Frontera at the mouth of the Grijalva River. Some 110–120 buccaneers disembarked and traveled 50 miles upriver through the marshy channels until coming within sight of the provincial capital of Villahermosa de Tabasco. At four o'clock on the morning of 24 February, they fell upon the sleeping city, capturing most of the inhabitants in their beds. A general sack ensued, after which booty and captives were loaded aboard a coaster lying in the river. The raiders then paused at nearby Santa Teresa ranch to release their women captives, retaining the

men, for whom they demanded a ransom of 300 head of cattle. Farther down the river they came upon a second coaster bearing flour, which they also seized.

Nearing the river mouth, they discovered their waiting ships had been captured by a Spanish naval patrol. Three Spanish frigates and 270 men had been sent out by Campeche's Lieutenant Governor Antonio Maldonado de Aldana, in quest of the prize seized from that port. This *armadilla* had sighted the interlopers' trio of vessels anchored off Santa María de la Frontera on 22 February, boarding two without a fight. A few Englishmen fled in the other vessel, abandoning their 10-gun flagship and 8-gun prize, along with seven buccaneers. These had revealed to their captors that the ships had been left unmanned because "Captain Mauricio [*sic;* Morris] and David Martin [*sic;* Martien]" had led the bulk of the raiders inland.

With their retreat cut off, the main body of freebooters released their remaining hostages and began moving westward with their two coasters, hoping to find another river channel whereby to escape. On the afternoon of 17 March they were overtaken by the *guardacostas* opposite Santa Ana Cay, this time sailing the privateers' former 10-gun flagship and 8-gun prize (the Spaniards having crewed these with 300 volunteer militia from Campeche). José Aldana, the Spanish commander, sent a messenger in a boat to call upon the buccaneers to surrender, but these pretended not to understand. When an interpreter approached shore the following morning, Morris and Martien replied they would not give up without a fight, and the Spaniards reluctantly disembarked. They then discovered the raiders had used the interval to entrench themselves behind a palisade reinforced with sandbags and bristling with seven small cannon from Villahermosa. The Spanish force, mostly armed civilians, showed little stomach for an assault and were easily repelled without incurring a single loss among the freebooters. The next day, 19 March, the Spanish ships were found conveniently run aground, thus allowing the raiders to exit undisturbed in their two coasters.

## CENTRAL AMERICAN CAMPAIGN
### (SUMMER 1665)

Morris and Martien proceeded northward hugging the coastline, capturing smaller boats and making occasional landings to obtain supplies. Off Sisal they looted a vessel laden with corn, whose crew they allegedly released with a message to the governor of Yucatán, vowing to return and lay waste his province. They then rounded Yucatán and traversed the Bay of Honduras as far as Roatan, where they paused to take on water. Striking next at Trujillo, on the north coast of Honduras, they overran this port and seized a vessel lying in the roads before continuing to Cape Gracias a Dios and the Mosquito Coast. Nine native guides joined them there, sailing southward to Monkey Point (Punta Mico, Nicaragua), where the buccaneers hid their ships in an inlet before heading up the San Juan River with their lighter boats. More than 100 miles and three waterfalls later, they emerged in the great Lago de Nicaragua. Crossing this by travelling at night and resting by day, they snuck up on Granada and took it by surprise on 29 June 1665, when they

marched undescried into the center of the city, fired a volley, overturned 18 great guns in the Plaza de Armas, took the *sargento mayor* [garrison commander's] house wherein were all their arms and ammunition, secured in the great church 300 of the best men prisoners, abundance of which were churchmen, plundered for 16 hours, discharged

all the prisoners, sunk all the boats [to prevent pursuit], and so came away.

Retracing their course across the lake, at the southeastern extremity "they took a vessel of 100 tons and an island as large as Barbados, called Lida [*sic;* Solentiname?], which they plundered."

Amazingly, the raiders then regained their anchored vessels and by the end of August, William Beeston was writing in his journal at Port Royal, "Captain Fackman [*sic;* Jackman] and others arrived from the taking of the towns of Tabasco and Villahermosa, in the Bay of Mexico." They had traveled almost 3,000 miles in seven months, assaulting five Spanish towns and undergoing countless lesser engagements.

## MORGAN'S LIEUTENANT
### (1668-1671)

Over the next few years, Morgan would be elevated to a position of prominence amongst the Jamaican privateers because of his military skills, as well as his excellent political connections with Modyford. When the next major sortie was made from that island in early 1668, Morgan bore a commission from the governor styling him "General," with instructions to unite the privateers "and take prisoners of the Spanish nation, whereby he might inform of the intention of that enemy to invade Jamaica." Because of this patent, veterans such as Morris suddenly found themselves serving under their former junior colleague, although apparently without much resentment. Morris in particular became a loyal subordinate in Morgan's expeditions, starting with the sack of Portobelo of July 1668, where he even went over among the Spaniards as a hostage during the negotiations for the ransom of that city.

Early the following year, Morris narrowly escaped death. On 12 January 1669, he was one of eight English and French corsair captains who met aboard Morgan's *Oxford* off Ile-à-Vache to decide on an enterprise against the Spaniards. Both Morris and his son of the same name were aboard, and since 900 freebooters had been mustered, this strength made the captains agree to try the great port of Cartagena on the Spanish Main, after which they began a feast to celebrate their voyage. Captains Aylett, Bigford, Edward Collier, Thornbury, and Whiting all sat down to dinner with Morgan and the Morrises on the quarterdeck, while the seamen caroused on the forecastle. "They drank the health of the King of England and toasted their good success and fired off salvoes," until suddenly the *Oxford's* magazine accidentally exploded. Ship's surgeon Richard Browne, who sat toward the foot of the officer's table on the same side as Morgan, later wrote:

> I was eating my dinner with the rest, when the mainmasts blew out and fell upon Captains Aylett, Bigford and others, and knocked them on the head.

Only six men—including Morgan and Morris—and four boys survived out of a company of more than 200, but not Morris's son. Despite his grief, Morris proceeded to serve in the subsequent campaign against Maracaibo.

## DEATH OF RIVERO PARDAL
### (OCTOBER 1670)

The following summer, Modyford attempted to rein in the privateers' activities, and Morris returned to his plantation, but the Spaniards then began issuing anti-English commissions of their own. One such was used by the Cartagena corsair Manoel Rivero Pardal to launch nuisance raids on Jamaica itself, prompting angry calls for retaliation. Morgan and Morris sortied to organize yet another strike against the Spaniards, hosting an assembly of buccaneers

off Hispaniola. Meanwhile, foraging parties were sent out to gather supplies and intelligence for the forthcoming expedition, one of these being commanded by Morris.

In mid-October 1670, his 10-gun ship *Dolphin* with 60 men was forced to put into a small bay at the east end of Cuba by a threatening storm. Two hours later, just before dark, Rivero Pardal sailed in for this same purpose with his 14-gun ship *San Pedro (alias Fama),* being delighted to see he had the smaller Jamaican ship embayed. Setting men ashore to cut off any escape, the Spaniards prepared to attack at dawn.

It was Morris who moved first the next morning, bearing down upon *Fama* with the land breeze and boarding at the first attempt. Rivero was shot through the neck and killed, his crew panicking and jumping into the sea, where some drowned and many others were finished off by the privateers, only five Spaniards being taken alive. Later that month the jubilant buccaneers beheld *Fama* being led into Ile-à-Vache, now peacefully renamed *Lamb.* Morris then accompanied Morgan on his successful campaign to reconquer Providencia Island, capture Chagres, and march across the isthmus to punish Panama. In the final assault, Morris seconded Laurens Prins in command of the vanguard, which routed the Spanish host before Panama's walls on 28 January 1671.

## LATER CAREER
### (1672)

Following the return of the privateers to Jamaica, Morris was spared the official opprobrium that descended on Modyford and Morgan, resulting in both being sent to England as prisoners for persisting in these hostilities against Spanish America. Morris instead was assigned by the new Governor Sir Thomas Lynch "to take up the straggling privateers that are to leeward [i.e., westward]" of that island, with the added recommendation that he was "a very stout fellow, good pilot, and we know he will not turn pirate."

*See also* Beeston, William; *guardacostas;* Huidobro, Mateo Alonso de; Jackman, Captain; Laguna de Términos; Maldonado de Aldana, Antonio; Martien, David; Modyford, Sir Thomas; Morgan, Sir Henry; Morris, John; Myngs, Sir Christopher; Prins, Laurens; Rivero Pardal, Manoel; Windsor, Thomas.

*References:* Cruikshank; *C.S.P., Amer. and W.I.,* Vol. IX; Earle, *Panamá;* Pawson, *Port Royal;* Pope; Zahedieh, *Contraband.*

# MORRO

Spanish word for large harbor castle or coastal fortification.

The term doubtless originated in medieval times when such defenses were needed in Spain against the seaborne raids of the fierce North African Moors. The term itself became confused by the English and other foreigners in the New World as the actual name of individual castles, leading to a profusion of ports ostensibly having a *morro* of their own: Havana, Santiago de Cuba, San Juan de Puerto Rico, etc. In fact, all of these castles, or *morros,* had different names, the one at Portobelo being called San Felipe, for instance.

# MOSELEY, SAMUEL

### ALSO MAUDSLEY
### (FL. 1667–1675)

New England privateer from Dorchester, Massachusetts.

In early life, Moseley was said to have served at Jamaica and "in the way of trade visited other parts of the West Indies, where the adventurous spirit was excited and

schooled, perhaps by Sir Henry Morgan and associate buccaneers, the result of which was his bringing home to Boston two prizes." In 1667, Moseley acted as attorney for his privateer friend Captain Thomas Salter of Port Royal, Jamaica, when a Spanish vessel the latter had taken in the "Bay of Campeche [Laguna de Términos]" was illegally carried off to New York by its prize crew.

During the Third Anglo–Dutch War, Moseley was given command of the ketch *Salisbury,* with a crew of 47 men, to patrol the Massachusetts coast in company with the ketch *Swallow.* On 15 February 1675 (O.S.), he was ordered by the council at Boston to sortie in quest of certain Dutch privateers who had captured the bark *Philip,* George Manning master, and several other English vessels. He fell in with a French ship that was also hunting the Dutchmen and soon came upon the enemy privateers. These were Captain Pieter Roderigo of the *Edward and Thomas* and Captain Cornelis Andreson of the shallop *Penobscot,* who had apparently been joined by Manning's *Philip,* as it was also flying Dutch colors. However, when Moseley and his French consort engaged Roderigo and Andreson, Manning turned his guns on the Dutch vessels as well and helped batter them into submission. Moseley returned to Boston with his prizes on 2 April 1675 (O.S.).

During the Indian conflict of 1675 known as "King Philip's War," Moseley formed a volunteer company made up of his crews and some of the released Dutchmen, called "Moseley's privateers."

*See also* Andreson, Cornelis; Laguna de Términos; Roderigo, Pieter; Salter, Thomas.

*References:* Chapin; Webster.

# MOSQUITO COAST

Nickname originally given to the eastern shores of present day Nicaragua by Spanish explorers, and which extends from Cape Gracias a Dios in the Honduran province of Mosquitia in the north to Monkey Point (Punta Mono) in the south. A torrid stretch of tropical mangroves and inlets, with few natural resources or arable farmland, it remained unsettled by the Spaniards and so became a natural sanctuary for runaway slaves, rovers and outlaws.

# MUM

Strong ale popular in the seventeenth century made from wheat and oat malts and flavored with herbs.

Its original name was *mumme,* from Brunswick in Germany where it was first developed; in Dutch, it was called *mom.*

**Reference:** Gehring.

# MUNRO, CAPTAIN

(FL. 1664–1665)

Renegade Jamaican privateer, who shortly after the installation of Sir Thomas Modyford as governor of Jamaica, "turned pirate and took the English merchant ships bound thither." After ransacked vessels began putting into Port Royal, about 21 December 1664 (O.S.), the Royal Navy's armed ketch *Swallow* was sent out under Captain Ensom, who met Munro off that coast, "fought him, killed many and took the rest of his men, being thirteen," which were carried back into Jamaica. Munro and his men were then swiftly tried and condemned, being hanged at Gallows Point in sight of all the vessels in the anchorage, where their bodies remained for several months, displayed in gibbets.

**See also** Modyford, Sir Thomas.

**References:** *Interesting Tracts;* Pope.

# MURPHY FITZGERALD, JOHN

ALSO JUAN MORFA
(C. 1620–C. 1680s)

Irish adventurer.

Despite beginning his career as a buccaneer on Tortuga Island, he rose to captain in the Spanish service on Santo Domingo and Knight of the Order of Santiago, in which capacities he fought against French *boucaniers* and helped repel William Penn and Robert Venables's invasion of 1655. It is believed Murphy may have then emigrated to Veracruz, where he apparently settled as a prosperous trader. In his declining years, Murphy underwent a harsh ordeal at the hands of Laurens de Graaf and Grammont during the great pirate raid of 1683.

According to Spanish records, this young adventurer was born in Glassely in County Kildare, Ireland. Murphy (his mother's surname was Fitzgerald) arrived on Tortuga Island as a boy soldier but deserted to the Spaniards with some companions in late 1633 after having killed a man in a dispute. He then agreed to lead the Spanish on an expedition to eliminate his former settlement. During the resultant fray, he was shot in the forehead. Such a serious wound, coupled with his extreme youth, Catholic faith, and an easy Spanish victory, ensured Murphy's stay on Santo Domingo, although he was never fully trusted by the Spaniards. Within a few years, he nonetheless became a captain of local militia, and by 1650 was in Madrid obtaining a knighthood in the Order of Santiago.

By December 1653, Murphy had returned to Santo Domingo, where he served as *maestre de campo,* or second-in-command, of the forces sent to again clear foreigners off Tortuga Island (this time those under the *boucanier* chieftain chevalier de Fontenay). Murphy performed with some distinction during this campaign, leading a

275

crucial charge of 200 men against Cayenne that helped ensure the Spanish triumph. However, even after all these years and service, he was still suspect—it was rumored that he secretly undermined his superiors and took too much of the spoils for himself. When the victors withdrew with their prisoners to Santo Domingo, Murphy was left behind in command of Tortuga, with a garrison 100 strong. However, Governor Juan Francisco Montemayor de Cuenca, leery of his ancient connections with pirates and uneasy at leaving him alone on that stronghold, soon sent a Spanish officer to replace him.

Such prejudice became even more marked after the failed English invasion of Santo Domingo in April and May 1655. Despite having been among the first defenders to sortie in opposition of the British advance, Murphy received no mention whatsoever in the official Spanish bulletins announcing victory. It is perhaps because of this that his name no longer figured on Santo Domingo after 1655; it is believed that, in disgust at such political intrigues, he may have transferred to Veracruz to start a new life. His timing may have proved fortuitous, for seven years later, on 30–31 October 1662, the authorities at Yucatán received an extraordinary deposition from a Portuguese captive. He declared that having been in London in early 1659, he learned through a fellow countryman who was a pilot that Parliament was secretly planning a second attempt on Santo Domingo

and for this they wished to avail themselves of an Irishman who had business dealings in England, and by means of Don Juan Morfa, *maestre de campo* of the city of Santo Domingo, who was a friend of said Irishman, achieve their goal.

This unfounded accusation was forwarded to the king in Madrid but evidently never acted

upon, as Murphy had long since left the island.

His new existence in Mexico was not only more tranquil than on the beleaguered Caribbean outpost, it also held infinitely better commercial prospects. Over the next two decades Murphy gradually became a well-to-do trader and owner of a fine two-story house and numerous slaves. He married and had a family, and by the late 1670s was able to maintain the city's only mounted militia troop entirely at his own expense. His days among the buccaneers must have seemed very remote indeed, when on a cloudless Monday afternoon, 17 May 1683, two sail were seen standing in toward the harbor. Despite the favorable wind, they did not draw appreciably closer, and Murphy became concerned. When he saw Governor Luis Bartolomé de Córdoba y Zuñiga strolling through the Plaza Mayor with his staff, Murphy hastened after him and said, "Sir, those ships cannot be good ones, for they have been able to enter and yet not done so." But the arrogant young governor brushed the Irishman off.

The next morning at daybreak, Veracruz's streets exploded with volleys of gunfire. During the night, several hundred pirates under Laurens de Graaf, Grammont, and Nikolaas van Hoorn had infiltrated the city, and begun a series of coordinated attacks. In addition to military objectives, the raiders targeted major households such as Murphy's; from the darkened street he heard a voice calling to him in English, saying "if he opened up he would be given quarter, but if not his throat would be cut." Outside was a band of a dozen buccaneers led by a vengeful English logwood cutter, who had been captured in the Laguna de Términos some years earlier and served a spell as convict laborer in the Irishman's home.

But for all his advanced age, Murphy had lost none of his fighting spirit, and he began distributing swords and lances to his 14 loyal black servants. When the pirates shot the lock off a small side entrance and forged through the gap into the darkened interior, they blundered into a deathtrap. The first three were so savagely hacked to pieces that the rest ran away in fright. Murphy's victory proved short-lived, though, for when he climbed onto his rooftop to scan the street, he saw another two dozen pirates hastening to the attack. Again he was ordered to open up or suffer dire consequences, and this time, "out of fear they might murder my wife and six children," he obeyed. The enraged buccaneers rampaged throughout his home "destroying whatever they could" after finding their fallen comrades, and Murphy's captivity promised to be a painful one.

At first, he and his family were shut up in Veracruz's principal church, along with the thousands of other captives. But the next morning at eight o'clock (Wednesday, 19 May), Murphy was led forth to endure the corsairs' wrath. Carried into a jeering mob of buccaneers in the Plaza Mayor, he "was received by Lorencillo [De Graaf] himself." The Irishman's hands were bound behind his back; then he was cruelly hoisted and swung suspended on the public scaffold by his arms. As he dangled there

with terrible pain and hurt, they told him to confess where he had his money and silver, to which he responded that those who had entered his house had taken everything.

This could not be, his tormentors insisted, but Murphy gasped out that he had been left penniless. Even his silver service, which had been cast down the well before the looters penetrated his home, had been retrieved. At this

Lorencillo slashed him in the head with his cutlass, opening up a serious wound, then clubbed him many times on the body,

almost killing him, before having him cut down and taken upstairs into the governor's palace, where a pirate surgeon attended him.

Nor was Murphy's ordeal over, for after being patched up, Grammont entered and "pointing a carbine" in the Irishman's face, ordered him to confess what monies he and his neighbors had. Again Murphy replied that he had lost everything and did not know his neighbors' wealth, at which the *flibustier* chieftain stormed out angrily.

Other prominent citizens underwent the same punishment, until more than a dozen had joined Murphy in his cell. They became the principal hostages, and were the last people released on Sacrificios Island when the pirates withdrew two weeks later. Murphy returned on foot to his gutted home to find his wife dead and his servants carried off into bondage. As a final blow, one of his daughters died three weeks later, and the Irishman was left to pick up the pieces of a shattered life.

***See also*** Córdoba y Zúñiga, Luis Bartolomé de; De Graaf, Laurens Cornelis Boudewijn; Grammont, "chevalier" de; Laguna de Términos; logwood; Van Hoorn, Nikolaas.

***References:*** Incháustegui; Marley, *Veracruz;* Peña Batlle, *Tortuga;* Rodríguez, *Invasión* (Montalvo); Walsh.

# MYNGS, SIR CHRISTOPHER

ALSO MINGS
(1625-1666)

Royal Navy officer who, as commander-in-chief at Jamaica, employed sizable contingents of freebooters.

Born into a prosperous Norfolk family, Myngs was an experienced fighter by the time he reached the New World, having first gone to sea in colliers and coastal traders. After joining the Cromwellian navy, his big break had come when he brought home the man o' war *Elizabeth* in May 1653. Its captain had been killed in a duel with a Dutch ship during the First Anglo–Dutch War while returning from the Mediterranean. Myngs was confirmed into this vacancy, then in October 1655 promoted to command the *Marston Moor,* recently returned from the disastrous Jamaican expedition.

Having witnessed calamitous sufferings in the West Indies, *Marston Moor's* crew mutinied upon finding itself unpaid and ordered back to Jamaica. Despite his popularity, Myngs was forced to imprison or dismiss many of the men before shifting anchorage from Portsmouth to Spithead, where he insisted on the remainder being paid, over the objections of the local admiralty agent. In November 1655 the *Marston Moor* sailed, joining Vice Admiral William Goodson at Jamaica on 25 January 1656. In May of that year, Myngs took part in Goodson's descent on Ríohacha, which ended disappointingly when little booty was found, and the squadron returned to Jamaica in June.

The fledgling colony continued to suffer because of hunger, slackness, and internal strife (there being doubts whether London would even maintain the outpost). Goodson and Myngs weighed in a vain attempt to intercept the Spanish treasure ships off Havana (which Admiral Stayner afterward took at Cadiz in September 1656) before passing across to Nevis to embark 1,400 planters who were willing to transfer to Jamaica. Having completed this mission, Goodson and Myngs cruised off the island till early the next year, when the admiral returned to England complaining of ill health.

Myngs followed a month later with a three-ship convoy, bringing *Marston Moor* into Dover in July 1657 after a brief stopover

at the Bahamas during his crossing (to buy 8,560 pounds of turtle meat as food). His crew were paid off, and Myngs was allowed a leave of absence to get married, but by December he was back on board, departing the Downs with three victuallers for Jamaica. He arrived on 20 February 1658 (O.S.), having captured the Dutch merchantmen *Charity (Barmhatigheid?)* of Amsterdam, *Marie* of Medemblik, *John the Baptist (Johannes de Doper?), Hopewell (Goede Hoop?),* the hoy *Three Cranes (Drie Kraanvogels?),* and a sixth unnamed vessel, for illegally trading at Barbados. He claimed all as prizes but was annoyed when eventually only one was so deemed, the rest being released on technicalities.

## DEFENSE OF JAMAICA AND EARLY SEABORNE CAMPAIGNS (1658)

Myngs was now the senior officer on that station and thus in command of the small trio of vessels that discovered four Spanish troop transports anchored off the north coast on 22 May 1658, having slipped 550 Mexican soldiers ashore. Returning a month later with Governor Edward D'Oyley and heavy reinforcements aboard ten ships, Myngs was able to land this force, which pulverized the invaders in a pitched battle. The Spanish artillery was conveyed back to Cagway (as the island capital was still called) and installed as part of the harbor defenses.

Shortly thereafter Myngs sailed on a counterraid against the Spanish Main, assaulting Santa Marta and Tolú in quick succession with the loss of only three men, then intercepting three Spanish merchantmen bound from Cartagena to Portobelo. Returning triumphantly to Jamaica six weeks later, he sold his prizes to men who would all prove formidable corsairs. The largest vessel, of 8 guns and 60 tons, was bought by Robert Searle and renamed

*Cagway;* one of 4 guns and 50 tons was purchased by the Dutch-born Laurens Prins and renamed *Pearl;* while the third later became John Morris's *Dolphin.*

## Second Descent against the Spanish Main
### (1659)

Having enjoyed good success on his first cruise, Myngs's frigates *Marston Moor, Hector,* and *Cagway* were joined by numerous freebooters for his next raid against the Spanish Main, which he launched early the following year. In order to surprise different targets, Myngs tacked hundreds of miles farther east than he or Goodson had previously operated. This paid handsome dividends when his formation burst upon an unprepared Cumaná, seizing and ransacking that port. Myngs hurriedly weighed and ran westward before the prevailing wind, falling upon Puerto Cabello before any alarm could be carried overland. He repeated this tactic a third time, racing still farther west to make a rich haul at Coro.

It is alleged that no less than 22 chests—and perhaps many more—were seized from two Dutch merchantmen flying Spanish colors at Coro; each chest contained 400 pounds of silver ingots belonging to the king of Spain. Myngs himself declared that there was "coined [i.e., minted] money" in the chests to the value of £50,000, besides bullion; but when the expedition returned to Jamaica four months after its departure, the chests were opened, and the authorities suspected that a great deal of silver had been plundered. Myngs did not deny that some looting had occurred, but dismissed it as customary among privateersmen. The officials took a dimmer view, believing Myngs was "unhinged and out of tune" because the Jamaican Court had refused to condemn his earlier Dutch prizes, and that he was therefore taking justice into his own hands. Governor D'Oyley suspended him and

ordered *Marston Moor* home, where Myngs was to stand trial for defrauding the state.

But upon his arrival in England in the spring of 1660, Myngs found the nation distracted by the restoration of Charles II, and—being an early public supporter of the monarch—was soon cleared of all charges after a sympathetic hearing that June. By the end of the year, he was restored, but because of many upheavals did not actually sail for Jamaica until late April 1662, when he conveyed the new royal governor, Lord Windsor, in the 46-gun *Centurion.* Shortly after reaching Port Royal on 21 August, a more vigorous line was implemented against the Spaniards. An uneasy truce had existed for the past three years, although Madrid still regarded all foreigners in the Americas as interlopers. In order to challenge this policy, Windsor had brought instructions that allowed him to issue a proclamation less than one month later, offering privateering commissions and calling on volunteers for a major operation against the Spaniards. Within three days, 1,300 men had been mustered (many of them former soldiers), and Myngs's *Centurion* was joined by ten privateering vessels, including a tiny craft commanded by a 27-year-old militia captain named Henry Morgan.

## Destruction of Santiago de Cuba
### (1662)

Myngs was to lead these men against Santiago de Cuba, which had been the Spaniards' advance base in their efforts to reconquer Jamaica and much loathed by the English. The flotilla quit Port Royal on 1 October 1662, slowly rounding Point Negril at the west end of Jamaica in light winds. Landfall was made east of their Cuban target, where the ship of Sir Thomas Whetstone was spotted at anchor in the lee of a cay. Joining him, Myngs obtained recent intelligence as to Spanish dispositions, then decided at a general conference held on board *Centurion* to burst directly into the enemy port, catching them by surprise. Reinforced by Whetstone and seven more Jamaican privateers who belatedly overtook the expedition, Myngs steered down the Cuban coast in scanty winds.

They came within sight of the towering harbor castle that guarded the approaches at daybreak on 16 October but could not close because of the faint, erratic breezes. Finally, late that afternoon Myngs decided to change plans—he would use the land breeze that sprang up every evening to steer directly toward the nearby village of Aguadores at the mouth of the San Juan River. By nightfall he had succeeded in putting 1,000 men ashore. In his own words:

> We decided to land under a platform two miles to windward of the harbor, the only place possible to land and march upon the town on all that rocky coast. We found no resistance, the enemy expecting us at the fort and the people flying before us. Before we were all landed it was night. We were forced to advance into a wood, and the way was so narrow and difficult, and the night so dark, that our guides had to go with brands in their hands to beat a path. By daybreak we reached a plantation by a riverside, some six miles from our landing and three miles from the town where being refreshed by water, daylight and a better way, we very cheerfully advanced for the town, surprising the enemy who hearing our late landing, did not expect us so soon. At the entrance of the town the Governor Don Pedro de Morales, with 200 men and two pieces of ordinance, stood to receive us, Don Cristopher [de Issasi Arnaldo] the old governor of Jamaica (and a good friend to the English) with 500 more being his reserve. We soon beat them from their

station and with the help of Don Christopher, who fairly ran away, we routed the rest. Having mastered the town we took possession of the [seven] vessels in the harbor, and next day I despatched parties in pursuit of the enemy and sent orders to the fleet to attack the harbor, which was successfully done, the enemy deserting the great castle after firing but two muskets.

Myngs spent the next five days pursuing the defeated Spaniards inland, "which proved not very advantageous, their riches being drawn off so far we could not reach it." In frustration, the freebooters razed the town, and Myngs used 700 barrels of gunpowder from the magazines to demolish the fortifications and principal buildings. After five days of calculated destruction, he reported that

> the harbor castle mostly lies level with the ground. It was built upon a rocky precipice, the walls on a mountain side some 60 feet high; there was in it a chapel and houses sufficient for a thousand men.

It would take the Spaniards more than a decade to repair their stronghold. Myngs returned to Port Royal on 1 November, where he found he had been elected to the council in his absence. The massive assault had only cost six men killed in the fighting and another 20 due to accidents or illness.

## SACK OF CAMPECHE
### (1663)

Encouraged by this success, "the privateers all went to sea for plunder." Myngs remained in port, and on 22 December 1662 issued a call for another expedition. *Centurion* refitted while freebooters once again began to marshal. Myngs was joined by Captains William James, Edward Mansfield, and many others. Soon a dozen ships were being made ready, and on Sunday, 21 January 1663, they got under way. Myngs quickly rounded Yucatán and worked past uncharted shoals, losing contact with his vice-flagship and several privateersmen. Nonetheless, he skillfully snuck almost 1,000 men ashore at Jámula beach, four miles west of Campeche, on the night of 8 February and began his advance on the sleeping city.

At first light the Spanish lookouts saw his smaller vessels lying opposite this disembarkation point, with two large men o' war farther out to sea. They sounded the alarm, but too late, as the freebooter army burst out of the nearby woods at eight o'clock and rushed the city. Despite being surprised and heavily outnumbered, the 150 Campeche militiamen put up a spirited resistance, especially from their "strong built stone houses, flat at top." A bloody firefight ensued, in which Myngs received serious wounds in the face and both thighs while leading the charge. He was carried back out to Centurion, and Mansfield assumed overall command. The Spanish defenders were eventually subdued after two hours' heated battle, suffering more than 50 fatalities as opposed to 30 invaders slain. Some 170 Spanish captives were then rounded up, while many of the city's thatched huts went up in flames.

The next morning Antonio Maldonado de Aldana entered and agreed to a truce in exchange for good treatment of the prisoners. (Because he dealt directly with Myngs's substitute, this raid has gone down as "Mansfield's assault" for Spanish historians; the few direct references to Myngs further misidentify him as "Christopher Innes.") Despite his injuries, Myngs remained sufficiently in control to order the release of four prominent captives on 17 February, with a message to Maldonado offering to spare the city and release the rest of his prisoners unharmed if the raiders could draw water from the nearby Lerma wells. He

also added his regrets at not coming personally to meet his Spanish counterpart "as he would have wished," being impeded by his wounds. The Spaniard acceded, and as a token of good faith, Myngs released all but six of his most important hostages before watering. On 23 February, his fleet got under way, carrying off great booty and 14 vessels found in the harbor, which were described by a Spanish eyewitness as "three of 300 tons, the rest medium or small, and some with valuable cargo still on board."

The heavily laden formation slowly beat back around Yucatán against contrary winds and currents, so that the Centurion, under the command of flag captain Thomas Morgan, did not reach Port Royal until 23 April 1663. It was followed "soon after [by] the rest of the fleet, but straggling, because coming from leeward every one made the best of his way." They had been gone so long that the Jamaicans had begun to despair. Myngs's wounds required a lengthy convalescence, so early in July Centurion sailed for England.

## LATER CAREER
### (1664-1666)

Myngs received widespread acclaim, and when the Second Anglo-Dutch War threatened in late 1664, he was promoted to vice admiral under Prince Rupert. Myngs served bravely at the Battle of Lowestoft in June 1665 and was knighted for his role in this engagement. After winter patrols, he commanded the vanguard as Vice Admiral of the Red aboard HMS Victory at the brutal "Four Days Fight" of June 1666, being engulfed by the Dutch fleet. With the battle raging, Myngs was shot through the throat but refused to leave his deck, remaining upright and compressing the wound with his fingers until a second bullet passed through his throat, and lodged in his shoulder. He lingered a few days, dying at his home in Goodman's Fields, Whitechapel.

The diarist Samuel Pepys would eulogize him as a "very stout man, and a man of great parts, and most excellent tongue among ordinary men."

**See also** Cagway; D'Oyley, Edward; Goodson, William; James, William; Maldonado de Aldana, Antonio; Mansfield, Edward; Morris, John; Prins, Laurens; Searle, Robert; Spanish Main; Whetstone, Sir Thomas; Windsor, Thomas.

**References:** *C.S.P., Amer. and W.I.*, Vol.IX; *D.N.B.;* Dyer, *Myngs;* Eugenio; Juárez; Pope.

# NARBOROUGH, SIR JOHN

## (1640-1688)

English Admiral who made a private voyage into the South Seas and died working Sir William Phips's Spanish shipwreck off Santo Domingo.

Narborough was born at Cockthorpe, Norfolk, England, in early October 1640. His first voyages were to the Guinea coast and Saint Helena aboard merchantmen, and his early naval career was spent as a protégé of Christopher Myngs, with whom he sailed to Jamaica in 1657. Returning to England five years later, Narborough followed Myngs onto a succession of warships during the Second Anglo–Dutch War, until the latter died at the "Four Days' Fight" (11–14 June 1666) against the Dutch under Michiel de Ruyter. Narborough himself was promoted to commander of HMS *Assurance* for his bravery during this battle.

In May 1669, following the cessation of hostilities, he was appointed to the 300-ton *Sweepstakes,* of 36 guns and 80 men, setting sail that autumn from the Thames to establish peaceful contact with Spain's colonists on the Pacific coast of South America. Narborough passed through the Strait of Magellan in November 1670, and by Christmas Day (15 December 1670, O.S.) the *Sweepstakes* came to anchor in Valdivia Bay, Chile. After an initially friendly reception, the Spaniards suddenly arrested a small landing party, and Narborough found the port closed to him. Unable to recover his men, and not authorized to take any offensive action, he returned through the strait in January 1671 and arrived home that June. (More than a decade later, Bartholomew Sharpe's men reported that Narborough's "lieutenant and nine or ten others" were still being held at Lima, Peru.)

In June 1672, Narborough served with some distinction aboard the flagship HMS *Prince,* of 100 guns, at the otherwise lackluster Battle of Sole Bay during the Third Anglo–Dutch War and the following year he was promoted to rear admiral and knighted. In October 1674, following England's withdrawal from the war against the Netherlands, he was sent to deal with the Tripoli corsairs, blockading their ports and capturing ships until the bey agreed to terms in early 1677. Within a few months, Narborough returned to the Mediterranean to visit a like treatment upon Algiers, which also submitted more than a year later. Thanks to these victories, Narborough was able to retire from the sea a wealthy man, being appointed as one of His Majesty's commissioners of the Navy in March 1680, and entering into a rich marriage the next summer with Elizabeth Hill of Shadwell. (His first marriage—to Elizabeth Calmady in spring 1677—had ended tragically when she died during that following winter "mightily afflicted with a cough, and big with child.")

Despite his retirement from active duty, newfound wealth, and growing family, Narborough continued to be interested in naval affairs, becoming William Phips's firmest backer in his attempts to locate a Spanish shipwreck in the West Indies. When these efforts were finally crowned with success in 1686 and a second expedition was organized in England the following year, Narborough could not resist visiting the site. He commanded this group from the frigate HMS *Foresight,* 48 guns, while Phips served aboard the 400-ton merchantman *Good Luck and a Boy,* and John Strong had the *James and Mary,* with the ship *Princess* and the smaller *Henry* rounding out the convoy.

The convoy set sail on 3 September 1687 from the Downs but soon encountered heavy weather. Phips's vessel was damaged and forced back into Plymouth, while

Strong became separated from the others off Cape Finisterre. Narborough reached Funchal at Madeira Island with the smaller two ships on 13 October, and Barbados by 16 November. There he found *James and Mary* awaiting him, and they departed again more than two weeks later for Samaná Bay on the northeastern coast of Hispaniola, arriving on 5 December. Two days later Phips joined him, and the expedition proceeded northward to the Ambrosian Bank (present-day Silver Bank) where the galleon lay.

By the time Narborough's flotilla arrived on 15 December, they found it surrounded by more than four dozen craft. These and many other local scavengers had been working the wreck for months, making away with an estimated £250,000. These interlopers were driven off, and Narborough's men settled in to resume their work, employing a total of almost 200 divers. But the gleanings now proved slender, hard labor resulting in relatively little silver. In February 1688 the site was visited by two Dutch warships, the 46-gun frigate *Noordhollandt* (North Holland) and a galliot hoy bearing the exiled English nobleman Lord Moraunt. *Foresight* cleared for action "not knowing his design," but he had allegedly come merely to view the wreck (although it was suspected his true intent was to sound out Narborough as to his loyalty to James II). After being rowed over the spot in a pinnace, Moraunt found the sea too rough for anything to be seen and withdrew.

Little more treasure could be raised, and an attempt to blast away coral with an underwater explosive failed. By the beginning of May 1688 morale aboard the flotilla was lagging, with the weather squally, men on half rations, and disease spreading throughout the ships. Narborough himself fell ill on 18 May and finally decided to give up any further efforts to salvage the wreck.

After a few days' preparation, *Foresight* attempted to weigh on the evening of 26 May 1688, but an anchor remained fouled on the bottom. Narborough's last action was to order divers to recover it before lapsing into unconsciousness. At three o'clock next morning he died. Being unable to embalm the corpse, *Foresight*'s surgeon removed Narborough's bowels, and the body was rowed over to the wreck site at five o'clock that same afternoon and slid over the side as the ships fired a salute. His entrails were then conveyed back to England and buried at the church of Knowlton, near his estate at Deal, with the rather misleading inscription: "Here lie the remains of Sir John Narbrough."

*See also* Myngs, Sir Christopher; Sharpe, Bartholomew; South Seas; Strong, John.

*References:* Bradley, *Lure; C.S.P., Amer. and W.I.,* Vol. XI; *D.N.B.;* Earle, *Treasure.*

# Nau l'Olonnais, Jean-David

## (FL. 1660s)

*Flibustier* from Saint Domingue who sacked Maracaibo.

Details are sketchy regarding his life, as Nau l'Olonnais apparently operated from Tortuga Island, well beyond the control of the French West Indies Company—the only official representation in that area during the 1660s. (A year after his death, the inhabitants of Tortuga were still so independently minded as to fire hundreds of rounds at Governor Bertrand d'Ogeron's ship, when he unwisely attempted to extend the company's monopoly against foreign trade to that island.) Most of what is known about Nau l'Olonnais stems from the chronicler Alexandre Olivier Exquemelin, who although a contemporary, apparently recorded much of his account secondhand, incorporating many lurid touches but otherwise few verifiable facts. Exquemelin further referred to the rover as "François l'Olonnais" throughout, while other sources indicate his real name was Jean-David Nau, but nicknamed "l'Olonnais" because he was originally from the port of Les Sables d'Olonne in the Vendée, France.

Nau l'Olonnais supposedly arrived at Saint Domingue as an *engagé,* or indentured servant, after which he earned his livelihood among the sharpshooting hunters known as *boucaniers,* then became a sea-rover, or *flibustier.* His early campaigns included cruises to Cuba and Campeche, where he was once shipwrecked but managed to escape. He reputedly had an abiding hatred of Spaniards and showed them little mercy, committing barbarous acts of cruelty. By early 1667 his reputation as a *flibustier* leader was such he was able to muster a large force of fellow captains for an assault against the Spanish Main.

## SACK OF MARACAIBO
### (AUTUMN 1667)

Nau l'Olonnais set sail from Tortuga at the end of April 1667 with a flotilla of eight small vessels and 660 men, pausing at Bayahá on the north coast of Hispaniola for an additional party of *boucaniers* and large stock of provisions. Three months later he stood into the Mona Passage and sighted a 16-gun Spanish vessel that had just departed Puerto Rico and gave chase. The Spaniard struck to Nau l'Olonnais's 10-gun sloop "after two or three hours' combat," proving to be bound for Veracruz with a rich consignment of cacao. Nau l'Olonnais sent this vessel back to Tortuga to unload, meanwhile taking up station with the rest of his flotilla off Saona Island.

While waiting for his first prize to return, Nau l'Olonnais took a second, an 8-gun Spanish ship carrying gunpowder and *situados* (payrolls) for the garrisons of Santo Domingo and Cumaná. When his first prize returned, Nau l'Olonnais made it his flagship and felt sufficiently strengthened to attempt a major descent on the Spanish Main, which he had combed the previous year.

Sailing into the Gulf of Venezuela, he disembarked his *flibustiers* near the battery guarding the Bar of Maracaibo, which consisted "of sixteen cannon surrounded by several gabions or earth-filled wicker cylinders, with a ramp of earth thrown against them to shelter the men inside." The buccaneers quickly overran this feeble fortification and passed their ships over the bar into the laguna. Next day they reached Maracaibo, which they found abandoned, and so occupied it uncontested for two weeks.

During this period buccaneer patrols were sent out into the outlying areas to bring in prisoners, a few being tortured by Nau l'Olonnais to reveal their riches with little results. He therefore crossed the laguna to the town of Gibraltar, which the Spaniards had reinforced with several hundred troops. The *flibustiers* believed this meant the enemy had something worth guarding and so elected to mount an assault. Nau l'Olonnais led them into battle with the roar, *"Allons, mes frères, suivez-moi, et ne faites point les lâches!"* (Come on, my brothers, follow me and let's have no cowards!)

Gibraltar fell after a brutal battle in which 40 buccaneers were killed and 30 wounded. The Spaniards suffered much heavier casualties, hundreds of their dead being loaded onto two old boats by the invaders, towed a mile out into the laguna, and sunk. The town was ruthlessly pillaged over the next month, after which Nau l'Olonnais demanded a ransom of 10,000 pesos to leave its buildings intact. Once paid, the *flibustiers* recrossed the laguna and extorted a ransom of 20,000 pesos and 500 head of cattle to spare that city as well. Nau l'Olonnais finally quit the laguna two months after he had entered and eight days later touched at Ile-à-Vache to divide the spoils. Shortly thereafter he apparently visited Jamaica, selling an 80-ton, 12-gun Spanish brigantine to Rok Brasiliano and Jelles de Lecat before reentering Tortuga in triumph a month afterward.

### CENTRAL AMERICAN CAMPAIGN
### (1668)

Some time later, Nau l'Olonnais sortied again with 700 *flibustiers,* 300 aboard the large Spanish prize he had brought from Maracaibo. In company with five smaller craft, he proceeded to Bayahá once more to take "on board salt meat for their victuals." The buccaneers then cruised southern Cuba as far as the Gulf of Batabanó, seizing boats to use in an ascent of the San Juan River, as they hoped to duplicate the feat of John Morris, David Martien, and Henry Morgan from three years previously of sacking Granada. But when Nau l'Olonnais attempted to clear Cape Gracias a Dios on the Mosquito Coast, he was prevented by a lack of wind and drifted along the north coast of Honduras. Running low on provisions, he sent foraging parties up the Aguán River and eventually prowled as far west as Puerto Cabellos.

At Puerto Cabellos he captured a Spanish merchantman armed with 24 cannon and 16 *pedreros,* or swivel guns, as well as occupying the town. He terrified two captives into leading him inland to the nearest city, San Pedro Sula, setting off with 300 *flibustiers* while leaving the remainder to garrison the tiny port under his Dutch-born lieutenant, Mozes van Klijn. Less than ten miles into the jungle they were waylaid by a party of Spaniards and learned from prisoners that more ambushes had been prepared. *"Mor'dieu,"* Nau l'Olonnais swore, *"les bougres d'Espagnols me le payeront!"* (God's death, the Spanish blackguards will pay for

this!) He gave the order for his men to give no quarter, for he believed the more they killed on the way, the less resistance they would find in the city. Despite this, the Spaniards sprang more ambushes and even fought off Nau l'Olonnais's initial assault on San Pedro Sula before being allowed to evacuate under flag of truce. The city and its outlying region were then pillaged over the next few days, being burnt to the ground when Nau l'Olonnais retired to the coast.

Upon returning into Puerto Cabellos, he learned a wealthy galleon was due to arrive soon from Spain "at the Guatemala river" (Bay of Amatique), so he posted a pair of lookout boats on the southern shore before crossing to the western side of the Gulf of Honduras to careen. Three months elapsed, until word was finally received that the galleon had come. Recalling his scattered forces, Nau l'Olonnais quickly attacked, although the Spaniard had 42 cannon and 130 men. His own 28-gun flagship and a smaller buccaneer consort were beaten off, but four boatloads of *flibustiers* carried the galleon by boarding. Its booty proved disappointing, however, as most of the cargo had already been unloaded and there only remained some iron, paper, and wine. Discouraged, Nau l'Olonnais's confederates Van Klijn and Pierre le Picard decided to quit his company, leaving him alone with his Maracaibo prize.

### DEATH
### (1669?)

The Spanish prize proved to be a heavy sailer and ran aground among the Pearl Islands "twelve leagues east" of Cape Gracias a Dios some time later. Nau l'Olonnais and his crew were forced to live ashore, planting crops and attempting to build a longboat from the ship's remains. When this was finally completed five or six months later, it was not big enough to accommodate all the survivors, so Nau l'Olonnais went with a group of men to the San Juan River to attempt to steal more boats. There they were defeated by the Spaniards and forced to flee, after which Nau l'Olonnais continued into the Gulf of Darien, determined to obtain more boats. Here his small band was set upon by natives, and according to the sole survivor, "l'Olonnais was hacked to pieces and roasted limb by limb."

**See also** Exquemelin, Alexandre Olivier; Hispaniola; Picard, Pierre le; Spanish Main.

**References:** Exquemelin; Lugo; Lussan; Sucre; Vrijman.

# NAVARRO, BALTASAR

## (FL. 1681–1685)

Spanish *guardacosta* who operated out of Campeche.

Navarro's activity was first mentioned in spring 1681, when he commanded a *piragua* sent on patrol into Mexico's Laguna de Términos. The previous year, a series of Spanish sweeps organized by Captain Felipe de la Barrera y Villegas had succeeded in clearing this region of English trespassers, who had established themselves ashore many years before to poach logwood. Campeche's authorities wished to maintain this advantage by dispatching regular patrols to cruise that shoreline, one such being Navarro's boat. In early April 1681, he spotted the 12-gun pink of John Hart lying inside the laguna, chasing it away and capturing twelve men who had been landed to fell trees.

Four years later, Navarro performed much more singular service in defense of Campeche. In early June 1685, the coast guard frigate *Nuestra Señora de la Soledad* (Our Lady of Solitude) hurried into port with a two-ship convoy, its captain, Cristóbal Martínez de Acevedo, reporting that they had been chased on 27 May by unidentified vessels off that coast. Rumors had already

been circulating of a pirate fleet gathering on the far side of the Yucatán peninsula near Isla Mujeres, and Lieutenant Governor De la Barrera decided to act. *Soledad* was ordered to anchor beneath the protection of Campeche's guns, while 25 of its crewmembers were transferred into Navarro's *piragua*. A further 25 soldiers were added from the city garrison, and he was commanded to proceed to the tiny advance port of Sisal to reconnoiter the enemy.

Upon reaching Sisal, Navarro was instructed to round Yucatán in search of strange sails. He probed as far as Isla Mujeres, where he saw a tall ship with 30 guns in the distance. Returning toward Sisal, his boat received a friendly hail from a sloop opposite Telchac, but Navarro refused to answer because he considered it suspicious. Next day he sighted more small craft to leeward, about five miles from land, who withdrew as his *piragua* approached, and joined two large ships and several smaller vessels farther out to sea. Alarmed, Navarro hastened toward Sisal to give warning, and at the entrance to its harbor heard from a coaster captain called Manzano that four more unidentified vessels were anchored inside the Gulf of Mexico. Twelve days after reporting these finds to the authorities at Sisal, Navarro and his men learned that more than a dozen sail had been sighted off Champotón, headed toward Campeche. At this his men became agitated, fearing for their loved ones left at home, insisting upon an immediate return. Navarro sent an urgent request to the governor of Yucatán, who soon authorized him to quit Sisal.

At four o'clock on the afternoon of 9 July 1685, Navarro's *piragua* arrived off the northern approaches of Campeche, and set a man ashore at the outlying village of Platanar to make inquiries. He returned at a run to report the pirate fleet of Laurens de Graaf and "chevalier" de Grammont had invaded the city two days earlier, although its citadel still held out. Lieutenant Governor de la Barrera, who had been driven out of Campeche during this fighting, now ordered Navarro's *piragua* directly into the roads to support the fort, whose guns prevented the pirate fleet from anchoring in the harbor. That night Navarro rowed up close to the citadel and hailed its commander, *Sargento Mayor* Gonzallo Borrallo. In an attempt to disconcert the freebooters, who were listening, Navarro shouted across the darkened water that Yucatán's Governor Juan Bruno Téllez de Guzmân, would arrive the next day with 800 troops, while Borrallo responded in a similar vein, loudly asserting he had 300 troops inside the citadel and no need of water or supplies.

Next day Navarro defended the roads, fending off pirate attempts to encroach upon the harbor, and that night neared the fort again, from where Borrallo asked him to make a disembarkation the following night to carry off the citadel's empty water casks, and refill them. During the night of 11 July the *piragua* was beached and these taken aboard, after which Navarro struck out through the darkness for the town of Lerma, southwest of the city—the nearest spot where he could safely complete this task. By eight o'clock on the morning of 12 July the casks were filled, but Navarro discovered three of his seamen had deserted. After a quick search failed to turn them up, he struck out toward Campeche. As his *piragua* approached the city, he and his crew could distinctly hear the boom of heavy artillery, as the pirates had landed guns from their ships and commenced bombarding the citadel at dawn.

While gliding past the outskirts, an Indian hailed and warned the men aboard the *piragua* that pirates had hidden two pieces close ahead, among the hides "behind the corner of the butcher shop" to ambush them. Navarro scoffed at this report, but his men refused to take up their oars again,

believing "they would be sunk and slaughtered as they waded onto the beach" because they were *guardacostas,* to whom the pirates traditionally showed no mercy. Navarro vainly shouted orders, then cajoled his crew, "and when some began to undress to dive into the water threatened them with a blunderbuss until they put on their clothes again" but could not persuade them to advance. Instead, they rowed directly in toward shore and abandoned the *piragua,* leaving him with only eight men. He attempted to row back to Lerma with these few, but the winds and tide were too much, and by that evening he was forced to scuttle his craft short of this destination.

Nevertheless, Navarro persisted with his efforts, marching toward the city with the handful of followers left him. But during that same day a Spanish relief column from Mérida de Yucatán had been defeated by Grammont, and that night the citadel's defenders deserted their posts. By the time Navarro drew near, resistance had ended and the enemy were fanning out into the countryside, so he made his way inland to the village of San Diego, where he found his wife and children among the refugees.

A report arrived a few days later that a column of mounted buccaneers was bearing down upon the nearby town of Zamulá, and Navarro was one who hastened to its aid. In the confusion he came upon the abandoned icon of Campeche's patron saint, Santo Cristo de San Román, which he helped defend until being shot in one leg. While the jubilant raiders pressed on to ransack the town, Navarro was able to crawl to a nearby Spanish company and be carried off. His wound was so severe it precluded any further participation in this campaign.

**See also** Barrera y Villegas, Felipe de la; De Graaf, Laurens Cornelis Boudewijn; Grammont, "chevalier" de; *guardacosta;* Laguna de Términos; logwood; *piragua.*

**References:** Juárez; Marley, *Pirates.*

# NEVILLE, EDWARD

### (FL. 1675-1678)

English privateer who served under French colors.

When England withdrew from the war against the Netherlands in early 1674, many of its West Indian corsairs shifted allegiance in order to continue privateering. One such captain was Neville, who obtained a commission from the French authorities on Saint Domingue to commit depredations against the Dutch and Spanish. On 26 March 1675 (O.S.), the new deputy governor of Jamaica, Sir Henry Morgan, drafted a letter promising Neville and his fellow rovers a friendly reception at Port Royal if they were to come in and cease their operations on behalf of foreign countries, which although legal, were an embarrassment to the English Crown. The retired buccaneer added that he hoped "their experience of him will give him the reputation that he intends not to betray them."

This proposal was never sent, though, as Morgan's superior, Lord Vaughan, preferred other measures to recall the privateers. Thus, Neville was still active three years later, taking part in George Spurre's assault on the Mexican town of Campeche. On 10 April 1678, Neville and his sloop lay in company with Spurre's frigate before Havana, where they intercepted the outward-bound dispatch vessel *Toro* (Bull) and made it their new flagship. Sailing across the Gulf of Mexico to the Laguna de Términos, they recruited additional men for an attempt on Campeche. Neville's sloop accompanied Spurre's *Toro* and eight *piraguas* up the coast, and on the night of 6 July 1678, Neville reconnoitered the port alone. At dawn he rejoined the main body to report that all was calm. That night, the pirates slipped ashore.

Before daybreak on Sunday, 10 July, the buccaneers entered the sleeping town and took it by surprise, suffering no casualties. They held it until the evening of Tuesday, 12 July, when they withdrew with their prizes: the ship *San Antonio,* a *barco luengo,* and a boat, plus a great deal of booty. They also carried off 250 blacks, mulattos, and Indians to be sold as slaves at the Laguna de Términos. That autumn, William Beeston noted in his journal at Port Royal, Jamaica:

> 18 October 1678 [O.S.].—Arrived Captain Splure [*sic*], who with one Neville about three months since, and 150 men, had taken Campeche, and with him a prize; for all of which he had his pardon, and leave to come in and spend their plunder.

***See also*** *barco luengo;* Beeston, William; Laguna de Términos; Spurre, George.
***References:*** *C.S.P., Amer. and W.I.,* Vol.IX; Eugenio; *Interesting Tracts;* Pope.

# NICHOLS, BERNARD

### (FL. 1664)

Minor English privateer who operated out of Jamaica.

On 23 November 1664 (O.S.), William Beeston noted in his journal at Port Royal, "Bernard Nicholas [*sic*] brought in a prize." This was exceptional in that the new governor, Sir Thomas Modyford, had some months previously issued a proclamation "that for the future all acts of hostility against the Spaniards should cease," yet Nichols was apparently allowed to retain this vessel.

On 20 February 1665 (O.S.), the governor himself informed London, "The Spanish prizes have been inventoried and sold, but it is suspected those of Morrice [*sic; Maurice Williams*] and Bernard Nichols have been miserably plundered, and the interested parties will find but a slender account in the Admiralty."

**See also** Modyford, Sir Thomas.

**References:** *Interesting Tracts;* Pawson, *Port Royal.*

# Norman, Richard

## (fl. 1669-1671)

English freebooter who operated out of Jamaica.

In summer 1669, Norman served under Henry Morgan in his campaign against Maracaibo and a year-and-a-half later sailed in the huge expedition against Panama. After recapturing tiny Providencia Island from the Spaniards on Christmas Day 1670, Morgan sent "Lieutenant Colonel" Joseph Bradley on ahead with 470 men aboard three ships (with Norman as his "Major") to capture the crucial San Lorenzo castle at the mouth of the Chagres River, which was to be used as the pirates's advance base for their overland march to the Pacific. This force landed within sight of that fortification at noon on 6 January 1671 and carried it the next day, after repeatedly being repulsed. Bradley was wounded during the final attack, being shot through both legs, and Norman assumed overall command.

Five days later, when Morgan's main body hove into view, Bradley died, and Norman was left in charge of Chagres with 540 men while Morgan crossed the Isthmus to attack Panama. During his absence Norman set two vessels to maintain watch off the coast under Spanish colors, which met a big Spanish merchantman and chased it into Chagres, where it was easily caught by Norman. This proved a valuable prize, being loaded with all kinds of provisions, of which the buccaneers were in sore need.

**See also** Bradley, Joseph.

**References:** Earle, *Panamá;* Exquemelin; Gosse, *Who's Who;* Pope; Vrijman.

# OGERON, BERTRAND D', SIEUR DE LA BOUÈRE
## (1613-1676)

Fourth French governor of Saint Domingue, who led its *boucaniers* to disaster.

Bertrand d'Ogeron was the third and last child born to a merchant of this same name at Rochefort, France, and baptized on 19 March 1613. In October 1653, a few months after his father's death, d'Ogeron was created squire *(écuyer)* and enrolled as captain in the Marine Regiment. By 1657 he was in the New World at Martinique, and two years later—following the end of the Franco-Spanish War—was discharged. He then joined some adventurers on a colonizing expedition to the west coast of Saint Domingue. D'Ogeron lost all his possessions when carried past this destination and shipwrecked, but he managed to struggle back to France the following year. While preparing to return to the Americas in 1662, d'Ogeron—as shareholder, or *interesé,* in one of the first French West Indian companies—laid claim to the Lucayan and Caicos Islands "from the 20th to 28th degree north latitude," then sailed to the Caribbean the following year. There he became one of 30 men who successfully settled on the west coast of Hispaniola in 1663, at Léogâne (a mispronunciation of its Spanish name *La Yaguana,* which became *l'Yaguane* in French, then "Léogâne").

In the spring of 1664, the *Compagnie des Indes Occidentales* was created by the Crown, and in October its directors in Paris named d'Ogeron governor of the *boucanier* stronghold of Tortuga Island, situated off the northwestern tip of Saint Domingue. Because of the usual delays in trans-Atlantic communications, d'Ogeron did not assume this new posting until 6 June 1665. He was rather coolly received by the *boucaniers,* who resented the company's attempts to monopolize their trade.

In 1668 d'Ogeron was granted leave to travel to France for a year on personal affairs, and deputized his nephew Jacques Nepveu, sieur de Pouançay, to serve during his absence. D'Ogeron left Paris to return to Saint Domingue on Easter weekend 1669, arriving at the colony in early autumn. He found the *boucaniers'* resentment against the company stronger than ever, and with extreme difficulty put down a serious revolt in the spring of 1670. This uprising exploded when d'Ogeron sailed from Cul de Sac to Tortuga with his *Irondelle,* encountering two Flushing ships of 300–400 tons who were bringing out goods for the *boucaniers.* D'Ogeron informed the Dutch captains, Pieter Constant and Pieter Marck, that such trade was prohibited, to which they replied "he would have to be stronger than they to prevent it." When the *boucaniers* learned of his threat, they mutinied and fired repeatedly upon d'Ogeron's ship. Order was restored many months later with the aid of ships and men sent by the governor general, Jean-Charles de Baas-Castelmore of the Windward Islands, plus a general amnesty issued by the Crown.

## DISASTER AT PUERTO RICO
## (1673)

News of the outbreak of the Franco-Dutch War reached the Caribbean during the latter half of 1672, and De Baas began organizing an expedition to attack the Dutch stronghold of Curaçao. He detached the 50-gun *Ecueil* (Reef) and smaller *Petite Infante* (Little Infanta or "Spanish Princess") to Saint Domingue, with orders for d'Ogeron to raise a large number of volunteers and join him off Saint Croix on 4 March 1673. At least 200 recruits boarded the *Petite Infante* at Léogâne, half transferring to the *Ecueil* at Petit Goâve, where another 200 had been mustered. This pair of ships then rounded Môle Saint Nicholas toward Tortuga, where they arrived on 18 February, and almost immediately got under way again, with further reinforcements plus half a dozen smaller privateer craft.

The night of 25 February 1673, through navigational error, d'Ogeron's *Ecueil* ran aground in the vicinity of Arecibo, on the northwest shores of Puerto Rico. "More than half the people were saved," he wrote later, 500 survivors struggling ashore through the surf. He sent his lieutenant Brodart and nephew De Pouançay with a message to the local Spanish authorities, informing them of the accident and requesting aid. However, the French had so long victimized the Puerto Rican coast that they were regarded as mortal enemies, despite the fact this particular band had arrived purely by chance and Spain was neutral in the European conflict. The two emissaries were thrown in jail, and a host of militia descended upon the French survivors, subduing them after a one-sided clash in which 10 Puerto Ricans died and 12 were wounded, as opposed to perhaps 40–50 fatalities among d'Ogeron's group.

Following this outburst, the island governor, a hard-bitten, surly veteran named Gaspar de Arteaga y Aunavidao (whose foul temper was made worse by the fact that he was dying from a lingering disease), ordered the Frenchmen detained. He informed his Spanish counterpart at Santo Domingo, who sent two officials to examine the prisoners. This done, 460 French captives were marched to Aguada and inland to San Germán, where they were settled and allotted cattle to sustain themselves, all the while loosely guarded by 60 Spanish soldiers. (d'Ogeron was apparently not among this first group, having been temporarily left behind. The chronicler Alexandre Olivier Exquemelin later reported that d'Ogeron duped his captors by concealing his true identity and feigning

madness, but the official records show the Spaniards knew exactly who he was.)

After several months' captivity, in which some of his men slipped away or were exchanged, and many others succumbed to sickness or neglect, d'Ogeron succeeded in escaping (perhaps with the barber-surgeon François La Faverye, as Exquemelin states). The two allegedly made a day-long walk from the internment area at Hato de Arriba to the coast, where they stole a small fishing boat after murdering its two-man crew and dropping the bodies into the sea. It took four days to clear Cape Rojo and reach the French settlement at Samaná Bay, during which neither man had anything to eat or drink. Having already been given up for dead, "the return of Monsieur d'Ogeron to this island is a miracle," a contemporary eyewitness noted.

Overtures had been previously made from Martinique for both him and his fellow captives, but d'Ogeron now insisted on a more impetuous approach. Despite the peace prevailing with Spain, he organized a force of 500 *flibustiers* at Tortuga and sailed for Puerto Rico on 7 October 1673. Pausing at Samaná for reinforcements, he appeared before Aguada in the middle of the month and learned—incorrectly—that De Arteaga might consider an exchange. D'Ogeron therefore blundered ashore with a landing party of 300 men and tried to seize some hostages. On his third day, he had marched as far as six miles inland, where he was ambushed and lost 17 men before retreating. It is alleged that the Spaniards lost double this amount, and in their wrath butchered the French wounded left on the field.

Nor did d'Ogeron's attack benefit his men at Hato de Arriba, who suffered for this temerity. When De Arteaga was informed of this latest outrage, he ordered 40 prisoners executed and the rest placed in strict confinement. D'Ogeron cruised helplessly off the coast for the next couple of months, until word arrived that France and Spain were at war, dashing his final hopes. The Spaniards would now be most unlikely to release their captives in the West Indies, and a discouraged d'Ogeron returned to Tortuga on 29 December 1673, requesting permission to visit France. He never saw his men again. By the spring of 1674, scarcely 131 were left alive, slaving on the fortifications at San Juan de Puerto Rico. From there they were transported in groups to Havana, to await deportation to Spain.

A curious sequel occurred two years later, when the Spanish vessel *Nuestra Señora del Pópulo* was captured by the French in the Mediterranean in the Strait of Messina between Sicily and Italy. The Spanish captain and two ensigns were carried to the border between southern France and Cataluña, where a message was dispatched to the Spaniards offering to exchange them for any of d'Ogeron's survivors in the New World. The Council of Indies in Madrid took this offer seriously, sending a circular dated 23 December 1676 to their officials at Puerto Rico and Havana, ordering that any such captives be forwarded to Cadiz. The matter languished on account of the slowness caused by naval blockades.

Meanwhile, the *Compagnie des Indes Occidentales* had been disbanded in 1674, and the following year, d'Ogeron reached Paris to determine what his new role might be. But being "afflicted by an incurable diarrhea [*lienterie*]" he never got to see either the king nor his minister Colbert before dying on 31 January 1676 at the *Rue des Maçons* (Masons' Street) in the Sorbonne. Two years later, Exquemelin's book appeared in Amsterdam, its final chapter dedicated to d'Ogeron's Puerto Rican ordeal.

*See also* Exquemelin, Alexandre Olivier; Hispaniola; Pouançay, Jacques Nepveu, sieur de.

*References:* Exquemelin; López Cantos; Lugo.

# ORANGE, PIERRE D'

## (D. 1683)

French freebooter from Martinique who helped sack Veracruz.

D'Orange may have been a descendant of the family that founded the French colony of Guadeloupe in 1635. On 5 March 1683, he sailed from Martinique with the tiny 2-gun *Dauphin* (Prince), accompanied by the equally small *Prophète Daniel* (Prophet Daniel) of Antoine Bernard, intending to go turtling at the Cayman Islands. A month after arriving, they heard of a great pirate assembly off the Central American coast preparing to attack the Spaniards. Crossing to Guanaja Island, they learned that this peacetime raid was being launched because a Dutch-born rover named Nikolaas van Hoorn had been defrauded of a consignment of slaves at Santo Domingo. Being a French subject, he had obtained a letter of reprisal from Jacques Nepveu, sieur de Pouançay and governor of Saint Domingue, to exact restitution from the Spanish. Van Hoorn had sortied with the "chevalier" de Grammont and other buccaneer captains to recruit men at Roatan to attempt the great Mexican port of Veracruz.

D'Orange and Bernard joined the expedition, which eventually swelled to 13 vessels and perhaps 1,400 men. Hurrying around the Yucatán peninsula, a landing party of 800 freebooters stole ashore near Veracruz the night of 17 May 1683, infiltrating and attacking the city at dawn. The Spanish garrison was quickly subdued and several thousand half-dressed citizens herded into La Merced Church, where some would later recall d'Orange as a jailer "who behaved most tyrannically, and whom the rest of the pirates greatly respected." After ransacking the city over four days, the raiders withdrew two miles offshore to Sacrificios Island with their hostages, transferring vast quantities of booty aboard the waiting ships. A fortnight later they weighed and staggered back around Yucatán to divide their spoils at Isla Mujeres.

The flotilla then broke up, d'Orange and Bernard being among the first to attempt to beat across to Petit Goâve, only getting as far the Caymans before the latter fell ill. D'Orange and his *Dauphin* persisted, gaining the French colony and making a brief cruise along the north coast of Cuba before rejoining his consort. On 4 August 1683, while lying at Little Cayman, the Armada de Barlovento suddenly hove into view and captured both. The two prizes were carried into Veracruz three weeks later, and a hearing convened aboard the flagship *Santo Cristo de Burgos* (Holy Christ of Burgos). According to Spanish law, pirate leaders were to be tried at the scene of their crimes, while followers were to be deported to serve in the galleys of Spain. Thus, when the plate fleet set sail for Cadiz a few days later, d'Orange remained behind to be judged in the still-devastated Mexican port.

At his trial he was asked "how he, being a Catholic, could violate temples, steal icons and profane holy places, actions only of heretics," to which he lamely replied that everyone else had been doing so. D'Orange was condemned to death, and on 22 November 1683 he was paraded through the streets as the town crier shouted, *¡Esta es la justicia que manda hacer el Rey nuestro señor!* (Behold the justice ordered by the king our lord!) The rover was then hanged in the main square, decapitated, and his head spiked at the wharf.

**See also** Barlovento, Armada de; Bernard, Antoine; Grammont, "chevalier" de; Pouançay, Jacques Nepveu, sieur de; Van Hoorn, Nikolaas.

**References:** Juárez; Marley, *Veracruz;* Sáiz; Torres.

# OUTLAW, JOHN
## (FL. 1665)

English privateer who commanded the ill-named *Olive Branch* of 6 guns in Colonel Edward Morgan's expedition against Dutch Sint Eustatius and Sabá during the Second Anglo-Dutch War. This force departed Jamaica in two divisions, five sail putting out of Port Royal on 5 April 1665 and Morgan himself following with another four on 28 April. There were 650 men in all, described in a letter by Governor Sir Thomas Modyford as

> chiefly reformed privateers, scarce a planter amongst them, being resolute fellows and well armed with *fusils* [Spanish word for muskets] and pistols.

The Crown official was particularly pleased they would be serving "at the old rate of no purchase, no pay, and it will cost the King nothing considerable, some powder and mortar pieces." Their landing was successfully made, but the colonel, "being a corpulent man," died from heat exertion during the chase, and his expedition disbanded shortly thereafter.

**See also** purchase.
**References:** Cruikshank; *Interesting Tracts;* Pope.

# OXE, ROBERT
## (FL. 1680)

English logwood poacher caught off Mexico's Laguna de Términos.

On Sunday, 12 May 1680, Oxe appeared at the mouth of the "Bay of Campeche" with his ship *Laurel* of London and other vessels, hoping to visit the English logging establishments and obtain a cargo of logwood before proceeding northward to Boston. A bark of about 35 tons accompanying him went over the bar to locate a pilot, little realizing the Spaniards under Captain Felipe de la Barrera had recently swept the entire lagoon and were now maintaining regular patrols into the area. The next day, *Laurel* stood in toward the mouth of the bay again but neither the bark nor pilot appeared. Instead, that evening a sail was seen approaching along the coast; when Oxe sent his pinnace to investigate, it was discovered to be a Spanish frigate, which gave chase.

Oxe immediately fired a gun to warn Captain James Browne's pink, *Recovery,* which was with him, and the two fled into the night. Not realizing that his bark had already been captured, Oxe returned to the mouth of the lagoon with Browne, where they were again surprised on 16 May by the same frigate and two more Spanish men o' war. Browne and his crew joined Oxe aboard the *Laurel,* setting the pink adrift and fighting the Spaniards for more than two hours ("four or five glasses") before the latter drew off to seize the empty *Recovery.* That night Oxe set ashore watering parties at the mouth of nearby San Pedro y San Pablo River before resuming his futile watch off the lagoon.

Finally he sailed away to "the Cays of Yucatán for water," where one night he was caught by the Spanish with most of his crew ashore. Two of his men were killed and Oxe himself mauled, the Spaniards "hanging him up at the fore braces several times, beating him with their cutlasses, and striking him in the face." When he proffered Governor Lord Carlisle's pass to the *guardacosta* captain—most likely Pedro de Castro or Juan Corso—the latter flung it away and boasted that *Laurel* "was the twenty-second ship he had taken that summer." Oxe and eight hands were put in a canoe with two days' provisions; they landed on the Turneffe Islands (opposite present-day Belize City), where they remained "15 days before any relief came." By the end of that year, Oxe was back in Port Royal, complaining of his mistreatment but lucky to be alive.

***See also*** Barrera y Villegas, Felipe de la; Castro, Pedro de; Corso, Juan; *guardacostas;* Laguna de Términos; logwood.

***Reference:*** *C.S.P., Amer. and W.I.,* Vols. X–XI.

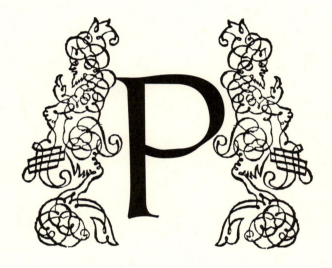

# PAINE, THOMAS

## (c. 1632-POST 1708?)

English privateer who roamed the West
Indies before emigrating to Rhode Island,
which he helped defend against the French.

### WEST INDIAN CAREER
### (1678-1682)

The first mention of Paine's activities
occurred in summer 1678, when he arrived
at Aves Islands with a 6-gun vessel to careen,
"intending to fit himself very well, for here
lay driven on the island masts, yards, timbers
and many things he wanted" from the vast
shipwreck of Vice Admiral comte d'Estrées
fleet, befallen only a few months previously.
Paine had evidently been cruising with a
French privateering commission, that
country being then at war with both Spain
and the Netherlands, while England
remained neutral. After hauling his ship into
harbor and beginning to unrig, Paine was
distressed to spot a 20-gun Dutch warship
materialize offshore, having been sent from
Curaçao to salvage among the wreckage.
The Dutchmen

seeing a ship in the harbor and knowing
her to be a French privateer, they
thought to take her first and came within
a mile of her, and began to fire at her,
intending to warp in the next day, for it
is very narrow going in. Captain Pain [sic]
got ashore some of his guns and did what
he could to resist them, though he did in
a manner conclude he must be taken.
But while his men were thus busied, he
spied a Dutch sloop turning to get into
the road, and saw her at the evening
anchor at the west end of the island. This
gave him some hope of making his escape, which he did by sending two canoes in the night aboard the sloop, who
took her and got considerable purchase

in her; and he went away in her, making
a good reprisal and leaving his own
empty ship to the Dutch man o' war.

Three years later, Paine was still operating
among the French, and in early June 1681
was lying at Springer's Key in the San Blas
Islands north of Panama with a ship of 10
guns and 100 men in company with John
Coxon, Jean Rose, Jan Willems, George
Wright, and four other captains. Together
they decided to make a descent on a Spanish
town along the Central American coast but
first sailed toward San Andrés Island to steal
boats for landing craft and advancing up
rivers. A gale scattered their formation en
route, and an *armadilla* of a dozen tiny men
o' war sent from Cartagena further dispersed
the rovers. Paine must have been one of
those captains blown to leeward into Bocas
del Toro (literally, "bull's mouths" or
"entrances of the bull") off the northwestern
shores of present day Panama. His ship was
damaged and the expedition disintegrated,
but apparently he decided to make repairs
there, during which he had an unpleasant
contact with the local natives, for

having built a tent ashore to put his goods
in while he careened his ship, and some
men lying there with their arms, in the
night the Indians crept softly into the tent
and cut off the heads of three or four
men, and made their escape; nor was this
the first time they had served the privateers so.

By late October 1682, Paine had
apparently tired of this renegade existence,
and put into Jamaica to obtain an English
commission. His moment was well chosen,
for Governor Sir Thomas Lynch—normally
no friend to the privateers—was issuing
commissions to recapture the 30-gun frigate
*Trompeuse* (Trickster), which had been seized
by a band of French cutthroats under Jean

Hamlin and committing depredations. Lynch later wrote:

> While busy at Port Royal over the despatch of [Johnson's] vessel one Captain Clarke, a very honest useful man, solicited me about one Payn, [*sic*] in a bark with 80 men. He told me Payn had never done the least harm to any and that if I would allow him to come in, he would engage to bring in or destroy these pirates.

The governor duly issued Paine a commission to "seize, kill and destroy pirates." Working his way northward with his bark *Pearl,* which was described by another correspondent as "a ship of 8 guns and 60 men," Paine reached the Bahamas in March 1683.

There he found the privateering vessels of Captains Conway Woolley, John Markham, Jan Corneliszoon (commander of a New York brigantine), and the French *flibustier* Capitaine Bréhal, who were jointly preparing "to fish for silver from a Spanish wreck." Instead, the five decided to raid the nearby Spanish outpost of Saint Augustine, Florida, supposedly authorized by Paine's commission. They landed flying French colors, only to find the Spaniards forewarned, so they withdrew after releasing some Spanish captives they had brought with them and looting the surrounding countryside. (The Spanish garrison commander later referred to Paine as "Tomás de la Peña" in his official report.) Paine, Markham, and Bréhal then returned to New Providence in the Bahamas, where Governor Robert Lilburne allegedly wished to seize the two Englishmen's ships "but failed for want of a force." The raiders were suffered to depart to the wreck site, which was being extensively worked, and Paine may have actually had the good fortune to raise some treasure (or possibly used this later

as an excuse to explain his illicit acquisition of Spanish silver). In any event, the governor soon manned a large ship that had arrived at New Providence and went out to the wreck site only to discover Paine and the rest dispersed. (Within a few months the Boston salvor William Phips would arrive to work this same site and find it largely picked clean.)

## ARRIVAL AT RHODE ISLAND
### (AUTUMN 1683)

Several weeks later, the *Pearl* entered Newport, Rhode Island, with its French consort, and Governor Edward Cranfield of neighboring New Hampshire wrote by mid-October 1683:

> During my stay at Rhode Island two pirates came in. Pain [*sic*] was one of them, with a counterfeit commission from Sir Thomas Lynch styling him [the Jamaican governor] one of the gentlemen of the King's Bedchamber, instead of his Privy Chamber, whereby I knew it to be forged. Colonel Dongan and I asked the government to arrest them, but they refused.

The *Pearl* was briefly detained at Boston in early December of that year "for breach of the Acts of Trade," then released, for indeed Paine's papers were quite legitimate. Next year, Paine was specifically mentioned in a circular from Charles II, written from Windsor on 13 April 1684 (O.S.) in the wake of numerous complaints from the Spanish Ambassador that West Indian rovers used British North America to dispose of their booty and recuperate. The monarch instructed all the governors of English America to "permit no succor nor retreat to be given to any pirates, least of all to Thomas Pain [*sic*], who with five vessels under Breha [*sic*], a Frenchman, is lately arrived at Florida." They were, the king added, "a race of evildoers and enemies of mankind."

Based on this new order, the deputy customs collector from Boston again attempted to impound Paine's vessel (now confusingly referred to as a frigate) at Newport on the evening of 26 August 1684 but with no better success. The next morning he had Paine hauled before Governor William Coddington of Rhode Island and in the "presence of Governor Dongan of New York and Cranfield of New Hampshire," insisted the privateer again exhibit his commission. Cranfield and the others affirmed "that it was not Sir Thomas Lynch's hand, nor were his titles correctly given, but Governor Coddington was of other mind" and found in Paine's favor. The Deputy Customs Collector returned angrily to Boston three days later, complaining that the Rhode Island governor refused to "see with eyes like other men."

Paine may have then—given this hostile reception—returned to the West Indies with Bréhal, as the *flibustier* commander was known to have been operating off southern Cuba in early November 1684 with a pair of English-looking sloops. A Royal Navy officer who visited Petit Goâve on the island of Saint Domingue on 16–17 December reported, "I saw in the port the ships commanded by Captain Yankey [*sic;* Jan Willems], Breha [*sic*], Thomas and Johnson." However, if true, Paine must have returned to Rhode Island within the next few years to settle at Jamestown, Rhode Island, where he built a house on an estate called Cajacet. He also married Mercy Carr, the daughter of Judge Caleb Carr (who would eventually become governor of that colony), and by 1688 Paine was being mentioned as serving on a Rhode Island grand jury.

## BATTLE OFF BLOCK ISLAND
### (JULY 1690)

The second summer following the outbreak of the War of the League of Augsburg (King William's War) against France, a flotilla of raiders appeared off that coast commanded by the veteran Pierre le Picard, former lieutenant to the ferocious Jean-David Nau l'Olonnais—and in better times, friend and privateering companion-in-arms to Thomas Paine. On 22 July 1690, Le Picard led a landing party ashore at Block Island, which he and his men plundered, seriously mistreating the inhabitants. News of this depredation quickly reached the mainland and warning bonfires were lit "from Pawcatuck to Seaconnet." A reconnaissance sloop set out from Newport the next day with 34 men, and the following night the French tried to penetrate Newport itself but drew off when they were discovered.

Three days later, on 27 July (17 July 1690 O.S.), Governor John Easton overrode his Quaker sensibilities sufficiently to order the 10-gun sloop *Loyal Stede* of Barbados, which was lying in Newport roads, impressed into the colonial service. (This vessel was named in honor of Edwin Stede, lieutenant governor of that West Indian colony.) Some 60 men were also hastily mustered, and Paine was put in command of this sloop and its smaller consort, under Captain John Godfrey. Three days later the two craft set out for Block Island with a contingent of soldiers on board.

Meanwhile, Picard had moved off to attempt New London (Connecticut), so Paine's force gained Block Island without sighting the French. The next day the two New England sloops beat about, until that afternoon they saw the enemy formation of one large bark, one large sloop, and a smaller sloop bearing down upon them. Paine retreated into a defensive position in the shallows off Block Island so as to be able to work the guns on only one side of his vessels. Believing the two retreating sloops to be coastal traders, the French made all possible sail and "sent a *piragua* before them, full of men, with design to pour in their small arms [fire] on them and take them, as their manner was." Unfortunately, Paine's gunner opened fire too soon, missing the advance boat and warning the French that their opponents were armed. The *piragua* retreated and its men reboarded their ships to bear down upon the New Englanders.

A brisk firefight erupted at five o'clock that afternoon, lasting until nightfall, in which the French suffered 14 killed, including their second-in-command, "a very violent, resolute fellow" who was shot in the neck while drinking a glass of wine and wishing damnation on the English. Paine only had one dead and six wounded, and the following morning Picard made off. The two New England sloops pursued, forcing the French to scuttle a merchant prize they had captured by firing "a great shot through her bottom." When Paine came up, he found this vessel standing straight up and down, so that none of its cargo of wine or brandy could be saved before it sank.

Paine returned triumphantly to Newport, where he learned that reinforcements had arrived from Boston under Captain Sugars, who was sent off after the retiring Picard.

### LATER CAREER
### (1692-1708)

Two years later Paine was appointed captain of the militia company, and in 1698 he was admitted as a freeman of the colony of Rhode Island. He was also one of the founders of Trinity Church in Newport and in June 1699 even visited briefly with the notorious Captain William Kidd aboard a sloop off Block Island, when the latter returned from his Red Sea cruise. Finally in 1708, Paine—although nearly 76 years of age—embarked on one final expedition when he seconded Major William Wanton in fighting against the French. Paine was eventually buried on the grounds of his Connecticut house, which still stands today.

*See also* Bréhal, Capitaine; careen; Corneliszoon, Jan; Coxon, John; De Graaf,

Laurens Cornelis Boudewijn; Hamlin, Jean; Johnson, George; Kidd, William; Lilburne, Robert; Lynch, Sir Thomas; Markham, John; Picard, Pierre le; purchase; Rose, Jean; Wanton, William; Willems, Jan; Woolley, Conway; Wright, George.

*References:* Chapin; *C.S.P., Amer. and W.I.,* Vol. XI; Dampier; Earle, *Treasure;* Ritchie.

# PARA

Dutch nickname for Paramaribo, capital of their South American colony of Suriname, whose approaches were guarded by Fort Zeelandia.

*Reference:* Shomette, *Raid.*

# PATACHE

Spanish word used to describe a fleet auxiliary or tender rather than a particular type of craft. *Pataches* occurred in every size and shape during the seventeenth century, depending upon individual circumstances.

# PEDRERO

Spanish name for a swivel gun, a weapon that they—unlike their English, French, or Dutch counterparts—more frequently took into account when assessing a vessel's defensive capabilities, especially aboard a small craft.

These portable weapons afforded additional protection against boarders or other hordes of men, although strictly speaking they were not part of the main batteries. Thus, the Spaniards often listed a small vessel's cannon and *pedreros* separately, a practice not observed by other maritime powers.

For example, in early February 1681 (27 January 1681 O.S.), Acting Governor Sir Henry Morgan wrote to the Lords of Trade and Plantation in London:

Since the beginning of November last, there has rid at anchor in this harbor one Captain John Crocker, commander of a small Spanish ship of ten guns and eight *patereras* [*sic*] and a hundred men, licensed by the Company of Seville to trade in the American seas for two years. It now waits for the Royal African Company's ships with Negroes, intending to sail next week to Cartagena.

In such an instance, these swivels would not only be a welcome defense in the pirate-infested Caribbean but also useful against any slave uprising.

The word *pedrero* itself is derived from the Spanish word *piedra* (stone), which was the most common type of ball fired by the earliest guns introduced in medieval times.

**Reference:** *C.S.P., Amer. and W.I.,* Vol. XI.

# PENNON, CAPITAINE

## (FL. 1682)

French *flibustier* named in a letter written by Governor Sir Thomas Lynch of Jamaica to his counterpart at Saint Domingue—Jacques Nepveu, sieur de Pouançay—complaining about the peacetime depredations committed by certain renegades. This communication, dated October 1682, specifically refers to the activities of "Pennon in a Spanish bark."

**See also** Pouançay, Jacques Nepveu, sieur de.

**Reference:** *C.S.P., Amer. and W.I.,* Vol. XI.

# PÉREZ DE GUZMÁN, JUAN

## (c. 1618-1675)

President of the Audiencia of Panama and knight of the Order of Santiago who organized the swift reconquest of Providencia Island after Edward Mansfield's attack in 1666, only to suffer a stinging defeat at the hands of Henry Morgan when Panama was sacked five years later.

Pérez de Guzmán was born in Seville around 1618 and entered the Royal Spanish Navy at age 20. He shipped out on a treasure fleet bound for the New World, twice seeing action against the Dutch off Havana. By 1640 he was back in Spain, where he was allowed to raise his own companies of troops before making a second trans-Atlantic voyage. Upon his next return to Europe, he was transferred to command a military company in Milan, where he remained from 1643 until 1647. In 1651 he was again appointed to duty on New World convoys and soon began making a reputation for himself as a likely candidate for administrative service in the empire of the Americas.

On 19 January 1657, Pérez de Guzmán was designated governor of Antioquia in New Granada (present-day Colombia), but he never occupied this post, becoming instead interim governor of Cartagena. He handled the affairs of this crucial port so well that he was promoted to *maestre de campo* and the governorship of Puerto Rico. He assumed the latter office on 26 August 1661, acquitting himself with some distinction. Because of this he was again promoted when his term expired three years later, this time to the presidency of the vital Audiencia of Panama and its surrounding province, called Tierra Firme.

He was installed on 11 January 1665, and thus had been in office almost a year-and-a-half when the Spanish survivors of Mansfield's assault on Providencia Island reached San Lorenzo castle at the mouth of the Chagres River in mid-June 1666. Pérez de Guzmán reacted quickly, ordering his subordinate José Sánchez Ximénez to lead an expedition to recapture this outpost before the English could arrange reinforcements from Jamaica.

However, when the *galeones* reached the isthmus the following year, bearing the new viceroy-designate of Peru, the conde de Lemus, Pérez de Guzmán's good fortune began to wane. He and the new viceroy took an immediate dislike to one another, after which Pérez de Guzmán was accused of defrauding the royal treasury of some silver bars.

Suspended from office and arrested in July 1667, Pérez de Guzmán was transported as a prisoner to Peru, his duties being assumed on an interim basis by Agustín de Bracamonte. The Council of Indies quickly exonerated him in January 1668, but this pardon did not reach Peru until a year later. Released from solitary confinement at Callao, he set sail on 4 February 1669 aboard the ship *Nuestra Señora de la Granada* to resume office, arriving in Panama more than two months later.

A year-and-a-half afterward, in January 1671, Pérez de Guzmán was ill in bed with "Saint Anthony's fire" (erysipelas, a contagious skin disease caused by streptococcus, whose symptoms included boils and high fever), when news arrived that a trio of buccaneer vessels under Joseph Bradley had captured the fortress guarding the mouth of the Chagres River on the north side of the isthmus. The governor rose from his sickbed to mobilize Panama's troops, and on 20 January heard that more raiders had arrived under Morgan and were advancing upriver.

Despite the large tumor on his right breast and repeated bleedings by his physician, Pérez de Guzmán rode forth with 800 militiamen next day and camped at Guayabal to await the enemy. These advanced inexorably, despite the Spaniards' hopes of delaying them in the jungle with ambushes, and on 24 January the governor awakened to find two-thirds of his men had deserted. Retreating to Panama, he gave the order for all able-bodied militiamen to muster at Mata Asnillos, a mile outside the city, while the civilians evacuated by ship.

On the evening of Tuesday, 27 January 1671, Morgan's 600-man vanguard appeared, still carrying the wine they had looted at Venta de Cruces during their march. "We have nothing to fear," a Spanish officer commented to the militiamen around him, "There are no more than 600 drunkards." But more companies continued to arrive, so that by next morning double that number of buccaneers had mustered.

Morgan began his advance at sunrise on 28 January with "red and green banners and flags clearly visible to the Spaniards who awaited them on the plain a couple of miles away." Pérez de Guzmán had 1,200 militia infantry drawn up in a long line, six deep, with two militia cavalry companies of 200 riders apiece on both flanks. But his inexperienced troops had few firearms and no artillery, while the governor pinned rather slender hopes on breaking the enemy formation by stampeding two great herds of cattle through their ranks.

Morgan, however, swung round the Spaniards' right flank, at which Pérez de Guzmán's unwieldly host launched an undisciplined dash against the buccaneer lines. Morgan's buccaneers received the Spanish charge with concentrated fusillades, and more than 100 Spanish militia were killed in the first volley. "Hardly did our men see some fall dead and others wounded," Pérez de Guzmán reported later, "but they turned their backs and fled." He himself rode into the press with his staff raised high "like a mast," hoping to rally his troops, but this was impossible. His staff shot from his hand, the Spaniards scattered pell-mell, leaving 400–500 killed and injured on the field as opposed to only 15 buccaneers.

Pérez de Guzmán rode back through Panama's streets, shouting all was lost, and buildings were set ablaze as the raiders entered in hot pursuit. He himself eventually fled as far as the town of Nata, 70 miles southwest of Panama on the Pacific coast, where on 4 February he called for a fresh muster of conscripts—but only a few hundred volunteers appeared, not enough to dislodge Morgan, who was left in undisputed possession of Panama for four weeks. Morgan then withdrew with what booty the buccaneers had been able to extort, leaving Pérez de Guzmán to creep back home. He found Panama devastated and his own house cruelly vandalized, with beds, mirrors, desks and priceless pictures smashed in a heap, his personal library of 500 books torn to pieces.

Pérez de Guzmán was again suspended from office on 9 October 1671, when the inspector or *visitador* Francisco de Marichalar arrived from Peru to conduct hearings into his government. This was a routine procedure for any outgoing official, and Pérez de Guzmán's term had now expired. The extraordinary circumstances created by the invasion, however, led to court-martial proceedings being instituted against him on 17 November and lasted until 20 February 1672 when Pérez de Guzmán was acquitted. Nevertheless, he was a broken man and died three years later, after having returned to Madrid.

**See also** *galeones;* Mansfield, Edward; Morgan, Sir Henry; Sánchez Ximénez, José.

**References:** Earle, *Panamá;* López Cantos; Pope; Sáiz.

# PETERSEN, JON

## (FL. 1659)

Privateer from Kolding, Denmark, who operated with a Jamaican commission.

On 1 November 1659, the Dutch slaver *St. Jan* (Saint John), Adriaen Blaes van der Veer master, ran aground "two hours before daybreak" on the northeast section of Los Roques, a dangerous group of cays 125 miles east of Curaçao. Ninety West African slaves were left aboard in heavy surf, while captain and crew took to an overcrowded boat. They stopped at Bonaire to lighten their craft by unloading some men and reached Curaçao on 4 November. The local West India Company officials provided them with two small vessels to rescue their comrades and slaves: the bark *Jonge Vogelstruis* (Young Ostrich) and sloop *Jonge Bontekoe* (literally "young spotted cow," or more properly, "spotted calf").

They set sail separately from Curaçao on 7 November, and the following afternoon *Jonge Vogelstruis* came within sight of Bonaire. As they approached, a 4-gun frigate stood out from shore "and ordered them to strike, threatening to fire if they did not do so at once." The Dutch complied and discovered this rover to be commanded by Petersen, with 30 "English, French and German" crew members aboard his *Kastel Fergat* (Fergat Castle). The Dutch told him they were visiting company personnel on Bonaire, but—despite the recent peace treaty between England and the United Provinces—Petersen put a prize crew aboard and ordered them into the roads. Upon dropping anchor, the bark was hailed by Blaes van der Veer's survivors on shore, asking whether they had already rescued "the Negroes who were left behind on the stranded ship, or whether they were just on their way."

Angry at being deceived, Petersen detained the Dutch and the next day

(Sunday, 9 November) sent *Jonge Vogelstruis* to Little Curaçao to recall his lieutenant and some men he had stationed there to monitor ship movements. They were aboard a Spanish *piragua* taken earlier off Caracas, but which they now abandoned at anchor in order to rejoin Petersen. Once reassembled, the privateers set sail from Bonaire the evening of 10 November, taking their captives with them. They tacked upwind in the direction of Caracas, where they spotted a 6-gun Spanish frigate and a *piragua,* chasing both until the quarry beached themselves in the shallows. Petersen then veered over onto the opposite tack and attempted to reach Los Roques but only got as far as Aves Islands against the currents.

*Kastel Fergat* dropped anchor, and Petersen detached 14 privateers aboard *Jonge Vogelstruis* to visit the wreck. When they approached on 16 November, they found that the sloop *Jonge Bontekoe* had already been at Los Roques for four days and at one point made a line fast to the remains of the *St. Jan.* However, because the weather was rough and there were so few hands on board, they had not proceeded with the rescue "for fear of the Negroes," preferring to wait until their consort arrived. Petersen's men subdued the Dutch salvagers and brought 82 adult slaves and two infants aboard the *Bontekoe,* sailing them to Aves to rejoin Petersen. Meanwhile, *Vogelstruis* remained at the site another day, pillaging equipment and goods, including elephants' tusks.

After a week's captivity, Petersen restored the *Bontekoe* to the Dutch but kept the *Vogelstruis.* In light of the peace prevailing with England, his actions were entirely illegal, although he offered to pay for their "services" during the salvage, which was refused. Angry, Petersen bluntly told his prisoners, "Don't mouth off too much or you shall all leave naked; and don't make sail until we have gone." On the evening of 23 November 1659, *Kastel Fergat* stood off

toward the Spanish Main, and *Bontekoe* returned to Curaçao two days later to lodge an official protest. The island governor noted that Petersen had "committed similar acts before this, under improper commission, and persists therein now as a public pirate." He wrote to warn Peter Stuyvesant in New York about the raiders, especially "a certain *Peeckelharinck* [literally, "pickled herring"] who previously sailed with Captain Beaulieu at the Cape, and now and then comes into Your Honor's area in New Netherland."

Petersen was doubtless the "Capt. Peterson" mentioned in the journal of Colonel Edward D'Oyley, governor of Jamaica, as having been issued a "let pass" on 31 December 1659 (O.S.).

**See also** D'Oyley, Edward; Spanish Main.
**References:** Gehring; Pawson, *Port Royal.*

# Peterson, Captain

## (fl. 1688)

Rhode Island privateer who served as lieutenant to Jan Willems and Jacob Evertsen.

In the summer of 1688, after the deaths of Willems and Evertsen in the West Indies, Peterson arrived at Newport, Rhode Island, with a *barco luengo* of 10 guns and 70 men. He traded some of his booty with the local New Englanders before proceeding northeastward to French-held Nova Scotia. The governor of Massachusetts dispatched HMS *Rose* to arrest him, but this warship did not reach Newport until after Peterson's departure. It succeeded only in detaining two local ketches for trading with the pirates; the ketches were then sailed into Salem. Also charged with receiving illicit goods were several private individuals, including a Boston merchant who had bought some hides and "elephants' teeth" (i.e., ivory tusks) from Peterson for £57. When the governor ordered a court to try them, a sympathetic grand jury threw out the bill.

Peterson meanwhile took a pair of French ships off the Nova Scotia coast, notwithstanding the fact that war had not yet been declared against France, then used them to surprise the garrison at Chebucto. According to a later report:

> The pirates said they took the fort easily, for all the soldiers were asleep. They plundered it, finding several chests of arms and other goods useful for the Indian trade and great store of provisions, some of which they left to the garrison at the Governor's entreaty; nor did they spike the guns when told that the garrison might otherwise be destroyed by the Indians. They took a ketch afterwards from a Frenchman, which had originally been taken from Piscataqua [New Hampshire]. This vessel Peterson sent back, saying that the French rogues had no business with other people's vessels.

Thus resupplied, Peterson apparently decided to cross the Atlantic to West Africa's Gold Coast, "being near a hundred men well armed and victualled for a year."

**See also** *barco luengo;* Evertsen, Jacob; Willems, Jan.

**References:** *C.S.P., Amer. and W.I.,* Vol. XII; Gosse, *Who's Who.*

# PETIT, CAPITAINE

## (FL. 1684)

French *flibustier* who in 1684 was in command of the *Ruze,* of 4 guns and 40 men, at Saint Domingue.

**References:** Gosse, *Who's Who;* Lugo; Juárez.

# PEZ Y MALZÁRRAGA, ANDRÉS DE

## (1657-1723)

Spanish naval officer and pirate hunter.

Of Basque origin and the son of a naval officer, Pez was born at Cadiz, Spain in 1657. He joined the navy at the age of 16 and three years later was present at the crushing defeat of the combined Hispano-Dutch fleets at Palermo, Sicily (2 June 1676), in which both his father and brother were killed by the French. In 1681, he transferred into the vessels that were being sent out from Spain as reinforcements for the Armada de Barlovento, the naval squadron assigned to permanent patrol duty in the West Indies. Two years afterward, in summer 1683, Pez was promoted to captain and apparently given command of the auxiliary vessel *Jesús, María y José* (alias *Sevillano,* of 8 guns), when Admiral Andrés de Ochoa detached this small man o' war along with the larger frigate *Santo Cristo de San Román* to strengthen north Panama's defenses. By December, Pez was lying at anchor inside Cartagena, when a flotilla of seven pirate craft were seen prowling outside the harbor.

### DEFEAT OFF CARTAGENA
### (CHRISTMAS 1683)

Determined to drive these pirates away, the local Spanish governor, Juan de Pando Estrada, commandeered the private merchant ships *San Francisco,* of 40 guns, *Nuestra Señora de la Paz* (Our Lady of Peace), of 34 guns, and a 28-gun galliot, placing a total of 800 soldiers and sailors under Pez's command. The armada captain exited on 23 December, half expecting his enemy to flee before this cumbersome force; but the blockaders were led by the boldest corsairs of that day—Laurens de Graaf, Michiel Andrieszoon, and Jan Willems—and they swarmed in to give battle. Pez's inexperienced crews were no match for the veteran rovers, who completely outmaneuvered and outfought them. In the confusion, *San Francisco* ran aground, after which both *Paz* and the galliot were forced to strike. Ninety Spaniards were killed in the engagement, as opposed to only 20 pirates. Pez and his survivors were deposited ashore on Christmas Day, with a humiliating note thanking the governor for the gift of these ships.

One year later, Pez had evidently rejoined the main body of the armada with his *Sevillano,* for in April 1685 this vessel sailed as part of the full squadron from Veracruz to Havana and by June had traversed the Caribbean again back into Cartagena. While lying there, word arrived that a huge *flibustier* fleet under De Graaf and the "chevalier" de Grammont had assaulted the Mexican port of Campeche, so the armada was ordered to intercept and punish them as they withdrew. Admiral Ochoa set sail on 2 August 1685 with his vessels, checking the Cayman Islands for raiders before touching at Trujillo (Honduras) on 17 August. The nearby buccaneer lair of Roatan was also inspected but found to be uninhabited, so the armada resumed its northerly heading on 8 September.

## DEBACLE OFF ALACRÁN REEF
### (SEPTEMBER 1685)

At dawn, three days later, five sail were sighted near Isla Mujeres off the Yucatán coast, and the squadron gave chase. Two of these vessels lagged behind and were captured, proving to be corsairs who had participated in the assault on Campeche. De Graaf's *Neptune* had been sailing with the stragglers, but Pez and the rest of the Spaniards had lost sight of it while securing their two prizes and dearly hoped to overtake it. At two o'clock the following afternoon more sails were spotted to leeward (i.e., in the northwest), so Captain Francisco

de Llanos's 335-ton *Nuestra Señora del Honhón* and Pez's *Sevillano* were sent downwind to investigate. Upon drawing near, they recognized the largest of the vessels as De Graaf's flagship, so while *Honhón* remained to shadow this enemy, *Sevillano* beat back upwind to report. The main body of the armada had disappeared over the horizon, so it was not until the next day that Pez was able to lead Ochoa's flagship *Santo Cristo de Burgos* and vice-flagship *Nuestra Señora de la Concepción* back toward De Graaf.

At four o'clock on the afternoon of 13 September, they found the corsair east of Alacrán Reef, *Honhón* having lost contact during the night and made off toward Veracruz. The two Spanish flagships gradually closed on the heavily laden *Neptune,* enjoying both the weather gauge and a two-to-one superiority, while Pez observed from a distance. The next day, the battle was resumed at dawn, ending in another embarrassing failure that evening—De Graaf fought his ship brilliantly throughout the day, outmaneuvering and outshooting the Spaniards until nightfall, after which he slipped past them upwind and left the battered armada behind. Ochoa died two days later, and the demoralized squadron limped back into Veracruz the night of 28–29 September 1685, to face a series of courts-martial. Pez was one of the few officers absolved of misconduct in this affair.

## SEARCH FOR LA SALLE
### (1687-1689)

From their prisoners, however, the Spaniards learned that a French colonizing expedition had settled on the north shores of the Gulf of Mexico that previous year, under René Robert Cavelier, sieur de La Salle. Alarmed at this encroachment upon their territories, the Mexican authorities dispatched a small party to make a reconnaissance, which returned to Veracruz on 13 March 1686 without sighting any settlement. A second pair of specially constructed *piraguas* was sent out next, and when these proved slow to reappear, a third enterprise was prepared in summer 1687 under Pez and his fellow armada captain, Francisco López de Gómara.

Meanwhile, *Sevillano* had sunk at anchor the previous year during a norther at Veracruz, while López de Gómara had lost his pink during a storm attempting to cross the Gulf of Mexico for a consignment of spars from Havana. The two officers were therefore provided with the armada frigate *Santo Cristo de San Román* and a *patache* that had accompanied that year's *azogue,* or quicksilver ships, each manned by 40 seamen and 30 infantrymen. Pez commanded the former and López de Gómara the latter, departing Veracruz on 30 June 1687 to proceed to Tampico and take on two large launches for exploration work close inshore. They arrived at four o'clock on the afternoon of 3 July to hear disturbing rumors that the previous expedition had been shipwrecked on the gulf coast and so hastened their departure. They set sail from Tampico at noon on 5 July, little realizing that the overdue expedition had returned safely into Veracruz three days previously. Over the next two months they combed the shoreline as far east as Pensacola without finding anything before reentering Veracruz on 4 September 1687.

In November, Pez attended a conference in Mexico City where a captive English buccaneer claimed to have sailed to the as-yet undiscovered French colony with the *flibustier* Jean Rose, and so *Santo Cristo de San Román* was prepared for another voyage. On 8 March 1688, Pez quit Veracruz with the veteran pilot Juan Enríquez Barroto and the English prisoner on board, crossing into the area of present-day Mobile Bay. No trace of any settlement was found, and the captive confessed he had lied in hopes of being released or finding an opportunity to escape. Pez sailed back into Veracruz with the man in irons on 24 April, and three months later suggested another cruise be made with the two original *piraguas,* which was approved. Pez did not accompany this particular mission, but eventually the remains of La Salle's colony were found with only two Frenchmen left alive.

## VISITS TO SPAIN AND PENSACOLA (1689-1695)

The immediate danger removed, Pez presented a memorial to the Mexican viceroy, suggesting a Spanish colony be established at Pensacola to preempt any future foreign occupations in that region. This was agreed to, and in summer 1689 Pez was authorized to travel to Spain and present his proposal to the Council of Indies. He arrived late that year to a frosty reception, for Spain had just declared war against France and the ministers were annoyed to find one of their naval officers returning home without prior permission. A rebuke was sent to the Mexican viceroy, and Pez's submission was received with scant sympathy. However, the deformed King Charles II was eventually won over, and Pez's plan was approved.

In July 1692, Pez set sail from Cadiz aboard the annual plate fleet with an additional commission promoting him *almirante,* or second-in-command, of the Armada de Barlovento once this position fell vacant. He returned to Veracruz that October and departed across the gulf again on 25 March 1693 accompanied by the eminent mathematician from the University of Mexico, Dr. Carlos de Sigüenza y Góngora, to conduct an accurate survey of Pensacola Bay for its future colonization. They were back at Veracruz by 13 May, having completed their mission, although no consensus could then be achieved as to a next step. Sigüenza and the Mexican authorities called for the immediate installation of a small garrison, but Pez objected, arguing its very weakness would invite attack, by either the French or pirates. Consequently, it was decided he should travel to Spain once more and obtain authorization for a large-scale occupation.

Pez set forth aboard the plate fleet in July 1693 and by December had reached Spain. After lengthy consultations his position was approved, and by September 1695 he was back in Mexico, with a new commission as *capitán general,* or commander-in-chief, of the Armada de Barlovento as well. He called on the viceroy in the capital, but the Pensacola project could not be implemented then for lack of funds, so Pez left Mexico City that December for Veracruz, to organize his new command.

## DEFEAT OFF SANTO DOMINGO
### (1697)

After lengthy delays, his armada finally sailed on 4 August 1696, consisting of the flagship *Santísima Trinidad* with 56 guns and 350 men, *Maracaibo* with 46 guns and 250 men, *Rosario* with 42 guns and 240 men, *Guadalupe* with 26 guns and 130 men, and *Jesús, María y José* with 22 guns and 100 men. These vessels escorted two combined plate fleets across to Havana, arriving on 25 August. Rather than wait to accompany these into the Straits of Florida, as was customary, Pez preferred sallying with his squadron alone after a long layover. Putting out to sea again on 11 November 1696, he stood toward Puerto Rico, which was reached on 15 December. On 29 December his armada departed for Santo Domingo, intercepting the French merchantmen *Saint Louis* and *Americaine* en route. Off Caucedo Point, four large sail were sighted the morning of 6 January 1697, and as the armada bore down, the strangers hoisted the colors of Spain's allies in that

conflict, England and Holland. After sending an officer aboard to make a brief inspection, Pez continued his cruise.

Pez had been duped; the ships actually were the French royal warships *Bourbon* of 58 guns, *Bon* of 52 guns, *Favorite* of 36 guns, and *Badine* (Playful) of 24 guns. Having gained the weather gauge and the advantage of surprise, these now stole down upon Pez's formation that night and opened fire. The armada scattered in panic, Pez himself making directly for Cuba while his vice-flagship *Maracaibo* was captured; *Guadalupe* and *Jesús María* fled inshore, and *Rosario* headed for Santa Marta. It was an embarrassed admiral who returned into Veracruz on 5 April 1697, having failed to deliver his *situados* or reach the Spanish Main.

Almost a year later, Pez sailed again, peace having meanwhile been reestablished in Europe. On 28 May 1698, he left Veracruz with *Trinidad, Rosario, Guadalupe,* and the 6-gun sloop *San José y las Animas,* with a total of 670 men, to escort another plate fleet across to Havana. He remained in the Cuban capital most of July before conducting the plate fleet out into the straits and intercepting a small English brigantine, which he carried into Santiago. From there his armada reconnoitered Saint Thomas before making a lengthy layover in San Juan, Puerto Rico. His squadron then visited Santo Domingo before heading for the Spanish Main, calling at Margarita, Araya, Cumaná, La Guaira, Ríohacha, and Santa Marta (where a small sloop was seized) before reaching Cartagena.

## DARIEN CAMPAIGN
### (1699)

Following his arrival, Pez received intelligence of a new Scottish settlement at Darien. After attempting to gather reinforcements at Cartagena to help drive the settlers out, he sailed for Portobelo, which he reached on 16 January 1699.

Convinced his four warships were inadequate for a seaborne assault, he instead proposed leading 500 men over the isthmus to Panama so as to use them to form the nucleus for a land attack. This was agreed to by the president of Panama, Conde de Canillas, who added two companies of regulars to his expedition. Pez and his men left Panama on 9 March, gathering volunteers as they advanced, but the jungle trails grew increasingly difficult, particularly when torrential rains set in, and so progress was halted two leagues short of their objective.

Pez soon retreated, being hastened by rumors of an English squadron approaching Portobelo, where he had left his armada careening its vessels. This threat never materialized, but he had lost 90 men through desertion and another 80 due to illness. Despite being ordered by Canillas to remain at anchor off the coast, Pez sailed away to Cartagena that summer, arriving late in July. The Scots had meanwhile abandoned Darien because of disease, so Pez was free to return to Veracruz. Upon reaching New Spain on 24 August 1699, he found he was to be court-martialed along with his second-in-command, Guillermo Murphy, for the loss of *Rosario* two years earlier. Both officers were incarcerated on San Juan de Ulúa to await transportation to Spain, while Francisco de Buitrón assumed command of the armada.

### LATER CAREER
#### (1701-1723)

The War of the Spanish Succession revived Pez's career, as he was quickly cleared at his trial in 1701. Two years later he was back in the West Indies commanding the Armada de Barlovento, and afterward made several successful trans-Atlantic crossings with the king's bullion, which won him great distinction. He served at the siege of Barcelona from 1712–1714 and was

appointed to Spain's Supreme War Council in August 1715. A year-and-a-half later he became *gobernador* of the Council of Indies and was made secretary of state in 1721. Pez died in Madrid two years later, where there is a street named after him.

***See also*** Andrieszoon, Michiel; Barlovento, Armada de; De Graaf, Laurens Cornelis Boudewijn; *patache;* plate fleet; *piragua; situados;* Spanish Main; Willems, Jan.

***References:*** Juárez; Prebble; Robles; Sáiz; Torres; Weddle, *Wilderness.*

# PHIPS, SIR WILLIAM
## (1650-1695)

New England salvor who rose to become governor of Massachusetts.

Phips was born in 1650 "at a despicable plantation on the river of Kennebeck" in Maine, one of many children of an immigrant gunsmith from Bristol, England. His father died when he was a small boy and he grew up poor. At the age of 18, Phips made his way to Boston, where he became apprenticed to a ship's carpenter. The young man succeeded in this trade, growing "tall beyond the common set of men, and thick as well as tall, and strong as well as thick." He was enormously ambitious and began making trading voyages to the Bahamas and West Indies, first as the employee of others, then on his own account. He married the widow of a well-to-do merchant, to whom he bragged "he should come to have the command of better men than he was now accounted himself, and that he should be the owner of a fair brick house" in the most fashionable quarter of Boston.

During his travels, Phips learned of numerous Spanish shipwrecks dotting the Caribbean, many with immense treasure still on board. He quickly acquired a reputation for "continually finding sunken ships" and grew skillful at underwater salvage. In particular, he visited a famous wreck site near New Providence in the Bahamas (perhaps *Nuestra Señora de las Maravillas,* lost in 1656), which was being worked by many other seafarers, and he also heard rumors of another lost galleon that lay undisturbed on the shoals north of Hispaniola. He tried to raise money in Boston for an expedition in quest of this latter wreck, and when this failed, sailed to England in the early 1680s to petition Charles II. Another semiofficial expedition was preparing there around this same time in an attempt to combine regular naval patrols with a search for the wreck, comprised of Captain George Churchill's HMS *Falcon* of 42 guns and Captain Edward Stanley's HMS *Bonito* of 4 guns.

While in London, Phips came into contact with the wealthy Sir John Narborough, commissioner of the Royal Navy and former serving officer in the West Indies, who shared Phips's enthusiasm for such projects. Thanks to his intervention, Phips was provided with the loan of an 18-gun Royal Navy vessel, *Golden Rose* (also known as *Rose of Algier,* having been captured in the recent campaign against that North African state), which he was to man with 100 men and sail to the Bahamas, working the known wreck there to raise the capital for a subsequent expedition north of Hispaniola.

Phips set sail from the Downs on 5 September 1683 for Boston to pick up his diving equipment, arriving there at the end of October. He was very proud of commanding a king's ship, although he exceeded his instructions when he insisted every vessel salute his flag and was fined £10 for firing five times at the *Samuel and Thomas* of London when it failed to do so. His men, who were serving for shares only and not wages, got into an altercation with the Boston constabulary, which ended when Phips ordered them back aboard ship. He then argued with the constables himself,

saying "he did not care a turd for the Governor" and invited the constabulary to kiss his arse. Again he was hauled into court, although released with the admonition "that everybody in Boston knew very well what he was and from whence he came, and therefore desired him not to carry it so loftily among his countrymen."

## Expedition to the Bahamas (1683-1685)

Phips also made agreements with Captain William Warren of the ship *Good Intent* and Captain William Davis of a Bermuda sloop to help him work the wreck. Warren sailed first from Boston on 28 November 1683, followed by the other two on 14 January. Phips arrived at New Providence in the Bahamas on 9 February, only three weeks after it had undergone a devastating attack from the Spaniards of Havana. He reached the wreck site on 16 March and discovered it had been largely picked clean over recent months by rovers such as Thomas Paine. Several weeks' work resulted in only disappointing returns, and after another Spanish attack on New Providence (this time by the Cuban corsair Gaspar de Acosta), Phips was forced to careen his ship on a desolate isle. His hard-bitten crew attempted to rise with the ship and try "a trade of piracy in the South Seas," but the massive Phips put them down with his fists.

In November 1684 he visited Port Royal, Jamaica, where he got into a dispute with a Spanish merchantman lying in the roads, firing upon it for some minor offense. Meeting the Spanish captain later in the street, Phips

with a rabble at his feet, told him that if he did not pay him for his shot, he would take his sword from him. The Spaniard was unwilling either to give up his sword or to pay the money, and the rabble was ready to have laid hands on him if a gentleman passing by had not taken ten shillings from his pocket and paid it for him.

A few days afterward, the truculent salvor departed, accompanied by the sloops of Davis and a local captain called Abraham Adderley. They paused at Puerto Plata on the north coast of Santo Domingo, where Phips met a very old Spaniard who claimed to have been "cast away in the [original] wreck" of the vice-flagship *Nuestra Señora de la Pura y Limpia Concepción* in 1641 and was willing to guide him out to the site. Together they traveled northeastward to the Ambrosian Bank but could not hit upon the galleon exactly.

Nevertheless, Phips realized he was close, but because of the growing unreliability of his men, decided to return to England for a new expedition. He paused at Bermuda from April–May 1685, where the colonists were in open rebellion against the royal governor, Richard Cony, because of the recent death of Charles II and his succession by James, Duke of York, whom they regarded as "a Papist." Phips helped uphold Cony's rule, carrying two of his most vociferous opponents back to England as prisoners aboard the *Rose* when he sailed. These prisoners brought charges against Phips once they arrived that August, so he was detained for a day within "the liberties of the Tower [of London]." His lack of profits also meant Phips would no longer receive royal patronage but had to seek out private investors. Fortunately, the wealthy Narborough and the hard-pressed Duke of Albemarle agreed to form a syndicate in March 1686, which attracted the necessary funds. The 200-ton merchantman *Bridgewater* of 23 guns was purchased and renamed *James and Mary,* in honor of the new king and queen, to which was added the 40-ton sloop *Henry* under Captain Francis Rogers, with a combined total of 70 crewmembers.

## TREASURE EXPEDITION
### (1686-1687)

On 12 September 1686, Phips set sail again from the Downs, parting company with his sloop during the trans-Atlantic voyage but reuniting at the end of November in Samaná Bay on the northeastern coast of Santo Domingo. The two vessels disguised their true intent by pretending to seek trade with the local Spaniards, meanwhile discreetly stocking up on supplies and waiting for the stormy season to pass before proceeding to the Ambrosian Bank. After visiting Puerto Plata and the Turks Islands, Phips and Rogers reached the bank on 12 January 1687, and eight days later one of their East Indian divers discovered the wreck, proving it by bringing up pieces of eight "by thousands, sticking together, the sea water having dissolved some of the alloy or copper next with the silver and made it into verdigris, which has fastened them together."

Phips worked the site feverishly until 2 May, when he set sail for England with more than 34 tons of silver on board, worth £200,000. He returned to a hero's welcome that June, a naval guard being placed aboard *James and Mary* to escort it to its anchorage at Deptford and prevent any treasure from being smuggled ashore. Phips himself was summoned to Windsor on 28 May to tell James II of his expedition, after which he was knighted and offered "a very gainful place among the Commissioners of the Navy, with many other invitations to settle himself in England, [but] nothing but a return to New England would content him." In honor of this desire, he was appointed provost marshal of New England on 4 August, a position second only to that of governor.

## NARBOROUGH'S EXPEDITION
### (1687-1688)

A second expedition was prepared, as much more silver still remained at the wreck site;

Narborough was to command the venture from the king's frigate *Foresight*, of 48 guns, with the 400-ton merchantman *Good Luck and a Boy* under Phips, *James and Mary*, under John Strong, and the ship *Princess* under Rogers, along with the former *Henry*. The five set sail on 3 September 1687 from the Downs but soon encountered heavy weather. Phips's vessel was damaged and forced back into Plymouth, while Strong lost sight of the others off Cape Finisterre. He nevertheless pressed on to Barbados, where he was eventually joined by Narborough on 16 November.

By the time the expedition finally reached the Ambrosian Bank (present-day Silver Bank) in mid-December, they found it surrounded by more than four dozen craft. These and numerous other local scavengers had been working the wreck for many months, making away with a further £250,000. These interlopers were driven off, and Narborough's men settled in to resume their work. But the gleanings now proved slender, and five months' labor resulted in little silver. In May, Phips sailed for New England, "to entertain his lady with some accomplishments of his predictions," and assume office as provost marshal. That same winter James was deposed in the "Glorious Revolution," and the next year the War of the League of Augsburg (King William's War) erupted against France.

## ACADIAN EXPEDITION
### (APRIL–MAY 1690)

The following spring, Phips exercised his newfound authority by impressing several private vessels and leading a raid against the French settlements in Acadia. His force consisted of:

*Six Friends,* of 42 guns and 120 men, Captain Gregory Sugars
*Swan,* of 16 guns, Captain Thomas Gilbert

*Mary,* of 8 guns and 12 [?] men, Captain Cyprian Southack
*Porcupine,* of 16 guns and 117 men
*Union,* of 4 guns and 15 men
*Mary Ann,* of 2 guns and 9 men
*Lark,* of 9 men
*Bachelor,* of 6 men

On 23 April 1690 (O.S.), 500 drafted soldiers went aboard these vessels at Nantasket and put out to sea five days later. On 1 May (O.S.) they anchored at Mount Desert and the next day attempted to rush Penobscot fort, although the wind died away and left them becalmed in the harbor. It was not until the day after that the soldiers could get ashore, and when they attacked the fort at dawn on the 4 May, found it deserted. Further reinforcements then joined Phips's expedition from Salem and Ipswich, which together on 6 May (O.S.) plundered the settlement of Passamequoddy and three days later captured Port Royal in the Bay of Fundy without resistance. Phips's triumphant fleet returned to Boston at the end of that same month, only to have to hasten back out again in early July in a vain attempt to counter the retaliatory raid of Pierre le Picard.

## QUEBEC CAMPAIGN
### (AUGUST–OCTOBER 1690)

That autumn Phips launched a much more ambitious enterprise when he sailed from Hull on 9 August 1690 (O.S.) with the following ships:

*Six Friends* (flagship), Captain Gregory Sugars
*John and Thomas,* Captain Thomas Carter
*Return,* (fireship), Captain Andrew Knott
*Lark,* Captain John Walley
*Bachelor,* Captain Thomas Gwynne
*Mary,* Captain John Rainsford

*Elisabeth and Mary,* Captain Caleb Lamb
*Mary Anne,* Captain Gregory Sugars, Jr.
*Hannah and Mary,* Captain Thomas
    Parker
*Friendship,* Captain Windsor
*Elijah,* Captain Elias Noe
*Swallow,* Captain Thomas Lyzenby
*Swan*(vice-flagship), Captain Thomas
    Gilbert
*Swallow,* Captain Small
*Samuel,* Captain Samuel Robinson
*Delight,* Captain Ingerston
*Mary,* four guns, Captain Jonathan
    Baulston, Jr.
*Beginning,* Captain Samuel Elsoe
*Speedwell,* Captain Barger
*Mayflower,* Captain Bowditch
*Boston Merchant,* Captain Michael Shute
*William and Mary,* Captain Peter Ruck
*America Merchant,* (rear admiral),
    Captain Joseph Eldridge
*Lark,* Captain Walk
*Union,* Captain Brown
*Adventure,* Captain Thomas Barrington
*Kathrine,* Captain Thomas Berry
*Fraternity,* Captain Elias Jarvis
*Success,* Captain John Carlisle
*Bachelor,* Captain Edward Ladd

and two transports, commanded by Captains William Clutterbuck and Febershear.

Eleven days later these 32 vessels sighted Cape Breton, and on 31 August (O.S.), Eldridge's *America Merchant* captured a French fishing boat near Ile Percé, where Phips landed and burned some houses on shore. A few more tiny craft were taken as the fleet slowly groped its way up the Saint Lawrence seaway, with Captains Clutterbuck and Ingerston taking soundings in the lead and waving "their jack respectively so many times as they had fathom."

On 6 October 1690 (O.S.), Phips finally anchored three miles below Quebec and demanded the surrender of that city. Not

surprisingly, Governor comte de Frontenac refused, being well prepared for the English attack, which he proved once Phips's fleet weighed and advanced against the batteries. A one-sided duel ensued between the wooden ships and stone ramparts, until the New Englanders cut their cables and drifted out of range.

Checked in his approach, Phips was left with no other choice than to retreat a few days later, pausing off the northern tip of Ile d'Orléans to repair his damaged ships. It was noted "Sir William worked as diligently as any among them, plying his former trade of ship's carpenter," before the fleet fortuitously intercepted the French bark *Nôtre Dame de la Conception* as it arrived from La Rochelle with a cargo of pork, flour, and salt. Three other French merchantmen were chased a few days afterward but disappeared "amid thick fogs and a howling tempest of snow" as winter set in. Captain Rainsford's *Mary* was wrecked on Anticosti Island with 60 men, and Phips limped back into Boston at the end of November with six ships missing, although all but three eventually reappeared. Nevertheless, his grand expedition against Quebec had ended in utter failure.

## LATER CAREER
### (1691-1695)

Notwithstanding this setback, Phips traveled to England in 1691 and won appointment as governor of Massachusetts. When he returned to Boston in May 1692, he found the province in the grip of the Salem witch hunts, which he relegated to Lieutenant Governor William Stoughton while he left to concentrate on throwing back the French and Indian counteroffensives along the borders of New England.

During his absence, twenty innocent men and women were hanged as a result of the witch trials, and when Phips finally returned from Pemaquid and Penobscot that fall, he found his wife among the accused. This promptly led him to decree that no more people were to be committed, and the hysteria abated. Two years later he was accused of maladministration and sailed to London to clear himself of these charges. He arrived in January 1695 but died suddenly on 18 February, not yet 45 years of age.

**See also** Hispaniola; Narborough, Sir John; Paine, Thomas; Picard, Pierre le; pieces of eight; Strong, John.

**References:** Chapin; *C.S.P., Amer. and W.I.,* Vol. XI; Earle, *Treasure.*

# PICARD, PIERRE LE

## (FL. 1668-1690)

French *flibustier* who apparently roamed the West Indies, South Seas, and North America.

The first notice of Picard's activities occurred in early 1668, when he left Saint Domingue as commander of one of five smaller craft supporting the freebooter Jean-David Nau l'Olonnais. These vessels proceeded to Bayahá to take on provisions, and then cruised the south Cuban coast as far as Batabanó, seizing boats for a projected ascent up the San Juan River into Nicaragua. When the buccaneer flagship failed to clear Cape Gracias a Dios on the Mosquito Coast, they probed along the north coast of Honduras instead. At Puerto Cabellos, a Spanish merchantman armed with 24 cannon and 16 *pedreros,* or swivel guns, was seized and the town occupied. Nau l'Olonnais led 300 *flibustiers* inland to attack San Pedro Sula, returning a few days later with little plunder. Meanwhile, it had been learned a wealthy galleon from Spain was due to arrive soon "at the Guatemala river" (Bay of Amatique), so the raiders continued into present-day Belize to await its arrival. Three months later it appeared, and Nau l'Olonnais led the assault. This galleon was

overrun by a horde of boarders, but again the booty proved disappointing, as most of its cargo had already been unloaded. Discouraged, Picard and others decided to quit Nau l'Olonnais's company and roam on their own account.

## VERAGUA RAID
### (1668-1669?)

Proceeding southward to the coast of Panama, Picard made a landing in the province of Veragua and pillaged its principal town, carrying off prisoners and "seven or eight pounds of gold" from the local mines. He had hoped to march across the isthmus and surprise the Pacific coast town of Natá—famed for its even greater gold production—but he had been unable to carry out this ambitious design because the alerted Spaniards awaited him in great numbers.

Retiring out to sea, little more was heard of Picard during the next few years, although he probably found gainful employment as a privateer during the decade of the 1670s, when France was continually at war with both Holland and Spain. Even after the Treaty of Nijmegen was signed in early 1679, local conflicts persisted with the Spaniards in the Caribbean, and Picard's name was once more mentioned. In October 1682, Governor Sir Thomas Lynch of Jamaica wrote to his French counterpart on Saint Domingue, Jacques Nepveu, sieur de Pouançay, complaining of the depredations of renegade French corsairs, "particularly one Picard in a brigantine." A little more than two years afterward, Picard was one of a group of captains who penetrated the Pacific Ocean.

## SOUTH SEAS CAMPAIGN
### (1685-1687)

In the company of Captains Jean Rose and Desmarais (as well as the chronicler Ravenau de Lussan), Picard left his ship at Golden

Island and marched with 264 mainly French *flibustiers* across the Isthmus of Panama, being met on the far side on 11 April by a boat which François Grogniet had sent back for them. This in turn conducted the new arrivals to a pirate assemblage off Isla del Rey, where they were incorporated into the fleet of the English Captains Edward Davis, Charles Swan, William Knight, and Francis Townley, who offered the *flibustiers* the 90-ton *Santa Rosa* they had recently captured from the Spaniards. All the French were to serve under Grogniet, including Picard, and the six vessels and almost 1,000 men of the freebooter fleet then settled down to blockade Panama in hopes of intercepting the anticipated Peruvian treasure fleet.

But these vessels slipped past, delivering their cargo and sallying to engage the buccaneers. Toward noon on 7 June 1685, the rovers were lying off Pacheca Island when a squadron of six Spanish men o' war and a tender unexpectedly bore down upon the pirates, catching them off-guard. An indecisive, long-range engagement ensued, with the buccaneers unwilling to close with the more heavily armed vessels of the Armada del Mar del Sur, who in turn feared being boarded by their more nimble opponents. Nevertheless, the next day ended with a Spanish victory, and the pirates driven off. The buccaneers then fell out amongst themselves along national lines, each group blaming the other for this defeat. A failed attack was jointly made on the coastal town of Remedios (Pueblo Nuevo) at the beginning of July, after which both contingents headed northwestward as separate groups.

Grogniet continued to command Picard and the other *flibustiers* aboard *Santa Rosa,* refusing to join the English raid on León (Nicaragua) in early August 1685, preferring to take 120 men in five boats for a repeat attempt against Remedios. This was repulsed

and Grogniet rejoined his remaining 200 men aboard *Santa Rosa* on 3 September. Realejo was entered on 1 November, but the French found it and the surrounding countryside already devastated from an earlier English assault and so obtained little booty. Reversing course, Grogniet hesitated to march inland and sack Esparta (in Costa Rica) on 9 December, pressing on instead into the Gulf of Chiriquí toward the end of that year.

On 9 January 1686 his *flibustiers* captured the tiny coastal town of Chiriquita (Panama), which was abandoned a week later. At the end of this same month a Spanish squadron passed by out at sea, and when Grogniet's men approached Remedios again the night of 5 March to forage for supplies, they were ambushed by a small frigate, *barco luengo,* and *piragua,* suffering more than 30 casualties. They roamed westward once more, anchoring off Esparto on 19 March and sighting Francis Townley's small flotilla four days later.

Despite some residual ill will, the two groups combined for a joint attempt against the inland city of Granada (Nicaragua), landing a force of 345 men on 7 April and fighting their way into the city three days later. Little loot was found, however; the Spaniards had been forewarned and had transferred their valuables offshore to Zapatera Island, so the pirates withdrew empty-handed five days later. They endured numerous ambushes before passing Masaya and regaining their ships, after which they traveled to Realejo.

Having enjoyed such limited success, on 9 June 1686 half of Grogniet's French followers voted to join Francis Townley in his eastward progress toward Panama. The remaining 148 *flibustiers* agreed to remain with Grogniet while he sailed westward, and the two contingents parted company a fortnight later. Grogniet operated for a time in the Gulf of Amapala (present-day Gulf of

Fonseca), until a majority of his men again voted to quit his leadership. These 85 *flibustiers* sailed *Santa Rosa* northwestward for New Spain and California to await the annual galleon from Manila, while Grogniet retraced his passage down the Central American coast with 60 followers aboard three *piraguas*. He rediscovered Townley's contingent, now commanded by George Hutt, in the Gulf of Nicoya on 23 January 1687. After ravaging that area for a month, they weighed together for a surprise attack on the equatorial port of Guayaquil.

It is not known whether Picard had remained with Grogniet or Townley throughout this period, but he was present for this particular assault, being chosen to command the vanguard. In the words of Lussan, "Fifty *enfants perdus* were to be led by Captain Picard, in command of our small frigate, and were to attack the large fort."

On 16 April 1687, the rovers arrived opposite Puná Island, and two hours before dawn on Sunday, 20 April, landed to march inland against Guayaquil. Picard led his company against the main fort, Hutt directed his 50 English buccaneers against another, while Grogniet advanced with the main body through a marsh toward the heart of the city. The Spaniards had earlier been advised of strange sails off Puná, but when no attack immediately developed, assumed this to be a false alarm. Between three and four o'clock on that rainy Sunday morning, however, they were disabused when buccaneers burst upon them and a vicious house-to-house melee ensued. Between 34 and 60 Spaniards were killed in eight hours of fighting, and many others captured, as opposed to only 9 pirates dead and 12 wounded. Among the latter was Grogniet, though, who died a few days after the raiders had retired to their ships to await the ransoming of hostages.

Picard now assumed command of the *flibustiers,* who along with Hutt were joined

a few days later by Davis. The latter brought word of a squadron of Peruvian privateers on their way to attack the raiders, who then fought an inconclusive engagement with these vessels off Puná Island between 27 May and 2 June. Although undefeated, Picard and his consorts were forced to abandon their prize *San Jacinto,* and ten days later held a meeting at Cape San Francisco, where they divided the spoils. Each proceeded on their separate ways, Picard sailing with five vessels as far north as Tehuantepec (Mexico), which he captured with 180 men on 30 August 1687, and then looked into Acapulco bay a few weeks later. Reversing course until he reached the Gulf of Fonseca, Picard scuttled his vessels there on 2 January 1688 and marched overland into Nueva Segovia province with some 260 followers. In the interior highlands the buccaneers constructed rafts and sped down the Coco River, emerging at Cape Gracias a Dios on 9 March. A Jamaican ship was persuaded to carry them to Saint Domingue, which they reached on 8 April.

Picard and his *flibustiers* were leery of any official sanction, peace having long since been declared between France and Spain, which they feigned not knowing about because of their lengthy absence. Governor Pierre-Paul Tarin de Cussy was not present at the capital of Petit Goâve, being on an inspection tour of that island's northern districts, so there were no immediate recriminations—although it became obvious the Crown's policy had changed drastically with regard to roving, despite the local officers' continuing distrust of their Spanish neighbors. Lussan and many other freebooters therefore elected to disperse even further afield, with Picard apparently choosing to emigrate with his booty to Acadia in French North America. A little more than a year later, when the War of the League of Augsburg (King William's War) erupted against England, Holland, and Spain simultaneously, Governor de Cussy was to lament he had ever been ordered to put a halt to privateering, as he now desperately required their services.

## RHODE ISLAND RAID
### (SUMMER 1690)

Meanwhile, Picard had established himself in North America, where during the second summer following the outbreak of the war he led a flotilla of raiders against the Rhode Island coast in retaliation for both Massachusetts Governor Sir William Phips's and Acting New York Governor Jacob Leisler's earlier strikes against the French colonies.

Stealthily, these raiders disembarked at Block Island on 22 July 1690, plundering the area and mistreating the inhabitants. News of this attack quickly reached the English mainland, and warning bonfires were lit "from Pawcatuck to Seaconnet." A reconnaissance sloop set out from Newport the next day, while the following night Picard boldly attempted to penetrate Newport itself, drawing off only when discovered.

Three days later, on 27 July (17 July 1690 O.S.), Governor John Easton commandeered the 10-gun sloop *Loyal Stede* of Barbados, which was lying in Newport roads, placing it and 60 men under the command of Picard's old West Indian counterpart, Thomas Paine. The latter sortied on 30 July, accompanied by a smaller consort under Captain John Godfrey with a contingent of soldiers on board.

Picard had meanwhile moved off to attempt New London (Connecticut), so Paine's force gained the offshore island without sighting the French. The next day the two New England sloops beat about, until that afternoon they saw Picard's formation of one large bark, one large sloop, and a smaller sloop bearing down upon them. Paine retreated into a defensive position in the shallows of Block Island, so as to be able to work his guns on only one side.

Mistaking the two retreating sloops for coastal traders, the French made all possible sail and "sent a *piragua* before them," but Paine's gunner opened fire too soon, missing the advance boat and warning the French that their opponents were well armed.

The *piragua* retreated, and Picard's ships then bore down upon the New Englanders. A brisk firefight erupted at five o'clock that afternoon, lasting until nightfall, in which the French suffered 14 killed, including Picard's second-in-command, described as "a very violent, resolute fellow," who was shot in the neck while drinking a glass of wine and wishing damnation on the English. Paine had only one dead and six wounded, and the following morning Picard made off. The two New England sloops pursued, forcing the raiders to scuttle a merchant prize by firing "a great shot through her bottom." When Paine came up, he found this vessel standing straight up and down, so that none of its cargo of wine and brandy could be saved before it sank, while the elusive Picard once more made a clean escape over the horizon before Governor Phips himself arrived with reinforcements.

*See also* Bréhal, Capitaine; Grogniet, Capitaine; Lynch, Sir Thomas; Mar del Sur, Armada del; Mosquito Coast; Nau l'Olonnais, Jean-David; Paine, Thomas; Phips, Sir William; Pouançay, Jacques Nepveu, sieur de; Townley, Francis.

*References:* Bradley, *Lure;* Chapin; *C.S.P., Amer. and W.I.,* Vol. XI; Exquemelin; Lugo; Lussan.

# PICAROON

Anglicized version of the Spanish word *picarón,* which means "great knave," "great rogue," or "great rascal."

*Pícaro* is the simple Spanish term for "knave," "rogue," or "rascal," with the accent falling on the first syllable; *picarón* is the stressed or augmented form, with the accent falling on the last syllable. In the seventeenth century, prior to the standardization of accents in the Spanish language, it was common for Spaniards to write this latter form as *picaroon,* from whence it passed directly into English. Governor Sir Nathaniel Johnson of Antigua, for example, complained to the Lords of Trade and Plantations in London on 22 October 1688 (O.S.), saying that he hoped

> by this time a frigate is on its way to us to preserve us from pilfering picaroons. Two sloops of this island have lately fallen into such hands, one of them, my own property, worth £300.

The spelling sometimes varied in English, as when a delegation of Jamaican merchants petitioned the Crown a year later for two Royal Navy frigates to be sent to that colony, because the "French at Petit Goâve, which is almost in sight of our island, are strong, and the place is a nest of pickeroons."
**Reference:** *C.S.P., Amer. and W.I.,* Vol. XIII.

# PICHILINGUE

### ALSO PECHILINGUE OR PECHELINGUE

Spanish nickname for any Dutchman, believed to be derived from the name of the great Zeeland seaport of Vlissingen (Flushing), from which so many ships sailed for the New World.

# PIECES OF EIGHT

English name for the silver coin known in Spanish as *peso de ocho reales* (literally, "*peso* worth eight *reales*").

These were minted in such vast quantities at both Mexico City and Lima, Peru, that they came to circulate all around the world from Europe as far away as China. They were a commonly accepted form of currency in England's colonies, being valued at four and a half shillings (or "four shillings sixpence") apiece, although oftentimes clipped or chopped into eight pieces—from which developed the expression "two bits" to mean a quarter. On 19 November 1691, the newly appointed governor of Massachusetts, Sir William Phips, wrote his friend Increase Mather: "There is practically only Spanish money in New England, and many of the people have been cheated by bad money."
**References:** *C.S.P., Amer. and W.I.,* Vols. XI and XIII.

# PIGNIER, CAPTAIN

### (FL. 1675-1676)

English freebooter who operated with a French commission.

When England withdrew from the Third Anglo-Dutch War in early 1674, many of its West Indian corsairs shifted allegiance in order to continue privateering. One such captain was Pignier, who obtained a patent from the French authorities on Saint Domingue against the Dutch and Spaniards. On 26 March 1675 (O.S.), the newly appointed deputy governor of Jamaica, Sir Henry Morgan, drafted a letter promising "Pryniar" [*sic*] and his fellow English rovers a friendly reception at Port Royal if they were to come in and cease their activities, which although legal were becoming an embarrassment to the English Crown. The retired buccaneer added that he hoped "their experience of him will give him the reputation that he intends not to betray them."

This proposal was never sent; Morgan's superior, Lord Vaughan, preferred sterner measures for recalling the privateers, but the failure of his approach can be judged from the fact that more than a year later, in a letter dated 24 June 1676 (O.S.) at Port Royal, it was being mentioned that

one Pignier, an Englishman with a French commission near our Island, with considerable "purchase" taken from the Spaniards, but understanding they [i.e., English privateers serving under foreign colors] were to be hanged if our governor could lay hold of them, made their way for [French] Tortugas, where they were assured of being better treated.

*See also* purchase.
*Reference: C.S.P., Amer. and W.I.,* Vol. IX.

# PINEL, CAPITAINE

## ALSO PINET
## (FL. 1694)

French *flibustier* who operated out of Martinique.

On 5 March 1694, the recently arrived priest Jean-Baptiste Labat assisted at a thanksgiving Mass celebrated in honor of Capitaine Pinel, who had captured two English vessels to windward of Barbados with his 6-gun corvette *Volante* (Flyer), alias *Malouine* (literally, "one from Saint Malo, France"). These prizes had carried 18 guns and 58 men, and 12 guns and 45 men, respectively, so that Labat was astonished at the outcome of the battle, which lasted three-quarters of an hour and resulted in more than 60 casualties on both sides. He spent the morning helping to confess the *flibustiers,* after which the service was held "with drums and trumpets" and broadsides fired from all three anchored vessels.

*See also* Labat, Jean-Baptiste.
*Reference:* Labat.

# PIRAGUA

Spanish-American term for any crude type of coastal craft or seagoing boat.

Originally, *piragua* appears to have been the Carib word for dugout canoe, which was made by felling a soft cotton or cedar tree, then hollowing this out with fire and axes. Many were quite large, measuring almost 40 feet in length and six in breadth, capable of travelling swiftly from one island to another with the aid of simple masts and numerous paddlers. Following the conquest of the Americas, the Spaniards continued to employ native carpenters in the construction of these and similar vessels, which they used as cheap port auxiliaries or coastal traders.

By the late seventeenth century these craft had become slightly more refined in their design, differing from canoes—according to the buccaneer surgeon Lionel Wafer—"as lighters and small barges do from wherries." The typical *piragua* had a shallow draft, no decking, and single mast, having to hug the coastline or travel with a larger ship whenever it put to sea. Nevertheless, its ability to work nimbly into any estuary, or land on any beach, made it highly popular with pirates and the West Indian squadrons that hunted them.

# PISTOLE

General English term for any foreign gold coin, especially of Spanish or French manufacture.

The name is believed to be derived from the same root as the word "pistol," originally meaning a small weapon designed for use with one hand rather than two (such as the famous *poignards* made at Pistoia near Florence, Italy). In this same sense, "pistole" came to be applied to any half-crown coin, as opposed to the full crown.

In early 1684, Captain Matthew Tennant of HMS *Ruby* traveled to Cartagena on the Spanish Main as escort for a slaving convoy. While lying outside the roads, he was approached by the employee of a rival slaving consortium, Santiago de Castillo, who delivered "a present of 2,000 pistoles from him and from Don Juan Coleman, an Irish priest." When the Spanish authorities learned of this money being smuggled out of their port, they demanded its return, but Tennant refused. When he reached Port Royal, Jamaica, a few weeks later, Governor Sir Thomas Lynch made him restore the sum, referring to it as both "pistoles" and "doubloons."

*See also* doubloon; Spanish Main; Tennant, Matthew.

*Reference:* C.S.P., Amer. and W.I., Vol. XI.


# PLATE FLEET

Convoy sent annually for the King of Spain's American *plata* or silver, hence its name.

Traditionally, two such fleets departed Seville and Cadiz every year, the first being the Mexican *flota,* which set sail early in spring and after touching at the Canary and Leeward Islands during its passage (to refresh water and provisions only), would traverse the Caribbean directly for Veracruz. The second was the Panamanian *galeones,* which got under way from Spain somewhat later in the year, and after following the same route across the Atlantic, stood into Cartagena, before making for Portobelo (Panama) to meet the rich merchants who had traversed the isthmus from Peru. Both convoys were usually comprised of two men o' war as flagship *(capitana)* and vice-flag *(almiranta),*

escorting roughly a dozen large merchant galleons and some smaller *pataches,* all bearing expensive cargos of European manufactured goods.

After celebrating their respective commercial fairs, the Mexican and Panamanian flagships received chests containing the king's annual silver production, and the galleons bales of American wares such as indigo, logwood, hides, and cacao. They would then rendezvous at Havana, sailing jointly up the coast of Florida and Carolina before heading out into the Atlantic toward the Azores and home.

These fleets were usually too large and powerful to be attacked by West Indian privateers, who had to content themselves with hunting individual galleons, such as the pair of ships which split off from the Mexican convoy every year to anchor in the Bay of Honduras and trade overland with Guatemala. Moreover, the Spaniards operated their plate fleets cautiously, almost like blockade runners, reconnoitering the sea before putting out from any port and delaying their departure if danger threatened. For all its slowness and inefficiency, this system seemed to serve Spain well—at least against piracy.

*See also* almiranta; capitana; flota; galeones; indigo; logwood; patache.

*References:* Robles; Sáiz; Torres.


# POINTIS, BERNARD-JEAN-LOUIS DE SAINT JEAN, BARON DE

## (1645-1707)

French admiral who assaulted Cartagena in 1697 supported by a large contingent of *flibustiers.*

Born in 1645, De Pointis entered France's Royal Navy as a senior midshipman *(enseigne de vaisseau)* in 1672, participating in the battles of Sole Bay, Walcheren, and the Texel within the next two years. In January 1677 he sailed to the New World as a senior lieutenant *(lieutenant de vaisseau)* in the Admiral comte d'Estrées's second expedition, taking part in the capture of Tobago.

He was made captain of a galliot in January 1684, winning promotion for his distinguished service during the bombardments of Algiers and Tripoli. He became a *capitaine de vaisseau* (senior captain) in January 1685, *commissaire d'artillerie* (artillery commissioner) in March 1687. The next year he made a mission to England and in 1689, following the outbreak of the War of the League of Augsburg (King William's War), served as artillery lieutenant general in James II's failed attempt to take Londonderry, Ireland. By July 1690 De Pointis had returned to sea, commanding *Courtisan* (Courtier) at the French victory over Lord Torrington's combined Anglo-Dutch fleet off Beachy Head, or Bévéziers. The following year he took part in the bombardments of Barcelona and Alicante, Spain, and in 1694 helped defend Havre against an English raid.

## CARTAGENA CAMPAIGN
### (APRIL-MAY 1697)

Two years later, De Pointis was given command of the 84-gun man o' war *Sceptre* and nine other ships, four frigates, and several troop transports with 2,800 soldiers on board to attempt a lucrative attack on the great Spanish American port of Cartagena before hostilities ceased. Because of the bankruptcy of the French Exchequer, the Crown provided only the ships, crews, and men, while wealthy patrons raised the financing and supplies through private subscription, expecting a handsome return.

Governor Jean-Baptiste Ducasse of the French colony of Saint Domingue was further instructed to raise as many *flibustiers* as possible to serve as West Indian auxiliaries for this force. Unfortunately, De Pointis's departure then became delayed, his fleet not being able to sortie Brest until 7 January 1697. He did not appear off Cap François until early March and on 16 March dropped anchor before Petit Goâve. When Ducasse came aboard, De Pointis was infuriated to learn only a few hundred buccaneers had awaited his long overdue arrival, the rest having instead dispersed on their own pursuits. Relations worsened a day later when a French naval officer arrested an unruly *boucanier* ashore, touching off a riot in which two or three others were killed. Only the arrival of Ducasse succeeded in calming the mob.

The *flibustiers* in turn were offended by the secondary role they were offered in the enterprise, the question of shares being kept deliberately vague and Ducasse excluded from any command position. Nonetheless, they enlisted in goodly numbers once De Pointis published a proclamation stating that they would participate "man for man" with the crews of the royal warships. Ducasse himself offered to go as a mere ship's captain with his 40-gun *Pontchartrain,* commanding only the island contingent.

A force of 170 soldiers, 110 volunteers, 180 free blacks, and 650 buccaneers was promptly raised, sailing aboard the *Serpente,* 18 guns; *Gracieuse* (Graceful), 20 guns; *Cerf Volant* (Kite), 18 guns; *Saint Louis,* 18 guns; *Dorade* (Golden One), 16 guns; *Marie; Françoise;* and one other vessel. These rendezvoused off Cape Tiburon with the fleet, and by 8 April 1697 were in sight of the Spanish Main. Five days later they dropped anchor before their intended target of Cartagena.

A landing was proposed for the buccaneers at Point Hicacos near the city but canceled once Ducasse and De Pointis reconnoitered the shore in a boat and found it lined with dangerous reefs. (Their own craft overturned, and they barely escaped drowning.) Consequently, it was decided to force the harbor entrance known as Bocachica farther south and on 15 April, Ducasse and De Pointis disembarked with 1,200 men. While preparing the siege operations, the buccaneers captured a coaster arriving from Portobelo and also drove off Spanish reinforcements that were stealing down in boats from Cartagena. During this latter action, the freebooters came under fire from the Bocachica fortress and immediately scattered. Mistaking this for military indiscipline, De Pointis fell upon them with a cudgel and treated them with ever-increasing contempt. Bocachica surrendered after the initial assault on 16 April, with 6 French soldiers and 7 buccaneers killed and 22 wounded, Ducasse among the latter.

The *flibustier* contingent was now under his second-in-command, Joseph d'Honon de Gallifet, a relative newcomer to Saint Domingue who was not well known. When De Pointis ordered them into the boats to seize the Nuestra Señora de la Popa high ground while the main army advanced overland, there was considerable hesitation among the buccaneers. Gallifet seized a buccaneer by the arm but was thrown off. De Pointis had the offender tied to a tree and blindfolded, in anticipation of being executed by regular musketeers. Gallifet publicly interceded, and in a contrived gesture, De Pointis released the man so as to ingratiate Gallifet with his followers. The buccaneers then occupied the heights unopposed and linked up with the army on 20 April.

A formal siege ensued, with approach trenches dug and heavy artillery landed from the fleet. Wounded in the leg by a sharpshooter's round, De Pointis supervised the works from a litter. On 28 April a heavy bombardment began against the Getsemaní suburb. During a lull on 30 April, Ducasse—recuperated from his injury—visited a

Spanish officer at the gate and noticed that a breach had been made. At his urging, De Pointis ordered an immediate assault that same afternoon, and in bloody fighting the French grenadiers and buccaneers battled their way through to the very edge of Cartagena itself. The defenders' morale collapsed, and on the evening of 2 May, white flags were hoisted on the walls. While finalizing terms, De Pointis allegedly received word that a Spanish relief column of 1,000 men was approaching, so he sent Ducasse and his buccaneers, along with several hundred soldiers, to oppose them.

They never appeared, and meanwhile De Pointis's regular troops occupied Cartagena on 4 May. By the time Ducasse and his men returned, they found the gates closed and so were billeted in the impoverished, devastated suburb of Getsemaní. The French commander-in-chief feared that they would violate his carefully arranged capitulation terms with their excesses, so he kept them outside the walls and away from where the booty was being tallied. The few remaining Spanish inhabitants were obligated to surrender a large percentage of their wealth as tribute, and the total plunder eventually came to eight million French crowns. The buccaneers expected a quarter of this but were outraged at the end of the month to discover they were only to receive 40,000 crowns. Unknown to them, the crews aboard De Pointis's warships had been serving for only a small percentage, which is what he had meant when offering them shares "man for man."

By now the plunder was aboard his men o' war, and De Pointis was ready to depart. Furious at being duped, the buccaneers swarmed back into Cartagena on 30 May, despite Ducasse's attempts to dissuade them, and rounded up every Spaniard they could find. The victims were herded into the principal church and sprinkled with gunpowder, the buccaneers threatening that it would be lit unless an additional ransom of five million crowns was raised. This was clearly impossible, but through torture and extortion the *flibustiers* raised a thousand crowns per man before weighing on 3 June.

De Pointis had meanwhile set sail, but four days later encountered a large Anglo-Dutch fleet under Vice Admiral John Neville, hastening to Cartagena's rescue. Outnumbered and with most of his crews dead or diseased, De Pointis reversed course and evaded his pursuers for the next two days, until finally shaking them off by dawn on 10 June. He then resumed his course northward but was forced to touch at Newfoundland for fresh provisions before continuing his voyage across the Atlantic. He had a brief encounter with an English squadron on 24 August 1697, reentering Brest five days afterward.

De Pointis found himself involved in a public controversy because of having cheated the buccaneers, even including lawsuits. This prompted him to publish a *Relation de ce qui s'est fait à la prise du Cartagene* (Relation of what was done at the taking of Cartagena) in Brussels the following year, once the war had concluded. He was eventually obliged to allocate a slightly larger share to the West Indian *flibustiers* from his booty, but this proved to give scant satisfaction.

In October 1699, De Pointis was promoted to rear admiral, and during the War of the Spanish Succession commanded *Magnanime* (Magnanimous) in the hard fought Battle of Vélez-Málaga of 24 August 1704. Seven months later his five ships of the line, separated by a gale while blockading Gibraltar, were chased by the fleet of Vice Admiral Sir John Leake with disastrous results. Three were captured and the other two, including De Pointis's own flagship, were deliberately beached to be burnt. He died at Champigny-sur-Marne two years afterward, on 24 April 1707.

**See also** Ducasse, Jean-Baptiste; Estrées, Jean, comte d'; Spanish Main.

**References:** Crouse; Lugo; *Piracy and Privateering;* Taillemite.

# PONS, JEAN
## (FL. 1683-1686)

*Flibustier* from Martinique, whose arrest by the Royal Navy heightened international tensions.

As early as 28 September 1683, Pons had been issued a commission at Fort Saint Pierre by Claude de Roux, chevalier de Saint Laurent and acting governor-general of the French West Indies, to operate in the Lesser Antilles. On 26 July 1686 this was renewed by his successor comte de Blénac, and Pons sailed from Martinique to Tobago with his brigantine *Françoise* (Francis) to fish and hunt. This island had been captured from the Dutch by the comte d'Estrées almost a decade earlier during the Franco-Dutch War and remained a French possession.

While lying at anchor, the frigate HMS *Mary Rose* of Captain Temple arrived nearby to make a peacetime visit. Some Dutch settlers informed the Royal Navy officer that Pons had boasted he held a commission "to confiscate all English vessels found in the harbors of that island," and moreover extended this authority to the English-claimed Saint Lucia, Dominica, and Saint Vincent as well. They added the French rover seemed to be "on some piratical design, being armed and manned for more than his ostensible business." These unsubstantiated charges were then apparently confirmed when the *Mary Rose's* pinnace

was attacked by two or three large *piraguas* full of Indians with some white men among them, who fired several arrows and killed two men. The pinnace put them to flight, took two of the boats, and some of the Indians. The rest, with the whites, saved themselves by swimming, but in the boat were found French arms and apparel such as Indians do not wear, also some boxes. Hence the white men were suspected to belong to this brigantine.

Consequently, Temple seized Pons's *Françoise* and carried it into Barbados for adjudication at the end of September 1686. Lieutenant Governor Edwyn Stede believed the Royal Navy captain correct in his suspicions, but for lack of evidence the *flibustiers* were released, and their vessel and goods restored. Stede nonetheless dispatched a letter to Blénac, asking him to clarify the clause in Pons's commission prohibiting "foreign ships in French anchorages," and also requesting that all Frenchmen be recalled from Saint Lucia, "for I cannot allow them to continue there." The lieutenant governor then dispatched *Mary Rose* and other English vessels to cut timber on Saint Lucia, with the express aim of maintaining "our claims and our possessions there."

When *Françoise* returned to Martinique one month later, Pons immediately lodged a formal protest. The governor-general in turn availed himself of this complaint to denounce all of Temple's proceedings, replying to Stede on 24 October, "I thought that I had to deal with a pirate, and that his credentials were forged, and but for your last letter I should think so still." He dismissed the lieutenant governor's request for clarification, saying merely, "You wish to know which are the French anchorages; no one has ever asked this before, and they are well enough known." But the real thrust of Blénac's letter was revealed when he wrote:

You say you have orders to retake Saint Lucia and Dominica; I have orders to hold them. The matter is for our masters to decide. You say you wish to keep the peace between the two nations; allow me to inform you that Captain Temple's proceedings are not best calculated to do so.

The following month word of Temple's descent on Saint Lucia reached Paris, and the minister de Seignelay informed his English counterpart Lord Sunderland:

I have laid this extraordinary proceeding before the King [Louis XIV], who is the more surprised at it since the Treaty of Neutrality between the two nations in America is but a year old. The King is convinced that both the [lieutenant governor of Barbados] and the [Royal Navy] captain have acted without orders. As to the property of Saint Lucia, it belongs incontestably to France.

Throughout the subsequent diplomatic exchange, the English side was handicapped by the unjustified seizure of Pons's *Françoise*, as well as by the fact not all the *flibustiers'* goods had been restored as promised, but rather embezzled by *Mary Rose*'s officers and crew. These and many other incidents eventually contributed to the outbreak of the War of the League of Augsburg two years later, known in America as King William's War.

*See also* Blénac, Charles de Courbon, comte de.

*Reference:* C.S.P., Amer. and W.I., Vol. XII.

# POUANÇAY, JACQUES NEPVEU, SIEUR DE

## (?-1683)

Fifth French governor of Tortuga Island and Saint Domingue and a great abettor to its *flibustiers*.

Pouançay was the eldest of two children born to Bertrand d'Ogeron's older sister Jeanne by her husband Thomas Nepveu. He served many years as his uncle's aide at Saint Domingue, on several occasions deputizing for him as governor of the colony, and enduring the 1673 shipwreck on Puerto Rico by his side. Pouançay was evidently also in Paris when d'Ogeron died; he was named as d'Ogeron's successor in a commission dated 16 March 1676 at Saint Germain en Laye. (Pierre-Paul Tarin de Cussy had been serving as interim governor during both men's absence in France.)

Upon assuming office as governor, Pouançay attempted to revive the colonial economy "by giving privateering commissions, on condition these return to the island" with their spoils, as otherwise he felt Saint Domingue had few possibilities of prospering. He felt justified in continuing this aggressive policy even after peace was declared in Europe three years later because of the continual frictions between the French and Spanish colonists.

At the end of July 1680, an envoy from the Spanish governor of Santo Domingo visited Pouançay, bearing a copy of the recently ratified Treaty of Nijmegen and a letter calling for peace, on condition that Pouançay "restrain and contain the subjects of France that inhabit Tortuga," prohibiting them from landing on the coasts of Hispaniola. Pouançay rejected this proposal, pointing out that the treaty contained "no article concerning the affairs of this government," and so like previous agreements, this treaty was deliberately designed by Madrid to avoid touching on the New World. Pouançay said he was willing to live in peace with the local Spaniards but would place no unreasonable restraints upon the movements of French citizens, who had been inhabiting large stretches of Santo Domingo's northern and western coasts for more than 40 years.

Pouançay privately wrote his superior, Colbert, that he believed the Spanish offer had been prompted only by the presence of Vice Admiral comte d'Estrées's squadron in the West Indies, which reached Petit Goâve in late August of that same year. The governor felt a profitable smuggling trade could eventually be developed with the Spaniards of Santo Domingo but doubted whether there was any sincerity in their offer of a truce. As proof of this, he pointed to the recent capture of a merchantman from Nantes off the Cayman Islands, which had been taken by the 40-gun ship of Francisco Galán and sent into Havana for adjudication.

Consequently, Pouançay was to maintain this hard line against the Spaniards, which gave ample employment to the 1,000 to 1,200 *flibustiers* who operated out of Saint Domingue under such captains as the "chevalier" de Grammont, Pierre le Picard, and Jean Rose. The French colony had a total population of 7,800 people, including *engagés* and slaves, so depended upon these raiders for their prosperity, as in the words of Pouançay, "What the *flibustiers* take is employed here, and their silver passes to France." He was equally disturbed to see corsairs retiring into "Jamaica, into some islands dependent on Curaçao, to the Virginias, to New England and the coast of Florida" to dispose of their booty, actively seeking to entice them to his coast.

Under such circumstances, it was hardly surprising that Pouançay issued a letter of reprisal to the Dutch rover Nikolaas van Hoorn in early 1683, after the latter had been cheated out of a consignment of slaves at Santo Domingo. The French governor was convinced the Spaniards intended to attack his colony anyway and believed such punitive raids kept them divided and off balance. Van Hoorn used his commission to mount a massive strike against Veracruz that May with the combined forces of Grammont and Laurens de Graaf; this was doubtless more retaliation than Pouançay had in mind, but he died before any recriminations could reach him from Paris. On 30 September 1683, De Cussy was appointed to succeed him.

**See also** De Graaf, Laurens Cornelis Boudewijn; *engagé;* Estrées, Jean, comte d'; Galán, Francisco; Grammont, "chevalier" de; Hispaniola; letter of reprisal; Ogeron, Bertrand d'; Picard, Pierre le; Rose, Jean; Van Hoorn, Nikolaas.

**References:** Crouse; Lugo.

# POUND, THOMAS
## (FL. 1687-1703)

Massachusetts privateer turned renegade.

In 1687, Pound was a loyal servant of the English Crown, being pilot aboard the Royal Navy sloop HMS *Rose,* which patrolled the New England coastline in search of illicit traders, smugglers, and pirates. The following year he was appointed captain of the new colonial sloop *Mary,* which Governor Sir Edmund Andros had built through public subscriptions. Pound's commission was dated 11 July 1688 (O.S.), but he was to operate this vessel only briefly, because the upheaval caused by the "Glorious Revolution" in England—when James II was deposed in favor of the Protestant rulers William and Mary—evidently led to his dismissal.

On 8 August 1689 (O.S.), amid reports that the former king had landed in Ireland with a French army to attempt to recoup his throne, Pound sailed out of Boston harbor with five men and a boy as passengers aboard a small vessel. When off Lovell's Island, five other armed men joined them and Pound seized command, declaring his intention of going on a self-proclaimed privateering cruise. The first vessel he and his partner Thomas Hawkins met—a fishing boat—was rushed, but at the last moment Pound

changed his mind and merely bought "eight pennies' worth of mackerel" from the surprised fishermen. The renegades then proceeded north to Falmouth, Maine, where the corporal and soldiers of the guard deserted their fort one night to join forces with Pound.

Meanwhile, the colonial sloop *Resolution* had been manned with 30 sailors in Boston and ordered out into Massachusetts Bay under Captain Joseph Thaxter to detain these rovers on a charge of piracy. Pound, however, circled past and around Cape Cod to take up station in Vineyard Sound, where over the next few weeks he attacked the sloop *Good Speed* off Cape Cod and took the brigantine *Merrimack* plus several other prizes.

### BATTLE OFF TARPAULIN COVE
#### (OCTOBER 1689)

On 30 September 1689 (O.S.), Pound's original sloop *Mary* was dispatched from Boston to again search for him, with 20 volunteer crewmembers under Captain Samuel Pease. This vessel reached Wood's Hole four days later, where a boat rowed out from shore and informed Pease the renegades were cruising off nearby Tarpaulin Cove. At this *Mary*'s crew gave "a great shout or hurrah," and shortly thereafter sighted their prey to westward, overhauling it in a stiff south–southeasterly wind. Pease had the king's Union Jack raised and a shot from the great gun fired across the renegades' forefoot, at which a man climbed Pound's mast and affixed "the red flag of piracy at the mainmast top." Pease responded with a single musket shot and then a full volley directly into the renegades' hull and as the distance narrowed, called upon them "to strike to the King of England." Such a sentiment must have inflamed Pound, who could be clearly seen on his quarterdeck, brandishing a sword and shouting back above the wind, "Come aboard, you dogs, and I will strike you presently!"

Pound then picked up his gun and led his men in firing a volley against *Mary,* which in turn touched off a heated exchange. Pease's sloop, being more nimble, ran down to leeward of the renegades, normally a tactical disadvantage but not on such a blustery day. The heeling caused by the strong wind raised *Mary*'s weather side as a bulwark for its marksmen, while further allowing the volunteers to fire down upon the more exposed renegades. Nonetheless, these resisted bravely, even after Pound was wounded in both arm and side and was carried below. Soon two of *Mary*'s men were also injured by an accidental detonation of gunpowder, which created a small fire and much billowing smoke. Seeing this, the renegades cheered and redoubled their efforts, soon shooting Pease in the arm, side and thigh, as well as wounding two other volunteers.

With Captain Pease below being tended, his lieutenant, Benjamin Gallop, assumed command and decided to board the enemy. *Mary* surged alongside the renegade craft, and a fierce hand-to-hand struggle ensued. Muskets were swung about viciously as clubs until four pirates lay dead and twelve wounded, forcing the remaining two to surrender. The weather had become so bad by then that Gallop sailed his two vessels into the Sakonnet River and anchored in the shelter between Pocasset and Rhode Island.

The next morning, 5 October 1689 (O.S.), the casualties were treated by doctors ashore, while six days later Pease resumed command and attempted to sail back to Boston. His wounds proved too severe, however, and he was carried back ashore to die in agony on 12 October (O.S.) and was buried at Newport. A week later, Gallop sailed *Mary* back into Boston with his prize, and the 14 prisoners were cast into jail.

## LATER CAREER
### (1690-1703)

Although Pound was tried on 13 January 1690 (O.S.) and found guilty of piracy along with his confederate Hawkins and several other crewmembers, the peculiar circumstances motivating his cruise meant that none were executed. Instead, he and Hawkins were sent to England for a determination (the latter dying en route in a fight against a French privateer). Pound arrived and was eventually set at liberty, even getting command of a ship afterward, and dying there in 1703.

**References:** Chapin; Gosse, *Who's Who.*

# PRINS, LAURENS
## (FL. 1658-1680)

Dutch corsair who served for many years among the English in the West Indies under the name "Lawrence Prince."

In summer 1658, Commodore Christopher Myngs returned to that island from a raid against the Spanish Main with three prizes, which were all sold to men who would eventually prove formidable corsairs: the largest, of 8 guns and 60 tons, was bought by Robert Searle and renamed *Cagway;* one of 4 guns and 50 tons was purchased by Prins, who changed its name to *Pearl;* while the third later became John Morris's *Dolphin.* Six years later, Prins had become so anglicized he was commissioned to mount an expedition against his former countrymen on the tiny Dutch West Indian outpost of Bonaire.

## BONAIRE RAID
### (FEBRUARY 1665)

By late 1664, trade rivalries between England and the Netherlands had become so intense that Governor Sir Thomas Modyford of Jamaica felt justified in issuing local licenses for attacks against Dutch possessions. One of these was granted to Prins, who sortied from Port Royal in command of Searle's 8-gun frigate *Cagway*, with a crew of 61 "mostly English" freebooters. After a long upwind beat into the Lesser Antilles, he fell upon the unsuspecting settlers of Bonaire four hours before daybreak on 11 February 1665.

Unaware of the danger that had been closing in upon them, the settlers naturally proved easy prey and were particularly outraged to discover the nationality of their captor. Prins openly bragged he had been born in Amsterdam "and acted with great insolence against the defenceless people," ordering them bound and forcing them to reveal the whereabouts of their livestock. The raiders remained on Bonaire for six days, causing considerable damage before withdrawing. It is believed Prins and his men then also plundered the galliot *Hoop* (Hope) of Jan Pietersz Poppen, removing a native pilot "in order to guide them in their villainous deeds." When news of these depredations reached Curaçao, an arrest order was issued by the Dutch West India Company for both Prins and his English frigate.

Little more was heard of his activities during the next few years, although Prins was known to have sold Henry Morgan his first Jamaican plantation toward the end of this same decade.

## SPANISH MAIN AND NICARAGUA RAIDS
### (SUMMER 1670)

In summer 1670, Prins and Captains Harris and Ludbury took it upon themselves to retaliate for the nuisance raids of the Spanish corsair Manoel Rivero Pardal. In a singularly bold stroke, the Dutchman led his small flotilla up Colombia's Magdalena River in an attempt to reach the important town of Mompós 150 miles from the sea. This daring attempt was checked by a fort that had recently been built on an island in that river.

In August, the trio headed westward to the Mosquito Coast, hoping to find better fortune there. Ascending the San Juan River (despite the fort that had been installed after Morgan's raid five years earlier), Prins and his cohorts stole across the Lago de Nicaragua and surprised the city of Granada. According to a Spanish account, Prins "made havoc and a thousand destructions," further driving home his demand for ransom by "sending the head of a priest in a basket and saying that he would deal with the rest of the prisoners in the same way, unless they gave him 70,000 pesos." A few weeks later he was back in Port Royal, William Beeston noting in his journal for 19 October 1670 (O.S.), "Arrived the ships that had taken Grenada [*sic*], who were Captains Prince, Harris and Ludbury." Governor Modyford allegedly reproved the trio for attacking the Spaniards without commissions but thought it prudent not "to press the matter too far in this juncture." Instead, he ordered them to go join Morgan's own retaliatory expedition that was gathering off Ile-à-Vache, "which they were very ready to do."

## PANAMA CAMPAIGN
### (1670-1671)

Prins incorporated his ship *Pearl*, of 10 guns and 50 men, into Morgan's fleet, and because of his fierce reputation and friendship with Admiral Morgan, was considered a senior officer. He served in the subsequent capture of Providencia Island, advancing overland from Chagres into the Isthmian jungles. When the 1,200-man buccaneer host confronted Juan Pérez de Guzmán's army outside the gates of Panama at daybreak on 28 January 1671, Prins commanded Morgan's 300-man vanguard with the rank of "lieutenant colonel," and John Morris served as his "major."

Prins's unit advanced on to a hillock off the right flank of the Spaniards, and when the enemy charged, smashed their will with a murderous fire that killed almost 100 militiamen with its opening volley. The city was captured quickly and looted over the next four weeks, producing a disappointingly small booty because much of its wealth had been evacuated prior to the occupation. Curiously, the Spaniards later reported that the invaders had "brought with them an Englishman, whom they called the Prince, with intent there to crown him King of Tierra Firme [i.e., the Spanish Main]."

Prins's *Pearl* returned to Port Royal in April 1671 along with Morgan aboard Joseph Bradley's *Mayflower;* Morris's *Dolphin* and Thomas Harris's *Mary* were also present. The Dutchman was spared the official opprobrium that subsequently descended on both Modyford and Morgan for these unauthorized hostilities against Spanish America and which resulted in their being sent to England as prisoners a few months later. Instead, Prins was assigned by the new governor, Sir Thomas Lynch, as deputy to the lieutenant governor, being described as "one of the great privateers." Lynch further described him as

a sober man, very brave and an exact pilot. I thought it not amiss for that reason to employ him, and to let the Spaniards see the privateers are subjects to the King's orders, and have not all left the island, but take it as an honor to serve the King in any capacity.

Prins apparently forsook roving, and by 1672 had become a considerable landowner on the Liguanea plain of Jamaica, which was then being opened up for new plantations. Eight years later, in January 1680, a man named Samuel Long brought charges against another Jamaican governor, the earl of Carlisle, asserting among other things that he had violated Crown policy by encouraging pirates. As proof of this, Long declared:

I have seen one Captain Prince, who is said to be a proclaimed pirate, with others said to be privateers, leading each his woman by the said Earl as he sat in his coach viewing affairs; many of the Council and Assembly standing by the said Earl, making some comment on them as they passed. I perceived he both saw and knew who they were.

*See also* Beeston, William; Harris, Thomas; Lynch, Sir Thomas; Modyford, Sir Thomas; Morgan, Sir Henry; Morris, John; Mosquito Coast; Myngs, Sir Christopher; Pérez de Guzmán, Juan; Rivero Pardal, Manoel; Searle, Robert; Spanish Main.

*References:* Exquemelin; Gehring; Gosse, *Who's Who; Interesting Tracts;* Pawson, *Port Royal;* Pope.

# PUNCH HOUSE

English nickname for a brothel, although originally applied to any low drinking establishment where "punch" or some other alcoholic concoction was sold.

A visitor to seventeenth-century Port Royal, Jamaica, described its punch houses as haunts of "such a crew of vile strumpets and common prostitutes that 'tis almost impossible to civilize" the town.

*Reference:* Pawson, *Port Royal.*

# PURCHASE

English euphemism for "booty" or "loot," much used by privateers and pirates.

In particular, the phrase "no purchase, no pay" was employed to advise recruits that if no prize money, or "purchase," resulted from a cruise, there could be no pay for the men, who otherwise received no regular wages (the exception being those sailing under letter of marque). Such an incentive made rovers eager to tackle any rich target they found, leading to acts of both astonishing bravery and low criminality.

Just as a potentially wealthy reward could draw privateers into almost any harebrained venture, the lack of good prospects could also deter them from even the most necessary enterprise. For instance, late in 1684 Acting Governor Hender Molesworth of Jamaica wished to dispatch a small expedition into the south cays of Cuba to protect English turtlers from the Spanish and French corsairs who were waging a bitter struggle in those waters. Despite the fact that Jamaica depended almost entirely upon this source of food, Molesworth found few volunteers forthcoming "on the conditions of no purchase no pay," as privateers thought the enemy *piraguas* elusive and worthless as prizes. The governor therefore entered into an arrangement with several prominent citizens of Port Royal, who agreed to hire sloops in exchange for a two-month monopoly over turtling. Molesworth found this "a cheap and reasonable demand," adding that

they have their choice of men (the lowest of whom gets 40 shillings a month), and so can depend on their crews, whereas if they had gone upon the first design as volunteers I should have been in constant fear of a mutiny, the damned privateering business reigning much in the minds of those people.

*See also* letter of marque.
*Reference:* C.S.P., Amer. and W.I., Vol. XI.

# REIJNIERSEN, CLAES

## (FL. 1673)

Dutch privateer who operated out of Suriname.

On 15 March 1673, Reijniersen was patrolling the eastern reaches of the Wild Coast when late that afternoon he saw the flotilla of Cornelis Evertsen (Kees the Devil) approaching with supplies from Zeeland. Knowing these to be desperately needed, as Suriname had been cut off from the Netherlands ever since the war with France and England had begun the previous year, Reijniersen went aboard Evertsen's flagship *Swaenenburgh* and piloted the formation into its anchorage opposite the principal town of Paramaribo, through a driving tropical downpour.

*See also* Evertsen de Jongste, Cornelis; Wild Coast.

*Reference:* Shomette, *Raid.*

# REINER, GEORGE

## (FL. 1691-1692)

English privateer who with his ship *Loyal Jamaica* captured the vessel of Jonathan Amory and carried it into Jamaica, where it was condemned as a legitimate prize (presumably for illicit trading). When *Loyal Jamaica* later visited Charleston, South Carolina, in April 1692, its crew was seized by the authorities, apparently on account of rumored irregularities but quickly released on bail.

*Reference:* Chapin.

# RETTECHARD, CAPITAINE

## (FL. 1685)

*Flibustier* commander who led the pirate vanguard against Campeche.

Late in June 1685, a pirate fleet of 6 large and 4 small ships, 6 sloops, and 17 *piraguas* rounded the Yucatán peninsula and bore down upon the Mexican port of Campeche. Among its captains were Michiel Andriesoon, Joseph Bannister, Laurens de Graaf, the "chevalier" de Grammont, Rettechard, Jan Willems, and quite probably Bartholomew Sharpe. This host materialized half a dozen miles off Campeche the afternoon of 6 July, and a landing force of 700 buccaneers took to the boats, rowing in toward shore. A company of Spanish troops exited and stationed themselves opposite the intended disembarkation point, forcing the raiders to remain offshore that night.

The next morning, the boats stood out to sea as if withdrawing before suddenly rushing the outskirts of the city. Before the startled Spaniards could react, the buccaneers swarmed ashore, forming four distinct columns. According to Spanish eye witnesses, Capitaine Rettechard commanded the vanguard of 100 men, while Grammont led 200 buccaneers in an encircling maneuver around the city. De Graaf marched at the head of another 200 up Campeche's principal avenue toward the central plaza, while Jean Foccard brought a like number along a parallel street. The pirates swiftly overran Campeche, although its citadel held out for another week. The invaders then remained in undisputed possession of the port for the next two months, but as most of the Spaniards' wealth had been withdrawn prior to the assault, relatively little plunder was found. Captives were threatened with death if ransoms were not forthcoming, but Yucatán's governor, Juan Bruno Téllez de Guzmân, prohibited any such payments. Finally, late in August 1685, Rettechard and the rest of the pirates abandoned the city after putting it to the torch.

*See also* Andrieszoon, Michiel; Bannister, Joseph; De Graaf, Laurens Cornelis Boudewijn; Foccard, Jean; Grammont, "chevalier" de; Willems, Jan.

*Reference:* Juárez.

# REYES, ANDRÉS DE LOS

## (FL. 1659)

Apparently a Cuban corsair.

In the first days of 1659, while operating out of the port of "Santa María" on Cuba's southern coast, De los Reyes seized the Dutch merchantman *Hoop* (Hope) of Nikolaas Direcksen, setting both master and crew ashore. They promptly lodged a complaint with the governor of Havana, Juan de Salamanca, who sent a frigate to pursue De los Reyes, eventually overtaking him near Campeche and bringing him back to Cuba.

In the meantime, Direcksen and his men had been issued special passes by the governor that February, permitting them to sail to Seville aboard the annual plate fleet. On the last day of that year, Governor Matthias Beck of Curaçao wrote his Spanish counterpart at Havana, thanking him for his intervention in this affair, adding that the *Hoop* and its cargo would be retrieved from the Cuban capital.

*Reference:* Gehring.

# REYNING, JAN ERASMUS

## (1640-1697)

Dutch adventurer who spent more than a decade roving the West Indies under four different flags.

He was born in Vlissingen (Flushing) in 1640, the son of a sailor from Copenhagen. Reyning first went to sea with his father at the age of ten and saw action against both the English and French in the North Sea. His father was killed in a naval engagement during the First Anglo-Dutch War

(1652–1654), and Reyning himself was captured and imprisoned in Ireland for 18 months during the Second Anglo-Dutch War (1665–1667). After a brief reunion with his wife and child, he signed on with a Middelburg ship bound for Suriname.

## ARRIVAL IN THE NEW WORLD (1667)

Once in the Antilles, Reyning was put ashore with six other men to attempt to reestablish the Dutch colony at Cayenne seized by the French three years previously. The French in turn had been dispossessed by the English but soon returned, carrying Reyning off to Martinique as a prisoner. He served briefly as boatman to the retiring governor, Robert Le Frichot des Friches, seigneur de Clodoré, accompanying him as far as Tortuga Island on his return passage toward France. Reyning deserted and became a plantation hand on Saint Domingue, then an indentured servant to a *boucanier,* quickly regaining his freedom.

Resuming his sea career, Reyning reached the Cayman Islands some time in 1668, where he found the Dutch privateer "Captain Casten of Amsterdam," holder of a Jamaican commission, careening his ship. Reyning joined his company and sailed on a cruise as far as Aruba. Taking a Spanish prize, they put into Port Royal to dispose of it, paying the requisite one-tenth of its value to the king of England and one-fifteenth to the duke of York. Shortly thereafter, Jean-David Nau l'Olonnais reached Jamaica with an 80-ton, 12-gun Spanish brigantine he had captured, in which Reyning allegedly bought a share. Rok Brasiliano was installed as captain, Jelles de Lecat as first mate. They prowled the Spanish Main between Cartagena and Portobelo, seizing another brigantine before returning to Port Royal, where Brasiliano took command of the new vessel while De Lecat and Reyning remained aboard the old one.

## LAGUNA DE TÉRMINOS
## CAMPAIGN
### (1669)

The two brigantines stole into the Gulf of Mexico in the spring of 1669, accompanied by the frigate [*Mayflower?*] of Joseph Bradley, to begin operations in and around the Laguna de Términos. Plunder proving scarce, Brasiliano and Reyning supposedly quarreled and separated. De Lecat's vessel began loading logwood, while Bradley and Brasiliano blockaded Campeche. The Spaniards finally sortied with three armed ships on 18 December 1669, chasing them away. A norther wrecked Brasiliano and his crew on the Yucatán peninsula, and they were rescued by De Lecat and Reyning, who transferred them to Bradley's frigate for return to Jamaica. Shortly thereafter, De Lecat and Reyning seized a Spanish merchantman, which they renamed *Seviliaen,* scuttling their brigantine and sailing this prize back to Port Royal.

Upon their arrival they found the colony in an uproar because of the nuisance raids of the Spanish privateer Manoel Rivero Pardal. In August 1670, Reyning sailed as part of Henry Morgan's retaliatory strike against Panama, pausing first at Ile-à-Vache for supplies and reinforcements. The corsair fleet then descended on Providencia Island, overwhelming the tiny Spanish garrison, before Morgan sent Bradley ahead to seize San Lorenzo castle at the mouth of the Chagres River as a foothold for their approach to Panama. Reyning, De Lecat, and Brasiliano all served in this advance force, which disembarked against heavy opposition. Reyning's company was so badly decimated that the wounded Brasiliano reported to Bradley that they had all been killed. This was disproved the following dawn when Reyning's survivors took part in the final assault, in which the Spanish defenders were massacred and Bradley was fatally wounded.

## SACK OF PANAMA
### (1670-1671)

Reyning then led his company on Morgan's epic march across the isthmus where, despite hunger, disease, and repeated jungle ambushes, the freebooters fought their way into Panama and looted the city for a month. Retiring to the Atlantic coast, they were disappointed at the division of spoils, and felt that Morgan had cheated them by making off with the lion's share. Sailing in his wake toward Jamaica, Reyning had a brush with the Cartagena coast guard vessel *Santa Cruz* (Holy Cross) and another Spanish vessel before gaining Montego Bay.

There at anchor, he found the Dutch merchantman *Witte Lam* (White Lamb) of Zeeland, which chanced to have his brother-in-law aboard with a letter for him. Nostalgic for his family, Reyning arranged passage home aboard this vessel, but his piratical minions held such riotous, drunken celebrations that the *Witte Lam*'s master grew frightened, and discreetly slipped away without him. Reyning thus had no choice but to proceed to Port Royal.

He found the political climate greatly altered, with the new governor, Sir Thomas Lynch, having arrived on 1 July 1671 (O.S.) with the warships *Assistance* and *Welcome* to arrest his predecessor and revoke all anti-Spanish privateering commissions. Reyning was asked to bring in the *Seviliaen,* but when he met up with De Lecat at their prearranged rendezvous off the Caymans, they simply joined forces and sailed away toward Cuba. There they rustled some cattle, but when a trio of Spanish warships sortied from Havana, the corsairs decided to cross the Gulf of Mexico to their old hunting grounds off Laguna de Términos. Immediately upon reaching the Mexican coast, they seized a small Spanish coast guard vessel, De Lecat assuming command of this prize, while Reyning captained the *Seviliaen.*

Shortly thereafter, HMS *Assistance* hove into view, having been detached under William Beeston to bring in rogue privateers. Reyning and De Lecat withdrew close inshore, beyond the reach of such a powerful antagonist, so the English commander sailed to nearby Campeche to hire shallow-draft vessels to cut them out of their anchorage. The wily Dutchmen frustrated this scheme by following the frigate into port, where the neutrality of the Spanish harbor offered protection against capture, until the Royal Navy grew tired of the game and left.

## SPANISH SERVICE
### (1671-1672)

Realizing how risky it was to continue prowling the Caribbean, Reyning and De Lecat purged their crews of English seamen, marooning them on the island of Tris, where they were eventually rescued by the former privateer *Lilly* in January 1672. Meanwhile, the two Dutchmen struck a deal with the Campeche authorities and were issued Spanish letters of marque. Desperate to stem foreign incursions throughout the region, but without funds for an adequate defense, the Spaniards overlooked the Flushingers' checkered past because they were willing to serve for prize money alone. Reyning and De Lecat, hunted by the English, agreed and further cemented the deal by taking indoctrination into the Catholic faith.

On their first patrol into the Laguna de Términos they captured four English vessels, which they auctioned off at Campeche. Soon a routine developed whereby Reyning remained in port attending to business, while De Lecat took care of the rough-and-tumble aspects of coast guard duty. Within a few months they had seized 32 prizes, and at Jamaica the logwood trade declined because of fears of "Captain Yellowes." On 28 April 1672, while De Lecat was patrolling in a captured sloop, Reyning exited Campeche with the *Seviliaen* to transport retiring

governor Don Fernando Francisco de Escobedo to Tabasco. Reyning then hired out the *Seviliaen* to convey a rich cargo of cacao and logwood toward Veracruz, departing Tabasco on 18 July. Five days later, he reached Veracruz, where his ship was briefly impounded because of irregularities regarding its ownership.

## HOSTILITIES WITH FRANCE
### (1672)

While awaiting adjudication, Reyning learned from the Spanish slaver and privateer Francisco Galesio that war had broken out among England, France, and Holland back in Europe. Thus, once the *Seviliaen* was released in late August 1672, Reyning hurried back to Campeche in ballast to pay off his Spanish hands and reassemble his Dutch crew. The *Seviliaen* was careened while hoping for De Lecat to rejoin, but Reyning eventually left Mexico without him. Proceeding past Yucatán toward Cape Tiburon, the *Seviliaen* made a few captures before going in pursuit of a lone French sail. This led them around a headland into the large formation that Governor Jean-Charles de Baas-Castelmore had sent from the Windward Islands to raise *flibustiers* on Saint Domingue for an assault against Curaçao. The wind died away, and Reyning was forced to abandon his prizes and break out the oars to escape from this superior force. He allegedly beat off several French boarding parties before returning to seize two of their vessels.

Upon reaching Caracas, Reyning again met up with Francisco Galesio and escorted his vessel across to Curaçao in early 1673. There Reyning secured a Dutch privateering commission and for the next two years helped maintain the island by bringing in numerous French and English prizes. During one of his cruises, the *Seviliaen* was wrecked in a storm off Hispaniola, but Reyning managed to get his crew safely ashore and to the Spanish capital of Santo Domingo. While awaiting passage from there, he and his men were supposedly used to man a ship and chase away a French privateer, for which the Spanish governor showed himself exceedingly grateful. Put aboard a ship bound for Puerto Rico and Caracas, the passengers instead ordered it directly to Curaçao.

Having lost his half ownership in *Seviliaen,* Reyning was given a quarter share in another Dutch privateer and returned to Puerto Rico for food and water before going on a cruise. The English ship *Laurel* of Portsmouth was captured, its captain furious at discovering how few Dutchmen had defeated him. Reyning then snuck ashore at English-occupied Sint Eustatius and seized its commander, only to learn that peace had been declared between Holland and England as of February 1674. Frustrated in this design, Reyning left for Curaçao, hijacking 60 slaves on Grenada and trading these for indigo at Montserrat while en route.

## SURRENDER AT GRENADA
### (1675)

He now concentrated his efforts in the Lesser Antilles. After numerous smaller raids and seizures, Reyning joined forces with Jurriaen Aernouts to attack Grenada in 1675. The Dutch raiders succeeded in occupying the fort, but were in turn besieged inside by the French and starved into submission. Upon surrendering, Reyning and Aernouts were carried to Martinique by the warship *Émerillon* of Captain Chadeau de la Clicheterre. Eventually, they succeeded in escaping from the plantation where they were being held by drugging the guards' wine and, along with five other men, stealing a *piragua.* They laid in a course for Curaçao but nearly died when their boat was carried westward by the winds and currents, landing them on Cora Island in present-day Venezuela. Eventually they reached Maracaibo, where they were briefly incarcerated by the

Spaniards (although common foes of the French, the Spaniards were suspicious of any foreign trespassers on their territory) before being restored to Curaçao.

## BINCKES'S CAMPAIGN
### (1676)

Early the next year, Reyning returned to Amsterdam and saw his family again after a nine-year absence. Shortly thereafter, he was given command of the tiny 8-gun frigate *Fortuyn* in Admiral Jacob Binckes's expedition, which sailed for the West Indies that March. On 4 May 1676, they dropped anchor off Cayenne, landing 900 men and taking Fort Saint Louis with almost no resistance. Garrisoning the island, the Dutch then sailed northward and did the same to Marie Galante, throwing down the fortifications and carrying off the French colonists. When Binckes sighted Guadeloupe on 16 June, he considered its defenses too strong and passed it by, instead pursuing (unsuccessfully) a trio of French vessels. A few days later, he landed 500 men and overran Saint Martin, killing the French governor and seizing 100 slaves.

From there, part of the expedition proceeded to Santo Domingo under its second-in-command, Pieter Constant, pausing at the Spanish half of that island for water and seizing a French vessel off the coast. Reyning was with this contingent, which then rounded to Petit Goâve on the French half of the island, where Constant attempted to persuade the *boucaniers* to "throw off the unbearable yoke" of the French West Indies Company in favor of the more reliable, competitive Dutch. Although disgruntled with their own traders, the French settlers nonetheless rejected this offer with musket fire, and the Dutch sailed away after seizing the merchantmen anchored offshore. Reyning got one of these prizes, and even fought a "duel" with another captain over possession of a drum.

## FIRST BATTLE OF TOBAGO
### (MARCH 1677)

As a counter to Binckes's efforts, the French government dispatched a large fleet of its own into the New World, under Vice Admiral Jean, comte d'Estrées. Reyning claimed to have captured a French vessel off Nevis with letters revealing that this force was on its way. In December 1676, d'Estrées appeared and recaptured Cayenne, then pressed on toward Tobago, which Binckes had transformed into a heavily fortified base. On the evening of 21 February 1677, the French landed 1,000 soldiers near Rockly Bay and sent 14 light vessels on ahead to make a feint against its harbor mouth. Reyning's *Fortuyn* was one of the Dutch auxiliaries attacked there and was forced to retreat into the inner roads when the outnumbered Binckes wisely refused to strip his land defenses to reinforce these ships.

Reyning transferred onto land, serving in the trenches when d'Estrées launched his major assault the morning of 3 March 1677. The fighting was fierce both on land and in the harbor, with the Dutch emerging victorious. However, they lost 10 of their 13 anchored vessels to spreading conflagrations (which also consumed four of the heaviest French men o' war). Two French vessels were also captured, Reyning claiming that some of his crew members were found aboard the dismasted *Précieux* and that the French commander-in-chief had narrowly eluded him in a rowboat. D'Estrées meanwhile retired to Grenada and Martinique with 1,000 losses, and by early July was back in Versailles reporting on his failure to King Louis XIV.

## SECOND BATTLE OF TOBAGO
### (DECEMBER 1677)

The Sun King immediately ordered his admiral to return to the West Indies and complete his mission. D'Estrées departed Brest again on 27 September 1677 with 17 more ships. He arrived off Tobago on 6 December, having paused en route to destroy the Dutch slaving station of Gorée, West Africa. The tropical weather was rainy, but despite this the French quickly threw a large contingent ashore and installed siege artillery, refusing to be drawn into a suicidal charge against the Dutch entrenchments like the last time. The defenders were much reduced by hunger and disease, with Reyning serving on board the *Précieux,* one of only two ships remaining in the harbor.

On 12 December 1677, the French chief gunner began firing ranging shots against the Dutch fortification, laying odds that he would blow it up at the third attempt. Incredibly, the third round landed squarely in the magazine, killing Binckes and 250 defenders with a mighty blast. The French swarmed exultantly over the ruins, while Dutch resolve collapsed. Reyning abandoned the *Précieux* to flee inland on foot, eventually escaping the island in a tiny craft with a sail made of two oars and a pair of shirts. It took him ten days to reach Curaçao, but he was so weakened by lack of food and water that he could not work into port, sailing past to Aruba.

Rescued and returned to Curaçao, Reyning helped brace for d'Estrées's inevitable appearance. On this occasion, though, fortune smiled on the Dutch, for when the French expedition confidently headed toward Curaçao five months later, it was shipwrecked on the Aves Islands. Hostilities with France ended shortly thereafter (10 August 1678), and Reyning sailed for Zeeland. He made a return trade voyage into the West Indies and was allegedly even offered a position on devastated Tobago, as well as in the Royal Spanish Navy, neither of which he accepted. Instead he served on commercial cruises between Holland and Spain, on one occasion delivering a man o' war built in a Dutch yard to the Spaniards.

## SLAVING VOYAGE
### (1687-1688)

After a number of years, Reyning obtained command of the Coymans Company's *Koning Balthasar* (King Balthasar), a large new ship that was to convey a cargo of slaves from Curaçao to the Spanish Main under terms of the *asiento,* or Crown monopoly, granted in Madrid to that Dutch firm. Reyning sailed with his son, picking up a Spanish priest named Francisco de Rivas, of whom he remained darkly suspicious, as supercargo at Cadiz. The *Koning Balthasar* seized a Portuguese slaver off Cumaná for violating the trade monopoly, but it was released by the corrupt local authorities, thus depriving Reyning and the Coymans Company of one-third its value in prize money.

At Curaçao the *Koning Balthasar* took on its consignment of slaves, depositing a portion of them at Cartagena, the rest at Portobelo. By now convinced that Rivas and the Spaniards were plotting to seize his vessel, Reyning slipped out of the roads one dark night without permission and was fired upon by the harbor defenses. (A few months later the *Koning Balthasar*'s sister ship, *Santiago de la Victoria,* was impounded and sold by the Spanish for smuggling, which persuaded Reyning that he had narrowly escaped the same fate.) On his return passage to Holland with 180,000 pesos in profits on board, he learned that war had again broken out with France, so he brought in three French prizes.

Presumably while lying at Curaçao he had also come in contact with David van der Sterre, the doctor for the slave depot on that island. The latter recorded Reyning's reminiscences in a rambling, heroic vein, producing an almost unreadable book that was published in Amsterdam in 1691. Meanwhile, Reyning had been appointed commander by the Dutch admiralty two years earlier and fought against the French in the War of the League of Augsburg

(King William's War). In 1694 he captained the *Drakesteyn,* of 44 guns and 170 men, in a fruitless Anglo-Dutch bombardment of Brest, losing 49 of his crew but being promoted to "extraordinaris-kapitein" for his bravery. More small actions ensued, but his name crops up again only in 1697, when he was wintering at Portsmouth with his ship *Nijmegen,* of 50 guns and 210 men.

## DEATH
### (4 FEBRUARY 1697)

From this English port, Reyning departed on his last voyage, joining Admiral Swaan of the *Vrede* to escort a convoy of Dutch merchantmen to Bilbao, Spain. Upon their arrival on 2 February 1697, the harbor pilot informed them that the two warships drew too much water to pass over the bar and would have to await high tide. Two days later, a sudden storm blew up out of the Bay of Biscay, parting the cables of the *Vrede* and *Nijmegen,* driving them onto the rocks. More than 400 seamen perished in this maelstrom, among them Reyning. His name was soon forgotten in Holland, but not on Curaçao, where local legend maintains that he left buried treasure in caves along that coast.

**See also** Aernouts, Jurriaen; Beeston, William; Binckes, Jacob; Bradley, Joseph; Estrées, Jean, comte d'; Hispaniola; Lecat, Jelles de; Laguna de Términos; letter of marque; logwood; Ogeron, Bertrand d'; Rivero Pardal, Manoel; Spanish Main.

**Reference:** Marley, *Pirates;* Vrijman.

# RHOADES, JOHN
## (FL. 1674-1678)

Boston pilot who assisted in the Dutch capture of French Acadia and was later tried for piracy.

In the summer of 1674, the privateer Jurriaen Aernouts arrived at New York from

Curaçao to conduct offensive operations. Learning that peace had been reestablished some months before between England and the Netherlands, he decided to attack the French settlements farther north in Acadia (present-day Maine and New Brunswick). While preparing for this expedition, Aernouts met Rhoades, an experienced pilot well versed with the waterways around the French outposts, who encouraged his plans. The Dutchman therefore enlisted Rhoades and several other Americans into his force, sailing into the Bay of Fundy at the beginning of August to land 110 men. They easily overran the stronghold at Penobscot (Pentagoët) on 11 August, after which Rhoades piloted the Dutch flagship *Vliegende Postpaard* (Flying Post Horse) up the Saint Jean River to seize the secondary French fort at Jemsec. Aernouts then renamed the province New Holland and retired into Boston.

Before returning to the Antilles, on 11 September, Aernouts appointed Rhoades acting governor of the newly conquered territory, furnishing him with two small armed vessels for this purpose. Left in charge after Aernouts sailed, Rhoades and his subordinates, Cornelis Andreson, Pieter Roderigo, and the Cornishman John Williams created friction with their New England neighbors by attempting to enforce a new "Dutch" authority. When vessels from Boston continued to ignore his jurisdiction, Rhoades ordered the patrols to begin impounding trading vessels and fishing boats. This provoked an angry reaction, and a retaliatory force emerged from Boston in early 1675 under Captain Samuel Moseley to capture the two coast guard vessels in the Bay of Fundy and carry their commanders to Cambridge, Massachusetts, to be tried for piracy. Although initially condemned to death, both Andrieszoon and Roderigo were eventually reprieved.

Rhoades, too, had been condemned to hang in June 1675, but his sentence was commuted on the condition that he leave Massachusetts. The Dutch authorities recognized his title to New Holland, although they appointed Cornelis Steenwyck of New York to be the actual governor. In fact, no effort was ever made by the Dutch to assert their hold, so the territory soon reverted to the French. In 1678 Rhoades was again arrested by the New Englanders for violating trade laws and sent as a prisoner to New York. The Dutch ambassador petitioned London on his behalf, and that October he was released. Rhoades then moved to Delaware, where he eventually became a justice of the peace.

**See also** Aernouts, Jurriaen; Andreson, Cornelis; Moseley, Samuel; Roderigo, Pieter.
**References:** Gosse, *Who's Who;* Webster.

# RIBAUT, ANDRÉ

## (FL. 1677)

French privateer who ravaged the Mexican province of Tabasco.

Ribaut apparently arrived in the Gulf of Mexico early in 1677 bearing a commission for hostilities against the Spaniards (France was then at war against Spain and Holland, while England remained neutral in this conflict). Although his frigate only bore 3 guns and 35 men, Ribaut had the good fortune to capture a fisherman who informed him that Campeche's coast guard frigate *Pescadora* (Fisher) had recently sunk near the entrance of the Grijalva River while returning from Veracruz with a rich cargo of silver and arms. Ribaut immediately visited the English logwood-cutters at the Laguna de Términos, obtaining a *piragua* and experienced pilots to go in search of the wreck; but when these reached the site they found the remains picked clean, and probing further upriver, they received reports that the goods had been carried into the inland town of Jalpa.

Convinced that this meant the Spaniards had already recovered all the treasure and were off guard, Ribaut returned to the laguna and recruited more men for a major descent. Baymen flocked to his side, especially an English captain called George Rivers (Jorge Riveros or Rivas as he is named in Spanish records). Together they set sail from the laguna on 1 March 1677 with more than 100 buccaneers on a frigate and 17 on a brigantine, both owned and commanded by Rivers, plus 70 crammed into Ribaut's frigate. The raiders anchored their three vessels near Barra de Dos Bocas (literally "two-mouth bar") and advanced stealthily up Río Seco (Dry River), guided by a mulatto prisoner called Bartolomé Saraos. Fording streams more than twenty times during this trek, they appeared outside Jalpa before sunrise on Sunday, 7 March 1677. Attacking at dawn, the Spanish citizenry were overwhelmed in their beds by the 150 heavily armed freebooters, who quickly secured the town.

It was then the raiders' turn to be surprised, for the treasure and arms had already been shipped back to the coast with the mule train of José Tenorio. A detachment of 40 buccaneers was sent in hot pursuit to the coastal town of Amatitlán but arrived too late. Despite killing three teamsters and capturing the rest of Tenorio's men, only the slow matches and powder flasks had not yet been sent aboard ship for transportation to Campeche. The treasure beyond their reach, the frustrated buccaneers evacuated Jalpa at ten o'clock on the morning of 8 March, taking with them whatever booty and prisoners they had been able to seize. Before Spanish militia units from outlying areas could react, Ribaut and Rivers's men were back aboard their ships, not having suffered a single loss during this incursion.

*References:* Eugenio; Sáiz; Robles.

# RINGROSE, BASIL

## (c. 1653-1686)

English buccaneer famous for his recorded observations of the South Seas.

Ringrose was apparently born in the parish of St. Martin-in-the-Fields, Westminster, London, England, in January 1653. He was the first of at least four boys born to Richard and Mary Ringrose. Their household was poor, located on the south side of High Street (close to present-day Charing Cross station), in a district where the Great Plague of London was to break out 12 years later. Ringrose traveled to the New World and early in 1680 took part in John Coxon's invasion of the South Seas, which later devolved into a two-year piratical cruise under Bartholomew Sharpe. Despite his lack of formal education (or perhaps because of it) Ringrose was a quick-witted, inquisitive man who recorded much of what he saw. He was a skillful navigator who could speak French, Latin, and Spanish, serving as the buccaneers' interpreter. William Dick, who was on the voyage, described him as "a good scholar and full of ingeniosity," adding that

> this gentleman kept an exact and very curious journal of all our voyage, from our first setting out to the very last day, took also all the observations we made, and likewise an accurate description of all the ports, towns and lands we came to.

When the buccaneers captured the *Santo Rosario* (Holy Rosary) on 29 July 1681, they also secured the dead captain's waggoner, or pilot book, a valuable source of navigational information on the Pacific coast.

Ringrose carried this book back to England after Sharpe's voyage concluded at Saint Thomas in the Danish Virgin Islands. Ringrose and 13 others departed Antigua in the *Lisbon Merchant* of Captain Robert Porteen, arriving at Dartmouth, England, on 26 March 1682. The waggoner proved so valuable that even Charles II and the Spanish ambassador, Pedro Ronquillo, became involved in its fate, which allegedly spared Sharpe from the noose. Ringrose spent his time preparing it for publication by cartographer William Hack, as well as persuading Captain Charles Swan and a group of London merchants to send a trade mission to the Pacific coast of South America. They outfitted the 180-ton *Cygnet*, 16 guns, with £5,000 worth of goods, and Ringrose agreed to join the 36-man crew as one of three supercargos. He later told his friend William Dampier, "He had no mind to this voyage, but was necessitated to engage in it or starve."

On 1 October 1683, *Cygnet* sailed from the Downs, but once in the South Pacific, they found the Spaniards hostile to their overtures. At Valdivia, Chile, the English were fired upon in their boat under flag of truce. Two were killed and several more were wounded, Ringrose and one other being the only ones to emerge unscathed. Swan became disillusioned with his supercargo, "for Mr. Ringrose being the proposer of the voyage, did demonstrate the thing being very feasible in England, which now Captain Swan found to be difficult." After wandering northward to New Spain, the interlopers landed at the Río Grande de Santiago, opposite the Tres Marías Islands (Mexico), advancing 15 miles upriver to capture the town of Senticpac. But while transferring loads of maize from horseback to their canoes, the buccaneers were ambushed by a large body of Spaniards. About 50 out of 200 were killed, among them, wrote Dampier, "my ingenious friend Mr. Ringrose."

*See also* Coxon, John; Dampier, William; Sharpe, Bartholomew; South Seas; Swan, Charles; waggoner.

*References:* Dampier; Howse.

# Rivero Pardal, Manoel

## (FL. 1670)

Portuguese corsair with a Spanish commission who provoked Henry Morgan's sack of Panama.

Little is known about Rivero's career prior to the last few months of his life. On 3 January 1670, he received a privateering commission from Pedro de Ulloa, governor of Cartagena. The queen regent Mariana of Spain had authorized such licenses on 20 April of the previous year, immediately following news of Morgan's assault against Portobelo. But the intervening months had seen a steady decline in such hostilities, including a public proclamation of peace at Port Royal on 24 June 1669, so Rivero's onslaught would become misconstrued as a Spanish breach of faith.

Rivero set sail from Cartagena on 6 January 1670 with 70 men in his ship *San Pedro*, more commonly known as the *Fama*. He hoped to raid Point Morant, Jamaica, for slaves, but unfavorable winds carried him past to the Cayman Islands. On Grand Cayman he burned down half the fishermen's shacks, taking a ketch, canoe, and four children captives to Cuba. There he learned of an English privateer lying at Manzanillo, the port of Bayamo.

This proved to be the *Mary and Jane*, commanded by an old Dutch rover named Bernard Claesen Speirdyke, known affectionately as "Captain Bart" to his English friends. He had been dispatched with a flag of truce to convey letters from Sir Thomas Modyford to the Cuban authorities "signifying peace between the two nations" and to restore some Spanish prisoners. This done, Speirdyke clandestinely sold his cargo to the locals, then stood out to sea. Just as he was quitting the bay, a ship flying English colors hailed and asked whence he came. "From Jamaica," Speirdyke replied.

"Defend yourself, dog!" Captain Rivero roared back. "I come as a punishment for heretics!" The *Fama* opened fire, and a brisk cannonade ensued until dark. The following day, the Spaniards closed to board, as the *Mary and Jane* held only 18 men. Despite such heavy odds, a staunch resistance was made, in which a third of Rivero's men were killed or wounded before the ship was carried. Five of the *Mary and Jane*'s crew lay dead, including Captain Speirdyke—that "obstinate, mad heretic," as Rivero labeled him. The victorious corsair sent nine prisoners back to Port Royal in their boat with a declaration that "he had letters of reprisal from the king of Spain for five years through the whole West Indies, for satisfaction of the Jamaicans taking Portobelo."

Rivero sailed his prize back to Cartagena, arriving on 23 March 1670. A grand fiesta was held to celebrate his triumph, and others adopted his example. Scarcely a month later, two more corsairs lay fitting out in the roads, with Rivero flying a royal standard as admiral to this motley force. Meanwhile, an ugly mood was brewing on Jamaica, where news of Speirdyke's death had been followed by reports of other Spanish aggressions. These were confirmed when a copy of Francisco Galesio's commission was forwarded to Modyford by Governor Willem Beck of Dutch Curaçao. Issued at Santiago de Cuba on 5 February 1670, it authorized Spanish privateers to "proceed against the English in the Indies with every sort of hostility." The Jamaican governor was hard-pressed to prevent retaliatory strikes by his own surly buccaneers.

At the end of May 1670, Rivero sortied again from Cartagena, accompanied by the *Gallardina,* a former French privateer seized by the Spaniards two years earlier. The two vessels appeared off Jamaica on 11 June, flying English colors. They pursued the

sloop of William Harris for an hour-and-a-half as he was arriving to trade on the north side of the island, getting close enough to shout that the English were "dogs and rogues." Harris eventually beached his sloop and escaped inland, firing at Rivero's men as they came ashore. The sloop was refloated and, along with a canoe found on the beach, sailed to Cuba.

A week later the *Fama* and *Gallardina* returned, landing 30 men at Montego Bay to burn the settlements before retiring to Cuba once more. On 3 July Rivero was back a third time, having manned his captured sloop with reinforcements from Santiago de Cuba. A company of 40 mounted militia watched the trio of Spanish corsairs for an hour before they stood off to leeward. The next day, the raiders landed 50 miles away and burned a couple more houses, then the following night posted a written challenge on shore. In it, Rivero bragged, "I come to seek General Morgan with two ships of 20 guns and, having seen this, I crave he will come out upon ye coast to seek me, that he might see ye valor of ye Spaniards."

Rather than oblige directly, Morgan and an outraged Jamaican council opted for a full-blown operation against Spanish America. Modyford felt constrained to agree, although his latest instructions still called for peace with the Spaniards. (Lord Arlington, secretary of state, had dismissed the governor's complaint about Speirdyke's death as "not at all to be wondered at, after such hostilities as your men have acted upon their territories.") Nevertheless, in late August 1670, Morgan sailed with 11 ships and 600 men for a rendezvous off Ile-à-Vache, where he expected to be joined by hundreds more freebooters, all eager to serve against the Spanish. Thus, Rivero's nuisance raids would be repaid a hundredfold.

While buccaneers were assembling off Hispaniola, foraging parties were sent out to gather supplies and intelligence for the expedition. One of these was the ship *Dolphin,* commanded by Captain John Morris, who was forced to put into a small bay at the east end of Cuba by a threatening storm in mid-October. Two hours later, just before dark, Rivero sailed in for the same purpose and was delighted to see that he had the smaller Jamaican ship embayed. Setting men ashore to cut off any escape, he prepared to attack at dawn. But it was Morris who moved first the next morning, bearing down upon the *Fama* with the land breeze and boarding at the first attempt. Rivero was shot through the neck and killed. His crew panicked and jumped into the sea, where some drowned and many others were finished off by the privateers.

Thus it was late October 1670 that a jubilant Ile-à-Vache assembly beheld the *Fama* being led in and learned that its despised commander was dead and his ship was renamed the *Lamb.* "This is that same vapouring captain that so much amazed Jamaica," an English observer crowed, "in burning the houses, robbing some people upon the shore, and sent that insolent challenge to Admiral Morgan." But despite his removal from the scene, Rivero's actions continued to redound: For four months after his death, 2,000 freebooters swarmed into Panama to exact further revenge.

*See also* Speirdyke, Bernard Claesen.
*Reference:* Earle, *Panamá.*

# ROCHE, GEORGE

## (FL. 1691-1697)

English rover based at Antigua.

According to the French chronicler Jean-Baptiste Labat, Roche took part in the English invasion of Guadeloupe in 1691, in which the governor's *aide mayor,* sieur Bordenave, was killed. Years later, after peace

was reestablished and Roche had resumed his practice of smuggling contraband across to the French colonies at night, he boasted to Labat of having slain Bordenave personally

> in proof of which he showed some buckles and a silver badge he had removed from his body. He gave me the badge, which I gave to Mademoiselle Radelin, daughter of the sieur Bordenave, who immediately recognized it as her father's.

Just prior to the official proclamation of the treaty of Ryswyck in 1697, both English and French corsairs redoubled their efforts in hopes of winning final booty.

Roche was one of these, and on the night of 14 October 1697, he appeared off Marigot, Martinique, with a vessel of eight guns and almost 80 men. He took more than 60 ashore in two boats, his approach undetected because the French had neglected their lookouts "on seeing the night so dark and the seas so agitated." Leaving two men to guard each boat on the beach, Roche infiltrated the town. He was discovered and driven off, with seven dead and one captured. Two-and-a-half weeks later, he reappeared off Fonds Saint Jacques, three miles up the Martinique coast and again attempted to land. The night being clear and moonlit, his boats were spotted and challenged by Labat himself and a party of armed black slaves while still offshore. Surprised to hear themselves hailed, the English "replied in good French that they were from Basse-Terre [Guadeloupe]" and seeking the Sainte Marie anchorage. Labat tried to lure Roche ashore, but when the English suddenly bent oars back out to sea, opened fire. Roche allegedly suffered another three killed and five wounded before getting out of range, in one of the very last actions of the War of the League of Augsburg (King William's War).

*See also* Labat, Jean-Baptiste.
*Reference:* Labat.

# RODERIGO, PIETER

## (FL. 1674-1675)

"Flanderkin" privateer of Flemish birth or descent who was charged with piracy along the disputed coast of Maine.

In the summer of 1674, a Dutch naval expedition out of Curaçao commanded by Jurriaen Aernouts conquered French Acadia, renaming it New Holland. Before returning to the Antilles, he appointed Captain John Rhoades of Boston as acting governor of the colony, furnishing him with two small armed vessels for coast guard patrol: the *Edward and Thomas* of Captain Pieter Roderigo and the shallop *Penobscot* of Captain Cornelis Andreson. New Englanders long accustomed to trading and fishing off Acadia requested permission from the new administration to continue doing so but were refused. Because England was neutral in the Franco-Dutch conflict, though, they ignored this ban until Roderigo and Andreson began impounding vessels.

Incensed, the New Englanders called upon the Massachusetts council to take action against what they regarded as acts of piracy. On 15 February 1675 (O.S.), Captain Samuel Moseley of the ketch *Salisbury* was ordered to sortie from Boston and apprehend the transgressors. Once at sea he fell in with a French ship that was also hunting the Dutch vessels as enemy privateers, and together they came upon the *Edward and Thomas* and *Penobscot* lying in the Bay of Fundy with their latest prize, the English bark *Philip* of Captain George Manning. Moseley and his French consort immediately engaged, and once the battle was joined, Manning turned the *Philip*'s guns on Roderigo and Andreson as well, so that between them they battered the Dutch pair into submission. Moseley triumphantly carried the *Edward and Thomas* and *Penobscot* into Boston on 2 April 1675 (O.S.).

Roderigo and Andreson were tried at Cambridge, Massachusetts; they were sentenced to death for piracy, although soon pardoned. During the Indian conflict of that same summer known as King Philip's War, both fought very bravely in defense of that English colony. Moseley even formed a volunteer company made up of his crews and some of the released Dutchmen, which was called "Moseley's privateers."

*See also* Aernouts, Jurriaen; Andreson, Cornelis; Moseley, Samuel; Rhoades, John.

*References:* Chapin; Gosse, *Who's Who;* Webster.

# RODRÍGUEZ, MANUEL

## (FL. 1683-1684)

Spanish island trader with a privateering commission who in peacetime captured an English sloop and boat off St. John in the Virgin Islands, carrying both into Puerto Rico.

On 11 September 1683, Rodríguez pursued and seized the sloop *Africa* and boat *Hopewell* with his tartan *San Pedro y San Pablo* (Saint Peter and Saint Paul). The English craft had sailed from Nevis the preceding month toward Danish Saint Thomas, where they joined Captain Charles Carlile of HMS *Francis* in an attempt "to recover a New England sloop captured by pirates and seized by Governor Esmit, but found it staved." They then parted company from the Royal Navy warship and shortly thereafter fell to Rodríguez. According to a survivor, the English crewmen were immediately "all put on board the Spanish ship and ordered into the hold until they came to Puerto Rico, when they were landed and imprisoned by the governor's order [Gaspar Martínez de Andino] for a fortnight. A few days later the sloop was sold. Two men were taken out and put to serve on board, five more were sent in a Spanish man o' war to Havana," and the remaining four sailed off to Santo Domingo on Rodríguez's tartan. They escaped and found their way back to Nevis in mid-July 1684, reporting on their misadventure.

*See also* Carlile, Charles.

*References:* *C.S.P., Amer. and W.I.,* Vol.XI; López; Cantos.

# ROGERS, THOMAS
## (FL. 1669-1675)

English freebooter who served under Henry Morgan at the assaults on Maracaibo and Panama, then joined the French.

Rogers was first heard of in 1669, when he commanded one of the minor vessels in Morgan's raid against Maracaibo (*Forlorn,* a seventeenth-century euphemism for "vanguard"). The following year while on a peacetime cruise Rogers was attacked by a Spanish corsair. He turned the tables by capturing the Spaniard instead and while examining the prisoners found that one was an English renegade who lived at Cartagena. This captive told him that "war against Jamaica" had been openly declared throughout the Spanish Caribbean in retaliation for Morgan's assault on Portobelo. Actually, the queen regent Mariana of Spain had published a *real cédula* or royal decree, on 20 April 1669, authorizing Spanish-American officials to issue privateering commissions against the English. While not open warfare, Rogers nonetheless realized the importance of this development and carried his prize into Port Royal to advise the English governor.

Soon this news was confirmed by other sources, as well as by the coastal attacks of Manoel Rivero Pardal. Thus, late in 1670, Rogers joined the buccaneer fleet gathering

at Ile-à-Vache off southwestern Hispaniola with his 12-gun ship *Gift,* of 40 tons, to take part in a retaliatory strike against the Spaniards. He sailed to Providencia Island and Chagres with Morgan's expedition and led his contingent across the isthmus as part of the main body, distinguishing himself at the Mata Asnillos battle before Panama City on 28 January 1671. Following the withdrawal, little more is heard about his activities, although presumably he continued roving during the Third Anglo-Dutch War (1672–1674). When England withdrew from the Anglo-French confederation against the Netherlands, many West Indian corsairs shifted allegiance in order to continue privateering. Rogers was one, obtaining a commission from the French on Saint Domingue against the Dutch and Spanish.

Thus it was as a French corsair that, in early March 1675, Rogers chanced upon the wreckage of the *Jamaica Merchant* off Ile-à-Vache. Stranded ashore were its survivors, including Morgan, who had been created a baronet and sent back out to Jamaica as lieutenant governor. The *Gift* bore him proudly into Port Royal the evening of 15 March, flying an English flag in honor of the occasion. Three weeks later, Morgan drafted a letter promising Rogers and other English rovers a friendly reception at Port Royal if they were to come in and cease serving foreign flags, as this was proving an embarrassment for the Crown. (Morgan added that he hoped "their experience of him will give him the reputation that he intends not to betray them.") Nevertheless, this proposal was never sent, as the new governor, Lord Vaughan, preferred other measures to recall these privateers.

*See also* Hispaniola; Rivero Pardal, Manoel.

*References:* *C.S.P., Amer. and W.I.,* Vol.IX; Earle, *Panamá;* Gosse, *Who's Who;* Pope.

# ROMEGOUX, JEAN-LOUIS, SEIGNEUR DE

## (FL. 1699)

French naval officer and son of the comte de Blenác.

Romegoux arrived at Saint Domingue with a royal frigate on 14 July 1699, having been sent out to conduct peacetime patrols along "the coasts of Indies against pirates" and supposedly to help the Spaniards expel the Scottish settlement from Darien. Romegoux further brought out intelligence from the French minister de Pontchartrain in Paris, alleging that the English intended to establish a colony of 500 people at Samaná Bay on the north shore of Hispaniola.

Jean-Baptiste Ducasse, the governor of the French half of the island, immediately forwarded this information to his Spanish counterpart, Don Severino de Manzaneda Salinas at Santo Domingo, ostensibly to ingratiate his government with its neighbor but more precisely to lay claim to this particular stretch of Santo Domingo's coastline for France. Ducasse added that Romegoux was preparing to "depart without delay for Tierra Firme" (the Spanish Main) to help against the Scots—neither overture being very warmly received by the Spaniard.

*See also* Blénac, Charles de Courbon, comte de; Darien Colony; Ducasse, Jean-Baptiste; Hispaniola; Spanish Main.

*Reference:* Baudrit; Lugo.

# ROSE, JEAN

## (FL. 1679-1685)

French *flibustier* who campaigned in both the West Indies and South Seas.

On 17 January 1680, Rose and his 20-ton brigantine, with a crew of 25 men and no guns, met the English privateers Coxon, Robert Allison, Cornelius Essex, Thomas Magott, and Bartholomew Sharpe as they were standing away from Port Morant off the southeastern tip of Jamaica. All five had agreed to unite under Coxon's leadership for an assault on Spanish Portobelo, and Rose joined the enterprise, being especially welcome as he bore a commission from the French governor of Saint Domingue to attack Spaniards. When the weather turned foul, Coxon hailed his vessels to make to Isla Fuerte, 90 miles south–southwest of Cartagena on the Spanish Main.

Only Essex and Sharpe failed to keep the rendezvous. Coxon led a party to the nearby San Bernardo, or "Friends," Islands to obtain landing craft for the disembarkation. The formation then proceeded toward Isla de Pinos (Island of Pines) 130 miles east of Portobelo in the Archipelago de las Mulatas, although only Coxon's bark was able to beat through the contrary winds and gain the isle, the rest being forced to put into Golden Island some miles due south. From there Coxon ordered 250 buccaneers into boats to row westward along the coast, hoping to surprise Portobelo before the Spaniards could learn of their presence.

Nearing this destination they came upon the ship of another *flibustier,* Capitaine Lessone, who added 80 men to the boat party. Shortly thereafter the buccaneers slipped ashore at the Gulf of San Blas, proceeding on foot to avoid any Spanish coastal lookouts. They marched three days, bursting into Portobelo unexpectedly and capturing it with only five or six minor casualties.

The city was ransacked over the next two days, after which the freebooters retired northeastward to be picked up by their ships. A brief blockade ensued, and after a couple of captures a general distribution of booty was held, resulting in shares of 100 pieces of eight per man. Afterward, the flotilla retired to Bocas del Toro (literally "bull's mouths" or "entrances of the bull") at the western extremity of present day Panama to careen. Once refitted, all the pirates except Rose and Lessone decided to return to Golden Island and avail themselves of their newfound friendship with the Indians "to travel overland to Panama" and attack the Spaniards on the Pacific side.

Little more than a year later, early in June 1681, Rose was again in Coxon's company, lying at Springer's Key in the San Blas Islands with his *barco luengo,* along with Thomas Paine, Jan Willems, George Wright, and four other captains. Together they decided to make a descent on the Central American coast, for which they sailed first toward San Andrés Island to procure boats. But a gale scattered the formation, and an *armadilla* of a dozen tiny men o' war appeared from Cartagena, leading to the disintegration of this proposed expedition.

By mid-January 1685, Rose was prowling off the Spanish Main with Captains Michiel Andrieszoon, Vigneron, La Garde, and an English trader, jointly lying in ambush for a Spanish *patache* called the *Margarita,* rumored to be about to pass. They sighted a ship the night of 17 January, which Rose challenged the following morning. The response came back in French, but the stranger's lines were Spanish, so he opened fire. In the growing light Andrieszoon recognized this vessel as the 14-gun Spanish prize of their chieftain Laurens de Graaf and so put an end to the engagement. The formation then captured a Flemish ship out of La Guaira and visited Curaçao on 20 January before crossing to Cape de la Vela (Venezuela) on 27 January, still hoping to intercept the Spanish merchantman off that headland. While De Graaf careened, Rose sailed down the coast to Ríohacha and attempted to deceive the Spaniards into believing that he was a peaceful English trader with no success. Returning empty-handed on 8 February, the pirate flotilla split up.

Some weeks later Rose learned that a large force of *flibustiers* had traversed the Isthmus of Panama from Golden Island under Captains François Grogniet and Lescuyer to join an even bigger contingent of English buccaneers who were already operating in the South Seas. Rose therefore decided to follow these first groups across, joining his contingent to those of Captains Pierre le Picard and Desmarais, so that on 1 March 1685, 264 mainly French *flibustiers* set off through the jungle on foot. They emerged on the far side of the isthmus on 11 April, being met by a boat which Grogniet had sent back for them. This in turn conducted them to a pirate assemblage off Isla del Rey, where the new arrivals were incorporated into the fleet of English Captains Edward Davis, Charles Swan, William Knight, and Francis Townley, who offered the *flibustiers* the 90-ton *Santa Rosa* they had recently captured from the Spaniards. All the French would henceforth serve under either Grogniet or Picard, so Rose's name was no longer mentioned in the records. Whether he died early during the campaign or lived to return to the Caribbean with the rest of his companions in 1688 is not known.

*See also* Allison, Robert; Andrieszoon, Michiel; Coxon, John; De Graaf, Laurens Cornelis Boudewijn; Essex, Cornelius; Golden Island; Harris, Peter (fl. 1671–1680); La Garde, Capitaine; Lessone, Capitaine; Lussan, Ravenau de; Magott, Thomas; Paine, Thomas; *patache;* Rose, Jean; Sawkins, Richard; Sharpe, Bartholomew; South Seas; Spanish Main; Vigneron, Capitaine; Willems, Jan; Wright, George.

***References:*** Bradley; Dampier; Lussan.

# RUM

Alcoholic beverage made by distilling a liquid product of sugarcane such as molasses.

The origins of this word are unknown, some believing it was a garbling of a term originally native to the West Indies, others asserting it was derived from an English adjective meaning anything excellent, valuable, or handsome. (The expression "rum booze," for example was recorded as early as the mid-sixteenth century in England to describe any fine wine, just as "rum mort" meant the Queen, "rum blower," a beautiful woman, etc.) Whatever the case, the term "rum" soon came to be applied to distilled spirits throughout the English Caribbean islands, where there was an abundance of sugarcane products.

The whole question of potables was a tricky one for the region, both because of questionable health standards, as well as the even more fundamental problem of preserving liquids in the stifling heat. Water supplies were viewed as suspect; for example, drinking water was transported into Port Royal, Jamaica, in great casks aboard wherries or canoes from the clear Rio Cobre to be sold. But a gentleman resident of the city wrote:

> our drink is chiefly Madeira wine, lem-onades, punch and brandy; for cool drinks, mobby we have, made of potatoes, cacao-drink, sugar-drink and rappe made of molasses.

Such light fare was hardly to the taste of hearty seamen, and the benders of some buccaneers were to become legendary. Alexandre Olivier Exquemelin has left the following description of Rok Brasiliano:

> When he was drunk, he would roam the town like a madman. The first person he came across, he would chop off his arm or leg, without anyone daring to intervene, for he was like a maniac.

William Dampier said of the English logwood-cutters at the Laguna de Términos:

> they had not forgot their old drinking bouts, and would still spend £30 or £40 at a sitting on board the ships that came hither from Jamaica; carousing and firing of guns three or four days together.

Indeed, Governor Sir Thomas Modyford of Jamaica was even moved to observe in November 1665, "The Spaniards wondered much at the sickness of our people, until they knew of the strength of their drinks, but then wondered more that they were not all dead."

The Royal Navy's long association with rum also dates from the seventeenth century. Prior to deploying in West Indian waters, sailors had been served spirits aboard warship, but some of these did not stand up well to torrid, tropical climes. As early as 24 July 1655 (O.S.), Vice Admiral William Goodson wrote to the commissioners of the Navy from recently conquered Jamaica "that no drink be sent but brandy in very substantial casks, and a little vinegar, for the cider wholly decays, and the beer grows flat or sour." But it was not until much later that the policy of substituting local spirits for European issue was made official, especially after Admiral Sir John Narborough visited Barbados in November 1687 aboard HMS *Foresight*. During his brief layover he shipped "600 odd gallons of rum to be served to our ship's company in lieu of brandy," and—being a commissioner of the Navy himself, responsible for the Victualling Department—evidently recommended this practice be adopted as standard usage. A few months later the Admiralty in London ordered rum issued instead of brandy on all men o' war of the Jamaican service, instructing the captains to take care "that the good or ill effects of this proof" be observed. The results appear to have been satisfactory.

**See also** *kilduijvel.*

**References:** *C.S.P., Amer. and W.I.,* Vol.IX; Dampier; *D.N.B.;* Earle, *Treasure;* Exquemelin; Pawson, *Port Royal;* Vrijman.

# RUYTER, MICHIEL ADRIAENSZOON DE
## (1607-1676)

Gifted Dutch admiral, one of the greatest ever to hoist a flag, but whose two West Indian campaigns met with only indifferent success.

De Ruyter first went to sea at the tender age of nine aboard Dutch merchantmen and by 1635 had risen to captain. Six years later he served briefly as rear admiral of a fleet assisting Portugal against Spain before rejoining the merchant service. He spent the next ten years skirmishing with the Barbary pirates of North Africa until the First Anglo-Dutch War broke out in 1652 and he accepted a regular naval command. After the 1653 Battle of the Texel, in which Maarten Tromp was killed, De Ruyter was promoted to vice admiral. After peace was reestablished with England, De Ruyter took a Dutch fleet to the Baltic in 1659 to support the Danes against Sweden in the First Northern War (1655–1660). During 1664, he patrolled the Guinea Coast of West Africa, clashing frequently with the English, who were disputing ownership of the slaving stations there.

## FIRST WEST INDIAN CAMPAIGN
### (1665)

De Ruyter climaxed this latter cruise with a bold decision to attack English establishments in the Caribbean. He was already familiar with the West Indies from earlier voyages, and despite the lack of any official declaration of war, hostilities were already so far advanced that he was able to set sail on his own in late February 1665.

On 29 April he sighted Barbados, and the next morning led his fleet directly into Carlisle Bay where an English convoy of 29 merchantmen and a single warship were preparing to weigh. De Ruyter did not return the fire of either the shore batteries nor vessels as he approached, choosing to wait until his ships had come to within point-blank range, at which he unleashed a devastating broadside, followed by a second. The two sides exchanged heated volleys for the next several hours, De Ruyter's flagship *Spiegel* (Mirror) and many others being damaged. He destroyed much of the English convoy but could scarcely dent the shore defenses, one eyewitness reporting later that his bombardment "killed only one Negro, one Christian and a dog" on land.

De Ruyter was forced to withdraw, sailing to the French island of Martinique, where he was well received. He departed again on 5 May 1665, and while sweeping through the Lesser Antilles learned that the Second Anglo-Dutch War had finally been proclaimed back in Europe. After seizing some small prizes off Montserrat and Nevis, De Ruyter paused at Sint Eustatius to deliver supplies before quitting the Caribbean on 17 May. He returned to Europe via Bermuda and Newfoundland to be made lieutenant admiral of Holland and play an effective role in the hostilities. He defeated Monck and Prince Rupert in the Four Days' Battle of June 1666, and then in turn was beaten a month-and-a-half later off the North Foreland. But in June 1667, with peace negotiations already being conducted at Breda, he led an exceptionally bold strike up the Medway to within twenty miles of London, destroying much of the Royal Navy's strength. Soon afterward, a treaty was signed, but conflict resumed five years later. De Ruyter campaigned brilliantly throughout 1672–1673 against the combined Anglo-French fleets in the North Sea, contributing to England's retirement from that war in early 1674.

## SECOND WEST INDIAN CAMPAIGN
### (1674)

Now able to concentrate solely on the French, De Ruyter set sail on 8 June 1674 at the head of a major expedition comprised of 10 ships of the line, 21 transports, 6 fireships, and 2 galliots, the whole conducting 4,300 sailors and 3,400 troops. After touching at Madeira, he appeared at three o'clock on the afternoon of 19 July before Martinique, France's largest colony in the Windward Islands. The defenders had known of his approach, but their strength was concentrated up the coast at Saint-Pierre. Instead, De Ruyter bore directly down upon the principal port of Fort Royal before becoming becalmed. During the night the French worked frantically to shore up their defenses, but in addition to the Marquis d'Amblimont's single 44-gun warship, there were only a 22-gun merchantman and four lesser vessels in the roads. A garrison of 161 men was hastily scraped together to work

the batteries, and booms were placed across the harbor mouth.

When De Ruyter disembarked his troops the following morning, they encountered a position of great natural strength. Fortifications sat high atop rocky cliffs, and the assault columns became embroiled in a crossfire between the batteries and d'Amblimont's anchored ships. The Dutch attackers had no artillery, scaling ladders, nor supporting bombardment, and discipline collapsed when a warehouse full of rum was breached. Their commanders attempted to regroup in the shelter of a nearby cliff, but d'Amblimont quickly landed half a dozen guns and opened fire on this new position. Dutch will broke and they drew off, returning that afternoon for a second try. Again, they suffered heavily from the combined fire and retired to their transports in defeat when De Ruyter hoisted the recall from his flagship *Zeven Provinciën* (Seven Provinces).

Returning to Europe, he continued to campaign against the French in the Mediterranean until being mortally wounded at the April 1676 Battle of Augusta, Sicily.

**See also** Amblimont, marquis d'; rum.

**References:** Buchet; Crouse; Goslinga, *1580–1680*.

# Sainte barbe or santa Bárbara

Seventeenth-century expression for a powder room or magazine, the first in French and the second in Spanish.

The origin of this rather curious name stems from early church history: Barbara was one of the first converts to Christianity, for which her heathen father Diosorus had her tried, tortured, and executed. He personally carried out the death sentence, but in an act of divine retribution was killed by lightning while returning home. For this reason, the young martyr became the patron saint of those who worked with explosives, such as gunners or miners. Because a votive image of Saint Barbara was commonly displayed outside any powder room, her name came to be associated with the structure itself.

# Salmigondis

French name for a communal stew or ragout made with a mixture of meats, to which vegetables and other items were added, the whole being highly seasoned.

During the seventeenth century—when salting, smoking, or pickling were the sole means of preservation—people often had to resort to extraordinary means to render their meals more palatable. *Salmigondis* (usually spelled *salmagundi* in English) became popular among West Indian buccaneers, not least because it entailed a shared contribution to a general pot, from which everyone would draw in true brotherhood fashion. In times of plenty, such meals could make for hearty eating; one such concoction began with whatever meats were available being

roasted, chopped into chunks and marinated in spiced wine, then combined

with cabbage, anchovies, pickled herring, mangoes, hard-boiled eggs, palm hearts, onions, olives, grapes and any other pickled vegetables that were available. The whole would then be highly seasoned with garlic, salt, pepper and mustard seed, and doused with oil and vinegar—and served with drafts of beer and rum.

*Reference:* Botting.

# Salt Tortuga

Seventeenth-century English nickname for Isla La Tortuga off the northern shores of present day Venezuela.

According to the buccaneer chronicler William Dampier, turtling was such a frequent activity among Caribbean seafarers, that this particular island came to be "so called to distinguish it from the shoals of Dry Tortugas, near Cape Florida, and from the isle of Tortuga by Hispaniola." Quite probably Salt Tortuga got its name from the nearby salt pans of the Araya Peninsula, opposite Cumaná, which were freely drawn upon by passing seamen as an abundant source of this natural preservative.

*Reference:* Dampier.

# Salter, thomas

## (FL. 1667)

English privateer who operated out of Port Royal, Jamaica.

In 1667, during the closing stages of the Second Anglo-Dutch War, Salter captured the Spanish ship *Cedar* [sic]in the Laguna de Términos, laden with a cargo of logwood. He put a seven-man crew aboard with orders for his prizemaster, William Smith, to sail into Port Royal for adjudication. However, Smith and his men instead absconded with the vessel to New York, where they sold it under the name *William*. When Salter learned of this, he retained his friend Samuel Moseley of Massachusetts to sue for its recovery.

**See also** Laguna de Términos; logwood; Moseley, Samuel.

**Reference:** Chapin.

# SÁNCHEZ XIMÉNEZ, JOSÉ

### (?-1666)

Spanish soldier who reconquered Providencia Island from the English, then was treacherously murdered by his own men.

Sánchez was a veteran of "experience and courage," who had served 24 years in Flanders before emigrating to the West Indies. He attached himself to the train of Juan Pérez de Guzmán, following his patron from Puerto Rico to Panama in 1665, where he was appointed *sargento mayor,* or garrison commander, at Portobelo. The next year he was entrusted with command of the expedition sent to recapture Providencia, which had been taken by a group of English raiders under Edward Mansfield. After a few months occupation, Sánchez was murdered by some of his disgruntled troops.

**See also** Mansfield, Edward; Pérez de Guzmán, Juan.

**Reference:** Earle, *Panamá.*

# SANTO Y SEÑA

Spanish system of passwords based upon the church calendar, frequently employed along the South American coast.

If a Spanish vessel or fortress were approached by strangers after nightfall, a saint's name might be randomly shouted out by a sentinel in challenge. The correct response was to name the corresponding place associated with each particular saint; for example, to a cry of "Santa Rosa?" the proper reply was "Lima!" To "San Francisco Javier?" the answer would be "Navarra!" and so on. This system had been introduced with foreign pirates—especially the heretic English or Dutch—in mind, as they would never have such pious answers ready on their tongues. Moreover, such a flexible system permitted Spanish vessels to depart on voyages without worrying about a password being altered in their absence.

**Reference:** Pérez.

# SARGENTO MAYOR

Seventeenth-century Spanish military rank, much more senior than its present-day English equivalent would imply.

A *sargento mayor* was second-in-command to a military governor of a city, or to the commander of a large garrison, or to a *maestre de campo* (field marshal) during a campaign.

# SAWKINS, RICHARD

### (FL. 1677?-1680)

English privateer who died bravely during John Coxon's incursion into the South Seas.

Sawkins may have also participated in Coxon's previous raid into the Bay of Honduras in September 1679 or in the 1677 sack of Santa Marta on the Spanish Main. However, the clearest reference to his activities occurs early in December 1679, when the 32-gun frigate HMS *Success* was dispatched by Governor Lord Carlisle of Jamaica to detain the renegade privateer Peter Harris off the south Cuba cays. Shortly after departing Port Royal, Captain Thomas Johnson of the *Success* encountered Sawkins's brigantine, which he captured and sent in for adjudication, as it was suspected of belligerence against the Spaniards despite the peace prevailing in Europe. Sawkins was remanded into the custody of the provost marshal, and his brigantine impounded for the Crown.

Within a few days, word arrived that the *Success* had run aground off the Cuban coast, and Sawkins's former vessel cleared with water and supplies for the survivors. That night Sawkins "made his escape in a wherry" and sailed after his brigantine, which lay becalmed to leeward of the island. He boarded and was able to resume command, standing out to sea with 36 men. Shortly thereafter, they sighted a large Spanish ship, which they attacked, but were bloodily repulsed. Sawkins returned to bury ten of his men on the Jamaican coast, then began a refit. While doing so, he was spotted by HMS *Hunter,* 28 guns, which sent its pinnace inshore to investigate. Sawkins roared a warning, then "powder'd upon 'em a volley of small shot." The *Hunter* retaliated by sending in its accompanying sloop, which engaged the renegade but could not subdue him.

The rover was next heard from in early March 1680, when he appeared at the maze of islands known as Bocas del Toro (literally "bull's mouths" or "entrances of the bull") located at the northwestern extremity of present-day Panama, with a 25-ton *barco luengo* of 2 guns and 40 men. He encountered Harris, who had also eluded the Jamaican authorities and was further joined by Coxon's flotilla, fresh from its sack of Portobelo. The raiders refitted their vessels, then suggested returning to Golden Island to avail themselves of their newfound friendship with the local Indians "to travel

overland to Panama" and attack the Spaniards on their vulnerable Pacific flank. Sawkins agreed to join the expedition, and on 2 April the freebooters weighed.

## PACIFIC INCURSION

Coxon, Sawkins, Harris, Robert Allison, Edmond Cooke, Thomas Magott, and Bartholomew Sharpe all anchored their ships close inshore at Golden Island, out of sight in a small cove. An anchor watch was left aboard each, with orders to rally to Coxon's and Harris's ships—the two largest—if any attack should occur. At six o'clock on Monday morning, 15 April 1680, 332 buccaneers went ashore and obtained guides to cross the isthmus. Ten days later, they came upon the Spanish stockade of Santa María at the confluence of the Chucunaque and Tuira Rivers. This fort had no artillery, so at dawn

> [Sawkins] runs up to the palisades with two or three men more, and hauls up two or three palisades by main strength, and enters in.

A brisk firefight ensued. Sawkins was wounded in the head with an arrow, and a companion was shot in the hand before the Spaniards surrendered. Seventy of the 200 Spanish defenders were killed outright, and the rest were massacred later by Indians.

Flush with their victory, the buccaneers determined to press on into the Pacific, although "Coxon seemed unwilling, but with much persuasion went." Henceforth other captains began to assume the lead, most particularly Sawkins, Harris, and Sharpe. Reaching the Pacific, the pirates traveled westward along the coast in their river boats, until one night they captured an anchored Spanish bark, of which Sharpe took command with 135 men. The next night Harris came upon a second and seized it as well. Soon the buccaneers had assembled a small flotilla, with which they bore down upon Panama. The Spaniards sent out a hastily mustered force to do battle, and the raiders overwhelmed it in a three-hour fight. During this action, Harris was mortally wounded, and afterward Coxon decided to retrace his steps to Golden Island with 70 loyal hands.

The remaining buccaneers elected Sawkins admiral, and installed him aboard the 400-ton *Santísima Trinidad* (Most Blessed Trinity) as their flagship. On 6 May 1680, a large ship was intercepted arriving from Lima, Peru, which became Sharpe's new command, while Cooke commanded a bark of about 80 tons. Sawkins suggested that the flotilla sail southward to Guayaquil "before they should have any knowledge of our coming, but our people being headstrong, would have meat to eat first." The squadron accordingly roamed westward past Coiba Island, until two days later Sawkins went aboard Cooke's bark with 60 men to attempt to forage near the coastal town of Remedios. They sailed as far as they could up the Santa Lucía River before anchoring, after which Sawkins led a boat party of approximately 45 men further upstream.

Coming upon some stockades, the pirate chieftain

> landed himself first and went into the savanna [plain] and saw abundance of people there. One mulatto met him, whom Captain Sawkins shot down.

Retreating to the boats, he asked if the party were all landed and ready. On being told they were, he said, "Follow me and do not lie behind, for if I do amiss, you will all fare the worse for it." He then advanced with the briskest men but was met by a host of mulattos and hunters bearing lances. One of his followers recorded Sawkins's final moments:

> He fired his pistol and shot down one mestizo, the rest [of the vanguard] firing and loading as fast as they could, but the Spaniards coming in upon them so fast that killed Captain Sawkins and three men more. They took one alive. We heard him make a dreadful noise but could not rescue him, but was forced to retreat to our canoes and go off as fast as we could, they coming down so fast upon us.

*See also* Allison, Robert; *barco luengo;* Cooke, Edmond; Coxon, John; Golden Island; Harris, Peter (fl. 1671–1680); Magott, Thomas; Sharpe, Bartholomew; South Seas; Spanish Main.

*References:* Bradley, *Lure;* *C.S.P., Amer. and W.I.,* Vol. X; Jameson; Pawson, *Port Royal.*

# SCOTT, LEWIS

## (FL. 1661?)

English buccaneer who made an early attack on Campeche.

According to *De Americaensche Zee-Roovers* of Alexandre Olivier Exquemelin (first published in Amsterdam in 1678), Scott was the freebooter who pioneered large-scale land assaults against the Spaniards in the Americas. Specifically, it was stated that Scott

> took the town of Campeche, plundered the place and forced the citizens to pay ransom before abandoning it. After him came [Edward] Mansfield.

As it is known that Mansfield assaulted that particular Mexican port early in 1663 (as second-in-command to Christopher Myngs), Scott's action must have preceded this event. Perhaps it was the raid of 27 January 1661, in which two valuable

Spanish merchantmen were burnt in the Campeche roads, or one of many earlier assaults.

Some Spanish historians have erroneously attributed the attack of 10 July 1678 to Scott, although this was clearly the handiwork of George Spurre and Edward Neville, as well as being too late for inclusion in Exquemelin's book.

*See also* Exquemelin, Alexandre Olivier; Mansfield, Edward; Myngs, Sir Christopher; Neville, Edward; Spurre, George.

*References:* Exquemelin; Gosse, *Who's Who;* Juárez.

# SCROOPE, ROBERT

## (FL. 1692)

English captain issued a privateering commission by the Council of Jamaica on 8 February 1692 (O.S.).

*Reference: C.S.P., Amer. and W.I.,* Vol. XIII.

# SEARLE, ROBERT

## (FL. 1658-1671)

One of the earliest and most active English privateers on Jamaica.

Searle was first mentioned in the summer of 1658, after Commodore Christopher Myngs returned to Jamaica from a raid against the Spanish Main with three Spanish merchantmen. These prizes were sold to men who would all prove formidable corsairs. The largest vessel, of 8 guns and 60 tons, was bought by Searle and renamed the *Cagway;* a vessel of 4 guns and 50 tons was purchased by Dutch-born Laurens Prins, who changed its name to *Pearl;* while the third craft later became John Morris's *Dolphin.*

Four years later, Searle sailed with *Cagway* as part of Myngs's expedition against

Santiago de Cuba. This force of 1,300 men and a dozen vessels quit Port Royal on 21 September 1662 (O.S.) and two-and-a-half weeks later disembarked to the east of their intended target. Santiago was overrun the following day, and a considerable amount of booty carried back to Jamaica. It is not known whether Searle then sortied again for more plunder or participated in Myngs's next operation against the Mexican port of Campeche a few months later.

He continued roving, however, for in September 1664 brought two rich Spanish prizes into Port Royal with his new 10-gun ship *Pearl,* despite the fact that a few months previously the new governor, Sir Thomas Modyford, had proclaimed that "His Majesty cannot sufficiently express his dissatisfaction at the daily complaints of violence and depredations done by ships, said to belong to Jamaica, upon the king of Spain's subjects," and so Searle's prizes were restored to their Cuban owners along with their treasure, and his rudder and sails were removed as an example to other privateers.

The outbreak of the Second Anglo-Dutch War the next year seemed to offer better possibilities. In early March 1666, Searle's *Pearl* sailed as one of nine ships and 500 soldiers raised by Colonel Edward Morgan (uncle to Henry) to attempt to conquer the Dutch colonies of Sint Eustatius and Sabá. This force departed Jamaica in two divisions, five sail putting out of Port Royal on 5 April 1665, and Morgan himself following with another four on the 28 April. They mustered 650 men in all and were described in a letter by Modyford as

chiefly reformed privateers, scarce a planter amongst them, being resolute fellows and well armed with *fusils* [Spanish word for muskets] and pistols.

They served "at the old rate of no purchase, no pay," but although landing successfully, the colonel, "being a corpulent man," dropped dead from heat exhaustion. Although Sint Eustatius and its neighbor Sabá were quickly subdued, the English force disintegrated because of lack of booty and differences over the succession. Most of the privateers chose to split up and follow their own devices, it being recorded that Searle, accompanied only by Captain Steadman and a party of 80 men, took the Dutch island of Tobago and destroyed everything they could not carry away.

Four years later, with peace restored, Searle was lying at New Providence in the Bahamas when that colony was attacked by a Spanish force. In retaliation, Searle led several angry privateersmen on a raid upon Saint Augustine, Florida. When he next traveled to Jamaica in the summer of 1670, he realized that this foray would meet with the governor's disapproval. Indeed, Modyford wrote:

> There arrived also at Port Morant the *Cagway,* Captain Searle, with 70 stout men, who hearing that I was much incensed against him for that action of Saint Augustine, went to Macarry Bay and there rides out of [my] command. I will use the best ways to apprehend him, without driving his men to despair.

Shortly thereafter, Searle ventured ashore and was arrested and imprisoned in Port Royal. However, the veteran's luck continued to hold, for this was the same summer when Spanish corsairs such as Manoel Rivero Pardal began harassing Jamaica, prompting Morgan's vengeful strike against Panama.

Searle was released to participate in this campaign, and after the advance through the jungle and burning of Panama City, was given command of the tiny flotilla of commandeered Pacific vessels sent to ransack its offshore islands. At Taboga he and his men found a large store of wine, which by evening they were well on their way to consuming. In their drunkenness they failed to post lookouts and so did not notice that the 400-ton *Santísima Trinidad* (Most Blessed Trinity) of Captain Francisco de Peralta had appeared off that island from further out in the gulf. This galleon had departed Panama earlier, along with *San Felipe Neri,* to carry away the Spaniards' valuables and noncombatants before the buccaneer assault. Unaware that the triumphant raiders had quickly spread this far out from the mainland, De Peralta now sent a seven-man watering party ashore for his suffering passengers.

These were captured and brought before Searle, who questioned them and thus belatedly discovered the presence of such a wealthy prize nearby. But by the time he and his befuddled men were able to react, De Peralta had become suspicious at the disappearance of his watering party, and the galleon vanished back into the night. When the main body of buccaneers eventually learned of this missed opportunity a few days later, they were outraged. The chronicler Alexandre Olivier Exquemelin, even writing several years after the event, scornfully related how when the watering party had been brought before Searle, the old rover

had been more inclined to sit drinking and sporting with a group of Spanish women he had taken prisoner, than to go at once in pursuit of the treasure ship.

*See also* Cagway; Exquemelin, Alexandre Olivier; Morris, John; Myngs, Sir Christopher; Prins, Laurens; Rivero Pardal, Manoel; Spanish Main.

*References:* Cruikshank; Earle, *Panamá;* Exquemelin; Gosse, *Who's Who; Interesting Tracts;* Pope.

# SENOLVE, CAPTAIN
## (FL. 1663)

Dutch privateer.

He was described in an English document of 1663 as commanding "three small ships full of men from Jamaica," perhaps 100 overall, with a total of 12 guns aboard his trio of vessels. The Dutchman's name appears somewhat garbled, and may actually have been "den Olde" (the Elder).

*Reference:* Pawson, *Port Royal.*

# SERGEANT, BENJAMIN
## (FL. 1668)

English privateer issued a commission by Governor Sir Thomas Modyford of Jamaica on 28 October 1668 (O.S.) to take any Spanish ship he "might encounter below the Tropic of Cancer in the region of Mexico only, and no other place." Most likely this was a letter of reprisal granted in retaliation for some specific local depredation.

*Reference:* Tribout.

# SHARPE, BARTHOLOMEW
## (C. 1650-C. 1699?)

English buccaneer who raided Portobelo and the South Seas.

Sharpe is believed to have been born in the parish of Stepney, London, England, about 1650. He became a privateer during the Second Anglo-Dutch War (1665–1667), and the chronicler William Dampier later suggested that he was one of the buccaneers who plundered the Central American town of Segovia in 1675. The first definite mention of Sharpe's activities occurred in the summer of 1679, when he was one of a mixed band of English, French, and other privateers who forayed into the Bay of Honduras. On 26 September they captured a Spanish merchantman laden with a valuable cargo of wine and indigo, which they hoped to dispose of at Jamaica. A month later it was being reported at Port Royal:

> There has been lately taken from the Spaniards by Coxon, Bartholomew Sharpe, Bothing and Hawkins [*sic;* Richard Sawkins?] with their crew, 500 chests of indigo, a great quantity of cacao, cochineal, tortoiseshell, money and plate. Much is brought into this country already, and the rest expected.

Later that December, Sharpe attended a gathering of privateers at Port Morant, off the southeastern tip of Jamaica, along with Allison, Coxon, Cornelius Essex, and Thomas Magott. All five agreed to unite under Coxon's leadership for an assault on Spanish Portobelo, despite having only the sketchiest authorization for such a venture. They quit Port Morant on 17 January 1680 and less than 20 miles out at sea met the brigantine of French *flibustier* Jean Rose, who also joined the enterprise. After surprising and sacking the Spanish port, a general distribution of booty was made, after which the flotilla retired to careen at Bocas del Toro (literally "bull's mouths" or "entrances of the bull" at the northwestern extremity of present day Panama).

## PACIFIC INCURSION
### (1680-1681)

Once refitted, Sharpe and the rest of the buccaneers decided to return to Golden Island and have the Darien Indians guide them over the Isthmus of Panama to attack the Spaniards on their Pacific flank. Coxon, Allison, Edmond Cooke, Peter Harris, Magott, Richard Sawkins, and Sharpe all anchored close inshore and at six o'clock on a Monday morning, 15 April 1680, went ashore with 332 buccaneers to penetrate the jungles. (Among their number were Dampier, Basil Ringrose, and Lionel Wafer, all of whom would later write accounts of these adventures.) The buccaneers overran the outpost of Santa María ten days later at the confluence of the Chucunaque and Tuira rivers and from there pushed on into the Pacific, although Coxon showed himself increasingly reluctant. They traveled westward along the coast in river boats, until one night they captured an anchored Spanish bark, which Sharpe took command of with 135 men. The next night Harris came upon a second and seized it as well. Soon the buccaneers had assembled a small flotilla, with which they bore down upon Panama.

The Spaniards sent out a hastily mustered force to do battle, and the raiders overwhelmed it in a three-hour fight. During this action Harris was mortally wounded, and afterward Coxon decided to retrace his steps to Golden Island with 70 loyal hands. The remaining buccaneers elected Sawkins their admiral and installed him aboard the 400-ton prize *Santísima Trinidad* (Most Blessed Trinity) as their flagship.

On 6 May 1680, a large ship was intercepted arriving from Lima, Peru, which became Sharpe's new command, while Cooke commanded a bark of about 80 tons. Sawkins suggested the flotilla sail southward to Guayaquil, but the crews wanted to prowl northeastward for meat first. The squadron accordingly roamed past Coiba Island, until two days later Sawkins went ashore to attempt to forage near the coastal town of Remedios but was killed.

Sharpe now assumed overall command, although he was not as popular as his predecessor and saw numerous desertions, eventually crowned—after wearisome

cruising up and down the South American coast—by being deposed as admiral in favor of John Watling. But when the latter was killed in an ill-conceived assault on Arica in February 1681, the other buccaneers reluctantly restored Sharpe as senior commander. Another contingent of about 50 buccaneers parted company that April to recross the isthmus under John Cooke, and Sharpe's luck improved, taking a few richer prizes. Eventually he sailed *Trinidad* around Cape Horn that November and concluded his voyage at Saint Thomas in the Danish Virgin Islands in February 1682. There he and his men dispersed, Sharpe sailing to England from Nevis aboard the *White Fox* of Captain Charles Howard, reaching Plymouth on 25 March 1682 (O.S.). He lodged at the Anchor Inn on Salpeter Bank, it being noticed that he and his ten followers had "several thousands of pounds and several portmanteaux of jewels and of gold and silver, coined and uncoined."

## SUBSEQUENT CAREER (1682-1699)

Less than two months later he was arrested on charges of piracy, and on 10 June 1682 (O.S.) brought before the High Court of Admiralty at Southwark to stand trial for piracy. (Among the judges were Sir Robert Holmes and Sir John Narborough.) These charges were quickly thrown out for lack of material witnesses, although Sharpe's extensive knowledge of Spanish America was also deemed useful to the Crown, and so weighed heavily in his favor. That November he was even commissioned to command the 4-gun Royal Navy vessel *Bonito,* which was to sail on a semiofficial treasure hunting expedition to the West Indies, although he was replaced at the last moment by Captain Edward Stanley. Nonetheless, Sharpe returned into the Caribbean in his own vessel, receiving a commission from the governor of Nevis in January 1684 "to take and apprehend savage Indians and pirates." On 31 October 1684 (O.S.) he seized a ship off Jamaica that he renamed *Josiah,* and in July 1685 was suspected of taking part in Laurens de Graaf and the sieur de Grammont's sack of Campeche, although this could never be proved.

Sharpe was tried at Nevis for piracy at the end of 1686 and again on 12 February 1687 (O.S.), being acquitted both times for lack of evidence. In 1688 he was reportedly the "commander" of the northernmost of the Leeward Islands, Anguilla, and by summer 1699 was being confined by the Danish authorities on Saint Thomas for unspecified "misdemeanors."

*See also* Allison, Robert; Cooke, Edmond; Coxon, John; Dampier, William; Essex, Cornelius; Golden Island; Harris, Peter (fl. 1671–1680); Magott, Thomas; Ringrose, Basil; Rose, Jean; Sawkins, Richard; Sharpe, Bartholomew; South Seas; Spanish Main; Wafer, Lionel.

*References:* Bradley, *Lure; C.S.P., Amer. and W.I.,* Vols. X–XI; Dampier; Howse; Jameson; Prebble; Ringrose; Wafer.

# SHIRLEY, THOMAS

## (FL. 1692)

English captain issued a privateering commission by the Council of Jamaica on 12 February 1692 (O.S.).

*Reference: C.S.P., Amer. and W.I.,* Vol. XIII.

# SIBATA, KEMPO

## ALSO SIBADA, SEBADA, AND SABADA (FL. 1643-1658)

Dutch privateer who settled in Connecticut and was present at the English conquest of Jamaica.

Sibata was probably Frisian in origin, judging by the garbled attempts to Anglicize his name (which may have actually been "Remco Siebstra" or another such variant). In 1649 he had been serving on the Dutch privateering vessel *Garse,* [*sic;* possibly *Gans* (Goose) is meant] when he came to settle in Pequott (present-day New London), Connecticut. Late in April 1653, Sibata was fined for selling ammunition to the Indians, and a few days later suffered further misfortune when his fully laden bark was seized at the mouth of the Connecticut River by Captain Edward Hull of the Rhode Island privateer *Swallow* (formerly *Admiral).* Hull had sortied upon receiving news of the outbreak of the First Anglo-Dutch War in Europe and claimed the bark and its cargo as legitimate prizes because of Sibata's Dutch origins. The latter, of course, brought suit and succeeded in recovering his vessel a few months later— although not its merchandise, which by then had been sold and dispersed. On the strength of Sibata's complaint, two of the officers of the *Swallow* were briefly incarcerated when they arrived at Boston on 25 October 1653 (O.S.).

Less than a year-and-a-half later, Sibata was lying at the West Indian isle of Antigua when the expedition of William Penn and Robert Venables anchored nearby at Barbados in anticipation of attacking the Spaniards. Commissioner Gregory Butler was detached from the fleet with *Marston Moor* and *Selby* to recruit additional men at the outlying islands, inviting Sibata "into the service of the state" along with his ship and crew. Sibata duly presented himself at the marshaling area off Saint Christophers and "was entertained by General Penn" when the main body rejoined on 17 April 1655 and was engaged as pilot aboard the flagship *Swiftsure.* When Santo Domingo was sighted a week later, Sibata transferred aboard Vice Admiral William Goodson's *Paragon,* along

SIR CLOUDESLEY

with Venables, to land the army. This operation was botched when the fleet sailed almost 30 miles westward before depositing its troops, thus dooming the enterprise.

Having failed to secure Santo Domingo, the expedition then proceeded to smaller Jamaica. (Sibata is believed to have participated in an even earlier English raid on this same island, under Captain William Jackson in 1643.) This time the landing was successful, and Jamaica was occupied. Sibata then settled among the English forces, fighting a protracted guerrilla war against the surviving Spaniards. On 14 February 1656, he led 100 soldiers ashore at Great Pedro Bay from his ship *Hunter,* hoping to surprise a nearby Spanish encampment. A herdsman spotted them and raised the alarm, so only a few captives could be found in several days' march to Parottee and back. However, they provided valuable intelligence as to a projected Spanish relief force expected from Cartagena, so Goodson sailed on a preemptive strike.

Sibata survived the terrible outbreaks of disease that decimated the early colonists and fought in Colonel Edward D'Oyley's final victory over the Spaniards at Rio Nuevo in the summer of 1658. Returning to Port Royal from this engagement, Sibata requested his official retirement from Jamaican service on 26 July. His certificate read, in part:

And now finding old age creeping apace upon him, and urgent occasions to go for his own country, has the General's leave to depart for England, where he desires to receive his pay.

To this D'Oyley added, "Sibada has been a very diligent and faithful man [who has] done good service, and hopes he will find respect suitable."

*See also* D'Oyley, Edward; Goodson, William.
*References:* Chapin; *C.S.P., Amer. and W.I.,* Vol. IX; Taylor.

# SIR CLOUDESLEY

Jocular English name for a seventeenth-century drink made of small beer and brandy, often with sweetening, spices, and nearly always lemon juice. This concoction was apparently named in honor of the famous mariner Sir Clowdisley Shovell (1650–1707), both for his services against the Barbary corsairs and his unusual—and dreamy—first name.
*Reference:* Penguin.

# SITUADO

Payrolls and subsidies dispatched annually from Mexico and Peru to the less wealthy Spanish American colonies.

The name was derived from the verb *situar,* which in commercial parlance meant to transfer funds. In addition to the silver bullion sent every year to Spain aboard the plate fleets, the exchequer in Madrid had standing orders for lesser payments to be made directly to coastal garrisons throughout the Caribbean Sea and Pacific Ocean.

Usually a warship from the Armada de Barlovento called at Veracruz to convey the Mexican contribution across to Havana, where it was met by the Peruvian shipment being brought by the *galeones.* The appropriate portion was then discounted and distributed amongst that city's officers and men, after which other predetermined amounts were redirected in smaller vessels to the frontline outposts of Saint Augustine and

Pensacola, Florida, while another man o' war conveyed those of Puerto Rico and Santo Domingo. The Armada del Mar del Sur performed a similar function on the Pacific coast of South America, conducting payments from the mint at Lima, Peru, as far south as Chile and as far north as Panama. The Manila galleon which visited Acapulco every year did the same, carrying the Philippine *situado* back on its homeward passage.

Oftentimes these payments became delayed, particularly during the seventeenth century when the Spanish Crown was beset by bankruptcies, so unpaid troops would either desert or riot. For this reason hired vessels were sometimes employed, to hasten shipments when men o' war were not available. Such was the case with the private frigate *Buen Jesús de las Almas* (Good Jesus of the Souls), under Bernardo Ferrer Espejo, which was chartered to convey 46,471 pieces of eight from Havana to Santo Domingo as that island's *situado* for 1675. His vessel was captured by the English rover John Bennett as it approached Hispaniola and—as he held a French commission—Bennett carried his prize into Saint Domingue that April. The Spanish authorities remained highly suspicious of this seizure, noting Bennett only had a small brigantine with 20 men, while Ferrer Espejo's 50-ton frigate held three times that number; this led them to believe the Spanish captain had colluded in the capture.

An even more notorious incident occurred in July 1682, when the 28-gun royal frigate *Princesa* (formerly the French *Dauphine,* or "Princess," and commonly called *Francesa* by the Spaniards) was captured in the Mona Passage by the pirate Laurens de Graaf. The Spanish vessel was bound from Havana under Captain Manuel Delgado to deliver 120,000 pesos in Peruvian silver as the *situados* for Puerto Rico and Santo Domingo, when it was

surprised by De Graaf's *Tigre* off Aguada, Puerto Rico, and 50 of its 250-man crew were killed or wounded in the battle. The triumphant corsair and his crew, most of them French *boucaniers,* continued to Samaná Bay on the northern shores of Hispaniola with their prize, where they allegedly "made 140 shares and shared 700 pieces of eight a man." The Spanish on Santo Domingo became so incensed when they learned of their loss, they retaliated by expropriating a consignment of slaves brought into port that November by Nikolaas van Hoorn, another Dutch adventurer with French ties. He in turn escaped and in February 1683 obtained a letter of reprisal from the French governor of Petit Goâve, leading to a retaliatory raid on Veracruz.

Madrid shortly thereafter altered the *situado* distribution system, and henceforth only Mexican silver was sent to the Caribbean outposts of Cuba, Florida, Santo Domingo, Puerto Rico, Santa Marta, and Cumaná.

**See also** Barlovento, Armada de; Bennett, John; *galeones;* Mar del Sur, Armada del; pieces of eight.

**References:** *C.S.P., Amer. and W.I.,* Vol. XI; López Cantos; Marley, *Pirates* and *Veracruz;* Robles; Sáiz; Torres.

# SKUTT, BENJAMIN
## (FL. 1688-1693)

Barbados settler who petitioned the Crown in mid-June 1693, the fifth year of the War of the League of Augsburg (known in America as King William's War) that

in consequence of the losses of West Indian merchants, he may have a license for his advice boat of 150 tons and 16 guns to sail to and from Barbados, also a commission for her as a private man o' war, and immunity from embargo or press gang.

*Reference:* C.S.P., *Amer. and W.I.,* Vol. XII–XIV.

# SMITH, SAMUEL

## (FL. 1666-1667)

One-time buccaneer who had served with the famous Edward Mansfield.

On 30 June 1666, Major Smith was commissioned by Governor Modyford of Jamaica to reinforce the troops that had recaptured Providencia, or Santa Catalina Island, from the Spaniards. The Spanish in turn swiftly reconquered the island from the English, and Major Smith was carried off in chains to Panama, where he was kept in a dungeon for 17 months.

*See also* Mansfield, Edward; Sánchez Ximénez, José; Whetstone, Thomas.

*References:* Earle, *Panamá;* Gosse, *Who's Who.*

# SOMERS ISLAND

Early English name for Bermuda, sometimes misspelled "Summers Island."

On 25 February 1675 (O.S.), for example, Charles II of England replied to a petition from "the Governor and Company of the City of London for the Plantations of the Somers Islands, alias Bermuda." The origin of this curious name dates from the shipwreck of Sir George Somers's expedition while bound for Virginia.

*References:* Crump; *C.S.P., Amer. and W.I.,* Vol. IX.

# SOUTH SEAS

Term originally applied to the Pacific Ocean by sixteenth-century *conquistadores.*

As the first Spanish explorers and conquerors crossed Central America and Mexico to emerge on the shores of this new body of water, their initial contacts gave them the impression it lay due south of the Gulf of Mexico and Caribbean. Therefore, they referred to their latest discovery as the *Mar del Sur,* or "Southern Sea," to distinguish it from the former two, which were supposed to become collectively known as the *Mar del Norte,* or "Northern Sea." This latter expression never really entered the popular lexicon, although "South Sea" remained in vogue among the Spaniards even after future explorations revealed the Pacific Ocean's true boundaries. Doubtless the presence of the wealthy viceroyalty of Peru due south of Panama did much to perpetuate this name, which then passed into the English language.

# SPANISH MAIN

Northern coasts of present-day Panama, Colombia, and western Venezuela.

This curious name dates from the earliest sixteenth century, when the first explorers ventured beyond the Caribbean isles in search of what they believed to be the nearby Asian continent. By coincidence, the first large land mass they charted contiguously proved to be that of northern South America, which the Spaniards dubbed *Tierra Firme*—the Mainland. Even after further explorations revealed this to be but a portion of a vast new continent, it remained customary to refer to this particular stretch of coastline by its original name. From Spanish, the expression passed into English, soon being shortened to the "Spanish Main" and occasionally misapplied to the waters lying off that coast, rather than the territory itself.

# SPEIRDYKE, BERNARD CLAESEN

## (FL. 1663-1670)

Dutch-born privateer who operated out of Jamaica.

Speirdyke was very popular among his English colleagues, being known affectionately as "Captain Barnard" or "Captain Bart." The earliest known reference to his activities occurred on 19 June 1663, when he set sail from Port Royal for the Orinoco River on the Wild Coast, "with an intent to take St. Thomas's." Evidently he was successful, returning with his ships on 16 March to report that he had plundered the Spanish town of Santo Tomás.

However, Speirdyke is most remembered for the circumstances surrounding his death. In January 1670 he was delegated by Governor Sir Thomas Modyford to carry letters to the Spanish authorities on Cuba, "signifying peace between the two nations" and restoring some Spanish captives to their countrymen. This conciliatory mission was part of Modyford's efforts to restrain the depredations of Jamaican privateers and establish better relations with the local Spaniards. For Speirdyke, it represented an opportunity to profit from the clandestine trade that usually accompanied such a voyage. He quit Port Royal with his *Mary and Jane,* of 6 guns and 18 men, crossing over to Manzanillo, the southeastern Cuban port for the province of Bayamo, where he was at first greeted with some suspicion. The Spaniards searched his vessel three times, "fearing she was a privateer," but once convinced of his sincerity allowed him to sell his goods undisturbed.

The very day he was quitting the bay, Speirdyke saw a ship approaching, which ran up English colors. He brought *Mary and Jane* to and sent two men across in a boat to hear the latest news. As the men were going up the side, they were asked whence their vessel hailed, and upon replying "Jamaica," were taken captive. The stranger was the 14-gun Spanish corsair *San Pedro,* alias the *Fama,* commanded by Manoel Rivero Pardal. He held a commission to attack English vessels and instantly hoisted a Spanish flag and bore down upon Speirdyke. "Defend yourself, dog!" Rivero roared as he closed. "I come as a punishment for heretics!" *Fama* then loosed a broadside, and the battle was joined.

A brisk cannonade ensued until dark, with Speirdyke defending himself well despite being outgunned and outnumbered. The night was clear, so he could not hope to escape, and the following day the Spaniards pressed in to board, having 70 men. Still a staunch resistance was made, in which many of Rivero's men were killed or wounded, before the *Mary and Jane* was carried. Five of the crew lay dead, including Speirdyke himself—that "obstinate, mad heretic," as Rivero called him. The victorious corsair then sent nine prisoners back to Port Royal in their boat, while he sailed the prize to Cartagena, arriving on 23 March 1670. A grand fiesta was held to celebrate his triumph, while outrage gripped Jamaica. The privateers wanted to take revenge for Speirdyke, but Modyford defused the situation. However, he too resented the nature of his emissary's death, and when later that summer Rivero raided Jamaica—posting a notice saying, among other things, "I am he that took Captain Barns [*sic*] and did carry the prize to Cartagena"—the mood was already set for Henry Morgan's retaliatory strike against Panama.

*See also* Rivero Pardal, Manoel.

*References:* Earle, *Panamá;* Gosse, *Who's Who; Interesting Tracts;* Pope.

# SPURRE, GEORGE

## (FL. 1678-1683)

English freebooter who sacked Campeche in 1678, then Veracruz five years later.

Spurre began his West Indian career sometime during the 1670s, obtaining a French privateering commission against the Dutch and Spaniards after England withdrew from the general European hostilities. He must have ignored the many recalls emanating from Jamaica, because by the summer of 1678 he was in command of a corsair frigate with a crew of 105 men off the Cuban coast, accompanied by the sloop of Edward Neville. On 10 April they sighted the Spanish *aviso* or dispatch vessel *Toro* (Bull), Juan de la Requista master, which had departed Havana that day for Veracruz. They intercepted and carried their prize to the Santa Isabel cays, where Spurre burned his frigate and transferred into *Toro*. All the Spaniards were released at Bahía Honda except a coastal pilot whom the buccaneers retained.

Spurre and Neville then crossed the Gulf of Mexico to the Laguna de Términos, capturing the ketch of Alvaro Sánchez en route. The raiders spent the next three weeks in the laguna recruiting additional men for an attempt against Campeche. A Spanish captive reported that they reached 180 men in total

> the majority of them French and English and some Spaniards, among the latter a friar, a mestizo and one who had been a slave at Campeche. Captain Jorge ["de Eslurra," as Spurre's name was confusingly rendered into Spanish] said if he had wished, he could have collected up to 400 men for the sack.

The buccaneers ventured northeastward in their two vessels, towing eight *piraguas*. They circled past Campeche and anchored near Jaina. On the night of 6 July 1678, Neville departed to reconnoiter the port from his sloop. He rejoined the main body at daybreak, reporting that all was calm.

## SACK OF CAMPECHE
### (JULY 1678)

That evening, 160 pirates slipped ashore. The anchor watches left aboard *Toro* and the sloop were instructed to bear down upon Campeche at dawn two days later. If two smoke columns were seen, this would be the signal that the town had been won and they could enter the roads. The landing party meanwhile approached Campeche stealthily from the landward side, capturing every person they met. Some were tortured to reveal the best access to the town, and an Indian named Juan "was tied up and threatened to have his head cut off by a cutlass which the pirate captain showed him," agreeing to lead a nocturnal march that brought the column to a small city gate an hour before daybreak on Sunday, 10 July. The captive also answered the sentinel's challenge, allowing the buccaneers to enter unrecognized in the gloom.

The attackers then advanced swiftly toward the central plaza, ignoring the few early churchgoers attending matins. Once in front of the governor's residence, the column was again challenged by a sentry, but this time "the pirates with a great shout fired a heavy volley." The garrison was taken utterly by surprise, only nine soldiers being on duty instead of the required 60. (The best troops, moreover—mulatto militia—were absent, patrolling the countryside.) The *sargento mayor*, or garrison commander, Gonzalo Borrallo, leapt over his back wall in a nightshirt with his sword, but after being fired at repeatedly "from point blank range" out of the darkness, retreated to his house where he was seized.

Virtually every prominent citizen shared this same fate; the only Spaniards who escaped were the four-man watch aboard Juan Ramírez's frigate. They got this vessel under way and quickly cleared the harbor, which so infuriated the buccaneers they turned on Ramírez—whom they held captive—and savagely hacked him to death, "giving him many sword thrusts and cutting off his nose." Other Spaniards were terrified into raising ransoms, and every building in Campeche was ransacked. The *Toro* and Neville's sloop appeared on schedule, two huts being fired down by the waterfront to signal them to enter. The freebooters remained in possession of the town until the evening of Tuesday, 12 July, when they began to withdraw with their loot. The ship *San Antonio*, a *barco luengo,* and a boat were among the spoils, as well as considerable money and foodstuffs. The raiders also carried off 250 black, mulatto, and Indian townspeople to sell as slaves at the Laguna de Términos.

That autumn, William Beeston wrote in his journal at Port Royal, Jamaica:

18 October 1678 [O.S.].— Arrived Captain Splure [*sic*], who with one Neville about three months since, and 150 men, had taken Campeche, and with him a prize; for all of which he had his pardon, and leave to come in and spend their plunder.

It is possible Spurre briefly settled down to a peaceable existence, as in early 1681 a pink headed northwestward from Jamaica encountered "a lugger commanded by one Captain Spargh [?] with a nine-man crew, who said he had been trading on the Cuban coast." However, if true, Spurre must have soon resumed roving, for in early October 1682, Governor Sir Thomas Lynch reported that an emissary from the Spanish governor of Portobelo "left his *barco luengo* at Tuana, a leeward port 25 leagues from Port Royal and came here in a sloop," because he had been "told that one Spurre, an English pirate with 60 men, was on the coast." The following year, Spurre took part in one of the greatest pirate coups of his era.

## SACK OF VERACRUZ
### (MAY 1683)

Dutch-born Nikolaas van Hoorn obtained a letter of reprisal from the French governor of Saint Domingue, Jacques Nepveu, sieur de Pouançay, in retaliation for the Spaniards having seized a consignment of his slaves at Santo Domingo. Reinforced with *boucaniers* commanded by the "chevalier" de Grammont and Jan Willems, he set sail into the Bay of Honduras to recruit further help from Laurens de Graaf and Michiel Andrieszoon. Spurre and his men were among this freebooter throng, which paused off Yucatán to gather greater strength before descending on the unwary city of Veracruz the night of 17 May 1683.

Just as happened in Spurre's previous assault on Campeche, the Spanish inhabitants were caught sleeping in their beds, resistance crumbling after a few heavy volleys. The city governor, Luis Bartolomé de Córdoba, disappeared in the melee but was found a few days later hiding in the stables, reputedly by Spurre himself, who "with great difficulty saved him from some of the French who had been prisoners there, and ill used." Veracruz was occupied for four days and utterly ransacked before the raiders retreated to a cay off the coast to divide their spoils. The pirates sailed back around the Yucatán peninsula to their rendezvous off Isla Mujeres before dispersing.

When word of this assault reached Port Royal in early August 1683, Lynch learned that among the pirate commanders were "no English, except one Spurre, and Jacob Hall in a small brig from Carolina." Six weeks later the governor gained further information when he interviewed an "Englishman that was in the action," to whom he promised a pardon "if he brings in Spurre's sloop, but I have heard no more of him or the sloop." Apparently the renegade had repaired to French Saint Domingue with the rest of the raiders, so that when Lynch dispatched Royal Navy Captain James Risby to Petit Goâve at the end of September with a list of demands, they included the return of "Spurre's shalloup [sic] as belonging to this island, and the goods aboard Laurens [de Graaf's flagship] that belong to Spurre, as the king claims them." The sloop, at least, seems to have been returned, for there exists an "account of the goods on Spurre's sloop" dated at Jamaica in mid-November 1683, totaling more than £1,000.

*See also* Andrieszoon, Michiel; *aviso; barco luengo;* Beeston, William; Córdoba y Zúñiga, Luis Bartolomé de; De Graaf, Laurens Cornelis Boudewijn; Grammont, "chevalier" de; Hall, Jacob; Laguna de Términos; Lynch, Sir Thomas; Neville, Edward; Pouançay, Jacques Nepveu, sieur de; *sargento mayor;* Van Hoorn, Nikolaas; Willems, Jan.

*References:* C.S.P., Amer. and W.I., Vols. IX and XI; Eugenio; *Interesting Tracts;* Juárez; Pope.

# STANLEY, GEORGE

## (FL. 1683)

Master of the Royal African Company sloop *Africa,* taken by a Spanish privateer while returning from delivering dispatches to Danish Saint Thomas on behalf of Sir William Stapleton, English governor of the Leeward Islands.

According to the report Stapleton submitted to London some months later, dated 30 November 1683 (O.S.), *Africa* had been scurrying back to Nevis "at the close

of the hurricane season" when it encountered the Spaniard between Tortola and Saint John in the Virgin Islands chain. Eyewitnesses later claimed that the Spaniard fired first, although he denied doing so; but even if Stanley had let fly the first round, the governor judged this "no crime, for there are so many rogues upon the sea." Nevertheless, the sloop was taken and carried into San Juan de Puerto Rico, and Stanley was eventually deported to Spain.

*Reference:* C.S.P., Amer. and W.I., Vol. XI.

# STARR, JOHN

## (FL. 1680)

English procurer who "appears to have operated the largest whorehouse" in Port Royal, Jamaica.

According to the official census of 1680, Starr maintained an establishment containing 21 "white women" and 2 "black women."

*Reference:* Pawson, *Port Royal.*

# STATE'S OR STATES' SHIPS

Mid-seventeenth-century expressions for Cromwellian and Dutch vessels, respectively.

Following the execution of King Charles I of England and the introduction of Sir Oliver Cromwell's Protectorate, the honorific term His Majesty's Ship was naturally dispensed with, being substituted by State's Ship. For example, Captain John Wentworth issued a receipt at Port Cagway, Jamaica, on 9 April 1658 (O.S.), "for seven puncheons of cocoa laden on board the State's Ship *Paul,*" which he was to deliver at London. This term also applied to other governmental properties as well, such as the "State's Storehouse at Jamaica," it being the commonly accepted name for the new administration. When Captain William Powell wrote to complain of the deplorable straits the Protectorate's soldiers had been reduced to on Jamaica by October 1656, he declared that

> they have had a very sad dispensation, and have wanted that comfort that the State allowed them. Most of the provisions sent were laid on shore and rotted and spoiled, while many poor souls perished for want.

Dutch warships, on the other hand—but not their private vessels—were referred to by the English as "States' Ships" throughout the seventeenth century, because they sailed under the orders of the United Provinces' mutual government, the *Staten-Generaal* or States-General.

*Reference: C.S.P., Amer. and W.I.,* Vol. IX.

# STEADMAN, CAPTAIN

### (FL. 1666)

English buccaneer who with Captain Robert Searle and a party of only 80 men, took and plundered the Dutch West Indian island of Tobago in 1666 during the Second Anglo-Dutch War.

Later that same year, when France entered the conflict on the side of the Netherlands, Steadman's vessel became becalmed off the island of Guadeloupe and was attacked by a large French frigate. He and his 100-man crew fought bravely for two hours, even attempting to board their larger opponent but were eventually overcome.

*See also* Searle, Robert.
*Reference:* Gosse, *Who's Who.*

# STEPNEY, ROBERT

### (FL. 1683-1684)

English privateer who operated out of Barbados.

Early in February 1684 (23 January 1684 O.S.), Stepney was arrested "on the complaint of Monsieur de Saint Laurens, for attacking a French sloop at sea." Presumably this was the incident referred to by the chevalier in his letter dated 13 November of the previous year at Fort Royal, Martinique, when France and England were officially at peace. In it, he charged

> that one of your armed barks fired several musket shots at the crew of one of our ships at Dominica. She fired first under French and then under English colors, and the master of your bark forced the French crew to give them some men, and a canoe to go and take three Caribs who had come to the shore under the French flag. I demand satisfaction for this misuse and insult to the French flag.

*Reference: C.S.P., Amer. and W.I.,* Vol. XI.

# STRONG, JOHN

### (FL. 1686-1694)

English privateer and treasure salvager who served in both Sir William Phips and Sir John Narborough's fabulously successful dives on a sunken galleon north of Hispaniola.

He launched a similar mission of his own into the South Seas; a fourth and final attempt at La Coruña, Spain, ended with his death—which unwittingly set the stage for Henry Every's mutiny and subsequent venture into piracy.

## PHIPS'S EXPEDITION
### (1686-1687)

On 12 September 1686, Strong set sail from the Downs, England, as first mate aboard Phips's tiny flagship *James and Mary.* Accompanied by the *Henry,* the two vessels proceeded to the Greater Antilles and pretended to trade with the local Spaniards while discreetly searching for the remains of the *Nuestra Señora de la Pura y Limpia Concepción,* a fleet vice-flagship that had been sunk in a storm in 1641 while conveying a vast quantity of Mexican bullion toward Spain. Although unable to salvage the wreck themselves, the Spanish authorities still naturally regarded this treasure as theirs, and kept its half-forgotten resting place a secret.

After a few weeks, however, the English located it on the Ambrosian Bank (present-day Silver Bank, directly north of Santo Domingo). They worked the wreck until 2 May 1687, when Phips set sail for England with more than £200,000 in silver on board. He returned to a hero's welcome that June; a naval guard was placed aboard the *James and Mary* to escort it to its anchorage at Deptford—and prevent any treasure from evading the royal taxes. (More than a year later, Strong and four other officers were arrested for allegedly smuggling £1,200 ashore without paying the requisite duties, although these charges were quickly dropped.)

## NARBOROUGH'S EXPEDITION
### (1687-1688)

Knowing that more silver remained at the site, a second expedition was prepared with Strong now promoted to commander of the *James and Mary.* His position nonetheless remained a junior one, as three larger vessels had been incorporated into the flotilla: Narborough himself headed the group aboard the king's frigate *Foresight,* while Phips commanded the 400-ton

merchantman *Good Luck and a Boy,* and the ship *Princess* had also been added, along with the former *Henry.* The five set sail on 3 September 1687 from the Downs but soon encountered heavy weather. Phips's vessel was damaged and forced back into Plymouth, while Strong lost sight of the others off Cape Finisterre. He nevertheless pressed on to Barbados, where he was eventually joined by Narborough on 16 November.

By the time the expedition finally reached the Silver Bank in mid-December, they found it surrounded by more than four dozen craft that had been working the wreck for months, making away with a further £250,000. The interlopers were driven off, and Narborough's men settled in to resume their work. But the gleanings now proved slender, five months' labor resulting in little silver. Phips sailed away for New England in May, after which Narborough died. His body was buried at sea, and the discouraged expedition weighed for England. Strong evidently returned with these vessels to London in early August 1688, because he was detained shortly thereafter for his alleged fraud.

## SOUTH SEAS EXPEDITION
### (1689-1690)

He was soon released and also weathered the upheavals surrounding the deposition of James II in favor of the Protestant rulers William and Mary (the so-called Glorious Revolution of the winter of 1688–1689). Strong was then able to obtain financial backing for a new, independent salvage operation of his own into the South Pacific. Information had been received "of a rich wreck or two, at or near to Santa Elena not far from the Bay of Puná," off Guayaquil, on Spain's Pacific shores, which Strong proposed locating with the same subterfuge as his mentor Phips—a vessel would be supplied with trade goods to visit this area and conduct clandestine commerce with the local citizens (who were starved for European goods anyway, on account of the Spanish monopoly). This not only might result in handsome profits, but more importantly would disguise the true intent of the voyage, which was to dive on the wrecks. Its timing was further favorable in that England and Spain were now united against France in the War of the League of Augsburg (King William's War).

Consequently, the 270-ton ship *Welfare* was prepared with 40 guns and a crew of 90 men and boys. A cargo of woolen fabrics, "stockings, arms and other ironworks, as hatchets, hoes, etc.," was loaded on board, it being speculated that this merchandise "would bring a return of sixteen hundred per cent." The *Welfare* also carried "bombs and carcasses for our defence, and to work on the wreck, if there should be occasion to blow up rocks." Thus prepared, Strong set sail from the Downs on 22 October 1689, touching at Plymouth, Madeira, and the Falklands before entering the Strait of Magellan on 20 February 1690. It took *Welfare* several tries over a span of three months and 12 days to claw its way into the South Pacific, in "desperate weather," according to Strong's log.

His first contacts with the coastal Spaniards were unpromising, being hostile on account of the numerous corsairs already prowling their shores. *Welfare* struck northward until it reached Puná on 20 August, where Strong had his first friendly meeting with two Spanish merchantmen bound from Guayaquil toward Payta. He learned of the location of the shipwreck, "about eight leagues within ye point of St. Helena, about half a mile from the shore in four fathom water, sandy ground." The vessel had been the flagship of the Armada del Mar del Sur, the 1,200-ton *Jesús María de la Limpia Concepción,* which had gone down the night of 26 October 1654 with "twelve millions of

pieces of eight, besides a great quantity of plate." Supposedly only a small amount had ever been raised by Spanish salvagers, but Strong could not find any trace of the remains when he anchored over the spot on 7 September 1690. The local inhabitants informed him it was 20 years "since they could see her, by reason she is buried in ye sand."

Disappointed, Strong stood away to Juan Fernández Island, where on 21 October he found four English sailors who had been left there three years earlier by "a privateer that were on these seas." (This rescue predated Woodes Rogers's discovery of Alexander Selkirk on this same island by 15 years; Selkirk's rescue provided the inspiration for Daniel Defoe's *Robinson Crusoe.) Welfare* continued down the Chilean coast, suffering 11 men killed when one of Strong's landing parties was slaughtered in the surf by Spanish lancers. His return passage through the straits was completed in a week, after which he headed northward into the Caribbean.

## BARBADOS
### (1691)

In late February of the following year (17 February 1691 O.S.), *Welfare* came to anchor at Bridgetown, capital of Barbados, where Strong quickly secured a contract to transport sugar to London. Twelve days later, however, the governor impressed his vessel "to go look after a [French] privateer which had taken several ships about this island." Strong sortied on 15 March but could not lure this raider close enough to engage nor overtake the swift French craft "which sailed too hard for us." Returning to Bridgetown, he finished his lading and departed at dawn of 15 April, escorting an outward-bound convoy of 18 sail.

Off northwest Ireland, Strong intercepted the Dutch flyboat *Kroonprins Frederik* (Crown Prince Frederick), with Danish papers but a cargo of French wine, as well as the Norwegian vessel *White Lion* "laden with pickled salmon" and other provisions destined for France. He seized both for trading with the enemy and carried them into Tynemouth in late June (14 June 1691 O.S.). *Welfare* had been absent a year-and-a-half, and one of its crew opined at the conclusion to this voyage, "A traverse of near 40,000 miles might have promised more, we for a long time, and to little purpose, conversed with beasts and men." The profits proving modest, Strong's investors failed to recoup their money.

### SPANISH SHIPPING EXPEDITION (1692-1694)

Nevertheless, Strong soon became involved in another project when in January 1692 a consortium formed to dive on other Spanish wrecks. An Irish-born officer named Arturo O'Byrne had been granted such a privilege by Carlos II of Spain, in honor of two decades' service in the Royal Spanish Navy, during which O'Byrne had risen to admiral. Armed with this patent, O'Byrne had sought financial and technical expertise in England, which was allied with Spain against the French. He had come into contact with a wealthy London merchant named Sir James Houblon, who had extensive dealings with the Spanish trade, and promptly organized a group of 68 investors to fund the expedition.

Because of his ample experience in this area, Strong was retained to command the flagship. Preparations proceeded slowly because of problems brought on by the war and an ever-expanding role for the expedition itself: soon it was designated to trade with Spanish America and raid French West Indian outposts in addition to its original salvage operation. By the time the flotilla finally prepared to quit Gravesend in August 1693, Strong had been superseded by Charles Gibson as senior captain. Now a major enterprise, the force consisted of the

46-gun flagship *Charles II* (named after the Spanish king), the frigates *James* and *Dove*, and the pink *Seventh Son*.

However, delays continued to plague its departure, so it was not until early February 1694 that the ships at last arrived in La Coruña, Spain. Strong died there within a few days, depriving the expedition of its salvage expert and spreading unease among the demoralized men. Gibson also lay ill within his cabin, and the crews, after three months of being unpaid, rose up under their first mate Henry Every. *Charles II* was carried out of the harbor the night of 7 May 1694, launching one of the most famous piratical careers.

*See also* Every, Henry; Hispaniola; Mar del Sur, Armada del; Narborough, Sir John; pieces of eight.

***References:*** Baer; Bradley, *Ships; C.S.P., Amer. and W.I.,* Vol. XIII; Dyer, *Strong.*

# SUIGARIZIPI, JEAN

### ALSO SUIGARICIPI (FL. 1689-1694)

Basque sea captain who served as a French privateer in the War of the League of Augsburg (King William's War) and operated out of the fortified harbor of Placentia on the south coast of Newfoundland.

According to the legend on his tombstone, Suigarizipi captured hundreds of English vessels during this conflict, probably mostly mere fishing vessels. However, among this number he also included a first-rate Royal Navy warship, "the one hundred-gun *Princess*," for which he was allegedly decorated by King Louis XIV. Suigarizipi apparently died in a French seaborne assault on the nearby English settlement of Ferryland in 1694, when the defenders took guns from their anchored ships in the harbor and mounted them on Isle aux Bois, beating back Suigarizipi's attack.

**Reference:** Horwood.

# SWAN, CHARLES

## (FL. 1671-1686)

English adventurer who roamed the South Seas.

As a young man, Swan had served under Henry Morgan at the sack of Panama. More than ten years later, he was residing in England when the sensational trial of Bartholomew Sharpe was held, revealing new knowledge about the Spanish Pacific. In particular, Swan met Sharpe's companion Basil Ringrose in London, and after exchanging reminiscences, they decided to raise a peacetime trading expedition to travel around the Horn into South America. Ringrose agreed to invest in this venture and accompany it, so the 16-gun *Cygnet* was soon being furnished with a crew of 60 men and £5,000 worth of merchant traders' goods, weighing on 1 October 1683. A few months later, at the entrance to the Strait of Magellan, they encountered the *Nicholas* of John Eaton, also out of London on a similar mission. However, the latter had been operating with a much more vigorous hand, leaving a trail of destruction down the Brazilian coast and capturing a Portuguese prize, which sank in a storm. Some of Swan's men wanted him to adopt the same policy; when he refused, nine deserted one night "after they saw they could not prevail with me to play the rogue." The two English ships continued around the Horn in company but became separated by bad weather.

On 2 April 1684, *Cygnet* entered the Spanish port of Valdivia, Chile, in an open attempt to establish trade relations, much as Sir John Narborough had done 14 years earlier. At first everything went well, with Swan even warning the Spaniards about the presence of more hostile Englishmen off the coast. But once the initial surprise wore off, the Spanish authorities ruthlessly reimposed their monopoly over trade. Two of Swan's men were killed and others captured while going ashore under flag of truce. ("An ambuscade of between 100 and 200 men came out and fired upon a poor eight of us in the yawl.")

Rebuffed at Valdivia, he wandered northward into the Gulf of Nicoya (off present-day Costa Rica), where on 3 August 1684 he met a small party of buccaneers under Peter Harris. They had sortied from Jamaica on a straightforward freebooter raid, crossing the Isthmus of Panama, sacking the town of Santa María, and defeating a Spanish flotilla off Panama's Pearl Islands. Swan's disgruntled crew now insisted on joining them, and he felt constrained to accede, else he would have been left with "no one to sail the ship." He sold some of his cargo to the buccaneers, retaining only the silks and muslins, and insisted that the *Cygnet*'s owners receive a share in any prize money. Reversing course southward, Swan and Harris reached Isla de la Plata (literally "Silver Island," also referred to as "Drake's Island") on 2 October, where they found the 36-gun *Bachelor's Delight* of Edward Davis.

Together they mustered close to 200 men, and on 20 October sailed for the mainland. Paita was assaulted the morning of 3 November 1684, but nothing much of value was found before the town was put to the torch. The Lobos Islands were visited next, where Swan encouraged his men to sample the local wildlife by "comparing the seal to a roasting pig, boobies to hens, and the penguins to ducks." A second abortive raid followed against Guayaquil in early December, which ended when the pirates' captive Indian guide escaped as they were marching overland. A few prizes were then taken off the coast, but the rovers realized that they were too weak for greater enterprises, so they headed northward for Panama in hopes of meeting other buccaneers crossing the isthmus. At the end of December, off Gallo Island, they captured an *aviso* bound for Callao, and although its correspondence had been flung overboard, some letters were retrieved from the water quickly enough to reveal that the annual plate fleet had arrived at Portobelo on 28 November, which meant that the Peruvian silver ships would have to sail very soon to meet it. On 8 January 1685, the buccaneers intercepted the 90-ton *Santa Rosa* and then repaired to the Pearl Islands to careen.

On 14 February a fresh contingent of 200 French *flibustiers* and 80 English buccaneers, under the command of François Grogniet and Lescuyer, reached the islands in coastal canoes. The *flibustiers* were offered the *Santa Rosa* by Swan and Davis, while the Englishmen were incorporated into *Cygnet* and *Bachelor's Delight*. In appreciation, Grogniet presented the two commanders with blank commissions issued by the French governor of Saint Domingue. Davis accepted, but Swan—vainly striving to maintain some semblance of legality—politely declined with the observation that

> he had an order from the duke of York neither to give offence to the Spaniards, nor to receive any affront from them; and that he had been injured by them at Valdivia, where they had killed some of his men and wounded several more, so that he thought he had a lawful commission of his own to right himself.

Apparently more buccaneers were on their way, so a party was sent to await them in the Gulf of San Miguel. On 3 March they met Captain Francis Townley with 180 men, mostly English, in two captured barks. A few days later, another bark bearing about a

dozen Englishmen entered the Gulf of Panama from the west, having separated from William Knight off the coast of New Spain. And on 11 April, another band of 264 mainly French *flibustiers* arrived across the isthmus under Rose, Pierre le Picard, and Desmarais. Swan a vailed himself of this opportunity to send letters back across the isthmus to his wife and owners, explaining his change of fortunes and beseeching them to intercede with the king

> for as soon as I can I shall deliver myself to the king's justice, and I had rather die than live skulking like a vagabond for fear of death.

On 7 June 1685, a fleet of six Spanish men o' war suddenly emerged from a morning shower off Pacheca Island and caught the pirates unprepared. An indecisive, long-range engagement ensued, with the lightly armed buccaneer craft unwilling to close with the mightier vessels of the Armada del Mar del Sur, who in turn could not overtake such nimble opponents. Nevertheless, the next day ended with a Spanish victory when the pirates were driven off. The buccaneers fell out among themselves, with Davis, Swan, Townley, and Knight sailing northwestward as a single group, raiding Realejo and León (Nicaragua) in early August 1685, for little gain. After maintaining a fruitless blockade of the Mexican coast until March 1686, Swan concluded that he would rather head across the Pacific for the East Indies. After making a few more minor captures in the Philippines, he died—possibly in an arranged accident—at Mindanao.

***See also*** *aviso;* careen; Davis, Edward; Eaton, John; Grogniet, Capitaine; Harris, Peter (fl. 1684–1686); Knight, William; Lescuyer, Capitaine; Mar del Sur, Armada del; Narborough, Sir John; Picard, Pierre le;

Ringrose, Basil; Rose, Jean; Sharpe, Bartholomew; South Seas.

**References:** Bradley, *Lure; C.S.P., Amer. and W.I.,* Vol. XII; Dampier.

# SWAYNE, PETER

## (FL. 1660)

Petty rover confined in Fort Cromwell prison at Port Royal, Jamaica, in late January 1660.

Swayne was charged with piracy because upon

meeting with a shaloupe [*sic*] at sea belonging to Hines of the island of Barbados, [Swayne] did feloniously rob and plunder the same, and has disposed and converted the goods thereout taken to his own use.

Weblinge, the garrison provost marshal, had been ordered "to take the body of the said Peter Swayne into your custody and him safely keep in the tower, until he shall be released or condemned by law." What that eventual verdict was is not known.

**Reference:** Pawson, *Port Royal.*

# TAVERNS

"The Dream is better than the Drink, which only feeds the sickly fire," wrote the English diplomat and poet Matthew Prior (1664–1721).

Some of the better-known taverns that dotted Port Royal, Jamaica, prior to its destruction in the great earthquake of June 1692 were the Black Dog, Blue Anchor, Cat and Fiddle, Cheshire Cheese, Feathers, Green Dragon, Jamaica Arms, King's Arms, The Salutaçon (Salutation), The Ship, Sign of Bacchus, Sign of the Mermaid, Sign of the George, Sugar Loaf, Three Crowns, Three Mariners, Three Tunns, and Windmill.

**Reference:** Pawson, *Port Royal.*

# TENNANT, MATTHEW

### (FL. 1682-1684)

Royal Navy officer who hunted pirates out of Jamaica.

Tennant was first heard from in late 1682, when the French pirate Jean Hamlin and a band of 120 "desperate rogues" seized the frigate *Trompeuse* (Trickster) in the Bay of Honduras, then cruised eastward to intercept merchantmen bound for Port Royal. They ensconced themselves at Ile-à-Vache, on the southwestern arm of French Hispaniola, and the Jamaican governor, Sir Thomas Lynch, began issuing privateering commissions to bring in *Trompeuse.* None was able to find the renegade until the last day of 1682 (21 December O.S.), when a merchant named Spencer reported having been looted by the pirates, whom he had left careening at "Jaqueene" (perhaps present-day Jacmel, Haiti).

That same day Tennant returned to Port Royal from Santiago de Cuba with HMS *Guernsey* and was immediately ordered to sail against Hamlin. He cleared a few days

later and beat to windward, so that on the morning of 25 January 1683, *Guernsey* stemmed the entrance, spotting the pirate frigate anchored inside. But the weather grew so calm that the man o' war could not close with Hamlin "for want of oars"; and when a wind finally did spring up, it quickly blew into such a gale that the freshly cleaned *Trompeuse* easily outdistanced Tennant, for "the pirate sailed three feet to his one." *Guernsey* returned to Jamaica in early February (24 January 1683 O.S.) to report on this failure and was angrily ordered by Lynch to return to the area, where the rovers were still making captures.

Tennant instead requested permission to have his ship careened, for without greater speed he could not hope to overtake *Trompeuse.* Lynch testily agreed, sending

about twenty carpenters on board him and plenty of seamen, and so got her careened in twenty days, which was more than ever was done before in this harbor. I gave him twenty more men and a month's provision, hired a satee to wait on him, and [on 15 February 1683 O.S.] he sailed with my positive orders not to stir from the coast till the pirate was gone or destroyed.

By the time *Guernsey* beat back to Saint Domingue, Hamlin had long since disappeared toward Danish Saint Thomas.

Frustrated, Tennant continued eastward and took on fresh provisions at Puerto Rico before patrolling past the Virgin Islands toward the Spanish Main without catching sight of Hamlin. Although he prowled the West Indies for three months, he never had the good fortune to meet any pirates. On 3 September 1683 he "redeemed eight English captives at Santa Marta, who were condemned to die that day," carrying them back to Port Royal.

At the end of that year, Tennant was promoted to command of the 540-ton HMS *Ruby* and sailed to Cartagena as escort for the slave *asiento* ships. Off that Spanish port he met the triumphant pirate flotilla of Laurens de Graaf who, along with Jan Willems and Michiel Andrieszoon, had captured a trio of warships sent out to fight them. Tennant paused to visit with the victors and later reported to Lynch "that Yankey showed him a commission from the [French] governor of Petit Goâve," which was apparently his authorization for committing these hostilities.

Tennant himself soon became embroiled in a dispute between the two rival Spanish slaving companies at Cartagena when he took delivery of 2,000 doubloons from one of them aboard the *Ruby* lying outside the port. This money had been illegally extracted, but Tennant refused to hand it back over when the local authorities discovered the truth and complained. Instead, he carried it with him when the *Ruby* returned to Port Royal on 13 February 1684, escorting the Spanish slaver *Santo Tomás* with 300 blacks on board. Governor Lynch said he had "been cruelly enraged with Captain Tennant for his behavior," (which the governor felt might jeopardize the growing trade relations with the Spaniards) and ordered him to deliver the money "which he had received from one Santiago de Castillo, forthwith to Captain Hender Molesworth." Tennant grudgingly complied, and Lynch was sufficiently mollified to take no further action against the captain, "for he promises amendment and I was unwilling to ruin a young man who is sailor enough."

*See also* Andrieszoon, Michiel; *asiento;* careen; De Graaf, Laurens Cornelis Boudewijn; doubloon; Hamlin, Jean; Hispaniola; Lynch, Sir Thomas; Spanish Main; Willems, Jan.

*Reference: C.S.P., Amer. and W.I.,* Vol. XI.

# Tew, Thomas

## (FL. 1684-1695)

Hard-bitten sea rover originally born in Newport, Rhode Island.

After long service in the West Indies, Tew became famous for a single spectacular raid into the Red Sea, which established a precedent that many other freebooters—such as Henry Every and Captain William Kidd—attempted to emulate.

Little is known about Tew's early career, except that he was apparently the son of a seaman and cousin to Henry Tew, who much later rose to become a lieutenant colonel and deputy governor of Rhode Island. Around 1684, Thomas Tew lived on Jamaica, where over the years he had gained considerable experience as a corsair. In December 1692, he purchased a privateering commission from Lieutenant Governor Isaac Richier of Bermuda to operate against the French (England then being involved against that country in the War of the League of Augsburg, or "King William's War," as it was known in the American colonies). Armed with this permit, Tew bought a partial share and obtained command of the 70-ton sloop *Amity* of eight guns, which the previous year had been serving at Barbados under Captain Richard Gilbert.

### FIRST RED SEA EXPEDITION (1693)

Tew recruited a crew of perhaps 60 seasoned veterans and set out from Bermuda in January 1693, accompanied by the privateer sloop of Captain George Dew. Ostensibly, both vessels were bound for an attack against the French slaving factory of Gorée in West Africa, but a few days out into the Atlantic, Dew's sloop sprang its mast in a storm and the two became separated. Now alone, Tew assembled his ship's company and proposed that they choose another destination farther afield, in the unprotected Far East,

> a course which should lead them to ease and plenty, in which they might pass the rest of their days. That one bold push would do their business, and they might return home, not only without danger, but even with reputation. The crew finding he expected their resolution, cried out, one and all: "A gold chain, or a wooden leg, we'll stand by you!"

Despite the impropriety of venturing against neutral shipping, Tew and his men altered their course so as to round the Cape of Good Hope and head into the Indian Ocean.

After several weeks' fruitless search, Tew intercepted an immensely wealthy merchant vessel belonging to the Great Mogul of India, which was making for the Arab ports in the Red Sea. His heavily armed privateersmen subdued the Indian troops it carried in a one-sided fusillade, suffering not a single loss. Tew then carried his prize to St. Mary's, a tiny island off the Madagascar coast, to divide the spoils and careen his ship. By December 1693 all was ready, and the *Amity* once again set sail for the New World.

Traversing the Atlantic, Tew deliberately bypassed Bermuda in favor of his home port of Newport, Rhode Island, where the *Amity* arrived in April 1694, having logged more than 22,000 miles on its epic 15-month cruise. The local citizenry was dazzled by this exploit, and the exotic plunder brought in—gold, silver, jewelry, elephants' tusks, ivory, spices, and silk—the whole valued at more than £100,000. Tew's seamen received shares ranging from £1,200 to an astonishing £3,000 apiece, and the formerly inconsequential captain now found himself a rich man. He was accorded a hero's welcome by the townspeople, although less so by honest John Easton, the Quaker

governor. When Tew approached him about obtaining a new privateering commission, Easton asked where he intended to use it. "Where perhaps the commission might never be seen or heard of," Tew replied darkly and offered to buy one for the astounding sum of £500; but the good Quaker refused.

Tew then traveled to New York with his family, where they were entertained by the much more pliable royal governor, Colonel Benjamin Fletcher. He later described Tew as "what they call a very pleasant man; so that at some times when the labors of my day were over, it was some divertissement as well as information to me, to hear him talk." But their relationship truly flourished on account of corrupt transactions, which included the purchase of a privateering commission on 18 November 1694 for £300. Meanwhile, Mrs. Tew and her two daughters attended gala functions at the governor's mansion, dressed in rich silks with glittering diamonds from the Orient, and Fletcher openly bestowed a gold watch on her husband.

Tew also took some pains to write to *Amity*'s majority owners on Bermuda, alleging he had not been able to return there because the sloop had sprung a mast, forcing him to pass by, although having "for two weeks beat unsuccessfully against head winds" in a vain attempt to arrive. He further bought their cooperation by sending them a large payment, reputedly equivalent to 14 times their original investment in *Amity*.

## SECOND RED SEA EXPEDITION (1694)

Returning to Newport, Tew began to prepare his sloop for another cruise. When news of this development spread, there was great commotion throughout the colony, with "servants from most places of the country running from their masters, sons from their parents," in the hopes of signing on with Tew. Some lads even snuck aboard *Amity,* trying to sail as stowaways.

By the end of November 1694 Tew was ready and got under way. He again worked his way around the tip of Africa and into the Red Sea. However, when another of the Great Mogul's treasure ships was finally encountered in September 1695, the results were very different; for in "the engagement a shot carried away the rim of Tew's belly, who held his bowels in his hands for some space. When he dropped, it struck such terror to his men that they suffered themselves to be taken without further resistance."

*See also* Dew, George; Every, Henry; Kidd, William.

**References:** Botting; Chapin; *C.S.P., Amer. and W.I.,* Vol. XIV; Gosse, *Who's Who.*

# THURSTON, HUMPHREY

## (FL. 1670–1672)

English privateer who participated in the sack of Panama and then turned rogue afterward.

Thurston was apparently a Jamaican privateer, who during the brief cessation of hostilities against the Spaniards in summer 1669 was reduced to finding a more peaceable employment. A year later he was about to sail as master of the 50-ton merchant sloop *Port Royal,* bound into the Laguna de Términos for a cargo of logwood. The sloop's owner, Dr. George Holmes, had no interest in privateering, but Thurston was caught up in the warlike preparations being made at Jamaica that summer to retaliate against the nuisance raids of the Spanish corsair Manoel Rivero Pardal. Consequently, Thurston brought *Port Royal's* strength up to an impressive

12 guns and 55 men before departing, much more than would be required on a logging expedition, and then captured an 8-gun, 50-ton Spanish vessel shortly after putting out to sea. He transferred into this vessel and renamed it *Thomas,* installing his mate James Delliatt as commander of *Port Royal,* for which he raised an additional 55 men.

Without returning to Port Royal, both sloops proceeded directly to Tortuga Island and so were among the first to incorporate themselves into the freebooter fleet Henry Morgan was organizing for his campaign against the Spaniards. *Thomas* and *Port Royal* sailed as part of this force against Providencia Island and Chagres, the latter vessel being one of four that crashed on the reefs astern of Morgan's *Satisfaction* while entering the roads. Perhaps because of this loss, Thurston refused to return to Jamaica following the sack of Panama in early 1671, preferring to continue roving with the French *flibustiers* of Saint Domingue. His owner, Dr. Holmes, demanded £300 compensation for his ship from the booty brought in by Morgan, pointing out such payments were authorized by the raiders' own charter party, and the admiral himself had received £1,000 for the wreck of *Satisfaction.* This was apparently paid after the doctor appealed his case to the Council of Jamaica.

Thurston continued to prey upon Spanish shipping and carry his prizes into Tortuga, so that by 1672 he was one of the few remaining privateers—along with the mulatto corsair Diego Grillo and Dutch-born Jelles de Lecat—who were still regarded as renegades by the new Jamaican Governor, Sir Thomas Lynch.

*See also Charte-Partie;* Laguna de Términos; logwood; Grillo, Diego; Lecat, Jelles de; Lynch, Sir Thomas; Morgan, Sir Henry; Rivero Pardal, Manoel.

**References:** Gosse, *Who's Who;* Pope.

# TOWERS, CAPTAIN

## (FL. 1684)

Dutch corsair mentioned in a letter of Governor Sir Thomas Lynch of Jamaica, dated 20 June 1684 (O.S.): "Two or three pirate [ships] have lately been taken, one Towers, a Dutchman, of 30 or 40 guns." Perhaps "Touwers" or "Turen" was meant.

**Reference:** *C.S.P., Amer. and W.I.,* Vol. XI.

# TOWNLEY, FRANCIS

## (FL. 1685-1686)

English buccaneer who raided the Spaniards in the South Seas.

Townley was first heard from at the beginning of 1685, when he led a party of 115 mostly English freebooters from Golden Island across the Isthmus of Panama into the Pacific Ocean to join the flotilla of Edward Davis and Charles Swan that had already penetrated those waters. A larger group of French *flibustiers* had set out later than Townley to do the same, under Capitaines François Grogniet and Lescuyer, but who nonetheless came up with Davis and Swan first. Grogniet therefore sent a boat back into the Gulf of San Miguel to await the others, which met Townley on 3 March 1685, now with a total of 180–190 men and two captured Spanish barks. Townley incorporated these vessels—manned with 110 and 80 buccaneers respectively—into the formidable array of pirate craft that then gathered under Davis's orders to blockade Panama and hopefully intercept the Peruvian treasure fleet.

Toward noon on 7 June 1685, the rovers were caught off guard near Pacheca Island by a squadron of six Spanish men o' war and a tender from the Armada del Mar del Sur. These bore down upon the pirates, and an indecisive, long-range engagement ensued, mostly involving Davis and Swan, whose vessels were the only ones among the buccaneer flotilla mounting cannon. Next day the freebooters were driven off, abandoning their blockade and falling out among themselves, each national group blaming the other for this defeat.

Another failed attack followed at the beginning of July against the coastal town of Remedios (Panama), and afterward both contingents headed northwestward as separate groups. The English under Davis, William Knight, Swan, and Townley raided both Realejo and León (Nicaragua) during the first two weeks of August 1685 but were disappointed at the spoils. Consequently, they too split up, Swan and Townley proceeding further northwest to sweep the coast of Mexico and await the Manila galleon, while Davis, Peter Harris, and Knight returned to attack Peru.

Swan and Townley made numerous disembarkations along the coast of New Spain, eventually reaching as high as the Gulf of California but missing the Philippine galleon *Santa Rosa* that December. Early next year they decided to part company, Swan remaining to set sail later across the Pacific with his *Cygnet,* while Townley immediately began working his way back down the Central American coastline. It was presumably Townsley's flotilla was spotted by the Spaniards near Acapulco in mid-February 1686, "burning one of their ships to redistribute the people around the four which remained, and setting our prisoners on land." By 23 March he was opposite Esparta (Costa Rica), where he encountered Grogniet's larger French formation. Despite some residual ill will between the two groups, English and French combined for a joint attempt against the inland city of Granada (Nicaragua). Grogniet and Townley landed a force of 345 men on the coast on 7 April and fought their way into the city three days later. Little loot was found, however, as the Spaniards had been forewarned of their approach and transferred their valuables across the inland lake to Zapatera Island, and so the pirates withdrew empty-handed five days later. They endured numerous ambushes before passing Masaya and regaining their anchored ships, after which they then traveled to Realejo.

Grogniet having had such limited success on his own, half his 300 French followers voted on 9 June 1686 to join Townley, who was determined to press southeastward for Panama. The remaining 148 *flibustiers* stayed with Grogniet while he sailed westward, and the two contingents parted company a fortnight later. Thus heavily reinforced, Townley made a sudden descent on the outskirts of Panama on 22 July, seizing merchandise estimated to be worth 1,500,000 pesos, but which was subsequently lost in a Spanish counterambush. Nonetheless, the raiders made off with 15,000 pesos in silver and 300 captives, which Townley used to extort a truce. After two captives' heads were sent to the President of the Audiencia of Panama, the latter reluctantly agreed to supply the pirates with cattle, sheep, and flour on a daily basis. Meanwhile, Townley was threatening to send another 50 heads ashore if the five buccaneers that were in Spanish hands were not released.

On 22 August 1686, after a month of this uneasy arrangement, the Spaniards attempted a surprise attack by slipping a force of three ships and 240 men from the island of Perico to fall upon the raiders. This assault was fiercely beaten off, two of the Spanish ships being captured and only 65 Spaniards escaping injury or death. A furious Townley, himself wounded in the battle, sent 20 more heads ashore as a protest against this violation of the truce. "This measure was in truth a little violent," the pirate chronicler Ravenau de Lussan piously noted, "but it was the only

means of bringing the Spanish to reason." Indeed, the Spanish promptly delivered an additional 10,000 pesos to Townley on 4 September, along with a conciliatory note from the archbishop of Panama saying all English prisoners would henceforth be considered Catholics and so enjoy the protection of the Church. But Townley did not savor this victory for long, as four days later he died of his wounds. His body was cast overboard, as he had wished, near Otoque Island and he was succeeded in command by George Hutt.

*See also* Golden Island; Grogniet, Capitaine; Lescuyer, Capitaine; Lussan, Ravenau de; Mar del Sur, Armada del; South Seas; Swan, Charles.

*References:* Bradley, *Lure; C.S.P., Amer. and W.I.,* Vol. XII; Dampier; *Interesting Tracts;* Lussan; Robles.

# TRISTAN, CAPITAINE
## (FL. 1681-1693)

French *flibustier* who settled on Jamaica.

Tristan was first mentioned on 24 May 1681 (O.S.), when his *barco luengo* was being careened at La Sound's Key among the San Blas Islands, "about three leagues from the mouth of the river Concepción" on the northeastern coast of Panama. While lying at anchor there, he was approached by native canoes bearing John Cooke's party (among them William Dampier and Edward Davis) who were returning from John Coxon's raid into the South Seas. These men bought beads, knives, scissors, and mirrors from Tristan's crew to repay their Indian guides and would have given more "but could not get any, the privateer having no more toys." Tristan then weighed two days later to rejoin a large raiding party he had been operating with, which had earlier shifted to nearby

Springer's Key, "about seven or eight leagues from La Sound's Key." These included Captains Coxon, Archaimbaud, Thomas Paine, Jean Rose, Tucker, Jan Willems, Williams, and George Wright, who were sailing under commissions issued by the French governor of Saint Domingue.

Tristan transferred Cooke's survivors into Archaimbaud's crew, and the buccaneer commanders decided to make a descent on the Central American coast, for which they hoisted anchor to gain San Andrés Island and steal boats to serve as landing craft. But a gale scattered the formation, and as they were struggling to regroup, a large Spanish *armadilla* appeared from Cartagena to chase the rovers away. Tristan, "having fallen to leeward," was making for Bocas del Toro (literally "bull's mouths" or "entrances of the bull") on the northwestern coast of Panama, when he sighted these vessels and assumed they were his corsair comrades. Instead, the Spanish warships fired upon Tristan when he approached "and chased him, but he rowed and towed," and so got away. Nonetheless, Coxon's flotilla dispersed, and Tristan was not heard of again until next year.

In May or June 1682, he arrived off Ile-à-Vache, at the southwestern tip of Hispaniola, homeward bound into Petit Goâve. Cooke's South Sea survivors were also there, now serving aboard Jan Willems's ship, and had just captured a Spanish vessel. Cooke and his men fitted this prize out as their own, despite having no commission, but according to Dampier, the French, "begrudging the English such a vessel, all joined together, plundered the English of their ships, goods and arms, and turned them ashore." Tristan then incorporated eight or ten of the Englishmen—including Cooke and Davis—into his own crew, before completing his voyage to Petit Goâve. He soon regretted this decision, for shortly after Tristan and the bulk of his French crew had gone ashore upon arriving, the English rose

and made off with his vessel, returning to Ile-à-Vache to rescue their companions.

Sometime during the ensuing decade of the 1680s, Tristan emigrated to settle on the English island of Jamaica, possibly because he was a Huguenot, or French Protestant, and like thousands of others felt constrained to flee following the revocation of the Edict of Nantes in 1685. Whatever the cause for his exile, when the War of the League of Augsburg (King William's War) erupted against France a few years later, he was considered a loyal English subject. Toward the end of 1692 he sailed with a 14-man crew on a smuggling voyage to the Spanish Main, presumably trusting to the alliance existing with that nation. But on 26 January 1693, the Marqués de los Vélez, President of the Audiencia of Panama, wrote to the Council of Jamaica:

Ever since peace was made between the two Crowns of Spain and England I have endeavored to preserve it, never doubting that the government of Jamaica would do the like. But recently a sloop has come from Jamaica manned by Frenchmen under Captain Tristan, with merchandise to trade on these coasts. I am surprised that you should have permitted this breach of the treaty. These men though bidden by the Lieutenant General of Portobelo to come to him would not do so, and he, understanding that they were French, seized the ship. The men resisted and were all killed. I cannot omit to point out to you the danger to which the arrival of such vessels, especially manned with Frenchmen, exposes me.

The new Jamaican governor, Sir William Beeston, replied toward the end of March:

What [Tristan's] business was on the coast, I know not, but he and all his men were British subjects, and therefore even if they were trading [illegally] I conceive that the utmost required by the Articles of Peace is the seizure of themselves and the condemnation of their goods. But to cut them all off in cold blood on pretence of friendship (you must pardon me for saying it) was sanguinary, and contrary to the good agreement between the two Crowns.

This protest prompted a somewhat different tone when the marqués next wrote:

I confess that Captain Tristan's business has troubled me much, for I have always endeavored that English vessels should have good passage in these harbors, and have given orders accordingly. Frenchmen have too often been allowed to come and prosecute unlawful trade, under pretence of being English. I was lying very sick when I first heard of the matter, and my grief over the deceit of these men went near to cause my death. I have put the guilty parties in close confinement with a view to proper punishment. But do not doubt that the vessel was lawfully seized, for most of her people were French and her captain known to be one of the greatest pirates in America. Had he been brought in alive, I should have punished him.

*See also* Cooke, John; Coxon, John; Dampier, William.
*References:* C.S.P., Amer. and W.I., Vol.XIV; Dampier; Gosse, Who's Who.

# TRYER, MATTHEW

## (FL. 1699)

A Carolina privateer accused and acquitted on a charge of having captured a sloop belonging to Samuel Salters of Bermuda in 1699.

*Reference:* Gosse, Who's Who.

# TUCKER, CAPITAINE

## (FL. 1680-1681)

Despite his name, a French *flibustier* from Saint Domingue.

Tucker apparently came out from France with the Marquis de Maintenon toward the end of 1680, when the latter had been granted exclusive privilege for four years to deal with Spanish America. Tucker carried this information into Petit Goâve, from where Governor Jacques Nepveu, sieur de Pouançay, in turn dispatched him to warn Captains John Coxon, Jean Rose, Jan Willems, and others who were already operating with French commissions off the Spanish Main. Tucker set sail with a vessel of 6 guns and 70 men and came up with these rovers off the northeastern shores of Panama.

In the first days of June 1681, English and French buccaneers held a series of conferences at Springer's Key in the San Blas island chain, during which William Dampier noted:

The French seemed very forward to go [attack] any [Spanish] town that the English could or would propose, because the Governor of Petit Goâve (from whom the privateers take commissions) had recommended a gentleman lately come from France to be general of the expedition, and sent word by Captain Tucker, with whom this gentleman came, that they should if possible make an attempt on some town before he returned again. The English when they were in company with the French seemed to approve of what the French said, but never looked on that general to be fit for the service in hand.

Eventually the corsair leaders decided to make a descent on the Central American coast, for which they weighed and made toward San Andrés Island, hoping to steal boats that they could use as landing craft. But a gale scattered the formation, and as they were struggling to regroup, a large Spanish *armadilla* appeared from Cartagena to further disperse the flotilla. Only Captains Archaimbaud, Tucker, and George Wright reached San Andrés Island, and after waiting there vainly for ten days, proceeded to Bluefields Bay on the Mosquito Coast to search for their consorts. Still not finding them, Archaimbaud and Tucker left Wright, making instead for Bocas del Toro (literally "bull's mouths" or "entrances of the bull") on the northwestern coast of Panama.

*See also* Coxon, John; Dampier, William; Maintenon, marquis de; Rose, Jean; Spanish Main; Willems, Jan.

*Reference:* Dampier.

# TURTLE

Along with wild cattle, which were hunted by the *boucaniers,* turtle was the other great source of meat for those living in or traveling through the West Indies during the seventeenth century.

In a letter written at Jamaica in late November 1684, Acting Governor Hender Molesworth declared that turtle meat "is what masters of ships chiefly feed their men in port, and I believe that nearly 2,000 people, black and white, feed on it daily at [Palisadoes] Point, to say nothing of what is sent inland." Aside from the fact that these creatures were plentiful and easily caught throughout the Caribbean, they could also be kept alive in a ship's hold, thus ensuring freshness in an era when smoking, salting, or pickling were the sole means of preservation. Because of the extent of this turtle hunting, numerous places still bear this name today, usually in its Spanish or French variants: the Dry Tortugas off the Florida Keys, Ile de la Tortue north of Haiti, Green Turtle Cay in the Bahamas, Isla La Tortuga off Venezuela, Tortuguero in Costa Rica, etc.

*Reference: C.S.P., Amer. and W.I.,* Vol. XI.

# UPDIKE, DANIEL

### ALSO UPDYCK OR UPDICK
### (FL. 1692)

English captain named as having been issued a privateering commission by the Council of Jamaica on 12 February 1692 (O.S.).

*Reference: C.S.P., Amer. and W.I.,* Vol. XIII.

# URABURRU, TOMÁS

### (FL. 1683)

Cuban corsair who helped drive the English out of the Bahamas.

In May 1683, Uraburru and Gaspar de Acosta led a party of 200 corsairs on a second major assault against the ravaged English settlements of the Bahamas, attacking the capital of Charles Town (New Providence) with a single *piragua* and the coast guard galliot *Nuestra Señora del Rosario.* The English, under Governor Robert Lilburne, had already endured several lesser invasions, following the devastating opening assault of January of that year. Uraburru and Acosta's operation effectively cleared the islands of Englishmen for the next two-and-a-half years.

*See also* Acosta, Gaspar de; Lilburne, Robert.

*References:* Craton, *Bahamas;* Sáiz.

# URCA

Spanish term for any large cargo ship or store ship.

# VAN DE VELD, ANDRIES

## (FL. 1683)

One of a trio of privateers, along with Dennis Dey and Laurens Westerband, commissioned in late 1683 by Sir William Stapleton, governor of the English Leeward Islands, "to look after pirates."

They were sent out specifically to hunt the English renegade George Bond, and learning that he had recently bought a Dutch ship at Saint Thomas in the Virgin Islands, they went there and seized it, over the objections of the Danish governor Adolf Esmit. The privateers then sailed this ship into Nevis.

*See also* Bond, George; Dey, Dennis; Westerband, Laurens.

*Reference: C.S.P., Amer. and W.I.,* Vol. XI.

# VAN HOORN, NIKOLAAS

## (FL. 1681-1683)

Dutch-born slaver and smuggler who became the prime mover behind the sack of Veracruz.

Little is known about Van Hoorn's early career, there being a somewhat garbled account in both French- and Spanish-language editions of Exquemelin that he served aboard French privateers against his compatriots in the North Sea during the Franco–Dutch War of 1672–1680. Whatever the case, Van Hoorn certainly moved easily among the French once he reached the West Indies, a Spanish eyewitness describing him as "Dutch, although he passes himself off as French." There is a legend that he once narrowly escaped detention by Admiral comte d'Estrées, presumably because of illegal activities.

In October 1681, Van Hoorn left London, England, in command of the merchantman *Mary and Martha* of 400 tons, 40 guns, and a crew of 150 men, "fifty of them English." He was supposedly bound on a trading run to Cadiz, Spain, accompanied by a smaller vessel of 160 tons, 12 guns, and 23 men owned by the governor of Dover Castle, Colonel Stroude, and captained by one John Mayne. During this brief crossing, Van Hoorn was forced by heavy weather into a French port in the Bay of Biscay, where 25 of his men, "seeing what a rogue he was," deserted. He then touched at La Coruña before reaching Cadiz, where further complications arose: Apparently the two vessels had hoped to surreptitiously obtain licenses to trade in Spanish America, but these were not forthcoming. Van Hoorn therefore put 36 seamen ashore without pay, flogged another to death, and then resorted to even more drastic expedients.

He abandoned two of his merchant representatives ashore, stole four brass *pedreros,* or swivel guns, from the Spanish defenses one night, and the next morning sailed away with the *Mary and Martha.* He landed at the Canary Islands to rustle goats before continuing to Cape Verde, where another five of his crew deserted. Van Hoorn reached the Guinea coast about March 1682 and began trading his powder and guns for gold, "having no other cargo." He chanced upon a Dutch ship near El Mina and, through plundering it and scavenging from others, succeeded in acquiring about 100 slaves. He then led an armed party ashore "with great guns" to join a tribal war and obtain blacks by force, returning 28 days later with 600 slaves. Such forays, as well as his earlier trading with powder and guns and robbing fellow slavers, were measures normally shunned by other captains.

Van Hoorn then visited the Portuguese station of Sao Tomé, stealing a cannon and two more blacks before running across the

Atlantic to the French colony of Cayenne. He renamed his ship *St. Nicholas* and disposed of some of his slaves as well as six more disgruntled English crew members before proceeding to Trinidad. He only had about 300 slaves left (many others having died) when he was contracted to deliver the remainder to the Spanish island of Santo Domingo. Van Hoorn arrived there in late November 1682 but, instead of being allowed to sell his captives, found his ship and most of its contents impounded on orders of the local governor, Francisco de Segura Sandoval y Castilla. Spurious charges were laid against him, but the real reason for his detention appears to have been revenge for Laurens de Graaf's recent capture of that island's *situados*, or payrolls. Although entirely innocent in that affair, Van Hoorn made a convenient scapegoat.

When the Spanish governor discovered that Van Hoorn had also stolen four swivels from Cadiz, he made him hand them over, and kept him confined aboard ship beneath the guns of the harbor fort. The English privateer Captain George Johnson saw the *St. Nicholas* lying there when he visited Santo Domingo in pursuit of the pirate Jean Hamlin but was prevented from speaking to Van Hoorn by Governor de Segura. When Van Hoorn complained to the Spaniards of being cheated, he was contemptuously advised to go collect from De Graaf. Finally, with only 20 crew members and 50 or 60 slaves left, Van Hoorn escaped one night in early 1683, outsailing the customs boat sent out in pursuit. He then laid out a course for Petit Goâve, the *flibustier* capital on the French half of the island.

Immediately upon his arrival, he lodged a complaint with Governor Jacques Nepveu, sieur de Pouançay, demanding his assistance to exact restitution from the Spaniards. The French official issued a letter of reprisal authorizing Van Hoorn to win compensation in the time-honored fashion, and put him in touch with the self-styled "chevalier" de Grammont, greatest of *flibustier* commanders, who became Van Hoorn's lieutenant and helped man the depleted *St. Nicholas*. Coming at a time when France and Spain were nominally at peace, Van Hoorn's license proved a godsend to idle freebooters such as Grammont. Hard-pressed for money as always, the "Chevalier" seized upon the offer with alacrity, even asking Van Hoorn to set out in the corvette *Colbert* to recall his flotilla from the Cuban coast. Just as this vessel was exiting Petit Goâve, Grammont's cohorts reappeared, bringing in a Spanish prize. Together, they then cleared—more than 300 strong—for Roatan on the Central American coast to seek further reinforcements.

Van Hoorn and Grammont paused outside Port Royal on 27 February 1683 to deliver letters from Governor de Pouançay, assuring the Jamaican authorities that no hostilities were contemplated against the English. Governor Sir Thomas Lynch sent out his French secretary, Charles de La Barré, to visit the *St. Nicholas*. He found Van Hoorn "so vain that he showed him a number of bags which he judged to hold six or eight thousand pieces of eight." High-strung and unsure of himself, Van Hoorn tried to impress the visitor with his importance; instead Barré came away with the impression that the French were beginning to "abhor him for his insolence and passion" and might well replace him with the much more popular and experienced Grammont, "who is an honest old privateer." Van Hoorn claimed to be on a pirate-hunting expedition, but the secretary was not deceived and noted that the *St. Nicholas* was provisioned for six months and traveling to leeward, neither of which would have been consonant with such a venture. From deckhands, Barré also learned of the vessel's English origins and illegal seizure, which he studiously ignored.

The *St. Nicholas* bore away to westward, and a few days later met the privateer Captain John Coxon, who was beating back to Jamaica after a fruitless search for the pirate Hamlin. Van Hoorn and Grammont were much more candid with their fellow corsair, telling him that they were "trying to unite all the privateers for an attack on Veracruz." Parting company, they proceeded into the Bay of Honduras, where both De Graaf and his Dutch lieutenant Michiel Andrieszoon were reputed to be, along with a group of freebooters. While Van Hoorn and Grammont prowled the bay, they spotted two Spanish merchantmen lying at anchor, the *Nuestra Señora de Consolación* and *Nuestra Señora de Regla,* which they promptly seized. Little did they realize that De Graaf had been patiently careening his flagship *Dauphine (Princess,* also known by its previous Spanish nickname of *Francesa)* at nearby Bonaco Island, waiting for the Spaniards to bring their profits back aboard these empty ships from the great commercial fair in Guatemala.

Annoyed at this clumsy intrusion into his plans, De Graaf made away for Roatan, where he was soon overtaken by the *St. Nicholas* with its two prizes. On 7 April 1683, a huge gathering met on the beach to hear Van Hoorn describe his ill treatment at the hands of the Spaniards, read out the letter of reprisal granted him by Governor de Pouançay, and ask for their help in exacting vengeance. The buccaneers were all eager, and despite some initial misgivings (and personal animosity from De Graaf), the plan to assault Veracruz was quickly endorsed. But with the inclusion of De Graaf, Van Hoorn's position became even more awkward: He, a rank amateur with a small following, was supposedly commanding two hard-bitten campaigners with large, loyal contingents.

At first things went splendidly, with De Graaf leading the pirate fleet to Guanaja

Island for more men, then swiftly around the Yucatán peninsula into the Gulf of Mexico. Thirteen vessels comprised the expedition, with perhaps 1,300 or 1,400 freebooters. De Graaf cunningly reconnoitered the port, then slipped a landing party of 800 men into Veracruz during the night of 17 May 1683. The following dawn they attacked, Grammont commanding the critical column that snuffed out Spanish resistance in the city center. Van Hoorn, a baton as "pirate general" in his hand, received the initial sweep of booty in the Plaza Mayor, then installed himself in Governor Luis Bartolomé de Córdoba y Zúñiga's vacated quarters in the palace.

Much treasure still remained hidden, though, and it fell to Van Hoorn to extort it from the Spanish captives while De Graaf and Grammont saw to the city's defenses. Late on the afternoon of 18 May, Van Hoorn sent four pirates to bring the royal accountant José de Murueta Otalora into his presence and demanded of him in passable Spanish, "Where were the many millions there had to be in such a large city, because all he had been able to find thus far did not come to fifty thousand pesos?" The prisoner insisted that there had been no time to hide much of anything and stuck by this story even when beaten. The next morning, however, De Graaf and Grammont orchestrated an ugly mob scene that terrified the captives into revealing many hidden riches, netting 80,000 pesos and establishing ransoms for all the city's leading personages. Once this ordeal was ended, Van Hoorn invited two captive Spanish merchants to lunch with him in the palace, bragging of his role in the expedition; but by then, it was becoming increasingly obvious who the real leaders were.

Three days later, De Graaf ordered a withdrawal to nearby Sacrificios Island, and an immense column of 4,000 ladened captives was marched out of the devastated city under the direction of Grammont. Once offshore with their hostages, the pirates were beyond the reach of any Spanish rescue attempts. They settled down to divide their booty and await the arrival of ransoms out of Mexico's interior. The ransoms were being deliberately delayed by the Crown authorities, so after waiting almost a week, Van Hoorn decided to act unilaterally.

He informed his Spanish contacts on the mainland that he was about to send them a dozen captives' heads and seemed ready to put this barbarous scheme into effect when a hastily summoned De Graaf arrived from his flagship. According to Spanish eyewitnesses, the pirate admiral confronted Van Hoorn on the beach and reproved him that "it was not right to behead any surrendered men who had been granted quarter." Furious at being balked, Van Hoorn drew his blade and advanced upon his countryman—which proved a grievous mistake, for the enormous De Graaf promptly drove his own sword deep into Van Hoorn's wrist, then kicked his disabled opponent into the sand. His wrath now fully aroused, De Graaf bellowed at his men to haul his bloodied opponent aboard his flagship and clap him in irons, thus ending any talk of beheading Spanish captives.

Van Hoorn's jealous resentment would seem to lie behind this intemperate outburst, which then took a fatal twist when the wound became infected a few days later. As the engorged pirate fleet slowly beat back around the Yucatán peninsula, Van Hoorn's life ebbed away. He died off Isla Mujeres on 24 June 1683, and his body was rowed ashore and buried in an unmarked grave near Mexico's Cape Logrete, where it presumably lies to this day. Grammont assumed command of the *St. Nicholas,* which he sailed back to Saint Domingue. In a final footnote, Governor Lynch of Jamaica noted a year later, "Van Hoorn's son is dead at Petit Goâve, so the French have divided what he leaves."

*See also* Andrieszoon, Michiel; Córdoba y Zúñiga, Luis Bartolomé de; Coxon, John; De Graaf, Laurens Cornelis Boudewijn; Estrées, Jean, comte d'; Exquemelin, Alexandre Olivier; Grammont, "chevalier" de; Hamlin, Jean; Johnson, George; *pedrero;* pieces of eight; Pouançay, Jacques Nepveu, sieur de.

*References:* *C.S.P., Amer. and W.I.,* Vol.XI; Exquemelin; Juárez; Marley, *Veracruz.*

# VAN KLIJN, MOZES
## (FL. 1668)

Dutch freebooter who served under French colors.

Van Klijn appeared as confederate to the *flibustier* chieftain Jean-David Nau, alias "l'Olonnais," materializing off the north coast of Honduras in 1668 among a force of half a dozen vessels and 700 buccaneers. This expedition had originally been raised at Tortuga and Bayahá (Santo Domingo) for an attempt to ascend the San Juan River into the Lago de Nicaragua and assault Granada, but after cruising southern Cuba as far west as the Gulf of Batabanó, had been unable to clear Cape Gracias a Dios on its southerly leg. Instead, Nau l'Olonnais and his consorts were obliged to veer westward along Honduras, sending foragers up the Aguán River and eventually reaching Puerto Cabellos. Here they captured a Spanish merchantman armed with 24 cannon and 16 *pedreros,* or swivel–guns, of which Van Klijn received command.

The town was also occupied, and Nau l'Olonnais decided to use it as a base to march inland to San Pedro Sula, the nearest city, with 300 *flibustiers.* Van Klijn was left to garrison the tiny port with the remaining buccaneers, and during Nau l'Olonnais's absence cruised the coast and captured some Indian fishermen, from whom it was learned a wealthy galleon was due to arrive soon from Spain "at the Guatemala river" (Bay of Amatique). When Nau l'Olonnais's contingent returned from the interior, the whole flotilla proceeded farther into the Gulf of Honduras, where a pair of lookout boats was posted on the southern shore while the rest crossed to the western side to conceal themselves and careen.

Three months elapsed until word was finally received that the galleon had arrived. Reuniting his scattered forces, Nau l'Olonnais quickly attacked, although the Spaniard had 42 cannon and 130 men. His own 28-gun flagship and Van Klijn's smaller vessel were beaten off, but four boatloads of *flibustiers* carried the galleon by boarding. Its booty proved disappointing, however, as most of the cargo had already been unloaded and there only remained some iron, paper, and wine. Discouraged, Van Klijn decided to quit this company, "setting his course for Tortuga, where he intended to cruise [perhaps the Salt Tortuga off Venezuela, or Dry Tortuga off Florida]."

*See also* Nau l'Olonnais, Jean-David.

*References:* Exquemelin; Gosse, *Who's Who.*

# VAUGHAN, JOHN, THIRD EARL OF CARBERRY

## (1640-1713)

Fifth governor of Jamaica, who sought to restrain its privateers.

Vaughan was born in Wales and most probably educated at home during the closing stages of the English Civil War. His father had been a prominent cavalier general but made his peace with Oliver Cromwell's new Protectorate once Charles I had been executed. Vaughan studied at Oxford, matriculating from Christ Church on 23 July 1656 (O.S.) and being admitted to the Inner Temple as a barrister two years later. Following the restoration of Charles II, Vaughan was knighted and elected Member of Parliament for the borough of Carmarthen in 1661, succeeding to the honorary title Lord Vaughan when his older brother Francis died six years later.

Vaughan was a particularly servile courtier to the king and also interested in literature, having become a patron to John Dryden from as early as 1664 and contributing some prefatory verse to that poet's "Conquest of Granada" in 1670–1672. In a wholly different vein, the young nobleman became a notorious libertine as well, being described by the diarist Samuel Pepys as "one of the lewdest fellows of the age"—no mean feat, in Restoration London.

In April 1674, at the conclusion of the Third Anglo-Dutch War, Vaughan was appointed to be the new governor of Jamaica when the earl of Carlisle turned down the post. Henry Morgan was to be his lieutenant governor (having been restored to favor after a brief detention following the sack of Panama), and although Vaughan objected to this, he was eventually overruled. By December of that year both men were preparing to depart the Downs, Vaughan (whose wife had recently died) aboard HMS *Foresight,* of 40 guns and 522 tons, while Morgan would be travelling on the smaller hired ship *Jamaica Merchant.* Distrustful of what his deputy might do if arriving first, Vaughan ordered Morgan "to keep me in company and in no case be separated from me but by stress of weather." *Foresight* weighed and departed before *Jamaica Merchant,* but nonetheless when Vaughan entered Port Royal on 15 March 1675 (O.S.), he found Morgan had beaten him by ten days despite being shipwrecked.

## GOVERNOR OF JAMAICA
### (1675-1678)

Vaughan immediately relieved Sir Thomas Lynch and on 3 April (O.S.) issued a proclamation offering amnesty to all Jamaica's privateers if they returned and renounced roving. This effort proved ineffectual, running directly counter to the fact that although England remained at peace, France was at war with both Holland and Spain, and all three belligerents were willing to grant commissions to any corsair. Vaughan therefore was annoyed to see Jamaican privateers such as William Barnes, John Bennett, John Coxon, William Crane, John Deane, Edward Neville, George Spurre, and George Wright continue their depredations under foreign flags, resulting in doubts as to England's neutrality.

Aware that virtually all his predecessors had also suffered in some degree from their inability to control the privateers, Vaughan was particularly disillusioned at Morgan's lack of influence, which he had assumed would overawe the rovers. When this did not occur, he became convinced that his deputy was conniving behind his back with these renegades and wrote to London that "Sir Henry, contrary to his duty and trust, endeavors to set up privateering, and has obstructed all my designs and purposes as to those who do use that curse of life."

This false accusation caused a bitter rift with Morgan, yet did nothing to alleviate the governor's problem. Moreover, Vaughan was soon feuding with Jamaica's assembly and council as well, whom he convened as seldom as possible so as to avoid being importuned by their demands. Finally, in spring 1677, he was compelled to do so, needing to pass a money bill, but which they refused to do until other business had been discussed, leaving a frustrated Vaughan without funds to run his administration. Relations worsened when he condemned the rover James Browne for plundering a

Dutch slaver under French commission, despite that individual's plea that he was exempt under the assembly's "Act of Privateers." When this was brought to that body's attention, the Speaker, William Beeston, requested a stay; Vaughan refused, at which the assembly drew up a writ of *habeas corpus,* directing the execution be delayed and the island's provost marshal produce Browne "notwithstanding any warrant issued." Angry, Vaughan ordered Browne's immediate hanging as soon as he learned the writ was on its way, and then dissolved the assembly after a bitter reproof on 26 July 1677 (O.S.).

That same day a ship arrived from London with the rumor that "the Earl of Carlisle was coming Governor to Jamaica." This was confirmed later that autumn, and after passing the minimum amount of legislation required with the reconvened assembly—one of his last acts was to cut Morgan's salary from £600 to £300 a year—Vaughan concentrated exclusively on his personal affairs. He had used his position to acquire 7,737 acres of land during his tenure, all in the parish of Saint Mary, which made him the island's largest landholder. On 11 March 1678 (O.S.), he assembled the surprised council and informed them that rather than wait for his successor, he intended to depart forthwith, leaving the administration to his lieutenant governor. Three days later Vaughan went aboard Captain Nurse's ship and sailed for England.

## LATER CAREER
### (1678-1713)

He returned to London a wealthy man and never again entered public service. He built a fine new home (Gough House) at Chelsea and distinguished himself as a member of the Kit-Cat Club. Dryden marked his patron's reappearance that August by dedicating the play *The Kind Keeper, or Mr. Limberham* to him, even though this was prohibited after only three representations as being too indecent for the stage.

In 1686, Vaughan succeeded as third Earl of Carberry when his father died and became President of the Royal Society. This title became extinct at his death in 1713, as he only left a daughter, despite having married three times.

*See also* Beeston, Sir William; Browne, James; Lynch, Sir Thomas; Morgan, Sir Henry.

*References: C.S.P., Amer. and West Indies,* Vols. IX–X; *Interesting Tracts;* Pope.

# VEALE, CAPTAIN

On 1 July 1685 (O.S.), he arrived at New London in a sloop but was compelled to hurry away after he was recognized as a pirate by one of the crew of a ship he had previously taken in Virginia.

*Reference:* Gosse, *Who's Who.*

# VENTURA SARRA, JUAN

## (FL. 1670)

Minor Catalan privateer who arrived in Mexico via Tierra Firme and Guatemala, and who in late August 1670 petitioned the viceroy of New Spain for a privateering commission against the enemies of the Crown "in service of God our Lord, the king, and common utility of the commerce of Indies."

Despite asking to retain the entire value of any prizes taken (including the king's fifth), Ventura Sarra's request was initially approved. When Madrid signed a new American peace accord with England in February 1672, his request was voided.

# VERCOUE, CAPITAINE

## (FL. 1693-1694)

French *flibustier* mentioned in the chronicle of Jean-Baptiste Labat as having traveled out from La Rochelle to Martinique aboard the *flûte Loire* at the end of 1693.

*See also* Labat, Jean-Baptiste.

*Reference:* Labat.

# VESPRE, CAPITAINE

## (FL. 1694)

French *flibustier* who in 1684 was listed as commanding the tiny boat *Postillion,* of 2 guns and 25 men, at Saint Domingue.

*References:* Gosse, *Who's Who;* Juárez; Lugo.

# VIGNERON, CAPITAINE

## (FL. 1684-1687)

French *flibustier* who operated out of Saint Domingue.

In 1684, Vigneron was listed as commanding the bark *Louise,* of 4 guns and 30 men. The following January, he was with Andrieszoon and Willems when he met the smaller vessels of Captains Jean Rose, Vigneron, La Garde, and an English trader off the South American coast, who were lying in ambush for a Spanish *patache* called the *Margarita* rumored to be about to pass. Joining forces, they sighted a ship the night of 17 January, which the following morning they challenged. Rose opened fire, but in the growing light, Andrieszoon then recognized the vessel as the 14-gun Spanish prize captured by Laurens de Graaf the year before and realized they were engaging their commander.

This exchange being halted, next day the formation headed toward Curaçao. At two o'clock that afternoon, while within sight of Bonaire, they sighted a Flemish ship out of La Guaira, which they chased and captured that evening. On 20 January 1685, De Graaf and his consorts anchored off Curaçao, departing four days later. On the 27 January they stood over toward Cape de la Vela (Venezuela), although Vigneron parted company during this passage, as he wished to return to Saint Domingue because, only having "20 men on board, they were not prepared for war."

More than a year and a half later, Vigneron was the officer on the watch overlooking the harbor at Petit Goâve when the Cuban corsair Blas Miguel made his attack. At first light on 10 August 1687, Vigneron beheld a large *piragua* gliding into the roads and challenged it with the cry: *"D'ou est ce canot?"* (Where is that boat from?) A French captive called Saint Antoine, whom the Spanish raiders held aboard, was made to reply, *"Saint Antoine, qui vient de Léogane."* (Saint Antoine, coming from Léogane.) But when the suspicious Vigneron hailed a second time, the prisoner bravely shouted out across the waves, *"Aux armes! Aux armes!"* (To arms! To arms!), thus altering the defenses. Miguel stormed ashore and caused considerable damage before being defeated and executed the following day.

**See also** Andrieszoon, Michiel; La Garde, Capitaine; Lussan, Ravenau de; Miguel, Blas; *patache;* Rose, Jean; Willems, Jan.

**References:** Gosse, *Who's Who;* Lugo; Lussan.

# VIGOT, GUILLAUME

## (FL. 1684)

French rover captured off the Cuban coast by Spanish *guardacostas.*

Vigot departed France in January 1684, bound for the West Indian island of Martinique. His 130-ton ship *Concorde,* of 12 guns and 43 men, was taken off the south coast of Cuba a few months later. Apparently, Vigot's ship was preparing to embark on a privateer campaign because of the renewed hostilities against Spain. Its captors later related that the ship was armed with "39 blunderbusses, four carbines, 12 cutlasses" and a ton-and-a-half of gunpowder.

**See also** *guardacostas.*
**Reference:** Juárez.

# VONCK, MAERTEN JANSSE

## (FL. 1673-1674)

Dutch privateer captain, originally from Middelburg in Zeeland, who operated out of Suriname during the Third Anglo-Dutch War; in a bizarre twist of events he came to be abandoned aboard Commodore Cornelis Evertsen's flagship by his own crew, then carried off to take part in the reconquest of New York.

On 20 April 1673, Vonck returned to Suriname's capital of Paramaribo to resupply, having been blockading the English island of Barbados with his ship *Goude Poort* (Golden Gate). As he worked his way up the treacherous channel, he passed the recently arrived Zeeland squadron of Commodore Evertsen, gingerly picking its way back out to sea. Eleven days later when Vonck exited, he again encountered the men o' war anchored outside, taking on the last of their water. He paused briefly to visit with his fellow countrymen before proceeding toward his station.

Two-and-a-half weeks later, on 18 May, Vonck sighted Evertsen's force approaching

Barbados and once more went aboard the flagship *Swaenenburgh*. This time, however, the commodore questioned him closely about two soldiers who had deserted from the naval force and allegedly found service with the privateer. Vonck at first denied this, then under pressure admitted it might be true. A search party was sent over to *Goude Poort* but could not find the missing men "as they had hidden themselves among the kaper's crew." Now angry, Evertsen threatened Vonck, who sent a note across to his mate ordering that the deserters be surrendered. With tensions at a breaking point, the crew of *Goude Poort* suddenly rushed Evertsen's emissary, who jumped back into his boat, leaving four oarsmen on board. The privateersmen then "made as much sail as possible," swiftly outdistancing the heavier men o' war.

Thus, Vonck came to be left aboard Evertsen's flagship and took part in the remainder of the Zeelander's campaign. By the time New Netherland (present-day New York, New Jersey, and Delaware) was reconquered that autumn, the privateer captain had so vindicated himself that Evertsen put him in command of the second ship bearing messages home. Vonck set sail from New York on 2 September 1673 with the prize *Expectation,* a very poor sailer that was dismasted in a storm and ran aground near Nantucket. It was found there on 3 November by the Boston privateer Thomas Dotson, who boarded, captured, and refloated it, sailing it away as his prize. Vonck was exchanged, and on New Year's Day 1674, he again quit New Netherland, this time commanding the ketch *Hope.* He succeeded in reaching Holland by the beginning of March and forwarded his messages to The Hague, where they were received the day before the final peace treaty with England was ratified.

*See also* Dotson, Thomas; Evertsen de Jongste, Cornelis; *kaper.*

*Reference:* Shomette, *Raid*.

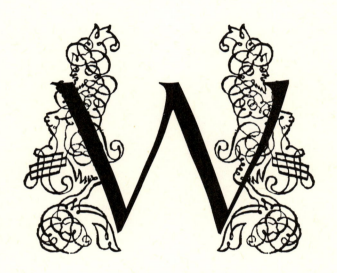

# WADE, CAPTAIN

## (FL. 1660)

English privateer mentioned in the journal of Colonel Edward D'Oyley, governor of Jamaica, as having been issued a "let pass" for his ship *Sea Horse* on 4 April 1660 (O.S.).

*See also* D'Oyley, Edward.

*References:* Pawson, *Port Royal.*

# WAFER, LIONEL

## (C. 1660-C. 1705)

Buccaneer surgeon and chronicler.

As a boy, Wafer apparently lived in the Scottish Highlands as well as Ireland, because he knew a bit of Gaelic. He first went to sea as a young surgeon's assistant or "loblolly boy" aboard the English East Indiaman *Great Ann* in 1677, traveling to Bantam in the Far East. Upon his return to England aboard the *Bombay* in 1679, he shipped out in a similar capacity aboard the 300-ton ship *John* of Captain Buckingham. Reaching Jamaica, Wafer remained on that island visiting his brother (who was employed at Governor Sir Thomas Modyford's "Angels" plantation), while the *John* crossed to Mexico's Laguna de Términos in an attempt to poach logwood, only to be captured by the Spaniards. Wafer then established a surgery in Port Royal but after four months shipped out with privateer Captain Edmond Cooke.

They sailed to Golden Island and there met the flotilla of John Coxon, which was about to assault Portobelo. After sacking this place, the pirates returned to Golden Island and crossed over the Isthmus of Panama, capturing a succession of Spanish vessels in the South Seas. Cooke was deposed, and Wafer remained under the overall command of Bartholomew Sharpe, prowling the Pacific coast, until a faction under John Cooke quit his company in April 1681. Wafer was among this latter group, which included William Dampier, and recrossed the isthmus toward the Caribbean. As they were traveling through the jungle with their Darien Indian guides on 15 May, Wafer

> was sitting on the ground near one of our men, who was drying off gunpowder in a silver plate; but not managing it as he should, it blew up and scorched my knee to that degree, that the bone was left bare, the flesh being torn away, and my thigh burnt for a great way above it.

Badly injured, Wafer was forced to fall out five days later and remain among the Indians. As his wound worsened,

> the Indians undertook to cure me, and applied to my knee some herbs which they first chewed in their mouths to the consistency of a paste, and putting it on a plantain [banana] leaf, laid it upon the sore. This proved so effectual, that in about 20 days' use of this poultice, which they applied fresh every day, I was perfectly cured.

For several months Wafer and some companions lived among the natives until early September 1681, when they reached the northern coast and heard guns fired out at sea.

Investigating, they spotted an English sloop and Spanish tartan lying off La Sounds' Key and went aboard from an Indian canoe. The tartan proved to be a captured vessel under the command of John Cooke. Wafer's companions were recognized and welcomed aboard, but he himself was dressed in native garb, so

> I sat awhile cringing upon my hams among the Indians, after their fashion,

painted as they were and all naked but only one about the waist, and with my nose-piece hanging over my mouth. I was willing to try if they would know me in this disguise, and 'twas the better part of an hour before one of the crew, looking more narrowly upon me, cried out: "Here's our doctor!"

Reunited with Dampier and his comrades, Wafer cruised the Spanish Main under Captains George Wright and Jan Willems until late April 1682, when the latter sailed for French Saint Domingue.

Cooke and Wafer were among Willems's contingent, which fell out with their commander over a prize near Ile-à-Vache, and the English faction was marooned. But Capitaine Tristan took eight or ten of them—including Cooke, Edward Davis, and Wafer—on board as part of his crew and carried them toward Petit Goâve. They repaid his kindness by running off with the ship when he and most of his men went ashore, returning to Ile-à-Vache to rescue their English companions. Cooke's band then seized a ship recently arrived from France with wines and another French ship "of good force," which they renamed *Revenge* and decided to use for a foray into the South Seas. They sailed these vessels to Virginia, disposed of their prize goods, reunited with Dampier, Ringrose, and other shipmates, then ventured to West Africa. Here they seized a 36-gun Danish ship, renaming it *Bachelor's Delight* and rounding the Horn to cruise the Pacific.

When Cooke died, Wafer remained under his successor, Davis, setting out southward from Realejo with three other vessels on 27 August 1685 (O.S.). They visited the "Gulf of Amapala" (present-day Golfo de Fonseca in Honduras) and the Galápagos Islands before raiding the Peruvian coast with Captain William Knight

in July 1686. The latter parted from them after careening at the Juan Fernández Islands, "making the best of his way round Tierra del Fuego to the West Indies," while Davis returned to Mocha Island around Christmas 1686. He and Wafer continued on that coast for another year before rounding the Horn themselves.

After touching at the River Plate, they passed Brazil and met a Barbados sloop commanded by Edwin Carter. He informed them of James II's "proclamation to pardon and call in the buccaneers" (probably of 22 May 1687 O.S.), and therefore sailed with Carter's sloop to Philadelphia, where they arrived in May 1688. Wafer remained there briefly before transferring to Virginia with Davis and other rovers, "but meeting with some troubles after a three years' [sic; two years'] residence there, I came home for England in the year 1690." In fact, Wafer had been arrested on suspicion of piracy immediately upon reaching Virginia in June 1688 and was deported aboard the *Effingham* to stand trial in England. Although eventually cleared, he was forced to cede part of his booty in March 1693 toward establishing the College of William and Mary in Virginia.

Three years later, Wafer was consulted by the Scottish investors contemplating the establishment of a Darien colony, and in 1697 by the Commissioners of Trade in London, also as to the feasibility of such a project. In the summer of 1698, Wafer was secretly smuggled to Edinburgh and pumped for information by the Scots before their own expedition departed, receiving a paltry £20 for his troubles. The following year, he published his *A New Voyage and Description of the Isthmus of Panama* in London, dying in 1705.

***See also*** Buckingham, Captain; Cooke, Edmond; Cooke, John; Coxon, John; Dampier, William; Davis, Edward; Golden Island; Knight, William; Laguna de Términos;

logwood; maroon; Ringrose, Basil; Sharpe, Bartholomew; South Seas; Spanish Main; Tristan, Capitaine; Willems, Jan; Wright, George.

**References:** Prebble; Shomette, *Chesapeake;* Wafer.

# WAGGONER

Seventeenth-century English term for any sea atlas or book combining charts and sailing instructions.

This expression is a corruption of Lucas Janszoon Waghenaer, a famous Dutch cartographer who in 1584 published the first such printed atlas systematically assembled in one volume. Generally known as the *Spiegel der Zeevaerdt,* it was translated into English four years later as *The Mariner's Mirror.* Such works soon became known in England as "waggoners," a noteworthy example being the *South Sea Waggoner,* based upon captured Spanish charts from the South Seas, that was compiled by the buccaneer Basil Ringrose in 1682.

**See also** Ringrose, Basil; South Seas.
**Reference:** Howse.

# WANTON, WILLIAM
## (1670-c. 1732)

Massachusetts seaman who supposedly fitted out ships on two different occasions to help defend New England against enemy blockaders.

Born at Scituate, Massachusetts, in 1670, Wanton was the third son of a Quaker shipbuilder named Edward Wanton. When he married the Presbyterian or Congregationalist Ruth Bryant in June 1691, family opposition drove the couple "to the Church of England and to the Devil

together," as Wanton later expressed it. They settled at Newport, Rhode Island, where Wanton became a successful merchant, sea captain, and shipbuilder.

In 1694, during the War of the League of Augsburg (King William's War), a large French vessel (allegedly of 300 tons and 20 cannon) appeared off the harbor mouth, establishing a blockade "between Block Island and Point Judith." Wanton and his younger brother John prepared a 30-ton unarmed sloop and went aboard with 30 of their friends, most hiding below decks. They stood out of port as if bound on a cruise and were soon intercepted by the French ship, which fired a round across their bow. Immediately Wanton "lowered the peak of the mainsail and luffed up" toward the enemy, as if in surrender. But rather than bring his sloop directly alongside as was customary, he drove it under the startled Frenchman's stern and grappled, further wedging the rudder. His friends then poured up on deck, and a firefight ensued until the enemy struck.

Three years later, at the very end of this same war, the two brothers allegedly captured another French ship using much the same trick. This time they sortied aboard two sloops and encountered their enemy off Holmes' Hole. While the younger John engaged the Frenchman from a distance, William again drove under his stern and wedged the rudder. The prize supposedly proved "very valuable, as she had the choicest spoils from the prizes she had taken, and the Wantons were greatly enriched." When the two brothers visited England in 1702, they were granted an addition to their coat of arms by Queen Anne; each was also presented with two pieces of plate—a silver punch bowl and salver—with their mottos inscribed in Latin.

In 1732, William Wanton became governor of Rhode Island.

**Reference:** Chapin.

# WATERS, SAMSON

## (FL. 1680s)

Minor Massachusetts privateer who was sent out in "Richard Pattershall's brigantine" in 1685 in a vain attempt to find the pirates Veale and Graham.

*See also* Veale, Captain.
*Reference:* Chapin.

# WEATHERBOURNE, FRANCIS

## (FL. 1671-1672)

English privateer who turned renegade after Henry Morgan's sack of Panama and who refused to give up roving even though the arrival of a new Jamaican governor, Sir Thomas Lynch, had heralded a reversal in Crown policy regarding Spain. When William Beeston was given command of HMS *Assistance,* 40 guns, in December 1671 and sent out to bring in rogue privateers, Weatherbourne became one of his captures. He was seized near Campeche for committing "great violence against the Spaniards," along with his ship *Charity* (which was described as having "been formerly Captain David Martyn's [sic; Martien's] man o' war.") Carried back into Port Royal, Weatherbourne was tried for piracy and condemned to death but then deported to England aboard HMS *Welcome,* 36 guns, the same vessel which was to transport Morgan as a prisoner to the Tower of London. This frigate set sail from Jamaica on 6 April 1672 (O.S.) and reached Spithead three months later.

*See also* Beeston, William.
*References: Interesting Tracts;* Pawson, *Port Royal;* Pope.

# WEATHERHILL, JAMES

## (FL. 1693-1694)

English privateer originally from Antigua, who commanded the Jamaican sloop *Charles,* with which he reputedly captured a Spanish merchantman of great value despite that country's alliance with England during the War of the League of Augsburg (King William's War). Several of the crew were killed and others reputedly "inhumanly abused."

*Reference:* Chapin.

# WENTWORTH, JOHN

## (FL. 1653-1665)

English privateer who operated out of Bermuda and captured Tortola at the beginning of the Second Anglo-Dutch War.

Wentworth was mentioned as a member of the Governor's Council of Bermuda for 1653 and 1655, representing the parish of Paget. Early in 1657 he commanded the frigate-galley *Martin,* and in October captained the man o' war *Paul,* which carried many new settlers to Jamaica. In late January 1665, he was in command of the small frigate *Charles,* which sailed from Montserrat with a Portuguese commission originally issued to Captain Robert Downeman. Wentworth used this to hunt Spanish vessels off Caracas until late June, when he proceeded to the island of "Salt Tortugas" [Venezuela] to careen. While doing so, he learned that war had broken out between England and Holland back in Europe. He laid in a course for the Windward Isles, hoping to secure an English commission against the Dutch.

The winds proved contrary, and on 13 July 1665 he was forced to round the west end of Saint Croix; two days later, he was anchored at St. Annes in the Virgin Islands. Although not yet legally licensed, Wentworth decided to attack the nearby Dutch settlement of Tortola, which one of his crew knew well. He later wrote that he hoped "the national war might bear out my doing so," and on the morning of 18 July landed 36 men who surprised the Dutch garrison of 130 men and seven guns and secured the island unopposed. The next day Wentworth raised the English flag, and roughly half the inhabitants swore fealty to Charles II. Later that same day, the brigantine *Hazewind* (Greyhound), belonging to the Dutch governor Willem Houten, came in and was seized.

On 24 July, Houten and his retinue were sent away in a bark, and Lieutenant Thomas Bicknell (or Bignoll) was appointed as commandant in his place. Four days afterward, *Charles* sailed for Bermuda, carrying 67 black slaves and *Hazewind* as prizes. It took Wentworth eight days to reach his destination, where he justified his actions by arguing that he had news there was "an open and national war betwixt His Majesty and the United States of Holland." After a lengthy inquiry, his capture was adjudged illegal and the slaves forfeit to England's Royal African Company. Wentworth was not actually issued a Bermudan commission until 21 October 1665.

*Reference:* Chapin.

# WESTERBAND, LAURENS

## (FL. 1683)

One of a trio of privateers, along with Dennis Dey and Andries van de Veld, commissioned in late 1683 by Sir William Stapleton, governor of the English Leeward Islands, "to look after pirates."

These were sent out specifically to hunt the English renegade George Bond, and learning that he had recently bought a Dutch ship at Saint Thomas in the Virgin Islands, went there and seized it, over the objections of the Danish governor Adolf Esmit. The privateers then sailed this ship back to Nevis.

***See also*** Bond, George; Dey, Dennis; Van de Veld, Andries.

***Reference:*** *C.S.P., Amer. and W.I.,* Vol. XI.

# WHETSTONE, THOMAS

## (FL. 1660-1667)

Nephew to Oliver Cromwell, although Whetstone himself remained a Royalist. He got heavily into debt in the heady days immediately following the restoration of Charles II in 1660 and was clapped into Marshalsea prison. He was eventually released by the king, receiving £100 to settle with his creditors before emigrating to the New World.

In the West Indies, Whetstone promptly became a privateer, whom Christopher Myngs met off the Cuban coast in October 1662 on his way to raid Santiago de Cuba. Whetstone's ship was sighted at anchor in the lee of a cay, where Myngs's force joined him. Myngs learned that Whetstone had been operating off that coast for some time (although without a commission), with a largely Indian crew. Whetstone was able to furnish Myngs with recent intelligence at a conference held aboard the flagship HMS *Centurion* and then took part in the successful English attack on that Cuban port a few days later.

In 1663, Whetstone's name was listed under "private ships of war belonging to Jamaica," commanding a seven-gun Spanish prize with a crew of 60. He afterward became Speaker of the Jamaican House of Assembly but in the summer of 1666 had the misfortune to be on Providencia Island when José Sánchez Ximénez's force arrived to reconquer that place. Surrendering against superior numbers at the end of August, the English were carried as prisoners to Portobelo, where the men were put to work on the fortifications. Whetstone, the island commander Major Samuel Smith, and an "honest old soldier" named Captain Stanley were marched overland to Panama. Their progress seems to have been a painful one, as they became the objects of public wrath and were flung into a dungeon upon reaching Panama. In late June 1667, Governor Juan Pérez de Guzmán wrote to the queen regent in Madrid, "I have the intention that they [the senior English captives] should never leave prison, because of the damage that one or other of them might do to us."

Whetstone was singled out especially, being described by the governor as "a man of much importance," responsible for planning "all the damage done on these coasts." Stanley further declared under interrogation that it had been Whetstone's ambition to arrange with "his friends and wealthy merchants" in London to fit out four frigates to attack the Armada del Mar del Sur of Peru. It appears Whetstone died during his incarceration, the only survivor of this captivity being Major Smith.

*See also* Mar del Sur, Armada del; Myngs, Sir Christopher; Pérez de Guzmán, Juan; Sánchez Ximénez, José; Smith, Samuel.

*References:* Earle, *Panamá;* Pawson, *Port Royal;* Pope.

# WILD COAST

Stretch of Atlantic shoreline along the northeastern side of South America, running from the Gulf of Paria to the Amazon River and home to the legendary El Dorado.

Its name apparently derived from the fact this region remained unsettled long after the rest of the Americas had begun to become populated by Europeans, partly because it fell along the boundary between the Spanish and Portuguese spheres of influence drawn by the 1493 Treaty of Tordesillas, but mostly because the emigrants from both Iberian nations preferred their wealthier viceroyalties of Mexico, Peru, and Brazil. Starting in the early seventeenth century, Dutch seamen began establishing trade settlements along the Wild Coast—particularly at the Guyanas—which they then used for further ventures into the Caribbean, thus driving Spain entirely out of this region. During the latter decades of the seventeenth century, Cumaná was considered a frontline garrison by Madrid, holding foreign interlopers at bay from spreading into the Spanish Main, just as Saint Augustine, Florida, did for the English settlers of the Carolinas. Both regions were frequently visited or used as havens by privateers and pirates.

*See also* Spanish Main.
*Reference:* Goslinga.

# WILLEMS, JAN

ALIAS JANTJE OR JANKE
(FL. 1680-1688)

Dutch corsair who prowled the Caribbean for many years.

Willems appears to have called himself "Jantje," a diminutive form of "Jan" or "John" traditionally associated with Dutch sailors (much as "Jack" was among the English); however, this nickname was most often rendered "Janke" or "Johnnie" by other nationalities he came into contact with. The French, for example, listed him as "Janchée," "Janquais," or "Jonchée," the chronicler Ravenau de Lussan mangling his name even further, into "Jean Quet"; the Spanish knew him as "Yanchée," "Yanquée," "Yonquée" or "Yunquée"; the English came the closest with "Yankey" or "Yankey Dutch," but referred to him more precisely as "John Williams, alias Yanky."

## DELIVERY OF THE PEACE OVERTURE (1680)

The first notice of Willems's activities occurred in spring 1680, when he played a modest role in the attempt to reestablish relations between the French *flibustiers* of Saint Domingue and their Spanish neighbors on that same island. On 16 May, Willems was lying with his ship *Saint Bernard* at Puerto Plata on the north coast of Santo Domingo, when Spanish scouts from the inland town of Santiago de los Caballeros surprised one of his crew on the beach, handing the seaman a letter asking if his captain would be willing to communicate with them concerning the peace. Willems sent a written message back to the Spaniards the following day, saying it would give him "great joy to see them."

At ten o'clock on the morning of 18 May, a company of Spanish cavalry appeared bearing a white flag. Willems sent two boats ashore to convey a deputation on board, from whom he received a copy of Madrid's *real cédula* of 6 July 1679, announcing ratification of the Treaty of Nijmegen that ended Franco-Spanish hostilities in Europe. The president of the Audiencia of Santo Domingo, Francisco de Segura Sandoval y Castilla, allowed sufficient time for Willems to convey the *real cédula* to the French governor of Saint Domingue, Jacques Nepveu, sieur de Pouançay, before dispatching another messenger with a copy of the treaty and a private letter dated 10 July 1680. Willems was at the French capital of Petit Goâve when this emissary

arrived, recognizing him as one of the persons who had come aboard his ship at Puerto Plata. Willems subsequently served as interpreter during his interviews with the French governor, at which the local frictions proved too deep-seated for anything other than a brief truce to be arranged.

## CRUISES (1681-1682)

Early in June the following year, Willems was lying at Springer's Key in the San Blas Islands north of Panama with a *barco luengo* of 4 guns and 60 English, Dutch, and French crewmembers, accompanying John Coxon, Jean Rose, George Wright, and five other captains. The buccaneers were joined there by Capitaine Tristan, who had just rescued John Cooke's band of rovers at nearby La Sound's Key after their adventures in the South Seas (among whom was the chronicler William Dampier). From there, the freebooter flotilla decided to make a descent on the Central American coast, for which they sailed toward San Andrés Island to procure boats. A gale struck the formation, however, and an *armadilla* of a dozen tiny men o' war sent out from Cartagena further scattered them. Willems put into Bocas del Toro (literally "bull's mouths" or "entrances of the bull") on the northwestern coast of present day Panama with Coxon, and two weeks later they were joined by Wright.

According to Dampier, Willems agreed to act as Wright's consort "because Captain Yanky [sic] had no commission, and was afraid the French would take away his bark." The two therefore sailed to Cartagena, seized some boats, then returned to the San Blas Islands to forage. Capturing some coastal traders laden with foodstuffs (as well as rescuing Lionel Wafer), they retired near Darien to careen. Afterward they prowled past Cartagena, Santa Marta, and Ríohacha, before reversing course and intercepting a 12-gun Spanish merchantman from Santiago de Cuba, which was just approaching the Spanish Main. During this chase Wright overtook the Spaniard first and engaged, followed half an hour later by Willems's slower craft. Because of this Wright claimed the entire prize but was persuaded to share it by his company. Nevertheless, Wright burnt his own bark and assumed command of Willems's ship, transferring the Dutchman and his crew into the Cuban prize.

After the buccaneers deposited their captives at Ríohacha, they made for Curaçao in mid-November 1681 to attempt to sell their Cuban cargo. No deal could be made, so Willems and Wright continued to Bonaire, where they met a Dutch sloop from Europe with Irish beef, which they exchanged for some of their captured goods. They then visited Aves Islands, where Wright careened his bark while Willems's was scrubbed, and two guns were fished from the wreck of the comte d'Estrées's fleet. In mid-February 1682 they crossed to Los Roques, where Willems's vessel was careened and ten tons of sugar sold to a passing French warship of 36 guns. By April 1682 they reached Tortuga Island (the Salt Tortugas off Venezuela) before attempting to tack upwind to Trinidad, only to be driven back to Blanquilla. Ten days later they returned to the Salt Tortugas, where Willems parted from Wright.

## CUBAN BLOCKADE
### (1682-1683)

Evidently he then laid in a course for Saint Domingue, as later that summer off Ile-à-Vache Willems had a falling out with Cooke, who had become his quartermaster or second-in-command. According to Dampier, after securing a Spanish prize, Cooke and the other survivors from the South Seas had been plundered and marooned ashore by their *flibustier* colleagues, who begrudged "the English such a vessel." These in turn sought to repay

this act by stealing Capitaine Tristan's ship while he was ashore at Petit Goâve and making off with a French merchantman laden with wine.

Willems meanwhile had begun serving as part of a French flotilla blockading the southern coast of Cuba under a commission issued to the legendary commander "chevalier" de Grammont. At the end of this year his force proceeded toward the Bahamas, where a Spanish ship was captured by Willems's consort Pierre Bot, and the survivors returned to Havana aboard a *barco luengo*. But Willems's own activities must also have been noteworthy, for his reputation soon reached Jamaica. In February 1683, Governor Sir Thomas Lynch, in a vain attempt to destroy the elusive pirate ship *Trompeuse* (Trickster) commanded by Jean Hamlin, sent Coxon

> to offer to one Yankey (who commands an admirable sailer) men, victuals, pardon, naturalisation, and £200 in money to him and Coxon if he will go after *La Trompeuse.*

Before any deal could be struck, Willems became involved in another more spectacular venture.

Late in March 1683 the flotilla began to sail back toward Petit Goâve with another Cuban prize, when upon approaching they were met by the Dutch rover Nikolaas van Hoorn, exiting in Grammont's corvette *Colbert* to recall them for a major enterprise against the Spaniards. Van Hoorn had earlier been cheated out of a large consignment of slaves at Santo Domingo, for which Governor de Pouançay had granted him a letter of reprisal against the Spaniards. Willems joined the freebooter force that crossed into the Bay of Honduras, searching for further reinforcements. In particular it was hoped to recruit the Dutch buccaneer Laurens de Graaf and his confederate

Michiel Andrieszoon, both of whom were persuaded to join in the projected attack against Veracruz at a meeting held on Roatan Island that April. The expedition of thirteen sail then rounded the Yucatán peninsula into the Gulf of Mexico.

## SACK OF VERACRUZ
### (MAY 1683)

On the afternoon of 17 May 1683, Willems's Spanish-built ship was one of two advance scouts used by the pirates to reconnoiter Veracruz's defenses from out at sea. That night a landing party of 800 buccaneers slipped into the sleeping city, attacking at dawn. The Spanish garrison and citizens were surprised in their beds, the entire city being seized and ransacked over the next four days. The pirates then withdrew offshore to Sacrificios Island with 4,000 captives, dividing their booty and awaiting the payment of ransoms out of Mexico's interior. Two weeks later these were paid, and after herding 1,500 blacks and mulattos aboard as slaves, the pirate fleet weighed. They encountered the annual Spanish plate fleet just as they were standing out from the coast, but its commander deferred combat, and so the raiders escaped.

The majority of buccaneer craft paused at Coatzacoalcos to take on water before shouldering back around Yucatán to Isla Mujeres, where by late June 1683 they had split the remaining spoils. Each went their separate ways, and by 26 July 1683 (O.S.) Governor Lynch was reporting:

> Yankey got first to Caimanos [sic; the Cayman Islands] and is bound for Hispaniola. A sloop that came in yesterday got this information from his men.

Lynch further identified the main perpetrators of this assault as "Van Hoorn, Laurens, and Yankey Dutch." Willems now subordinated himself to his famous compatriot, so that after a few months spent enjoying their loot, De Graaf led a pirate contingent of Andrieszoon, Willems, François Le Sage, and several other captains for the Spanish Main, arriving near Cartagena by late November 1683.

## VICTORY OFF CARTAGENA
### (CHRISTMAS 1683)

When the local Spanish governor, Juan de Pando Estrada, learned these rovers had appeared before his harbor, he commandeered the private merchant ships *San Francisco,* of 40 guns *Nuestra Señora de la Paz* (Our Lady of Peace), of 34 guns, and a 28-gun galliot to chase them away. This trio exited on 23 December 1683, manned by 800 soldiers and sailors under the command of Captain Andrés de Pez. The result was scarcely as the Spaniards had anticipated, for the seven nimble pirate ships swarmed all over them. In the confusion *San Francisco* ran aground, *Paz* struck after four hours' fight, and Willems took the galliot. Ninety Spaniards were killed in the battle, as opposed to only 20 buccaneers.

*San Francisco* was refloated and became De Graaf's new flagship, renamed *Fortune* (later *Neptune*); Andrieszoon received command of the *Paz,* calling it *Mutine* (Rascal); while Willems was given De Graaf's old flagship *Francesa* or *Dauphine* (Princess). On 25 December the triumphant buccaneers deposited their prisoners ashore, then settled down to blockade the port. In mid–January 1684 a small convoy of English slavers arrived, escorted by the frigate HMS *Ruby,* 48 guns, of Captain Matthew Tennant. This officer visited Willems, reporting "that Yankey showed him a commission from the Governor of Petit Goâve." The freebooters proved friendly, letting the English slavers pass and even entering into a contract with one of their passengers, a Dutch slave factor called Diego Maquet, to have a large supply of wine and meat delivered from Port Royal, Jamaica, to Roatan.

Shortly thereafter the pirates quit their blockade and headed northwestward. En route De Graaf captured a 14-gun Spanish vessel, then touched at Roatan with his flotilla before continuing to the south coast of Cuba. There he and his consorts intercepted a Spanish *aviso,* or dispatch vessel, bearing news that Spain and France were once again at war. Realizing this meant they could renew their French privateering commissions, De Graaf left Andrieszoon and Willems to prowl the Cuban coast, while he sailed his 14-gun prize into Petit Goâve to obtain new patents.

### RANSACKING OF THE DUTCH WEST INDIAMEN
#### (MAY 1684)

After parting company with their leader, Andrieszoon and Willems rounded western Cuba and took up station in the approaches to Havana. On 18 May 1684, while opposite the tiny hamlet of Santa Lucía, they saw two large vessels approaching, which they stood out to intercept. The strangers proved to be the Dutch West Indiamen *Stad Rotterdam* (City of Rotterdam) and *Elisabeth,* and despite Holland's neutrality in the conflict, Andrieszoon led an 80-man boarding party across in two boats to inspect their cargos. He discovered they had sailed from Cartagena three weeks earlier, and because of the protection afforded by Dutch colors, the Spaniards had shipped a great deal of money and passengers on board, including a bishop. Andrieszoon laid claim to half the 200,000 pesos and all the Spanish nationals, removing these over the masters' objections.

### NEW ENGLAND VISIT
#### (AUGUST 1684)

After this lucrative haul, the pair of buccaneer vessels worked their way up the Atlantic seaboard, and by the end of August

1684, Governor Edward Cranfield of New Hampshire was informing London that

> a French privateer of 35 guns has arrived at Boston. I am credibly informed that they share £700 a man. The Bostoners no sooner heard of her off the coast than they dispatched a messenger and pilot to convoy her into port in defiance of the King's proclamation [of March 1684, prohibiting aid and abetment to rovers]. The pirates are likely to leave the greatest part of their plate [i.e., silver] behind them, having bought up most of the choice goods in Boston. The ship is now fitting for another expedition.

This was Andrieszoon's *Mutine.* Two days later the governor wrote again, adding that a second French privateer—Willems's *Dauphine*—had appeared off that coast. Spanish escapees told the governor they had been taken off Cartagena "by the men who plundered Veracruz" and identified the ship refurbishing in Boston's yard by its former Spanish name *La Paz,* while the second they called *Francesa* (which the governor misheard as *Francis).* "They are both extraordinarily rich ships," Cranfield concluded, "chiefly through spoil of the Spaniards, though they have spared none that they have met at sea." Once Andrieszoon's ship had completed refitting, Willems's was to be repaired. However, a couple of weeks later the king's latest proclamation against piracy was promulgated in Boston, leading Governor William Dyre to attempt to seize the *Mutine.* This was restored to Andrieszoon after a brief impoundment but apparently convinced Willems to sail away alone.

### RETURN TO THE WEST INDIES
#### (OCTOBER 1684)

He was off the Spanish Main again by 14 October, for on this day Willems intercepted the English sloop *James* as it approached that coast with a cargo of goods for the Spaniards. In the words of its master John Thorp:

> we met Captain Yankey in the ship *Dolphin* [*sic; Dauphine*] off Cartagena, who fired a volley of small shot into our sloop, in spite of our showing our [English] colors, and ordered us on board him, while his men plundered our sloop. We were kept prisoners for six weeks till he came to Petit Goâve where the Intendant [Chevalier de St. Laurent] and Council voted her good prize.

This condemnation occurred on 22 November 1684, and when Thorp and the sloop's owner, James Wale, protested against this verdict, the Intendant replied with "reviling language, and told us to go complain to the King of England." The sloop had been taken entering a Spanish port, with Spanish goods and three Spanish factors on board, who furthermore had been tortured to reveal their ownership of the cargo. All this evidence rendered the *James* forfeit, France being then openly at war with Spain, and the disgruntled English captives noted how "Laurens the pirate, who gave Yankey his commission, took three barrels of flour from our ship."

When news of this capture reached Port Royal early in December, Acting Governor Hender Molesworth instructed the new captain of the *Ruby*, David Mitchell, to "forthwith sail to Petit Goâve and deliver my letter to the Governor, demanding satisfaction for a sloop of this island unlawfully seized by Captain Yankey." Mitchell arrived the morning of 16 December 1684, where he "saw in the port the ships commanded by Captain Yankey, Bréhal, Thomas and Johnson." *Dauphine* was the largest of this group, described in a contemporary French document as mounting 30 guns and carrying 180 men.

The Royal Navy officer referred to it by its former Spanish nickname when he sent his protest ashore, alleging piracy against "Captain Yankey of the *Francis*."

The French governor, Pierre-Paul Tarin de Cussy, was absent, but his deputy Capitaine Boisseau returned a polite rejoinder, disputing the characterization of Willems as a pirate. "I assure you that we know him to be incapable of such a thing," he wrote, explaining the *James* had been condemned as a lawful prize after examination at "the little river Léogane," where it had been found to be laden with Spanish merchandise. The next day Mitchell persisted, arguing the sloop "was *bona fide* the property not of Spanish but English subjects," to no avail. In a conciliatory gesture, Boisseau sent out three English seamen who had been serving aboard Willems's ship—it being technically illegal for them to sail under foreign colors, while England was at peace—but otherwise took no further action. *Ruby* returned to Port Royal empty-handed four days later.

Willems next was heard from in April 1685, when he was sighted at a huge pirate gathering off Isla de Pinos on Cuba's southern coast. Mitchell and HMS *Ruby* stumbled upon this vast assemblage of 22 sail, which included De Graaf, Grammont, Willems, George Bannister, and Jacob Evertsen, but could not discover their design, despite speaking with several of the captains. In fact, the buccaneers were preparing for a descent on the Mexican port of Campeche.

## ASSAULT ON CAMPECHE
### (JULY 1685)

Shifting to Isla Mujeres and Cape Catoche to gather more recruits, the raiders began their advance late in June, so that on the afternoon of 6 July the pirate fleet of 6 large and 4 small ships, 6 sloops, and 17 *piraguas* appeared half a dozen miles off Campeche. A landing force of 700 buccaneers took to the boats and began rowing in toward shore, and the following day they overran the city. The citadel held out for a week, after which the invaders were left in undisputed possession of the port for two months; little plunder was found by the buccaneers, as most of the Spaniards' wealth had been withdrawn prior to the assault. Captives were threatened with death if ransoms were not forthcoming, but Yucatán's Governor Juan Bruno Téllez de Guzmân prohibited such payments, so finally the pirates evacuated the city in late August after putting it to the torch.

Disappointed with their results, the pirate host scattered. Willems was not mentioned again for more than a year, but in October 1686 Molesworth received word that

> Yankey, the privateer, has taken a Spanish vessel with fifty thousand dollars off Havana. If we could meet with him, this would be a good time to call him to account for the English sloop [*James*] that was condemned at Petit Goâve, but he is said to be bound northward.

Almost another year would elapse before the Jamaican lieutenant governor got his opportunity, during which time Willems apparently visited North America once more.

## JAMAICAN OVERTURE
### (SEPTEMBER 1687)

In autumn the following year Willems reappeared off the northwestern shores of Jamaica with his consort Evertsen, their armament being described as follows:

> Yankey has a large Dutch-built ship with 44 guns and 100 men; Jacob has a fine bark with ten guns, 16 "patararoes" [*sic;* *pedreros,* or swivel guns] and about 50 men. They have also a small sloop.

Hoping to obtain supplies, Willems smuggled a letter ashore to a man he had dealt with previously; this individual in turn requested authorization from the governor. Molesworth declared he could not permit the rover to be supplied "with anything whatever, but that if he was ready to come in and live honestly among us, giving security for the same, he might be received." At the same time the governor secretly directed Captain Charles Talbot of the frigate HMS *Falcon* to circle round the north coast of the island and take Willems by surprise, but this scheme came to naught when the frigate turned back into Port Royal for want of sails.

Unaware of this treachery, Willems and Evertsen entered Montego Bay and drafted a formal petition before the local authority, Ensign William Geese, which read:

> Captains Yankey and Jacob to Lieutenant Governor Molesworth, Montego Bay, 3 September 1687 [O.S.].
>
> We have arrived from Carolina and brought several people thence who have been driven from the colony by the trouble with the Spaniards. In all sincerity we present ourselves, our ships and company to the service of the King of England, and hope for your assurance that our ships and men shall not be troubled or molested, as we are ignorant of the laws and customs of this island. We can satisfy you that we have never injured any British subject.
>
> (Signed) John Williams, Jacob Everson

Before this proposal was sealed, "the whole company agreed to it," according to Geese.

The governor replied nine days later, offering the rovers a royal pardon and letters of naturalization if they would break up their ships and renounce privateering. Willems and Evertsen responded in late September that to do so would leave them "destitute of all livelihood in present and future," and that neither had "money to purchase an estate ashore." Molesworth was unmoved, writing on 19 October, "If you will accept the condition, make the best of your way to Port Royal; if not, leave the coast at once, for I shall consider the treaty to be at an end." Willems and his confederate chose to make off, although a number of their men deserted ashore. The last Molesworth heard of the two captains, they were standing "away to leeward [westward], their vessels being much in want of repair."

## FINAL COUP
### (FEBRUARY 1688)

Nonetheless, Willems and Evertsen remained sufficiently strong to attack one of the annual Spanish galleons a few months later that had crossed the Atlantic to trade with Guatemala and Honduras. In mid-February 1688, the new Jamaican governor, the Duke of Albemarle, was told

that the pirates Yankey and Jacobs have fallen upon a great Spanish ship in the Bay of Honduras called the Hulk [sic; urca, or cargo ship], and that they had been in sight of her twelve hours. If Yankey failed in this attempt he is ruined, for it is said that he was very ill provided before. Had I the honor of pardoning pirates, which formally was usual here, I could have done the King good service [by granting amnesty to these two rovers].

Evidently the buccaneers succeeded in their aim, for two months later Albemarle learned they had fought the Spanish ship "in the port of Cavana [sic; Puerto Cabello?] from seven in the morning till three in the afternoon, and took her."

This was to be both commanders' last hurrah, however, for later that summer Captain Peterson led "the remainder of Yankey's and Jacobs's company" to New England, it being revealed they were dead. Twenty-five years afterward the director of

the French slaving *asiento* at Havana was one "Jean-Baptiste Jonchée," who may possibly have been a descendant of Willems, from those early halcyon days on Saint Domingue.

***See also*** Andrieszoon, Michiel; *asiento;* Bréhal, Capitaine; careen; Cooke, John; Coxon, John; Dampier, William; De Graaf, Laurens Cornelis Boudewijn; Estrées, Jean, comte d'; Evertsen, Jacob; Grammont, "chevalier" de; Hamlin, Jean; Hispaniola; Le Sage, François; letter of reprisal; Lussan, Ravenau de; Lynch, Sir Thomas; Paine, Thomas; Peterson, Captain; Pez y Malzárraga, Andrés de; Pouançay, Jacques Nepveu, sieur de; Rose, Jean; Spanish Main; South Seas; Tennant, Matthew; Van Hoorn, Nikolaas; Wafer, Lionel; Wright, George.

***References:*** *C.S.P., Amer. and W.I.,* Vols. XI–XII; Gosse, *Who's Who;* Juárez; Le Blant; Marley, *Veracruz.*

# WILLIAMS, MAURICE
### (FL. 1659-1664)

English privateer who operated out of Jamaica.

The earliest known mention of Williams's activities occurred in May 1659, when he bought the Spanish prize *Abispa* (erroneously rendered *Rabba Bispa* in English sources, a misreading of its proper Spanish name *La Abispa* or "the Wasp"), which had been brought into Cagway by the state frigate *Diamond* and sold by the authorities to Williams at auction for a bid of £120. He renamed it *Jamaica* and further acquired a privateering commission. To help him fit out his new vessel, Governor Edward D'Oyley sold him five cannon from the state storehouse and issued a proclamation that allowed Williams to recruit seamen from the government frigate *Marston Moor.*

Five years later Williams was still plying this same trade, for on 23 November 1664 (O.S.), William Beeston noted in his journal at Port Royal that the rover had that day "brought in a great prize with logwood, indigo and silver." This was unusual in that the new governor, Sir Thomas Modyford, had some months previously announced that "for the future all acts of hostility against the Spaniards should cease"; yet Williams was still allowed to keep this prize. On 20 February 1665 (O.S.), Modyford himself wrote to London, "The Spanish prizes have been inventoried and sold, but it is suspected that those of Morrice [sic; Maurice Williams] and Bernard Nichols have been miserably plundered, and the interested parties will find but a slender account in the Admiralty."

That spring Williams participated in a more legitimate venture, when his 18-gun *Speaker* served as flagship of Colonel Edward Morgan's expedition against Dutch Sint Eustatius and Sabá, upon the English receiving news of the outbreak of the Second Anglo-Dutch War back in Europe. This force departed Jamaica in two divisions, five sail putting out of Port Royal on 5 April 1665, and Morgan himself following aboard Williams's *Speaker* with another three on the 28 April. They mustered 650 men in all and were described in a letter by Modyford as

> chiefly reformed privateers, scarce a planter amongst them, being resolute fellows and well armed with *fusils* [Spanish word for muskets] and pistols.

The Crown official was particularly pleased they would be serving "at the old rate of no purchase, no pay, and it will cost the King nothing considerable, some powder and mortar pieces." Their landing was made successfully, but the colonel, "being a corpulent man," died from heat exertion during the chase, and his expedition disbanded shortly thereafter.

*See also* Beeston, William; D'Oyley, Edward; purchase.

**References:** Cruikshank; *Interesting Tracts;* Pawson, *Port Royal;* Pope.

# WINDSOR, THOMAS, SEVENTH BARON WINDSOR OF STANWELL, FIRST EARL OF PLYMOUTH

## (c. 1627-1687)

First Royalist governor of Jamaica, who authorized privateering raids against Spanish America even in peacetime.

Windsor was born in Kew, Surrey, England, around 1627, descended from an ancient Norman line. He served as a youthful cavalier during the English Civil War, although apparently without distinction. Upon the defeat of the Royalist forces, he fled to Flanders, but a few years later returned to England and posted a surety "not to do anything prejudicial" against Cromwell's Protectorate. He lived quietly in the country, "absorbed in a fruitless scheme to render the river Salwarpe navigable by means of locks, for the benefit of the salt trade at Droitwich." After the restoration of Charles II in the spring of 1660, he was reinstated, becoming 7th Baron Windsor and lord lieutenant of Worcestershire. The following summer, on the recommendation of the Committee for Foreign Plantations, he was appointed to succeed Colonel Edward D'Oyley as governor of Jamaica with a salary of £2,000 a year. Windsor did not set out to occupy this post until April 1662, but despite such a delay—not all his fault—he was well prepared to carry out the Privy Council's latest policies and quite enlightened regarding the colonists' needs.

He sailed with the veteran West Indian commander Christopher Myngs on HMS *Centurion,* 46 guns, accompanied by the frigate *Griffin* of Captain Smart.

Arriving in Barbados in July, Windsor sent *Griffin* with letters to the Spanish governors of San Juan de Puerto Rico and Santo Domingo, asking if they would admit English ships to trade. He meanwhile resumed his voyage to Port Royal a few weeks later, arriving in August 1662. Having brought out the back pay for the English garrison, he was able to release over a thousand soldiers from unhappy servitude with full wages and a gratuity. He replaced them with five militia regiments distributed throughout the island. Work was also accelerated on the harbor fort, renamed Fort Charles in honor of the king. Thirty acres of land was offered to "every person, male or female, being twelve years old or upwards" on the island. A local assembly was convened, and an admiralty court established, so cases need no longer be appealed to the far side of the Atlantic.

But Windsor's most surprising innovation followed reappearance of the *Griffin* with dispatches from the Spanish governors denying trade. According to Windsor's instructions, if "the King of Spain shall refuse to admit our subjects to trade with them, you shall in such case endeavor to procure and settle a trade with his subjects in those parts by force." Although Madrid had grudgingly accepted peace three years earlier, Spanish ministers refused to acknowledge English claims in the New World, hoping to eventually reassert their monopoly over the entire continent. In light of such a policy, the new royal governor launched a highly aggressive strategy. Privateering commissions, which had been recalled at Jamaica, were once more available "for the subduing of all our enemies by sea and by land, within and upon the coast of America." During the next few days, Windsor publicly called for volunteers for a major expedition against the

Spaniards to be led by Commodore Myngs. Many old hands, still feeling surrounded by hostile Spaniards, were delighted at this unexpected development. Within three days, 1,300 men mustered (many of them former soldiers), and *Centurion* and *Griffin* were joined by ten privateering vessels, including Robert Searle's *Cagway* and a tiny ship commanded by a 27-year-old militia captain named Henry Morgan.

This flotilla set sail late in September 1662, bound for Santiago de Cuba, which had been the advance Spanish base in the attempts to reconquer Jamaica. In a quick campaign, Myngs surprised the garrison and threw down its defenses while suffering only a handful of casualties. He returned heavily laden with booty and half a dozen prizes a month later, to find Windsor about to embark on the ship *Bear* for England. "Being very sick and uneasy," the governor had decided to go home, leaving Sir Charles Lyttelton to rule in his place, along with the Council of Jamaica. The real reason for Windsor's abrupt departure on 28 October 1662 (O.S.) may have been financial rather than medical, as he later complained that "he came back £2,000 worse off than when he went out." His apparent abandonment of royal duties was disapproved of upon his arrival in London, where Samuel Pepys noted in his diary, "Lord Windsor being come home from Jamaica unlooked for, makes us think these young Lords are not fit to do any service abroad." Windsor's appointment was revoked in February 1663, and Sir Thomas Modyford sent out as his successor. Windsor was not employed again until 1676, when he was made Master of the Horse to the duke of York. Five years later, he became governor of Portsmouth. He died an earl in November 1687 and was buried at Tardebigg, Worcestershire, England.

*See also* Myngs, Sir Christopher; Searle, Robert.

*References: D.N.B.; Interesting Tracts;* Pope.

# WOOLLERLY, THOMAS

## ALSO WOOLERLY
### (FL. 1687)

English rover who plied the South Seas.

In early June 1687, a large ship appeared off New Providence in the Bahamas and sent a boat ashore to say it was come from the South Seas under Woollerly. The local Bahamian magistrate, Thomas Bridge, instructed one man to remain ashore while the boat returned to the ship, then learned that the notorious Christopher Goffe and some of his cohorts were also aboard. Bridge therefore advised the strangers:

> it was the King's order that they [pirates] should not be entertained, and as she continued standing in, I fired a shot across her forefoot. She then anchored, and next day Woolerly [sic] told me that he was come to wood and water, that he had Colonel Lilburne's commission and had done nothing contrary to it, and that he had taken in Goffe and his companions in extremity of distress. I refused him leave to come in, and he sailed away next day. I am told that they burnt the ship at Andrew's Island and dispersed, leaving only six or seven men in the Bahamas.

Despite Bridge's apparent compliance with the king's instructions, the suspicion remained that Woollerly's prize had been allowed a place to scuttle and his men the opportunity to disappear into civilian life, most likely in exchange for a hefty bribe. This impression was reinforced when Bridge delayed writing to his immediate superiors at Jamaica over the next three months, by which time Woollerly had long since left the islands.

In fact, Lieutenant Governor Hender Molesworth of Jamaica learned of Woollerly's presence in the Bahamas through secondhand sources, and on 17 August 1687 (O.S.) was informing London he had heard the buccaneers

> quarrelled and burnt the ship, but some of them had bought a vessel and intended to sail for New England, but were detained by want of provisions. It is said that some of these pirates have [so much money] at times [they pay] half a crown a pound for flour.

Molesworth consequently dispatched Captain Thomas Spragge of HMS *Drake* to the Bahamas with specific orders "to take the pirate Woollerly," but he arrived only to find the pirate gone. It is presumed the rovers had sailed to Boston, where Goffe is known to have obtained a royal pardon in November of that year.

***See also*** Goffe, Christopher.

***References:*** *C.S.P., Amer. and W.I.*, Vol. XII; Gosse, *Who's Who*.

# WOOLLEY, CONWAY

### (FL. 1683)

English privateer who in March 1683 was lying at New Providence in the Bahamas along with Captains Markham, Jan Corneliszoon (commanding a brigantine out of New York), and the French *flibustier* Bréhal, preparing to go "fish silver from a Spanish wreck."

Then Captain Thomas Paine's bark *Pearl*, of 8 guns and 60 men, arrived with a license from Governor Sir Thomas Lynch of Jamaica to hunt pirates. The five decided instead to raid the nearby Spanish outpost of Saint Augustine, Florida, using Paine's commission. They landed under French colors, but, found the Spaniards alerted and withdrew after merely releasing some Spanish captives they brought with them, and looting the outlying countryside.

Returning to the Bahamas, Woolley and Corneliszoon apparently proceeded to the Spanish wreck site, while the other three reentered New Providence. When Governor Robert Lilburne visited the site a few weeks later, he found all the rovers gone.

*See also* Bréhal, Capitaine; Corneliszoon, Jan; Lilburne, Robert; Markham, John; Paine, Thomas.

*Reference: C.S.P., Amer. and W.I.,* Vol. XI.

# WRIGHT, GEORGE
## (FL. 1675-1682)

English privateer who served under French colors.

When England withdrew from the war against the Netherlands in early 1674, many of its West Indian corsairs shifted allegiance in order to continue privateering. Wright was one such commander, obtaining a commission from the French authorities on Saint Domingue to serve against the Dutch and Spaniards. On 26 March 1675 (O.S.), the new deputy governor of Jamaica, Sir Henry Morgan, drafted a letter promising Wright and his fellow rovers a friendly reception at Port Royal if they were to come in and cease their attacks on behalf of France, which although legitimate were embarrassing the English Crown. Morgan further added that he hoped "their experience of him will give him the reputation that he intends not to betray them," suggesting that Wright may have known Morgan from his Panama days.

This proposal was never sent, however, the Jamaican authorities preferring other measures to recall English subjects from foreign service. Wright continued under French colors and in early June 1681 was at Springer's Key in the San Blas Islands north of Panama along with John Coxon, Jan Willems, Jean Rose, and four other captains. Wright was sent with his *barco luengo* of 4 guns and 40 men to gather intelligence at Chagres for a possible attack against Panama. He captured a *piragua* laden with flour and returned with this prize and prisoners to report. An hour after his arrival, the ship of Capitaine Tristan joined Coxon's formation, having rescued John Cooke's band of buccaneers at nearby La Sound's Key, after their adventures in the South Seas. Among this group was William Dampier, who noted, "All the commanders were aboard of Captain Wright when we came into the fleet."

The buccaneers decided to make a descent on the Central American coast, for which they first sailed to San Andrés Island to procure boats. A gale scattered the formation, and Wright chanced upon a Spanish tartan armed with four *pedreros,* or swivel guns, and 30 men, capturing it after an hour-long fight. He learned that it was part of a larger *armadilla* sent from Cartagena to drive the pirates away. Cooke, Dampier, and the other English rovers who had arrived from the South Seas were now serving with Capitaine Archaimbaud, who

> desired Captain Wright to fit up his prize the tartan and make a man o' war of her for us, which he at first seemed to decline, because he was settled among the French in Hispaniola, and was very well beloved both by the governor of Petit Goâve and all the gentry; and they would resent it ill that Captain Wright, who had no occasion of men, should be so unkind to Capitaine Archembo [*sic*] as to seduce his men from him.

Nevertheless, when the English insisted, Wright relented on condition that they "should be under his command, as one ship's company."

Ten days later, Wright quit San Andrés, as no one other than Archaimbaud and Capitaine Tucker had reached the rendezvous. Returning to Bocas del Toro (literally "bull's mouths" or "entrances of the bull") located on the northwestern coast of present-day Panama, Wright discovered from Willems that the rest had been scattered by the Spanish *armadilla*. The two captains therefore sailed together to Cartagena, seized some boats, then returned to the San Blas Islands for forage. Capturing some coastal traders laden with "corn, hog and fowls," as well as rescuing Lionel Wafer, they repaired near Darien to careen. They then prowled past Cartagena, Santa Marta, and Ríohacha before reversing course and intercepting a 12-gun Spanish merchantman from Santiago de Cuba as it approached the Spanish Main. Wright burned his bark and assumed command of Willems's ship in exchange for the Cuban prize. The buccaneers deposited their captives at Ríohacha and in mid–November 1681 made toward Curaçao to dispose of their cargo of Cuban sugar, tobacco, "and 8 or 10 tons of marmalade."

Arriving off the Dutch island,

Captain Wright went ashore to the governor [Nikolaas van Liebergen] and offered him the sale of the sugar, but the governor told him he had a great trade with the Spaniards, therefore he could not admit us in there; but if we could go to Saint Thomas, which is an island and free port belonging to the Danes and a sanctuary for privateers, he would send a sloop with such goods as we wanted, and money to buy the sugar, which he would take at a certain rate; but it was not agreed to.

Instead Wright and Willems sailed to Bonaire, where they met a Dutch sloop come from Europe with Irish beef, which they bought for some of their cargo. They then visited Aves Islands, where Wright careened his bark, Willems's was scrubbed, and two guns were fished from the wreck of the comte d'Estrées's fleet. In mid–February 1682 the buccaneers crossed to Los Roques, where Willems's vessel was careened and ten tons of sugar sold to a passing French warship of 36 guns. In April 1682 they reached Tortuga Island (or Salt Tortugas, off Venezuela) and attempted to tack upwind to Trinidad but were driven back to Blanquilla. Ten days later, they returned to the Salt Tortugas, where Willems left Wright's company.

In a quarrelsome mood because of this inactivity, Wright and his remaining men raided the coast of Caracas, capturing three barks with assorted goods. They repaired to Los Roques to divide the booty, then separated.

*See also* Archaimbaud, Capitaine; *armadilla; barco luengo;* careen; Cooke, John; Coxon, John; Dampier, William; Estrées, Jean, comte d'; Hispaniola; *pedreros;* Rose, Jean; South Seas; Spanish Main; Tristan, Capitaine; Wafer, Lionel; Willems, Jan.

*References: C.S.P., Amer. and W.I.,* Vol.IX; Dampier; Pope.

# WROTH, PETER
## (FL. 1660s-1670s)

English privateer who operated out of Barbados during the Second and Third Anglo-Dutch Wars.

Wroth was the younger brother of Sir John Wroth of Kent, England, and emigrated to seek his fortune in the Lesser Antilles. When news of the Third Anglo-Dutch War reached Barbados during the latter half of 1672, Governor Sir William Stapleton of the Leeward Islands issued him a privateering commission to go seek "purchase in the Dutch plantations of Guiana." Wroth was already familiar with campaigning on the Wild Coast, having fought in the conquest of Suriname during the previous conflict.

Late in March 1673, he approached the mouth of the Suriname River with his 20-ton sloop *Little Kitt,* six guns, manned by 30 men. Wroth's intention was to obtain supplies by raiding the turtling camp at Three Creeks, but he found this waterway blocked up by the Dutch. However, from conversations with several colonists, he also learned that a small Dutch naval squadron had just arrived with reinforcements, "which next spring tide intended to go to Virginia to do what mischief they could." Realizing that this was important military intelligence, he immediately departed with a 15-year-old captive named Jan Madder, pausing at Isakebe on the Demerara coast to take on provisions. After obtaining supplies from the Carib Indians of the Amecouza River, he proceeded to Barbados with his report. It was eventually forwarded to London and brought to the attention of Charles II and the Lords of the Admiralty.

***See also*** purchase.

***Reference:*** Shomette, *Raid.*

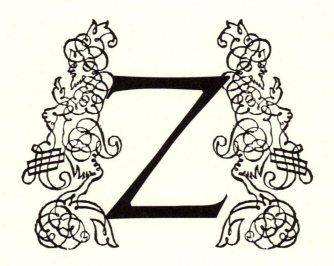

# ZOBY, JOSEPH
## (FL. 1678-1683)

English merchant adventurer victimized by the Spaniards in South America, for which he sought letters of reprisal.

In 1678 Zoby departed on a trading voyage, allegedly for the West Indies, although he actually traveled much further south and eventually put into *Río de la Plata* "to victual." There his ship was seized for violating Spain's trade monopoly and sold off as a legitimate prize. Zoby returned to England to complain and even traveled to the English embassy in Madrid to seek restitution from the Spanish Crown, remaining there many months. His suit did not prosper despite the support of the ambassador, and Zoby was further galled when his former ship arrived at the port of San Sebastián from South America, flying Spanish colors. He again petitioned for its release but was denied, leading him to conclude "no justice is to be looked for from Spain." He therefore sought letters of reprisal from the English government to extract his own compensation, which were apparently granted.

*See also* letter of reprisal.

*Reference: C.S.P., Amer. and W.I.,* Vol. XI.

# Select Bibliography

Alsedo y Herrera, Dionisio de. *Piraterías y agresiones de los ingleses y de otros pueblos de Europa en la América Española desde el siglo XVI al XVIII.* Madrid: Manuel G. Hernández, 1883.

Auffret, Pierre-Jean. "Le Père Labat: 'Critique sous toutes les formes, il n'a que peu de temps à vivre,' 1663–1738." Lyon: *Documents pour Servir à l'Histoire de Saint Domingue en France,* 1973 (8):11–24.

Baer, Joel H. "'Captain John Avery' and the Anatomy of a Mutiny." *Eighteenth-Century Life* 18 (February 1994): 1–23.

Barbour, Violet F. "Privateers and Pirates of the West Indies." *American Historical Review* XVI (1911): 529–566.

Baudrit, André. *Charles de Courbon, Comte de Blénac, 1622–1696; Gouverneur Général des Antilles Françaises, 1677–1696.* Fort de France: Annales des Antilles, Société d'Histoire de la Martinique, 1967.

Bensusan, Harold G. "The Spanish Struggle against Foreign Encroachment in the Caribbean, 1675–1697." Unpublished Ph.D. thesis, University of California at Los Angeles, 1970.

Bernal Ruiz, María del Pilar. *La toma del puerto de Guayaquil en 1687.* Seville: Escuela de Estudios Hispano-americanos, 1979.

Blanc, Gérard. "Dampier, ou la relation des îles aux tortues." *Dix-huitième siècle* 22 (1990): 159–170.

Bodge, Rev. George M. "The Dutch Pirates in Boston, 1694–5." *Bostonian Society Publications* VII (1910): 31–60.

Botting, Douglas. *The Pirates.* Alexandria, VA: Time-Life Books, 1978.

Bradley, Peter T. *The Lure of Peru: Maritime Intrusion into the South Sea, 1598–1701.* New York: St Martin's Press, 1990.

———. *Society, Economy and Defence in Seventeenth Century Peru: The Administration of the Conde de Alba de Liste (1655–61).* Liverpool, United Kingdom: Institute of Latin American Studies, University of Liverpool, 1992.

———. "The Ships of the Viceroyalty of Peru in the Seventeenth Century." *The Mariner's Mirror* 79, no. 4 (November 1993): 393–402.

Bromley, John Selwyn. *Corsairs and Navies, 1660–1760.* London: Hambledon, 1988.

Buchet, Christian. *La lutte pour l'espace caraïbe et la façade atlantique de l'Amérique centrale et du Sud (1672–1763).* Paris: Librairie de l'Inde, 1991.

Buisseret, David J. "Edward D'Oyley, 1617–1675." *Jamaica Journal* (1971): 6–10.

Calderón Quijano, José Ignacio. *Historia de las fortificaciones en Nueva España.* Seville: Escuela de Estudios Hispano-americanos, 1953.

*Calendar of State Papers, Colonial Series, America and West Indies IX–XIV.* London: Her Majesty's Stationery Office, 1893–1899.

Camus, Michel-Christian. "Une note critique à propos d'Exquemelin." *Revue française d'histoire d'outre-mer* 77, no. 286 (1990): 79–90.

Carr, H. Gresham. "Pirate Flags." *The Mariner's Mirror XXIX* (1943): 131–134.

Chapin, Howard Millar. *Privateer Ships and Sailors: The First Century of American Colonial Privateering, 1625–1725.* Toulon: G. Mouton, 1926.

Cordingly, David, and John Falconer. *Pirates.* New York: Abbeville Press, 1992.

Craton, Michael. *A History of the Bahamas.* London: Collins, 1968.

Crouse, Nellis M. *The French Struggle for the West Indies, 1665–1713.* New York: Octagon, 1966.

Cruikshank, E. A. *The Life of Sir Henry Morgan.* Toronto: Macmillan, 1935.

Crump, Helen J. *Colonial Admiralty Jurisdiction in the Seventeenth Century.* London: Longmans Green, 1931.

Dampier, William. *A New Voyage Round the World.* New York: Dover, 1968.

De la Matta Rodríguez, Enrique. *El asalto de Pointis a Cartagena de Indias.* Seville: Escuela de Estudios Hispano-americanos, 1979.

De Ville, Winston. *Saint Domingue: Census Records and Military Lists (1688–1720).* Ville Platte, Louisiana: Published by author, 1988.

*Dictionary of National Biography.* London: Oxford University Press, 1937–1938.

Dow, George Francis, and John Henry Edmonds. *The Pirates of the New England Coast, 1630–1730.* Salem, Massachusetts: Marine Research Society, 1923.

Driscoll, Charles B. "Finale of the Wedding March." *American Mercury* (July 1928): 355–363.

Ducéré, E. *Journal de bord d'un flibustier (1686–1693).* Bayonne, 1894.

Dunn, Richard S. "The Barbados Census of 1680: Profile of the Richest Colony in English America." *William and Mary Quarterly,* Third Series, 26 (1969): 3–30.

Dyer, Florence E. "Captain Christopher Myngs in the West Indies, 1657–1662." *The Mariner's Mirror XVIII* (April 1932): 168–187.

———. "Captain John Strong, Privateer and Treasure Hunter." *The Mariner's Mirror XIII* (1927): 145–158.

Earle, Peter. *The Sack of Panamá: Sir Henry Morgan's Adventures on the Spanish Main.* New York: Viking, 1981.

———. *The Treasure of the* Concepción: *The Wreck of the Almiranta.* New York: Viking, 1980.

Eugenio Martínez, María Angeles. *La defensa de Tabasco, 1600–1717.* Seville: Escuela de Estudios Hispano-americanos, 1971.

Exquemelin, Alexandre Olivier. *The Buccaneers of America.* Translated from the Dutch by Alexis Brown with an introduction by Jack Beeching. London: Penguin, 1969.

Fuller, Basil, and Ronald Leslie-Melville. *Pirate Harbours and Their Secrets.* London: Stanley Paul, 1935.

Galvin, Peter R. "The Pirates' Wake: A Geography of Piracy and Pirates as Geographers in Colonial Spanish America, 1536–1718." Unpublished Ph.D. thesis, Louisiana State University, 1991.

García Fuentes, Lutgardo. *El comercio español con América (1650–1700).* Seville: Escuela de Estudios Hispano-americanos, 1980.

Garmendia Arruabarrena, José. "Armadores y armadas de Guipúzcoa (1689–1692)." In *Boletín de Estudios Históricos de San Sebastián,* 259–277. San Sebastián: Biblioteca de la

Sociedad Bascongada de los Amigos del País, 1985.

Gehring, Charles T. and Jacob A. Schiltkamp, trans. and eds. "New Netherland Documents." In *Curaçao Papers, 1640–1665.* Vol. XVII. New York: Heart of the Lakes, 1987.

Gemelli Careri, Giovanni Francesco. *Viaje a la Nueva España.* Mexico City: Universidad Nacional Autónoma de México, 1976.

Gerhard, Peter. *Pirates on the West Coast of New Spain, 1575–1742.* Glendale, California: Arthur H. Clark, 1960.

———. *The Southeast Frontier of New Spain.* Princeton, New Jersey: Princeton University Press, 1979.

Goddet-Langlois, Jean, and Denise Goddet-Langlois. *La vie en Guadeloupe au XVIIe siècle, suivi du Dictionnaire des familles guadeloupéennes de 1635 à 1700.* Fort de France: Editions Exbrayat, 1991.

Goslinga, Cornelis Ch. *The Dutch in the Caribbean and in the Guianas, 1680–1791.* Dover, New Hampshire: Van Gorcum, 1985.

———. *The Dutch in the Caribbean and on the Wild Coast, 1580–1680.* Gainesville: University of Florida Press, 1971.

Gosse, Philip Henry George. *The History of Piracy.* London: Longmans Green, 1932.

———. *My Pirate Library.* London: Dulau, 1926.

———. *The Pirates' Who's Who.* London: Dulau, 1924.

———. "Piracy." *The Mariner's Mirror,* XXXVI (1950): 337–349.

Guijo, Gregorio M. de. *Diario, 1648–1664.* Mexico City: Editorial Porrúa, 1952.

Hamshere, C. E. "Henry Morgan and the Buccaneers." *History Today* XVI (1966): 406–414.

Haring, Clarence Henry. *The Buccaneers in the West Indies in the XVII Century.* London: Methuen, 1910.

Harvey, John H. "Some Notes on the Family of Dampier." *The Mariner's Mirror* XXIX (1943): 54–57.

Hasenclever, Adolf. "Die flibustier Westindiens im 17 jahrhundert." *Preussische Jahrbuch* CCIII (1926): 13–35.

Horwood, Harold, and Ed Butts. *Bandits and Privateers: Canada in the Age of Gunpowder.* Toronto: Doubleday, 1987.

Howse, Derek, and Norman J. W. Thrower, eds. *A Buccaneer's Atlas: Basil Ringrose's South Sea Waggoner. A Sea Atlas and Sailing Directions of the Pacific Coast of the Americas 1682.* Berkeley: University of California Press, 1992.

Hussey, R. D. "Spanish Reaction to Foreign Aggression in the Caribbean to About 1680." *Hispanic American Historical Review,* 9 (1929): 286–302.

Incháustegui Cabral, Joaquín Marino. *La gran expedición inglesa contra las Antillas Mayores.* Mexico City: Gráfica Panamericana, 1953.

*Interesting Tracts Relating to the Island of Jamaica, Consisting of Curious State Papers, Councils of War, Letters, Petitions, Narratives, etc., which Throw Great Light on the History of That Island from Its Conquest Down to the Year 1702.* St. Jago de la Vega (Kingston, Jamaica): Lewis, Lunan and Jones, 1800.

Jameson, John Franklin. *Privateering and Piracy in the Colonial Period: Illustrative Documents.* New York: Macmillan, 1923.

Juárez Moreno, Juan. *Piratas y corsarios en Veracruz y Campeche.* Seville: Escuela de Estudios Hispano-americanos, 1972.

Kemp, Peter K., and Christopher Lloyd. *The Brethren of the Coast: The British and French Buccaneers in the South Seas.* London: Heinemann, 1960.

Labat, Jean-Baptiste. *Viajes a las islas de la América.* Havana: Casa de las Américas, 1979.

Laburu Mateo, Miguel. *Breve vocabulario que contiene términos empleados en documentos marítimos antiguos.* San Sebastián: Departamento de Cultura y Turismo, Diputación Foral de Gipuzkoa, 1990.

Le Blant, Robert. "Un Officier Béarnais à Saint-Domingue: Pierre-Gédéon Ier de Nolivos, Chevalier de l'Ordre Royal et Militaire de Saint-Louis, Lieutenant du Roy, puis Major du Petit Goave et commandant la partie Ouest de Saint-Domingue, 1706–1732." Extrait de la *Revue Historique & Archéologique du Béarn et du Pays Basque.* Pau: Lescher-Moutoué, 1931.

Le Pelley, John. "Dampier's Morgan and the Privateersmen." *The Mariner's Mirror* XXXIII (1947): 170–178.

Lepers, Jean-Baptiste. *La tragique histoire des Flibustiers: Histoire de Saint-Domingue et de l'le de la Tortue, repairs des flibustiers, écrite vers 1715.* Edited by Pierre-Bernard Berthelot. Paris: G. Crès, 1925.

Lloyd, Christopher. *William Dampier.* London: Faber and Faber, 1966.

López Cantos, Angel. *Historia de Puerto Rico (1650–1700).* Seville: Escuela de Estudios Hispano-americanos, 1975.

Lugo, Américo. *Recopilación diplomática relativa a las colonias española y francesa de la isla de Santo Domingo, 1640–1701.* Ciudad Trujillo, Dominican Republic: Editorial "La Nación," 1944.

Lussan, Ravenau de. *Journal of a Voyage into the South Seas.* Cleveland, Ohio: Arthur H. Clark, 1930.

McJunkin, David M. "Logwood: An Inquiry into the Historical Biogeography of *Haematoxylum campechanium L.* and Related Dyewoods of the Neotropics." Unpublished Ph.D. thesis, University of California at Los Angeles, 1991.

Marcus, Linda C. "English Influence on Belize and the Petén Region of Northern Guatemala, 1630 to 1763." Unpublished Ph.D. thesis, Southern Methodist University, 1990.

Margolin, Samuel G. "Lawlessness on the Maritime Frontier of the Greater Chesapeake, 1650–1750 (Smuggling, Wrecking, Piracy)." Unpublished Ph.D. thesis, College of William and Mary, 1992.

Marley, David F. *Pirates and Engineers: Dutch and Flemish Adventurers in New Spain (1607–1697).* Windsor, Ontario: Netherlandic Press, 1992.

———. *Sack of Veracruz: The Great Pirate Raid of 1683.* Windsor, Ontario: Netherlandic Press, 1993.

Mitchell, David. *Pirates.* London: Thames and Hudson, 1976.

Moya Pons, Frank. *Historia colonial de Santo Domingo.* Santiago, Dominican Republic: Universidad Católica Madre y Maestra, 1977.

Pawson, Michael, and David J. Buisseret. *Port Royal, Jamaica.* Oxford: Clarendon Press, 1975.

———. "A Pirate at Port Royal in 1679." *The Mariner's Mirror,* LVII (1971): 303–305.

Peña Batlle, Manuel Arturo. *La isla de la Tortuga: Plaza de armas, refugio y seminario de los enemigos de España en Indias.* Madrid: Ediciones Cultura Hispánica, 1951.

Penguin. *Dictionary of Historical Slang.* New York: Penguin, 1972.

Pérez Mallaína Bueno, Pablo Emilio, and Bibiano Torres Ramírez. *La Armada del Mar del Sur.* Seville: Escuela de Estudios Hispano-americanos, 1987.

*Piracy and Privateering.* Catalog 4, National Maritime Museum Library. London: Her Majesty's Stationery Office, 1972.

Poirier, M. "Une grande figure antillaise: le R. P. Labat, aventurier, aumônier de la flibuste." *Annales de la Société des Lettres, Sciences et Arts des Alpes-Maritimes* 61 (1969–1970): 83–94.

Pope, Dudley. *Harry Morgan's Way: The Biography of Sir Henry Morgan, 1635–1684.* London: Secker and Warburg, 1977.

Prebble, John. *The Darien Disaster.* London: Secker & Warburg, 1968.

Rediker, Marcus. *Between the Devil and the Deep Blue Sea: Merchant Seamen, Pirates and the Anglo-American Maritime World, 1700–1750.* Cambridge: Cambridge University Press, 1987.

Ritchie, Robert C. *Captain Kidd and the War against the Pirates.* Cambridge, Massachusetts: Harvard University Press, 1986.

Robles, Antonio de. *Diario de sucesos notables (1665–1703).* Mexico City: Editorial Porrúa, 1972.

Rodríguez Demorizi, Emilio. *Invasión inglesa de 1655; notas adicionales de Fray Cipriano de Utrera.* Ciudad Trujillo, Dominican Republic: Montalvo, 1957.

———. "Acerca del tratado de Ryswick." *Clio* 22, no. 100 (July–September 1954): 127–132.

———. "Invasión inglesa en 1655." *Boletín del Archivo General de la Nación* [República Dominicana] 20, no. 92 (January–March 1957): 6–70.

———. *La era de Francia en Santo Domingo; contribución a su estudio.* Ciudad Trujillo, Dominican Republic: Editora del Caribe, 1955.

Rubio Mañé, José Ignacio. "Las jurisdicciones de Yucatán: la creación de la plaza de teniente de Rey en Campeche, año de 1744." *Boletín del Archivo General de la Nación* [México], Segunda Serie VII, no. 3 (July–September 1966): 549–631.

———. "Ocupación de la Isla de Términos por los ingleses, 1658–1717." *Boletín del Archivo General de la Nación* [México], Primera Serie XXIV, no. 2 (April–June 1953): 295–330.

Saint-Yves, G. "La flibuste et les flibustiers. Documents inédits sur Saint Domingue et la Tortue." *Bulletin de la Société de Géographie de Paris* 38 (1923): 57–75.

Sáiz Cidoncha, Carlos. *Historia de la piratería en América Española.* Madrid: Editorial San Martín, 1985.

Serrano Mangas, Fernando. *Los galeones de la carrera de Indias, 1650–1700.* Seville: Escuela de Estudios Hispano-americanos, 1985.

———. "El proceso del pirata Bartholomew Sharp, 1682." *Temas americanistas* 4 (1984): 14–18.

Shomette, Donald G. *Pirates on the Chesapeake: Being a True History of Pirates, Picaroons, and Raiders on Chesapeake Bay, 1610–1807.* Centreville, Maryland: Tidewater, 1985.

Shomette, Donald G., and Robert D. Haslach. *Raid on America: The Dutch Naval Campaign of 1672–1674.* Columbia: University of South Carolina Press, 1988.

Sigüenza y Góngora, Carlos de. *Infortunios que Alonso Ramírez, natural de la ciudad de San Juan de Puerto Rico, padeció*. Reprinted in *Obras históricas*. Mexico City: Porrúa, 1960.

———. *Relación de lo sucedido a la Armada de Barlovento*. Reprinted in *Obras históricas*. Mexico City: Porrúa, 1960.

———. *Trofeo de la justicia española en el castigo de la alevosía francesa*. Reprinted in *Obras históricas*. Mexico City: Porrúa, 1960.

Sucre, Luis Alberto. *Gobernadors y capitanes generales de Venezuela*. Caracas: Litografía Tecnocolor, 1964.

Taillemite, Étienne. *Dictionnaire des Marins Français*. Paris: Editions Maritimes et d'Outre-Mer, 1982.

Taylor, S. A. G. *The Western Design: An Account of Cromwell's Expedition to the Caribbean*. London: Solstice Productions, 1969.

Thornton, A. P. *West-India Policy under the Restoration*. Oxford, 1956.

———. "The Modyfords and Morgan." *Jamaican Historical Review* 2 (1952): 36–60.

Torres Ramírez, Bibiano. *La Armada de Barlovento*. Seville: Escuela de Estudios Hispano-americanos, 1981.

Tribout de Morembert, Henri. "A Saint-Domingue, Le Major Bernanos, capitaine de flibustiers." Paris: *Connaissance du Monde* 78 (1965): 10–19.

Vrijman, L. C. *Dr. David van der Sterre: Zeer aenmerkelijke reysen door Jan Erasmus Reyning*. Amsterdam: P. N. van Kampen and Zoon, 1937.

Wafer, Lionel. *A New Voyage and Description of the Isthmus of America*. London: Hakluyt Society, 1933.

Walsh, Micheline. *Spanish Knights of Irish Origin: Documents from Continental Archives*. Dublin: Irish Manuscripts Commission, 1960–1970.

Ward, Eliot D. C. "Imperial Panama: Commerce and Conflict in Isthmian America, 1550–1750." Unpublished Ph.D. thesis, University of Florida, 1988.

Webster, John Clarence. *Cornelis Steenwyck: Dutch Governor of Acadie*. Ottawa: Canadian Historical Association, 1929.

Weddle, Robert S. *Spanish Sea: The Gulf of Mexico in North American Discovery, 1500–1685*. College Station: Texas A&M University Press, 1985.

———. *Wilderness Manhunt: The Spanish Search for La Salle*. Austin: University of Texas Press, 1973.

Wright, Irene Aloha. *Spanish Narratives of the English Attack on Santo Domingo, 1655*. London: Royal Historical Society, 1926.

Young, Everild, and Kjeld Helweg-Larsen. *The Pirates' Priest: The Life of Père Labat in the West Indies, 1693–1705*. London: Jarrolds, 1965.

Zahedieh, Nuala. "'A Frugal, Prudential and Hopeful Trade': Privateering in Jamaica, 1655–89." *Journal of Imperial and Commonwealth History* 18, no. 2 (1990): 145–168.

———. "The Merchants of Port Royal, Jamaica, and the Spanish Contraband Trade, 1655–1692." *William and Mary Quarterly* 43, no. 4 (October 1986): 570–593.

# INDEX